Building Construction Details

Building Construction Details

Practical Drawings

Hans Banz

CBS

CBS Publishers & Distributors Pvt. Ltd.

New Delhi • Bengaluru • Chennai • Kochi • Kolkata • Mumbai

Hyderabad • Nagpur • Patna • Pune • Vijayawada

ISBN: 81-239-1263-3

First Published in Paperback in 1983
First Indian Edition: 1987
Reprint: 2001

Reprinted in India by CBS Publishers & Distributors in arrangement with Van Nostrand Reinhold Company, Inc., USA

Library of Congress Catalogue Card No. 82-70513

Published by **Satish Kumar Jain** and produced by **Varun Jain** for
CBS Publishers & Distributors Pvt. Ltd.,
4819/XI Prahlad Street, 24 Ansari Road, Daryaganj, New Delhi - 110002
delhi@cbspd.com, cbspubs@airtelmail.in • www.cbspd.com
Ph.: 23289259, 23266861, 23266867 • Fax: 011-23243014

Corporate Office: 204 FIE, Industrial Area, Patparganj, Delhi - 110 092
Ph: 49344934 • Fax: 011-49344935
E-mail: publishing@cbspd.com • publicity@cbspd.com

Branches:

- ***Bengaluru:*** 2975, 17th Cross, K.R. Road, Bansankari 2nd Stage, Bengaluru - 70 • Ph: +91-80-26771678/79 • Fax: +91-80-26771680 E-mail: cbsbng@gmail.com, bangalore@cbspd.com
- ***Chennai:*** No. 7, Subbaraya Street, Shenoy Nagar, Chennai - 600030 Ph: +91-44-26681266, 26680620 • Fax: +91-44-42032115 E-mail: chennai@cbspd.com
- ***Kochi:*** Ashana House, 39/1904, A.M. Thomas Road, Valanjambalam, Ernakulum, Kochi • Ph: +91-484-4059061-65 Fax: +91-484-4059065 • E-mail: cochin@cbspd.com
- ***Kolkata:*** 6-B, Ground Floor, Rameshwar Shaw Road, Kolkata - 700014 Ph: +91-33-22891126/7/8 • E-mail: kolkata@cbspd.com
- ***Mumbai:*** 83-C, Dr. E. Moses Road, Worli, Mumbai - 400018 Ph: +91-9833017933, 022-24902340/41 • E-mail: mumbai@cbspd.com

Representatives:

- Hyderabad: 0-9885175004
- Patna: 0-9334159340
- Jharkhand: 0-9811541605
- Nagpur: 0-9021734563
- Pune: 0-9623451994
- Uttarakhand: 0-9716462459

Printed at:
J.S. Offset Printers, Delhi (India)

Foreword

This basic work shows, in clear form, the technical planning and graphical working processes necessary for the professional management of a project in all areas of building practice.

The individual working areas, sub-divided into groups, provide a wealth of suggestions and details for a co-ordinated planning process for both architectural and trade purposes.

The descriptive material attached to the individual sections of the book provides information on the sequence and execution of work.

Contents

Perspective

In order to achieve a balanced representation of the object and one that is as close to the original and as accurate as possible, the following points should be observed in the construction of perspectives.

The direction of view or view point should not lie on the main measuring axis, but, if possible, be fixed to left or right at a suitable distance from the object, i.e. the distance from the viewpoint to the furthest edge of the object should be approximately twice the distance to the picture plane, (or 11/2-2 × the diagonal length of the object parallel to the picture plane).

The line of the picture plane should always be tangential to the front edge of the object, so that the plotted units of dimension remain the same. If the picture plane is moved towards the view point, the image is reduced in size; by moving the picture plane away from the view point, the image is enlarged.

Bird's eye view
(aerial perspective): object below horizon
Front perspective: horizon lies within the object

Ground level perspective: object above horizon.

There are two main forms of perspective construction: single point or central perspective, and two- or multiple-point perspective.

To facilitate an understanding of the means of representation, all construction lines have been shown.

Aerial perspective, fundamentals

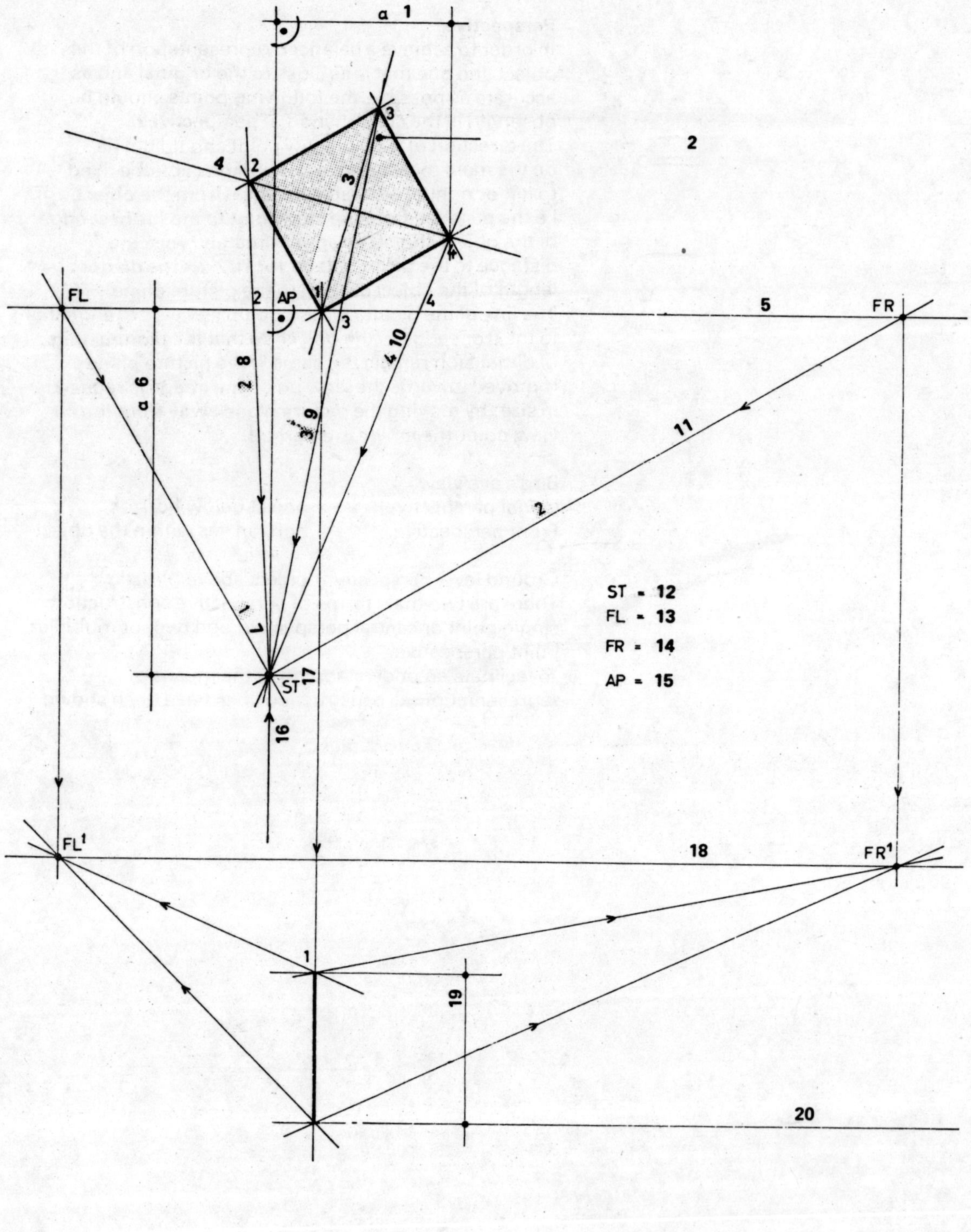

1 length a
2 object-plan, top view
3 diagonal
4 diagonal line
5 picture line - plane
6 distance approx. 2-times length a
7 parallel ray 1
8 ray 2
9 ray 3
10 ray 4
11 parallel ray 2 to the object
12 ST = station point
13 FL = vanishing point left
14 FR = vanishing point right
15 AP = center of vision
16 main direction of view
17 main measuring line
18 horizon
19 object elevation, true to scale
20 ground line - plane

Aerial perspective, object presentation

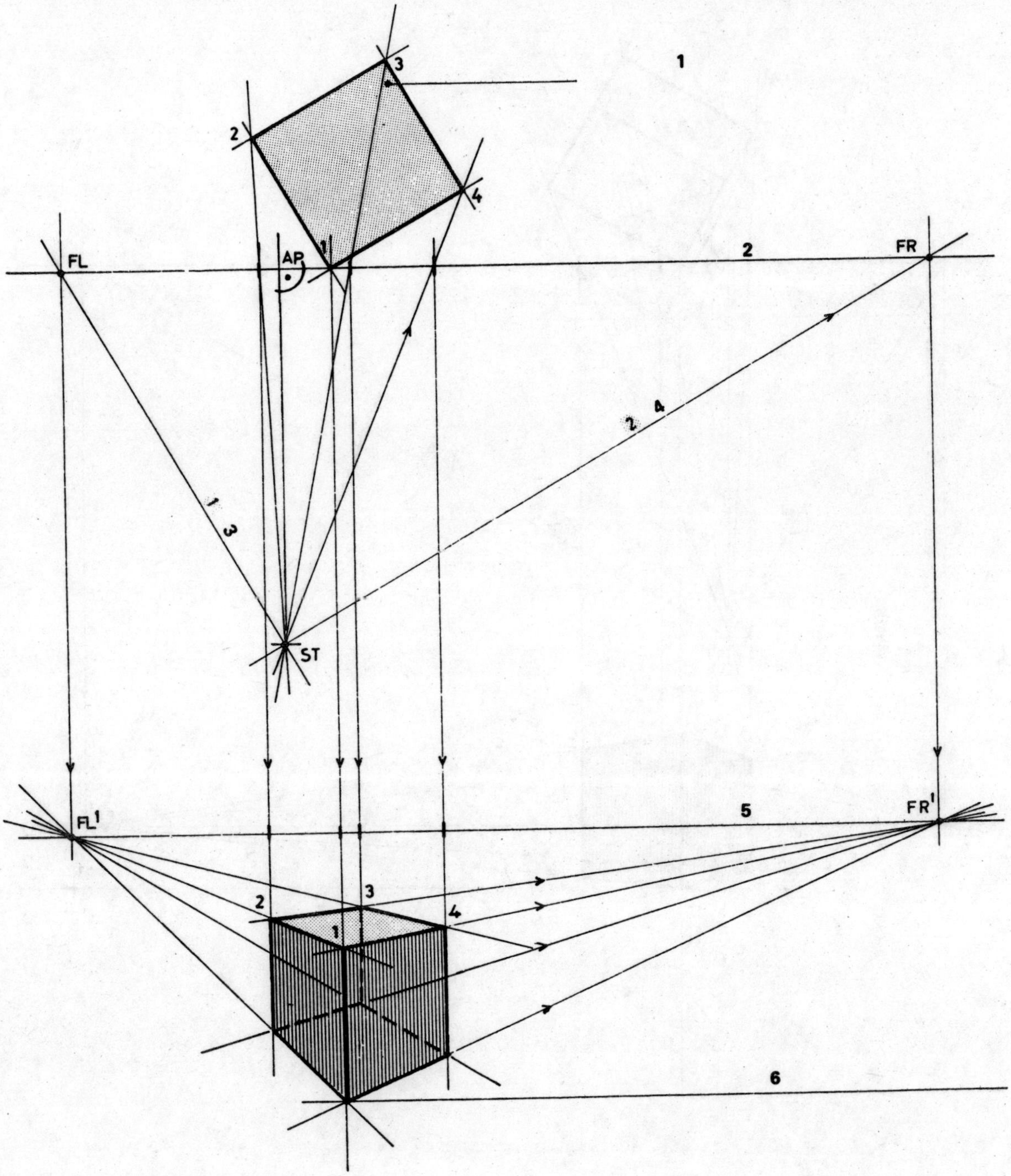

1 object, top view
2 picture plane
3 parallel ray 1
4 parallel ray 2
5 horizon
6 ground plane

Front perspective

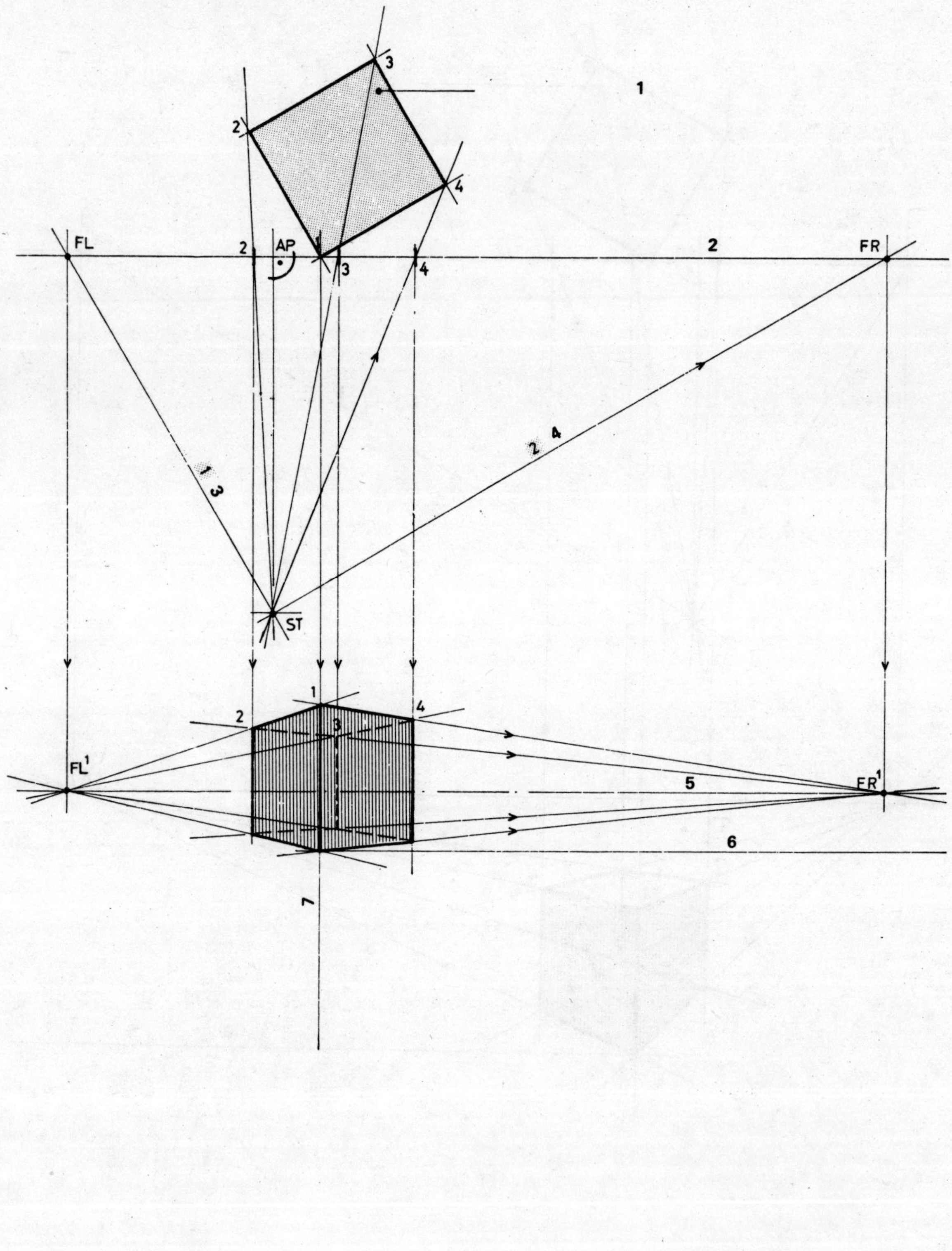

1 object, top view
2 picture plane
3 parallel ray 1
4 parallel ray 2
5 horizon
6 ground plane
7 main measuring line

Ground-level perspective scale 1:1

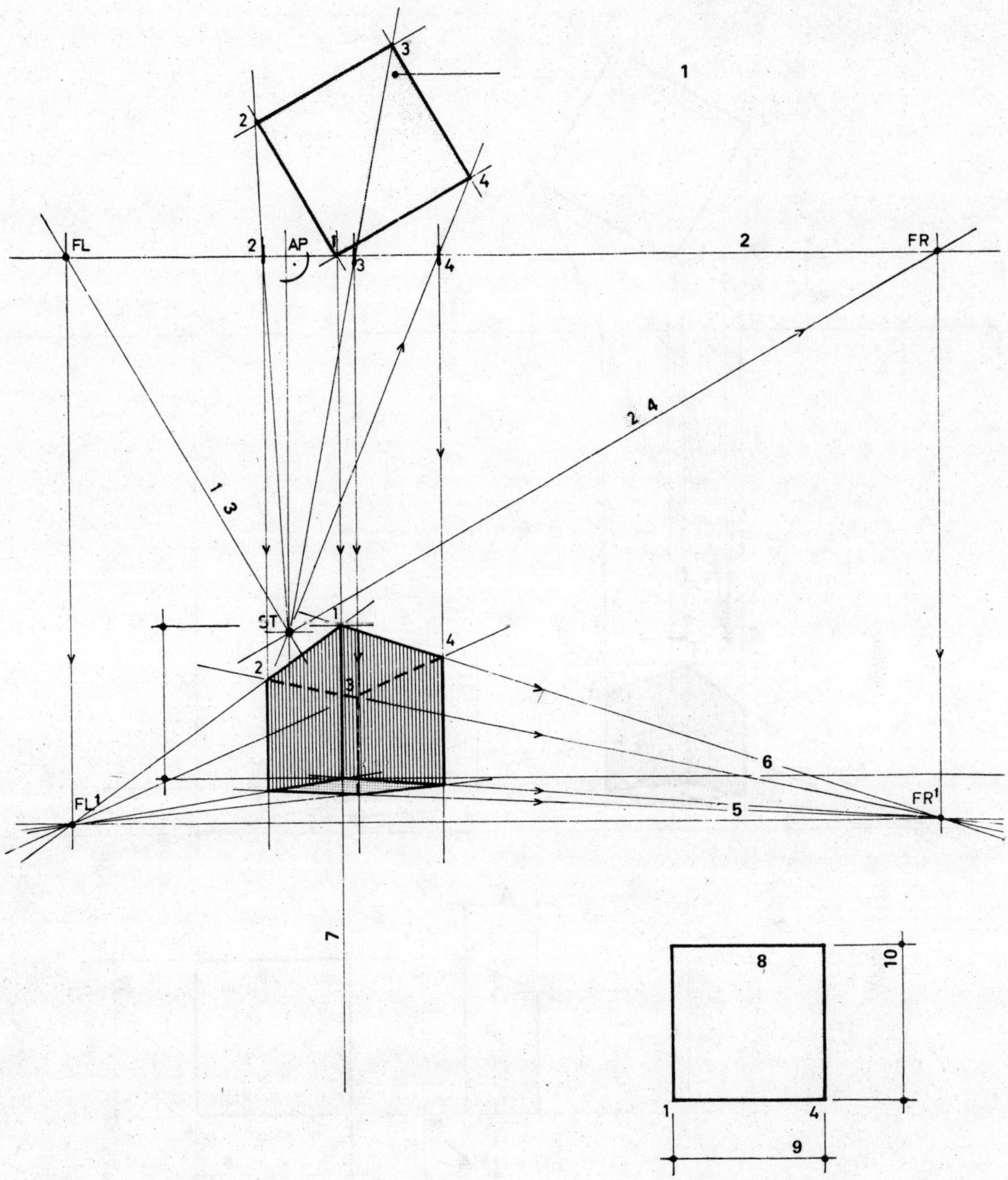

1 object, top view
2 picture plane
3 parallel ray 1
4 parallel ray 2
5 horizon
6 ground plane
7 main measuring line
8 cube
9 ground line
10 cube elevation

Ground-level perspective reduced scale

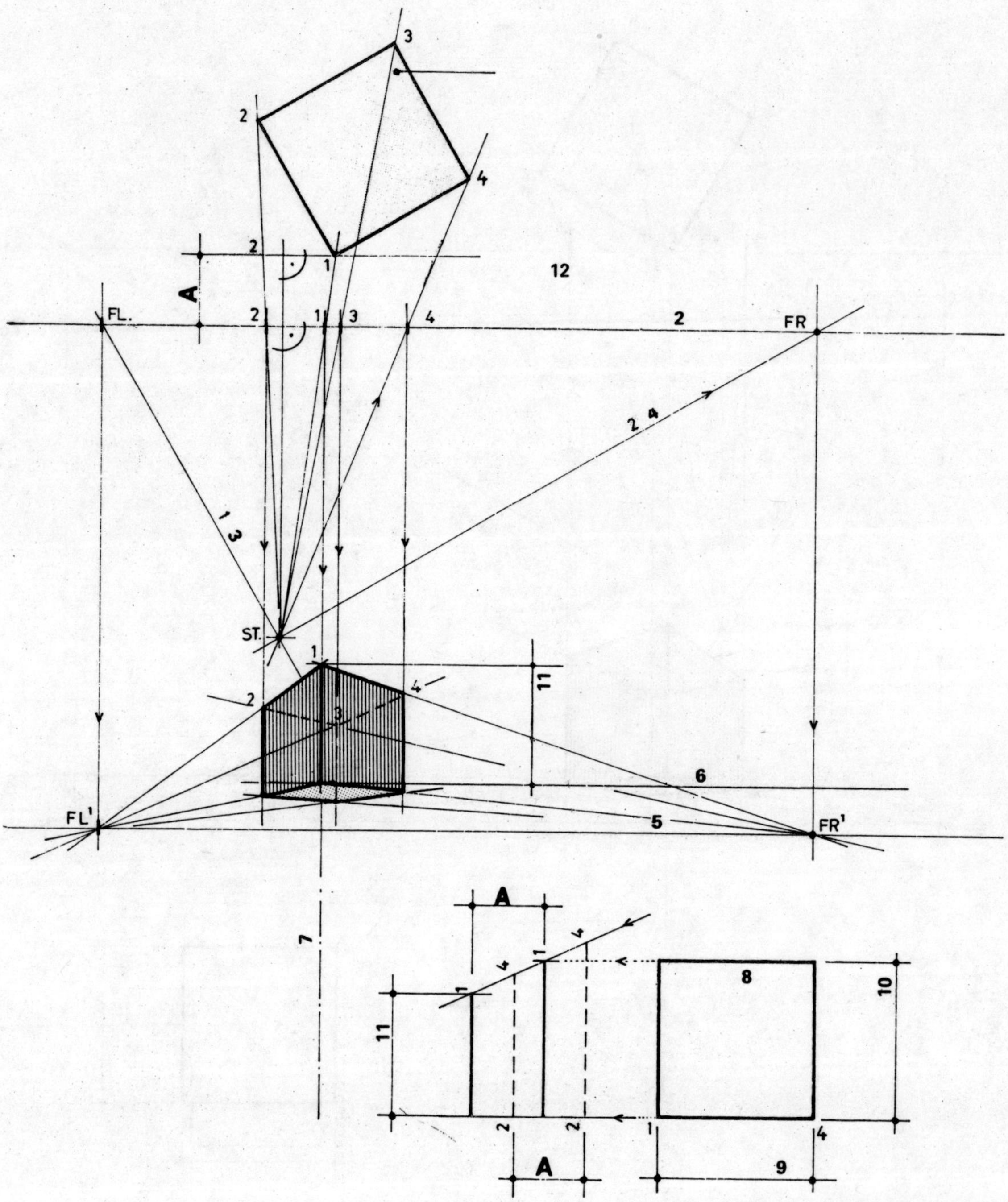

1 cube, top view
2 picture plane
3 parallel ray 1
4 parallel ray 2
5 horizon
6 ground plane
7 main measuring line
8 cube
9 ground line
10 cube elevation
11 proportional elevation
12 ground trace of picture plane

Ground-level perspective enlarged scale

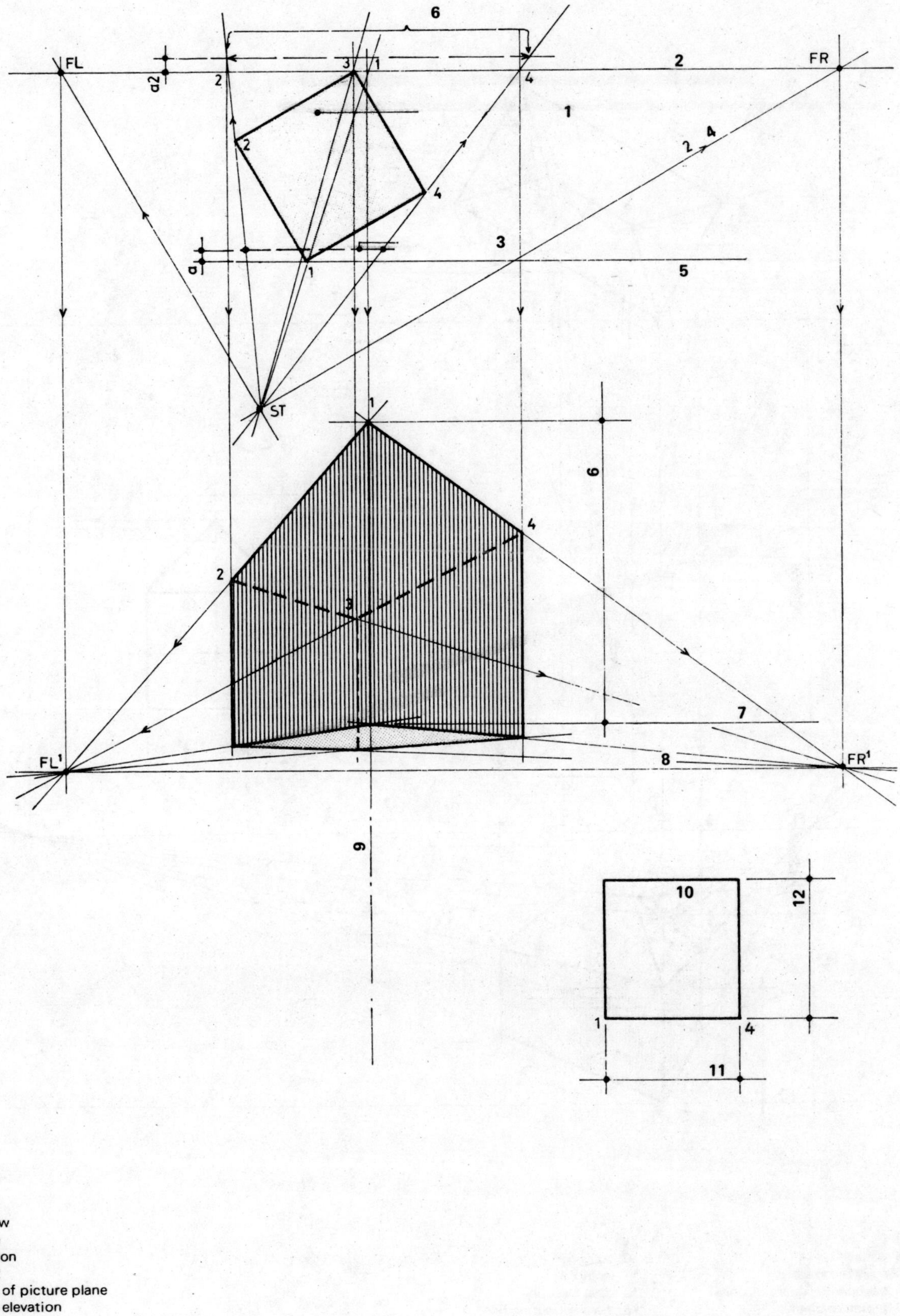

1 cube, top view
2 picture plane
3 actual elevation
4 parallel ray 2
5 ground trace of picture plane
6 proportional elevation
7 ground plane
8 horizon
9 main measuring line
10 cube
11 ground line
12 actual cube elevation

Vanishing-point perspective, object with rectangular ground area

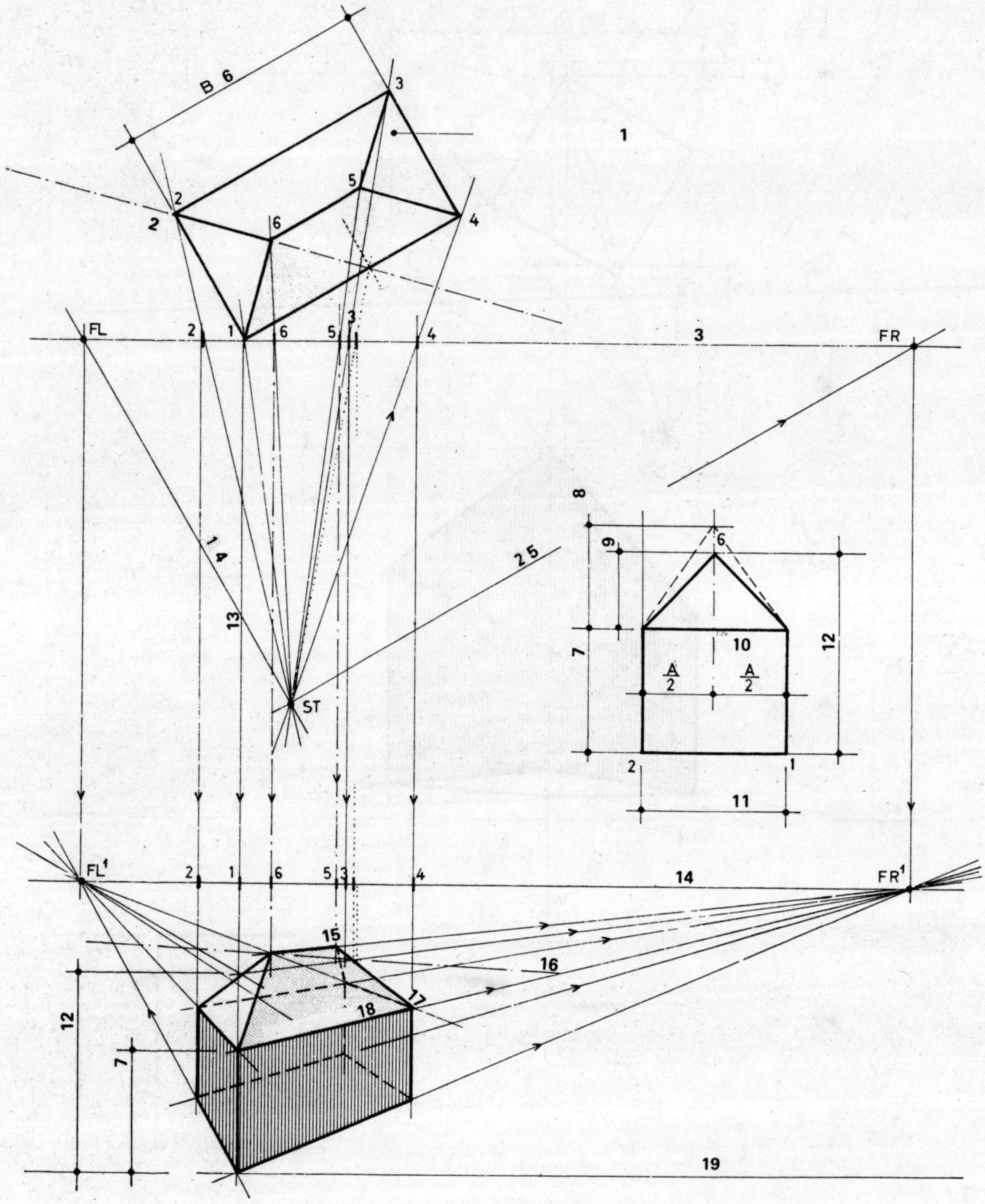

1 roof, top view
2 auxiliary square diagonal
3 picture plane
4 parallel ray 1
5 parallel ray 2
6 length B
7 eave elevation
8 rendered elevation
9 roof elevation
10 building
11 length A
12 total elevation
13 main measuring line
14 horizon
15 ridge
16 HQ diagonals
17 arris
18 eave line
19 ground plane

Vanishing-point perspective, object with displaced ground area

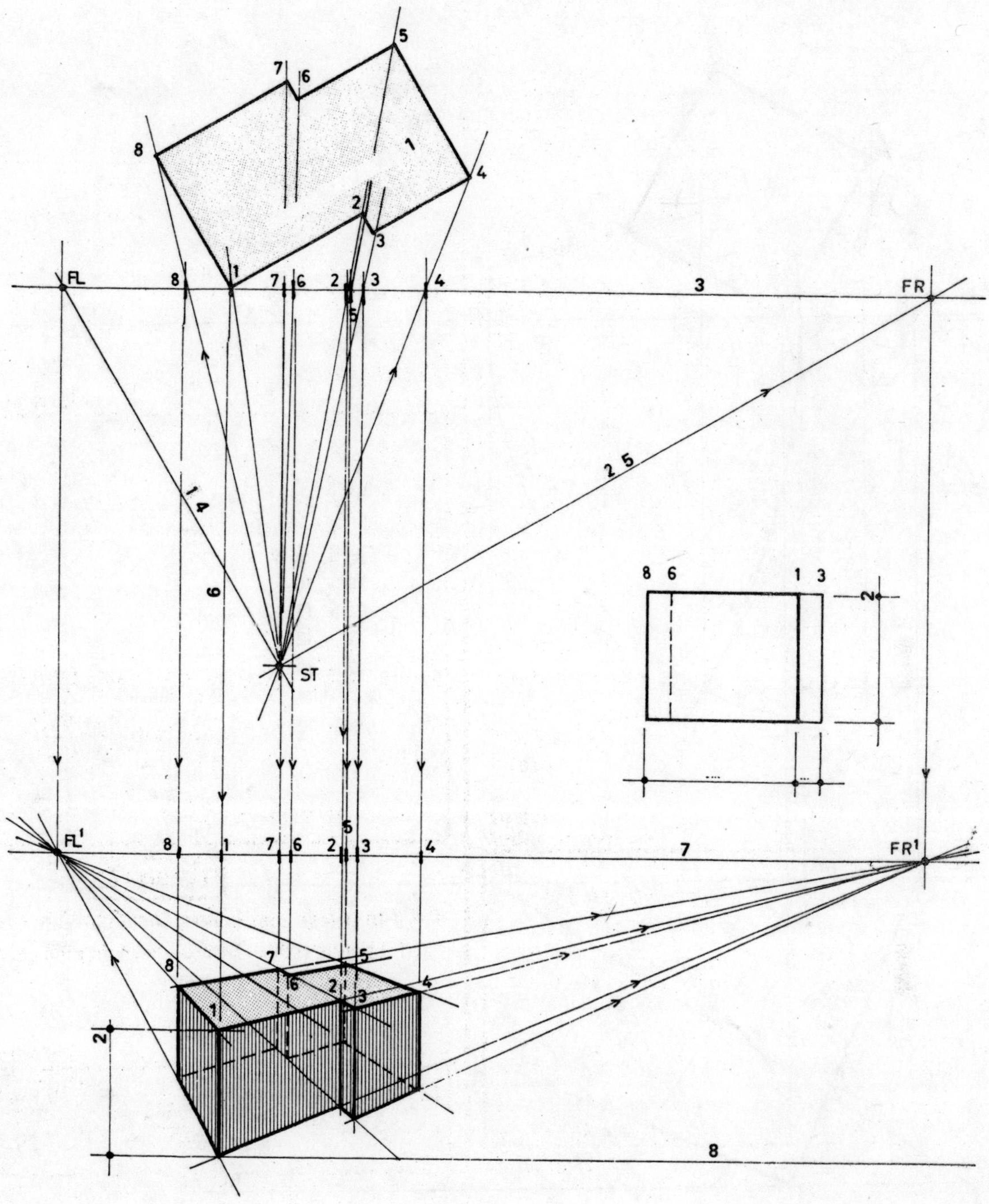

1 object, top view
2 object elevation
3 picture plane
4 parallel ray 1
5 parallel ray 2
6 main measuring line
7 horizon
8 ground plane

Division-point method fundamentals

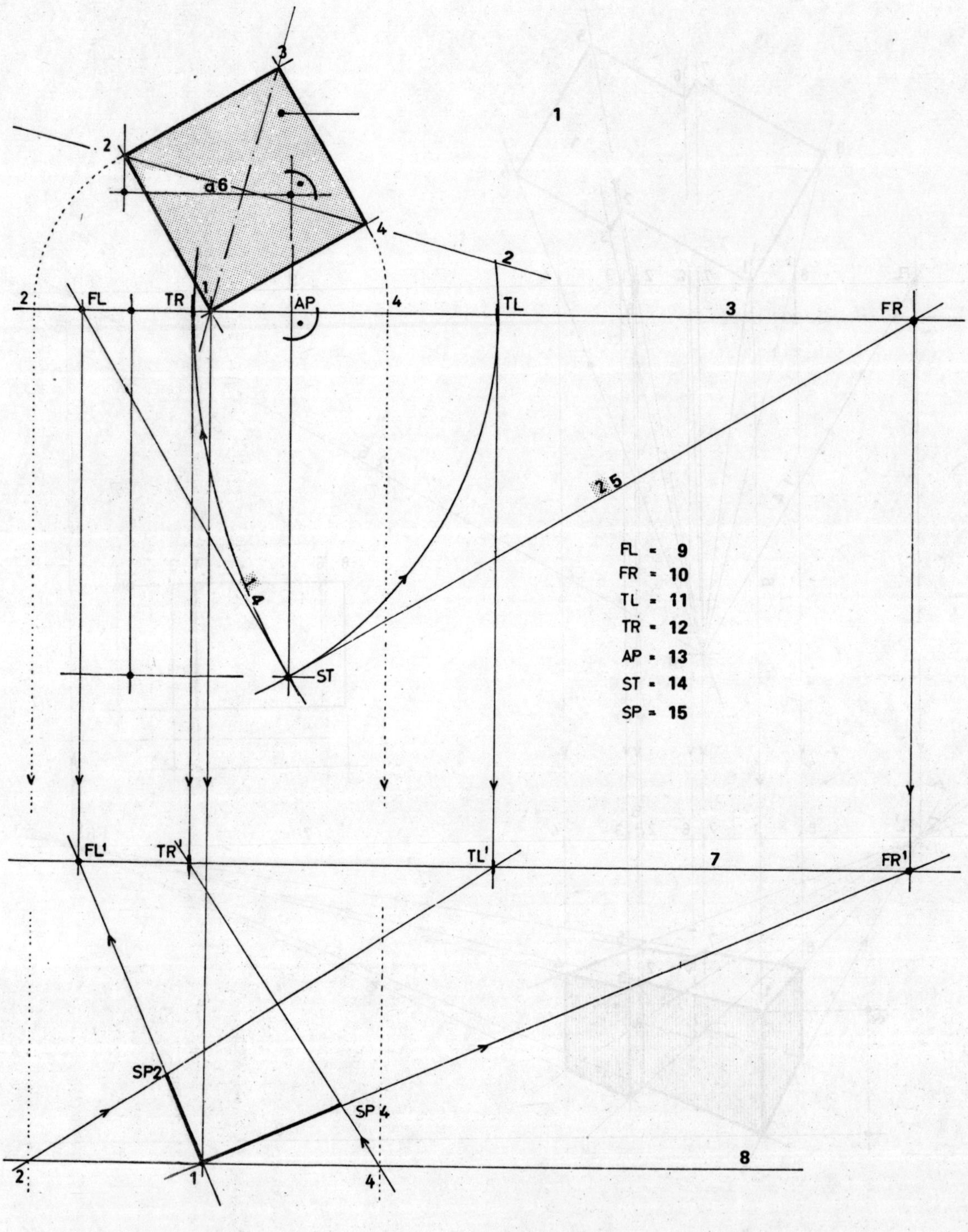

1 object, top view
2 diagonal
3 picture plane
4 parallel ray 1
5 parallel ray 2
6 length a
7 horizon
8 ground plane
9 FL = vanishing point left
10 FR = vanishing point right
11 TL = division point left
12 TR = division point right
13 AP = center of vision
14 ST = station point
15 SP = intersection point

Division-point method, object presentation

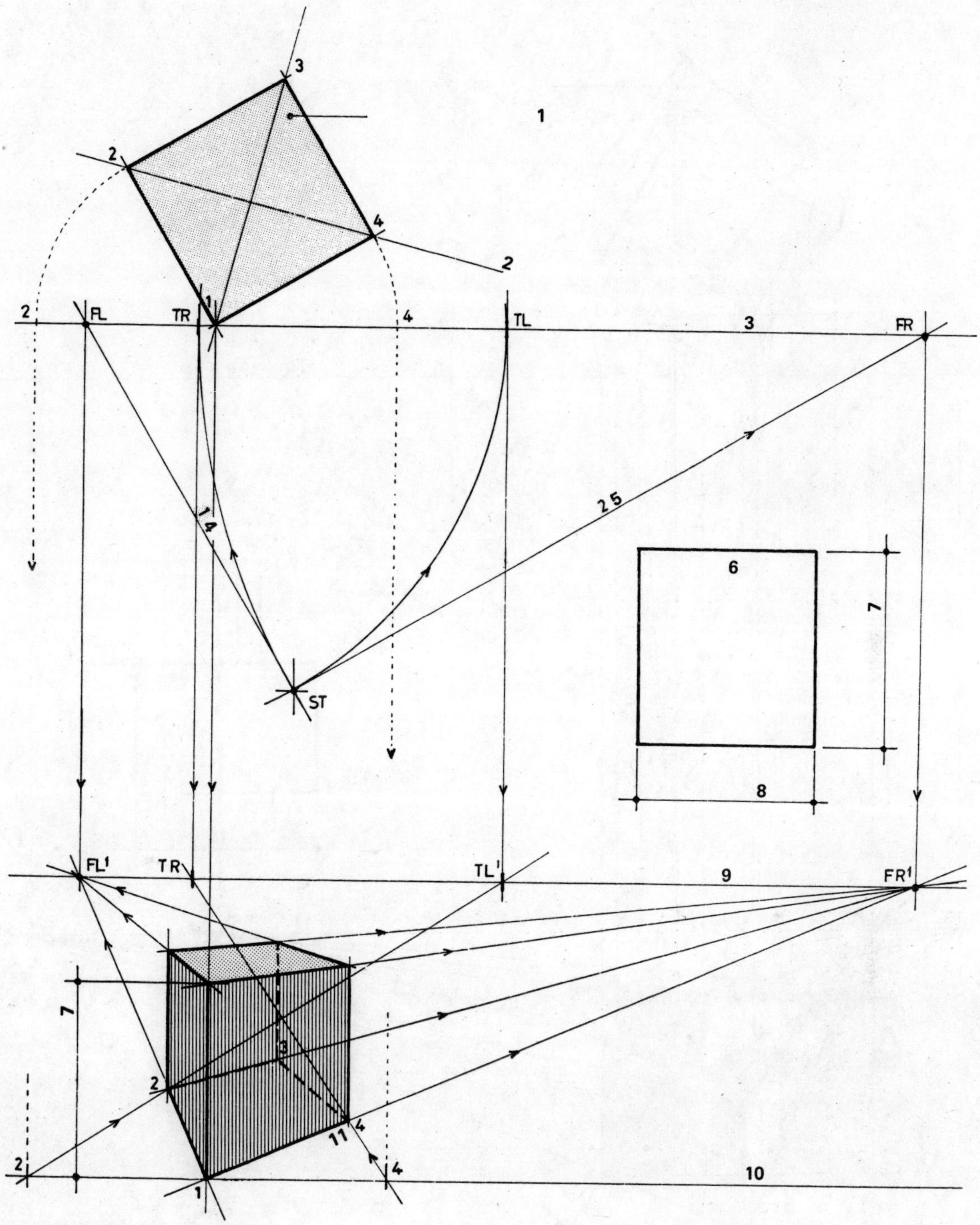

1 object, top view
2 diagonal
3 picture plane
4 parallel ray 1
5 parallel ray 2
6 object
7 object elevation
8 ground line
9 horizon
10 ground plane
11 base edge

Vanishing-point method

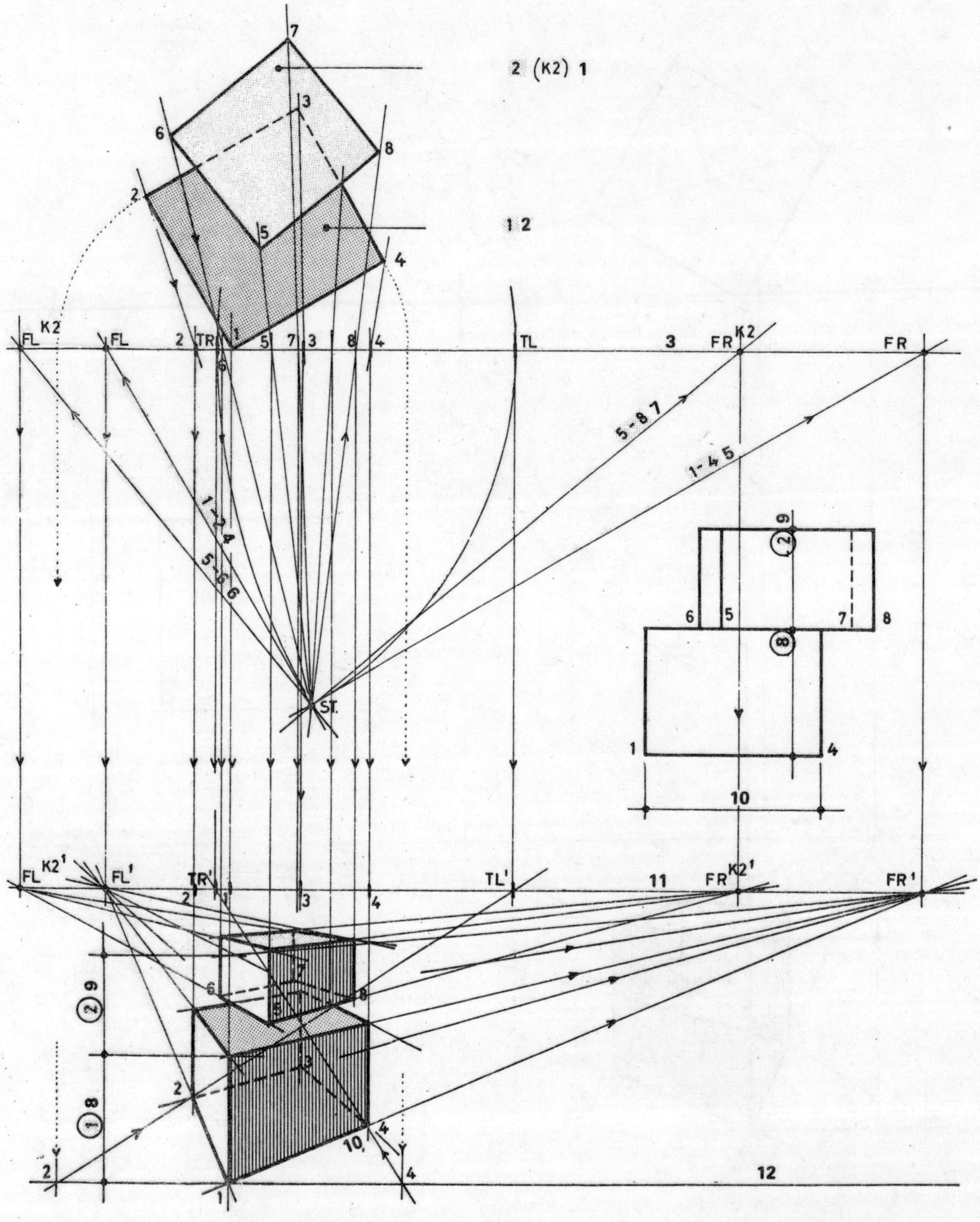

1 block 2
2 block 1
3 picture plane
4 parallel ray to 1-2
5 parallel ray to 1-4
6 parallel ray to 5-6
7 parallel ray to base edge 5-8
8 block elevation
9 block elevation 2
10 base edge
11 horizon
12 ground plane

Interior perspective, basic construction

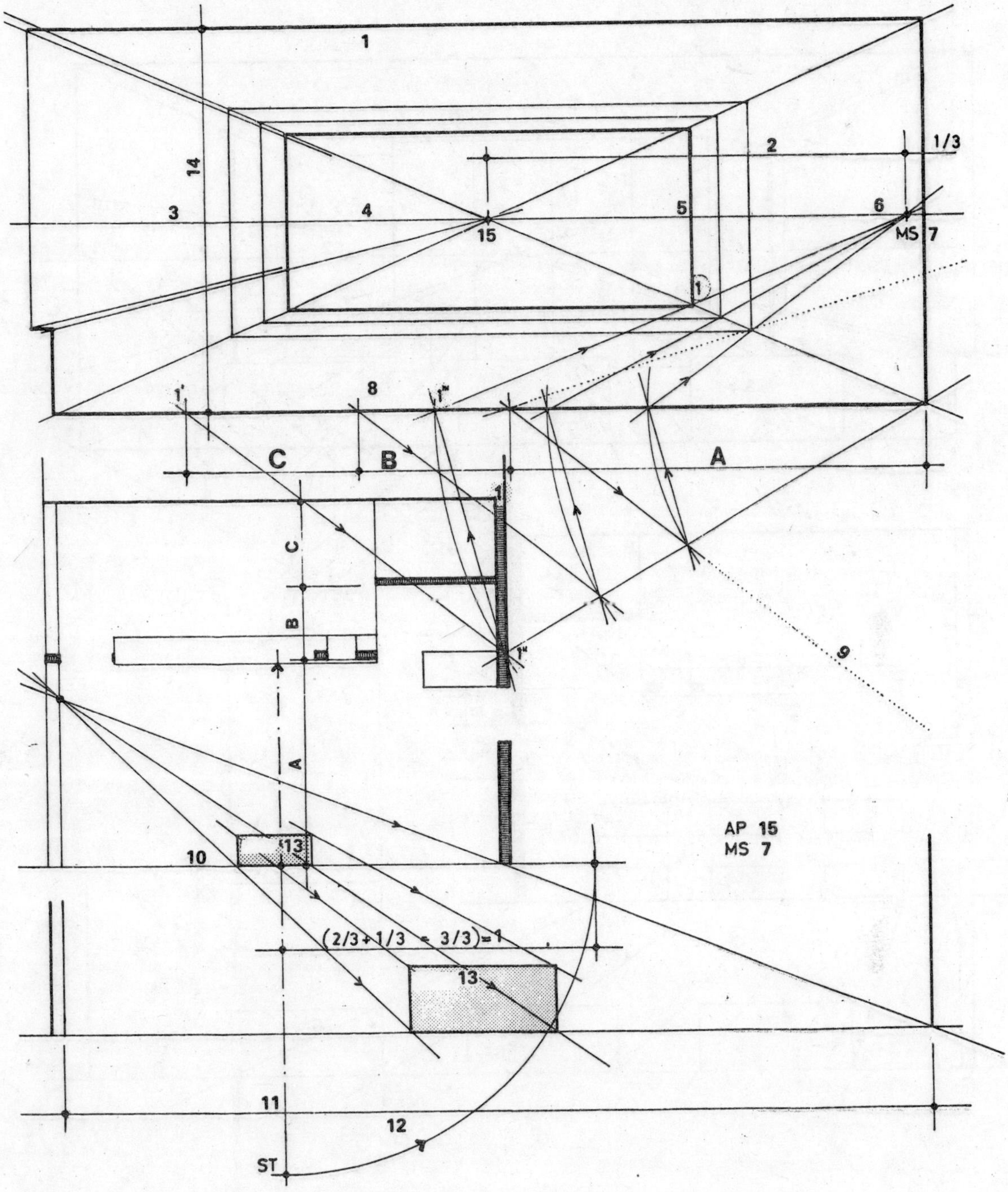

1 ceiling
2 2/3 (shortened dimension)
3 window front
4 front
5 horizon
6 side wall
7 MS = measuring point
8 floor
9 initial line
10 ground line
11 plotting line
12 desired scale ratio
13 desk
14 room elevation
15 AP = center of vision

Interior perspective, development stage

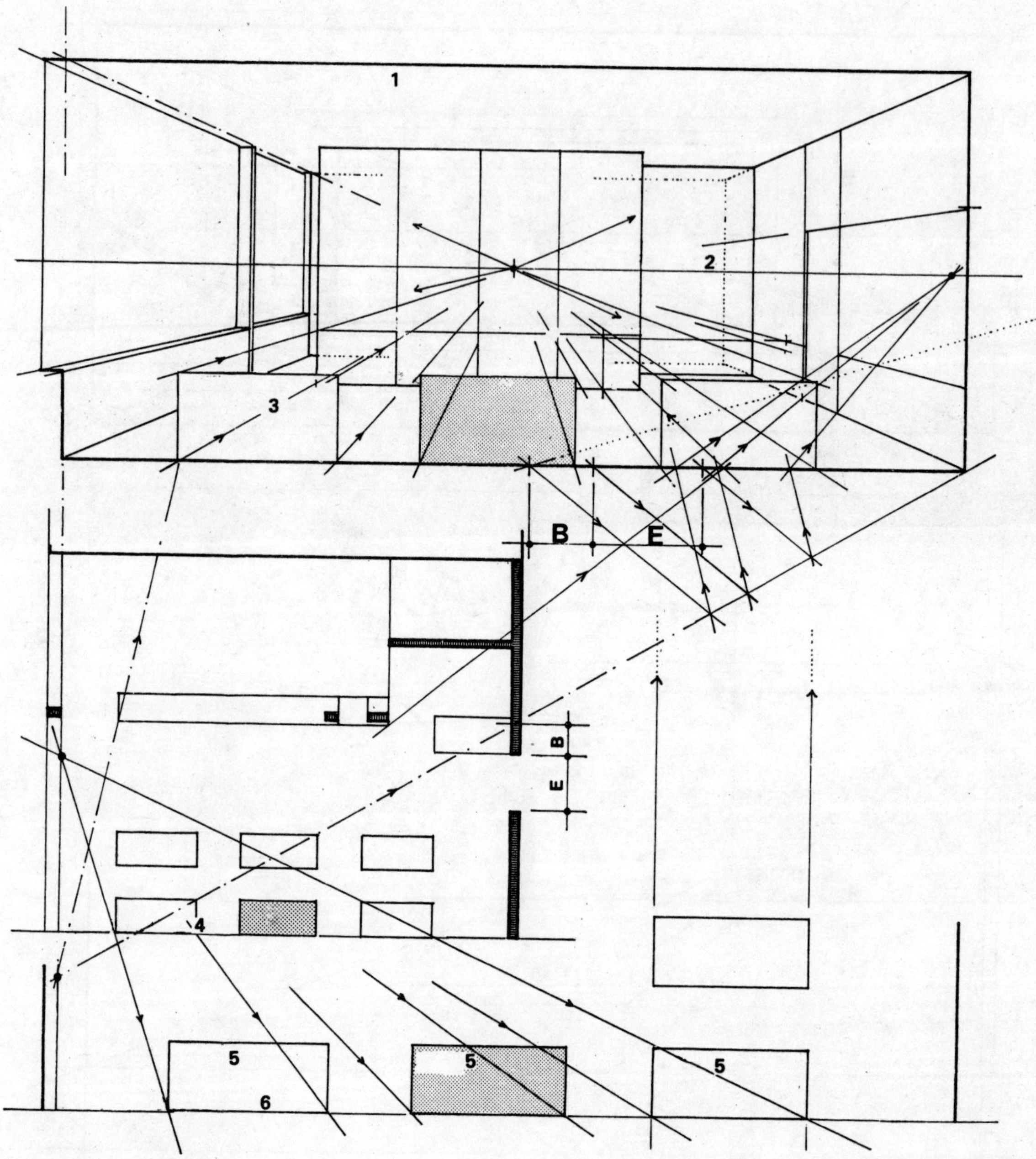

1 ceiling
2 horizon
3 desk - side view
4 ground line
5 desk
6 plotting line

Interior perspective, seating plan

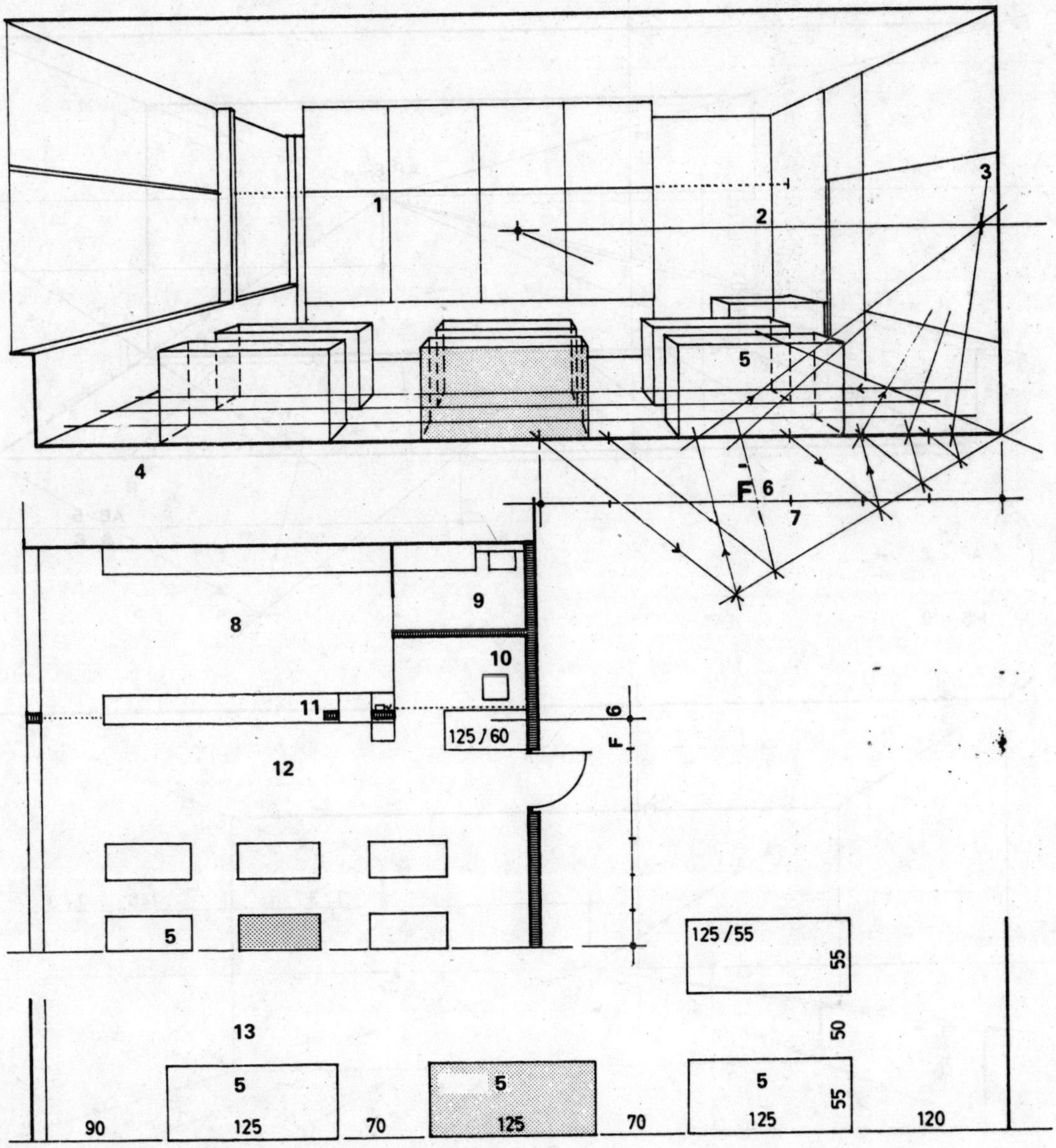

1 blackboard
2 horizon
3 wall panel
4 side view
5 desk
6 grouping line
7 for depth plot
8 material - groups - instruction
9 teacher, private
10 teacher
11 experiment table
12 classroom
13 plan

Interior perspective, variants

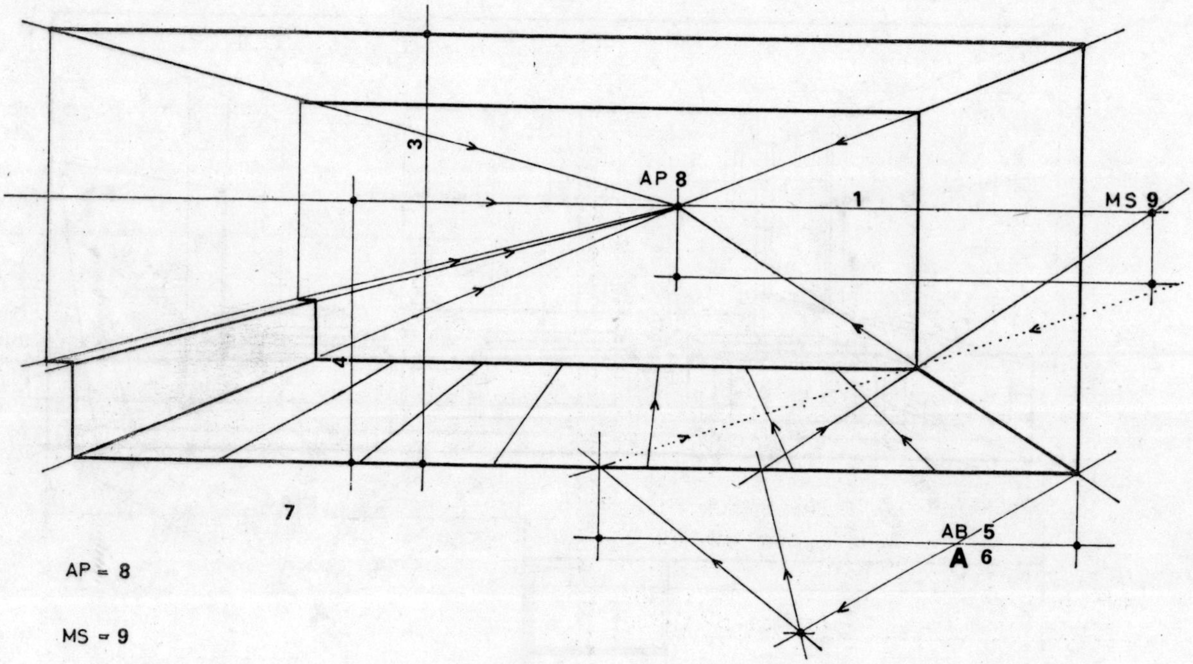

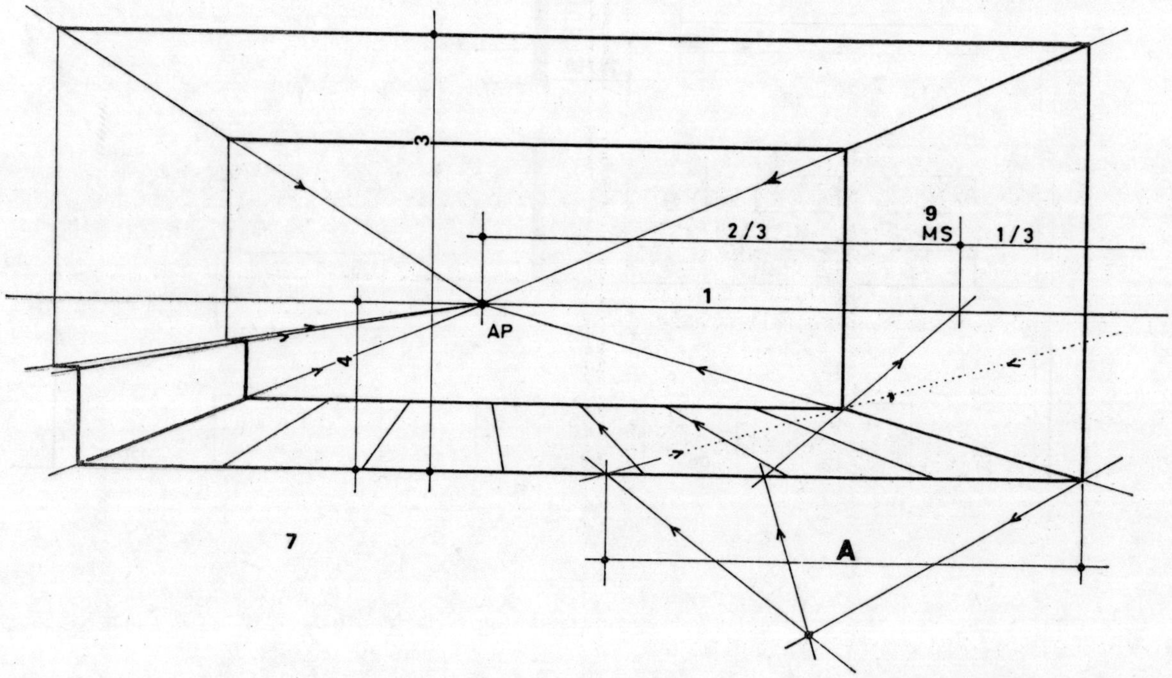

1 horizon
2 dimension tapered to 2/3
3 room elevation clearance
4 height of vision
5 dimension length AB
6 picture plane
7 side view of interior
8 AP = center of vision (location selected at will)
9 MS = measuring point

Construction of geometrical forms
Under this heading, the most common curve derivatives used in building will be dealt with.
The ellipse has a major and minor diameter, intersecting at right angles to each other at the mid-point. The outer circle limits the lateral or horizontal axis; the inner circle, the vertical axis.
From the centre of the ellipse, guide lines are subtended. The points of intersection with the inner and outer circles are then joined by construction lines parallel to the horizontal and vertical axes.
By joining these points of intersection, the regular, closed curve of the ellipse is obtained. The more guide lines one draws, the more accurate will be the ellipse.
For the construction of a three-centre or compound arch, draw a diagonal from the crown of the arch to its base, or abutment.
The point of intersection of the compass radii, or the halving of angles will give the starting point for the construction line, which is drawn from this point at right angles through the diagonal line. Mark the compass points for the curved arch along the base line and mid-point line of the arch.
For a five-centre construction draw a guide-line from the crown of the arch downwards at an angle of 45°.
The distance E of the point of intersection from the centre line serves as unit of measurement for fixing further points.
Semi-circular, segmental, pointed and ogee arches conclude this section.

Construction of ellipses

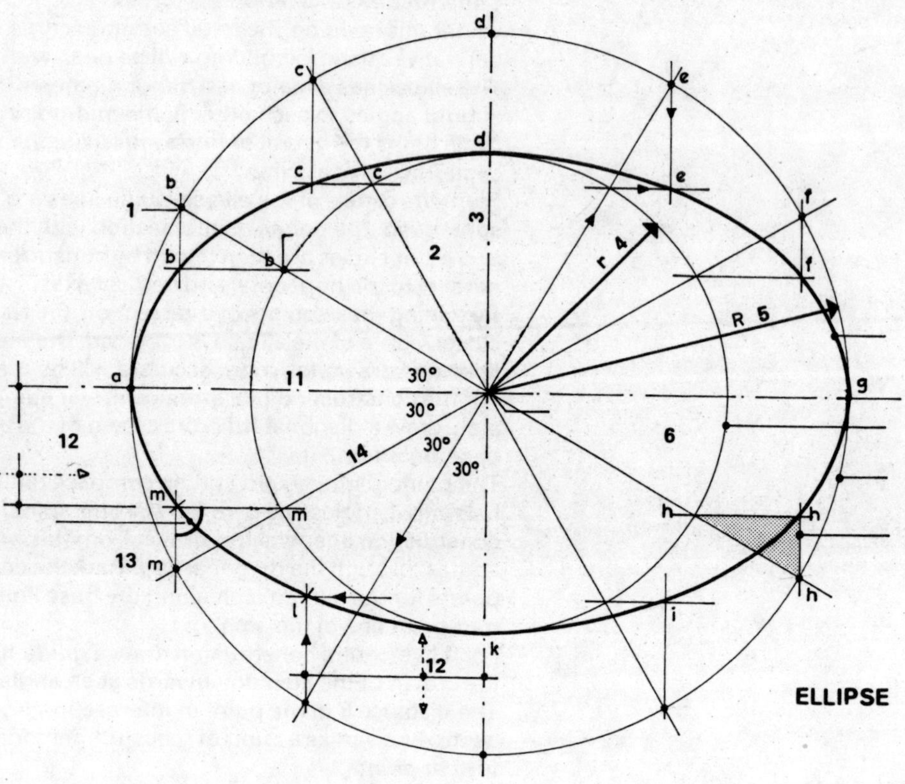

ELLIPSE

A 15

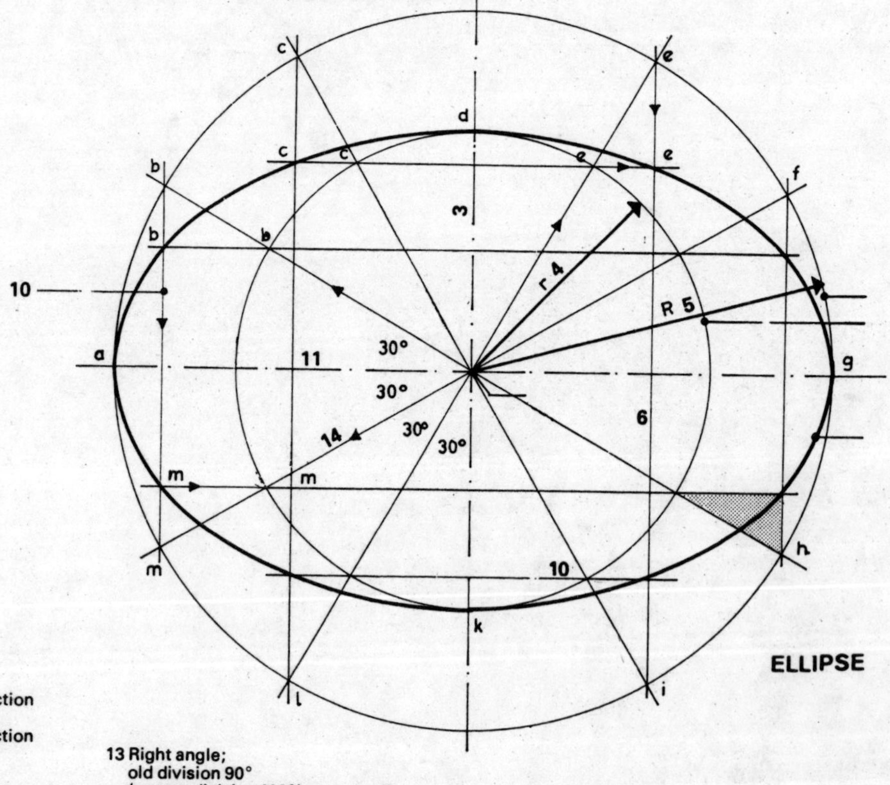

ELLIPSE

B 17

1 Point of intersection on outer circle
2 Point of intersection on inner circle
3 Vertical axis
4 Inner radius, r.
5 Outer radius, R
6 Mid point (centre)
7 Circumference of ellipse
8 Circumference of inner circle
9 Outer circle
10 Construction line
11 Horizontal axis
12 Parallel
13 Right angle; old division 90° (or new division 100°)
14 Guide line
15 Ellipse, constructional alternative A with guidelines (2×4)
16 Inner circle
17 Ellipse, constructional alternative B with guide and construction lines

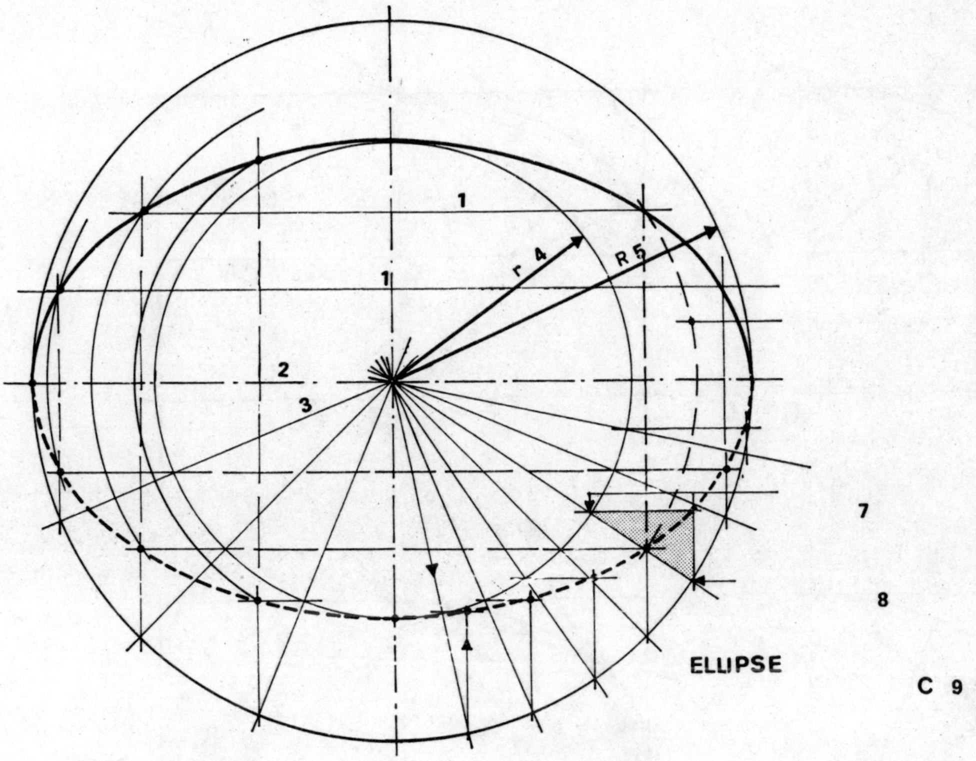

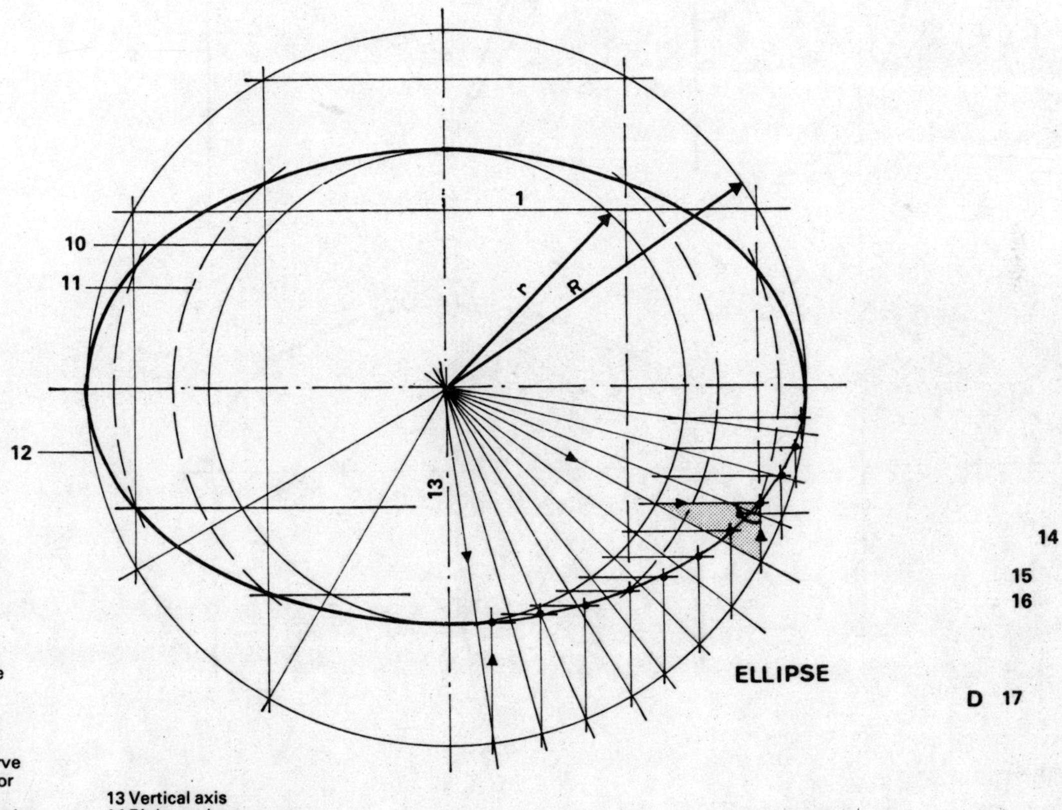

1 Construction line
2 Horizontal axis
3 Guide line
4 Inner radius r
5 Outer radius R
6 Construction curve for plotting mirror image
7 Points of intersection with inner circle
8 Points of intersection with outer circle
9 Ellipse, constructional alternative C with guide lines (4×7)
10 Inner circle
11 Construction curve
12 Outer circle
13 Vertical axis
14 Right angle (old division 90°) (or new division 100°)
15 O. D. = old division: (360° circle)
16 N. D. = new division: (400° circle)
17 Ellipse, constructional alternative D with guide lines (4×11)

3-Centre or compound arch

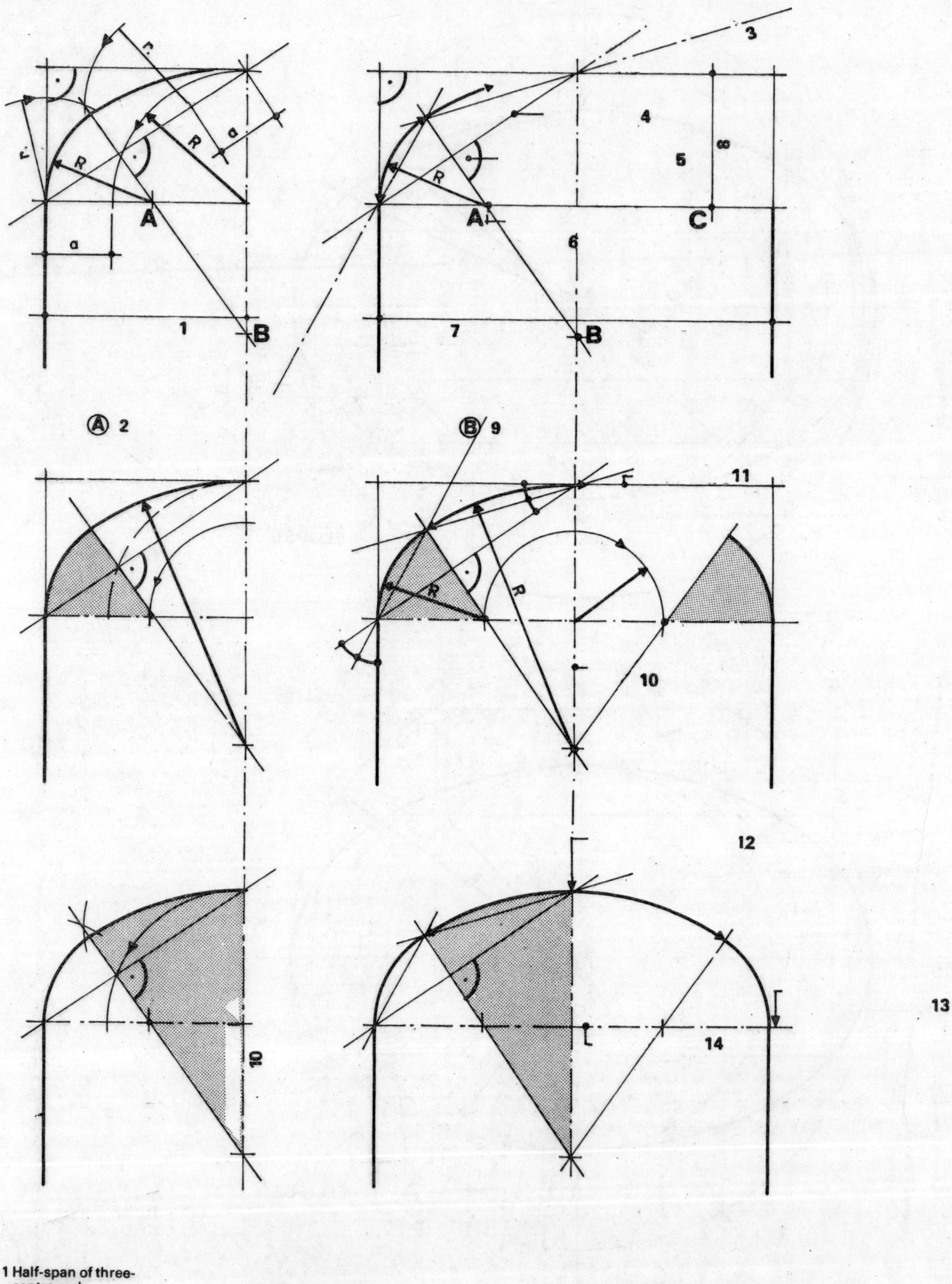

1 Half-span of three-centre arch
2 Constructional steps using compass, Alternative A
3 Construction line bisecting angle
4 Diagonal line
5 Right angle, 90°
6 Compass centre
7 Span of three-centre arch
8 Height of arch
9 Constructional steps: plotting by angles, alternative B
10 Centre line of arch
11 Guide line
12 Crown of arch
13 Base or abutment of three-centre arch
14 Base line

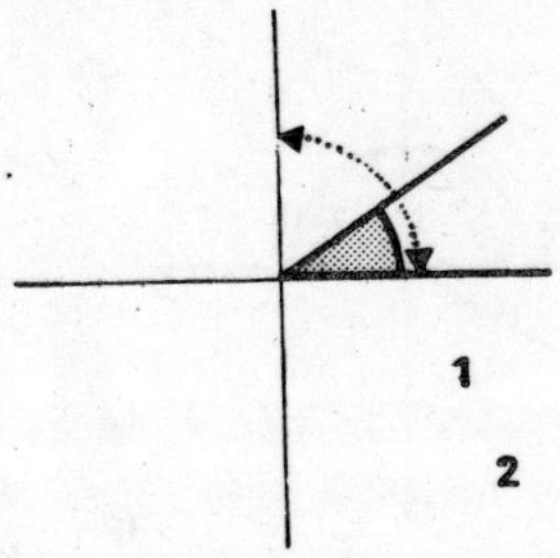

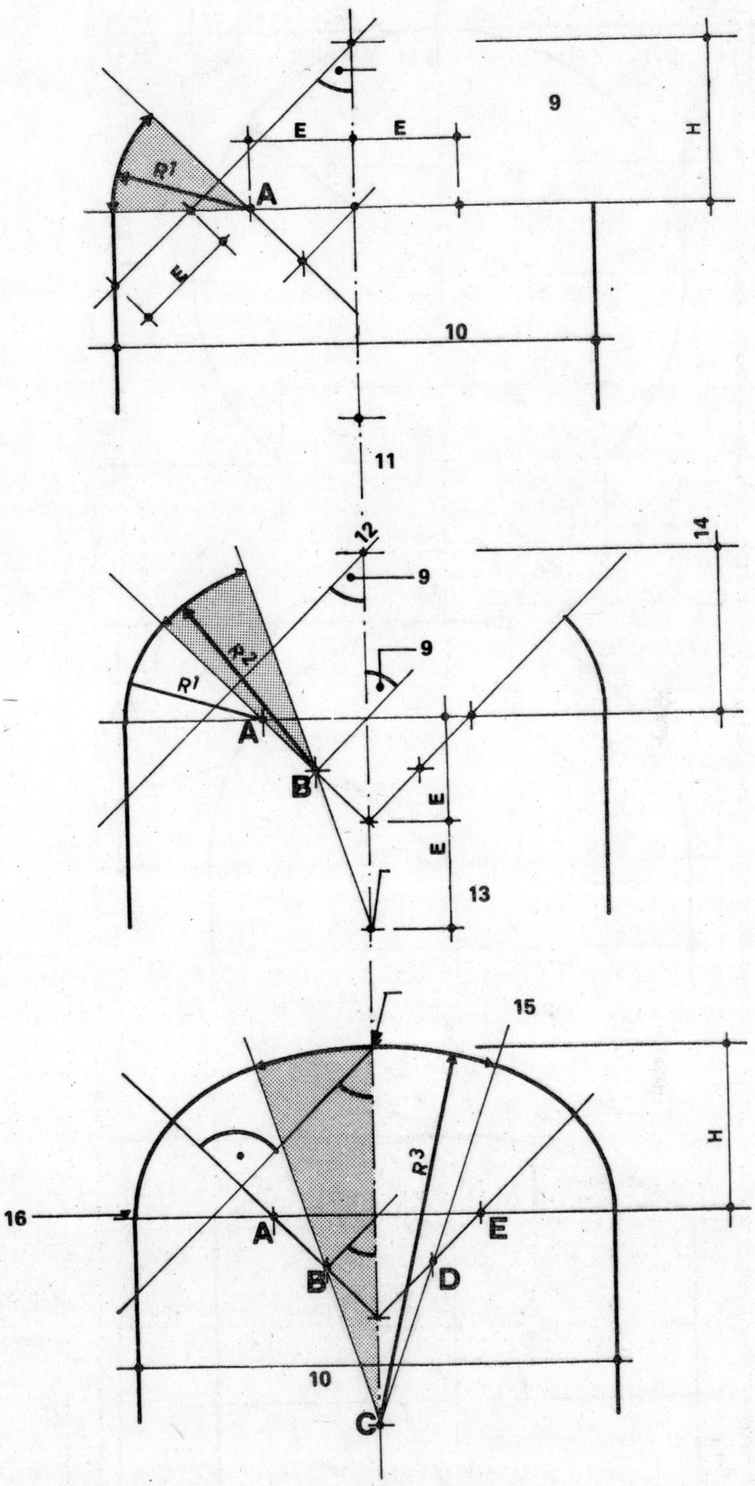

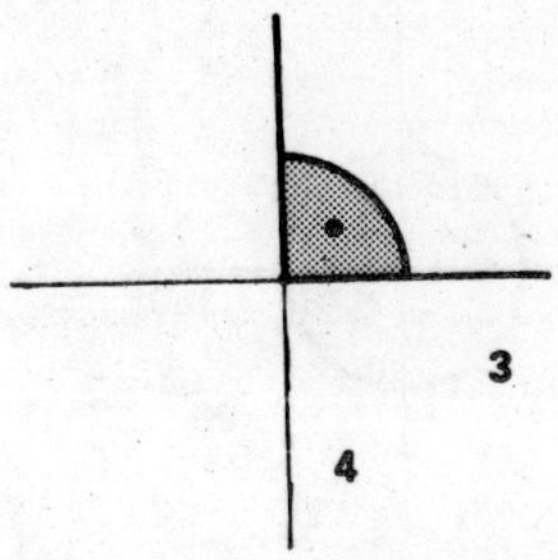

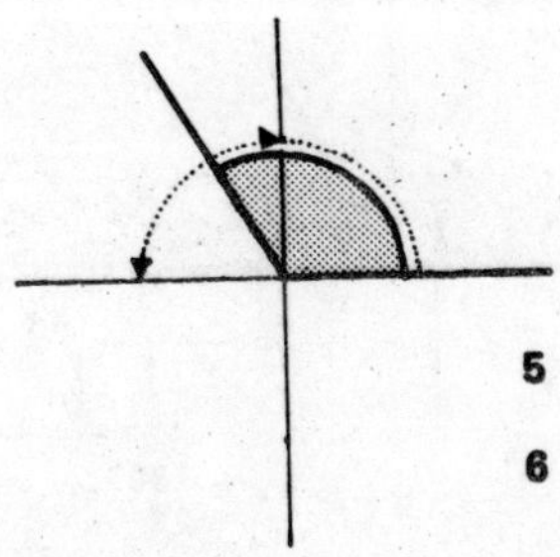

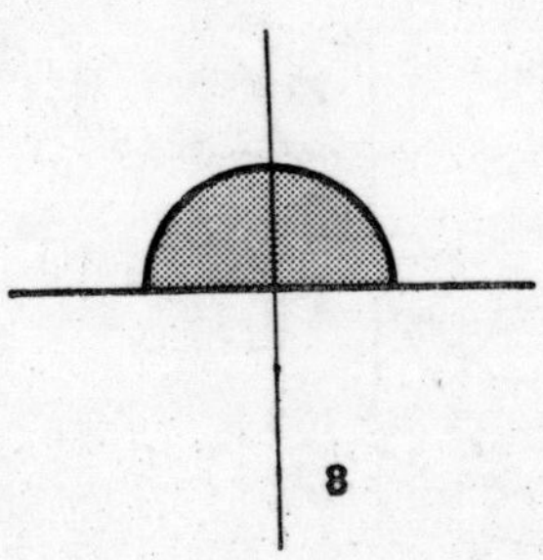

1 Acute angle
2 0°–90° OD
   or 0°–100° ND
3 Right angle
4 90° OD, 100° ND
5 Obtuse angle
6 90°–180° OD
   100°–200° ND
7 Flat or 180° angle
8 180° OD, 200° ND

9 Plotting angle
   (45° OD, 50° ND)
10 Span of compound arch
11 Compound arch,
   constructional steps
12 Guide line
13 Compass point
14 Height of arch = H
15 Crown of arch
16 Base of arch

Arch construction and names of angles

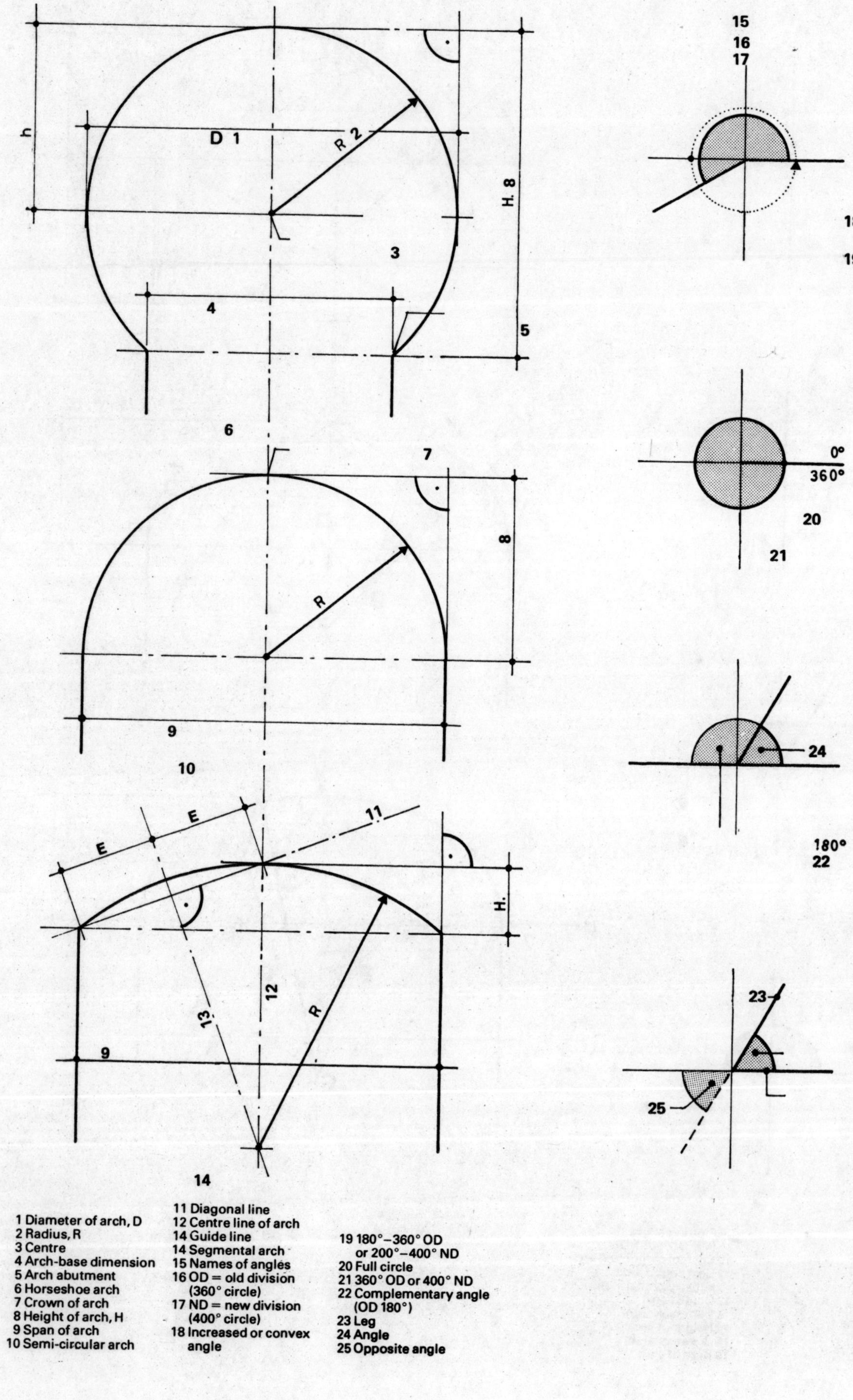

1 Diameter of arch, D
2 Radius, R
3 Centre
4 Arch-base dimension
5 Arch abutment
6 Horseshoe arch
7 Crown of arch
8 Height of arch, H
9 Span of arch
10 Semi-circular arch
11 Diagonal line
12 Centre line of arch
14 Guide line
14 Segmental arch
15 Names of angles
16 OD = old division (360° circle)
17 ND = new division (400° circle)
18 Increased or convex angle
19 180°–360° OD or 200°–400° ND
20 Full circle
21 360° OD or 400° ND
22 Complementary angle (OD 180°)
23 Leg
24 Angle
25 Opposite angle

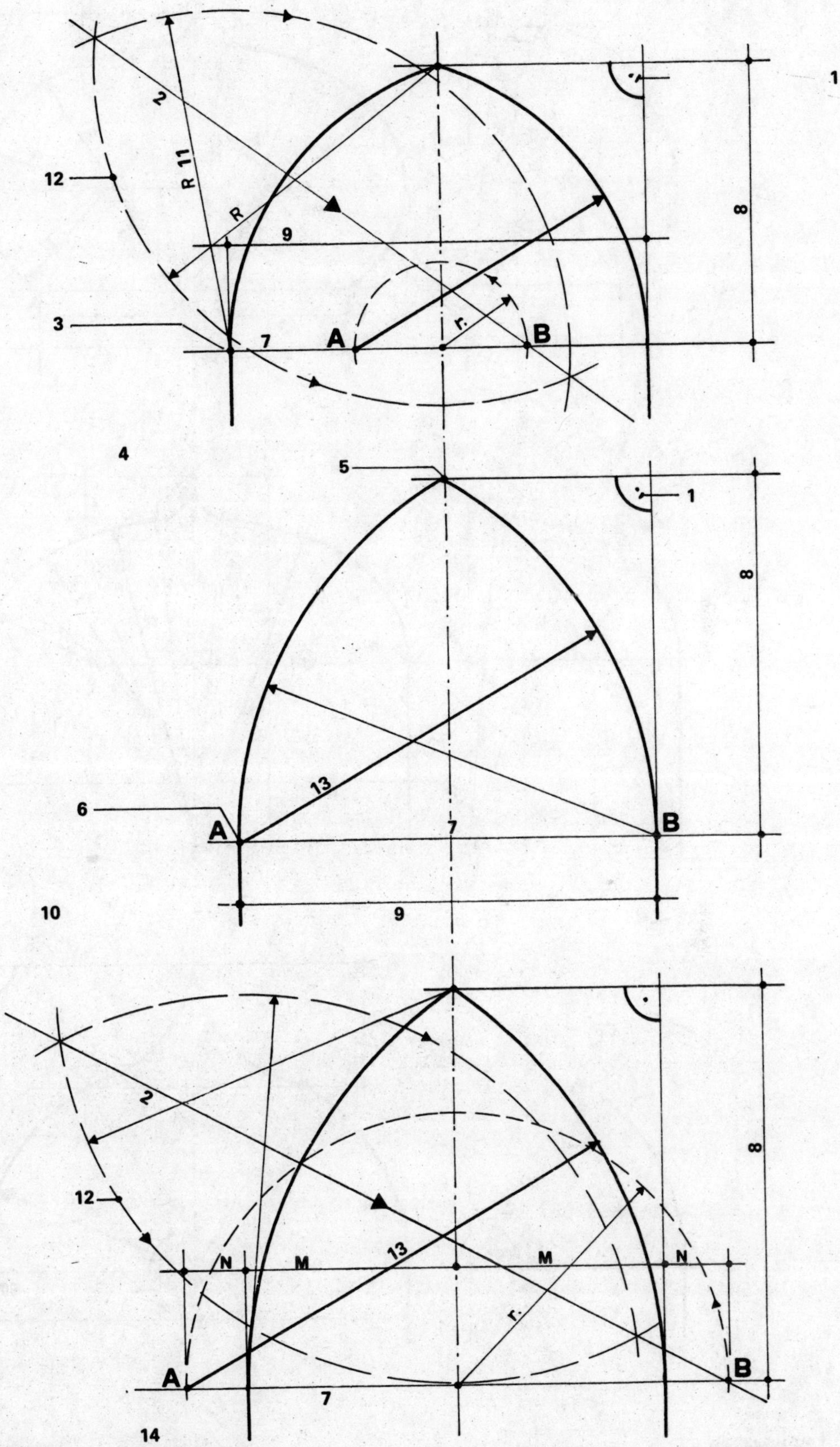

1 Right angle
2 Construction line
3 Compass point
4 Pointed arch with interior radius
5 Head of pointed arch
6 Base of pointed arch
7 Base line
8 Height of pointed arch = H
9 Span of pointed arch
10 Equilateral pointed arch (radius on curve)
11 Plotting radius
12 Guide curve
13 Radius of arch
14 Pointed arch with exterior radius

Arch variants

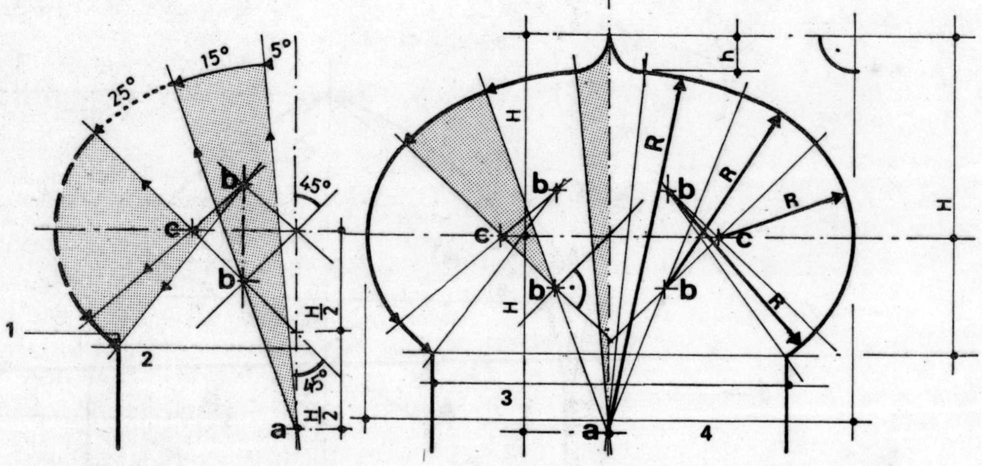

5

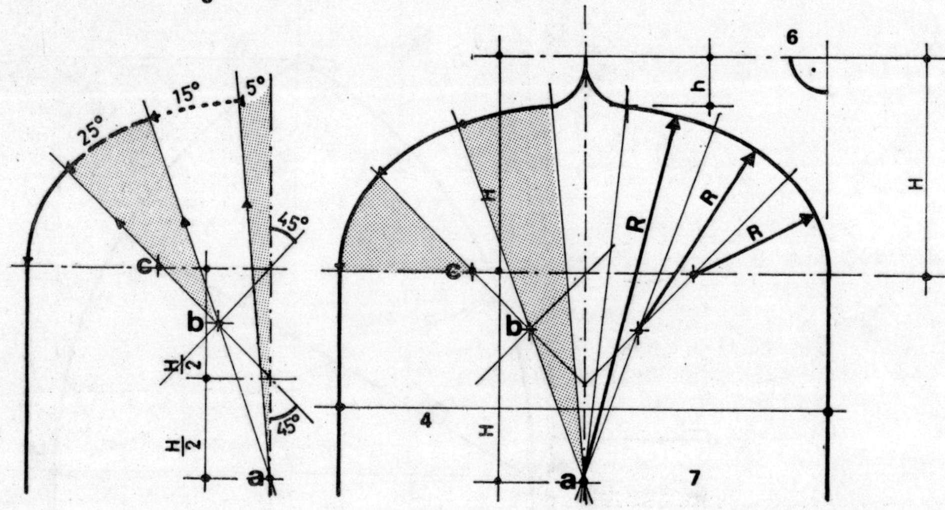

8

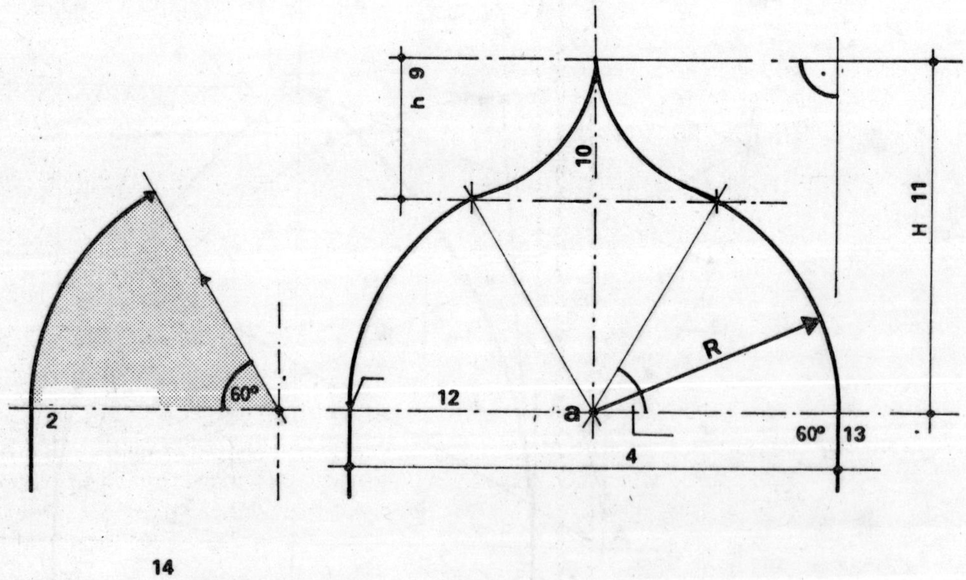

14

1 Arch abutment
2 Base line
3 Arch base dimension
4 Span of arch
5 Persian arch
6 Head of pointed arch
7 Compass point
8 Tudor arch
9 Height of head or point of arch = h
10 Centre line of arch
11 Height of arch = H
12 Arch abutment
13 Angle 60°
14 Ogee arch

Changes of scale

Where finite forms are to be reduced or enlarged in size, care should be taken in fixing the focal point that all radial construction lines can be drawn without creating confusing intersections. In the enlargement of an area or a volume, it is of advantage to fix the focal point in the middle of the sheet. When reducing in size, the focal point is best set outside the object. The distance should be 1 1/2 times to twice the side length of the area, in order that the reduction can be drawn clear of the original form.

After setting out the construction grid, the first parallel line should be drawn true to scale. Subsequent lines do not have to be measured out, but merely have to be kept parallel to the lines of the original. An accurate setting out will ensure that the first and last lines meet, creating a closed form.

As a check, it is advisable to measure diagonal lines to see whether they correspond to scale.

Plot enlargement, variant A

A

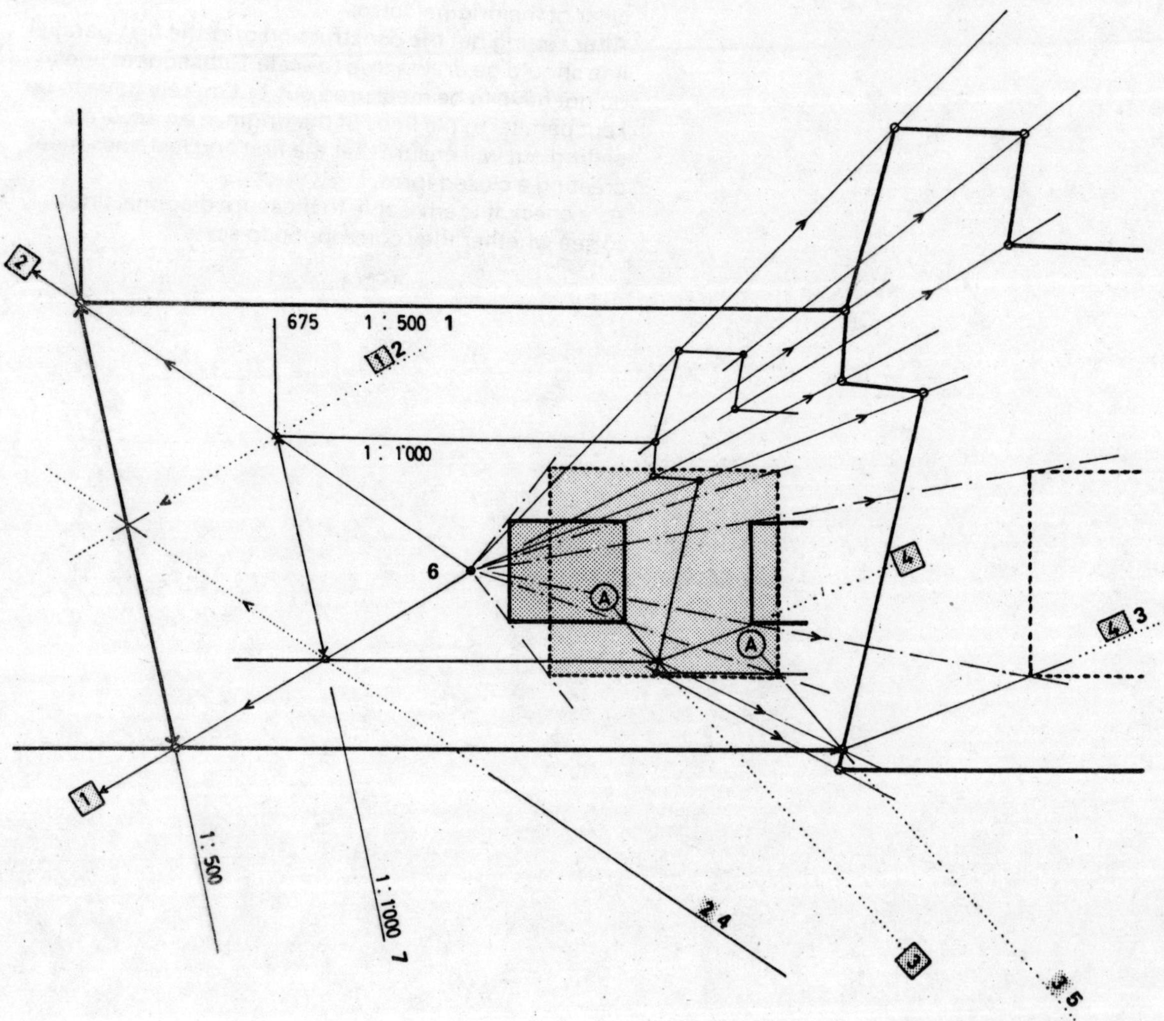

SP = 6

1 plot no. 675, scale 1 : 500
2 parallel ray to 1
3 parallel ray to 4
4 parallel ray to 2
5 parallel ray to 3
6 SP = ray point, selected at will but as central as possible
7 scale 1 : 1000

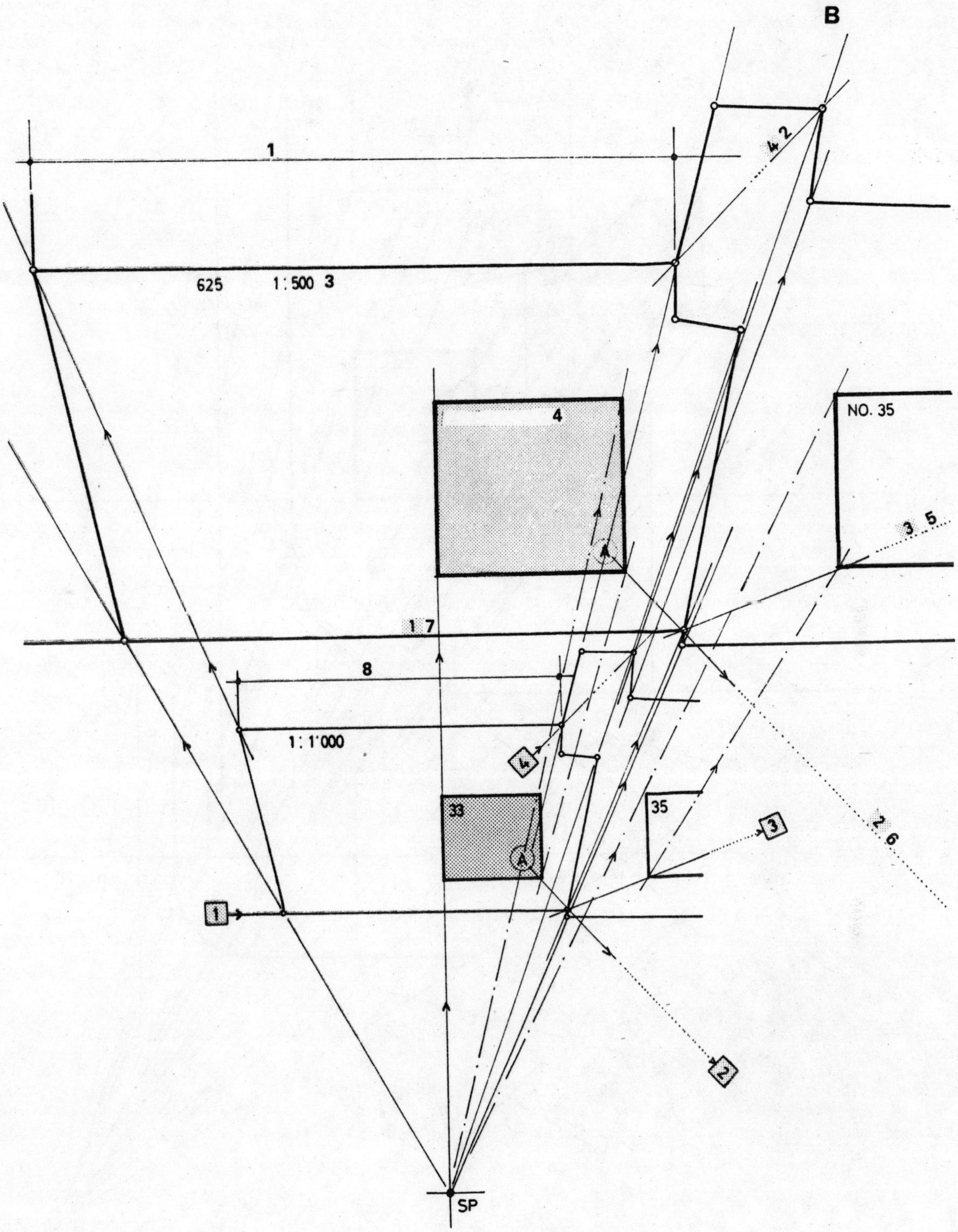

1 plotting length
2 parallel to 4
3 plot no. 625, scale 1 : 500
4 building No. 33
5 parallel ray to 3
6 parallel ray to 2
7 true to scale for distance 1
8 base length

Reduction or enlargement in size of building sites

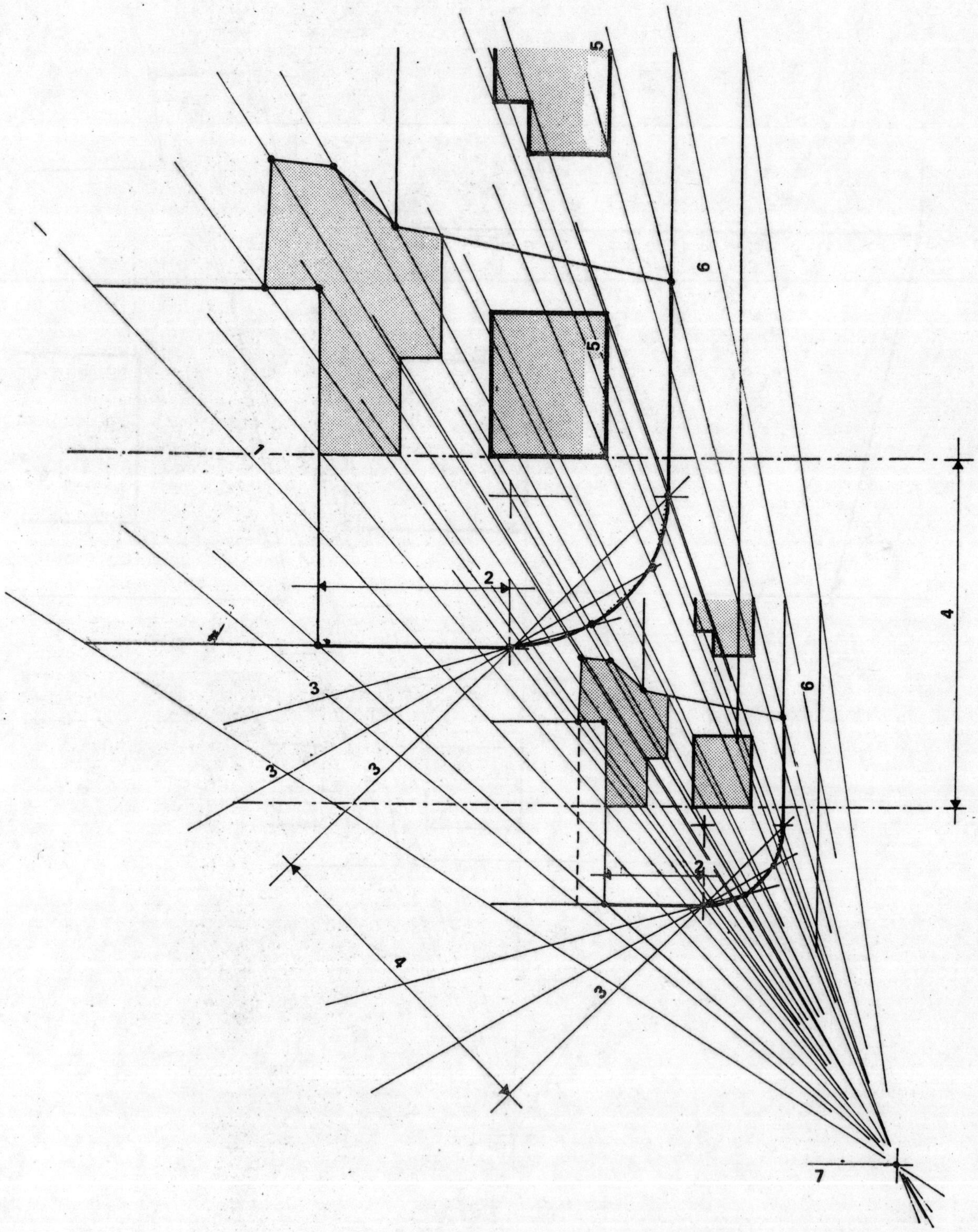

1 Radial construction line
2 Base measurement
3 Guide line
4 Parallel lines
5 House no.
6 Street
7 Focal point
(fixed where required)

Foundations

Choice of foundations is dependant on the load to be borne and the permissible load-bearing capacity of the ground. It is the function of foundations to prevent subsidence, by distributing the building load equally over the ground. In areas where frost is common, foundations should be taken down to a frost-free zone, 80-120 cm below ground level. In southern regions, where great fluctuations in temperature can occur, the same dimensions are applicable.

The cheapest and most common kinds of foundation are pad and strip foundations. With a relatively narrow bearing width and with a pressure distribution angle of less than 60° from the edge of the foundation projection, concrete of 150 kp/cm² nominal crushing strength (tamped or lean-mix concrete) is adequate. To keep the thickness of the foundation within economical limits, it is advisable to use reinforcement even with these kinds of foundation. Where greater loads and poorer ground occur, the choice of a raft foundation is essential. In the event of a flat slab foundation still not being strong enough, and where even soil consolidation with concrete injection is not satisfactory, pile foundations may be the only solution. Piles transmit the load to the ground as end bearing or friction piles.

The following pile types can be distinguished: the insitu pile, bored or driven direct into the ground; and pre-fabricated piles, which can be of wood or reinforced concrete. The latter type of pile is independant of the water table, but where aggressive, acidic water is likely to occur, a protective concrete additive is necessary.

Foundations: depths and types of construction

1:20/50

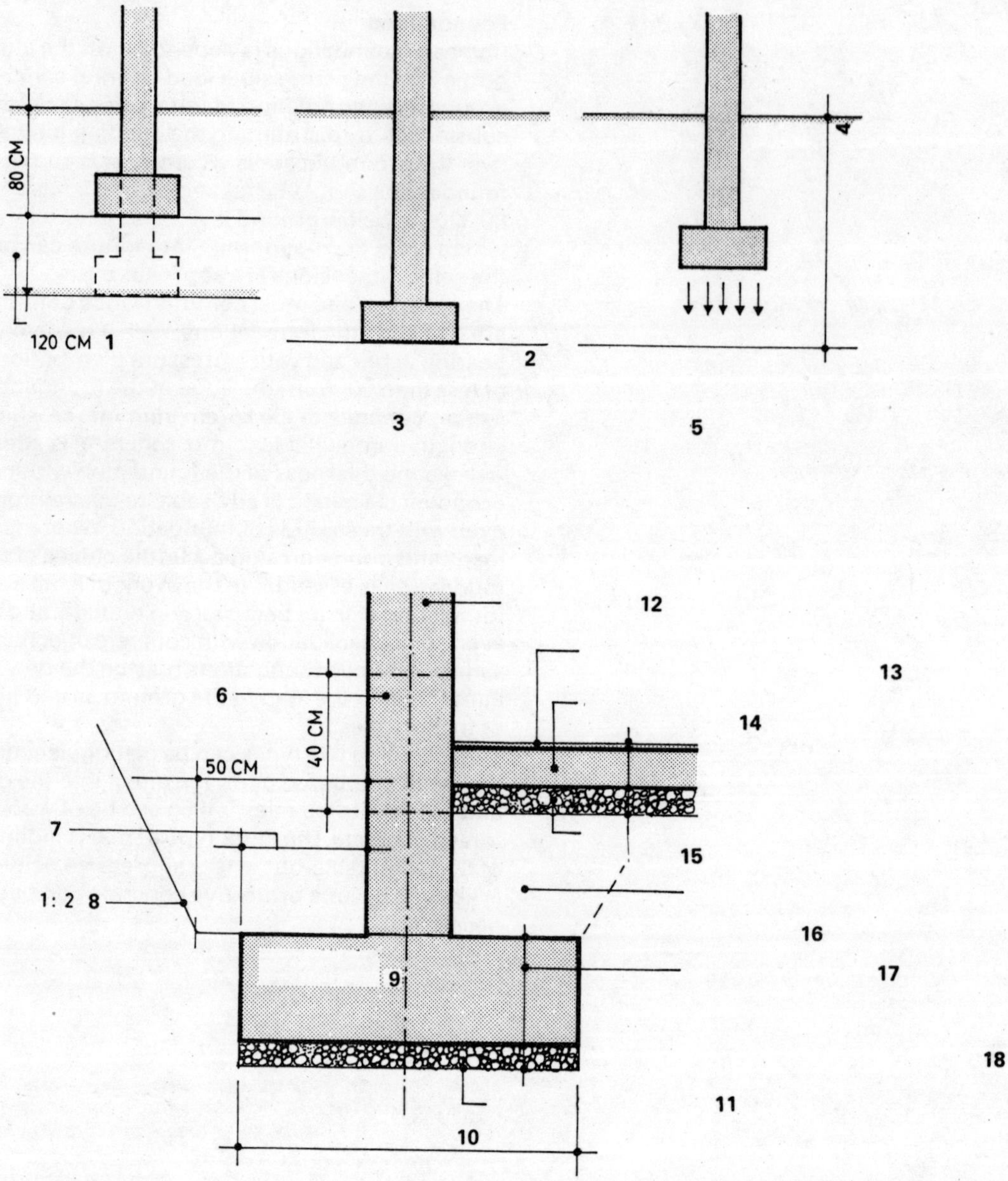

1 Frost zone, up to 120 cm deep
2 Load-bearing excavated bed
3 Correctly laid foundations
4 Load-bearing capacity of soil insufficient
5 Wrongly laid foundations
6 . . . Additive against rising moisture. Thickness of wall × ca. 40 cm height
7 Foundation projection
8 Sand or gravel soil, slope of excavation 1:2
9 Reinforced foundation
10 Foundation width
11 Levelling layer (hardcore, blinding)
12 Concrete wall
13 2 cm cement and sand screed laid on concrete when green
14 Concrete floor slab 10- . . . cm (possibly reinforced)
15 Hardcore bed 5- . . . cm
16 Gravel back-fill or compressible excavated material
17 Foundation thickness
18 Reinforced concrete foundation, commonest form

1:20

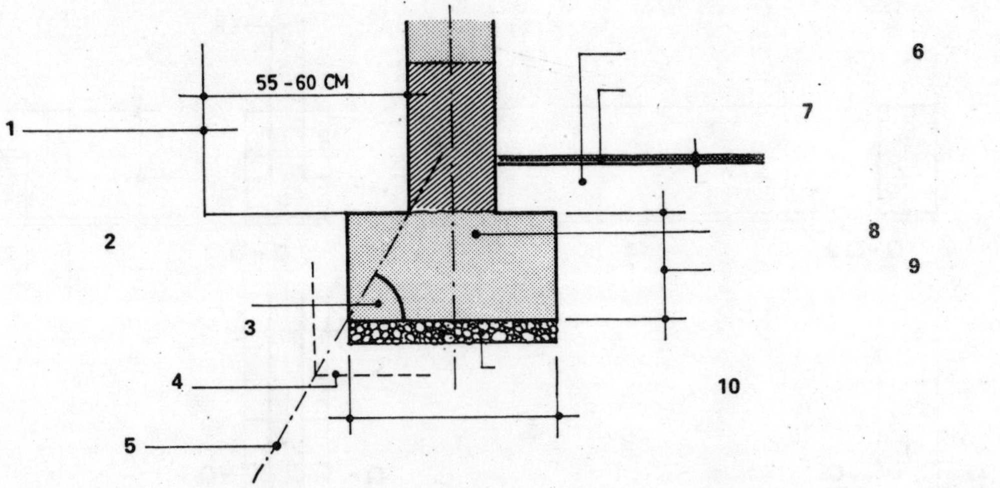

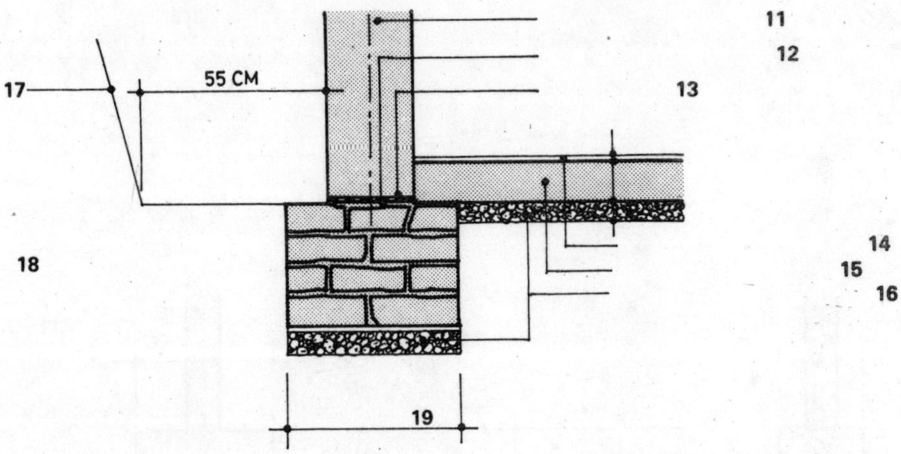

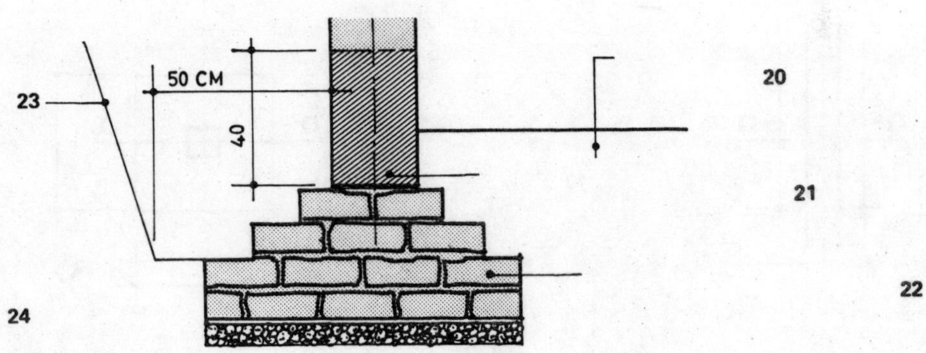

1 Firm soil, sides of excavation vertical up to 2 m depth
2 Tamped concrete foundation
3 60° angle
4 Possible foundation line
5 Pressure distribution line
6 Natural bottom, compacted
7 River gravel up to 4 mm diameter
8 Construction joint
9 Foundation thickness
10 Hardcore or mass concrete layer
11 Concrete external wall
12 Mortar bed
13 Bitumen felt d.p.c.
14 2 cm cement screed
15 12 cm concrete slab
16 Lean concrete blinding
17 Dry clay soil, sides of excavation 1:4
18 Rubble foundation
19 50 cm min.
20 Natural bottom, levelled and rammed
21 ... Additive against rising dampness
22 Rubble, only stones of large area used
23 Gravel soil, sides of excavation 1:3
24 Rubble foundation with footings

Beam, strip and pad foundations

1:50

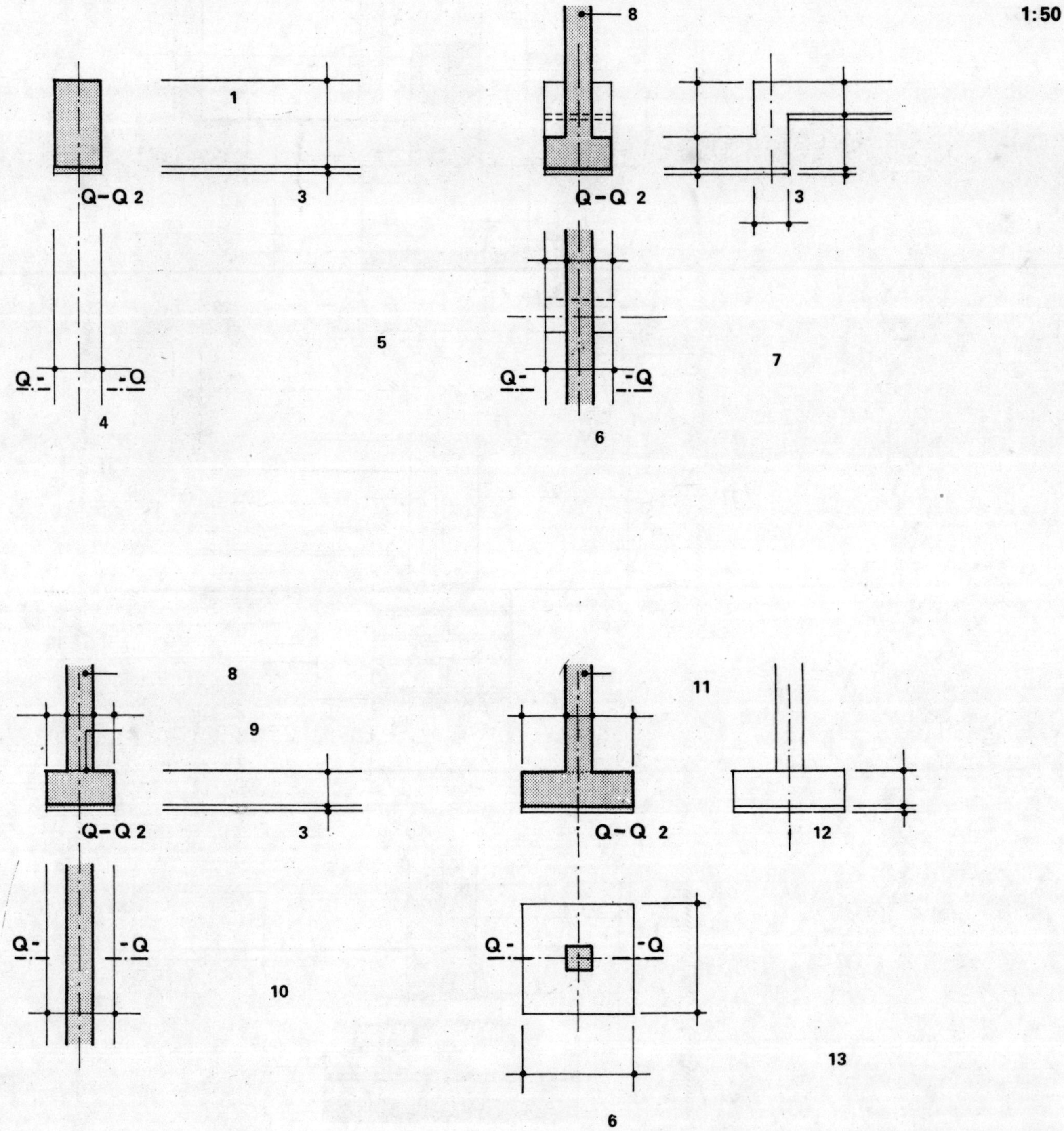

1 Beam
2 Section Q – Q
3 Elevation
4 Plan
5 Beam foundation
6 Plan view
7 Stepped foundation
8 Concrete wall
9 Construction joint
10 Strip foundation
11 Column (pier)
12 Elevation
13 Pad foundation

1:50

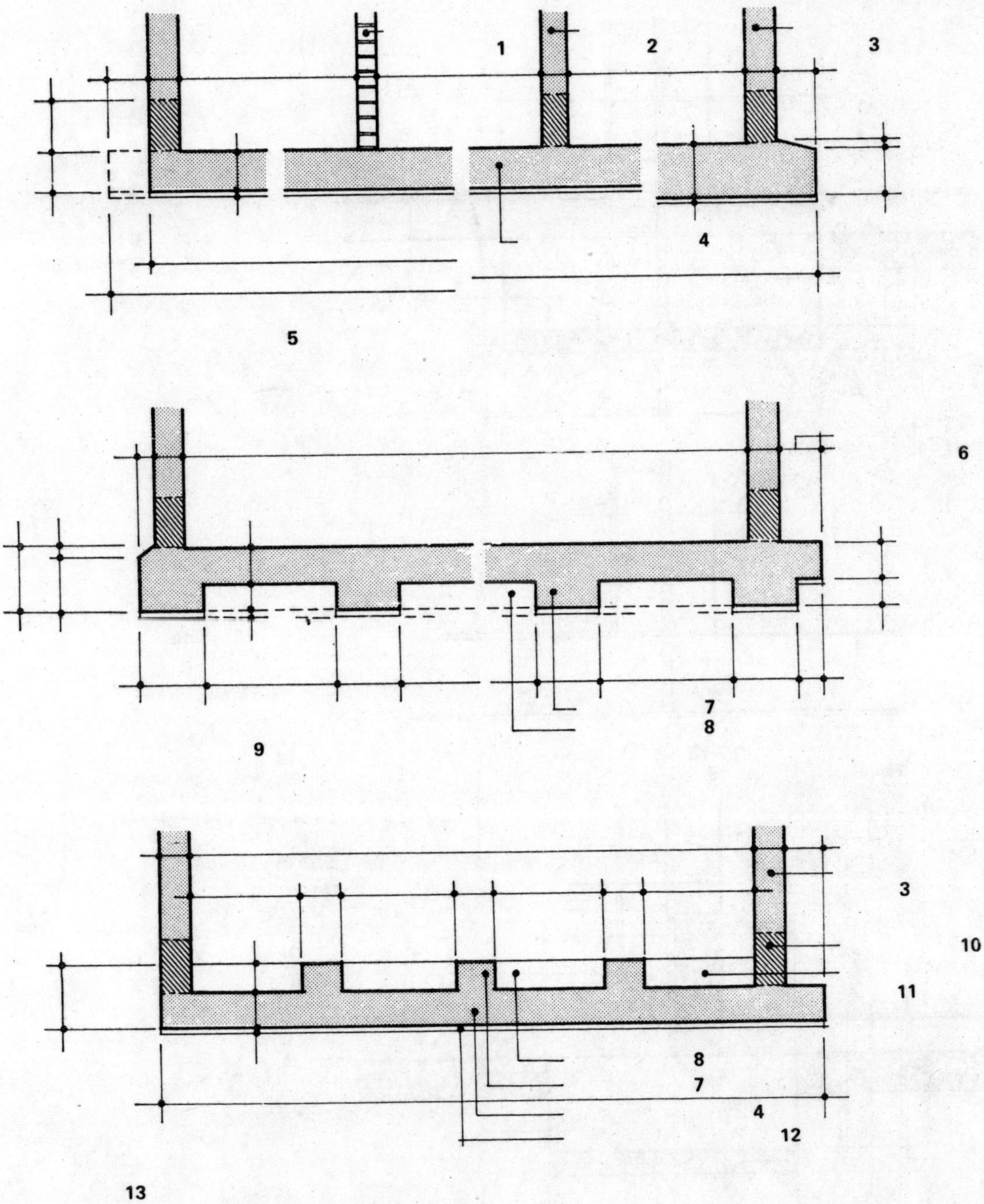

1 Sand-lime brick
internal wall
2 Concrete internal wall
3 Concrete external wall
4 Foundation slab
5 Raft foundation
6 Foundation projection
7 Longitudinal rib
8 Laterial rib
9 Raft foundation
with ribs on underside
10 . . . Additive
11 Lean concrete filling
12 Levelling layer
13 Raft foundation
with rib lattice on top

Expansion joints in foundations

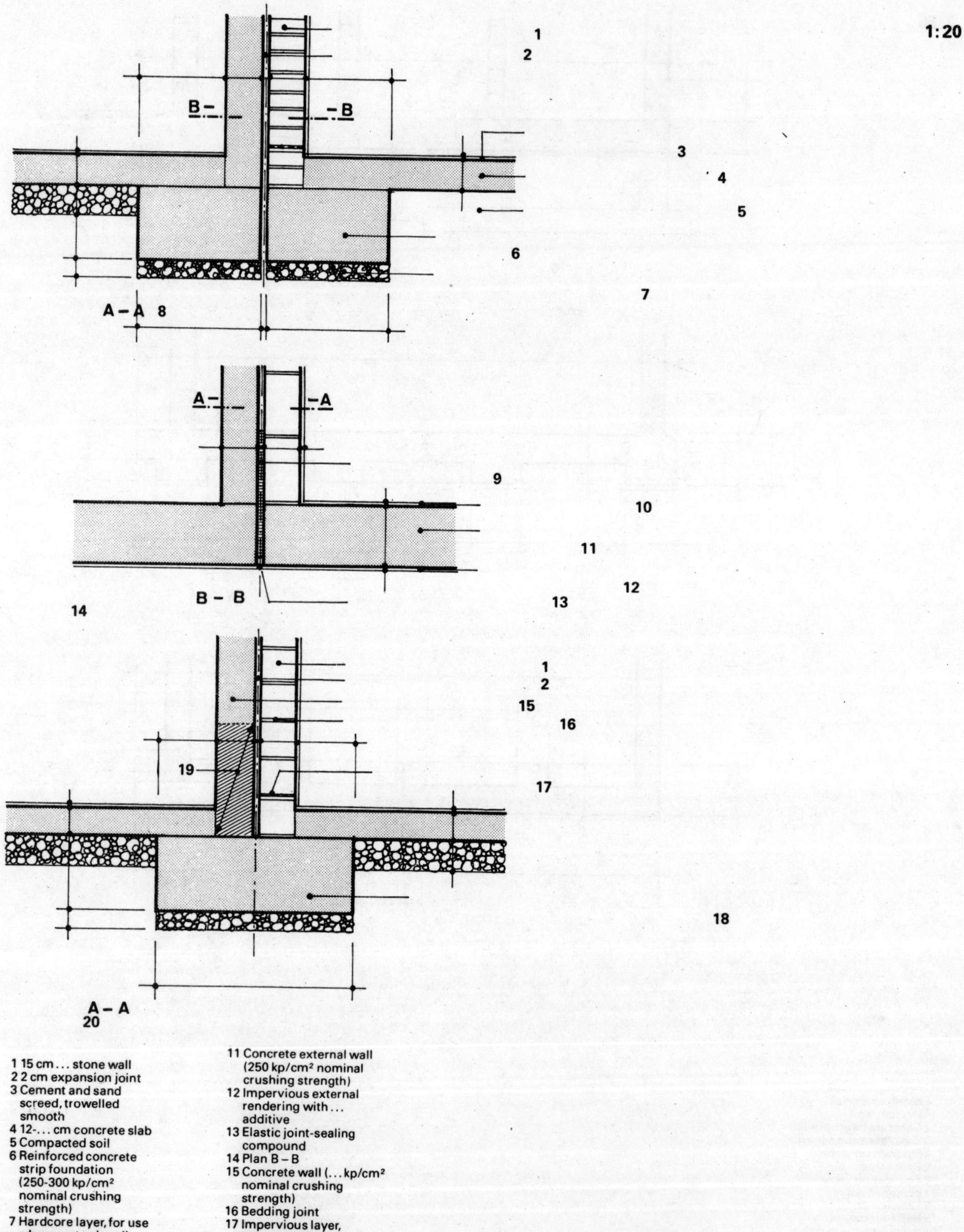

1 15 cm . . . stone wall
2 2 cm expansion joint
3 Cement and sand screed, trowelled smooth
4 12-. . . cm concrete slab
5 Compacted soil
6 Reinforced concrete strip foundation (250-300 kp/cm² nominal crushing strength)
7 Hardcore layer, for use where wet sub-soil
8 Section A – A
9 2 cm insulation board strip 50 cm wide for full height of wall
10 1,5 cm wall plaster
11 Concrete external wall (250 kp/cm² nominal crushing strength)
12 Impervious external rendering with . . . additive
13 Elastic joint-sealing compound
14 Plan B – B
15 Concrete wall (. . . kp/cm² nominal crushing strength)
16 Bedding joint
17 Impervious layer, bitumen felt d.p.c.
18 Foundation, common support, – only where expansion joint
19 . . Additive
20 Section A – A, alternative

1:20

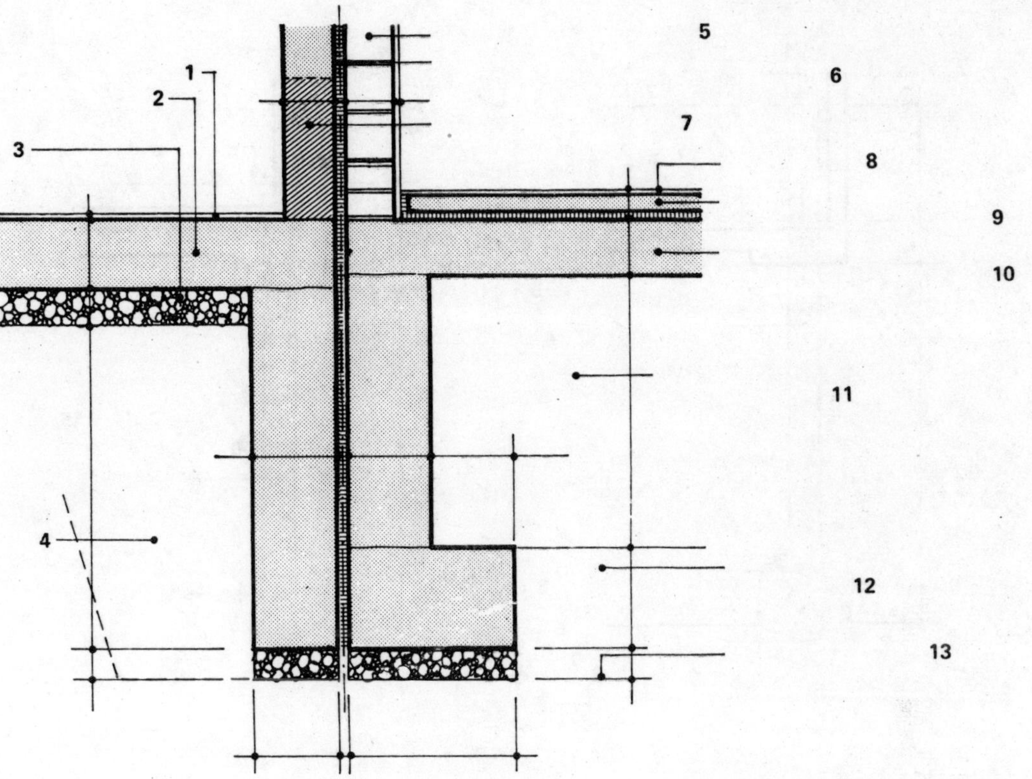

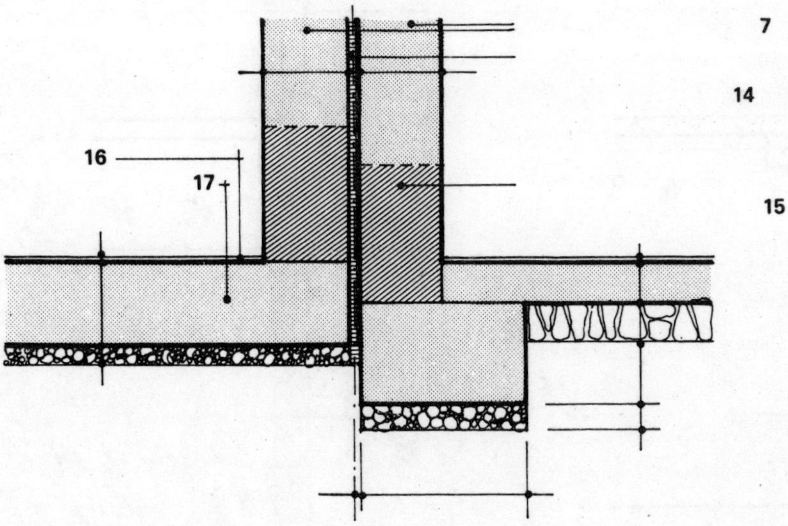

1 Cement and sand screed
2 Reinforced concrete foundation slab
3 Blinding (pit gravel) or lean concrete
4 Back-fill or pit gravel
5 ... cm brick wall
6 2,5 cm expansion joint with 2 cm insulating board insert, K-value 0....
7 Concrete wall (250 kp/cm² nom. crushing strength)
8 Floor finish
9 Floated screed
10 Concrete slab (350 kp/cm² nom. crushing strength) or hollow tile slab
11 Ventilated void, height 80-120 cm
12 Sub-soil, back-filled and compacted
13 Load-bearing sub-soil
14 3 cm expansion joint with 2.5 cm insulating board impervious layer against second wall
15 ... Additive and battering concrete (... kp/cm² nom. crushing strength
16 Cement and sand screed
17 Reinforced raft foundation

Timber or concrete pile foundations

1:100

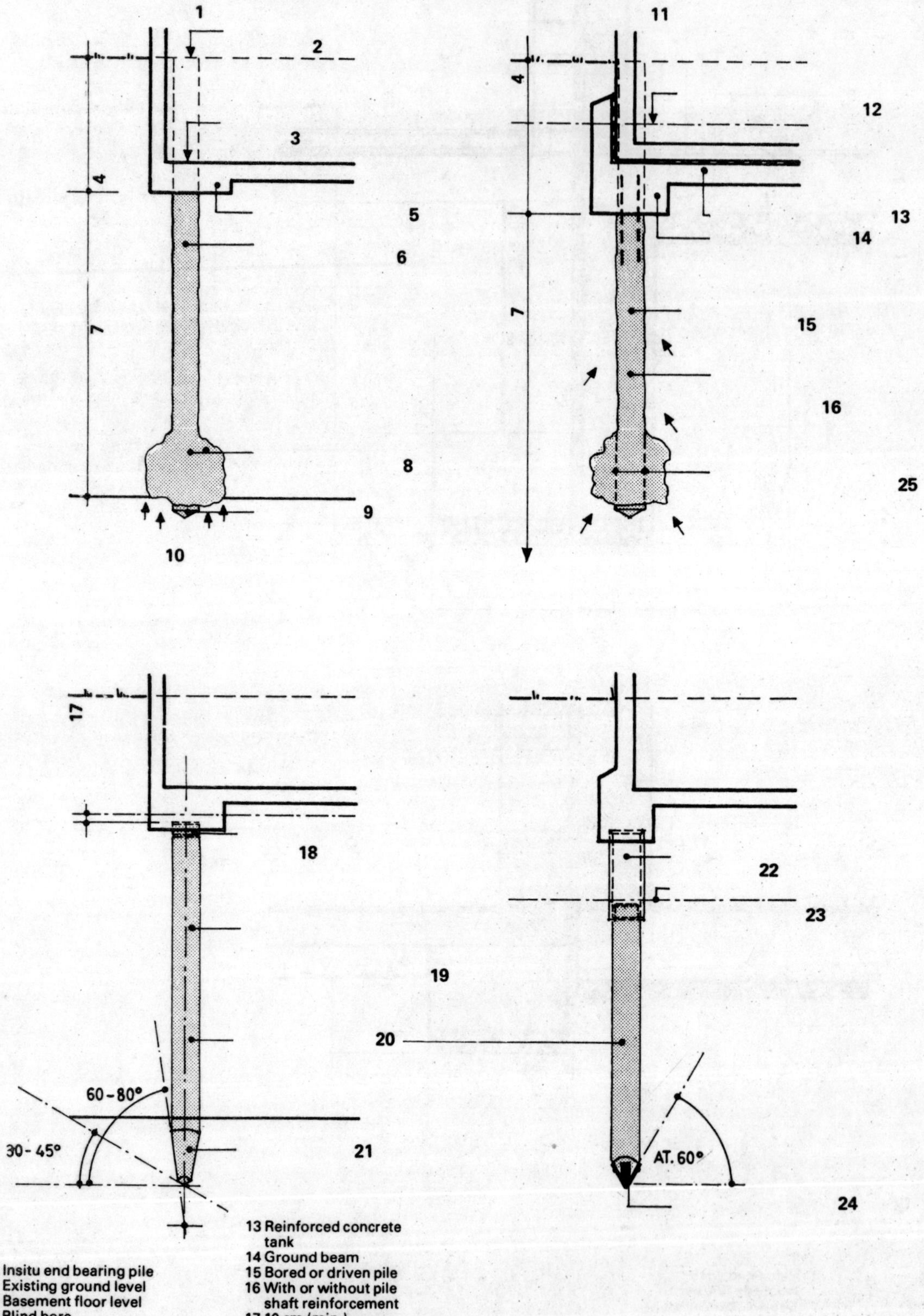

1 Insitu end bearing pile
2 Existing ground level
3 Basement floor level
4 Blind bore
5 Pile cap
6 Pile shaft or case
7 Sub-soil with poor load-bearing capacity
8 Bulb foot
9 Toe of pile
10 Sub-soil with good load-bearing capacity
11 Insitu friction pile
12 Water table, highest level
13 Reinforced concrete tank
14 Ground beam
15 Bored or driven pile
16 With or without pile shaft reinforcement
17 10 cm (min.)
18 Steel cap or helmet
19 Timber pile of oak or larch, 5 - 10 m long = 20 - 25 cm dia.
20 Timber pile
21 Timber pile toe
22 Concrete pile cap
23 Water table, lowest level
24 Steel shoe to pile
25 Precast pile, without bulb foot, reinforced

Insulation Against Capillary Moisture

Exterior walls lying on the earth can be insulated against capillary moisture at the floor connection with a sealing additive and increased concrete proportioning (depending on the brand). (Do not use corrosive additives which could damage the reinforcement or the sand/cement mixture or which could affect the setting process!) Installation height approx. 40 cm per wall thickness. The same execution should be used for all concrete interior walls.

In extreme cases, additional precautions in the ceiling area are necessary. If water may penetrate at wall height, the entire surface must be compacted. Outer sides of the exterior walls are to be covered with a water-proof cement coating or asphalt paint, all pockets in the concrete are to be filled in flush before applying this coating.

Brickwork (dividing) partition walls should be protected from capillary moisture with a layer of cardboard approx. 3 mm thick directly above the concrete or the 1 or 2-layer stone floor. The cardboard panels should overlap 10 cm. A smooth cement base is necessary to protect the cardboard. Two layers of cardboard used together must have the same material quality as tarred board.

Coated, continuous moisture shielding in floors fulfills its purpose only if it forms a closed unit with the brickwork insulation.

If the lower-floor rooms lie completely or partially in ground water, a continuous concrete base up to the appropriate height is unavoidable. The interior of the basin must also be sealed with continuous asbestos felt or mastic asphalt. This must be applied before the actual (lower) cellar floor is placed.
If these guidelines are followed, grey mold and moisture-saturated walls can be avoided.

Pavement light details

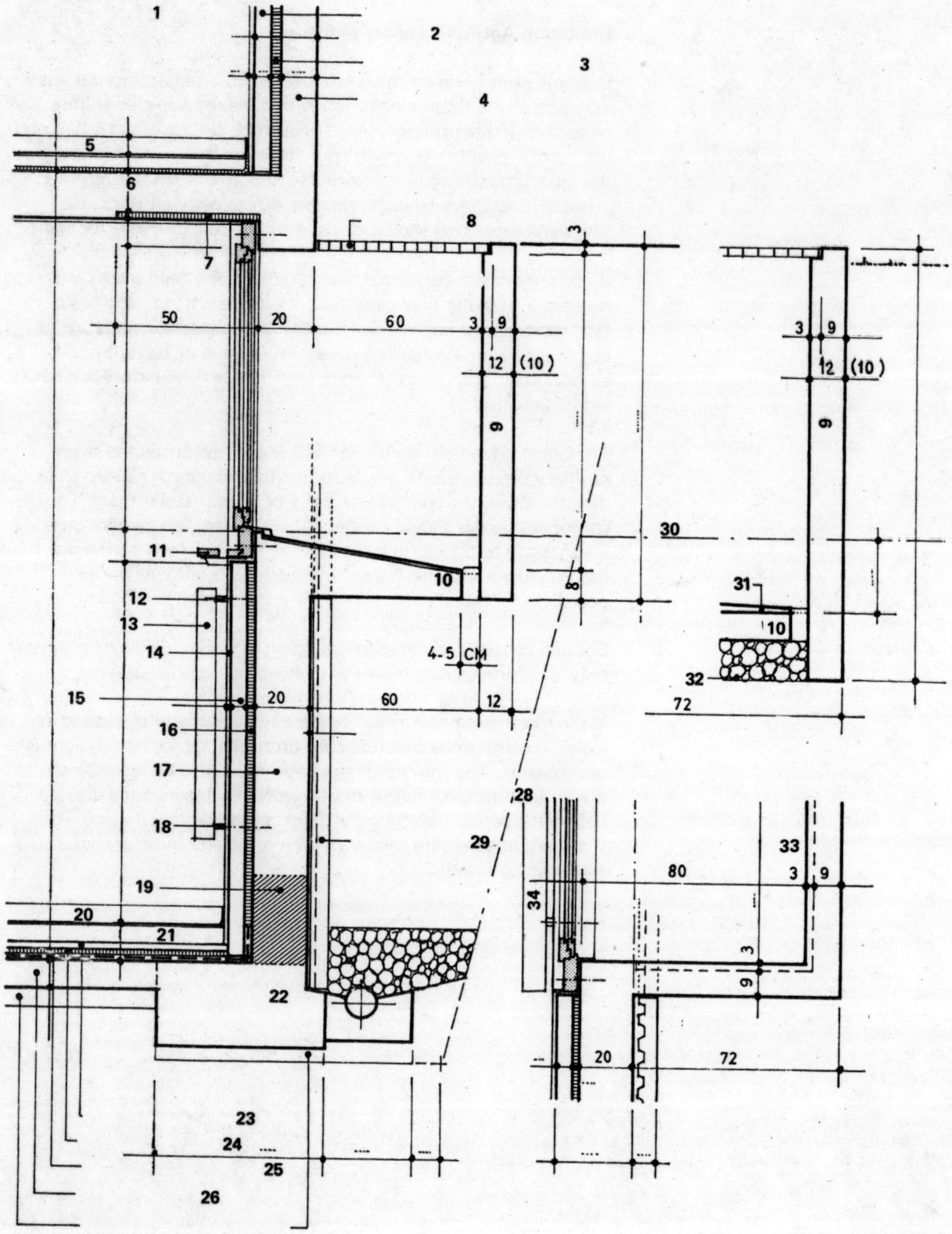

1 ground floor
2 . . . lightweight panel
3 . . . insulation panel
4 exposed concrete
5 base course
6 concrete floor
7 . . . insulation panel
8 grating
9 wall
10 concrete floor
11 molding, . . . wood
12 retainer
13 heating element
14 interior wall plaster
15 . . . lightweight panel
16 . . . insulation panel
17 concrete PC . . . normal concrete
18 radiator mount
19 . . . additive
20 base course
21 subfloor
22 strip footing
23 cement coating
24 cork insulation panel
25 asbestos felt layer
26 concrete floor
27 lean (tamped) concrete substructure, PC 100 (poss. 150) normal
28 2 x asphalt (cross coating) on smooth surface, or water-tight cement coating 2 cm
29 filter slab, system . . .
30 upper edge of breast
31 cement coating on slope
32 gravel bed
33 light shaft
34 moldings

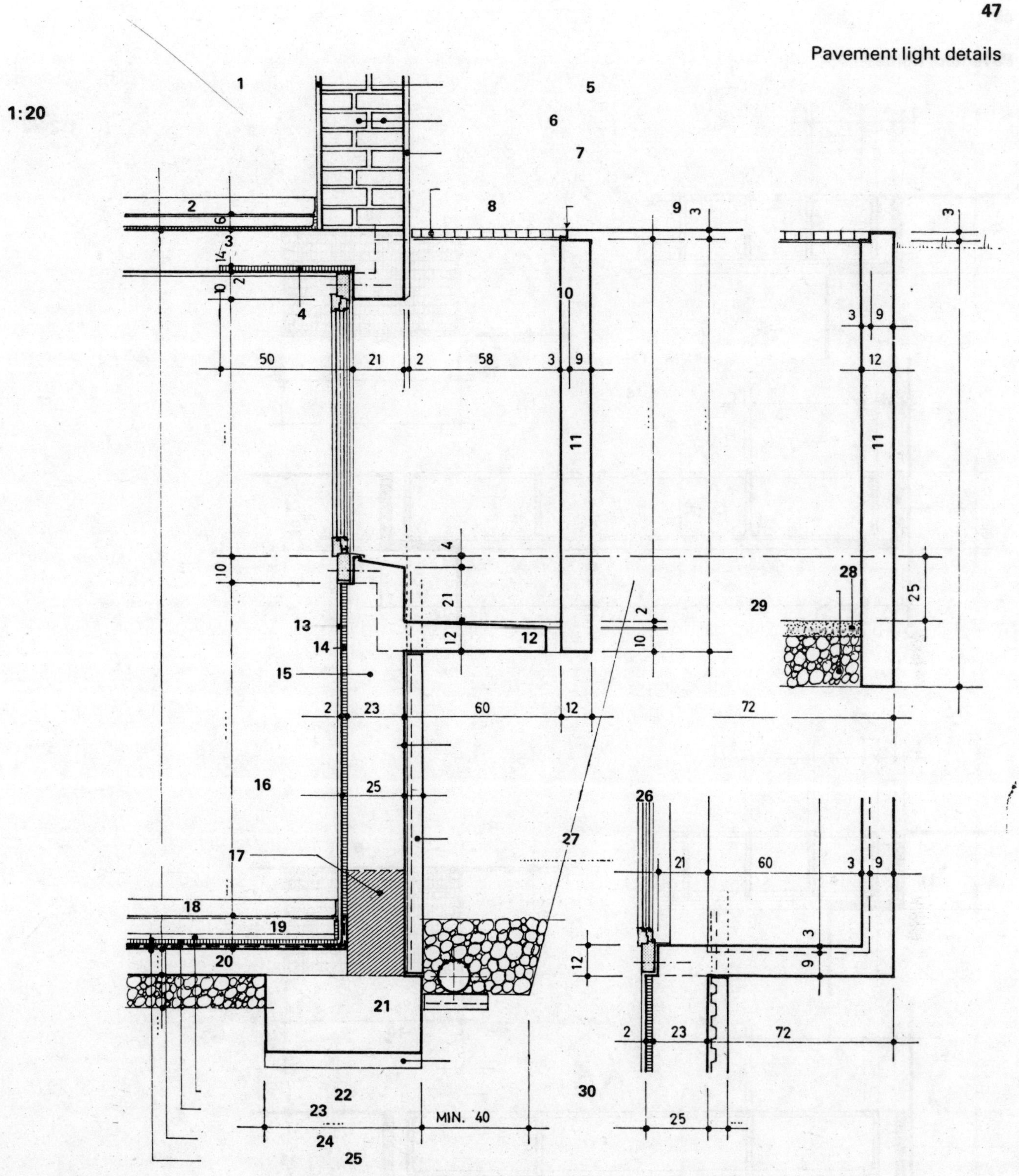

1 ground floor
2 base course
3 concrete floor
4 . . . insulation panels
5 interior wall plaster
6 brickwork
7 exterior plaster
8 light-shaft grating
9 rabbet frame
10 element - light shaft
11 wall
12 floor
13 wall plaster 0.5 - 1,5 cm
14 . . . insulation panels
15 concrete PC . . . normal concrete
16 basement
17 . . . additive
18 base course
19 subfloor
20 concrete flooring
21 strip footing
22 cement coating
23 cork insul. panels
24 mastic asphalt
25 separation layers
26 2 x asphalt (cross coating) on smooth surface, or water-tight cement coating
27 filter panel, system . . .
28 round gravel 3 cm
29 ballast bed 22 cm
30 lean concrete substructure PC 100 normal (poss. PC 150 normal)

Pavement lights

1:20/2

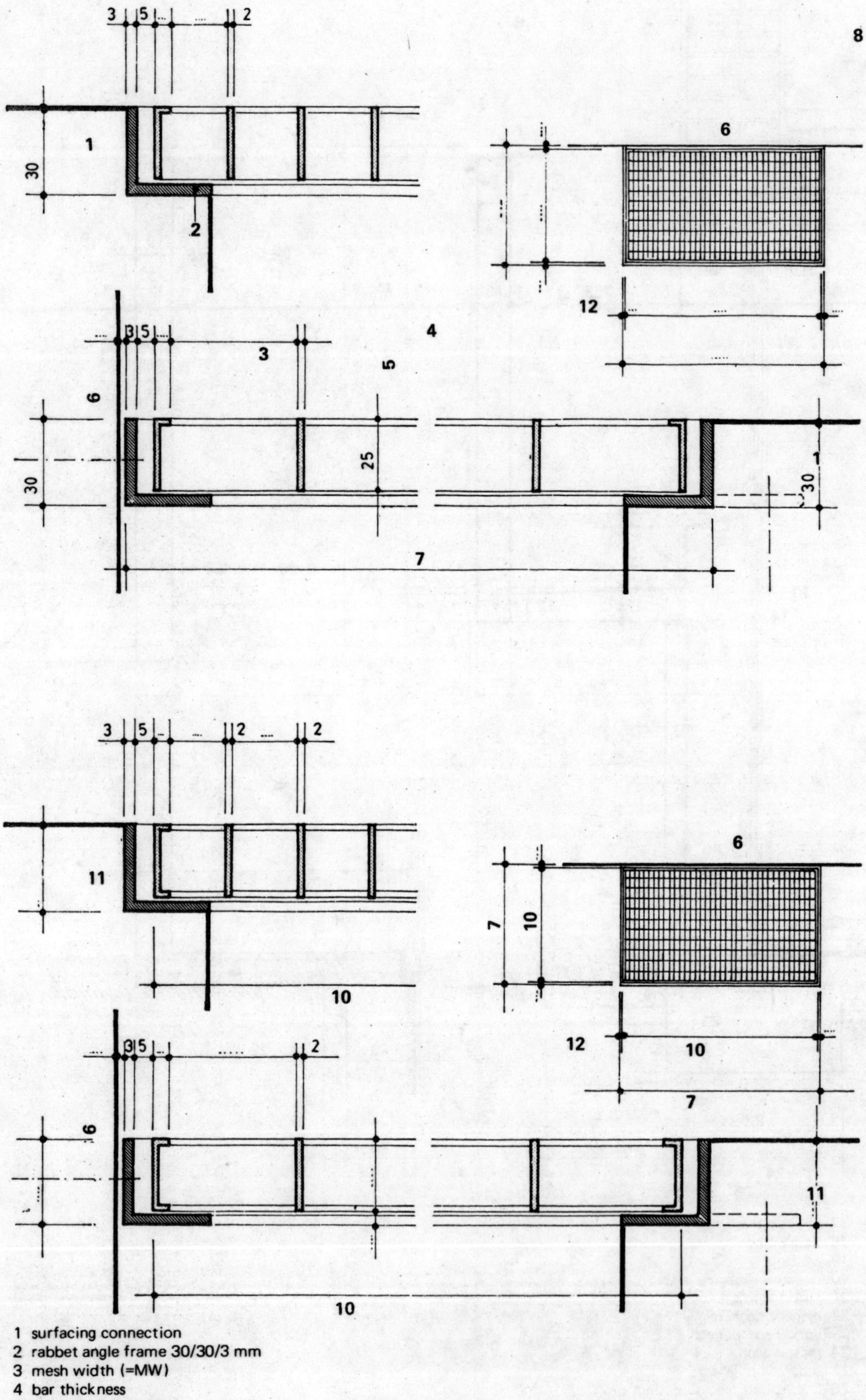

1 surfacing connection
2 rabbet angle frame 30/30/3 mm
3 mesh width (=MW)
4 bar thickness
5 grating height (=RH)
6 wall connection
7 rabbet angle, outer dimension (=FAM)
8 with angle iron frame - mounting
9 with c-section frame
10 grating outer dimension (=RAM)
11 surfacing or crest connection
12 grating, top view

1:20/2

8

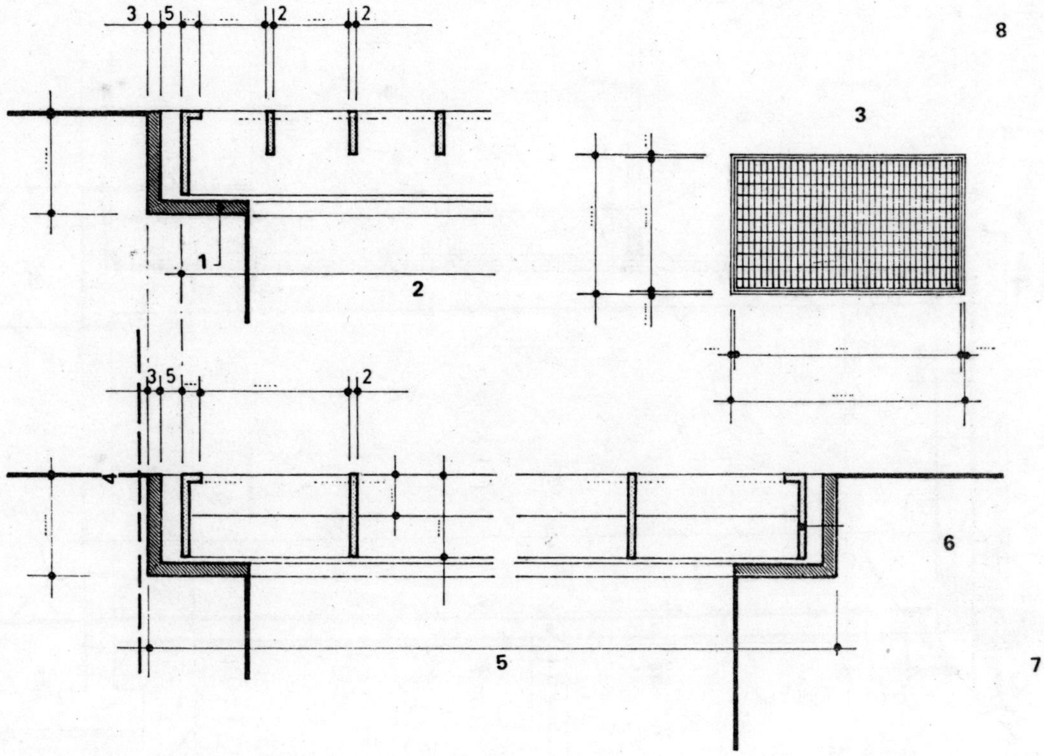

9

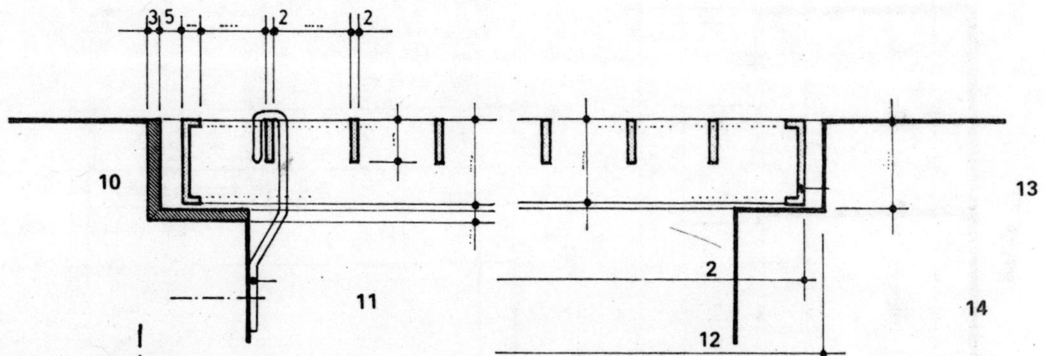

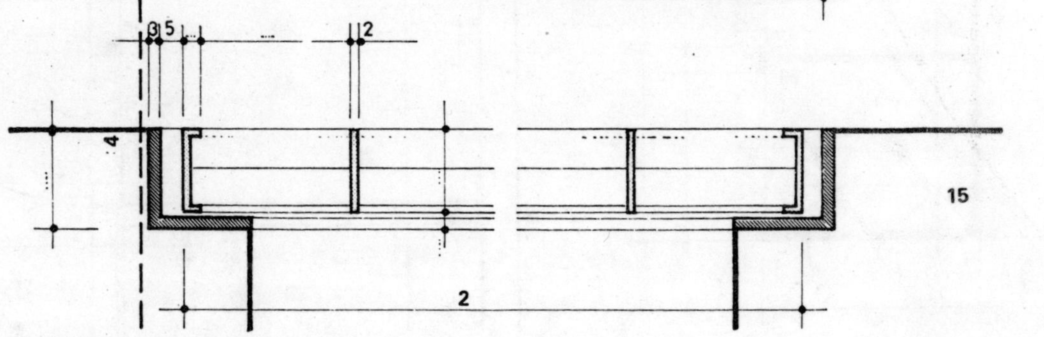

16

1 rabbet angle frame . . . / . . . / . . . mm
2 grating outer dimension
3 grating top view
4 wall connection
5 rabbet angle, outer dimension
6 angle mounting
7 shaft wall
8 with angle iron frame - mounting
9 with c-section frame
10 surfacing or crest connection
11 poss. clamp strap
12 rabbet outer dimension
13 c-section frame
14 design variant with concrete rabbet
15 surfacing or crest connection
16 execution variant with rabbet angle frame

Cellars, garages below ground level

1:50/200

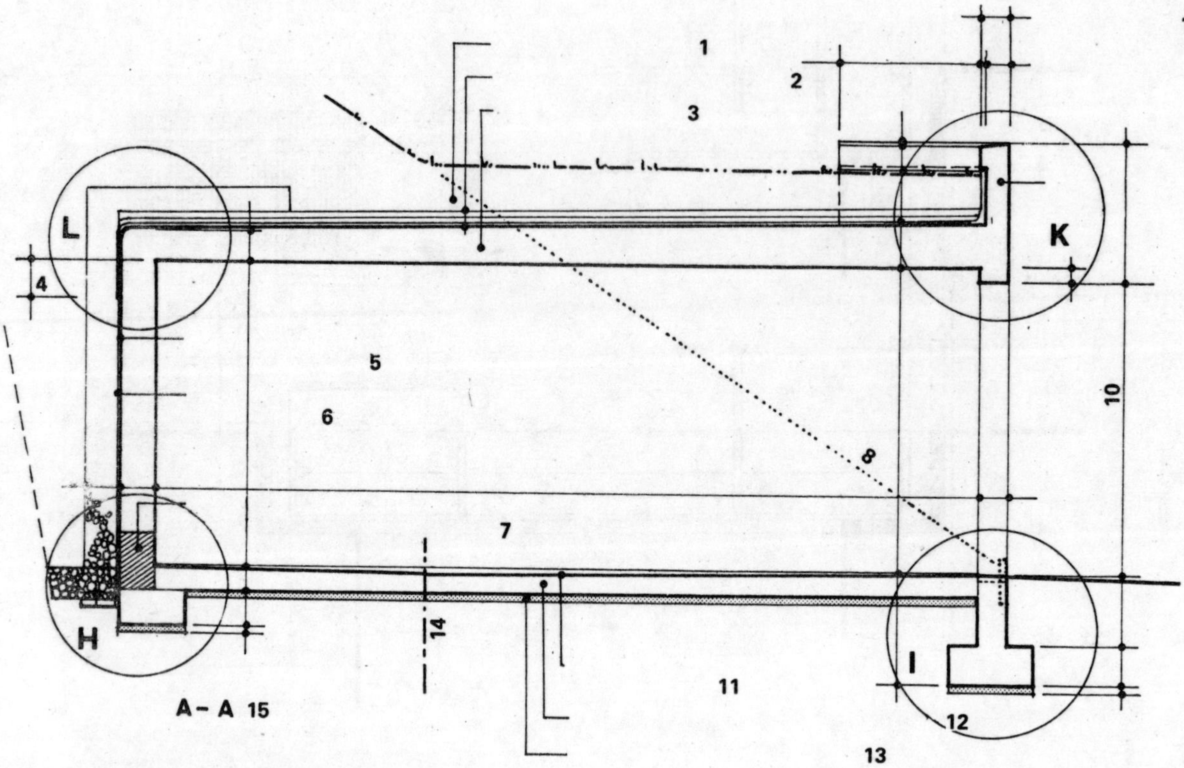

A – A 15

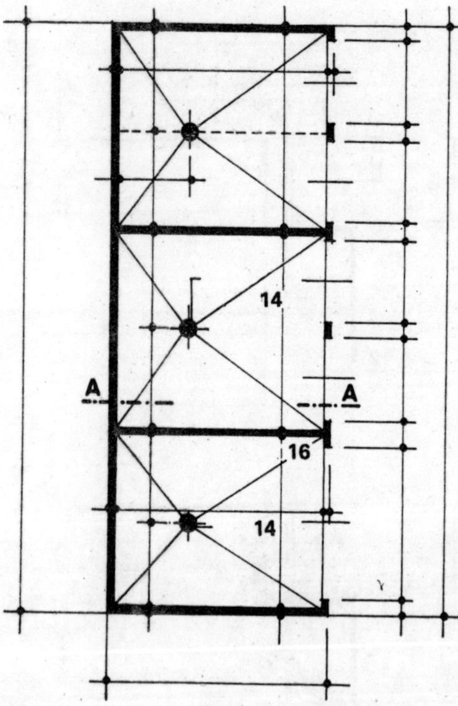

17

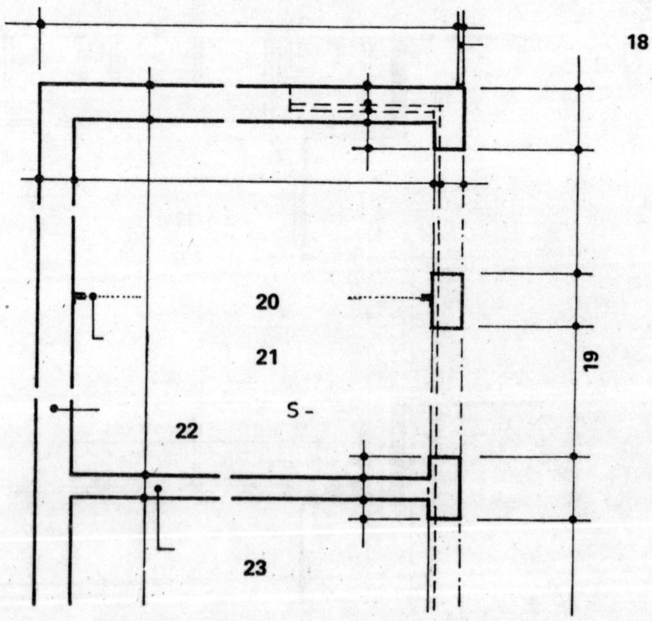

1 Earth filling
2 Insulation against water penetration
3 Reinforced concrete slab
4 Min. 10 cm
5 Impervious cement and sand rendering
6 2 Coats bitumen applied in 2 directions
7 ... Additive against rising moisture
8 Slope of ground at sides
9 Exposed face concrete upstand
10 Height of door opening
11 2 cm cement and sand screed to falls
12 12 -15 cm reinforced concrete floor slab
13 5 -7 cm blinding concrete
14 Floor gully
15 Section A – A
16 Double garage
17 Layout plan
18 Adjusting strip
19 Width of door opening
20 Detail of plan
21 Wire netting division
22 External concrete wall
23 Concrete dividing wall

1:20

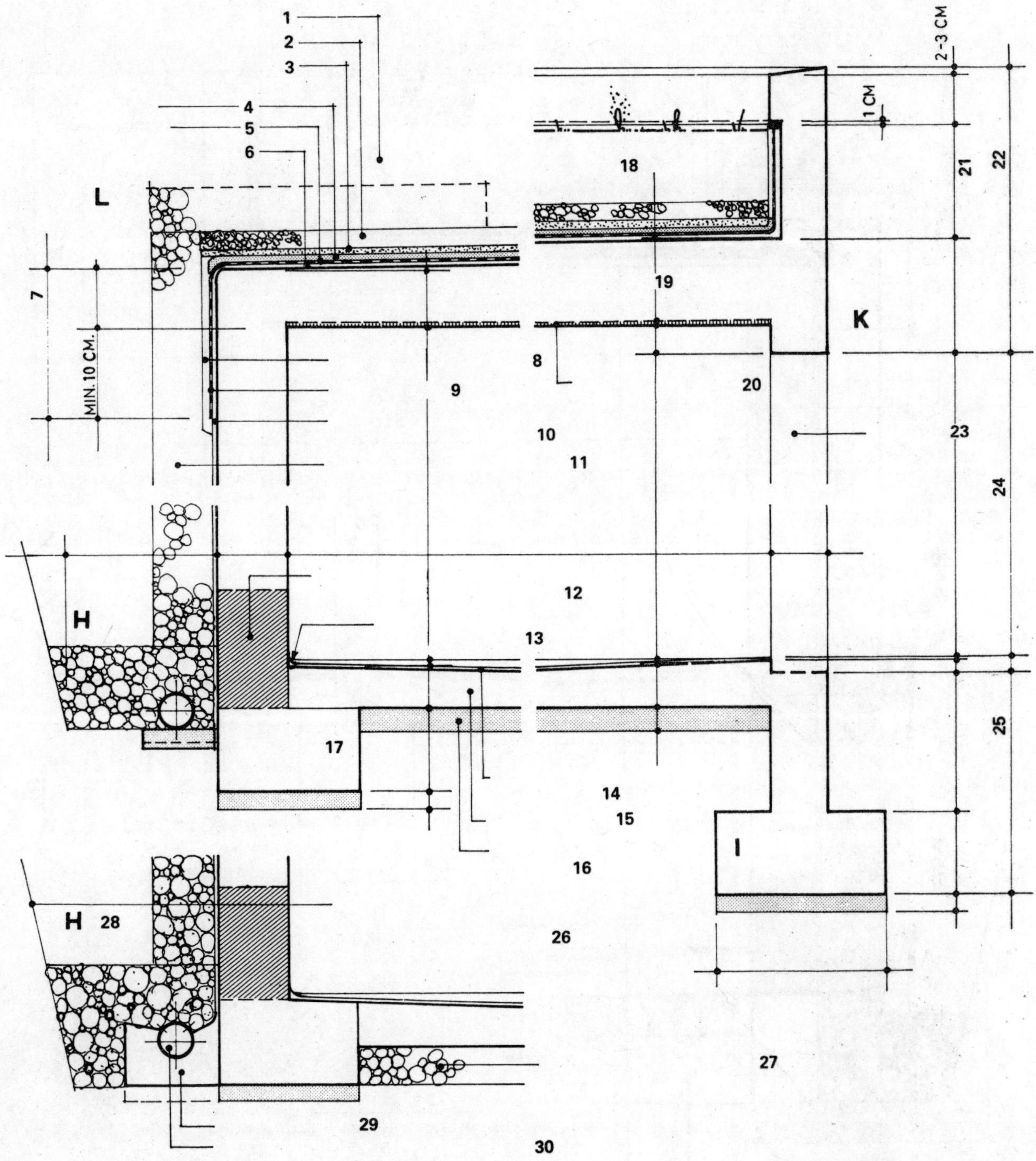

1 Earth filling
2 4-6 cm River gravel
3 2 cm sand bed
4 1,5-2 cm single layer of asphalt
5 Impervious sandwich layer
6 2 cm cement and sand screed
7 Down-turn to wall
8 1-2 cm protective rendering
9 Asphalt – jute fabric
10 2 cm impervious cement and sand rendering
11 20-30 cm gravel filter layer
12 . . . Additive against rising moisture
13 Angle fillet
14 2 cm cement and sand screed laid to falls
15 Concrete floor
16 5-7 cm concrete blinding layer
17 Strip foundation
18 Top soil (humus)
19 Reinforced concrete slab
20 Insulation to soffit
21 Up-turn against wall
22 Height of upstand
23 Column
24 Height of door opening
25 Depth of foundation
26 Angle of slope – depending on type of soil
27 12-15 cm hardcore bed
28 H. alternative
29 Drain bed
30 10,12 or 15 cm diameter agricultural drain

Foundations and waterproofing: alternative forms of construction

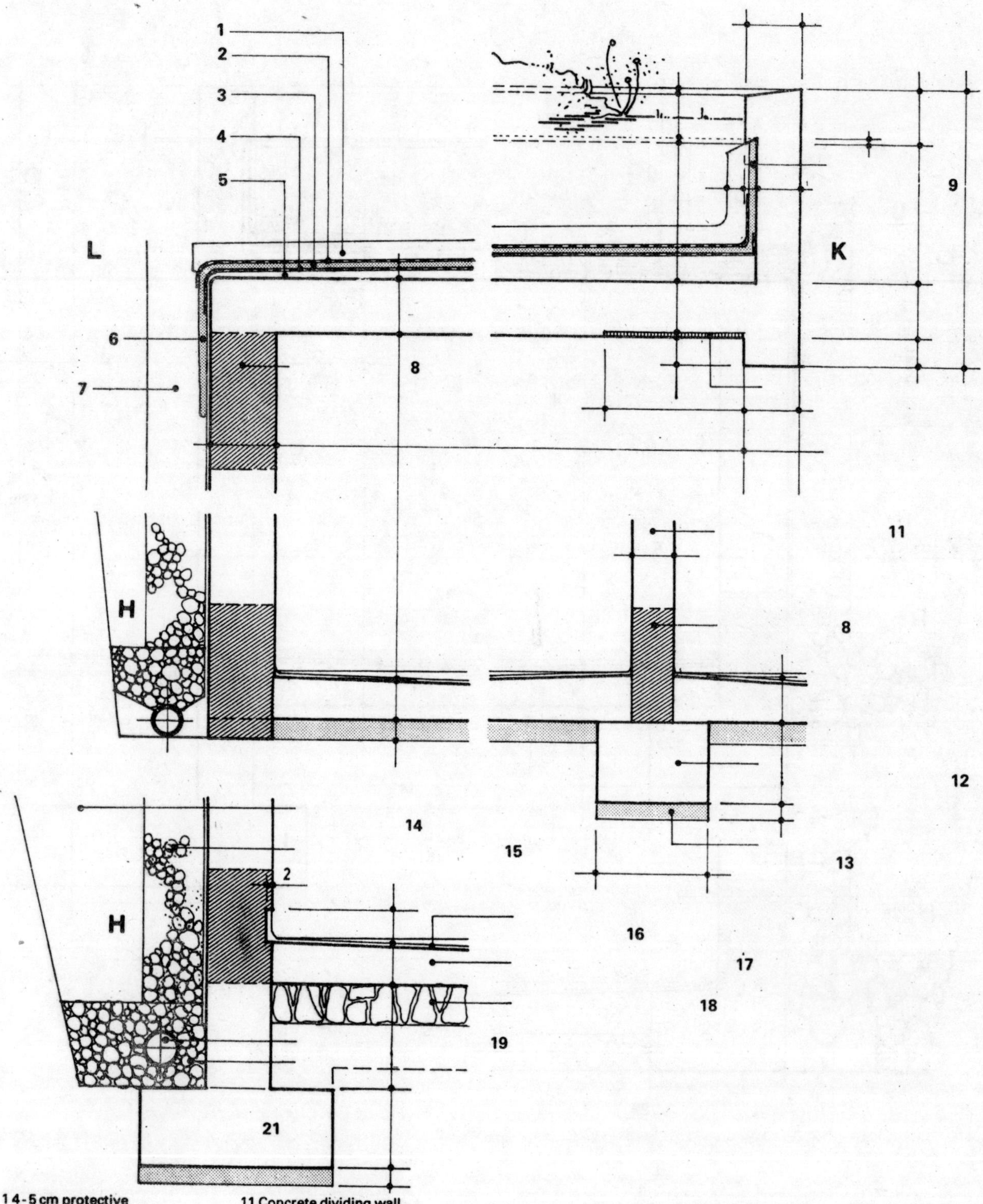

1 4-5 cm protective mortar bed
2 Impervious sandwich layer
3 Mastic asphalt or adhesive waterproofing (2-3 layers)
4 Sandwich layer, (where asphalt used)
5 2-...cm concrete bed finished to falls (falls ca.1-2%)
6 Asphalt down-turn to wall
7 Gravel filter layer
8 ... Additive
9 Asphalt up-turn
10 2 cm ... insulation board
11 Concrete dividing wall
12 Strip foundation (where structurally necessary)
13 5-7 cm blinding concrete
14 Earth back-fill compacted
15 ca. 20 cm porous concrete
16 2-3 cm cement and sand screed laid to falls
17 Reinforced concrete floor
18 12-15 cm rubble stone bed
19 Agricultural drain
20 Filter gravel
21 Strip foundation

1:50

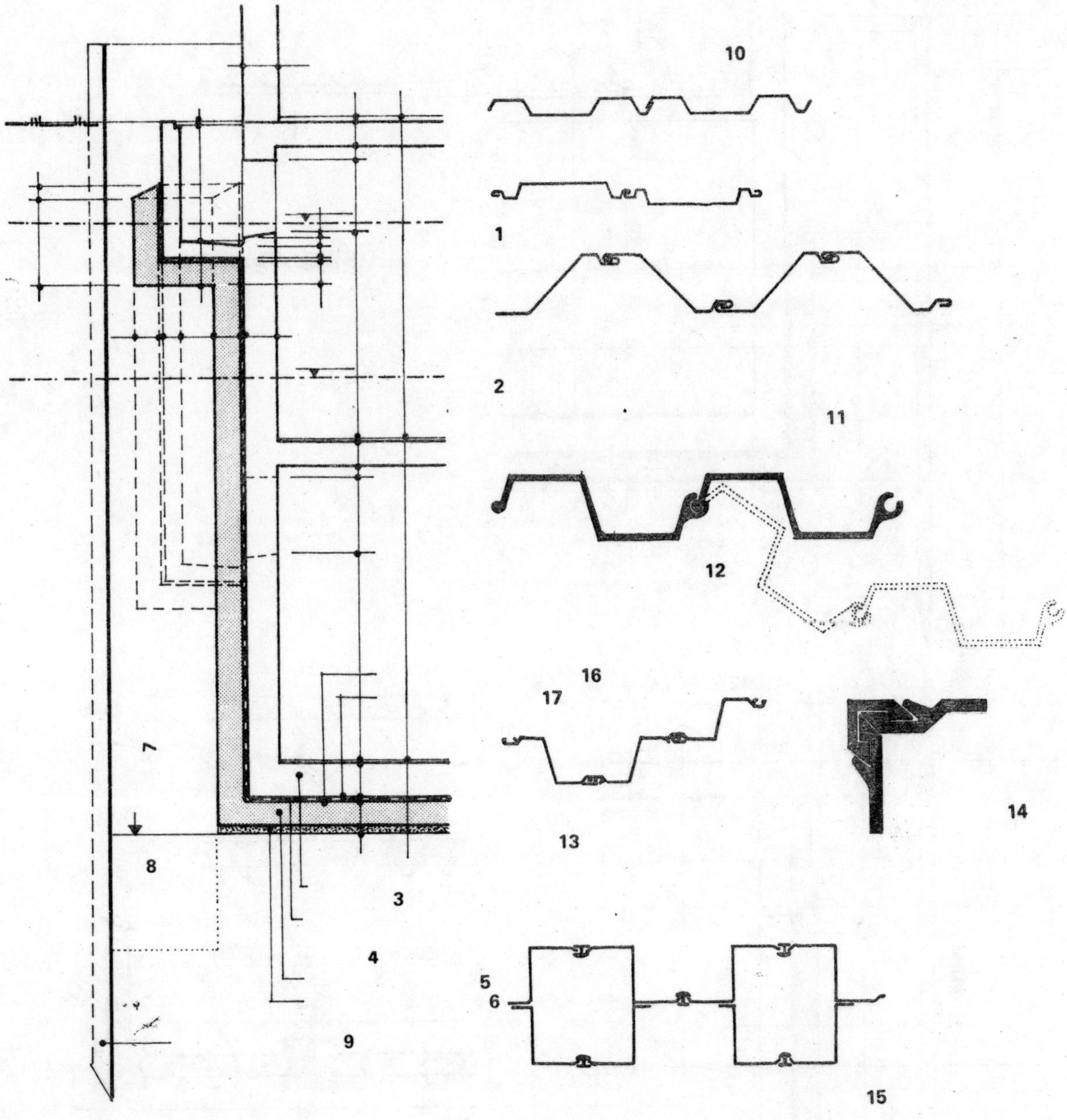

1 Water table, highest level
2 Water table, lowest level
3 Reinforced concrete floor
4 Asphalt or PVC sheet tanking
5 Reinforced concrete tank
6 Blinding
7 Bottom of foundation excavation
8 Pumping trench
9 Steel sheet piling
10 Trench walling and lightweight sheet piling profiles (height of sheet piling 2 - 5 m)
11 Sheet piling profiles for trenching
12 Double corrugated section
13 Z-section with claw grip joint
14 Corner detail
15 Box section for extreme situations
16 Levelling bed of mortar
17 Protective layer of mortar

Reinforced concrete tank construction and timber sheet piling

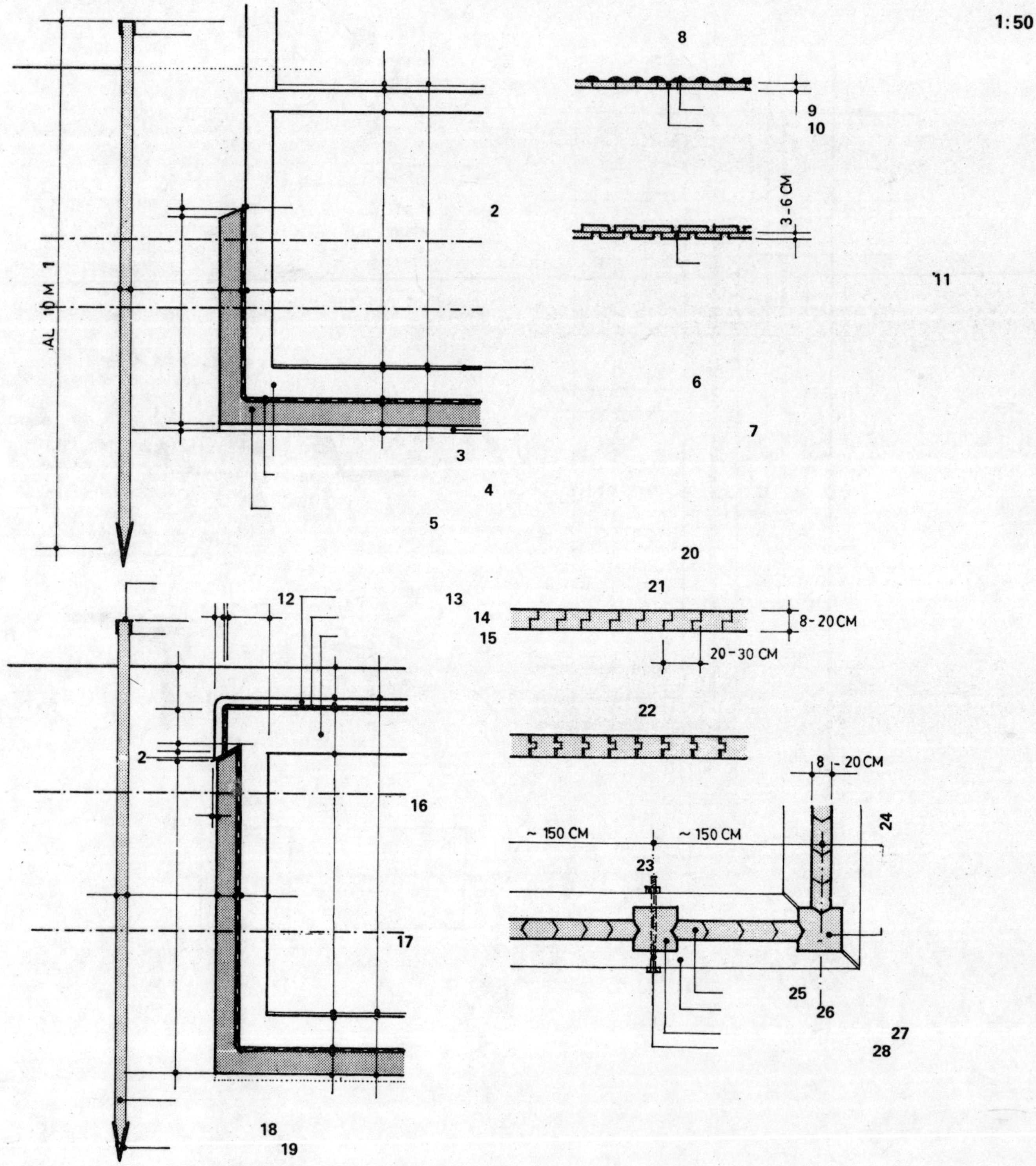

1 Height of poling max. 10 m
2 Elastic joint sealant
3 Reinforced concrete floor
4 Asphalt or PVC sheet tanking
5 Reinforced concrete tank with additive (water repellent)
6 Cement and sand screed
7 Blinding
8 Poling board sheeting 2-3 m high
9 Off-cut planks
10 Edge board
11 Bevel cut planks pointed
12 U-section driving cap
13 Protective concrete layer
14 Tanking layer
15 Reinforced concrete slab
16 Water table, highest level
17 Water table, lowest level
18 Timber sheet piling, thickness approx. 2% height of poling (min. 8 cm)
19 Steel shoe
20 Sheet trench-piling sections. Horizontal section
21 Lapped timbering
22 Tongued and grooved timbering
23 Double splay cut timbering
24 Corner pile or puncheon
25 Plank
26 Walings
27 Stiffening pile
28 Bolt with head and nut

Brickwork and stone walling

The strength of brickwork or stone walls is dependent on the quality of stones, mortar and the bonding used. The best results in terms of bearing capacity are achieved by pressing the bricks into the bed or mortar, without further rocking into position. Window and door openings should be co-ordinated as accurately as possible with brickwork dimensions.
Nowadays bricks or blocks used on building sites are almost invariably manufactured units: in general, clay or sand lime bricks, clinker or concrete blocks.
Bricks are made of clay or marl in brickworks. They can be hand made or machine pressed, air dried or artificially dried, and finally baked in tunnel or circular kilns.
In the production of insulating blocks or clay tiles sawdust is added, which burns during the process of vitrification.
Sand lime bricks are made from lime and quartz sand, and are pressed in a steam pressure process. Light-weight concrete solid or hollow blocks are manufactured from cement and mineral aggregates.
Walling using natural stone occurs in the form of dry walling, cyclopean walling, uncoursed and coursed random rubble, squared rubble and dressed stone walling.

Brickwork construction

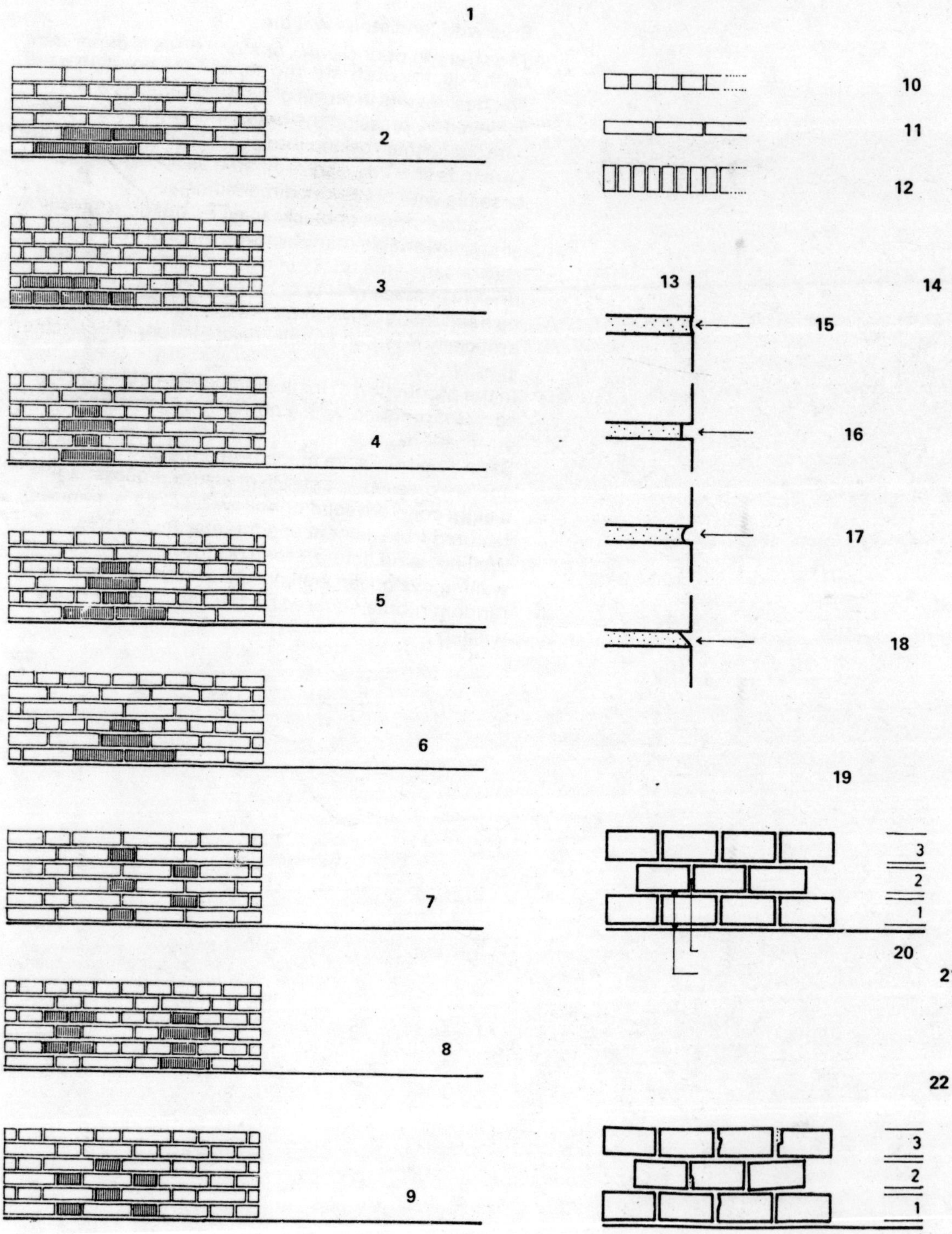

1 most common masonry bonds
2 stretcher
3 bondstone
4 block
5 cross bond
6 English
7 Scotch bond
8 Dutch
9 Gothic
10 fitting course
11 stretcher course
12 barge course
13 brick
14 pointing methods
15 fair-faced
16 recessed
17 filleted
18 bevelled
19 correct brickwork
20 vertical joint approx. 1 cm
21 supporting joint 1 - 1.5 cm
22 incorrect: irregular joints

Stretcher, header and English bond walling, diagrammatic representation

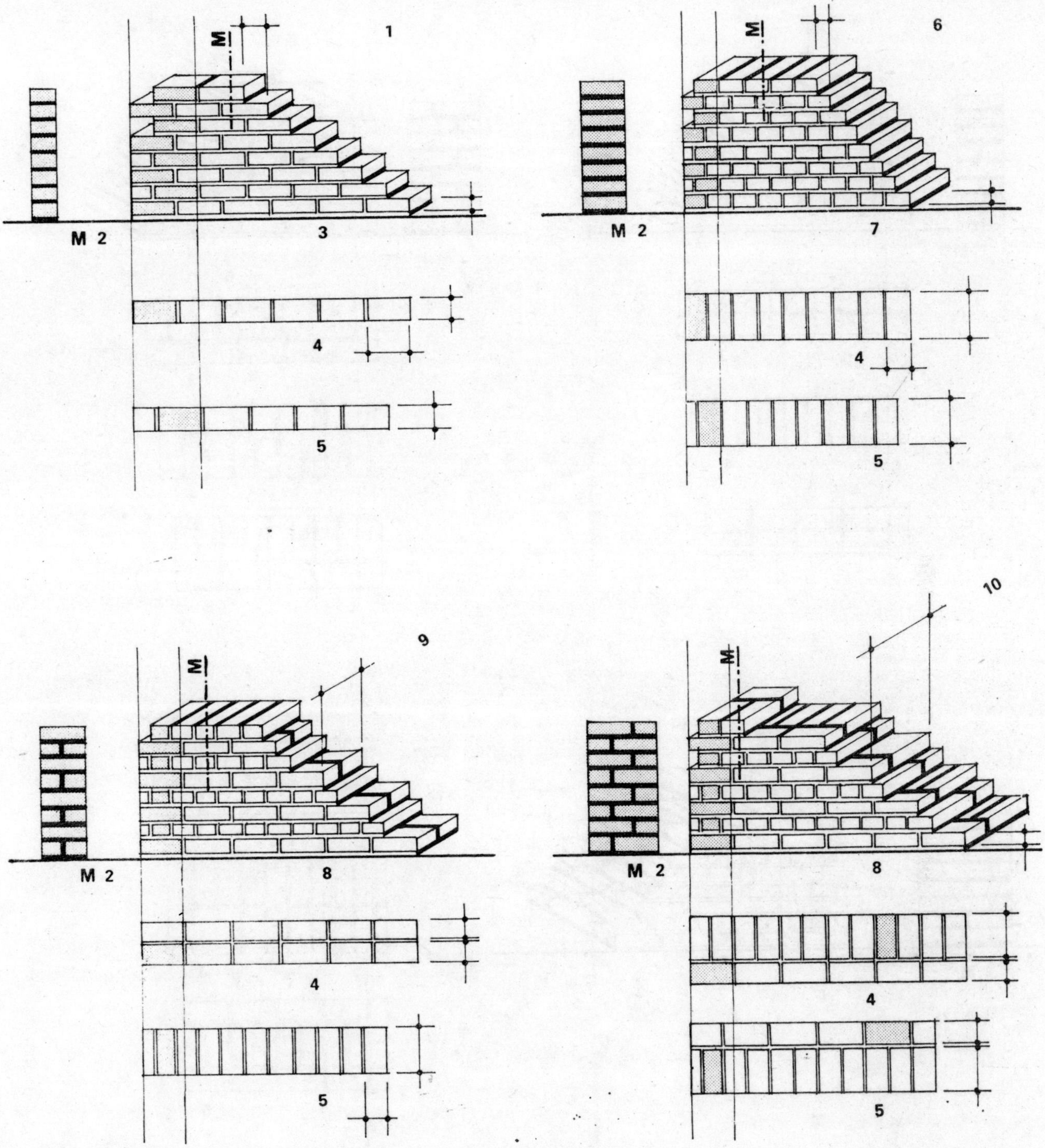

1 Lap, 1/2 brick
2 Section M
3 Stretcher bond
4 Courses 1, 3, 5, etc.
5 Courses 2, 4, 6 etc.
6 Lap: 1/4 brick
7 Header bond
8 English bond
9 One brick thick
10 1 1/2 brick thick

Cross-bond walling, wall thicknesses, diagrammatic representation

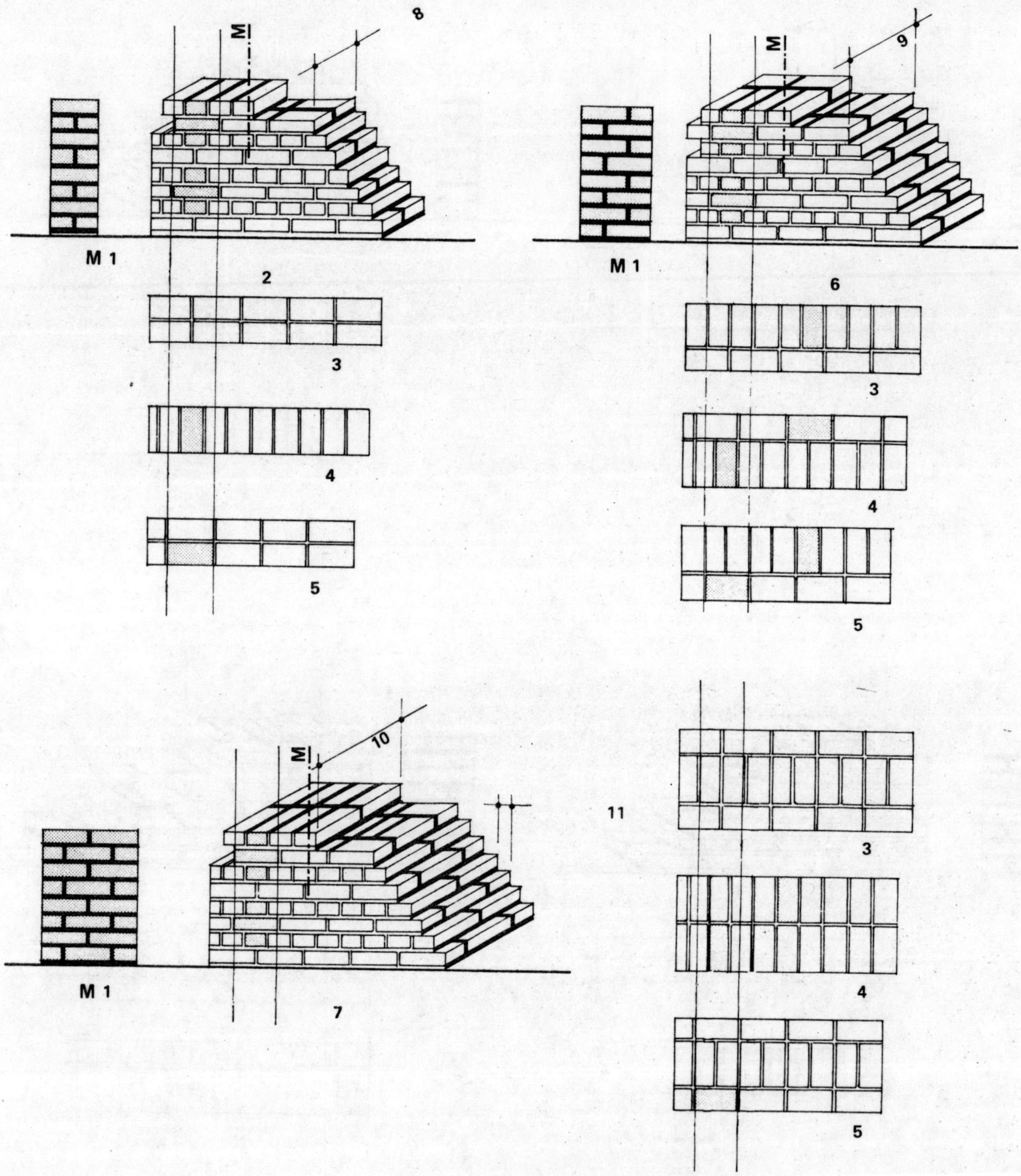

1 Section M
2 Cross bond, one brick thick
3 Courses 1, 5, 9, etc.
4 Courses 2, 4, 6, etc.
5 Courses 3, 7, etc.
6 Cross bond, 1 1/2 brick thick
7 Cross bond, 2 brick thick
8 One brick thick
9 1 1/2 brick thick
10 2 brick thick
11 Lap, 1/4 brick

1:20

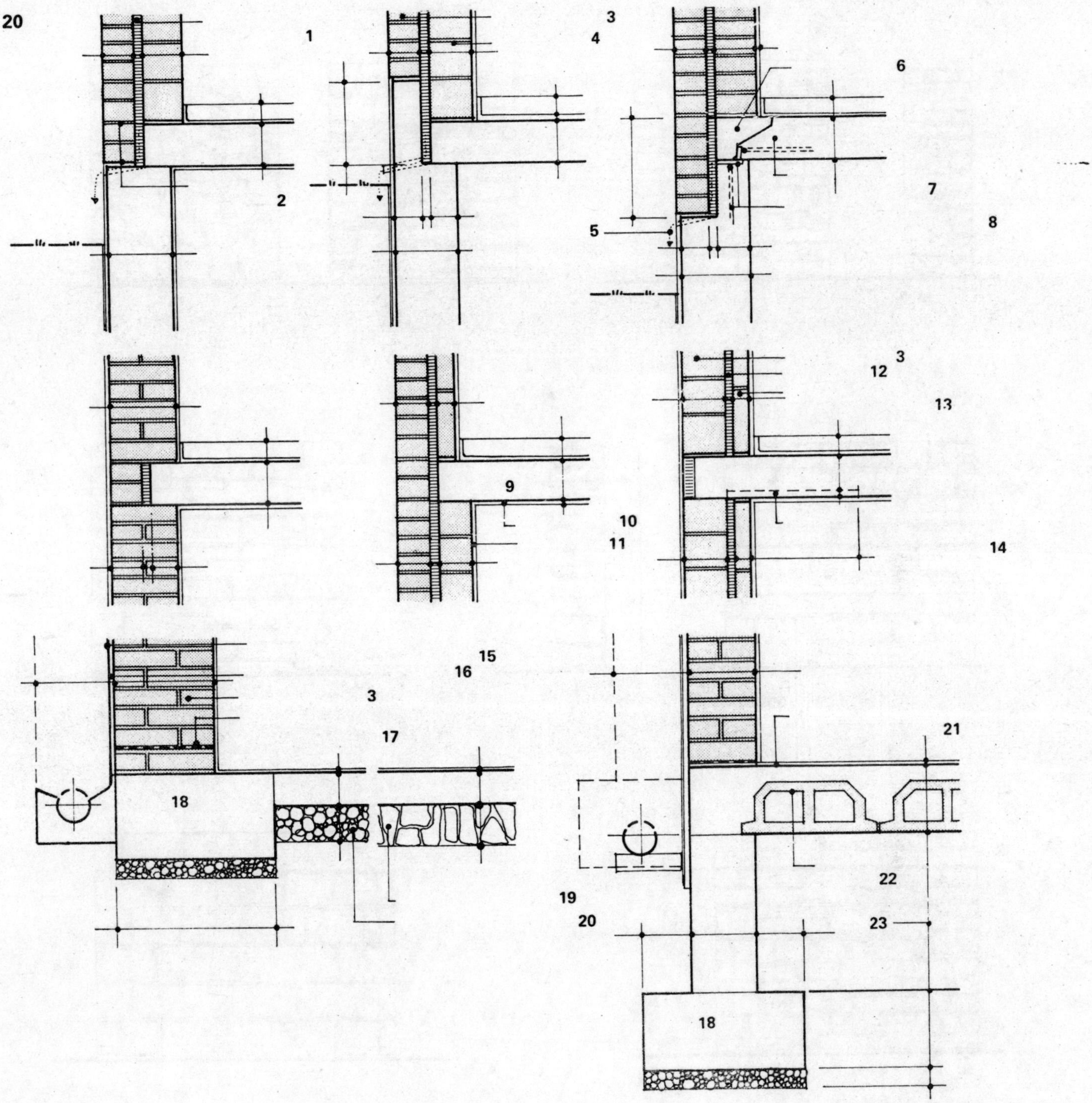

1 Insulation board . . . cm
2 Brick facing to edge of slab
3 External skin
4 Internal skin
5 Condensation
6 Concrete filling
7 Precast reinforced concrete slab units
8 Bearing plate with anchor
9 Reinforced concrete floor slab
10 Ceiling plaster
11 Wall plaster
12 Insulation
13 Inner skin wall, lightweight building blocks
14 Insulation not recommended, – discolouring of ceiling
15 Vertical impervious layer, 2 × bitumen brush-applied coating
16 Cement and sand rendering trowelled smooth
17 Horizontal bitumen felt d.p.c.
18 Strip foundation
19 15 - 20 cm hardcore bed
20 12 -15 cm gravel bed
21 Cement and sand screed
22 Hollow block floor
23 Ventilated void

Stone walling

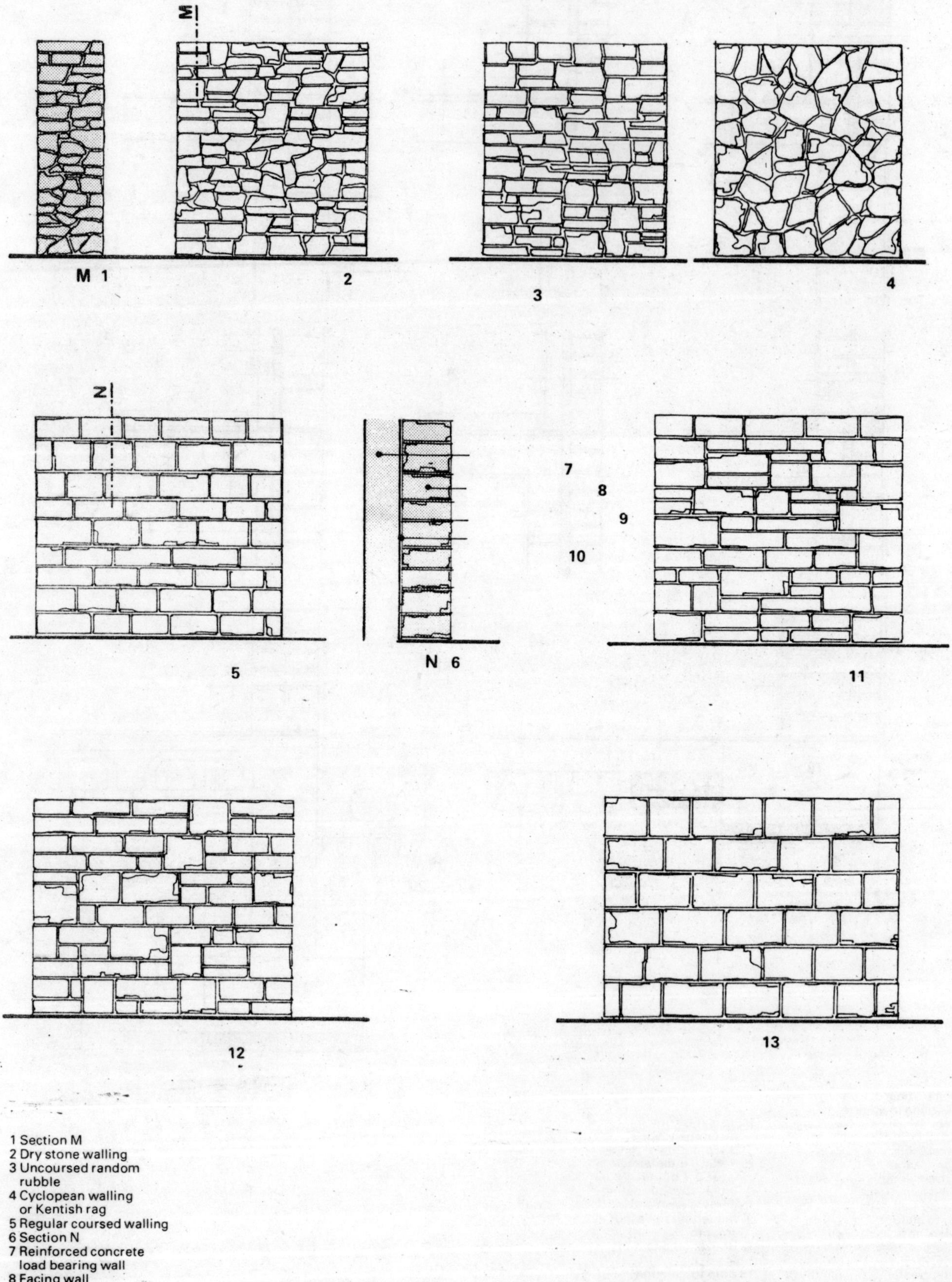

1 Section M
2 Dry stone walling
3 Uncoursed random rubble
4 Cyclopean walling or Kentish rag
5 Regular coursed walling
6 Section N
7 Reinforced concrete load bearing wall
8 Facing wall
9 Mortar bed
10 Insulation board . . . cm
11 Irregular coursed walling
12 Squared rubble walling laid to courses
13 Squared stone walling

Timber construction

To facilitate manufacturing processes, it is advisable to use structural timbers with standard cross-sectional dimensions, which should always be of even numbers, e.g. 12, 14, 16 cm, etc.

In general, untreated or air-dried fir, pine or other softwoods are used, or possibly, where beams are to be visible, oak or other high grade timber, wrought (planed), or rough gauged. Normally, the spacing of beams, (joists, etc.), is between 60 and 80 cm, depending on the distance spanned, the effective load and the floor construction to be used. To avoid torsional distortion in the length of the timber, wall plates should be spaced 2 cm from external and internal walls.

In order that calculated timber cross-sections correspond to the loading, building timber with as few knots as possible should be used in the various cutting classes: sharp edged, and with permissible defects, in accordance with the relevant standards. Timber for building should also be impregnated against all kinds of rot and infestation and against fire.

As a rule of thumb for the calculation of beam dimensions: (L = length spanned by beam; H = depth of beam);

Depth of beam = 16 cm + (L/100)

Thickness of beam = H/2 (min. thickness = 12 cm)

Timberfloor joist construction, plan and details

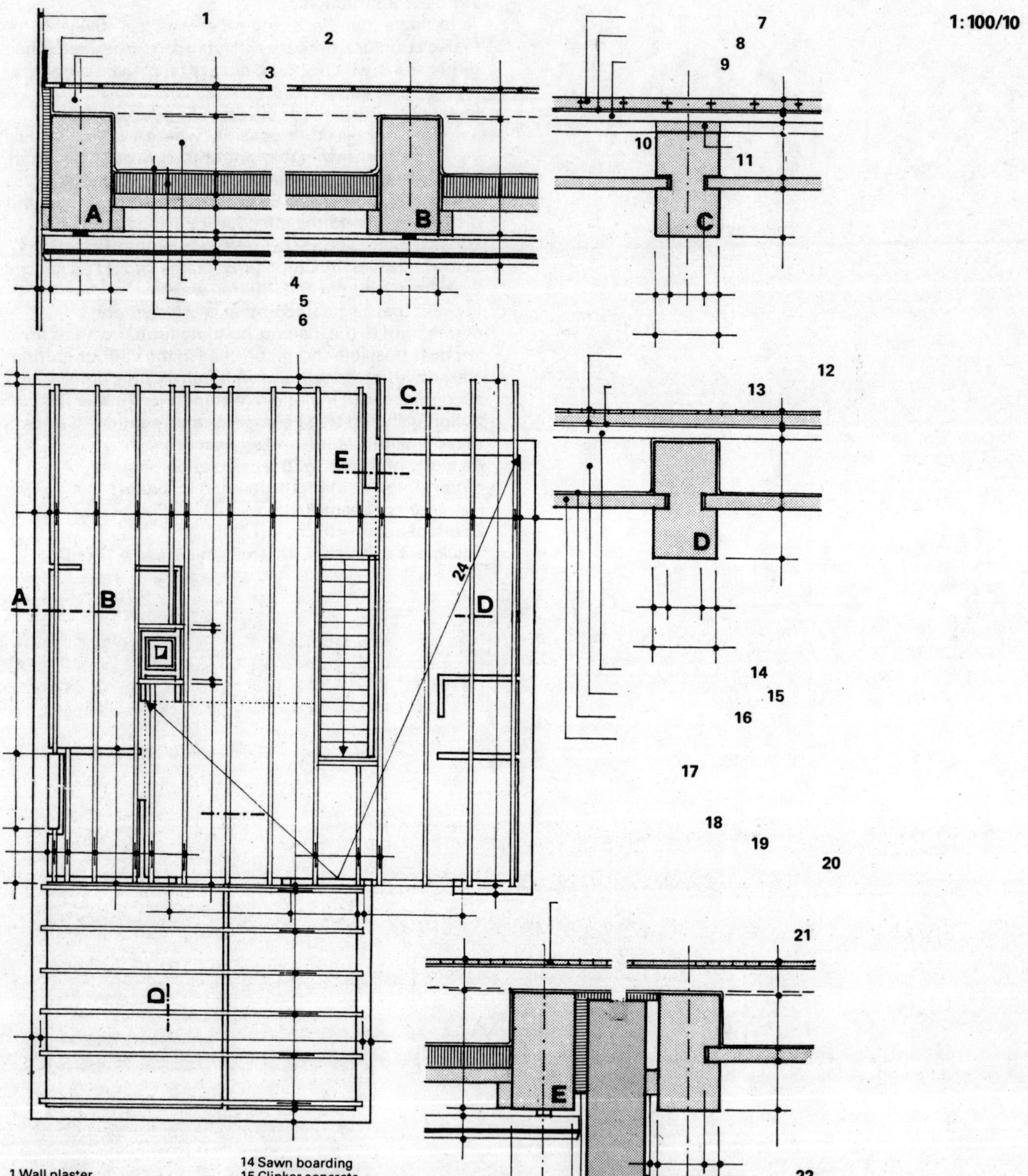

1 Wall plaster
2 Tile flooring
3 Mortar bed with wire netting reinforcement
4 Concrete filling
5 Insulating board
6 Felt-backed paper
7 Floor boarding
8 Felt-backed paper
9 Timber boarding
10 Void
11 Wedge shaped firring
12 Wood mosaic (parquet) flooring with softwood lining
13 Felt-backed paper
14 Sawn boarding
15 Clinker concrete
16 Felt-backed paper
17 Soffit lining let in, grade 1 wrot soffit
18 Timber joist construction, plan 1:100
19 Level of top of beams...
20 Joist dimensions .../...cm
21 Parquet flooring fixed with adhesive
Size of blocks 120/24/8 mm
Size of sheets 48/48 cm
22 Plaster
23 Wall

Solid floor and timber joist construction with alternative details

1:100/10

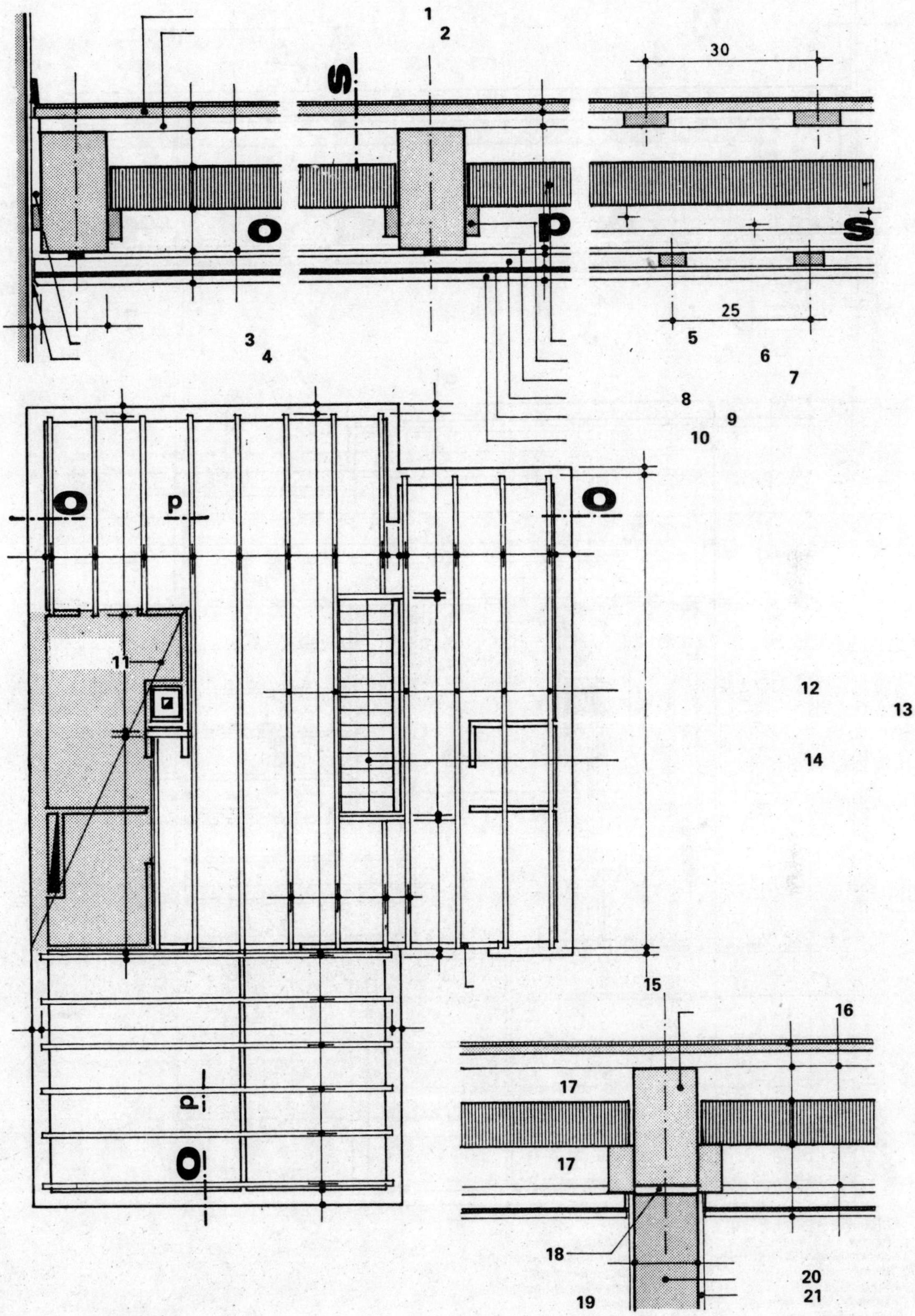

1 Chipboard ... mm
2 Sawn boarding 24/80 mm
3 Expanded polystyrene sheets
4 Splay cut/ chamfered edge
5 Insulating board
6 Bearer .../... mm
7 Firrings 8/22 mm
8 Studding
9 Insulating reed mat
10 Soffit plaster
11 Solid floor slab
12 Joist layout, level of top of joists ...
13 Joist dimensions .../... cm
14 Single flight staircase
15 Sill or plate .../... cm
16 Joist .../... cm
17 Void
18 Firring
19 Alternative
20 Wall
21 Plaster

Timber floor construction, alternatives

1:100/10

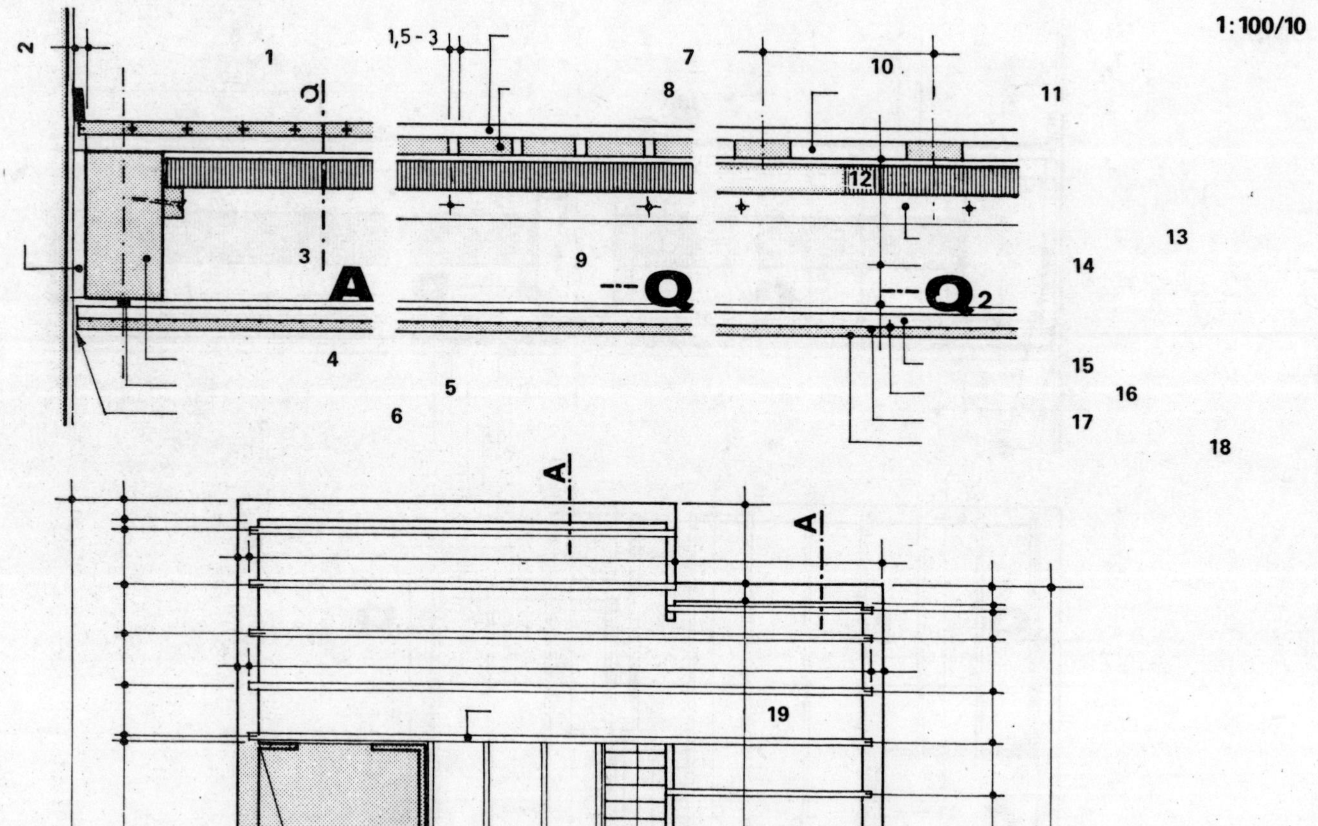

1 Distance of joists from wall, 2 - 4 cm
2 Expanded polystyrene sheet
3 Void
4 Timber joist
5 Firring 8/22 mm
6 Splay cut edge
7 Wood strip flooring, tongued and grooved
8 Hollow sub-floor
9 Elevation of joists
10 Centres 25 - 30 cm
11 Sub-floor
12 Insulating board
13 Bearer 24/48 mm
14 Depth of joist
15 Insulating board
16 Expanded metal lathing
17 Plaster base coat
18 Trowelled or finishing plaster
19 Trimming joist .../... cm
20 Sill .../... cm
21 Reinforced concrete or hollow tile floor
22 Services and ventilation duct
23 Timber joist construction level of top joists = ...
24 Joist dimensions .../... cm

Timberfloor joist construction, alternative floor and ceiling details

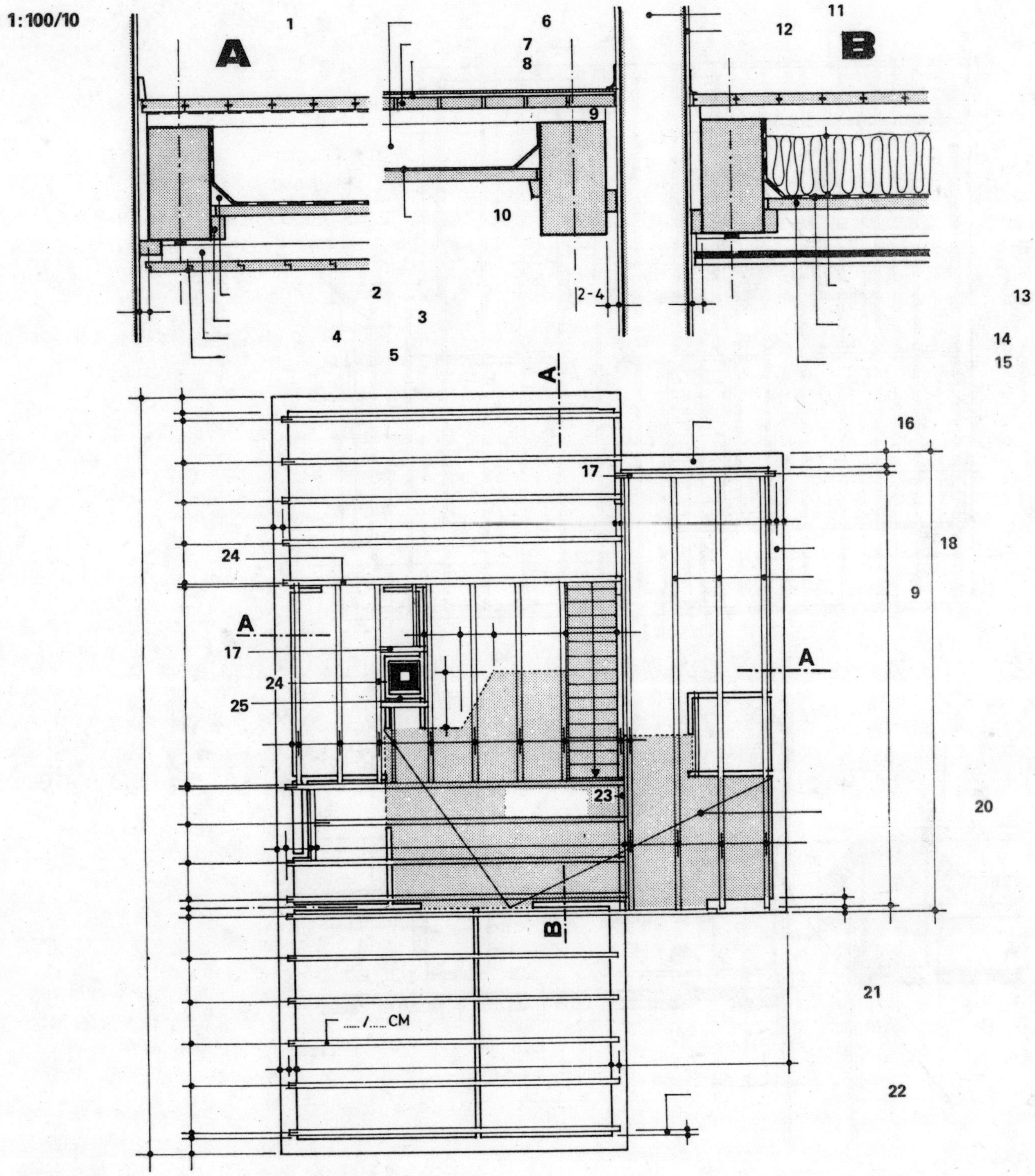

1 Section
2 Triangular fillet
3 Bearer …/… cm
4 Studding
5 Soffit boarding
6 Sand filling
7 Sub-floor
8 Hardboard flooring
9 Bearers, 30 cm centres
10 Oil impregnated paper
11 Internal wall
12 Plaster
13 Insulation … cm
14 Layer of PVC or building paper laid loose
15 Intermediate or false floor
16 Non-load-bearing wall
17 Trimming joist …/… cm
18 External wall
19 Timber joists …/… cm
20 Exposed joists
21 Timber joist construction Plan 1:100
22 Spacing of joist from wall
23 Plate …/… cm
24 Trimming joist …/… cm
25 Chimney casing

Timberfloor joist construction with sectional details

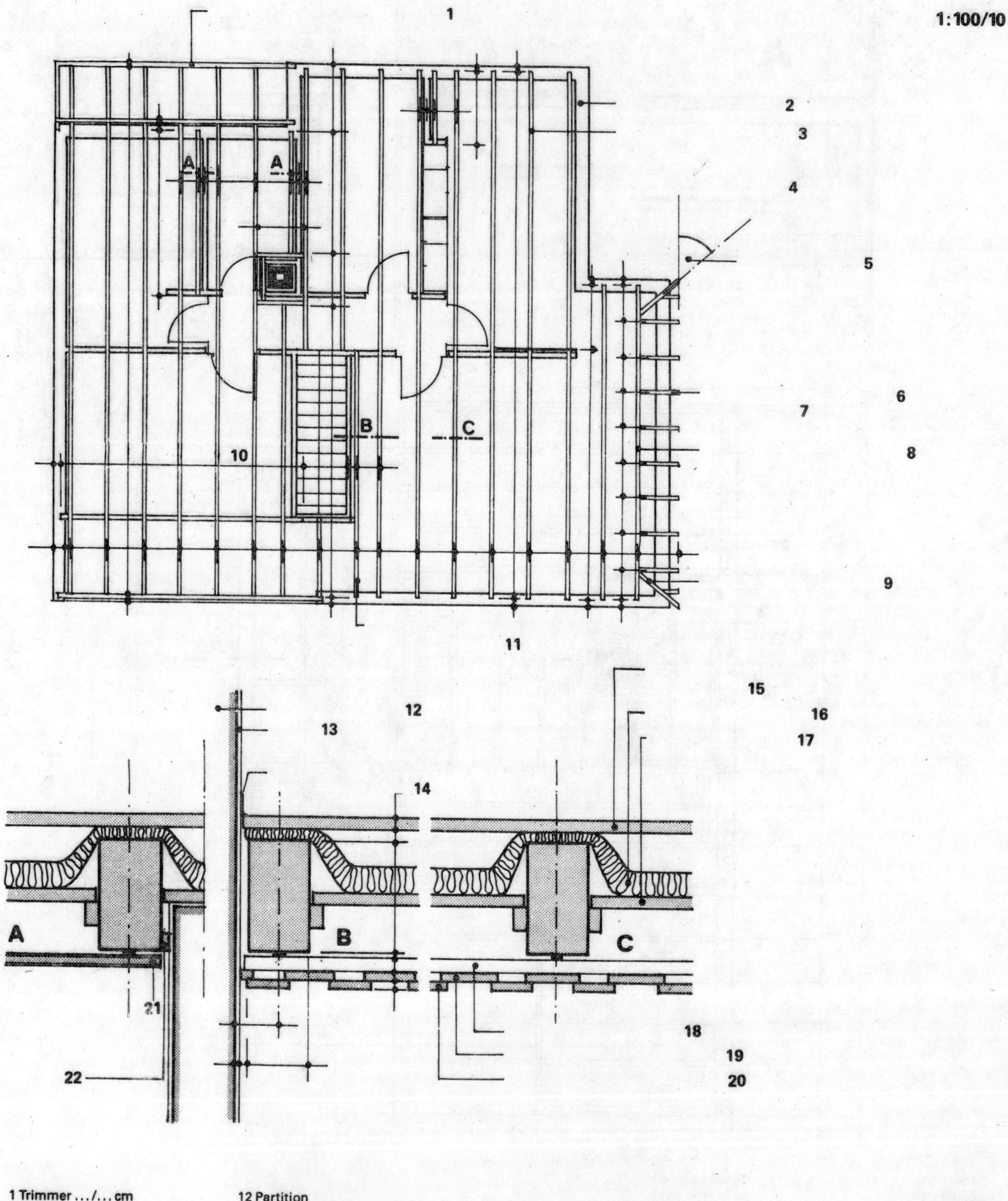

1 Trimmer .../... cm
2 Perimeter wall
3 Timber joist .../... cm
4 Joist construction
Level of top of joists...
5 Angle = ...°
6 Spur joist .../... cm
7 (Trimmed)
8 Trimming joist .../... cm
9 Corner spur joist
.../... cm
10 Sill .../... cm
11 Joist next wall .../... cm
12 Partition
13 Plaster
14 Plastic or timber skirting
15 Strip flooring,
tongued and grooved
16 Building quilt
17 Intermediate
or false floor
18 Cross bearer .../... mm
19 Base boarding .../... cm
20 Top boarding .../... cm
21 Wood lining
22 Shadow bead

1:20

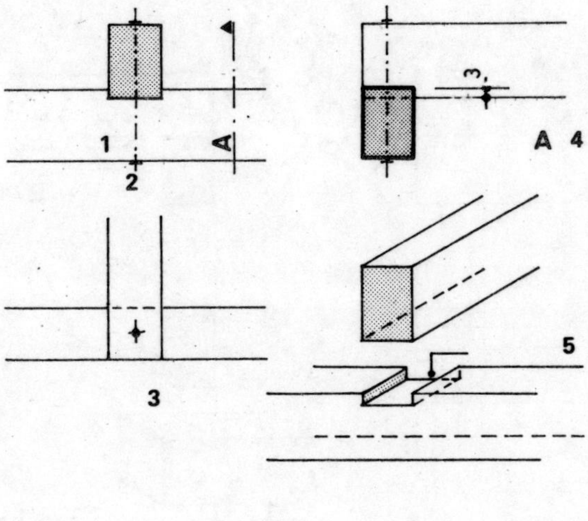

9

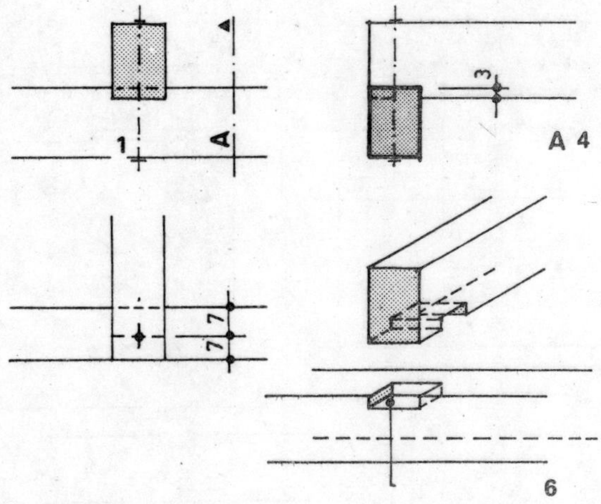

10

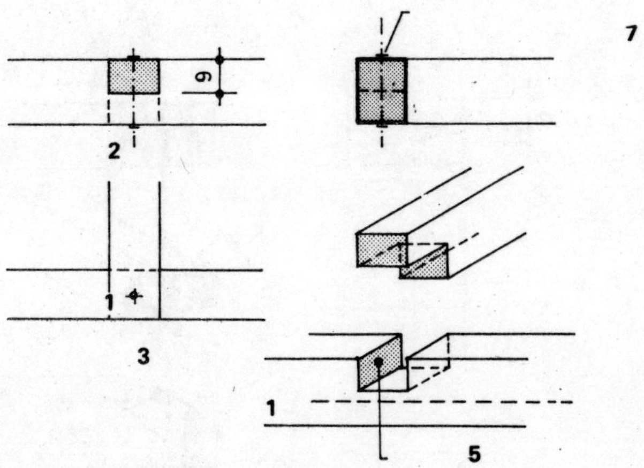

11

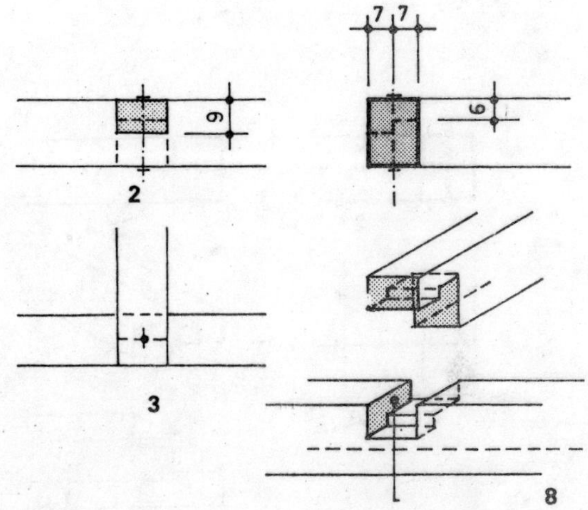

12

1 Beam
2 Elevation
3 Plan
4 Section A
5 Groove
6 Stopped groove
7 Hexagonal head nut and bolt
8 Notched groove
9 Full notching
10 Housed joint
11 Halved lapped joint
12 Notched and housed joint

Beam joints and connections

1:20

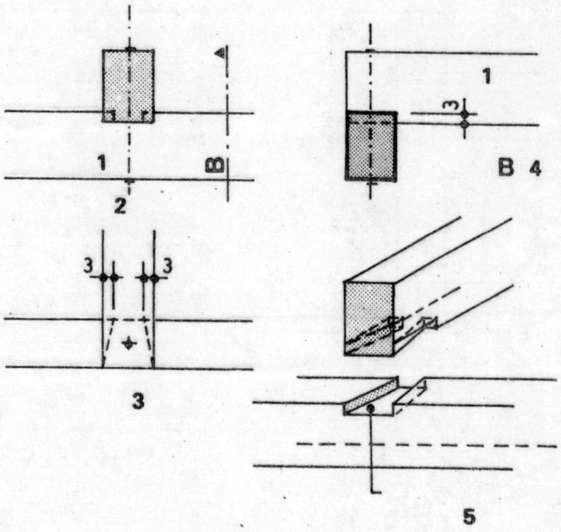

7

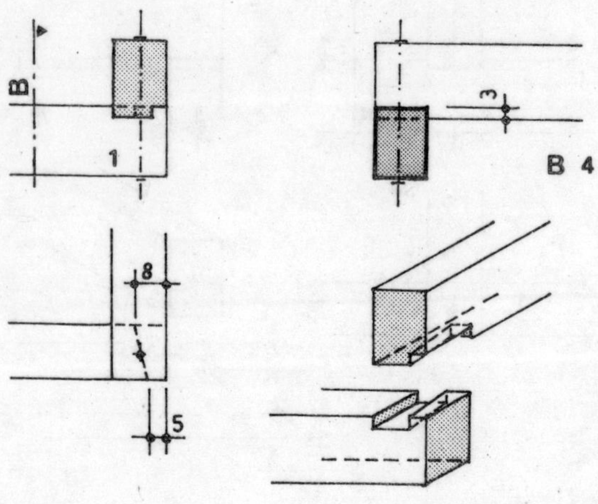

8

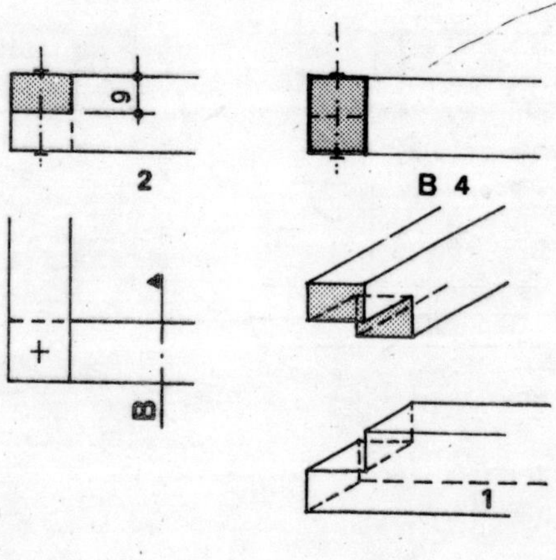

9

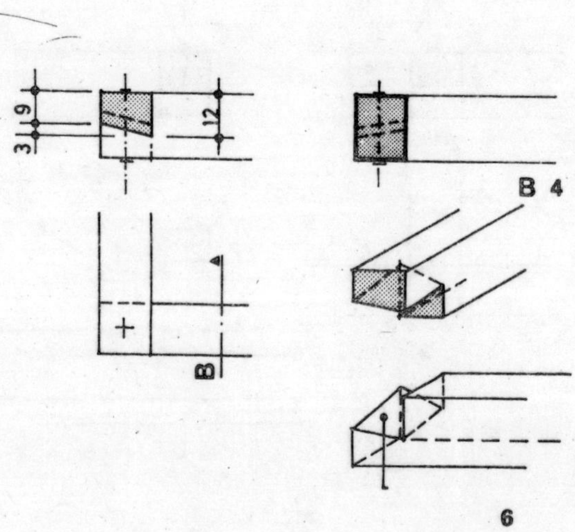

10

1 Beam
2 Elevation
3 Plan
4 Section B
5 Dovetail notching
6 Bevelled face
7 Dovetail notched joint
8 Notched halved joint
9 90° halved joint
10 Bevelled halved joint

1:20/1

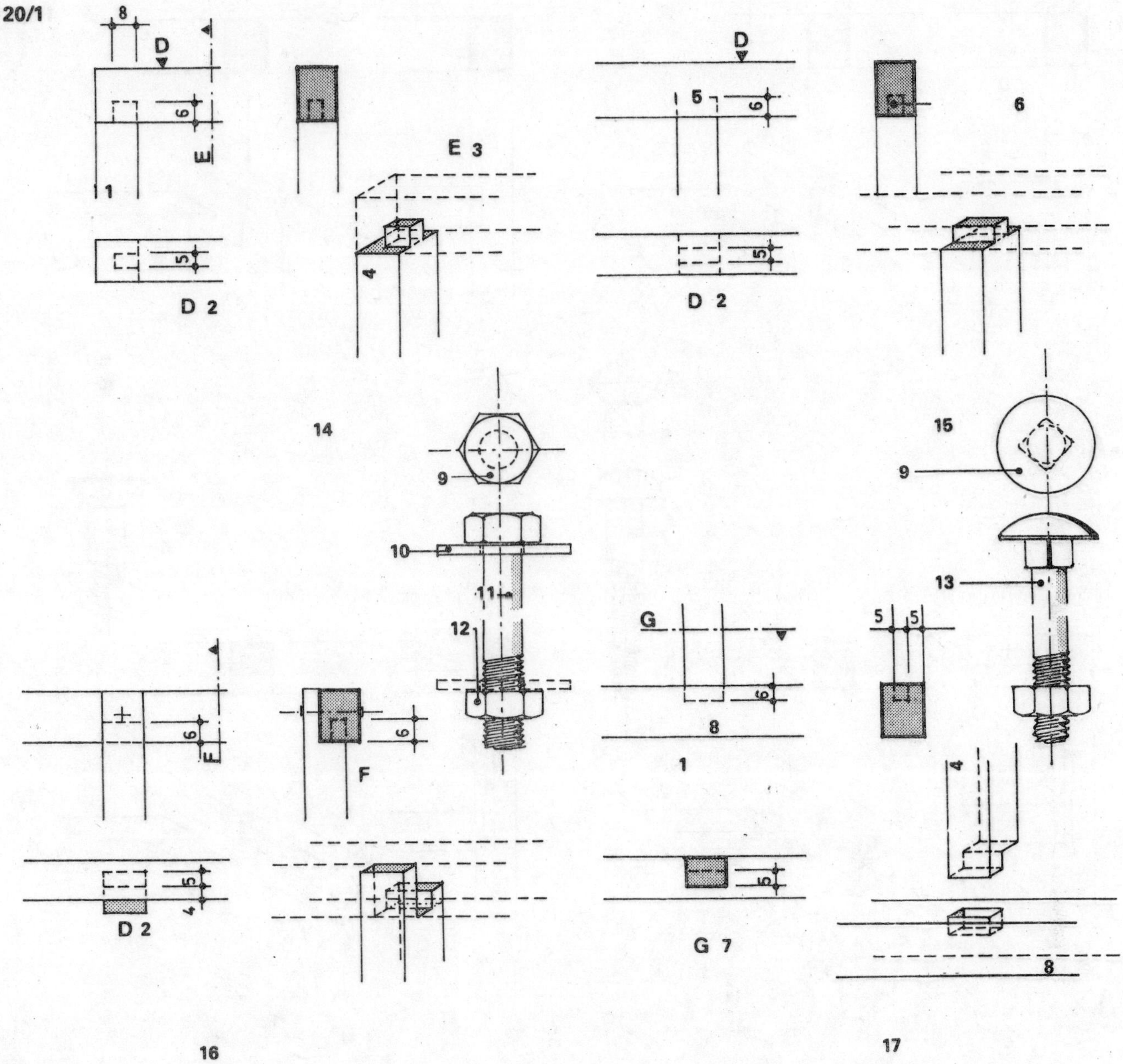

1 Elevation
2 Plan
3 Cut away view
4 Post
5 Beam, purlin or sill
6 Tenon
7 Section/plan G
8 Beam or sill
9 Bolt, view of head
10 Washer
11 Hexagonal head bolt
12 Hexagonal nut
13 Dome-headed bolt with square neck
14 Stub tenon
15 Tenon
16 Chase tenon
17 Side tenon

Trimming joints

1:20/1

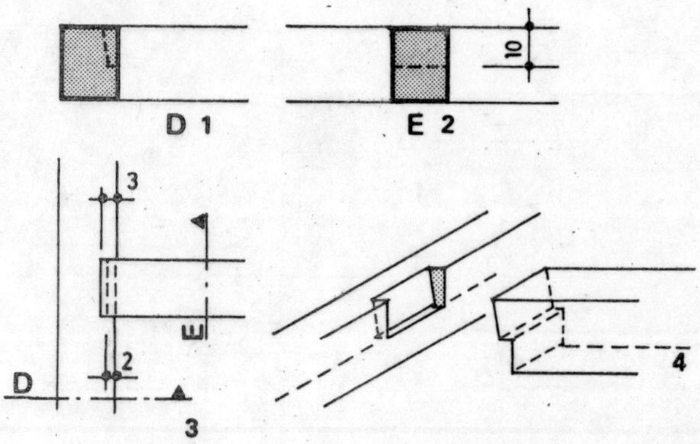

9

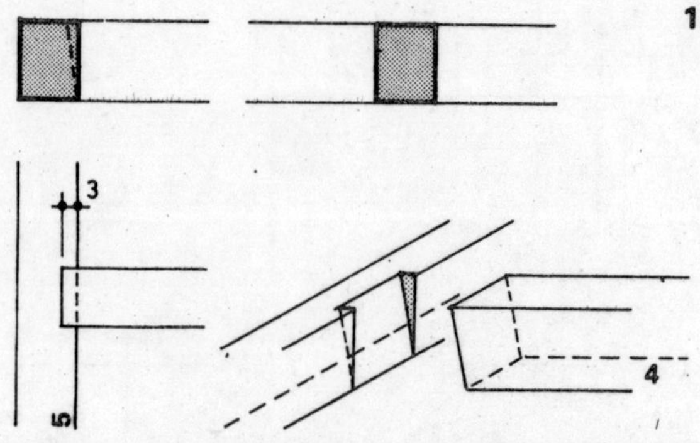

10

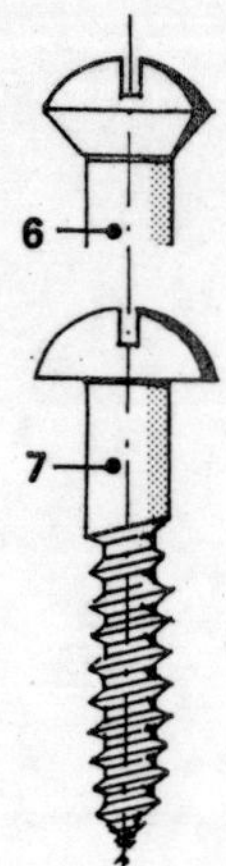

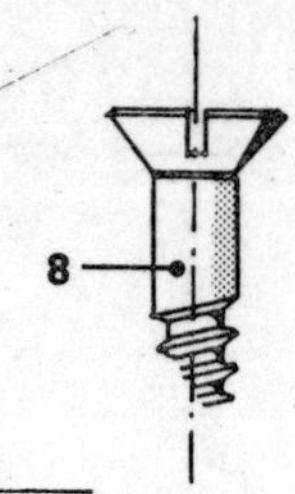

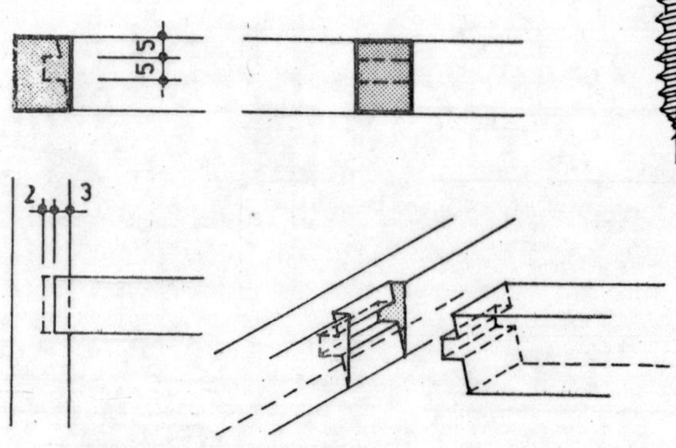

11

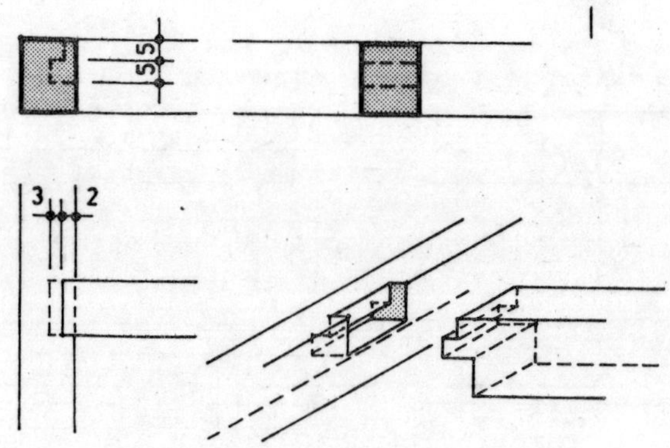

12

1 Section D
2 Section E
3 Plan
4 Trimming joist
5 Joists or rafters
6 Countersunk dome-headed wood screw
7 Dome-headed wood screw
8 Countersunk-headed screw
9 Halved trimming joint
10 Simple trimming joint
11 Trimming joint with tenon
12 Trimming joint with stepped tenon

1:20

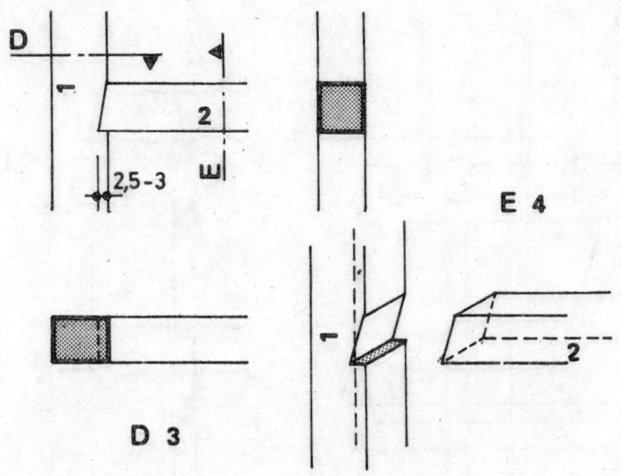

10

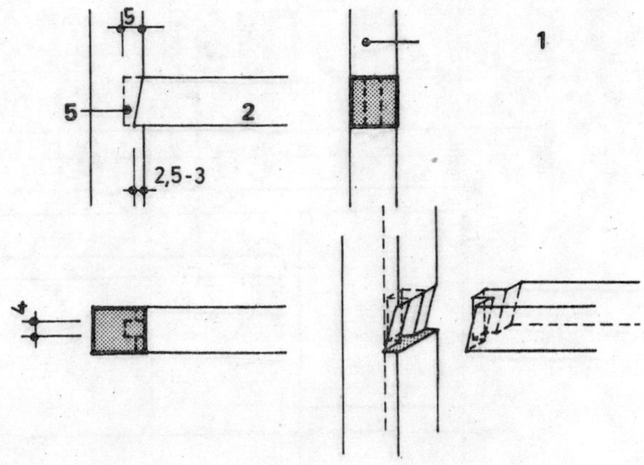

11

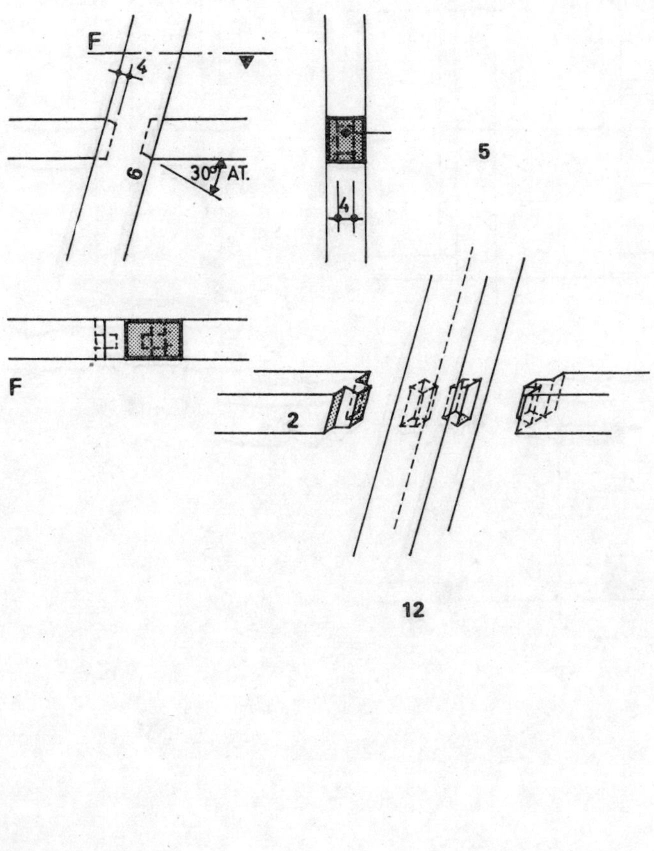

12

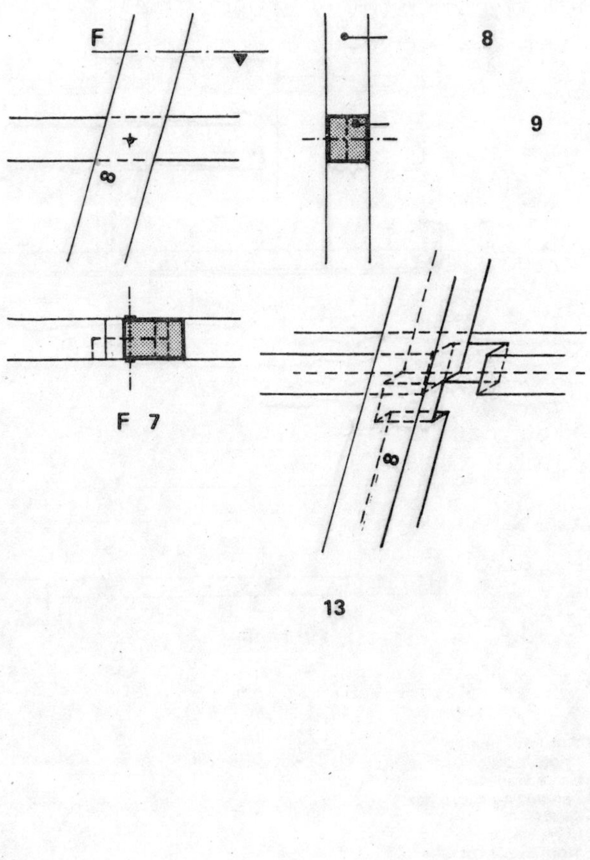

13

1 Post
2 Rail
3 Section/plan D
4 Section/elevation E
5 Tenoned rail
6 Framed strut
7 Section/elevation F
8 Brace or strut
9 Halved joint in rail
10 Splayed rail joint
11 Bridle mortice joint
12 Mortice joint of rail with raking member
13 Halved rail joint

Framed timber construction, plan, section, elevation

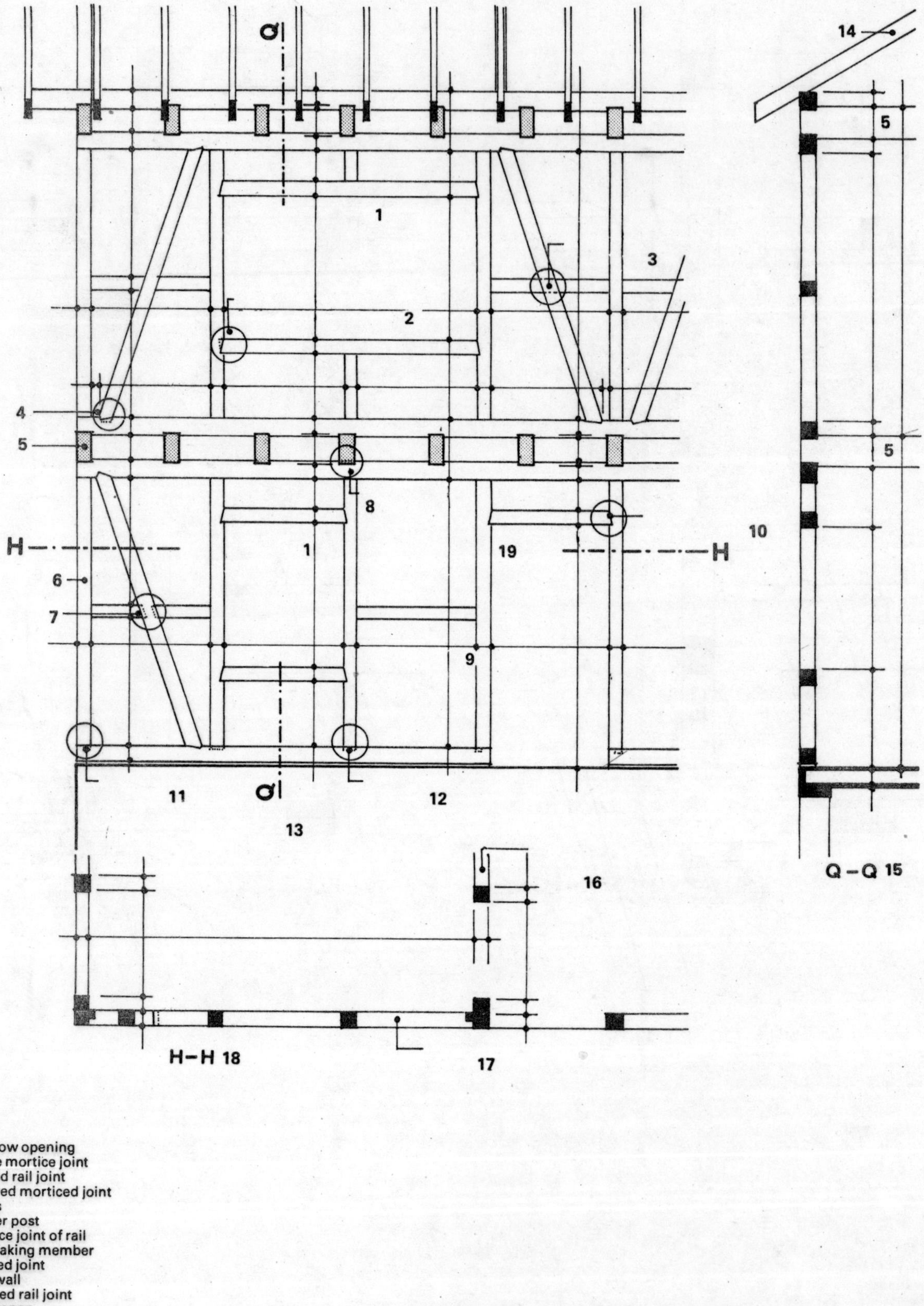

1 Window opening
2 Bridle mortice joint
3 Halved rail joint
4 Splayed morticed joint
5 Joists
6 Corner post
7 Mortice joint of rail with raking member
8 Housed joint
9 Infill wall
10 Splayed rail joint
11 Stub tenon
12 Tenon
13 External elevation
14 Rafters .../... cm
15 Section Q – Q
16 Framed partition
17 Framed timber external wall
18 Plan at H – H
19 Door opening

Framed timber construction, double rail construction, plan, section, elevation

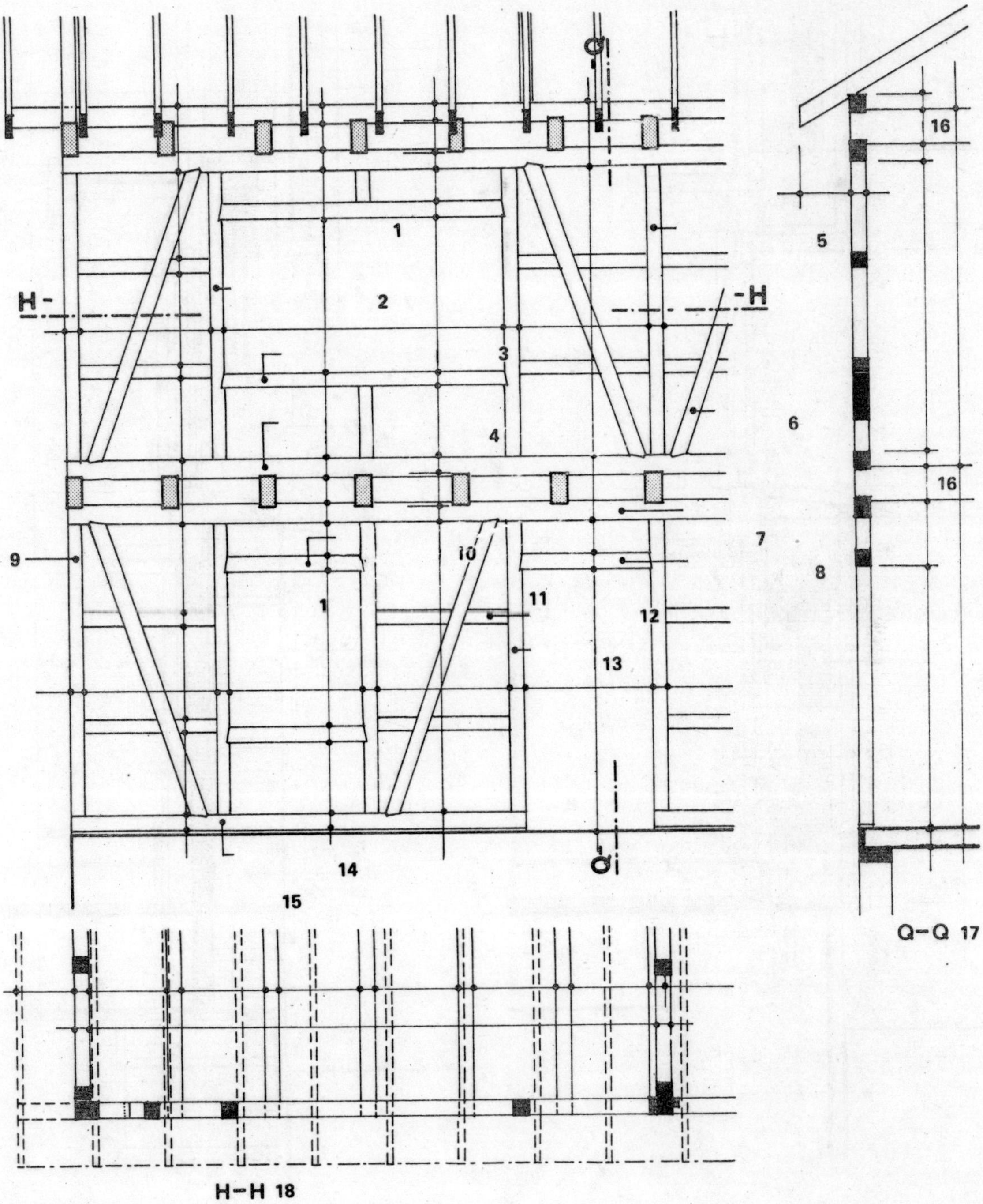

1 Window opening
2 Window post .../... cm
3 Rail .../...
4 Sill or plate .../... cm
5 Intermediate post .../... cm
6 Brace .../... cm
7 Head beam .../... cm
8 Door head .../... cm
9 Corner post .../... cm
10 Window head .../... cm
11 Door opening
12 Rail .../... cm
13 Door post .../... cm
14 Sill or base plate .../... cm
15 External elevation
16 Joists
17 Section Q – Q
18 Plan at H – H

Framed timber wall construction, details

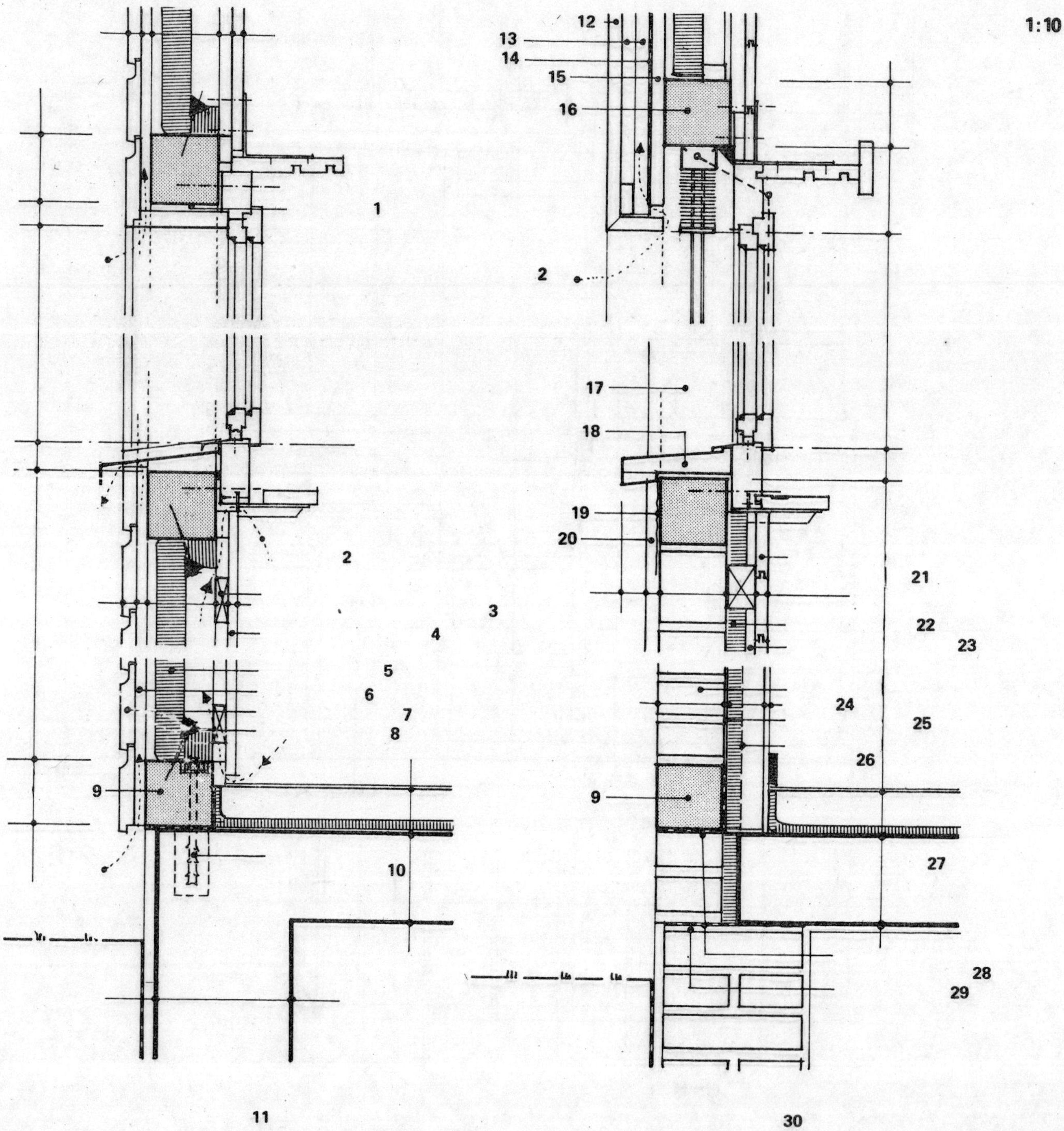

1 Grounds
2 Air circulation slit
3 Radiator bearer
4 Vertical boarding
5 Insulation quilt
6 Studding
7 Weatherboarding
8 Fixing fillet
9 Sill or base plate
10 Sill anchor bolt
11 Section, upstand under window
12 External boarding
13 Studding
14 Impervious membrane
15 Diagonal boarding
16 Window head
17 Plaster to reveals
18 Oak window sill, glued
19 Bitumen felt impervious layer
20 External rendering
21 Horizontal tongued and grooved boarding
22 Insulation board
23 Studding (double)
24 Facing brickwork panels
25 Possible studding
26 Two-layer insulation boarding
27 Reinforced concrete floor slab
28 Horizontal d.p.c.
29 Level bed
30 Alternative construction

Lintel, Threshold and Breast Design

We usually distinguish between the following types of construction: conventional, mixed or elemental system.

With Venetian blind (folding) shutters, a solid lintel (with or without frame stop) or a design without lintel is necessary. An external lintel (facing) is sufficient for gathered lamellas. A one or two-part box design – location depending on frame distance to outer facade line and/or shutter retraction device – is recommended for roll shutters.
The outer lintel margin requires insulation only if 1) the front lintel forms a unit with the ceiling and the (topping) subfloor does not offer sufficient temperature insulation or 2) if the underside of the ceiling is not appropriately insulated to a depth of 25 to 50 cm from the frame or the rear lintel with vertical side. With present-day facade paints (dispersion paints, etc.) weather has little effect on the various types of construction. This is not the case with earlier types of paints (lime base).

Breast height is determined according to local regulations and requirements and the bricks selected (and their dimensions). Among breast types we distinguish between the full and niched design. In either case, the insulation value must match that of the exterior walls.

Facade plaster layers in normal design according to work procedure:
Cement impact spray saturated; base leveling plaster with sealing finish plaster in desired texture – abrasion, trowel plaster, broom finish, combed stucco, etc. – with grain according to sample.
Two-layer interior plastering consisting of base plaster finished with clean abrasion or smoothing. For certain types of base constructions, application of a cement spray plaster beforehand is unavoidable. Under the proper conditions and using present-day bonding additives, single-layer plaster with self-smoothing can be recommended.

Lintel

1:10

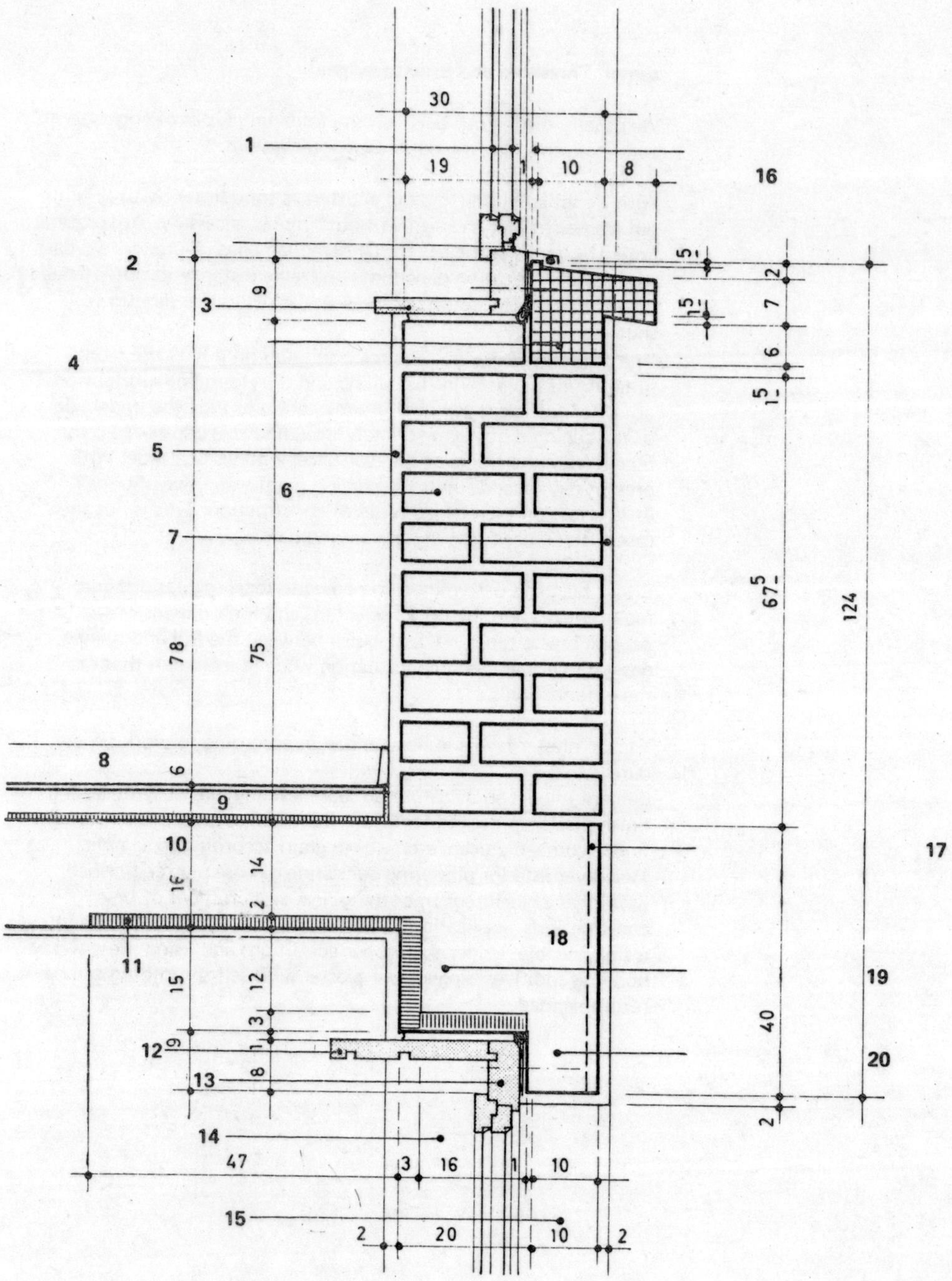

1 double glazing
2 aluminum weather stripping
3 window sill
4 artificial stone window ledge
5 interior plaster
6 breast brickwork
7 exterior plaster
8 base course
9 subfloor
10 solid floor
11 insulation
12 lintel board
13 window frame
14 interior reveal
15 exterior reveal
16 leveling plaster
17 clay brick inlay (not necessary with water-repellent outer coating)
18 lintel
19 rear lintel
20 front lintel

1:10

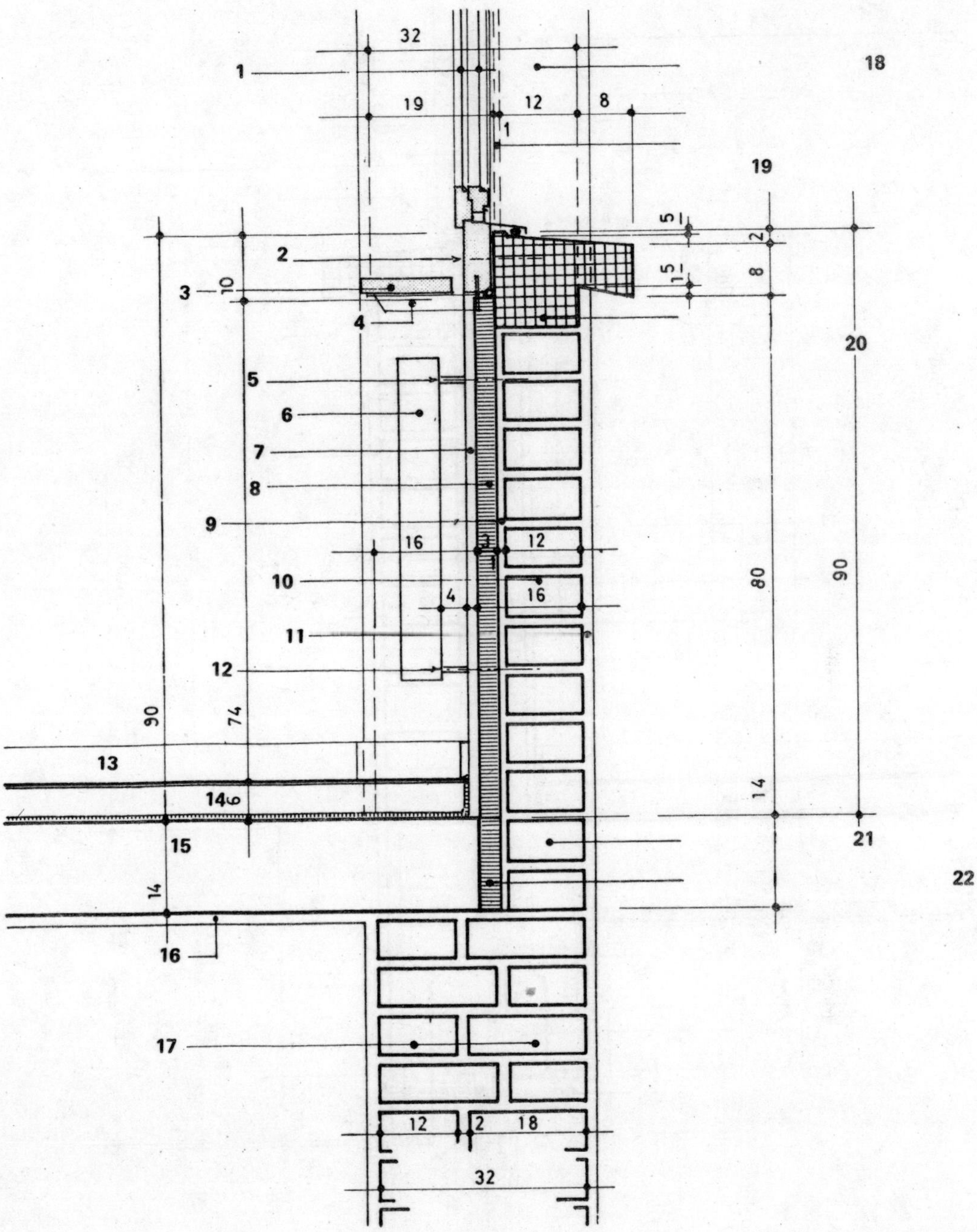

1 double glazing
2 patent stone screw
3 window sill
4 bracket
5 radiator retainer
6 radiator (heating element)
7 interior plaster 1.5 - 2 cm
8 breast insulation
9 leveling plaster
10 breast brickwork
11 exterior plaster 2 - 2.5 cm
12 radiator bracket
13 base course
14 subfloor
15 solid floor
16 ceiling plaster
17 exterior brickwork
18 reveal plaster
19 leveling plaster
20 artificial-stone window ledge
21 facing brickwork
22 floor face insulation

Roller shutter lintel/spandrel niche

1:10

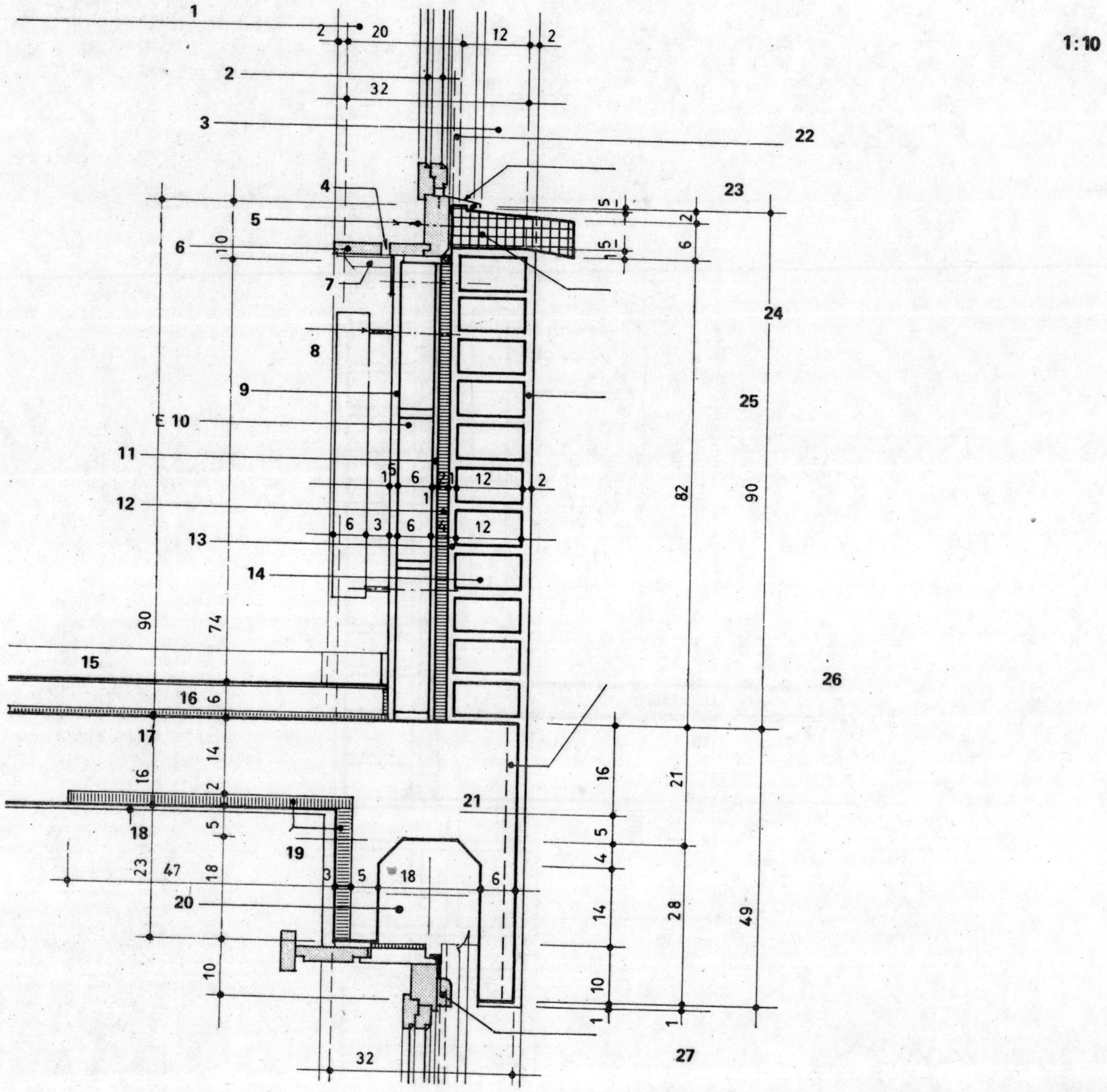

1 interior reveal
2 double glazing
3 exterior reveal
4 vent slot
5 patent stone screws
6 window sill
7 bracket
8 retainer
9 interior plaster 0.5 - 1 cm
10 lightweight panel
11 hollow space
12 insulation
13 leveling plaster
14 breast brickwork
15 base course
16 subfloor
17 solid floor
18 ceiling plaster
19 insulation
20 roll shutter box, size according to window height and system
21 lintel
22 leveling plaster
23 aluminum weather stripping
24 artificial stone window ledge
25 exterior plaster
26 poss. brick clay inlay
27 frame and ledge slip

Face stone window sill

1:10

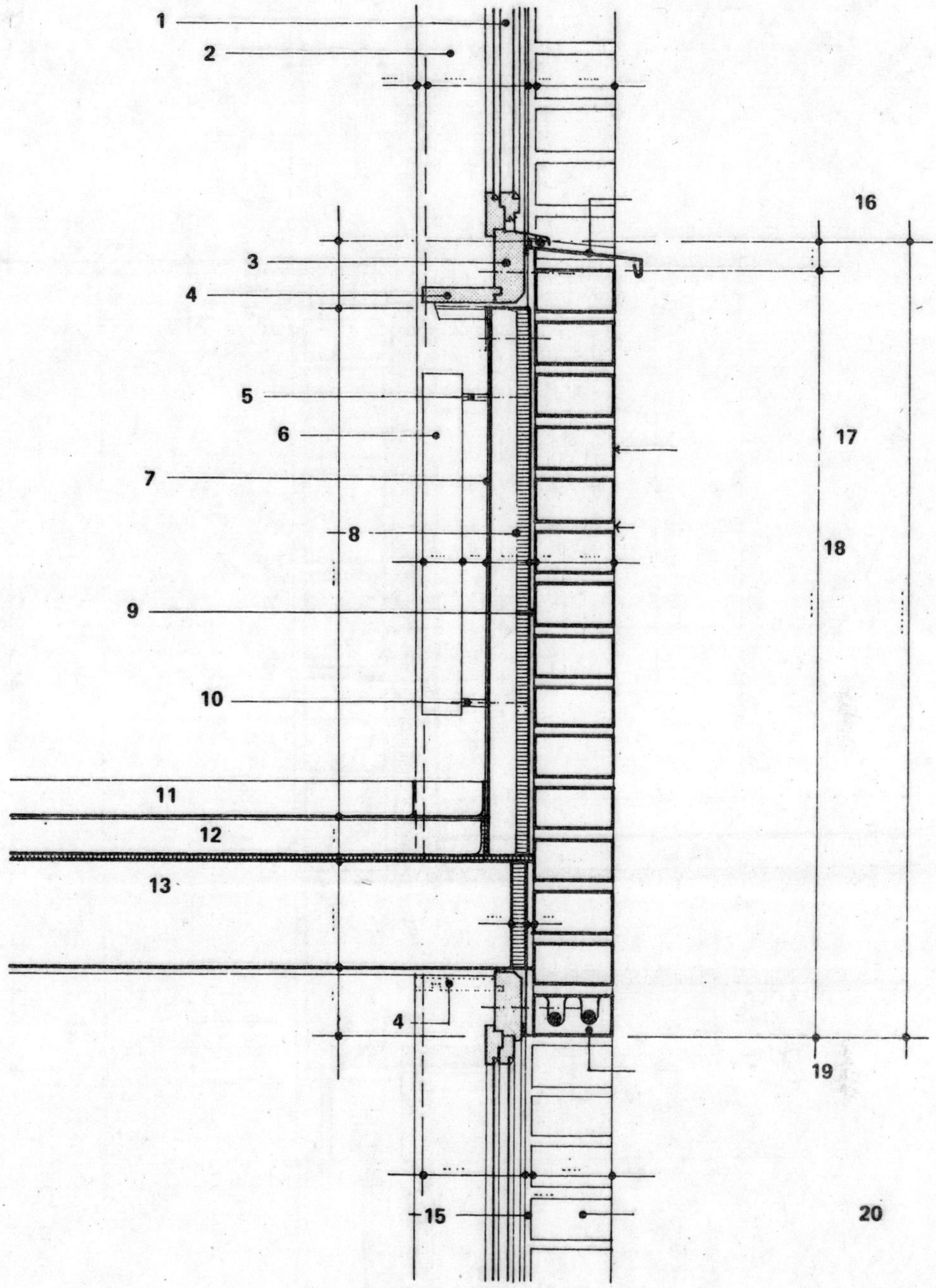

	10 radiator bracket
1 double-glazed window	11 PVC base course
2 interior reveal	12 subfloor
3 wooden window frame	13 concrete floor
4 window sill	14 curtain plank
5 radiator retainer	15 leveling plaster
6 radiator (heating element)	16 metal window ledge
7 smoothing	17 exposed brickwork
8 two-layer insulation panel system . . . 4 + 2 cm	18 joints filled flush
	19 prestressed clay plank
9 hollow space	20 face stone reveal

Lintel/spandrel

1:10

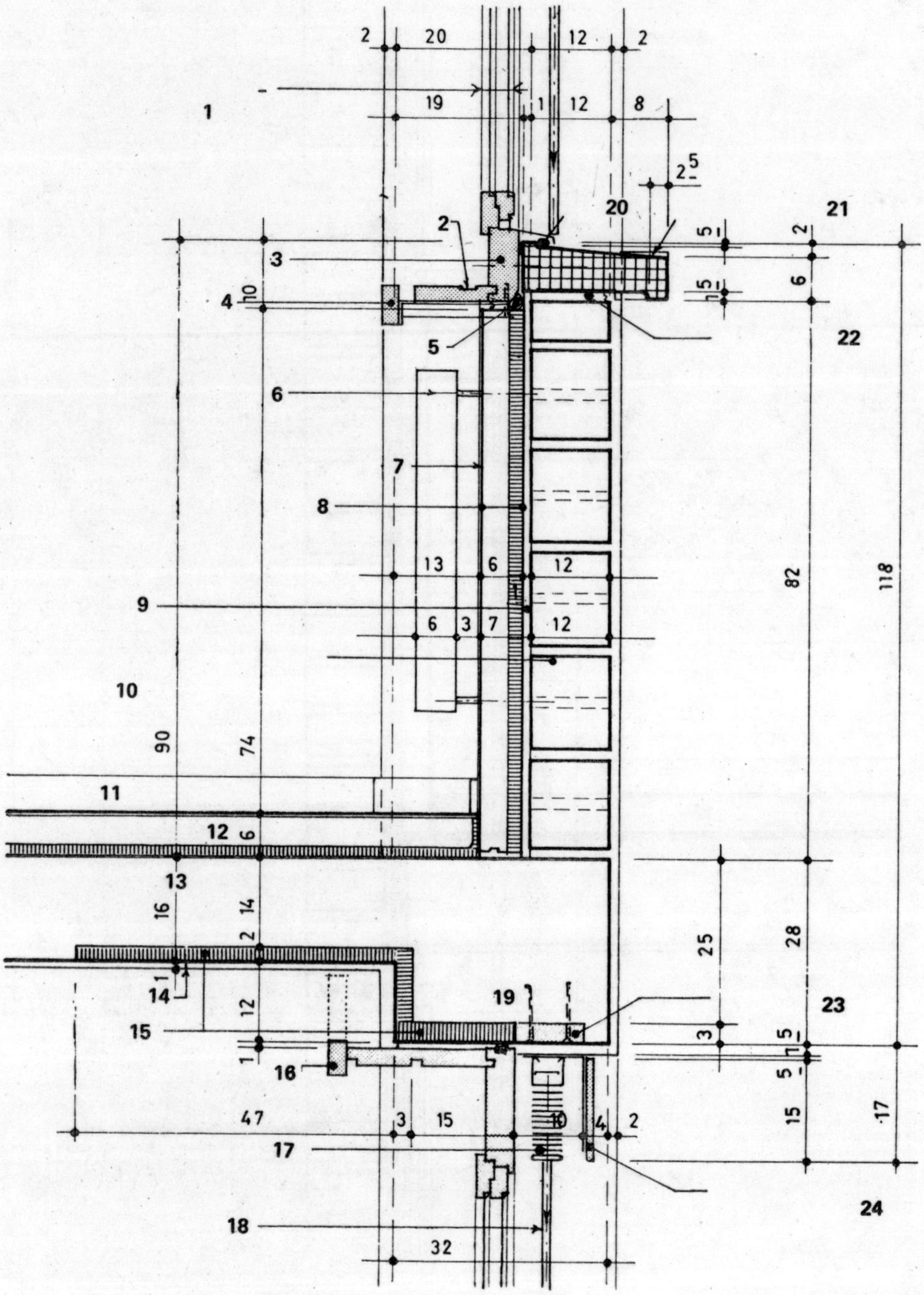

1 double glazed - window casement
2 condensation water trough
3 wooden window frame
4 sill facing panel
5 glass-silk braid insert
6 radiator retainer
7 smooth plaster layer (smoothing)
8 two-layer insulation panel system . . . 4 + 2 cm
9 hollow space
10 breast brickwork of normal or double normal bricks
11 base course
12 lower layer
13 solid floor
14 ceiling plaster
15 insulation
16 lintel facing panel
17 gathered lamella blinds
18 guide track
19 lintel
20 putty
21 side batter
22 sand bed
23 dowel-pin plank inlay
24 blind cover panel facing

1:10

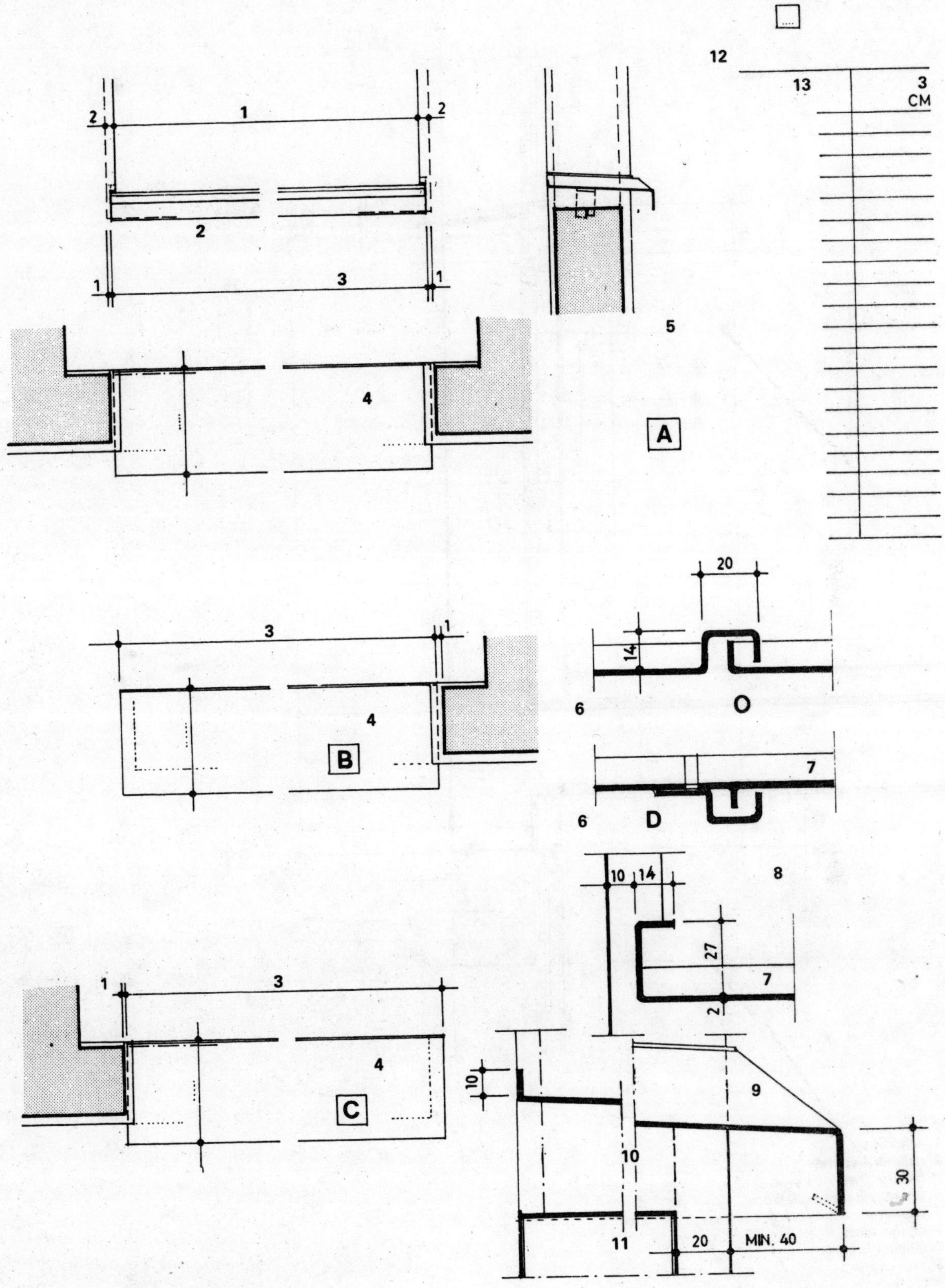

1 window clearance
2 side view
3 length of metal window sill
4 top view
5 cross section
6 expansion joint
7 raised border
8 side plaster connection
9 plaster connection border
10 mortar bed
11 spandrel
12 window sill - parts list
13 piece

Lintel/exposed concrete breast

1:10

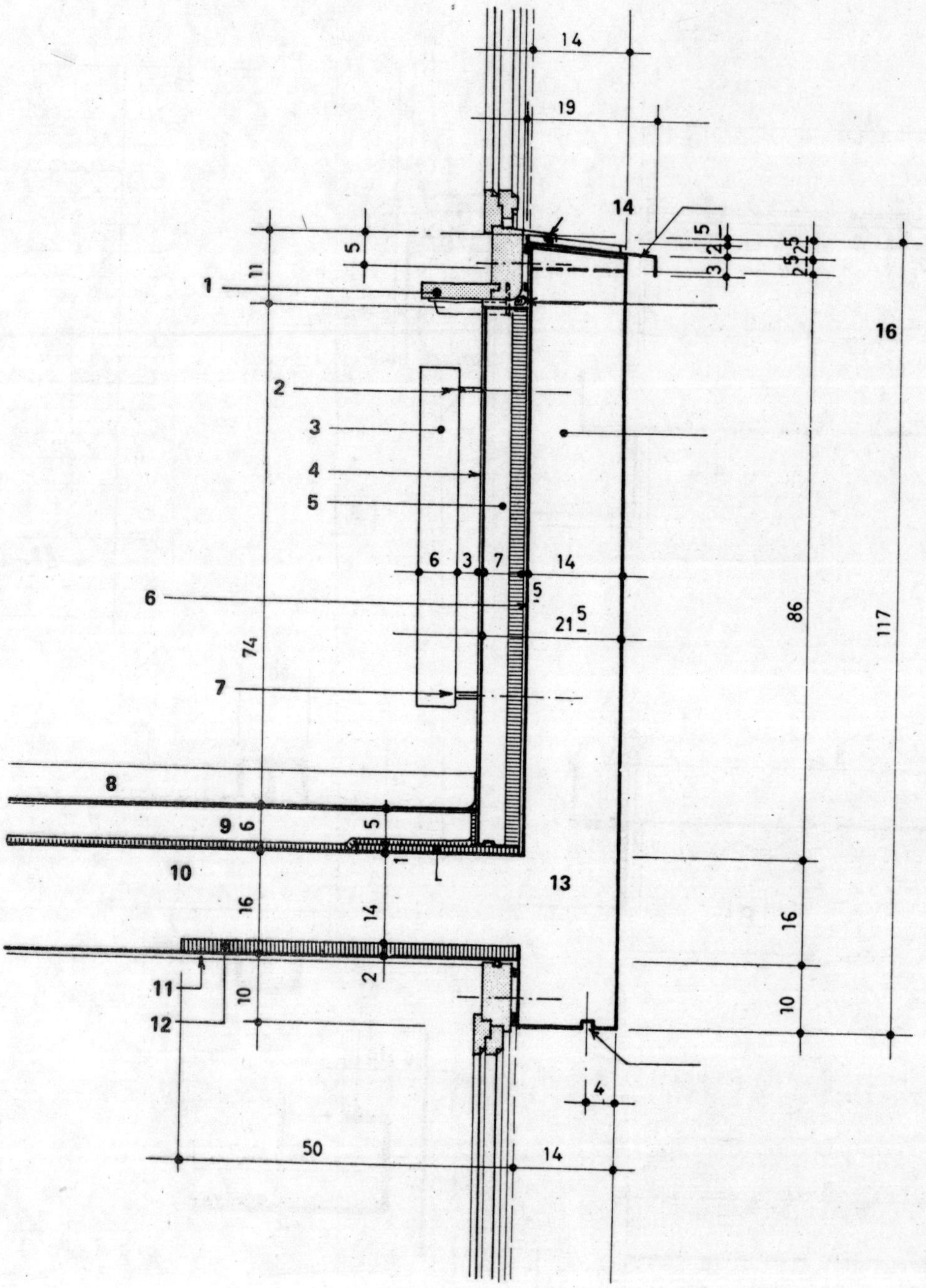

1 window sill
2 radiator (retainer)
3 radiator (heating element)
4 smoothing approx. 0.5 cm
5 two-layer insulation panel system . . . 4 + 2 cm
6 hollow space
7 radiator bracket
8 base course
9 subfloor
10 solid floor
11 ceiling plaster
12 insulation
13 back-up insulation
14 putty
15 metal window ledge
16 glass silk braid inlay
17 exposed concrete breast
18 plastic water insert

Exposed concrete window breast

1:10

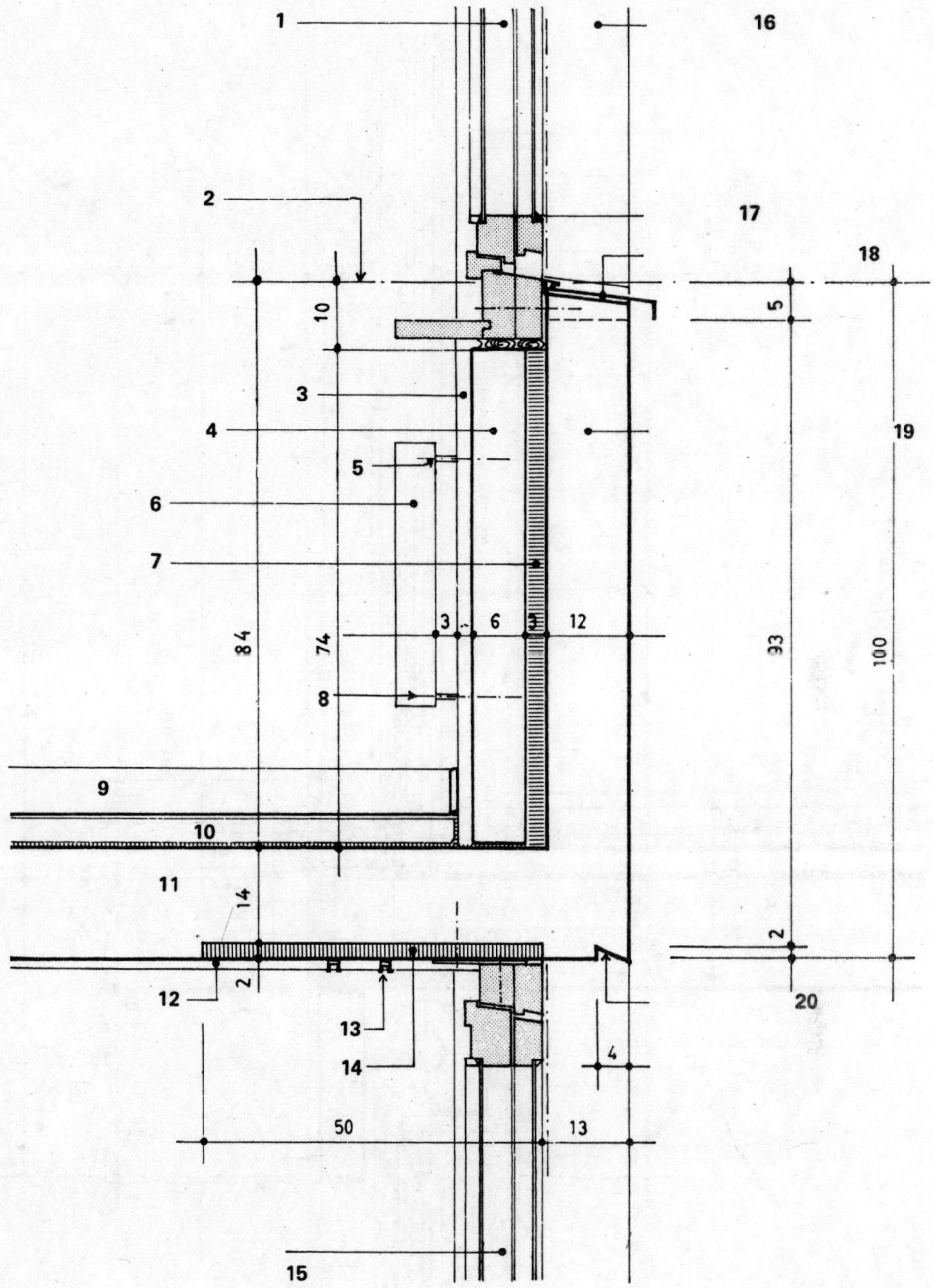

1 swing casement window
2 upper edge window ledge
3 interior plaster or smoothing
4 lightweight panel
5 retainer, system . . .
6 heating element
7 . . . insulation panel
. . . mm thick
8 bracket, system . . .
9 base course
10 subfloor
11 solid floor
12 ceiling plaster
13 curtain tracks, double sections only where curtains are extended sideways
14 . . . insulation,
. . . mm thick
15 swing casement window with built-in gathered-lamella blinds
16 reveal
17 fillister
18 metal window ledge
19 exposed concrete breast
20 water nib

Roll shutter lintel/balcony door threshold

1:10

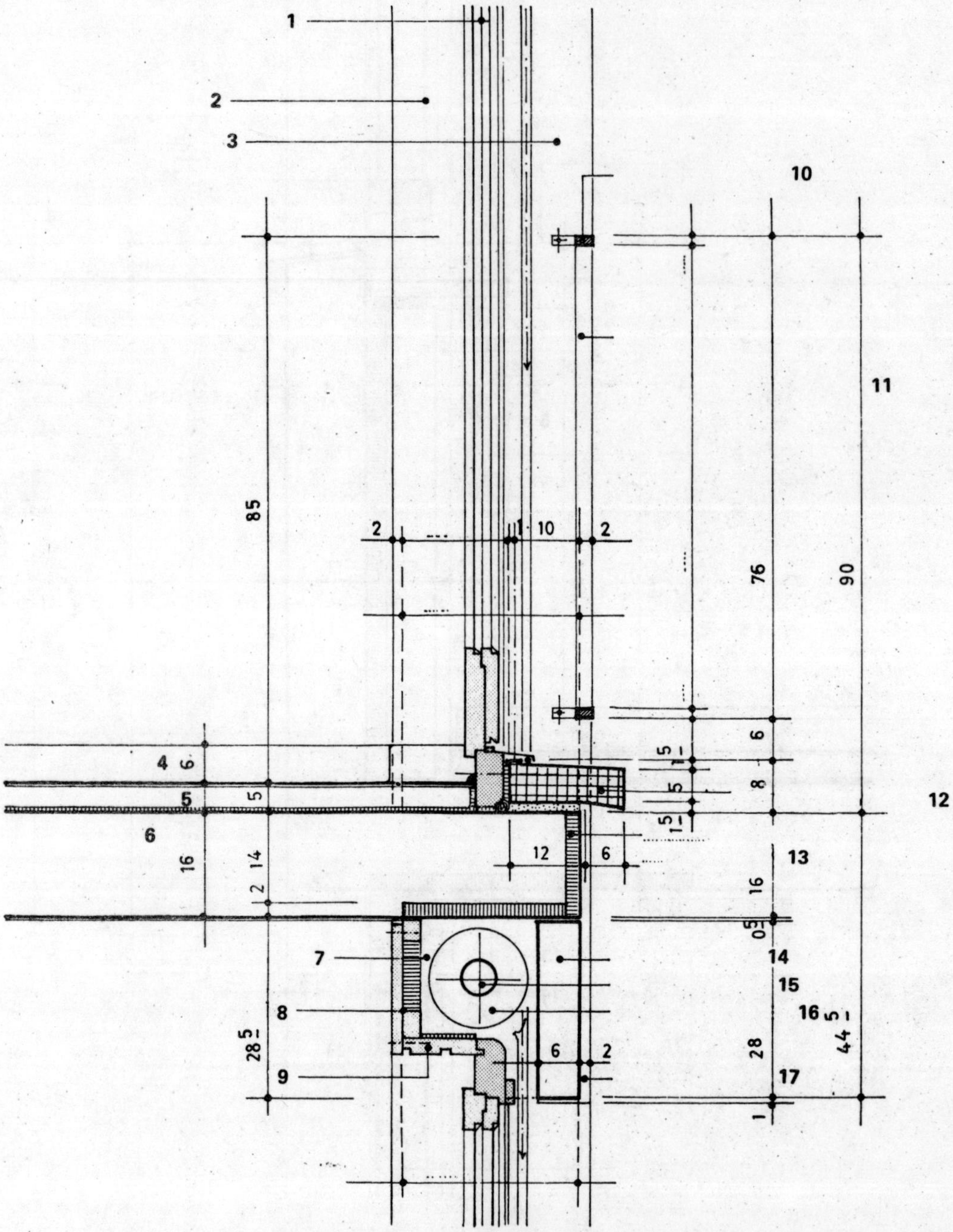

1 double-glazed door
2 interior door reveal
3 exterior door reveal
4 PVC base course
5 lower layer
6 solid floor
7 roll shutter box
8 roll shutter insulation, removable
9 curtain plank
10 flat iron rod
11 bar-grating balustrade, balusters . . . / . . . mm thick at intervals of . . . cm
12 artificial stone threshold
13 . . . insulation panel, . . . mm thick
14 lintel element
15 roll shutter drum
16 roll shutter guard
17 facade plaster

Artificial stone window sills

1:10

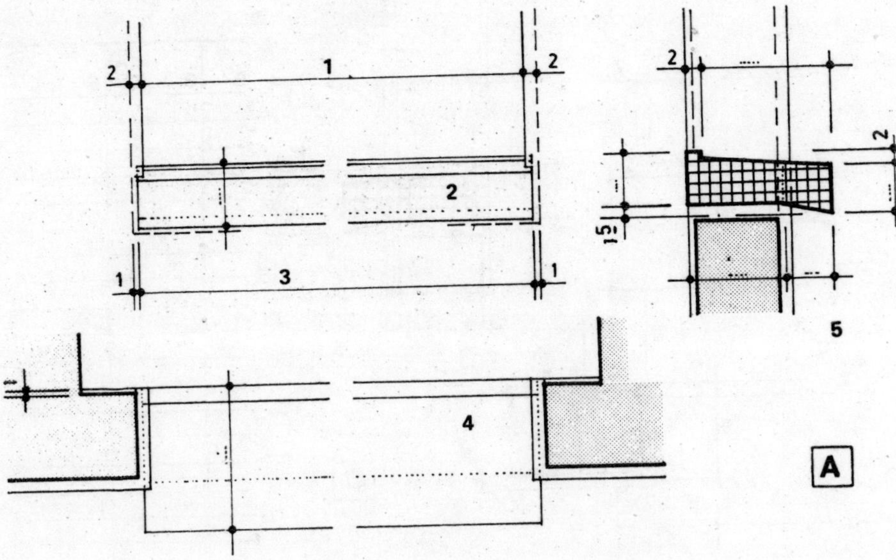

7

9	3 CM

9

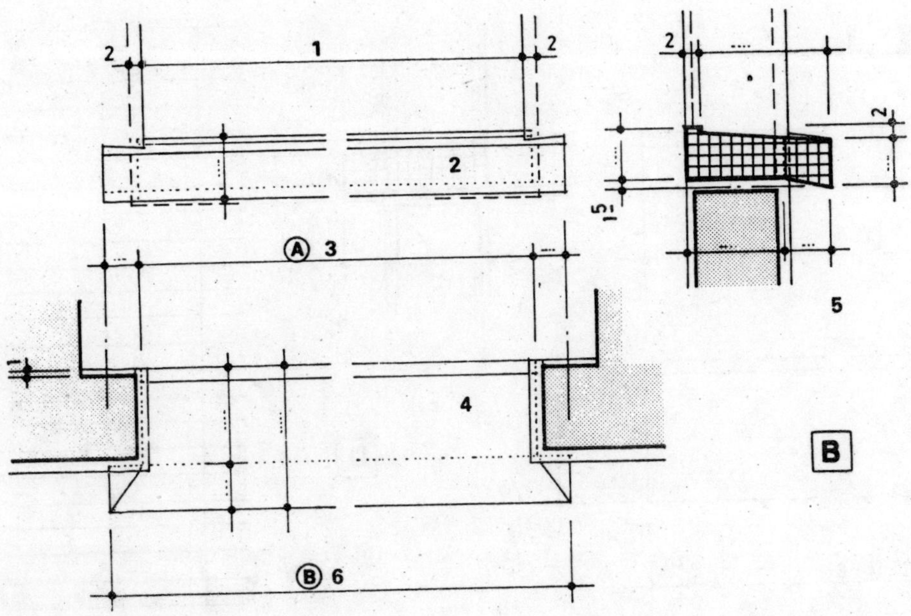

7

9	3 Ⓐ CM	6 Ⓑ CM

1 window clearance
2 side view
3 ledge length
4 top view
5 cross section
6 ledge length B
7 window ledge, parts list
9 piece

Artificial stone window sills

1:10

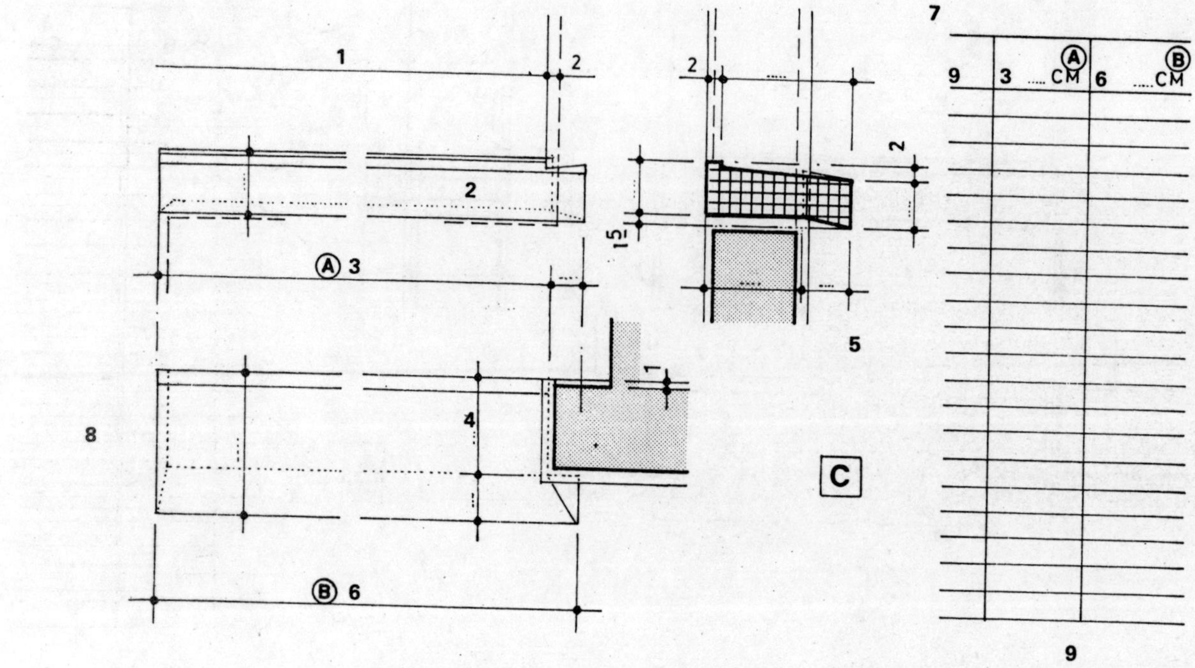

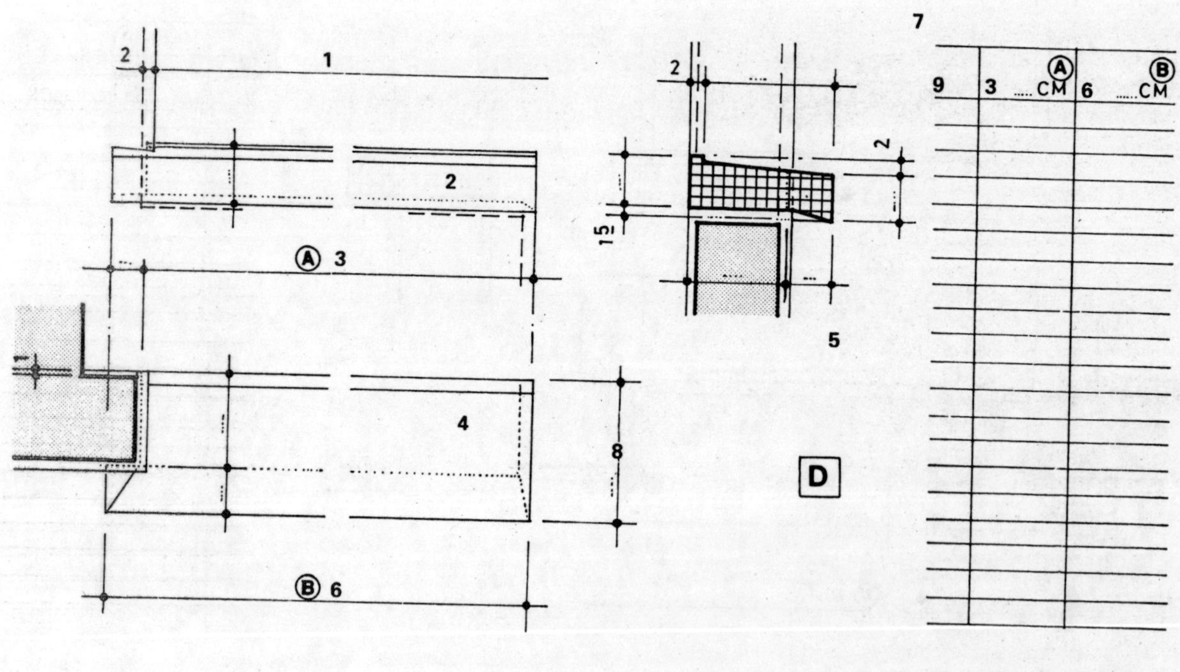

1 window clearance
2 side view
3 ledge length A
4 top view
5 cross section
6 ledge length B
7 window ledge, parts list
8 balcony door, side
9 piece

1:10

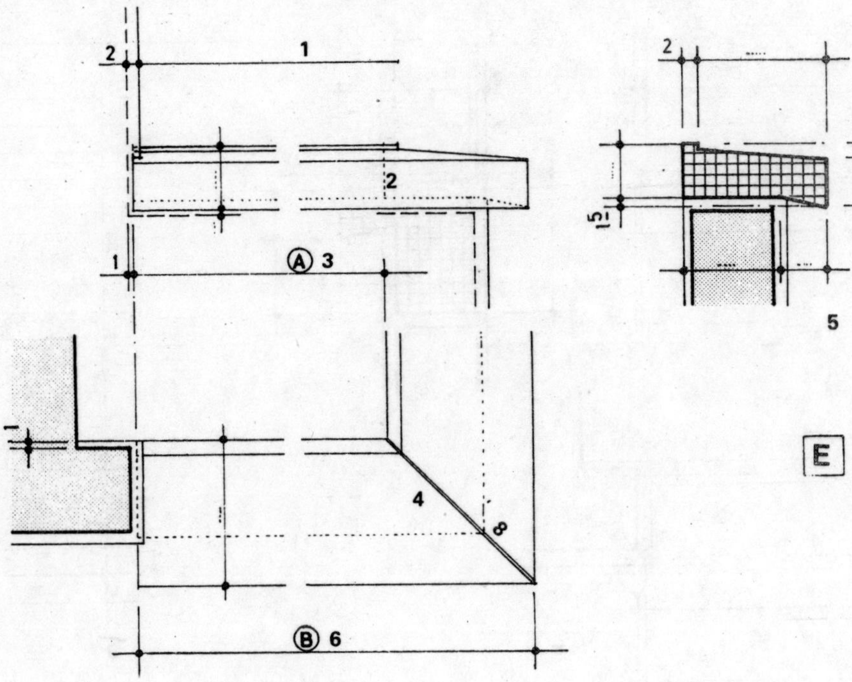

7

9	3 (A) .....CM	6 (B) .....CM

E

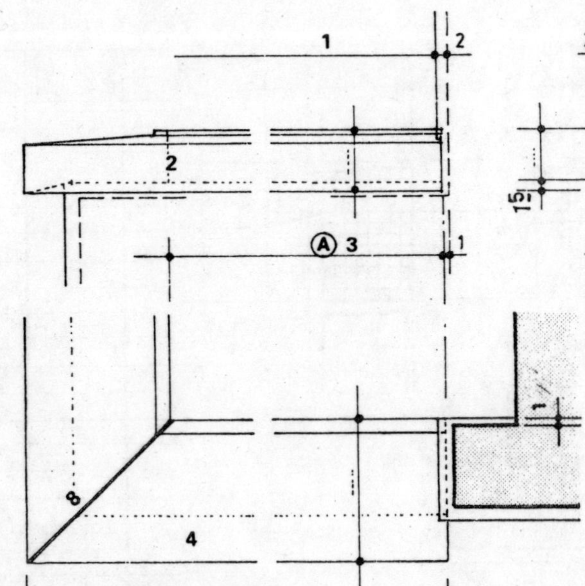

7

9	3 (A) .....CM	6 (B) .....CM

F

1 window clearance
2 side view
3 ledge length A
4 top view
5 cross section
6 ledge length B
7 window ledge, parts list
8 mitre
9 piece

Artificial stone window sills

1:10

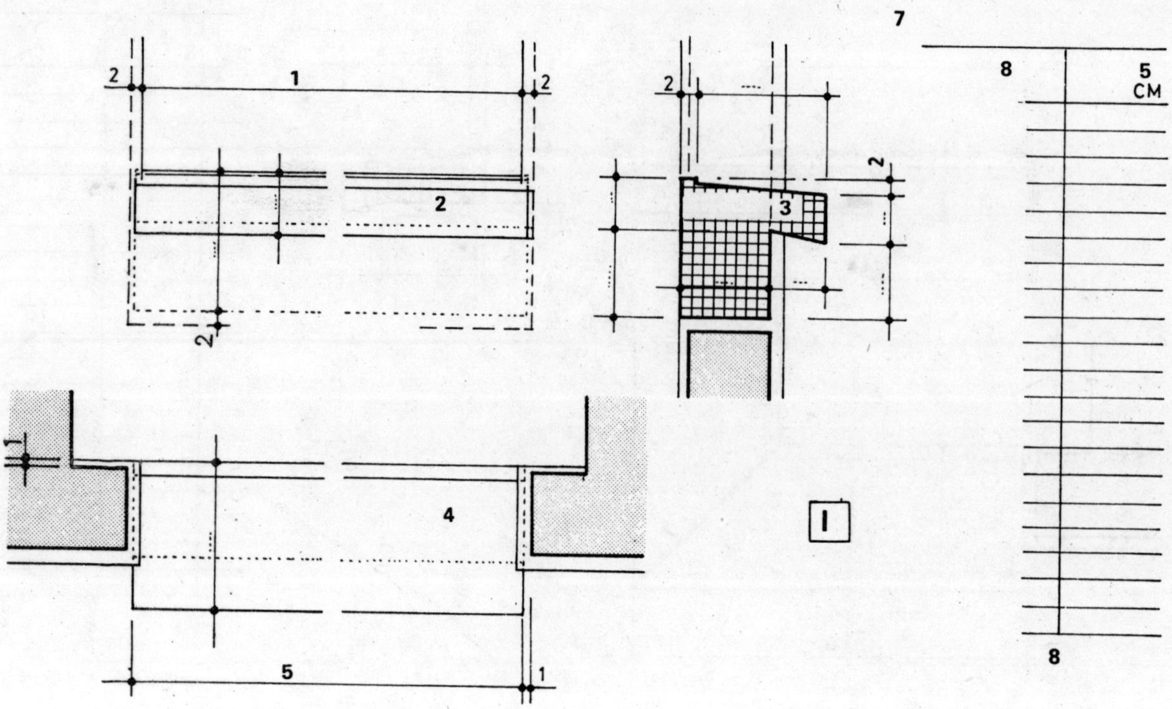

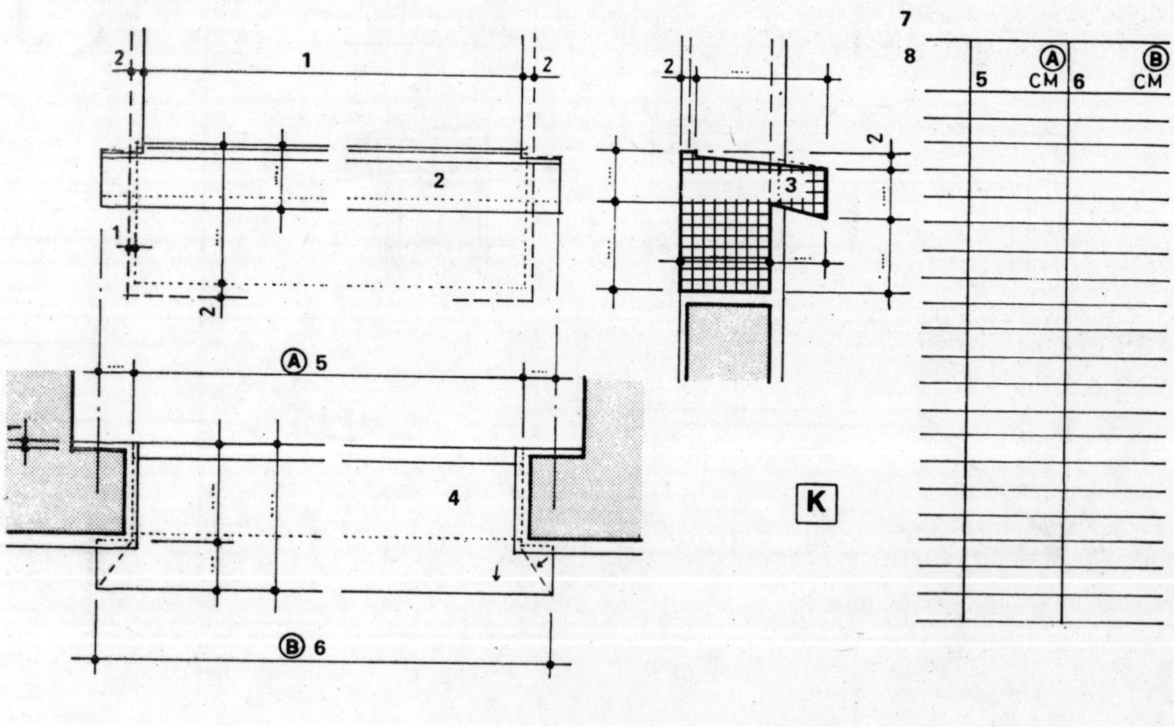

1 window clearance
2 side view
3 section
4 top view
5 ledge length A
6 ledge length B
7 window ledge, parts list
8 piece

1:10

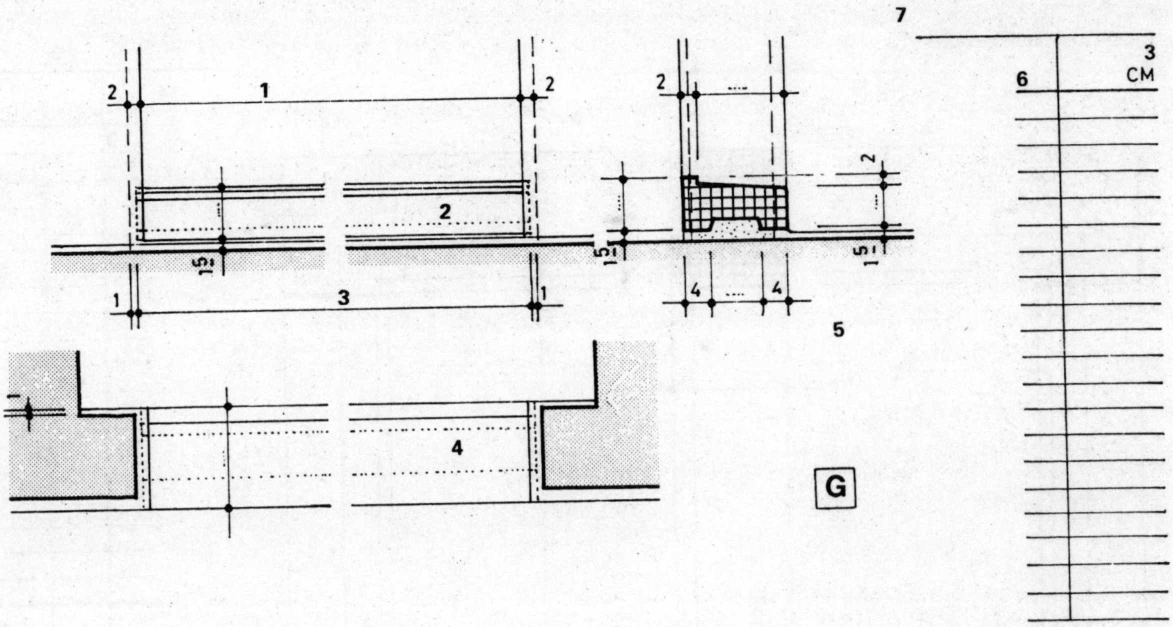

G

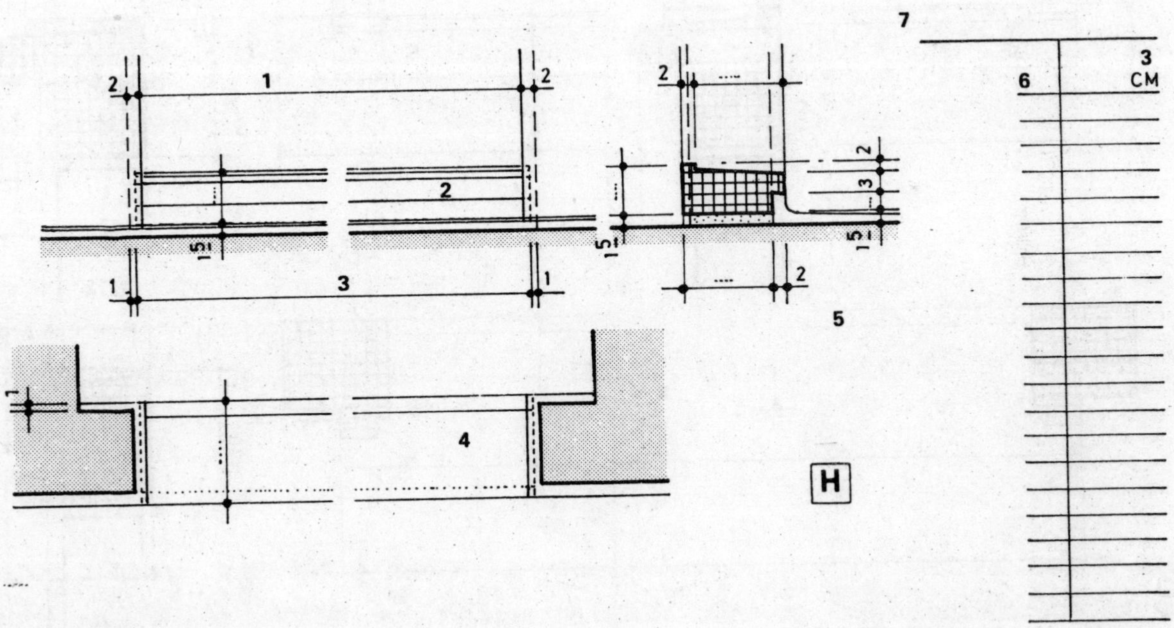

H

1 door clearance
2 side view
3 threshold length
4 top view
5 cross section
6 piece
7 door threshold, parts list

Window surround with shutter rebate

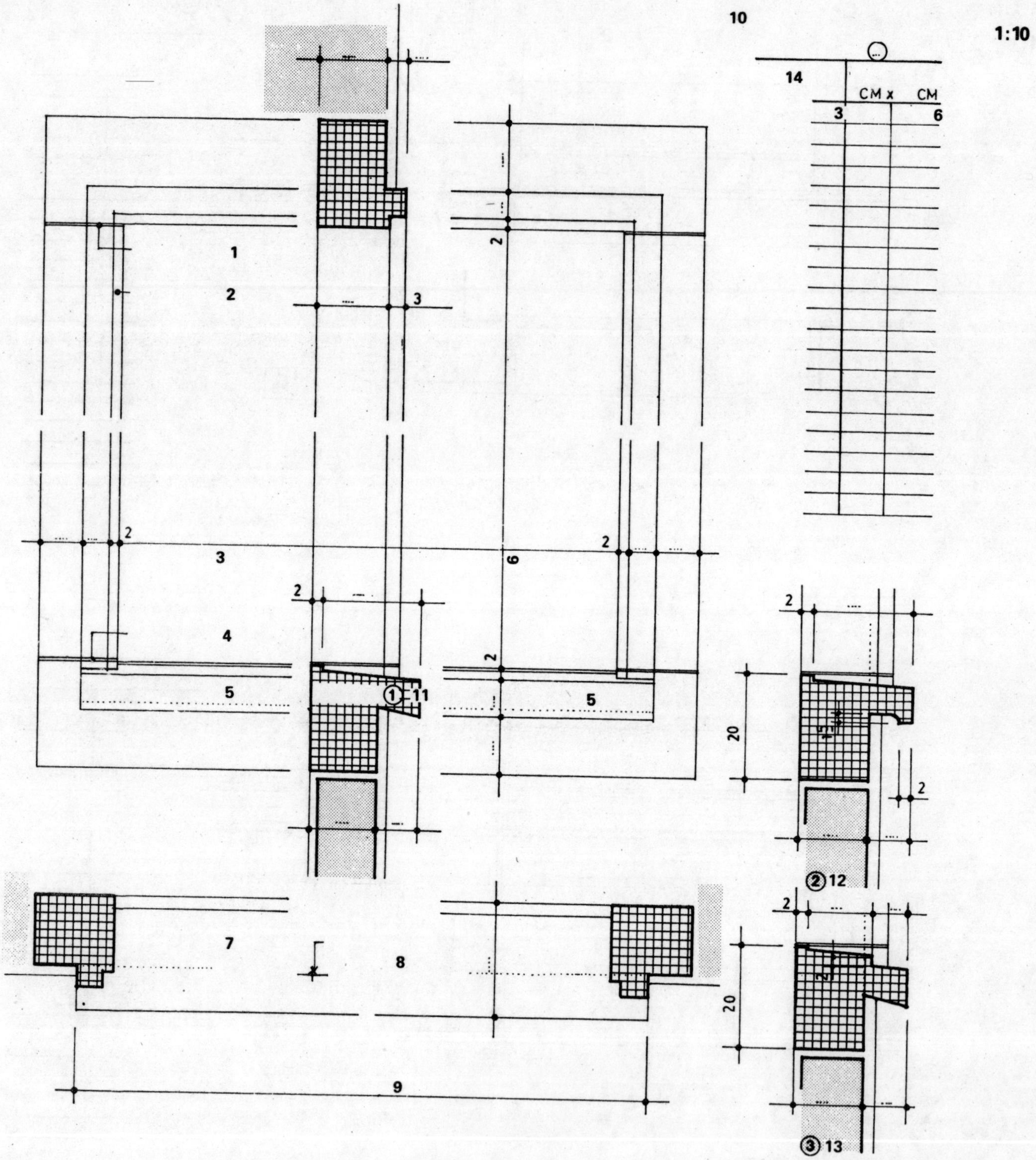

1 pressure joint
2 shutter rabbet
3 window clearance, width
4 standing joint
5 side view
6 window clearance, height
7 ledge, top view
8 shutter stop cam
9 window ledge length (exposed part)
10 parts list, window mounting with ledge variants
11 section 1
12 section 2
13 section 3
14 piece
15 clearance cm x cm

Door surround for roll shutter design

1:10

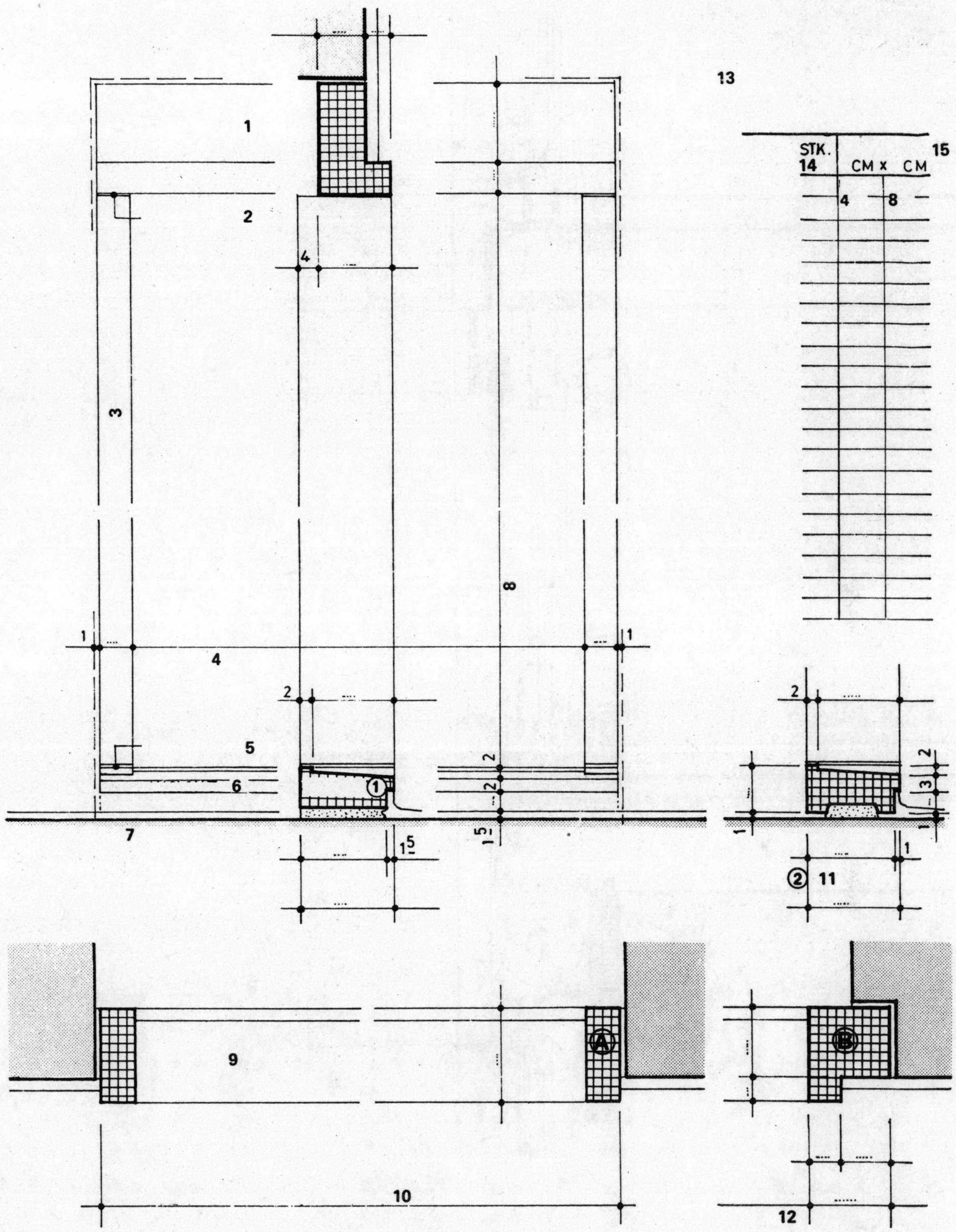

1 lintel, supporting
2 press joint
3 walls
4 door clearance, width
5 stand joint
6 side view
7 balcony slab
8 door clearance height
9 threshold, top view
10 threshold length (exposed part)
11 section 2
12 door clearance, width
13 parts list, door mounting with ledge variants and walls
14 piece
15 clearance cm x cm

Facing elements

1:10

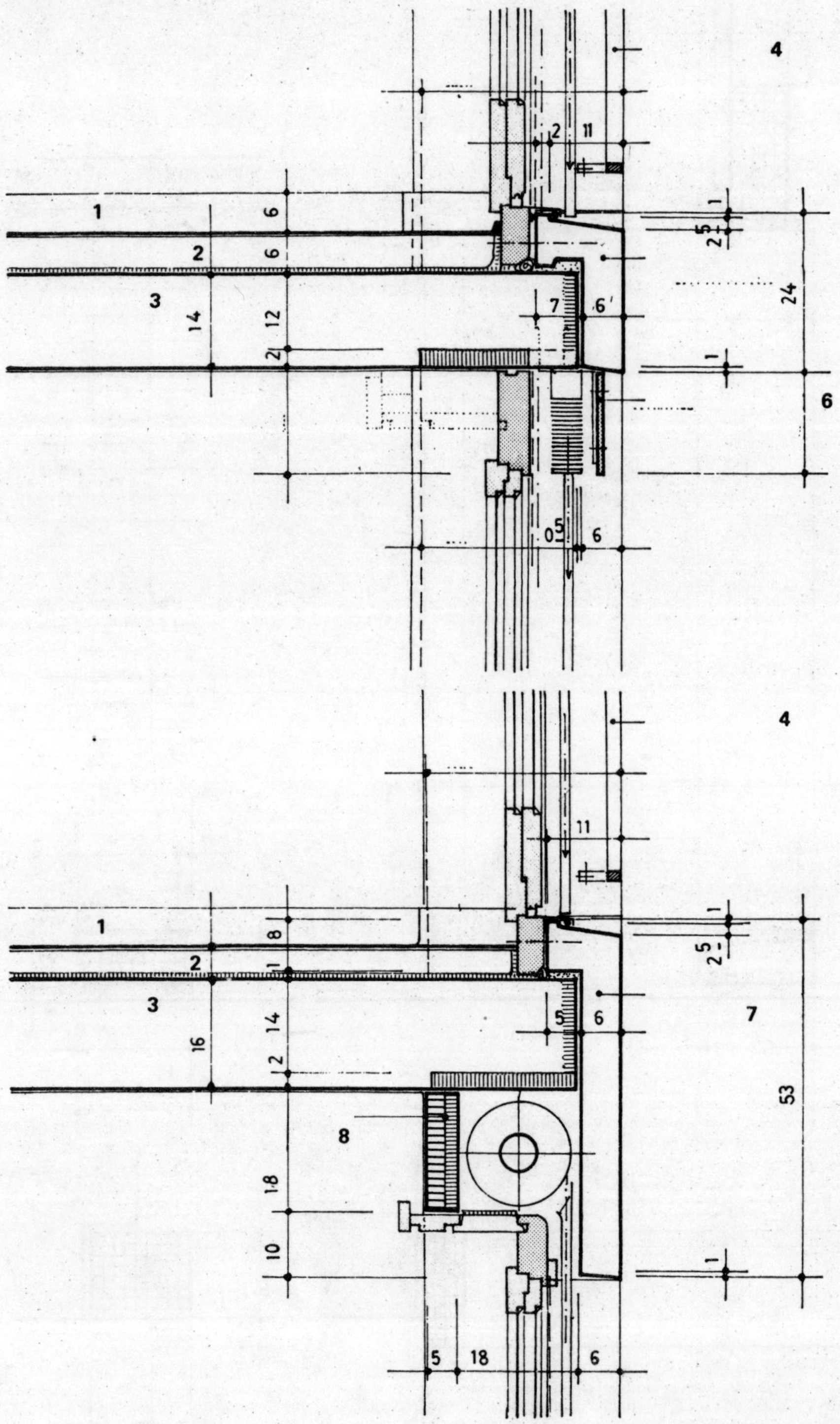

1 base course
2 subfloor
3 concrete floor
4 bar grating
5 front facing element in . . .
6 . . . apron
7 facing cover - lintel element
8 rear lintel, non-supporting

1:10

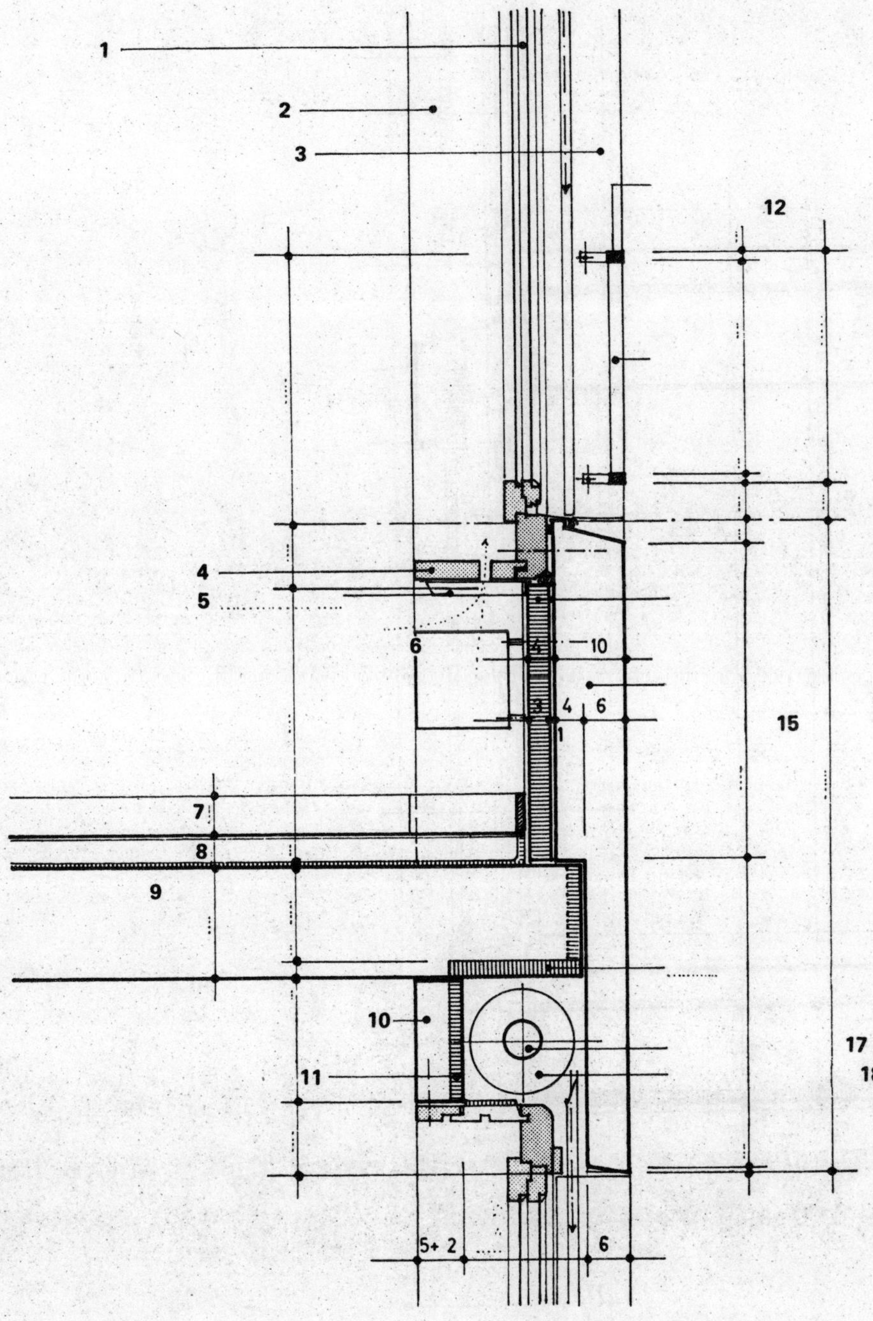

1 double-glazed window
2 interior window reveal
3 exterior window reveal
4 window sill
5 bracket system . . .
6 vent slot
7 base course of . . .
8 subfloor
9 concrete floor
10 . . . rear lintel
11 insulated with . . . panel . . . cm thick
12 . . . flat-iron rod . . . / . . . mm
13 bar railings, balusters . . . / . . . mm at intervals of . . . cm
14 . . . insulation panel bonded to the element
15 . . . breastwork element, exposed surface treatment according to sample
16 . . . insulation panel
17 roll shutter drum
18 roll shutter guard

Frame timber/floor connections

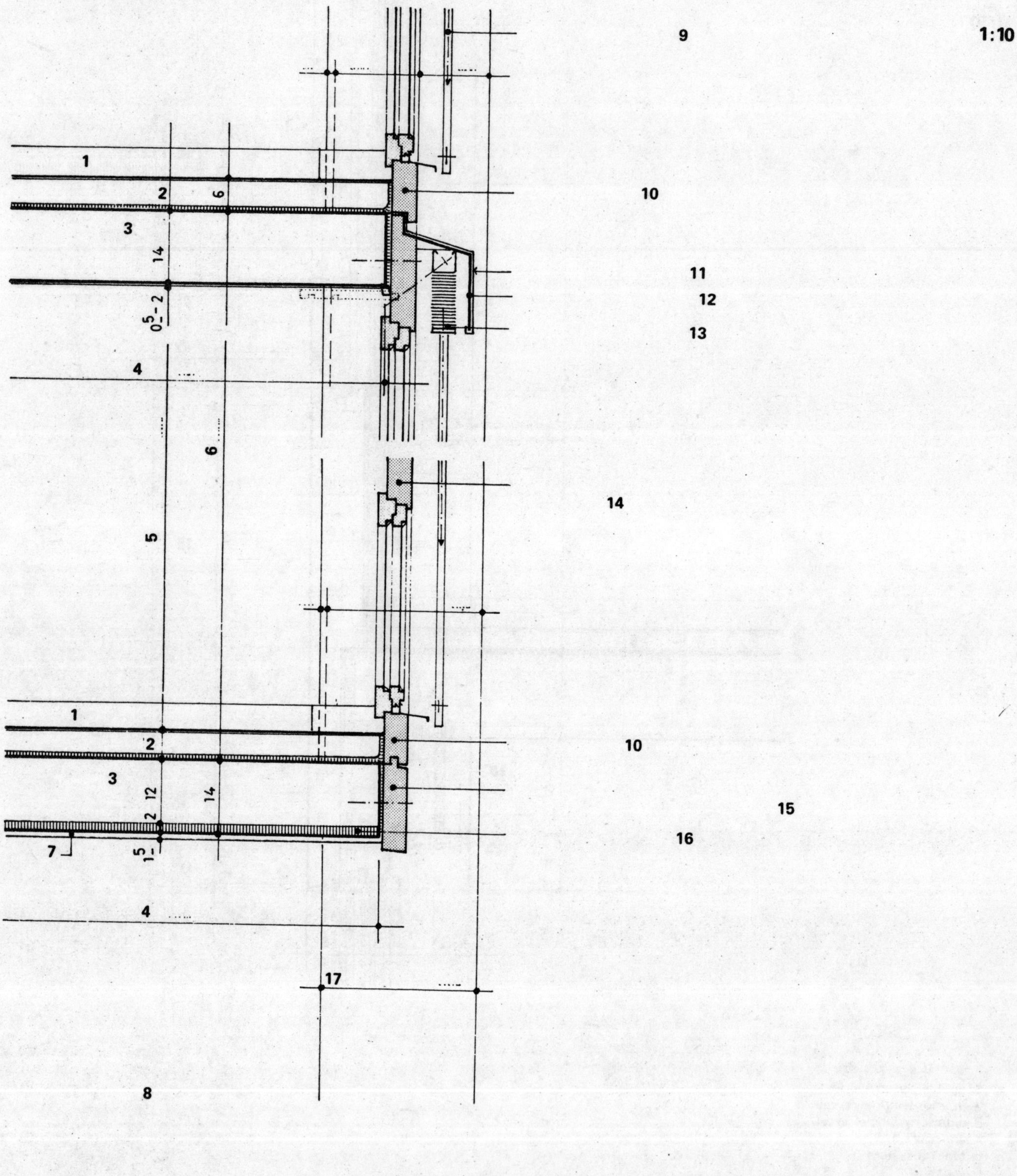

1 base course
2 lower layer
3 concrete floor
4 ceiling plane
5 room clearance height
6 story clearance height, unplastered-unplastered
7 plaster
8 entrance hall
9 guide tracks
10 frame timber
11 . . . sheet-metal box
12 . . . flat-iron . . . / . . . mm
13 gathered-lamella blinds
14 breast wood (transom)
15 lip timber with cocking for grooved connection
16 . . . insulation panel
17 pillar

1:10

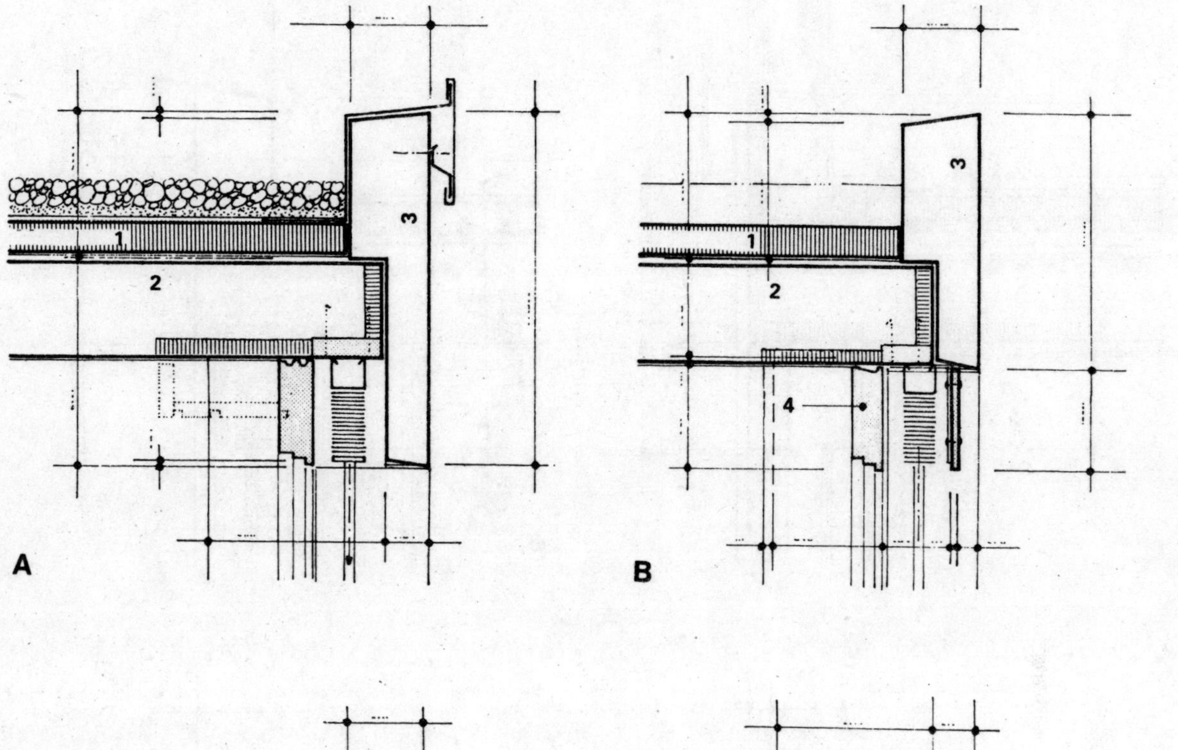

1 insulation
2 concrete floor
3 border element
4 wood frame
5 rear lintel insulated
6 flat-roof border element
7 element height, lower edge to upper edge
8 dowel pin plank
9 roll shutter box element 1, 2, or 3-part

Flat roof/edging elements

1:10

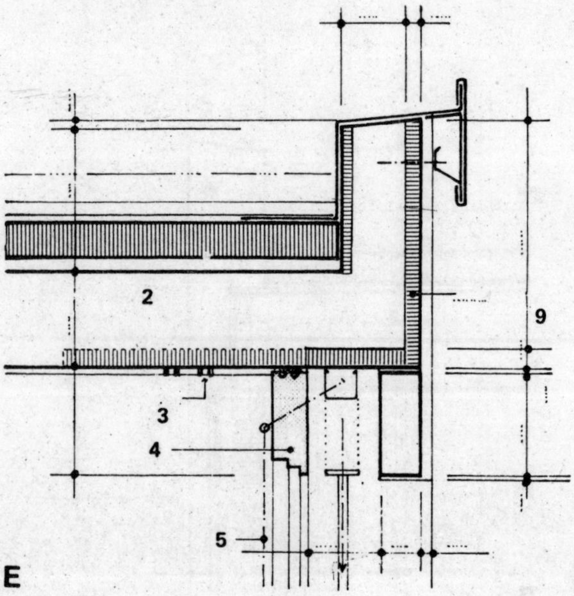

E

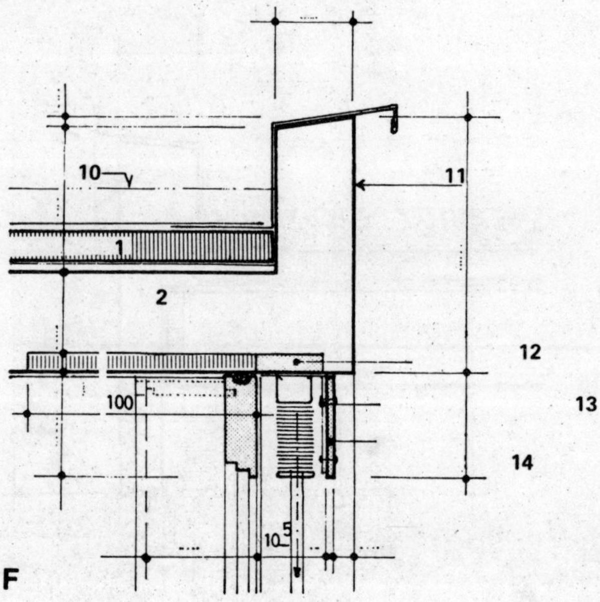

F

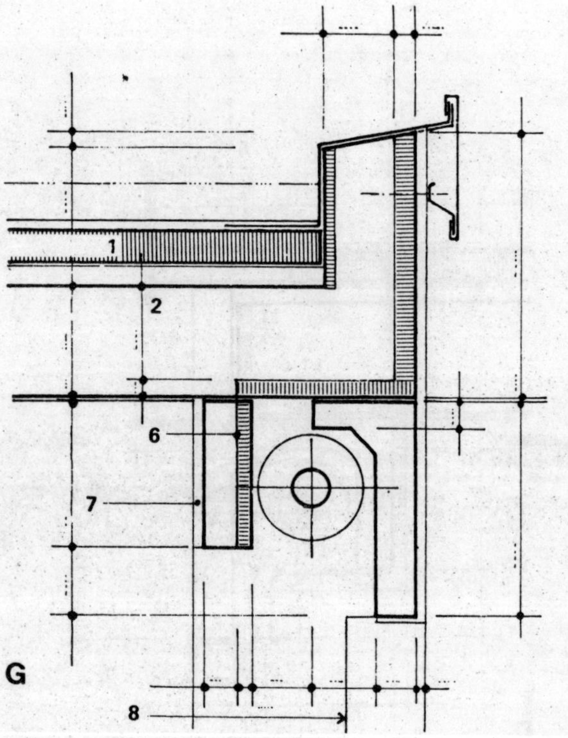

G

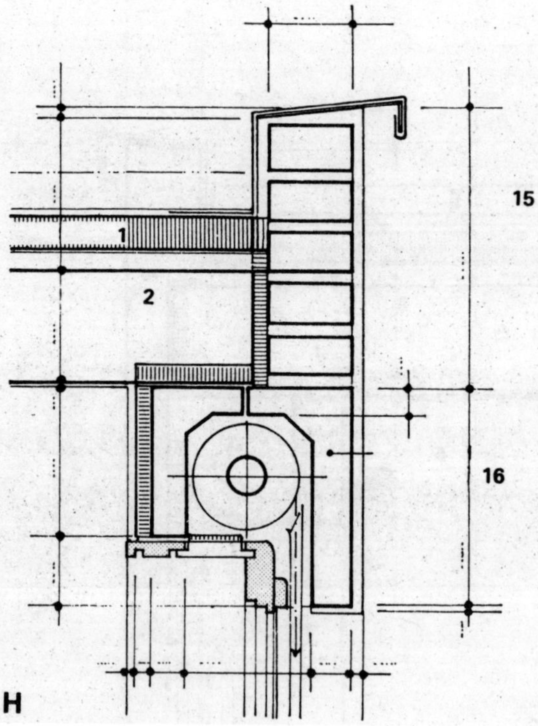

H

1 insulation
2 concrete floor
3 curtain track, double section
4 wood frame
5 crank rod
6 rear lintel insulated
7 plaster
8 rabbet
9 . . . insulation panel
10 upper edge flat roof covering
11 exposed concrete border
12 assembly with dowel pin plank
13 flat iron tie
14 eternit slab facing
15 roof curb
16 roll shutter box element 2-part

Balcony, Terrace and Loggia Parapet walls

In conventional design, joints at the roof connection must be neatly formed, possibly with shade strip inlays. Elements should have anchor reinforcement for strong floor connection. All horizontal and vertical traverses must be well executed. The slope of the breast surface should be directed inwards and the top side neatly smoothed so that water does not flow outwards.

Around the balcony slab, the breast should be recessed so that the cover surface can be applied approx. 6 - 12 cm on the interior wall. In order for the water to drip off the element directly, the underside must slope toward the outside.

With normal types of concrete on concrete, a de-watering nib must be mounted parallel to the outer line. (The inlay strip is to be removed immediately after dismantling.)
Rain or wash water falling on the floor of the balcony is drained outwards at the lowest point in the slope by spouts or by a direct connection to the roof drainage system. (If possible, it should not be routed into the sewage drain; however, if there is no other possibility, a conduit siphon must be installed.)

The inner sides of flower troughs are to be neatly smoothed. One or two coats of asphalt are necessary. Trough drainage or overflow is provided by a sieve.

The 8 - 15 cm-deep seepage bed and humus may be inserted approx. ten days after coating, otherwise plants will die prematurely.

If the flower troughs are not accessible, a pipe sprinkling system should be installed over the entire length.

Brackets, support attachments, etc. are best secured with patent stone screws, thus eliminating all plaster closing work.

Cast-in-place exposed concrete balcony parapet wall

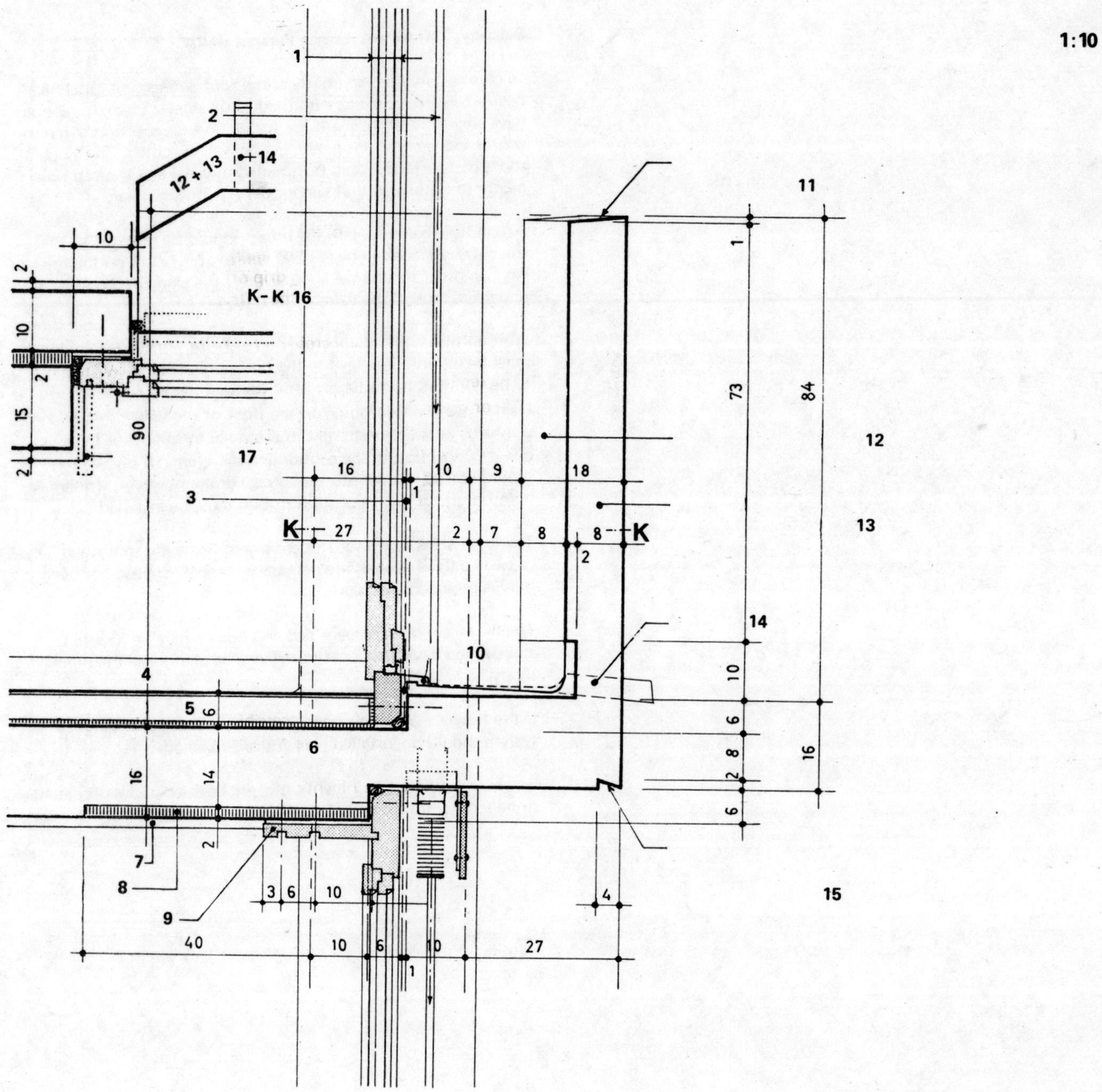

1 double glazing
2 guide track
3 leveling plaster
4 PVC base course
5 lower layer
6 concrete floor (solid floor)
7 ceiling plaster
8 insulation
9 curtain plank
10 putty
11 smooth cement coat on slope
12 side batter
13 exposed concrete balcony breast
14 spout
15 triangular lathe inlay (water nib)

1:10

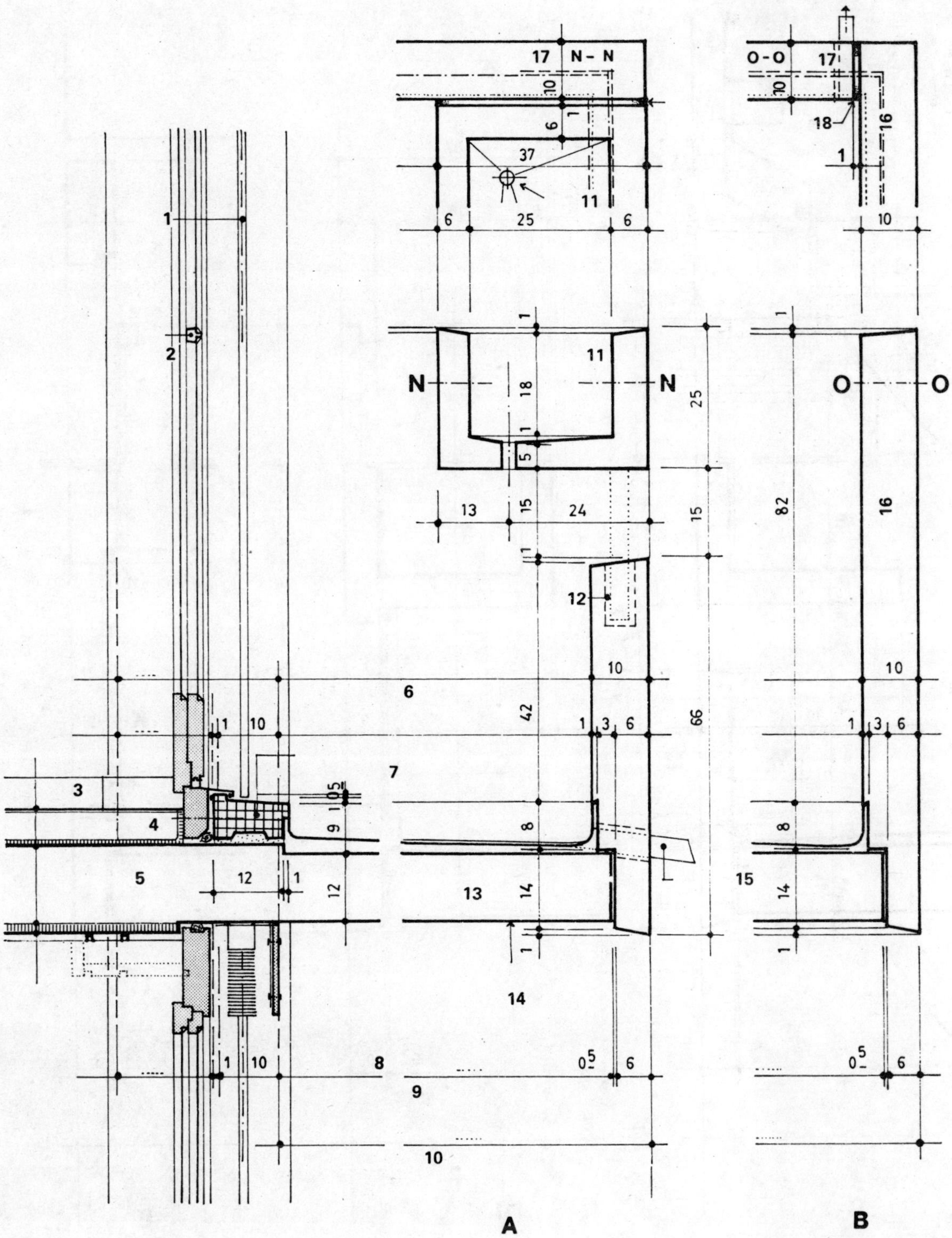

1 guide track
2 poss. crossbar, double glazing
3 base course
4 lower layer
5 solid floor
6 balcony, interior dimension
7 artificial stone threshold
8 balcony
9 interior dimension
10 exterior dimension
11 flower trough
12 recess 5/8/12 cm
13 balcony slab
14 underside, formwork-smooth exposed concrete
15 spout
16 element
17 side element
18 joint cement groove

Balcony breast elements

1:10

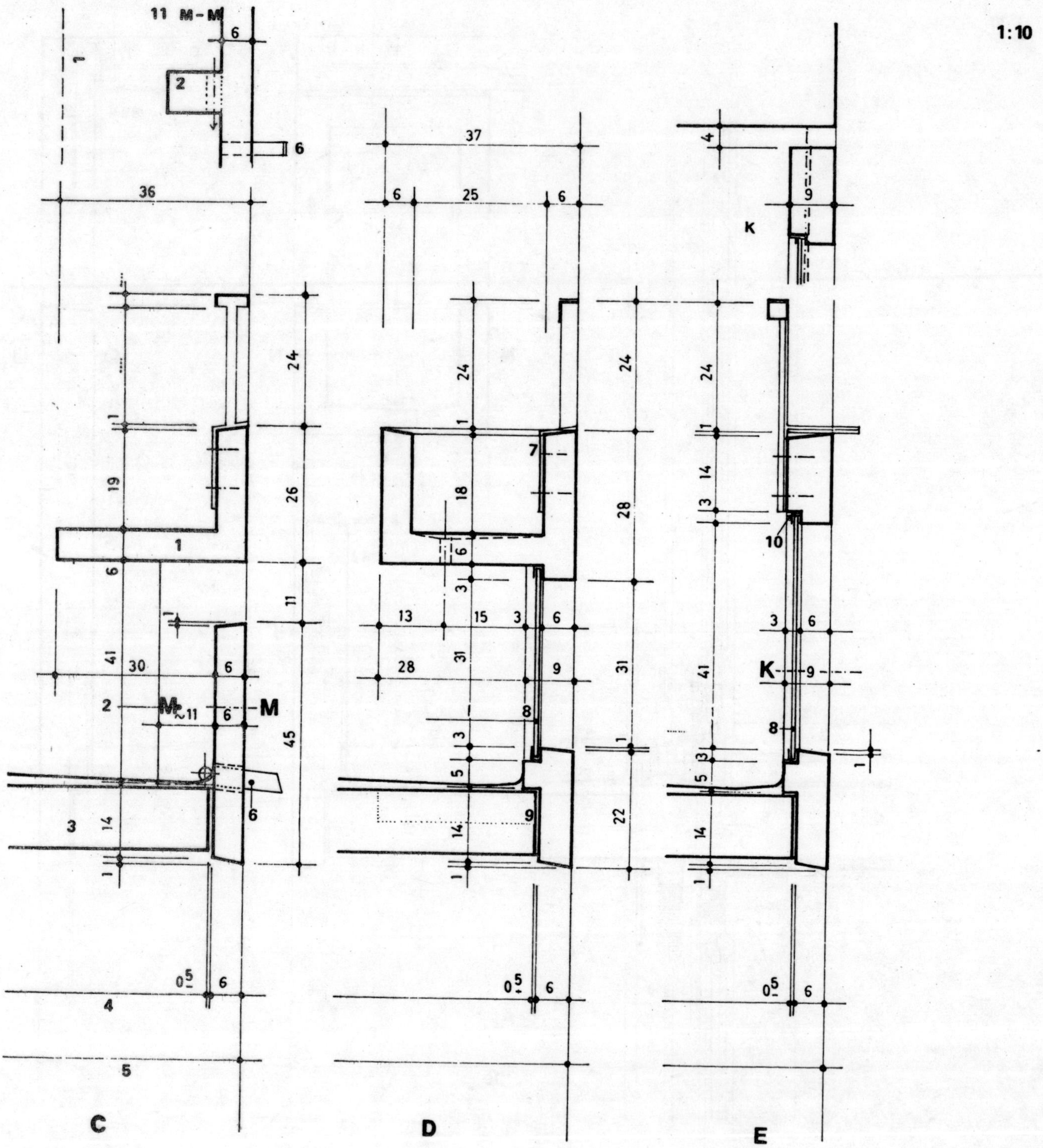

1 base plate
2 supporting rib
3 balcony slab
4 balcony, interior dimension
5 balcony, exterior dimension
6 balcony spout . . . / . . . mm
7 flower trough
8 wired glass . . . mm thick
9 poss. recess for connection fitting
10 clamping flange
11 section

1:10

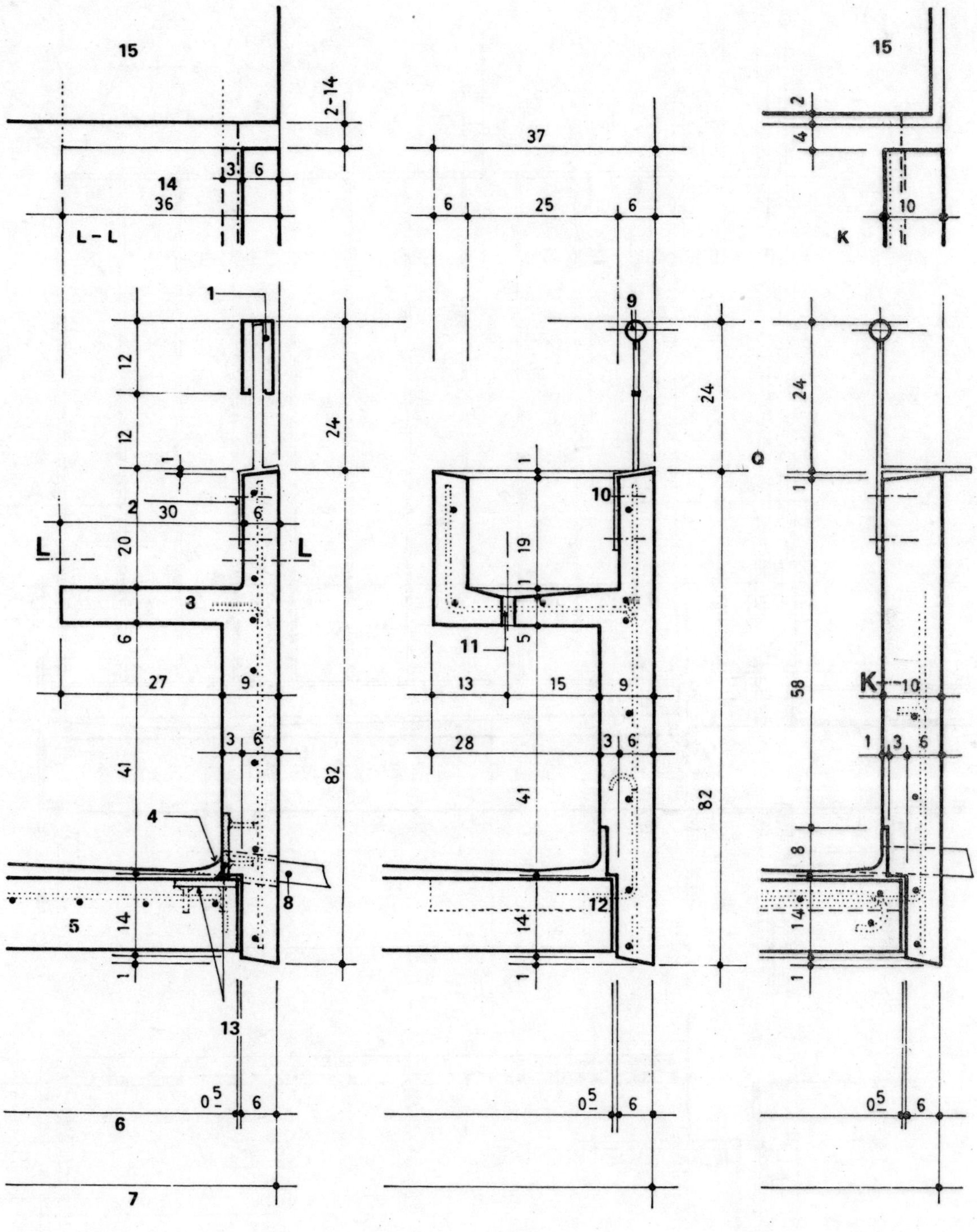

F G H

1 block section
2 patent stone screw - fastening
3 base plate
4 hollow molding r. ∿ 4 cm
5 balcony slab
6 balcony, interior dimension
7 balcony, exterior dimension
8 spout
9 tube railing Ø . . . mm
10 flower trough
11 drain Ø . . . mm
12 poss. recess for connection fitting
13 anchor plate imbedded in concrete, welded
14 base plate, top view
15 facade connection

Balcony breast details

1:10

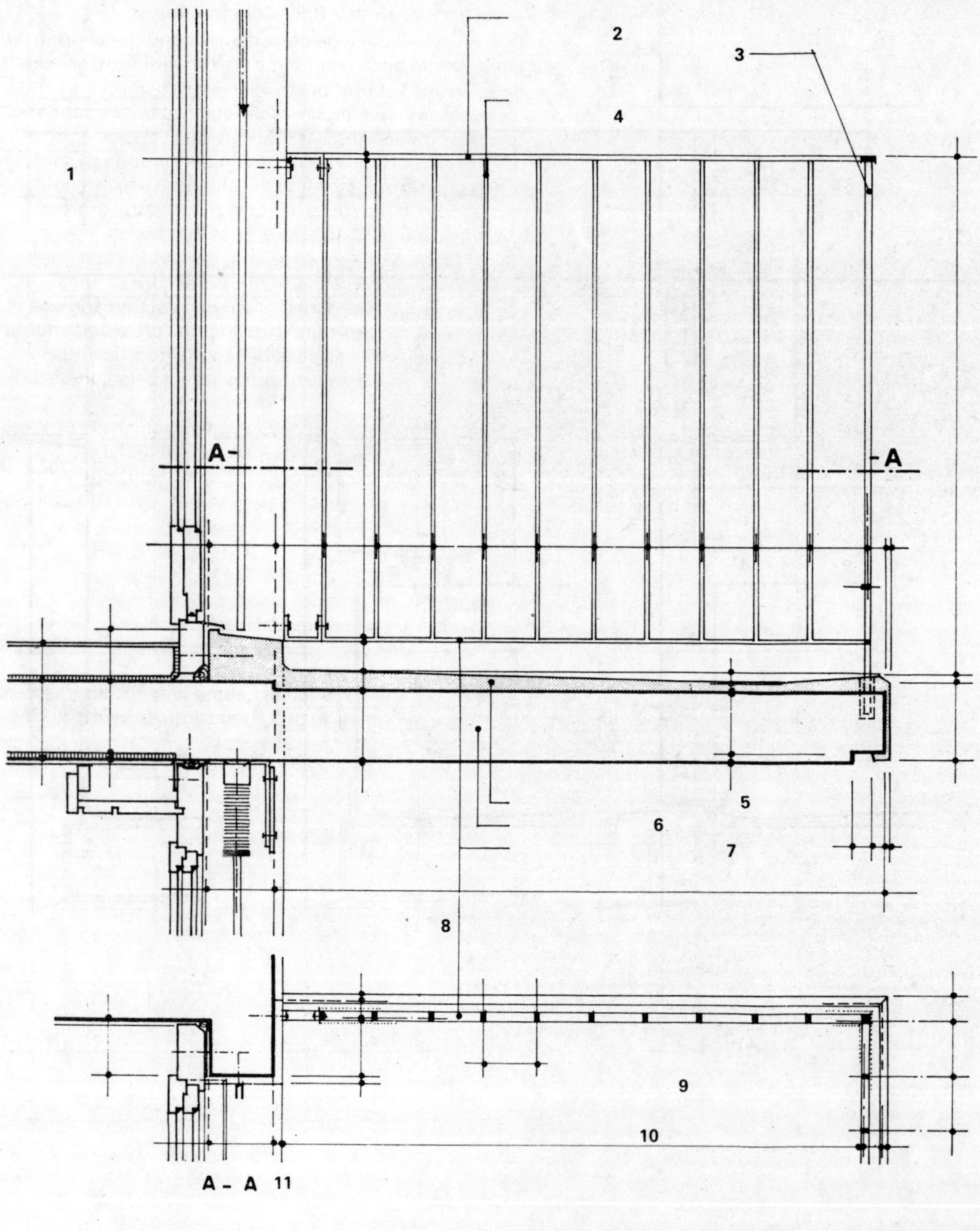

1 .../... mm Fixing stirrup with arms ... + ... + ... cm)
2 .../... mm Balustrade top rail
3 .../... mm Angle post
4 .../... mm Flat balusters
5 3-7 cm concrete finished to falls
6 Balcony slab
7 .../... mm bottom rail
8 Section through balcony, steel flat balustrade
9 Max spacing 12 cm (danger of children's accidents)
10 Clear cantilever of balcony
11 Plan A – A

Roof Forms, Timber Roof Construction

The choice of the type of roofing is conditional upon the appropriate pitch resulting from the roof form selected. In the choice of roof the formal relationship between architectural mass and elevational treatment must be considered.

In the interests of rationalization only woods should be used which conform to the standard sections customary in the trade. In general structural timbers are pine, fir and spruce, rarely oak and beech.

Timber to be used for structural purposes must have the following properties: naturally air-dried, bevelled or square-edged of varying section and size in accordance with standards. In principle wood should be as free of knots as possible, so that tensile and compressive stresses are sufficient for calculated static requirements.

Timber joints are nowadays almost exclusively effected with bolts, screws, tie rods, nails, etc. of metal, in contrast to former practice, in which carpentry and joinery joints were accomplished by means of wooden elements (nails, pegs and dowels).

As a rule rafters are spaced at about 60-70 cm. Their disposition depends upon the type of substructure, the span of rafters and type of roofing and snow load, etc. Trusses are placed at approx. 4-4,5 m centres.

The truss braces are set on the main load-bearing walls of the building.

Structural timbers must be treated with the appropriate wood-preservative agents against attack by every kind of pest.

Rule-of-thumb calculations for timber sections (L = span, H = height)

Rafter height: 8 cm + 2 × L : 100
Rafter width: min. 8 cm
Purlin height: 12 cm + 2 × L : 100
Purlin width: min. 12 cm
Post section: 10 cm + 2 × H : 100

Flat and Pent Roofs

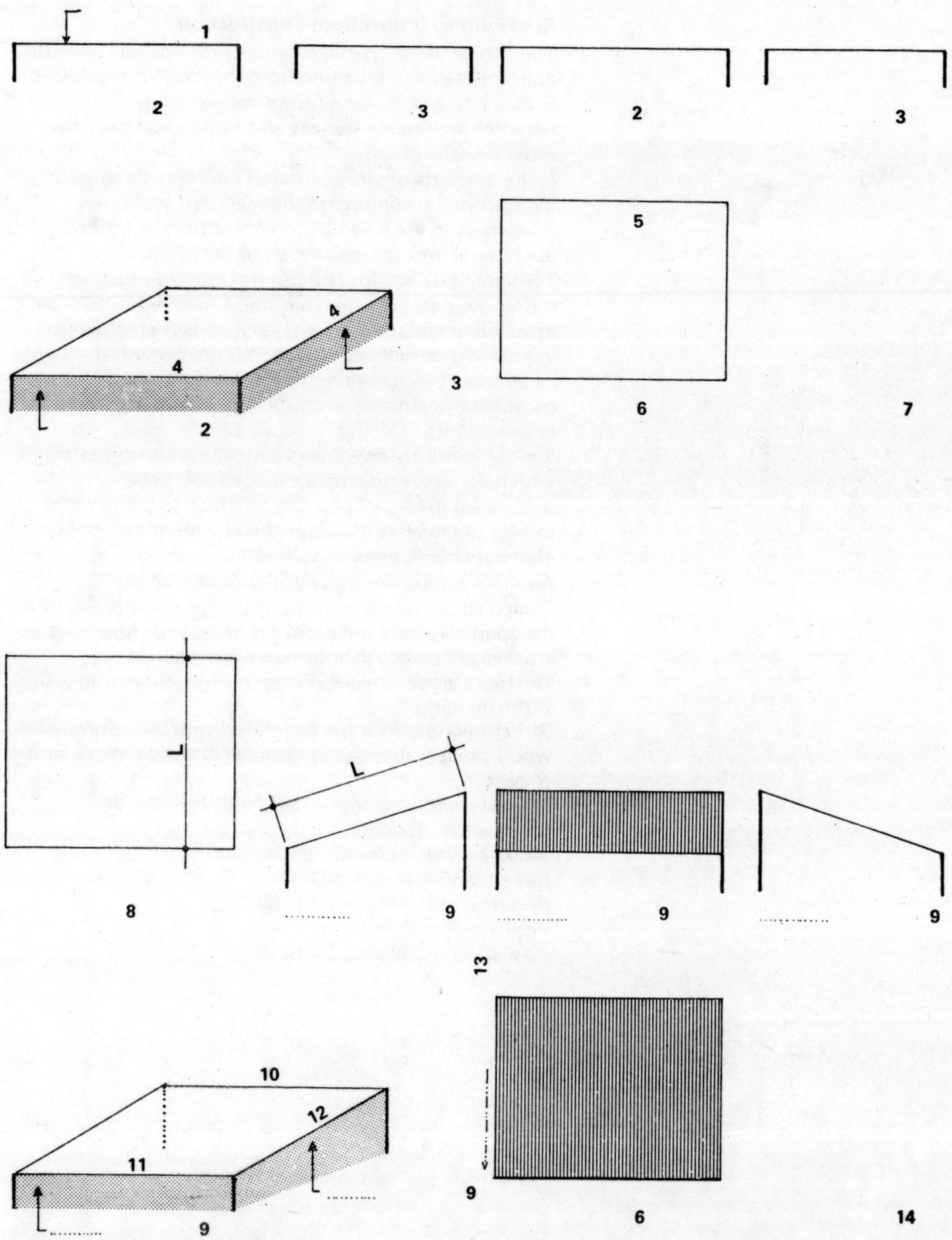

1 Top edge, Flat roof
2 Longitudinal view
3 Transverse view
4 Cornice
5 Roof fall
6 Roof elevation
7 Flat roof
8 True roof-surface
9 Elevation
10 Ridge of single-slope roof
11 Eaves
12 Verge line
13 Fall direction
14 Pent (single-slope) roof

Saddle Roofs of similar and dissimilar pitch

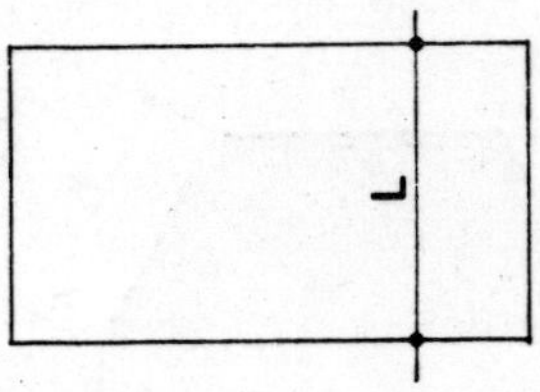

1

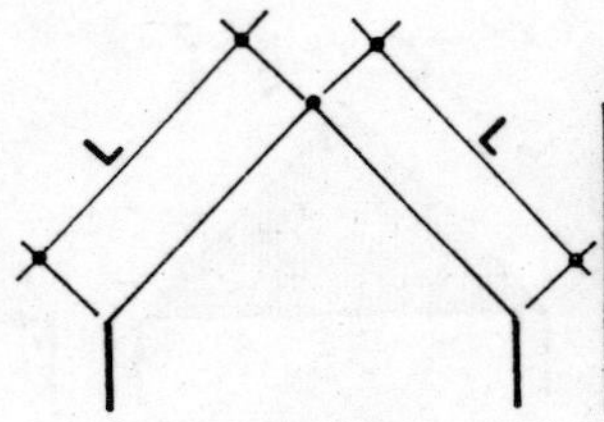

R 2

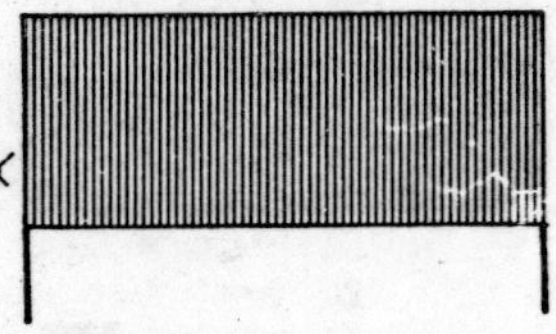

3

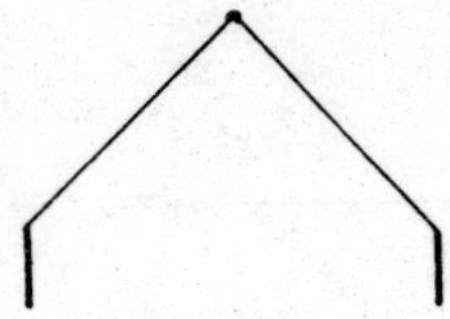

F 4

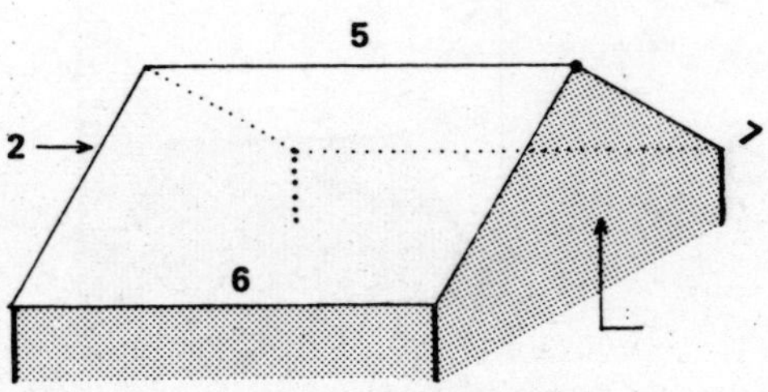

F 4

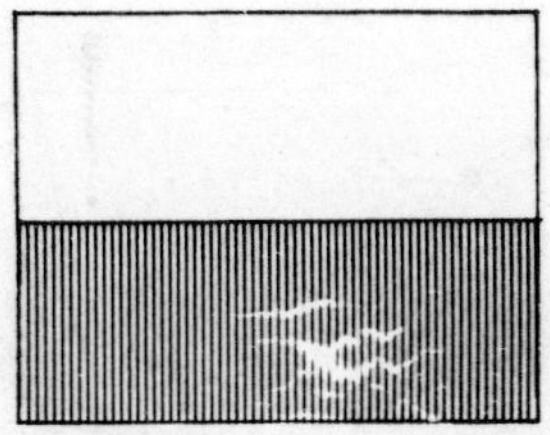

8

9

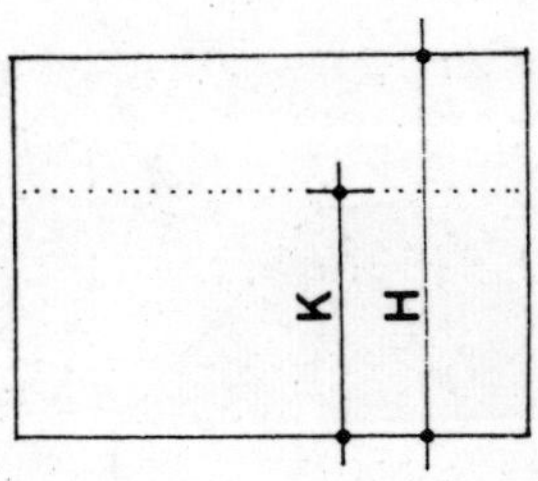

12

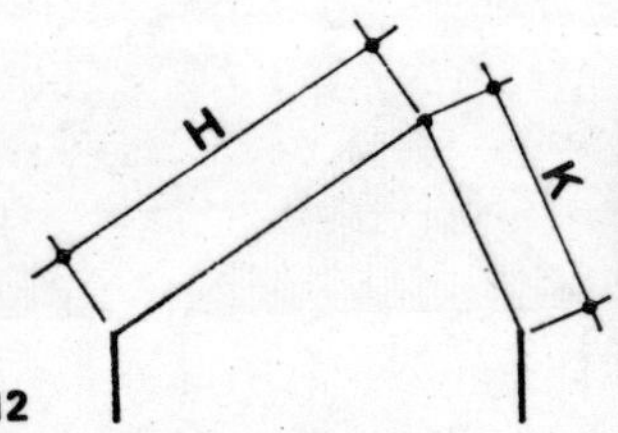

R 2

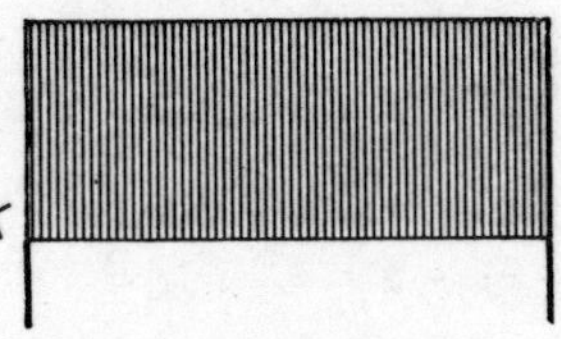

13

10

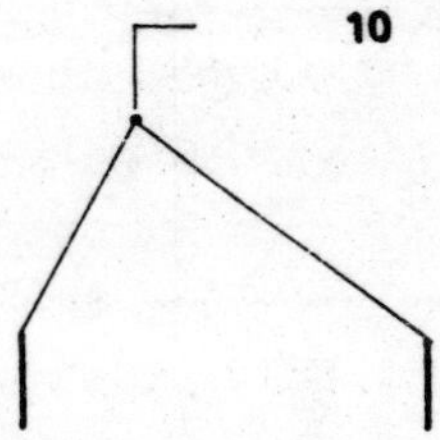

F 4

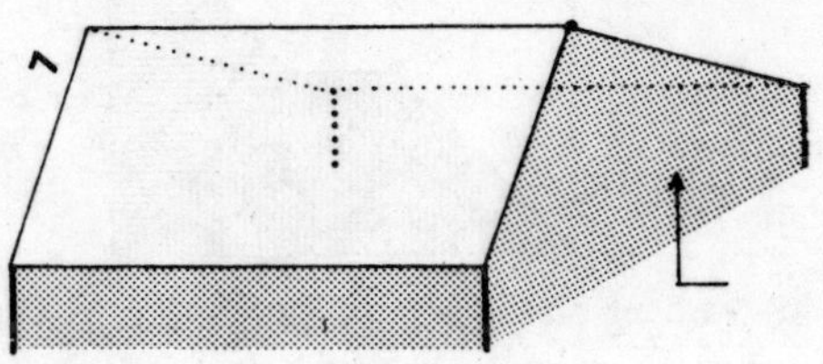

F 4

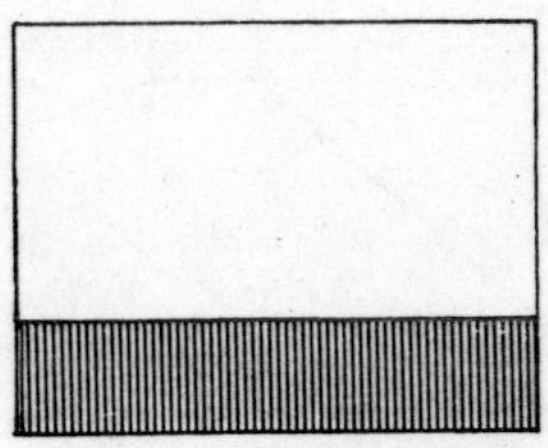

8

11

1 True roof surface
2 Gable R
3 Roof elevation, frontal
4 Gable F
5 Ridge line
6 Eaves
7 Verge line
8 Roof top-view
9 Saddle-back roof of similar pitch
10 Ridge
11 Saddle-back roof of dissimilar pitch
12 True roof surfaces
13 Principal roof

Hipped Roofs of similar and dissimilar pitch

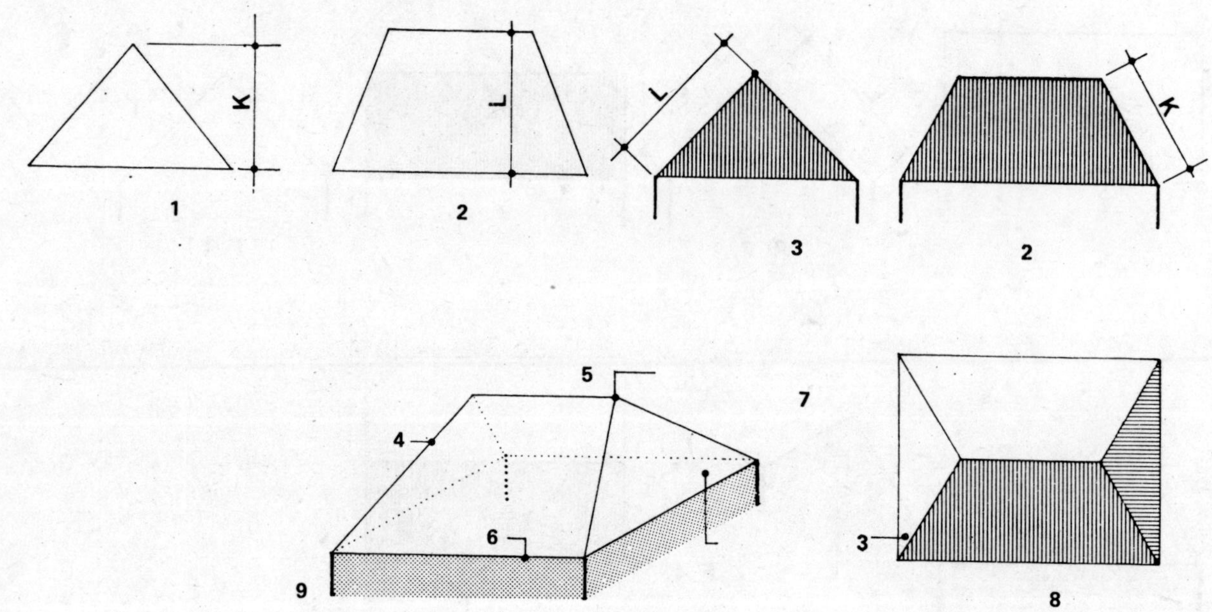

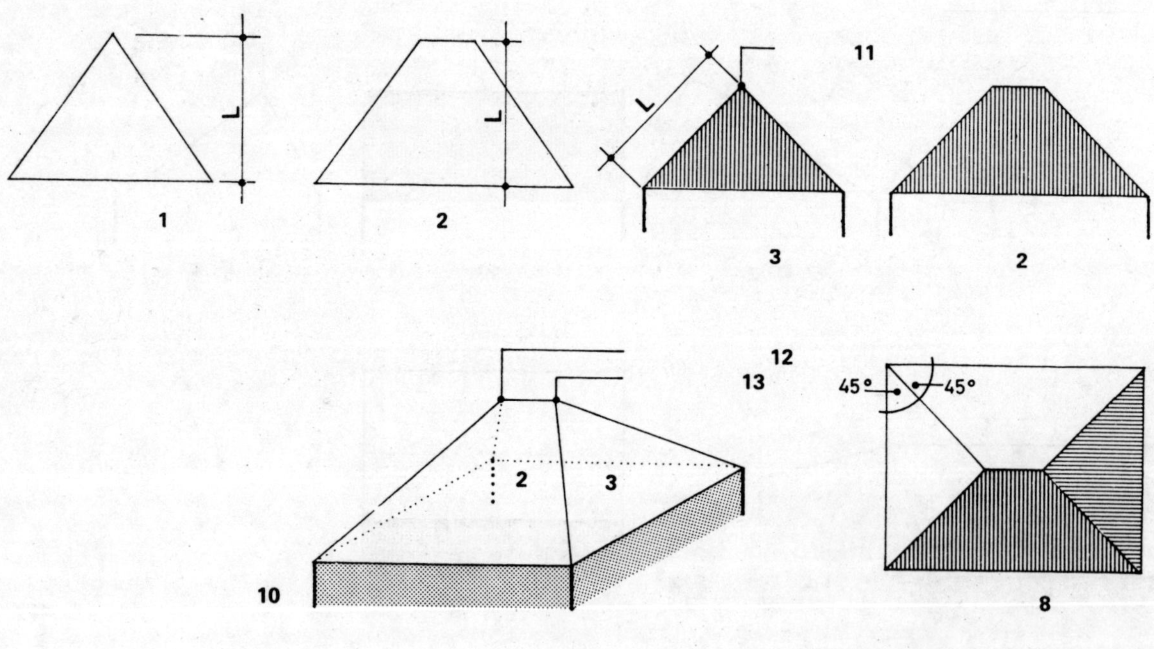

1 True surface of side roof
2 Principal roof
3 Side roof
4 Hip line
5 Ridge line
6 Eaves line
7 Ridge hip-capping
8 Roof, view from above
9 Hipped roof of dissimilar pitch
10 Hipped roof of similar pitch
11 Ridge
12 Ridge beginning
13 Ridge end

Half-hipped and Cross-ridge Roofs

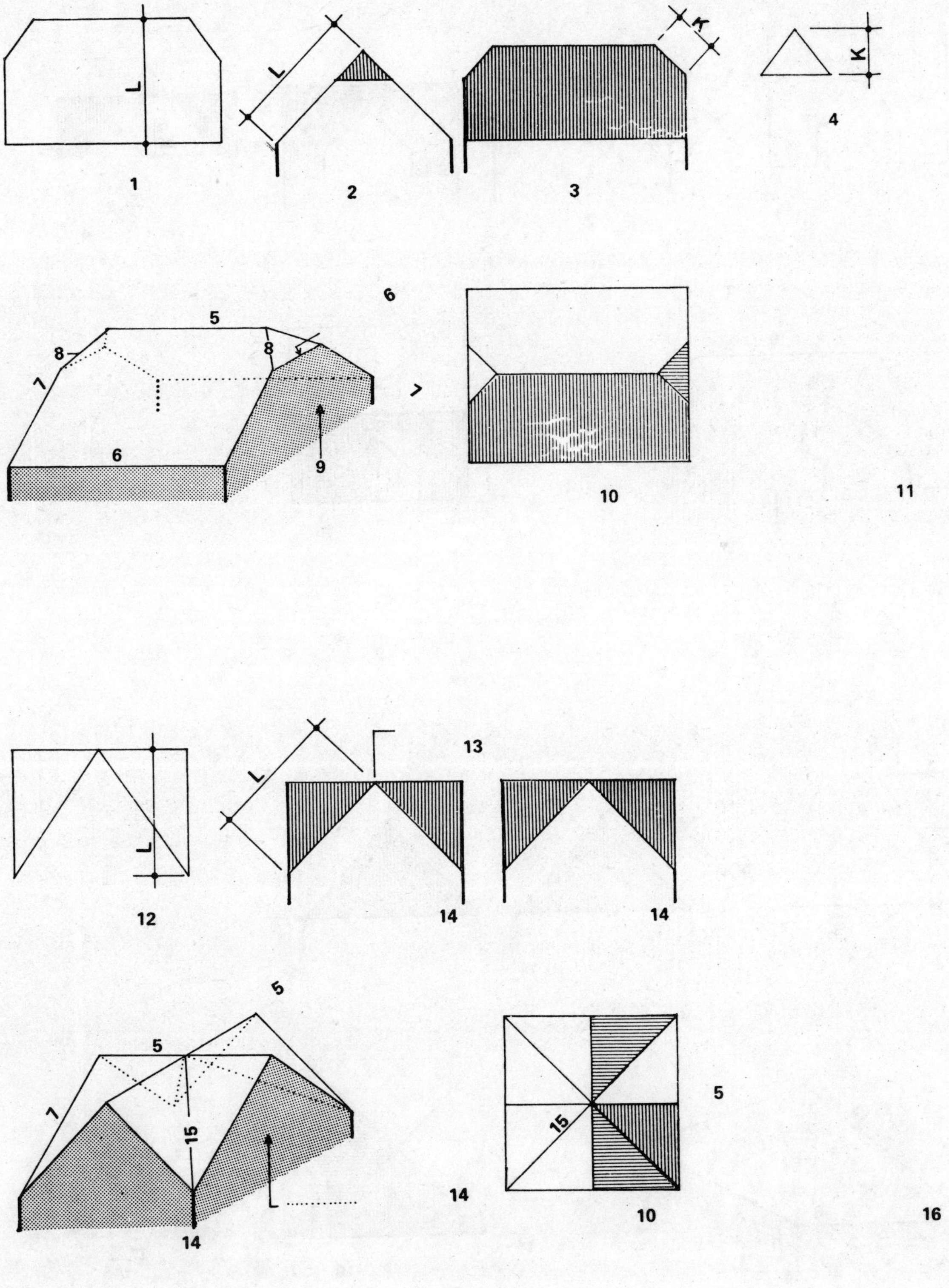

1 True surface
of principal roof
2 Gable
3 Principal roof
4 Half-hipped roof,
true surface
5 Ridge line
6 Eaves
7 Verge line
8 Hip line
9 Gable end (verge)
10 Roof top-view
11 Half-hipped roof
12 True roof surfaces
13 Ridge (middle)
14 Elevation
15 Valley
16 Cross-ridge roof

Two-level Cross-ridge and Pavilion Roofs

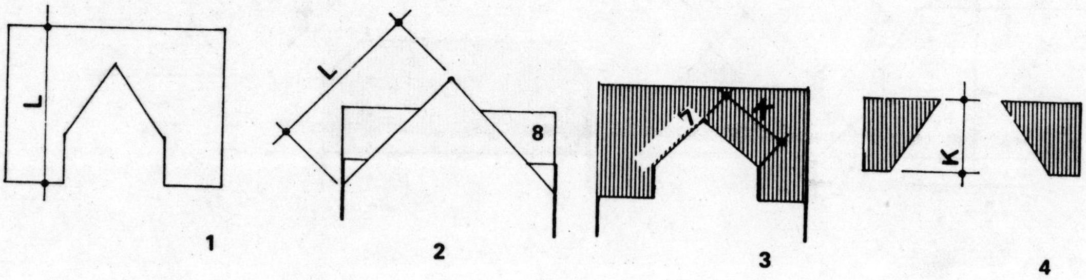

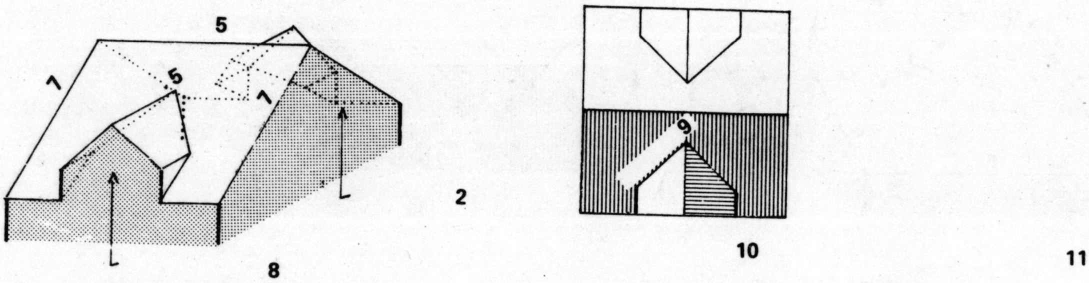

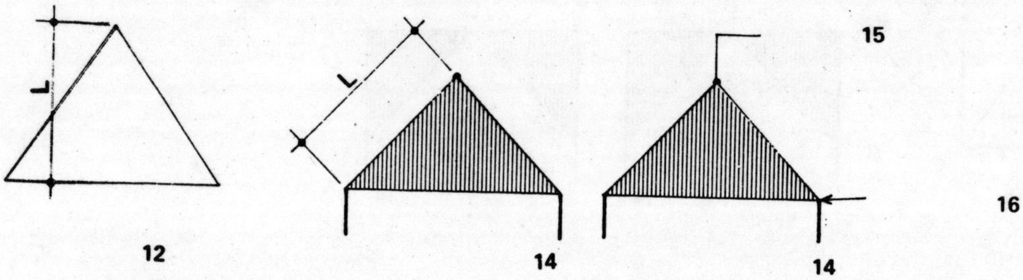

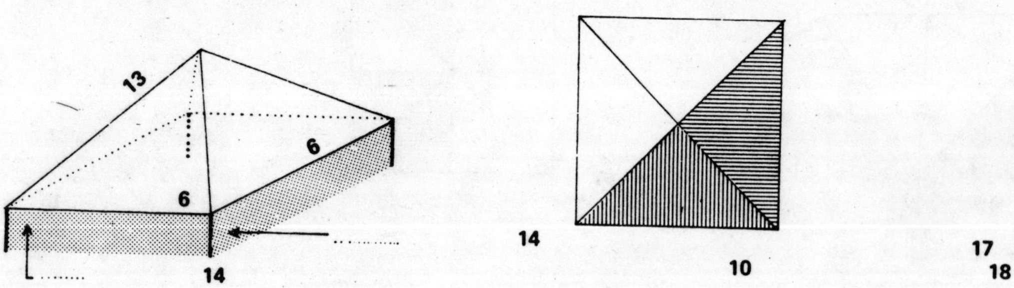

1 True principal roof surface
2 Gable
3 Main elevation
4 True roof surface of roof projection
5 Ridge line
6 Eaves
7 Verge line
8 Roof construction
9 Valley
10 Roof top-view
11 Two-level cross-ridge roof
12 True roof surface
13 Hip line
14 Elevation
15 Ridge
16 Eaves, wall plate
17 Tower roof
18 Pavilion roof

Pitched purlin roofs, cross-sectional representation

1:100

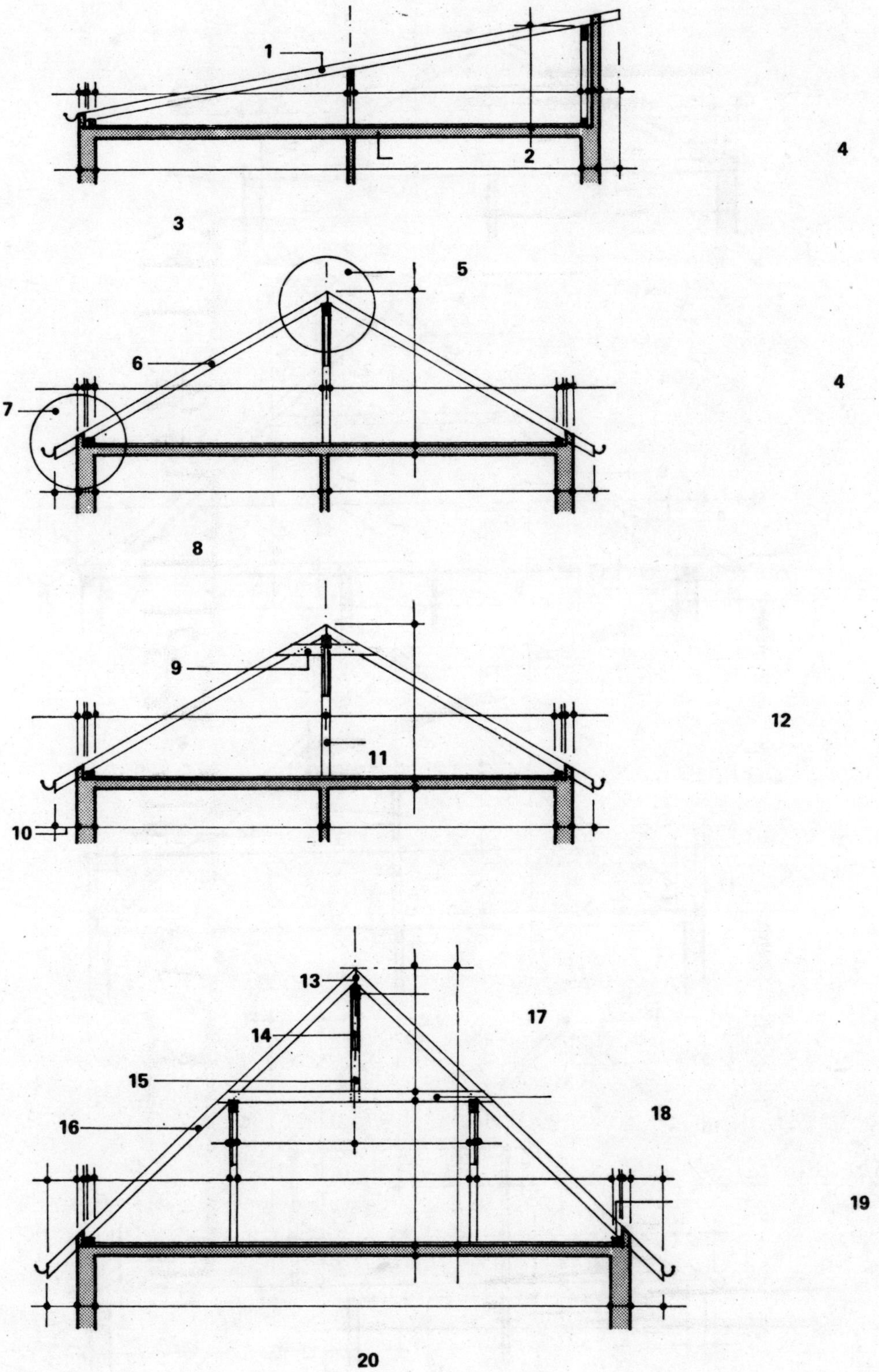

1 Normal rafters 8/16 cm
2 Solid slab
3 Section through lean-to roof
4 Simple purlin roof
5 Ridge
6 Roof pitch corresponding to situation and coverings
7 Eaves
8 Section through pitched roof
9 Single or double collar
10 Eaves projection
11 Post .../... cm
12 Purlin roof with simple roof truss
13 Notching
14 Strut
15 Suspension post .../... cm
16 Rafters .../... cm
17 Ridge plate or purlin .../... cm
18 Double collar 2 × .../... cm
19 Plate .../... cm
20 Purlin roof (double rafter roof)

Pitched roofs, cross-sectional representation

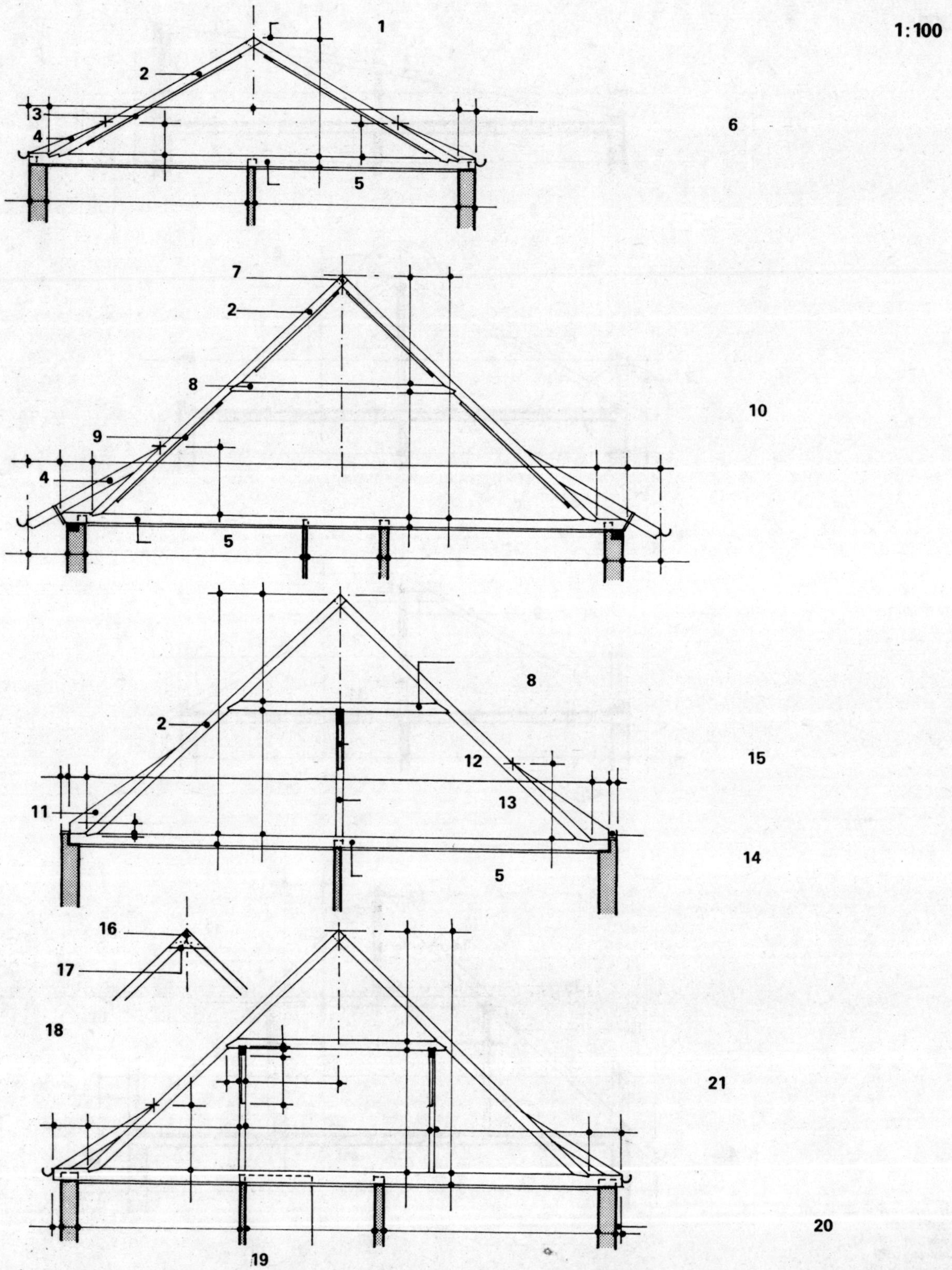

1 Ridge line
2 Rafters 8/16 cm
3 Wind bracing
4 Sprocket piece
5 Joists
6 Simple rafter roof
7 Forked mortice and tenon
8 Collar beam .../... cm
9 Diagonal wind bracing
10 Collar roof
11 Sprocket board ... cm thick
12 Strut
13 Post .../... cm
14 Box gutter construction
15 Post and collar roof
16 Notching
17 Triangular cleat, nailed
18 Alternative ridge construction
19 Section through building
20 Joist projection
21 Double rafter roof with collar

1:100/20

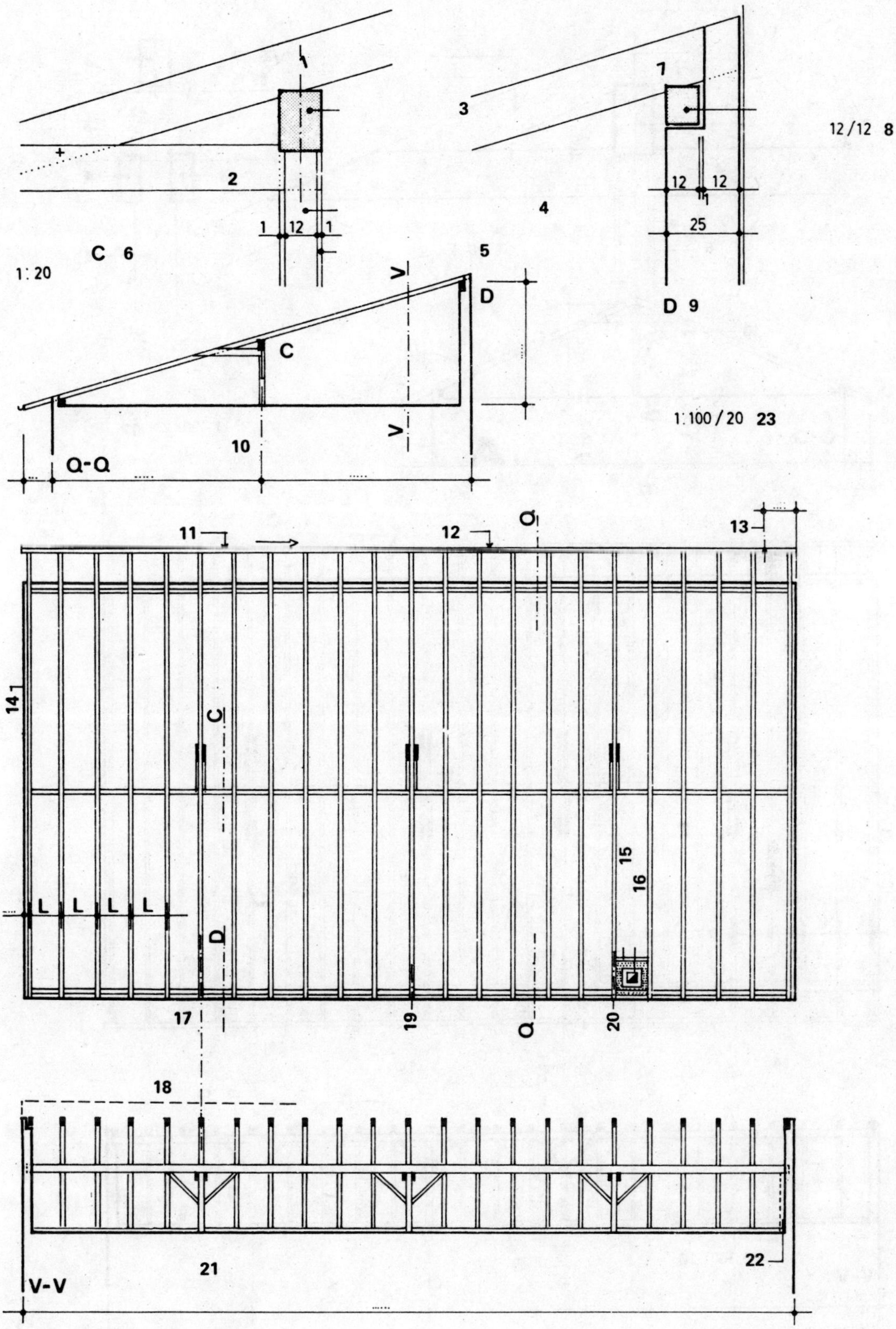

1 Principal Rafter
2 Double tie, collar beam
3 Purlin
4 Strut, (angle) brace
5 Post
6 Section
7 Common Rafter
8 Pent roof ridge-purlin
9 Section
10 Cross-section Rainwater
11 Gutter
12 Eaves line
13 Rainwater outlet
14 Verge
15 Joist
16 Chimney
17 Rafter top-view
18 Lean-to ridge line
19 Truss
20 Truss
21 Longitudinal section
22 End posts
23 Rafter plan, Pent roof

Saddle-back Roof, construction details

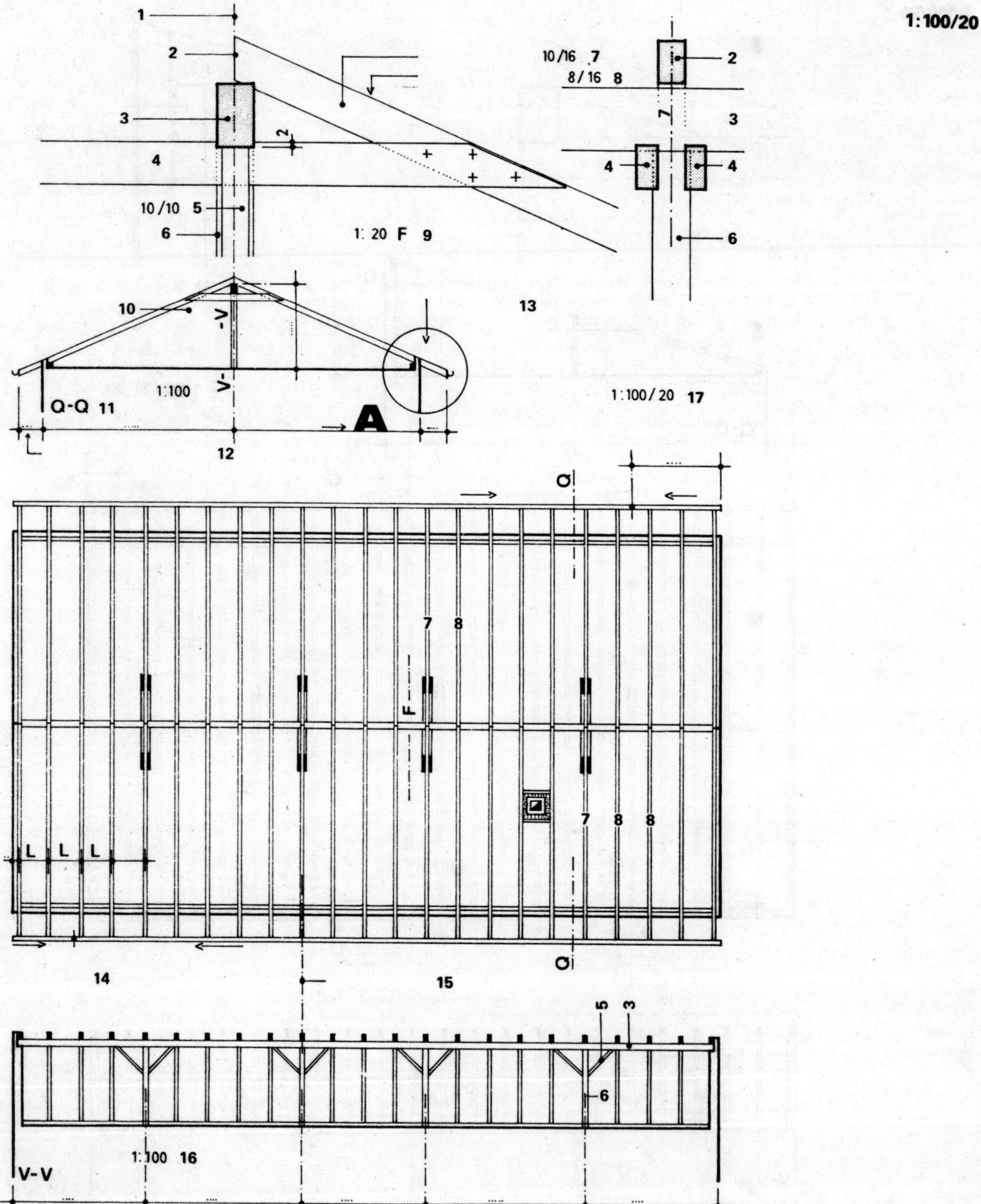

1 Ridge axis (centre)
2 Ridge section
3 Ridge purlin
4 Collar beam
5 (Angle) brace
6 Post
7 Principal rafter
8 Common rafter
9 Ridge section
10 Roof space (loft)
11 Cross-section
12 Rafter overhang
13 Eaves
14 Rafters top-view
15 Truss axis (centre)
16 Longitudinal section
17 Rafters plan, saddle back roof

1:100/20

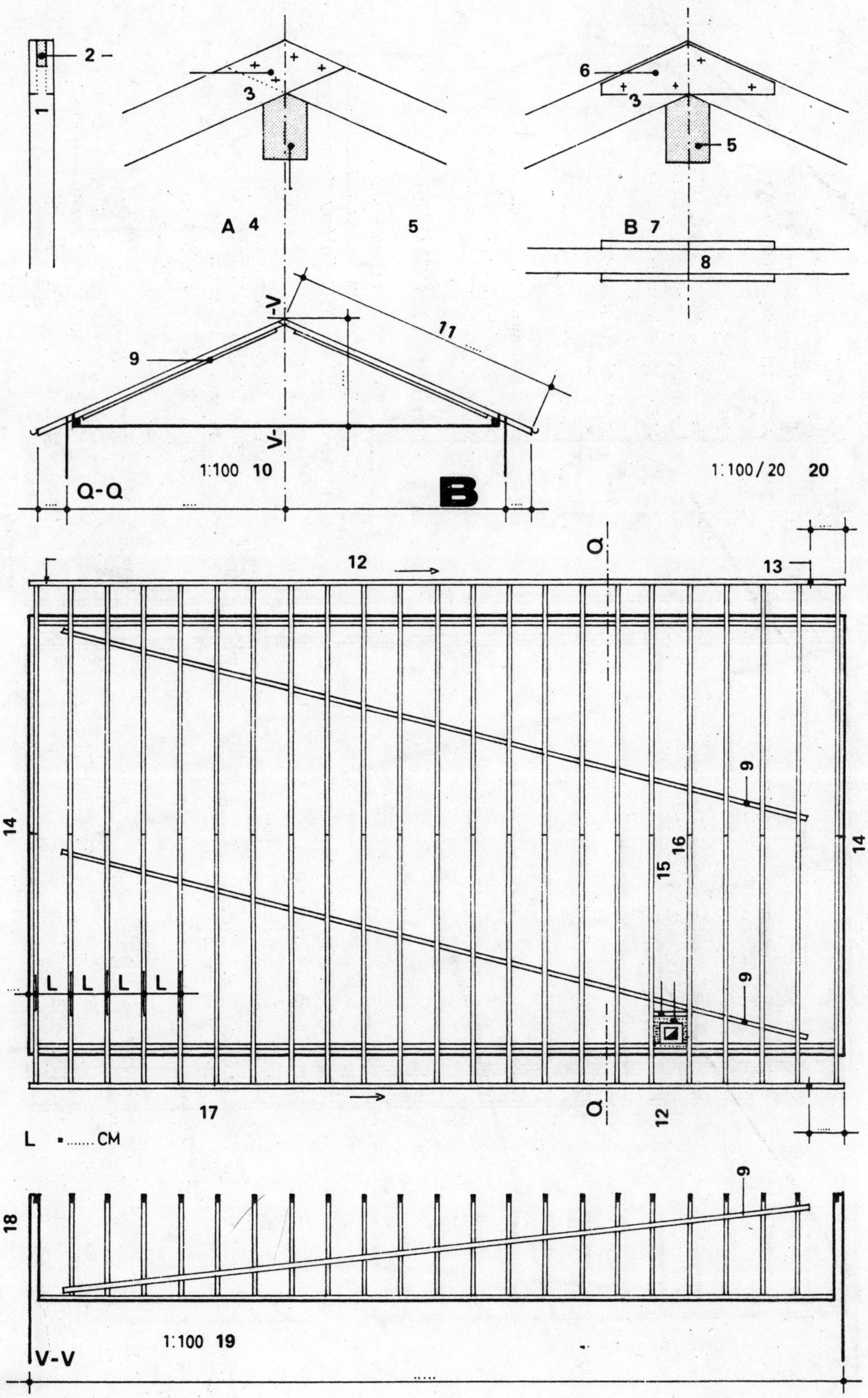

1 Rafter view
2 Forked joint
3 Rafters
4 Ridge design, variants
5 Temporary timber: removed after completion
6 Triangular board (stiffening)
7 Ridge design, variants
8 Rafters top-view
9 Diagonal counter (wind) batten
10 Cross-section
11 Rafter length
12 Rainwater gutter, elbow
13 Outlet pipe
14 Gable end
15 Trimmer
16 Flashing
17 Rafters top-view
18 Gable
19 Longitudinal section
20 Rafter plan, hipped roof

Saddle-back Roof, construction details

1:100/20

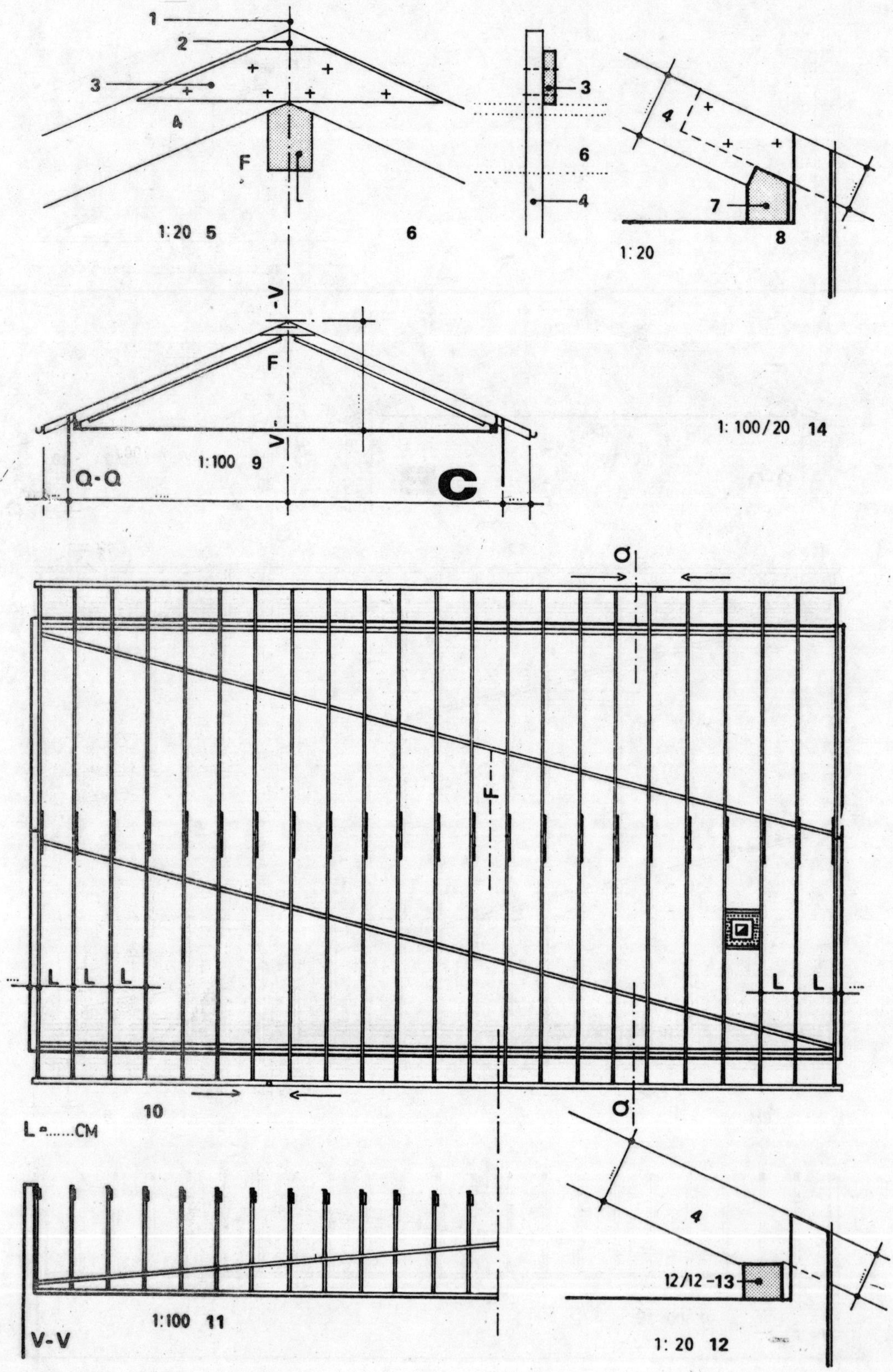

1 Ridge axis (centre).
2 Ridge section
3 Stiffening timber
4 Batten
5 Ridge section
6 Temporary timber: removed after completed erection
7 Foot purlin, variants
8 Eaves, detail
9 Cross-section
10 Batten layout
11 Longitudinal section
12 Detail variants of eaves
13 Foot purlin
14 Batten plan, saddle(-back) roof

1:100/20

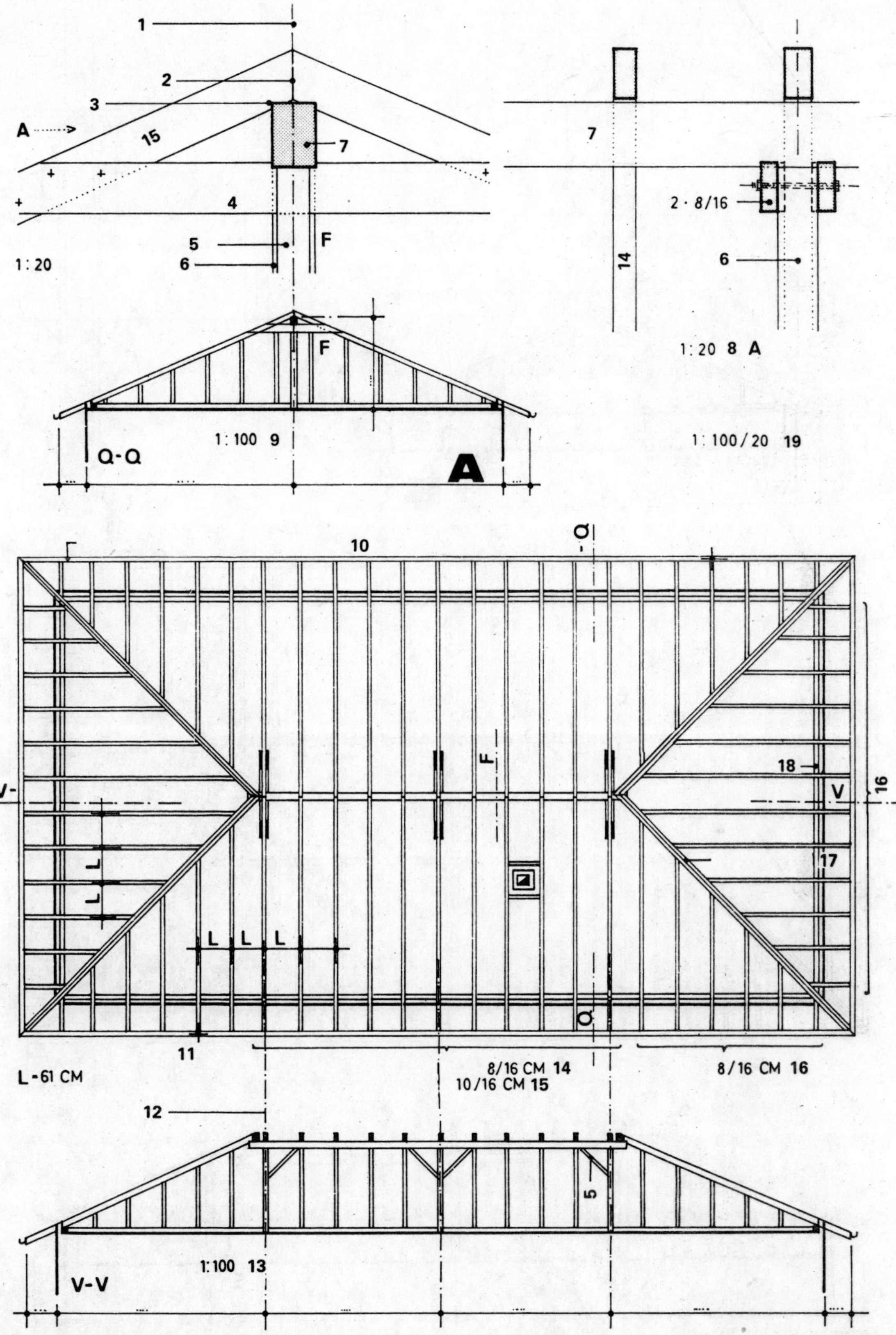

1 Ridge axis (centre)
2 Ridge section
3 Notch
4 Collar beam
5 (Angle) brace, strut
6 Post
7 Ridge purlin
8 View in section
9 Cross-section
10 Rainwater gutter, elbow
11 Rafters top-view
12 Truss axis (centre)
13 Longitudinal section
14 Common rafters
15 Principal rafters
16 Jack rafters
17 Hip rafters
18 Foot purlin
19 Rafter plan

Hipped Roof, construction details

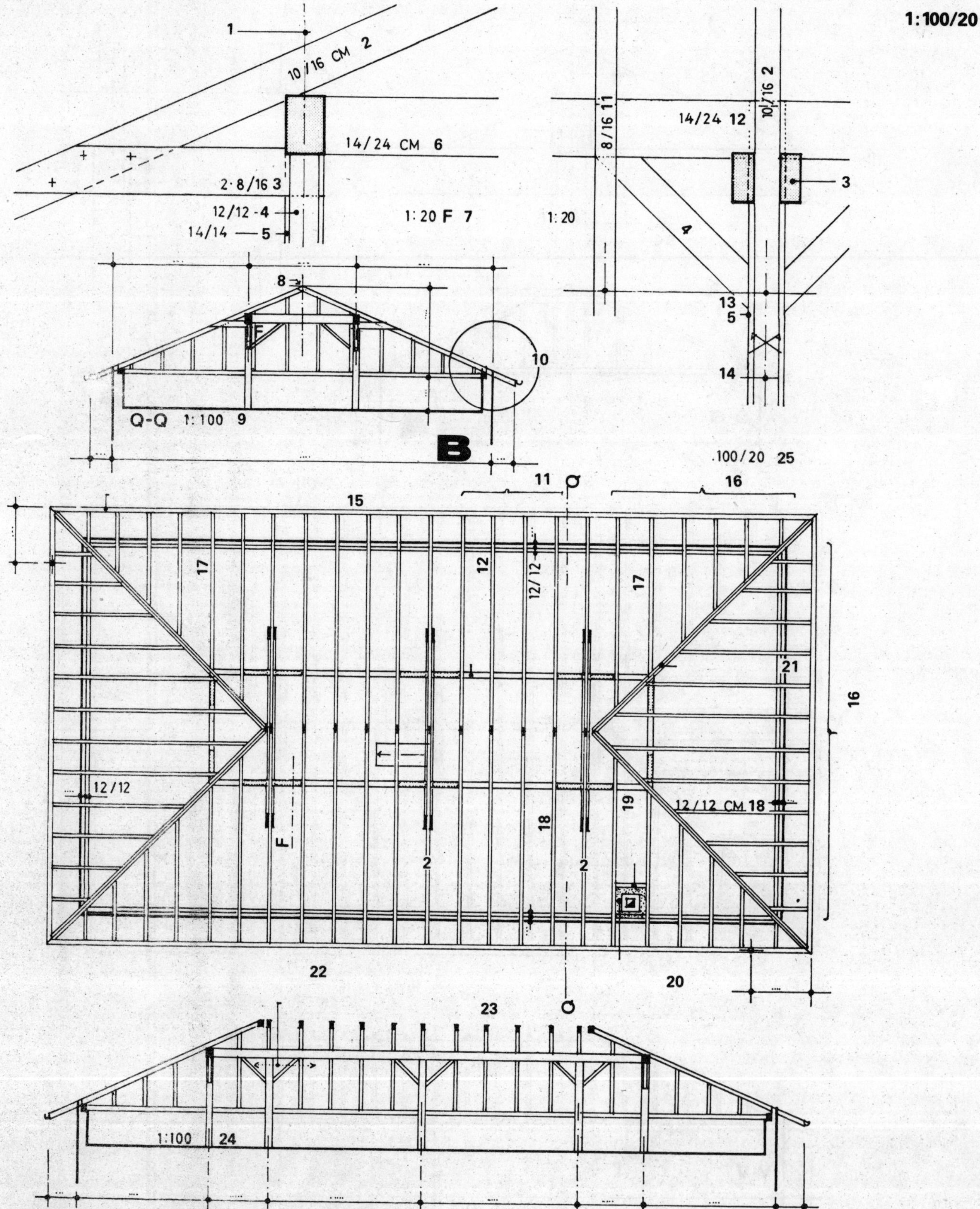

1 Purlin axis (centre)
2 Principal rafter
3 Collar beam
4 Strut, angle-brace
5 Post
6 Distance piece
7 Section
8 Forked joint
9 Roof-space (loft), cross-section
10 Eaves
11 Rafters
12 Purlin
13 Rafter-jackrafter spacing
14 Truss centre
15 Rainwater gutter, elbow
16 Jack-rafter
17 Angle timber
18 Foot purlin
19 Trimmer
20 Chimney flashing
21 Hip rafter
22 Top-view of rafter-distribution
23 Triangulated framework
24 Roof, longitudinal section
25 Rafter plan, hipped roof

1:100/20

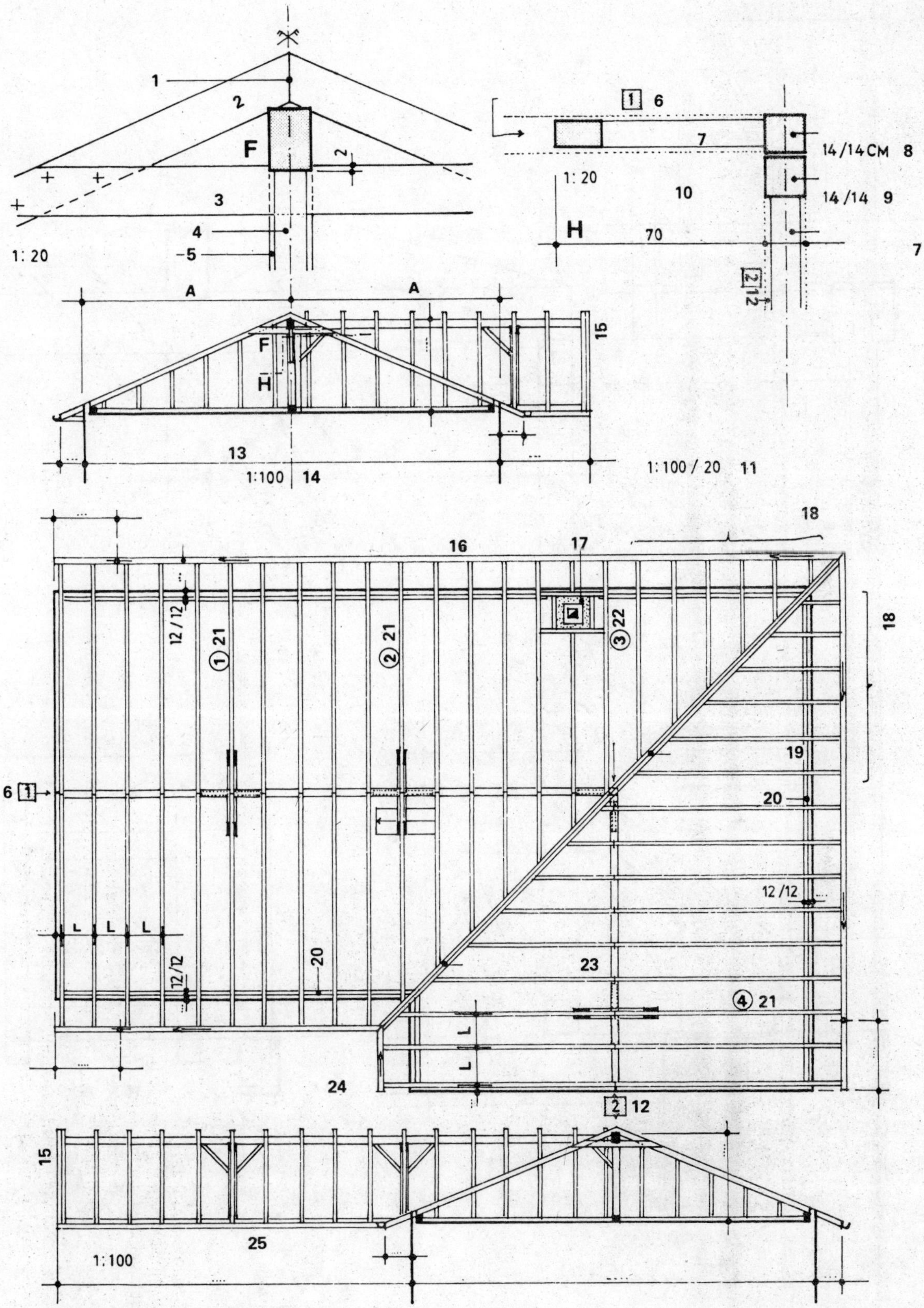

1 Ridge section
2 Principal rafter
3 Collar beam
4 Strut, angle-brace
5 Post
6 Ridge purlin
7 Angle-brace from above
8 Angle-post (corner-post)
9 Post
10 Brace (splayed)
11 Angle-truss: horizontal section
12 Ridge purlin
13 Building width
14 Roof (cross-section)
15 Gable end
16 Rainwater gutter, elbow
17 Chimney flashing
18 Trimmer
19 Hip rafter
20 Wall-plate
21 Truss
22 Angle-truss
23 Valley rafter
24 Rafter-distribution from above
25 Rafter view (elevation)

Dormer, construction details

1:20

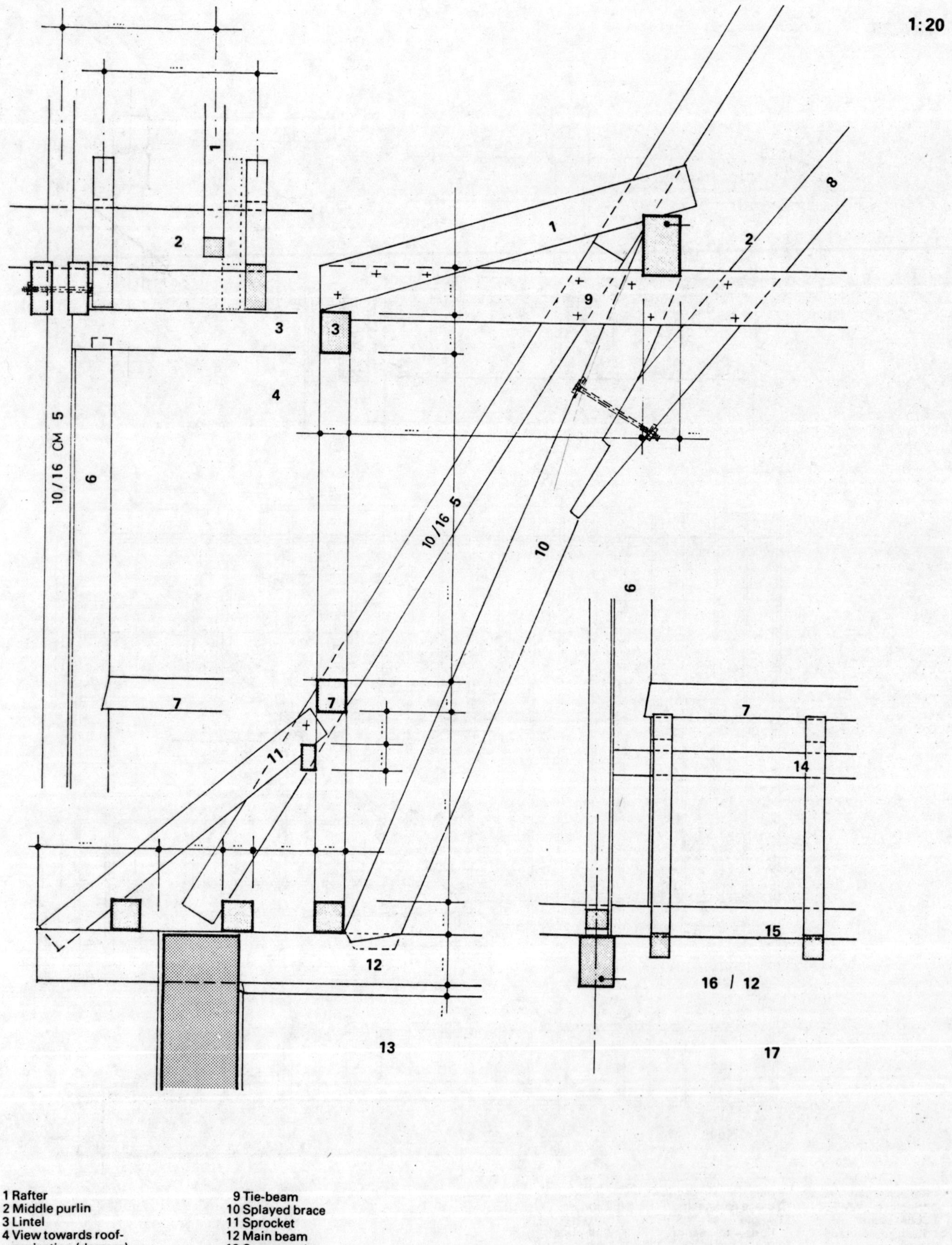

1 Rafter
2 Middle purlin
3 Lintel
4 View towards roof-projection (dormer)
5 Principal rafter
6 Post
7 Sill
8 Ridge-brace
9 Tie-beam
10 Splayed brace
11 Sprocket
12 Main beam
13 Cross-section
14 Bearer
15 Wall-plate
16 Beam
17 elevation

1:20

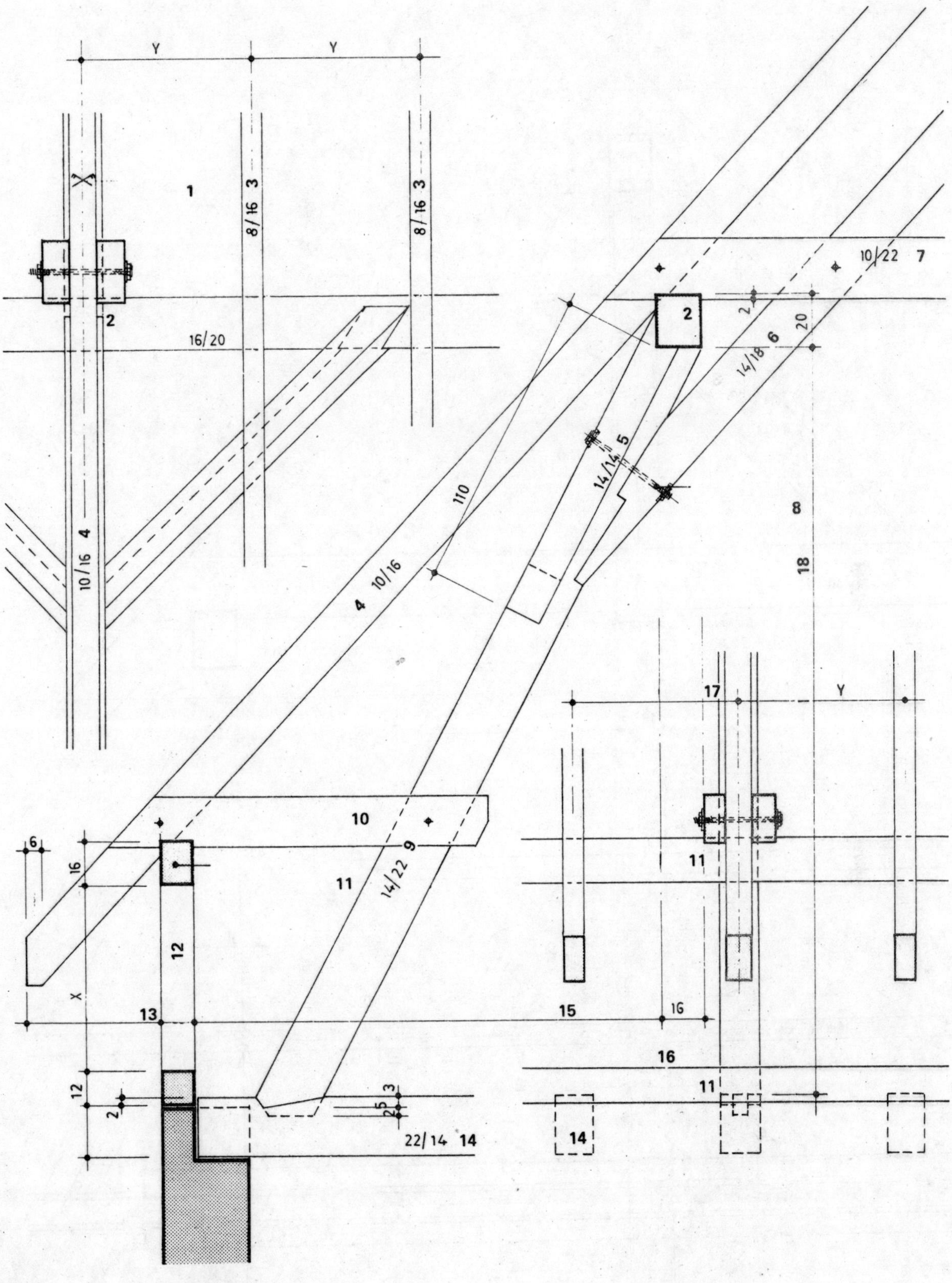

1 Truss axis (centre)
2 Middle purlin
3 Common rafter
4 Principal rafter
5 Fork-jointed strut
6 Ridge brace
7 Collar beam
8 Bolt
9 Brace
10 Collar beam

11 Wall-plate
12 Post (wall-post)
13 Overhang
14 Main beam
15 Purlin spacing
16 Knee-brace tie
17 Rafter spacing
18 Height to purlin under-edge

Knee-braced Truss, construction details

1:20

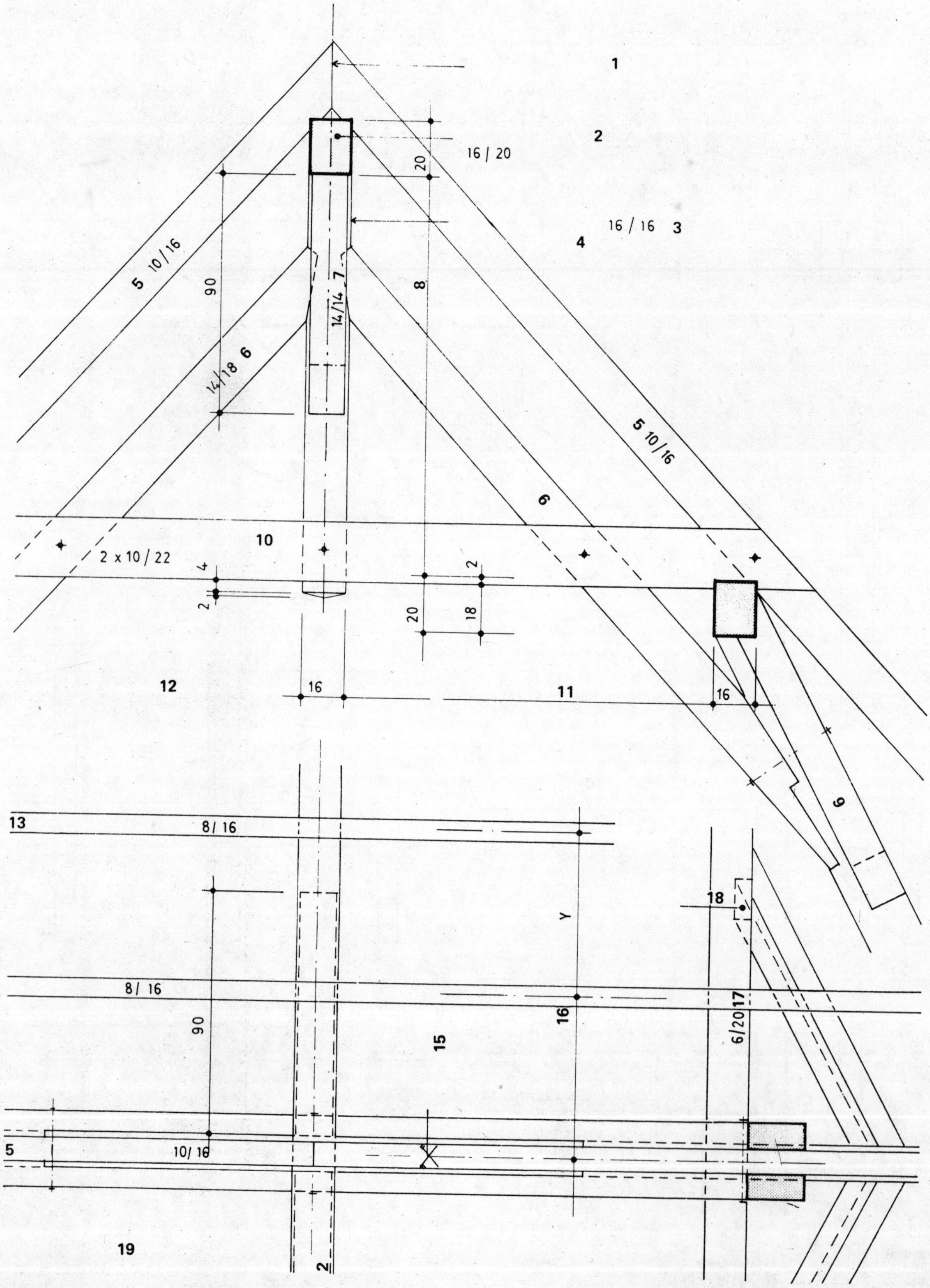

1 Ridge section
2 Ridge purlin
3 King-post
4 King-post
5 Principal rafter
6 Ridge brace
7 Angle-brace
8 Purlin spacing top-edge to bottom-edge
9 Fork-jointed brace
10 Tie beam
11 Purlin spacing
12 Cross-section
13 Common rafter
14 Rafter
15 Truss axis
16 Rafter spacing
17 Middle purlin
18 Forked joint
19 View from above

1:20

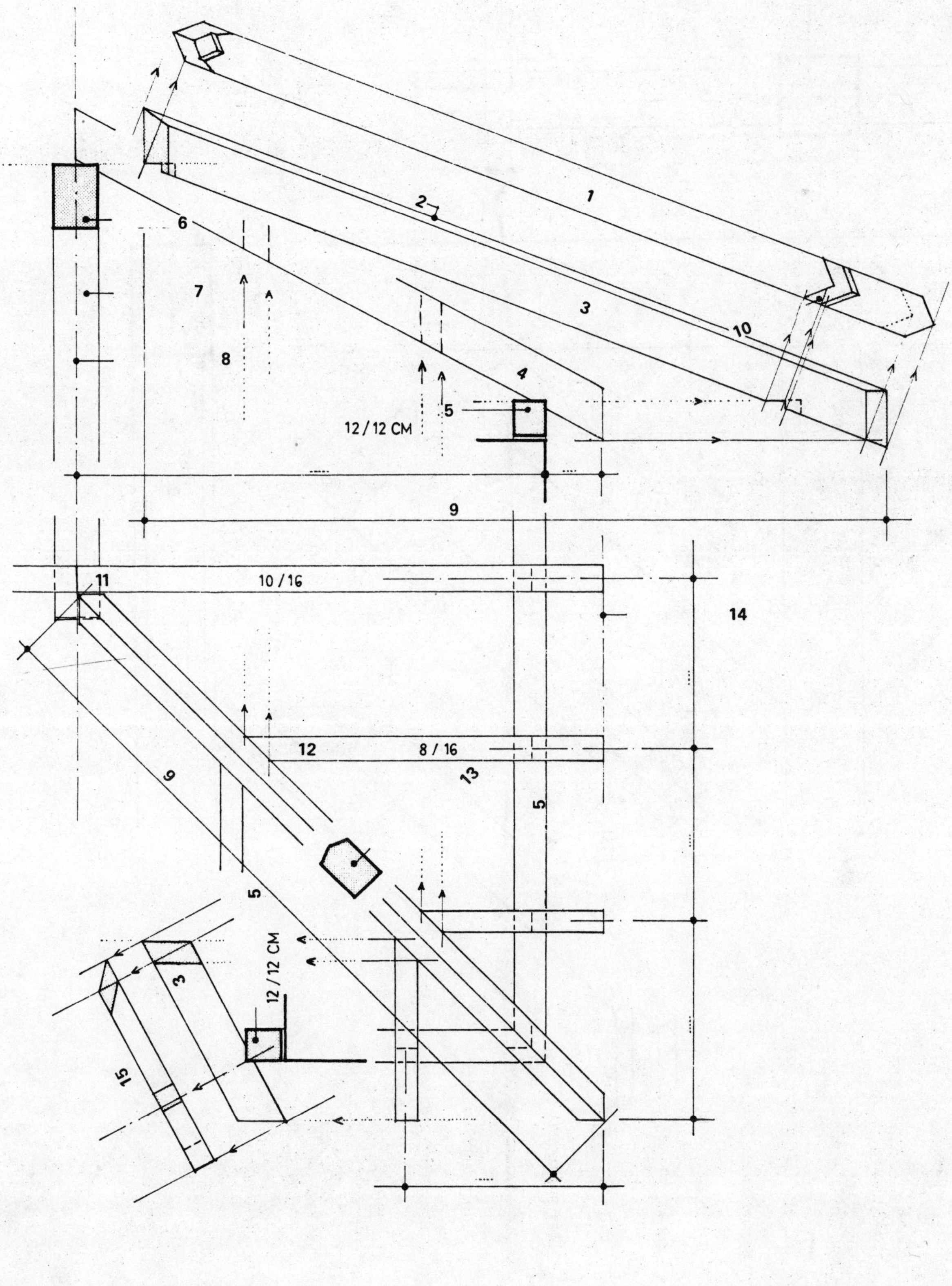

1 Hip rafters from below
2 Hip line
3 Side view
4 Rafter (elevation)
5 Wall plate
6 Purlin
7 Post
8 Ridge axis (centre)
9 Base line
10 Valley
11 Principal rafter
12 Jack rafter
13 Hip rafter (cross-section)
14 Eaves line
15 Underside

Angle-braced Post-connection construction

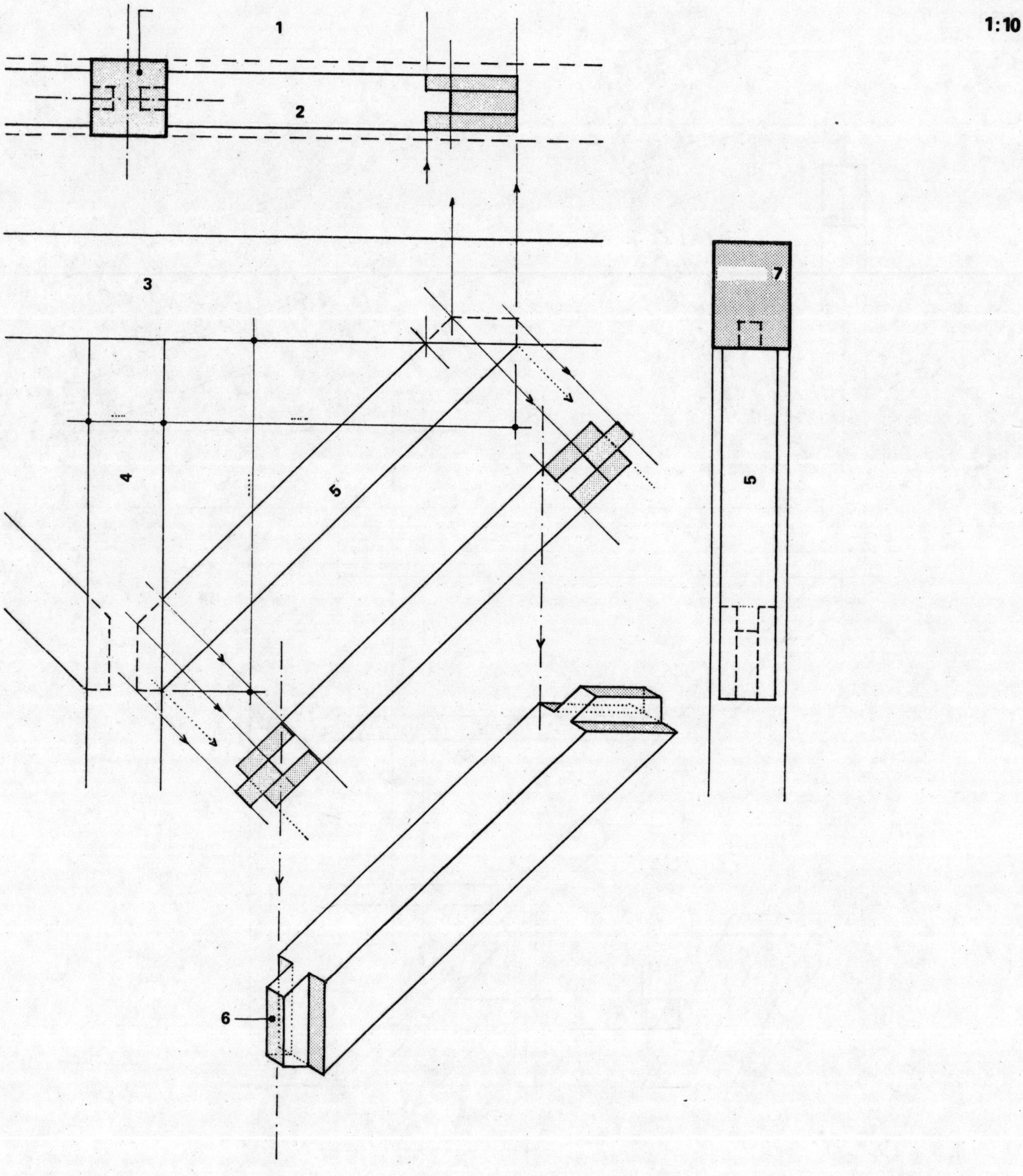

1 Post (cross-section)
2 Angle-brace from above
3 Purlin side-elevation
4 Post (king-post)
5 Angle-brace
6 Tenon
7 Purlin

1:10

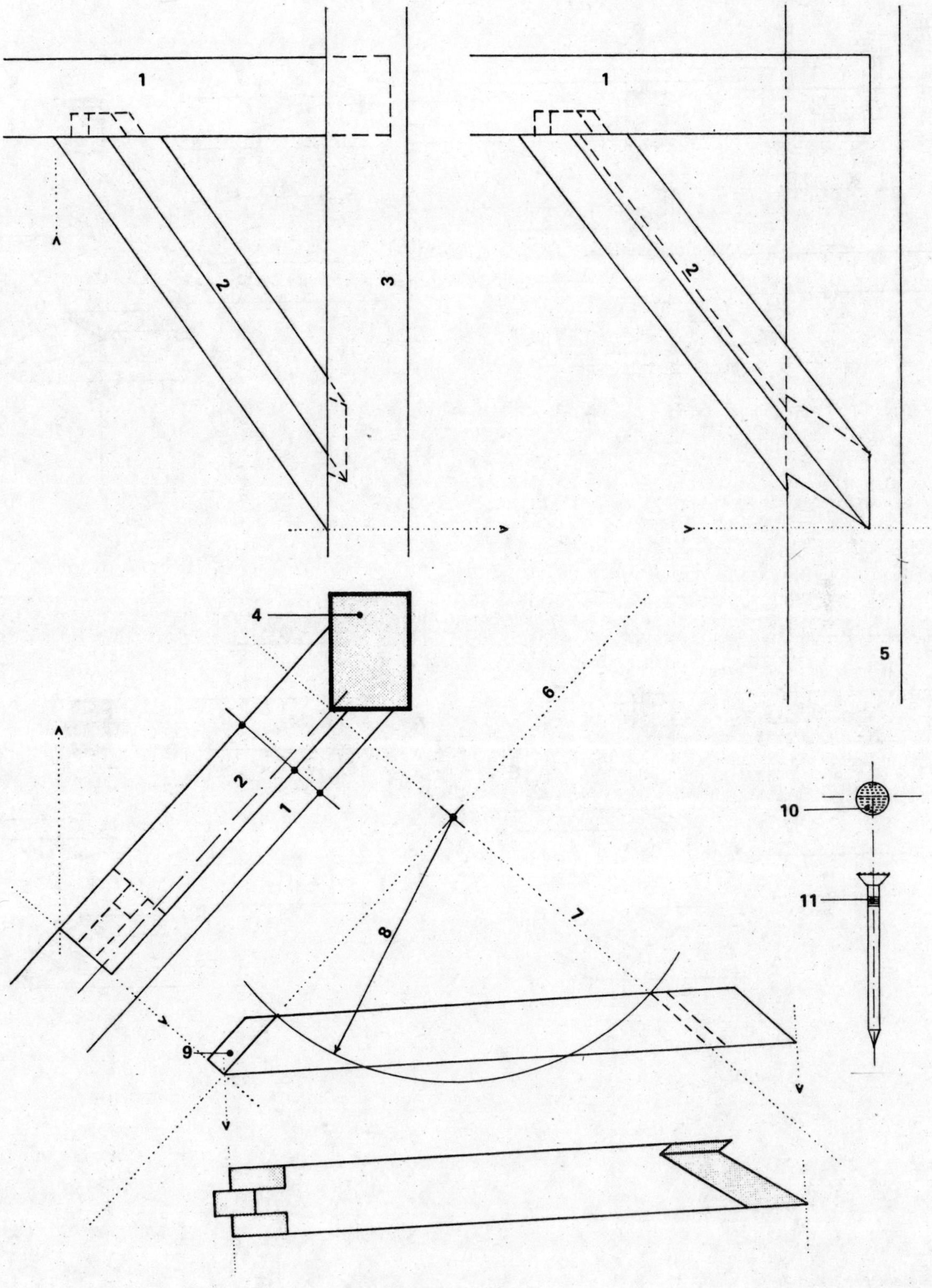

1 Diagonal stay
2 Angle brace
3 Purlin from above
4 Middle purlin
5 Purlin side-view
6 Line of splayed brace
7 Line of purlin
8 Radius
9 Tenon
10 Nail-head from above
11 Wire nail with
countersunk head

Beam and purlin connections

1:20

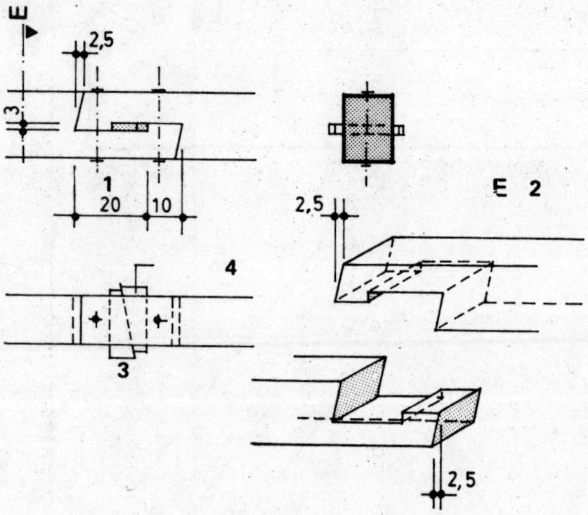

9

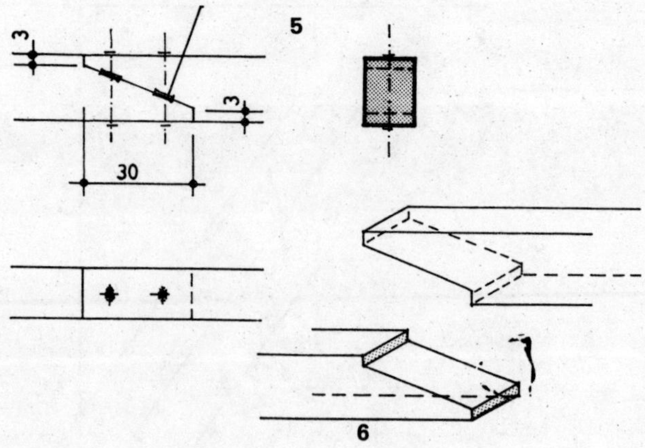

10

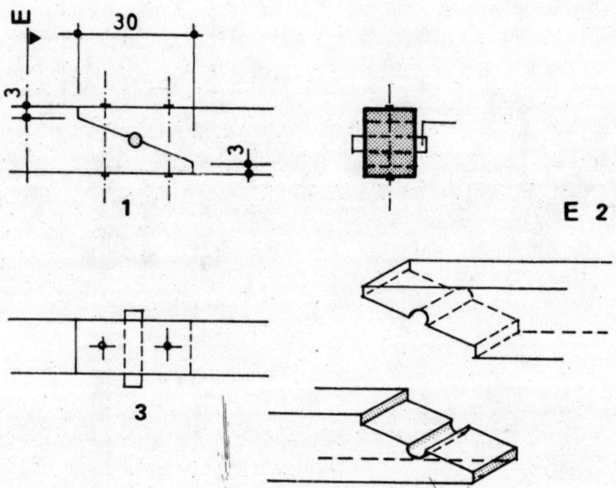

11

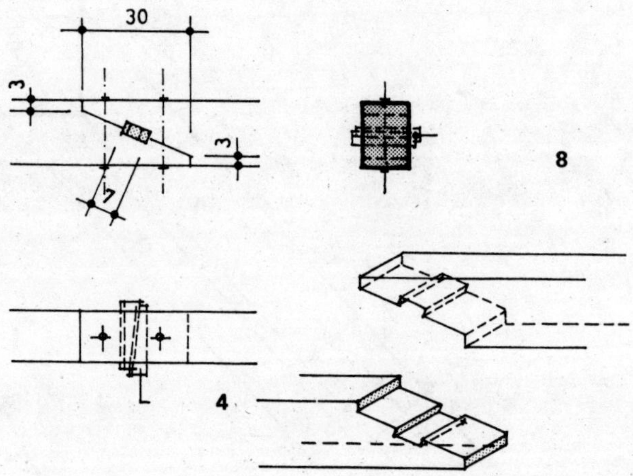

12

1 Elevation
2 Section E
3 Plan
4 Wedge
5 Metal ring inserts
6 Beam or purlin
7 Round timber peg ∅4 - 4.5 cm
8 Double wedge inserts
9 Wedge tabled joint
10 Scarf joint
11 Scarf joint with round timber peg
12 Scarf joint with double wedges

1:20

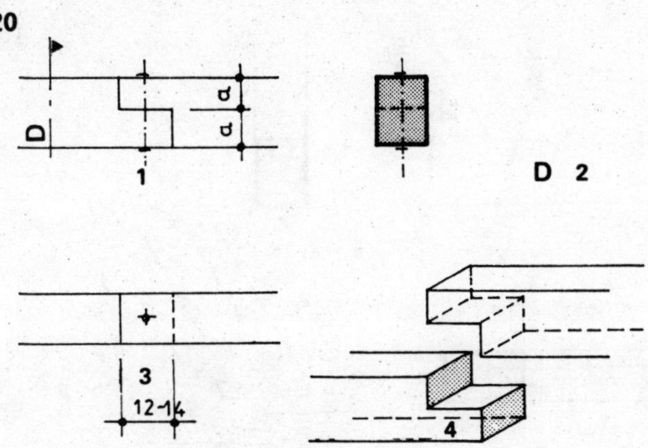

11

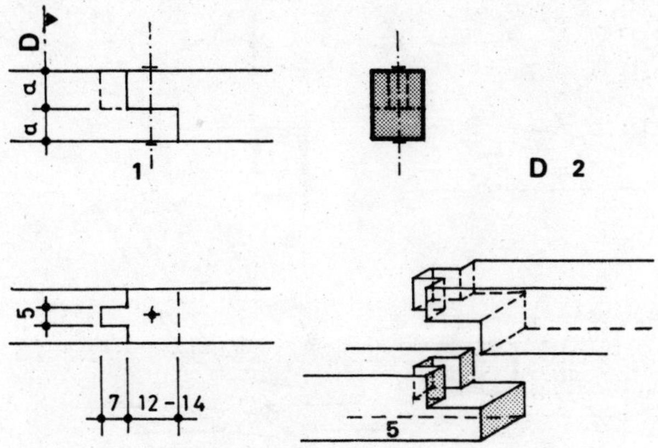

12

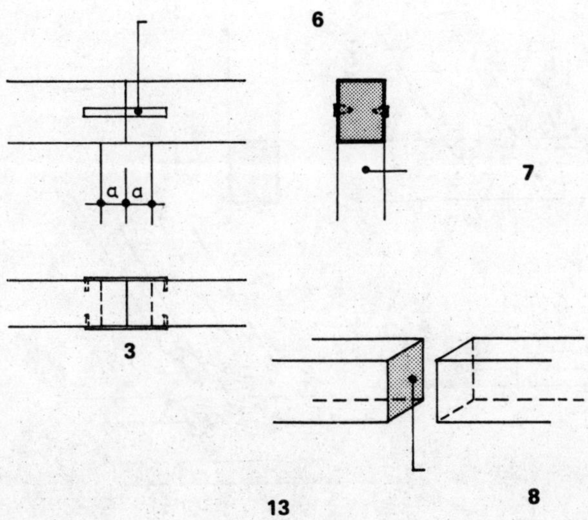

13

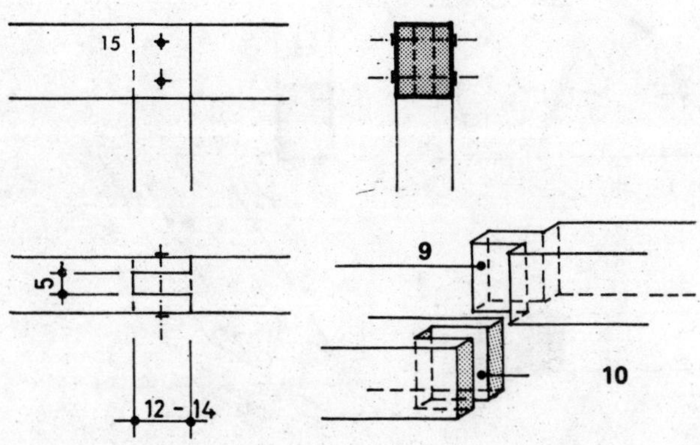

14

1 Elevation
2 Section D
3 Plan
4 Beam or plate (sill)
5 Beam or purlin
6 Timber connector (cramp)
7 Post
8 Surface of abutment
9 Tenon
10 Groove
11 Tabled joint in length of timber
12 Tabled joint with tenon
13 Butt joint
14 Groove and tenon joint
15 Purlin

Beam and brace joints

1:20

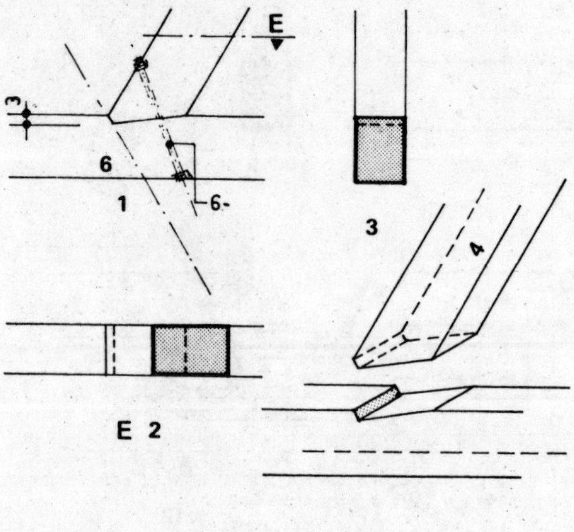

10

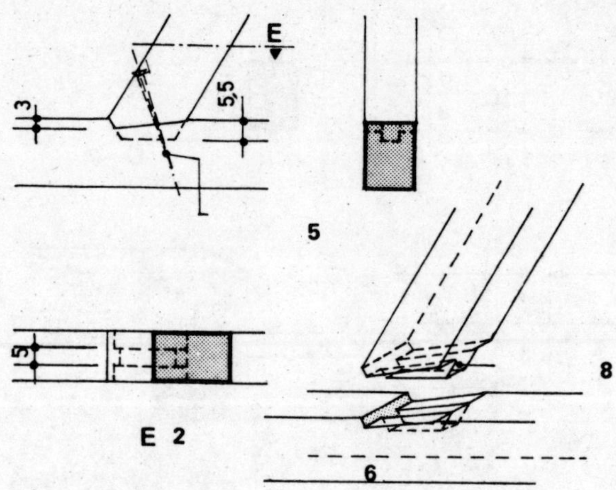

11

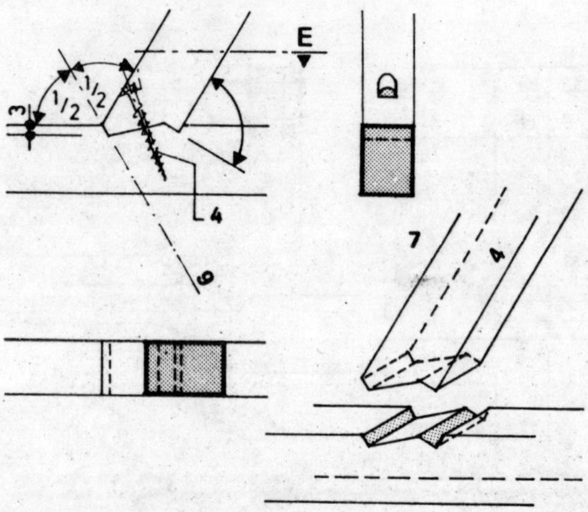

12

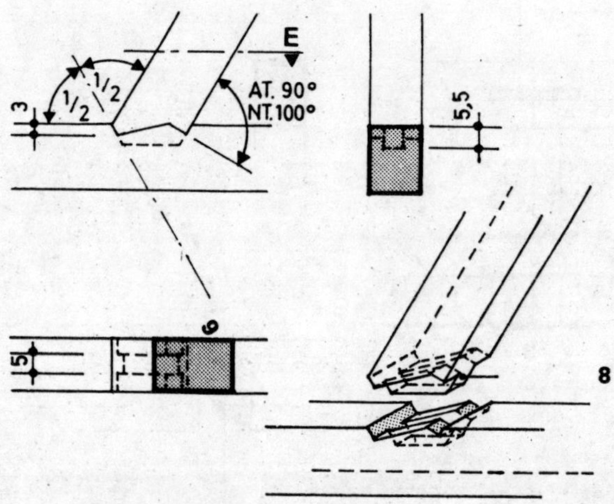

13

1 Elevation
2 Section/plan E
3 Hexagonal head nut and bolt
4 Strut or brace
5 Carpentry nail
6 Beam
7 Square or hexagonal head lag screw
8 Tenon
9 Bisecting angle
10 Simple notched joint
11 Simple notched joint with tenon
12 Double notched joint
13 Double notched joint with tenon (bridle joint)

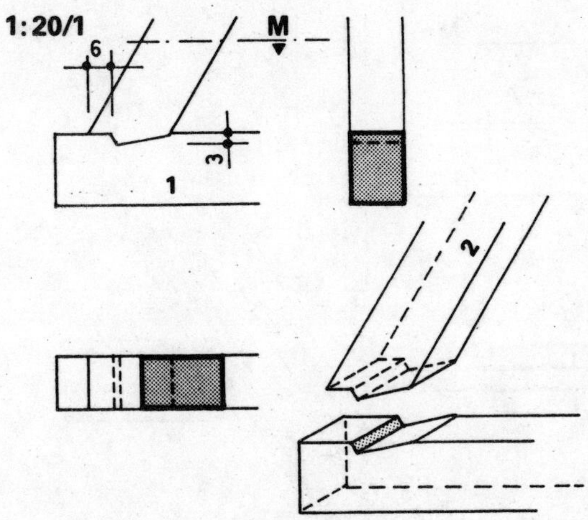

16

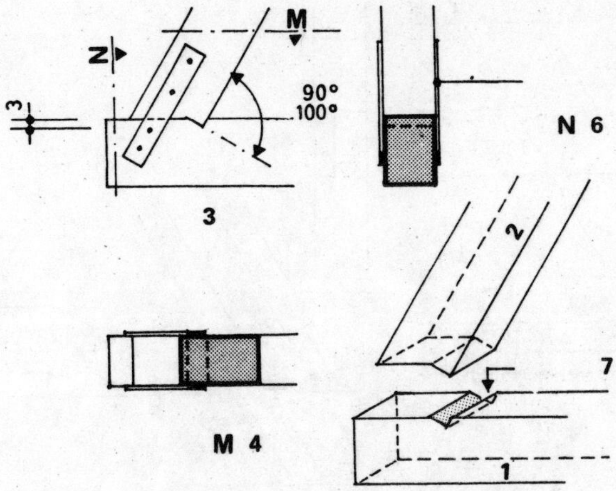

17

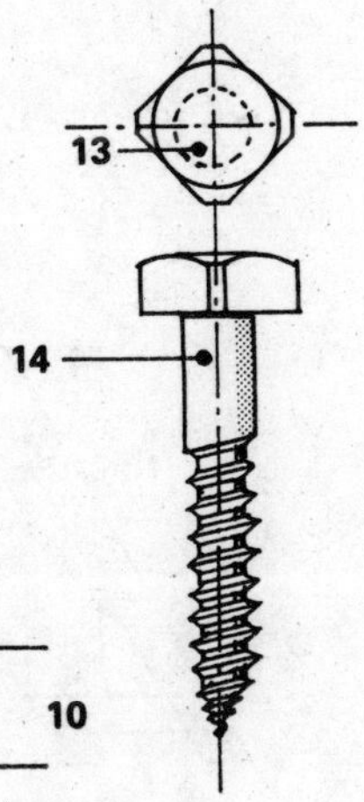

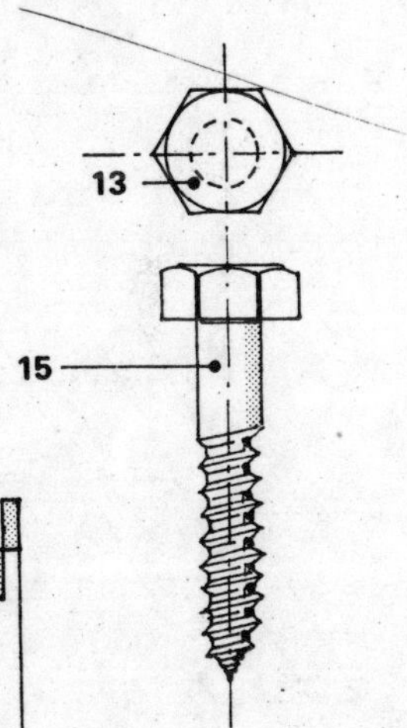

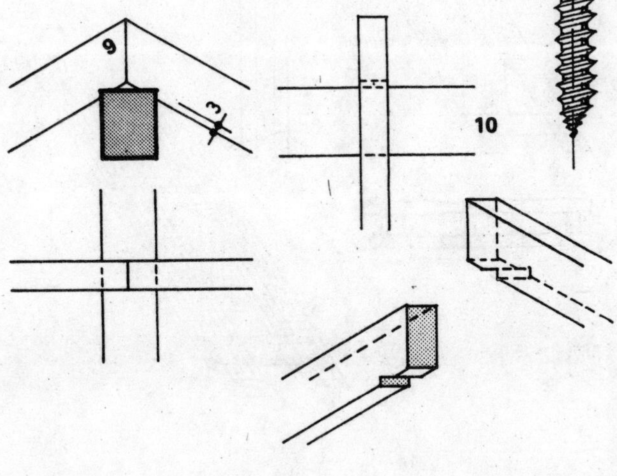

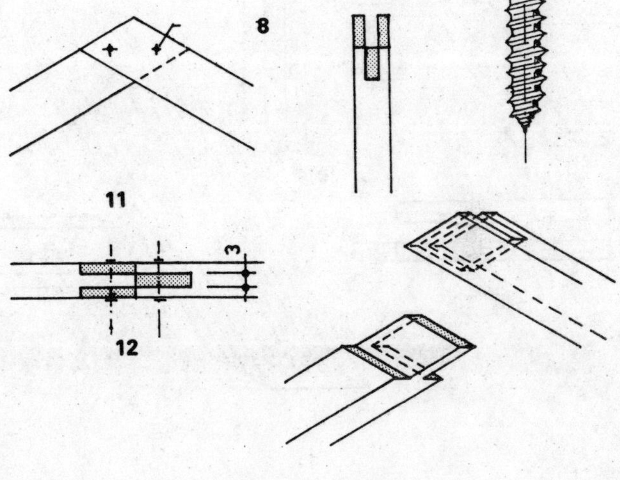

18

19

1 Beam
2 Strut or brace
3 Elevation
4 Section/plan M
5 Flat iron, screwed
6 Section N
7 Notching
8 Nail
9 Rafter
10 Ridge plate
11 Elevation of rafters
12 Plan of rafters
13 Plan of head of screw
14 Square head wood screw
15 Hexagonal head wood screw
16 Simple notched joint
17 Wedge joint
18 Notching
19 Forked mortice and tenon

Dovetail halved joints and simple timber connections

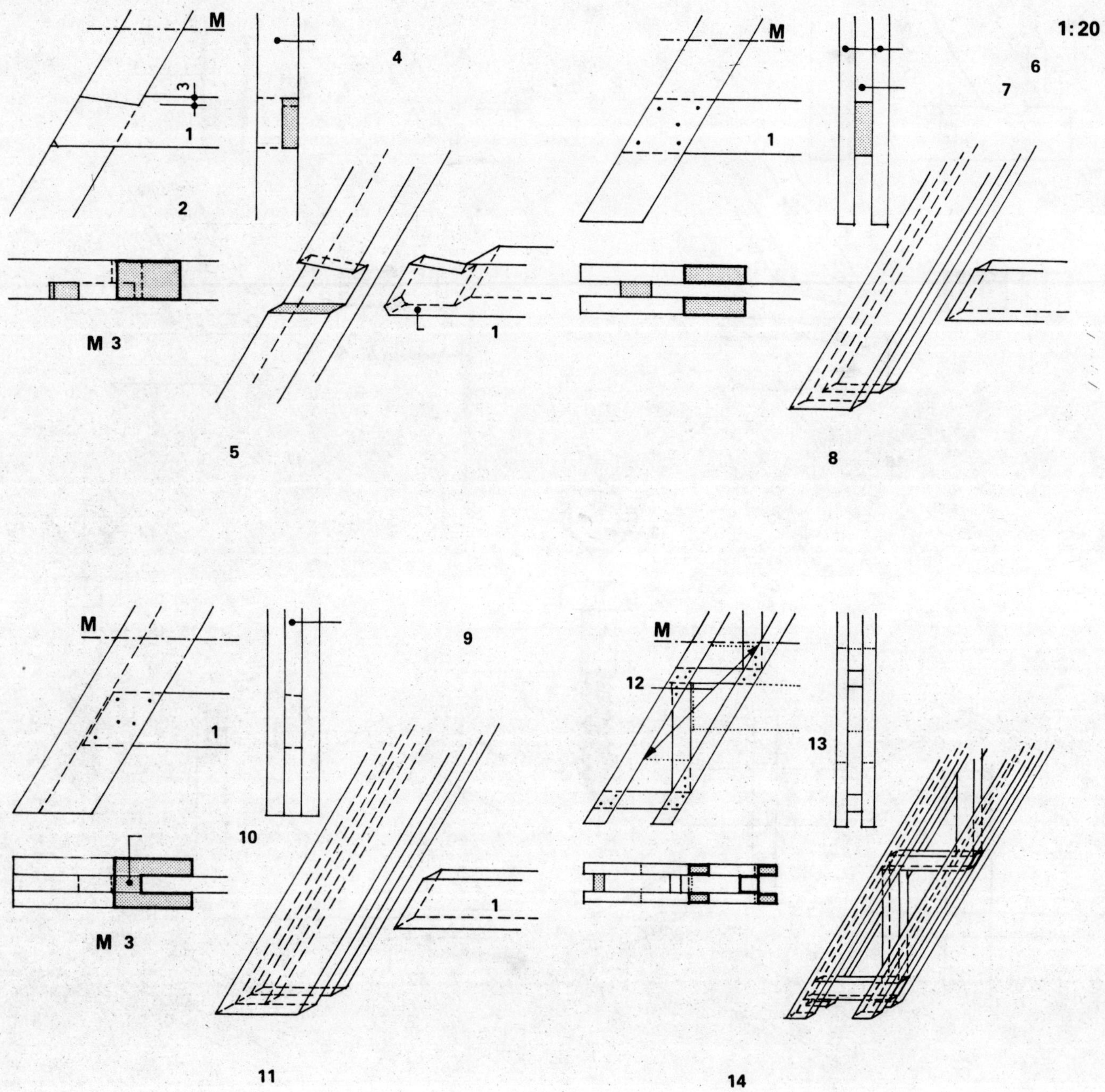

1 Collar or tie beam
2 Side elevation
3 Sectional plan
4 Rafter or brace
5 Dovetail halved joint
6 Double plank rafters
or brace
7 Void
8 Simple plank connection
9 Rafters or brace glued
10 Blocking piece
11 Glued plank connection
12 Plank stiffening
13 Possible brace
14 Triangulated plank truss

Pitched Roof Drainage

The material must be free from flaws and should not distort when bent. Gutter bearers are to be fixed in the gutter fall and screwed solid into the rafter- or fascia-board flush with the top-edge. In all fastenings the free movement of the sheet-metal material in fluctuations of temperations must be ensured. For reasons of price copper will often have to be dispensed with, and zinc, aluminium or galvanized sheet used instead.

Movement joints have to be arranged according to the type of material and in the forming of angles the continuous length should not exceed the permissible dimension. Sheet thicknesses are given in kg/m^2 or mm.

As a general rule for calculating rainwater amounts, a pipe-diameter of 10 cm is acceptable for approx. 80-100 m^2.

Tile Roofing

The pitch of a roof is decided by the type of roofing, as well as the situation in relation to wind and weather conditions, especially rainfall and snow. For heated rooms built in the roof a continuous shingle protective skin or, as is usual today, an overall under-roof lining as a second roof is necessary. Every third tile at the gable ends must be anchored by means of stormcramps. In deciding the precise length of rafters the appropriate spacing of timbers must be considered by the roofer.

Thermal insulating boards or other cladding should never be laid directly under the rafters or collar-beams, as otherwise flaws in the timber are transferred to the ceiling-surface and lead inevitably to cracks. Distance pieces or patent nails should be used.

Half-round Eaves-gutter with pipe/arched-offset

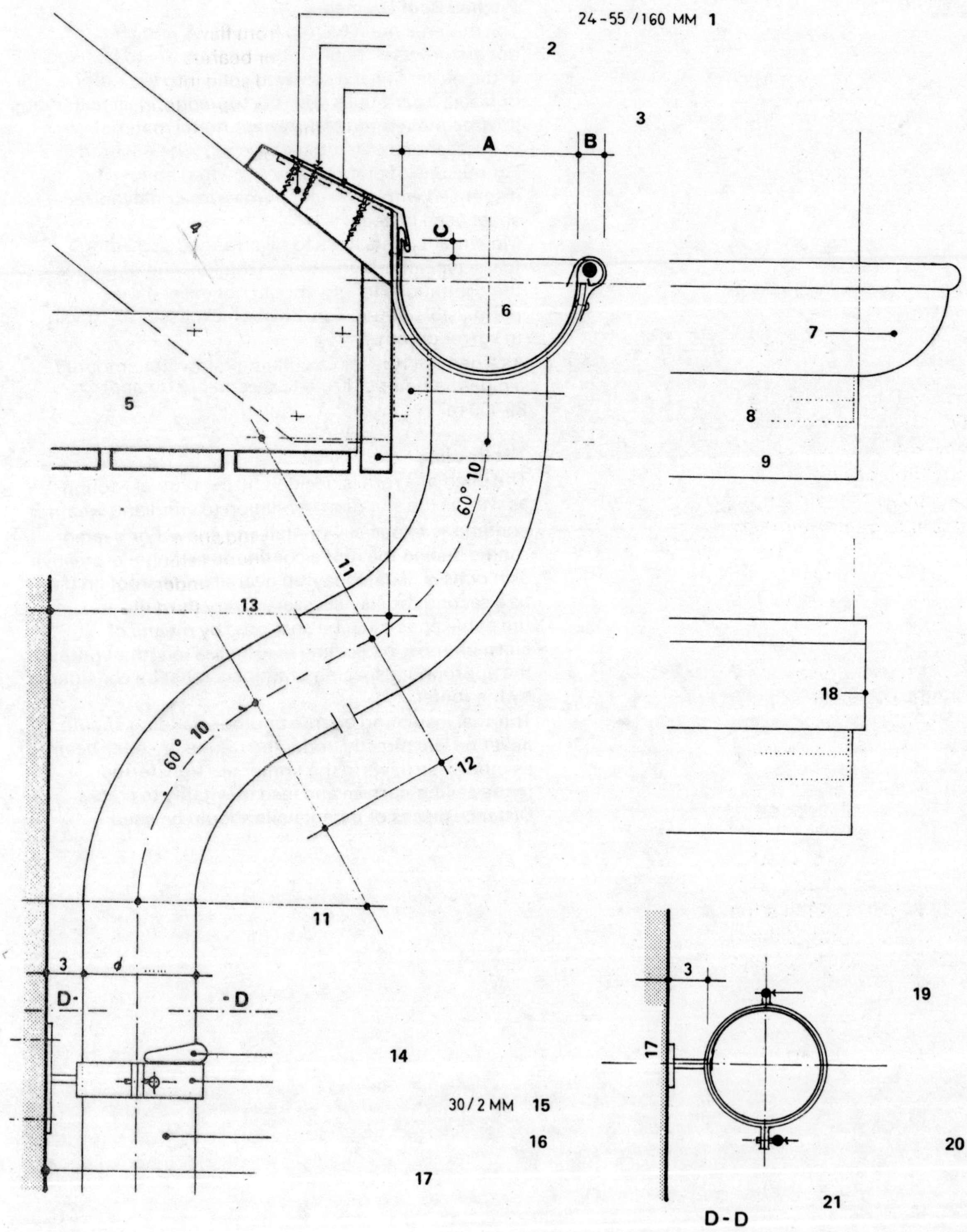

1 Eaves board
2 Wood screws
3 Inlet plate with provision for expansion
4 Rafter (spar)
5 Cleat
6 Gutter
7 Gutter head (round type)
8 Gutter batten (to equalize fall)
9 Fascia
10 S-profile
11 2 × pipe-diameter
12 Length according to overhang
13 Roof-overhang
14 Pipe packing
15 Pipe-clamp with hinged collar
16 Rainwater outlet-pipe
17 Wall line
18 Gutter head (rectangular)
19 Hinge
20 Eye-bolt
21 Section through outlet-pipe

Half-round Eaves-gutter with down-pipe variants

1:5

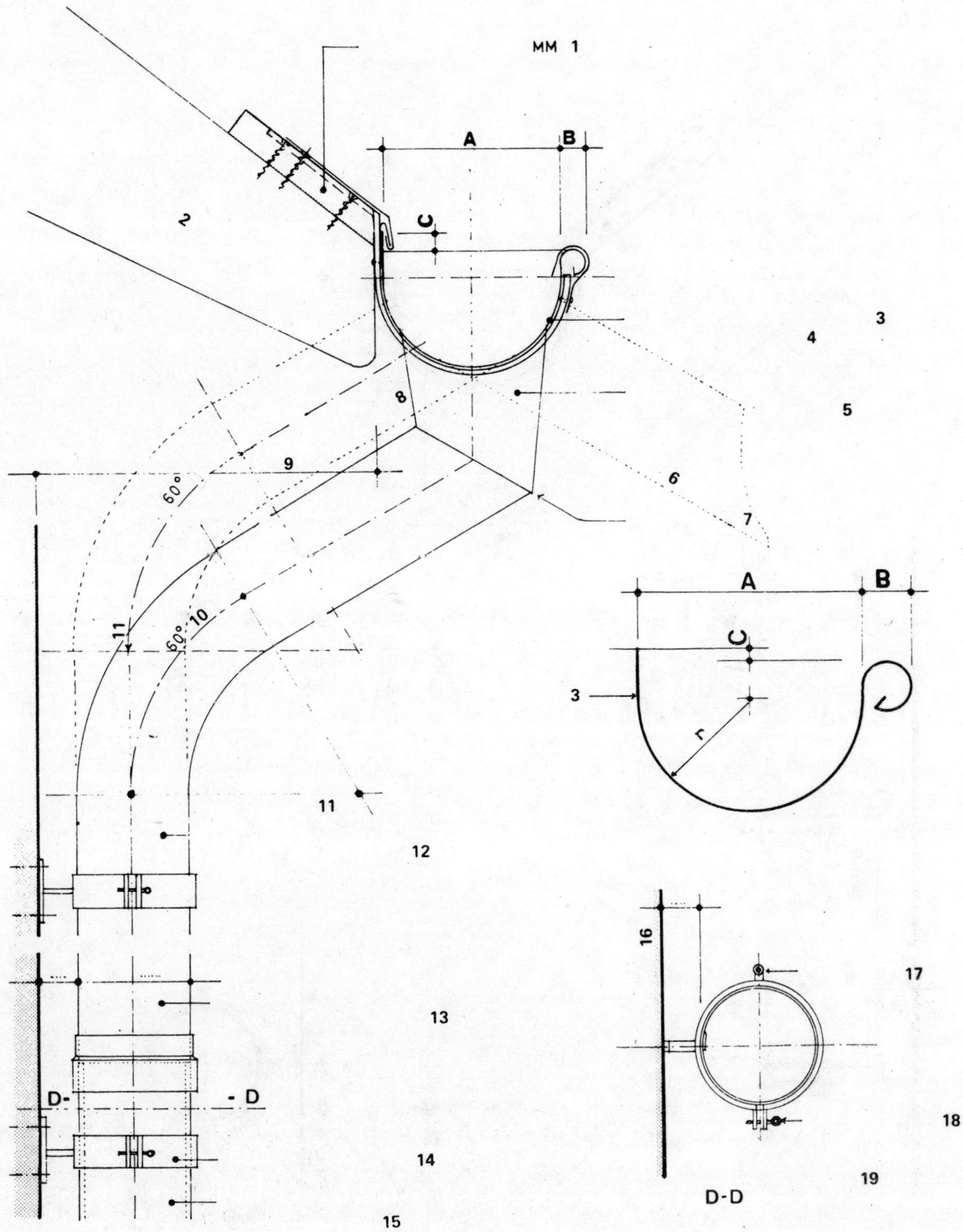

1 Eaves board
2 Rafter foot, tapered
3 Half-round eaves gutter
4 Elbow
5 Outlet connexion
6 Down spout
7 Pipe angle
8 Sloping outlet
9 Roof overhang (soffit), variable
10 Bend
11 2 × pipe-diameter
12 Rainwater downpipe
13 Continuous bead
14 Pipe bracket (hoop) with anti-slip fitting
15 Downpipe, straight form
16 Wall-fixing detail
17 Hinge
18 Eye-bolt
19 Section through downpipe

Half-round Eaves-gutter with pipe elbow-connection

1:5

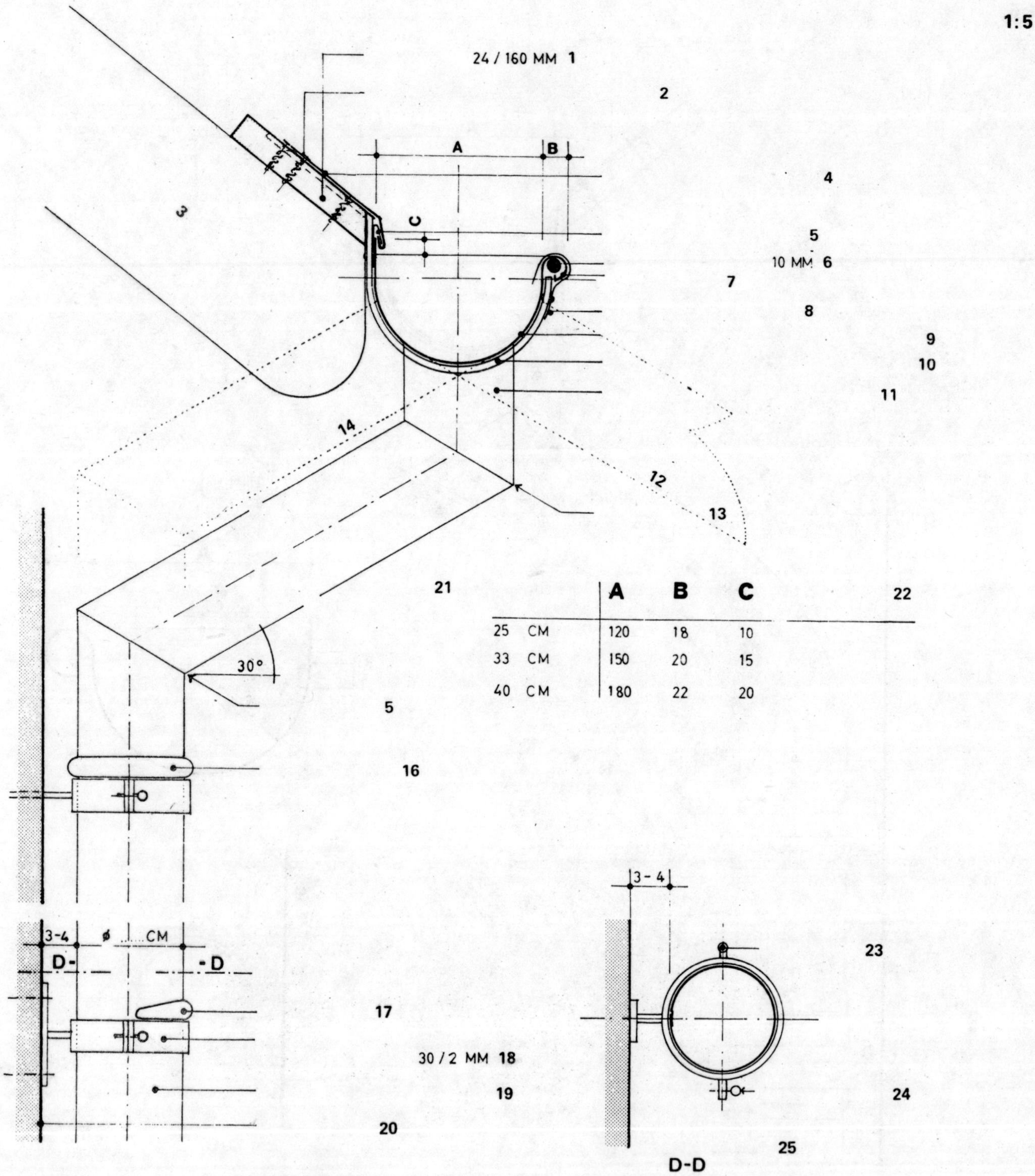

	A	B	C
25 CM	120	18	10
33 CM	150	20	15
40 CM	180	22	20

1 Eaves board
2 Wood-screws with long holes
3 Rafter
4 Inlet plate
5 Holdfast
6 Round-bar
7 Gutter bead
8 Beading
9 Half-round eaves-gutter, elbow
10 Gutter-bearer, section
11 Outlet connexion, straight form
12 Down spout
13 Pipe angle
14 Top outlet
15 Pipe angle, 30°
16 Continuous (ring) bead
17 Pipe bead
18 Pipe-holder (bat) with hinged collar (hoop)
19 Down-pipe
20 Wall line
21 Gutter angles
22 Dimensional unit mm
23 Hinge
24 Ring-screw
25 Section through down-pipe

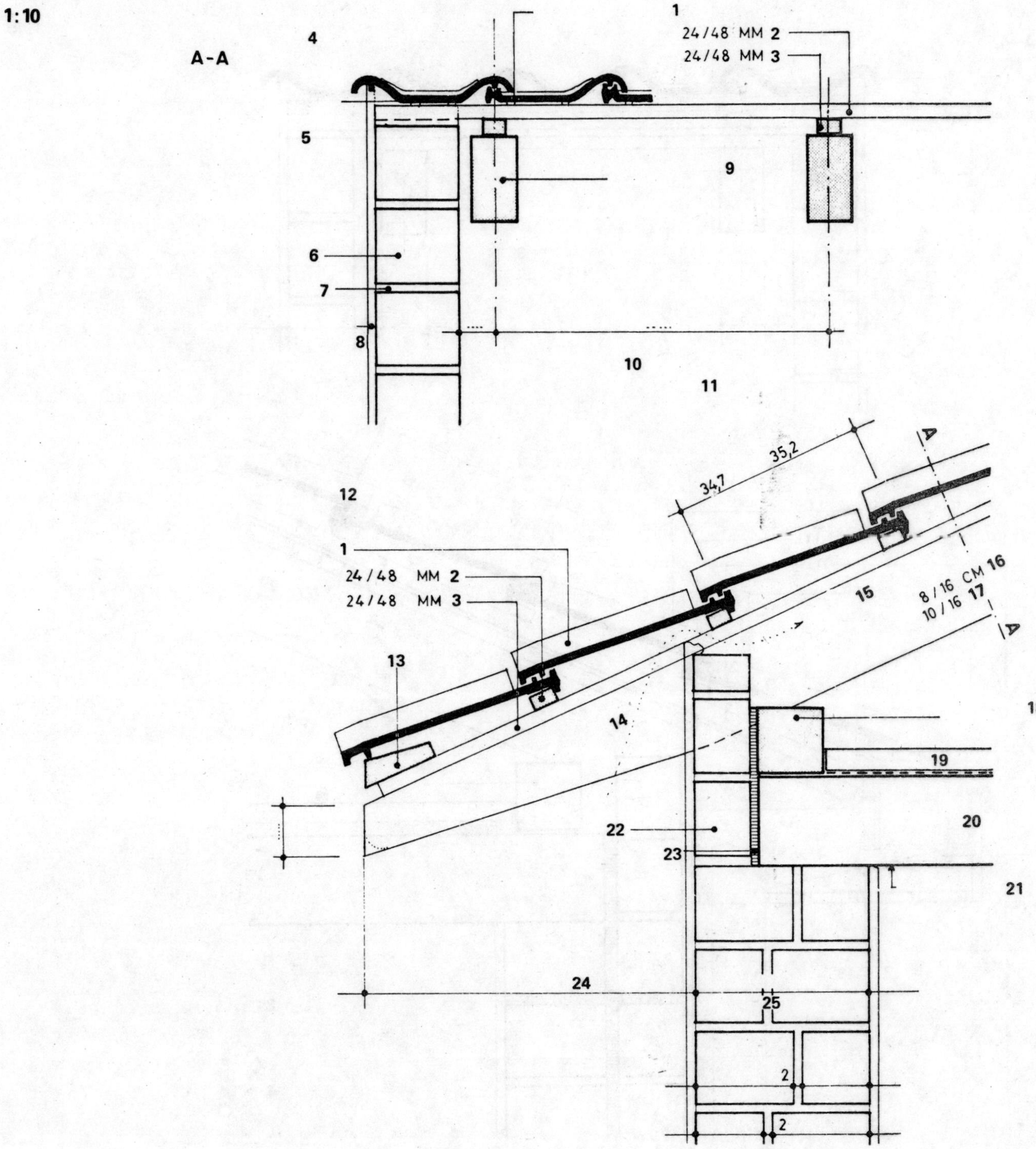

1 Pantile
2 Batten
3 Counter-batten
4 Verge detail
5 Verge tile (tile-and-a-half) pointed in mortar
6 Gable-slate
7 Bearing joint
8 External rendering, roughcast
9 Rafter (section)
10 Roof space
11 Effective surface (roof)
12 Eaves detail
13 Eaves board, conic
14 Rafter foot, tapered
15 Air space
16 Common rafter
17 Principal rafter
18 Wall-plate
19 Cement surface
20 Reinforced concrete ceiling
21 Exposed concrete
22 Outer wall
23 Insulation
24 Roof overhang
25 External masonry

Pantile Roofing, fixing details

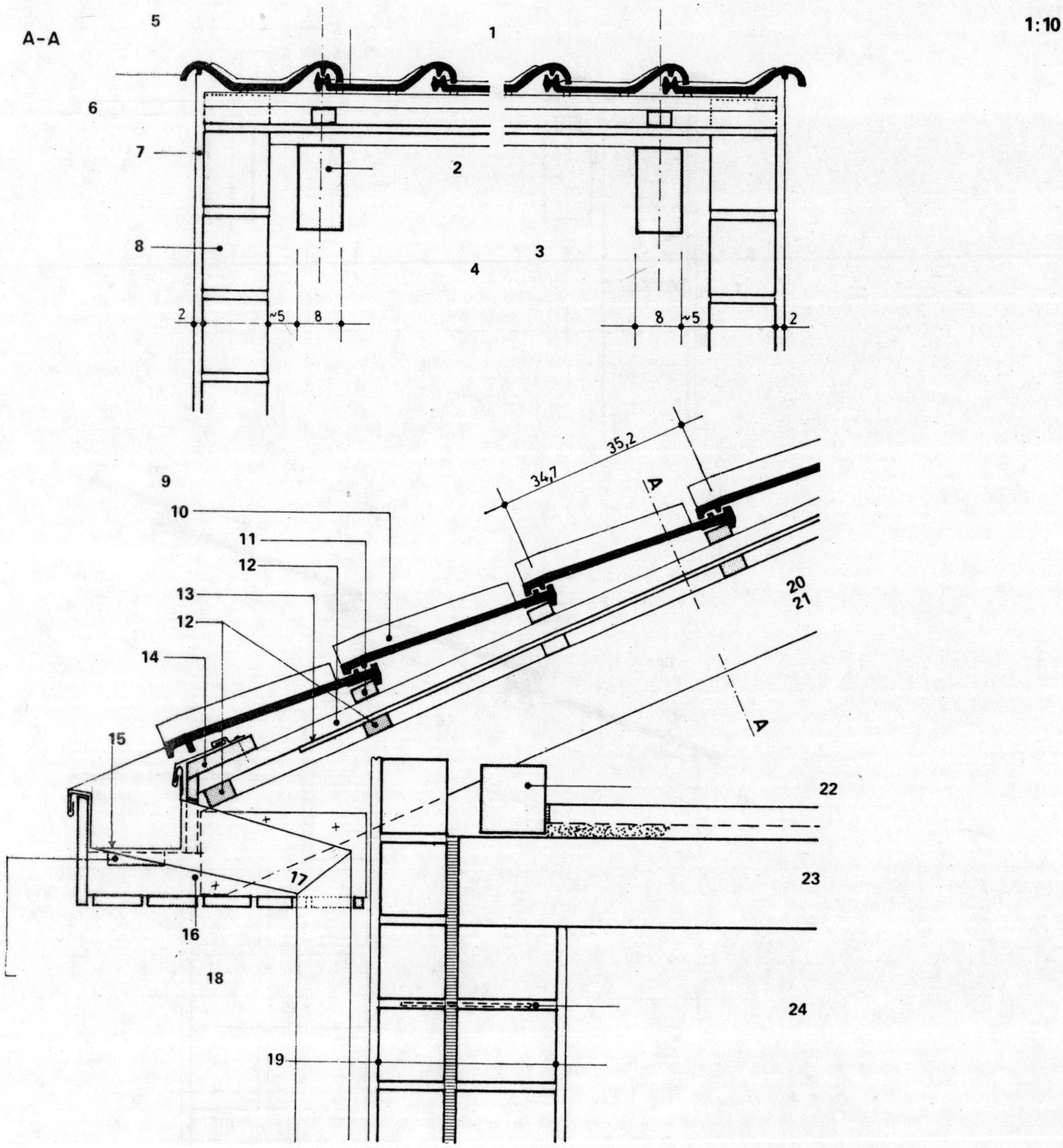

1 Plain (Roman) tile
2 Rafter
3 Effective roof surface
4 Roof space
5 Verge details
6 Verge tile (tile-and-a-half) pointed in mortar
7 External rendering
8 Gable wall
9 Eaves details.
10 Pantile
11 Batten
12 Counter-batten
13 Undercloak
14 Eaves detail
15 Box-gutter
16 Cleat
17 Outlet, conic
18 Gutter stiffening
19 Cavity wall
20 Common rafter
21 Principal rafter
22 Wall-plate
23 Reinforced concrete ceiling
24 Steel wall-tie

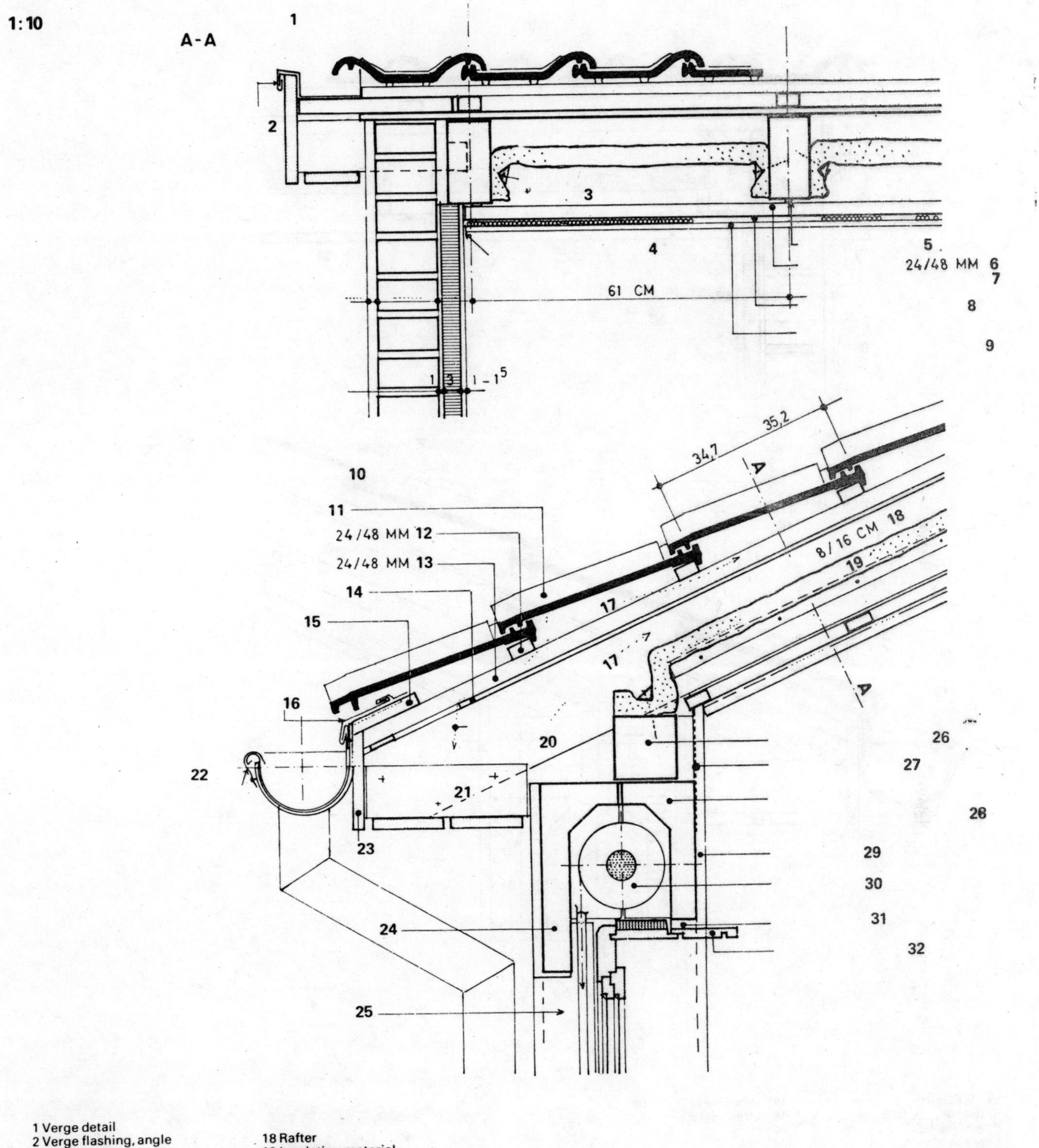

1 Verge detail
2 Verge flashing, angle
3 Triangular fillet
4 Fillet
5 Distance piece
6 Batten grid
7 At 30 cm centres
8 Stramit
9 Ground + final coat or one-coat
10 Eaves detail
11 Pantile
12 Battening
13 Counter-battens
14 Undercloak
15 Eaves board
16 Inlet plate, angle
17 Air space
18 Rafter
19 Insulating material
20 Condensation
21 Cleat
22 Holdfast
23 Fascia
24 Front lintel
25 External jamb
26 Wall-plate
27 Expanded metal
28 Back lintel
29 Plaster finish
30 Roll shutters
31 Trimmer
32 Curtain board
33 Internal jamb
34 Jamb edge

Pantile Roofing, fixing details

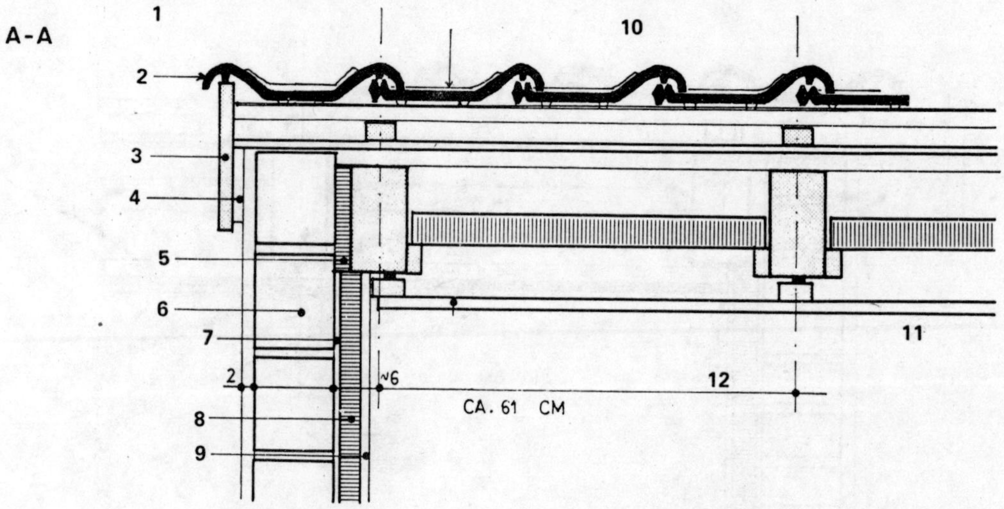

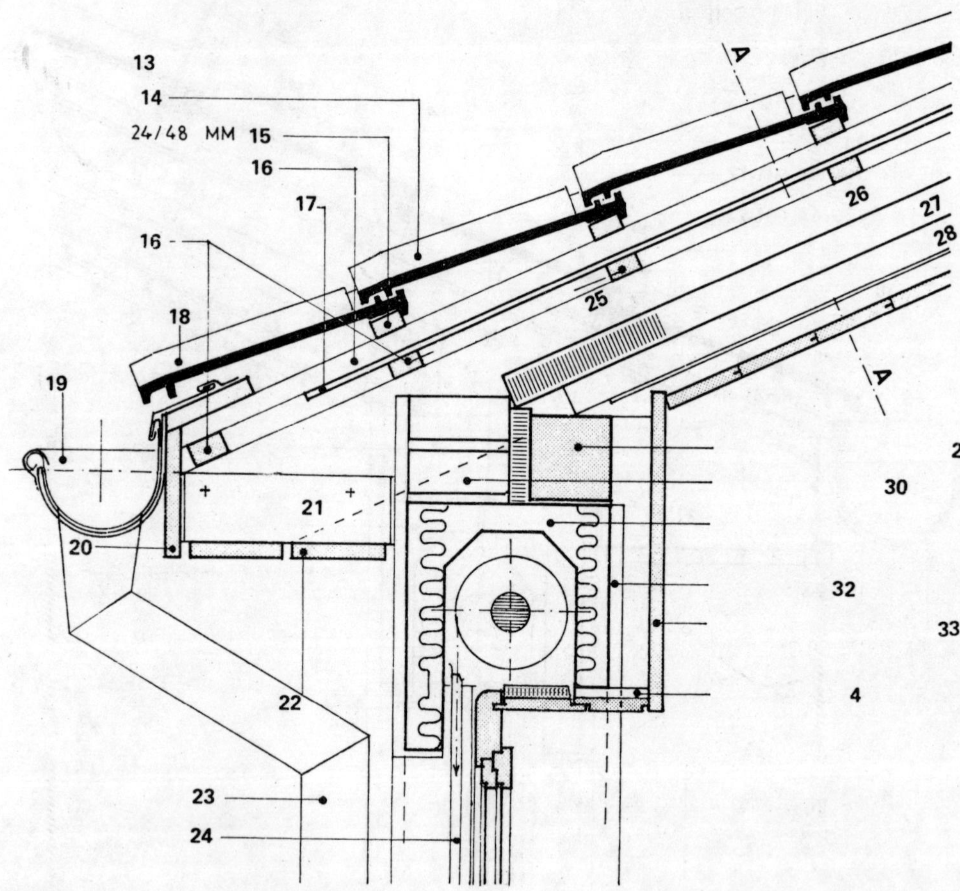

1 Verge detail
2 Verge tile (tile-and-a-half)
3 Barge board
4 Trimmer
5 Cork insulation
6 Gable wall
7 Plaster infill
8 Insulation
9 Internal plastering
10 Plain tile
11 Plaster-board
12 Rafter centres, about 61 cm
13 Eaves detail
14 Pantile
15 Battening
16 Counter-battening
17 Undercloak
18 Eaves-course (joint) tile
19 Gutter, angle
20 Fascia
21 Cleat
22 Soffit cladding, in wood
23 Down-pipe
24 Guide-band
25 According to roof-type
26 Rafter
27 Insulation, . . . cm thick
28 Supporting piece
29 Wall-plate
30 External masonry
31 Roll-shutter lintel
32 Plaster
33 Lintel cladding
34 Curtain board (rail)
35 Assembly covering
36 Composite window

1:10

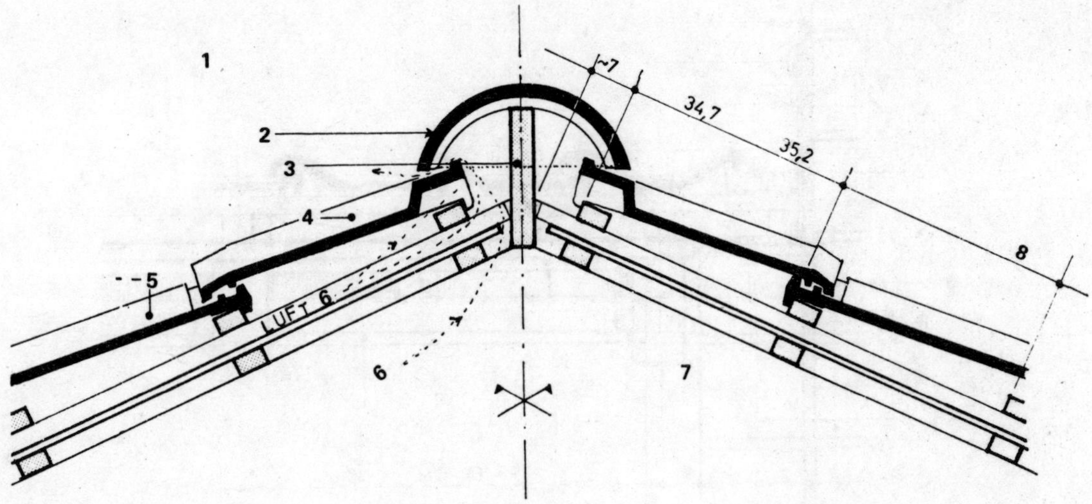

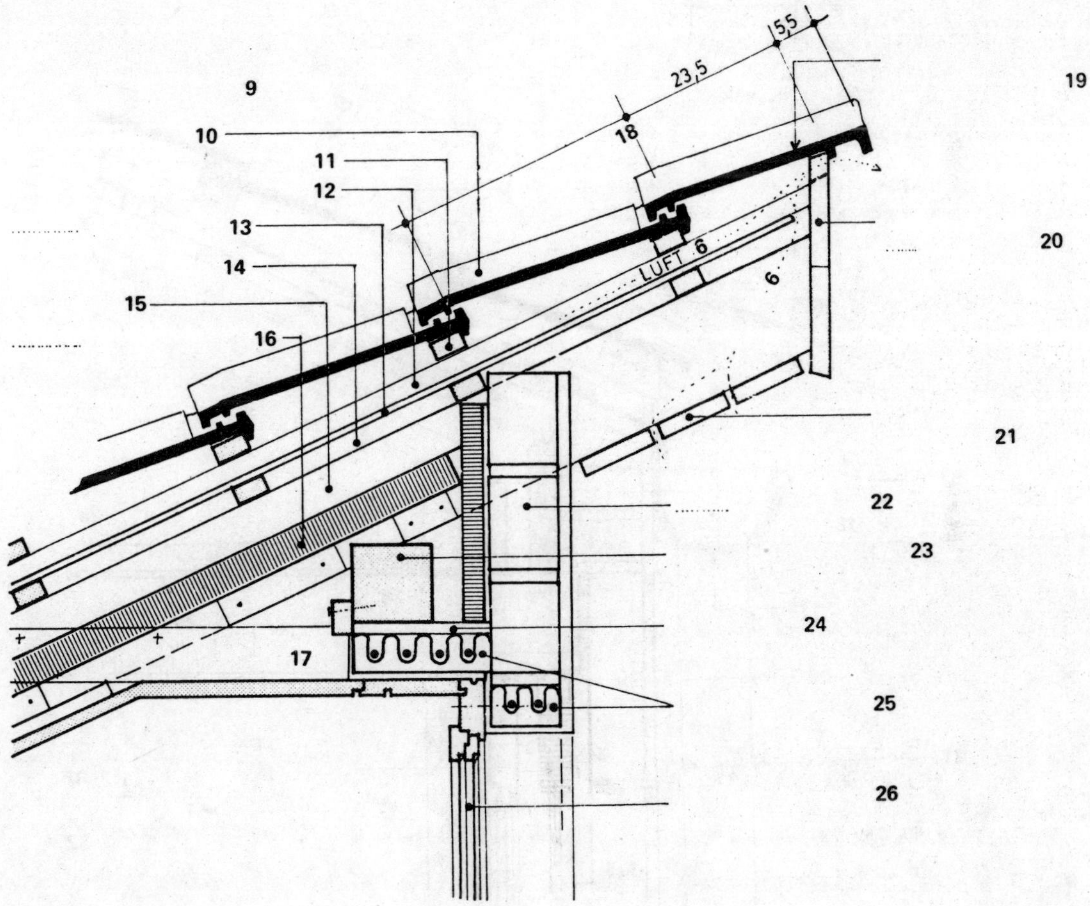

1 Ridge detail
2 Ridge capping tile
3 Ridge piece
4 Ridge (top course) tile
5 Common pantile
6 Air space
7 Ridge axis
8 Gauge
9 Pent-roof ridge detail
10 Pantile
11 Battening
12 Counter-battening
13 Undercloak
14 Optional counter-battening
15 Rafter
16 Insulation (sarking)
17 Cleat
18 Standard spacing (battening gauge)
19 Pent-roof top-course tile
20 Fascia
21 Soffit cladding
22 Masonry wall
23 Ridge purlin
24 Trimmer
25 Reinforced concrete lintel

Pantile Roofing, wall fixing and eaves details

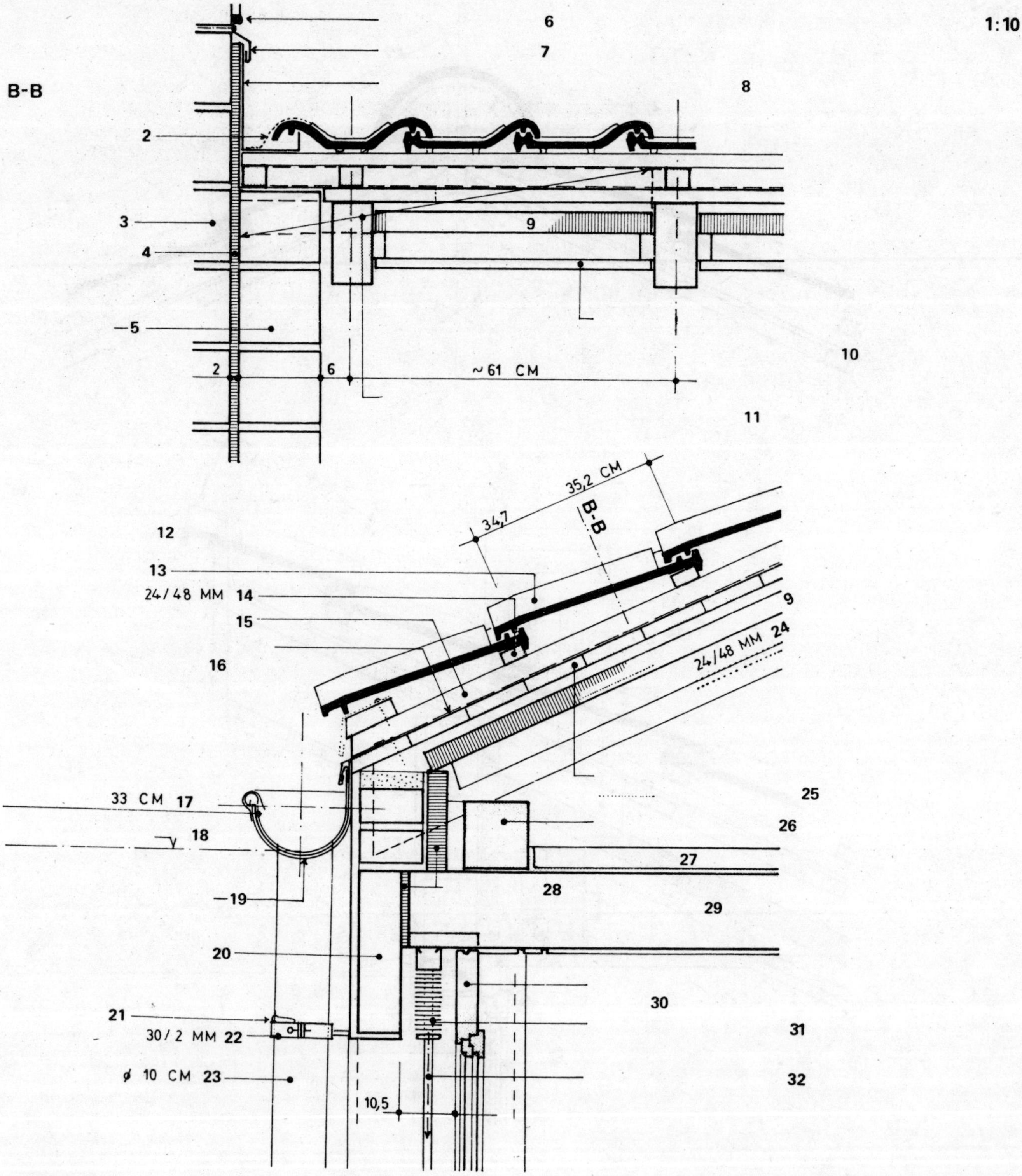

1 Wall-jointing detail
2 Lead lap
3 Fire-proof masonry
4 Expansion joint with … insulation panels, … mm thick
5 Fire-proof wall
6 Mastic filler
7 Flashing (weather-strip)
8 Angle plate (inc. flashing)
9 Insulation panel
10 Soffit cladding between rafters
11 Concrete fire-protection slab in accordance with by-laws
12 Eaves detail
13 Pantile
14 Battening
15 Counter-battening
16 Roofing felt, 10 cm overlap
17 Half-round eaves-gutter, angle
18 Lowest point
19 Eaves bearer including bracket
20 Concrete lintel
21 Pipe bead
22 Holderbat
23 Down-pipe
24 Supporting batten
25 Close-boarding
26 Wall-plate
27 Loft-floor
28 Insulation
29 Reinforced concrete ceiling
30 Window-frame (wood)
31 Folded (gathered) slatted blind
32 Guide-band

1:10

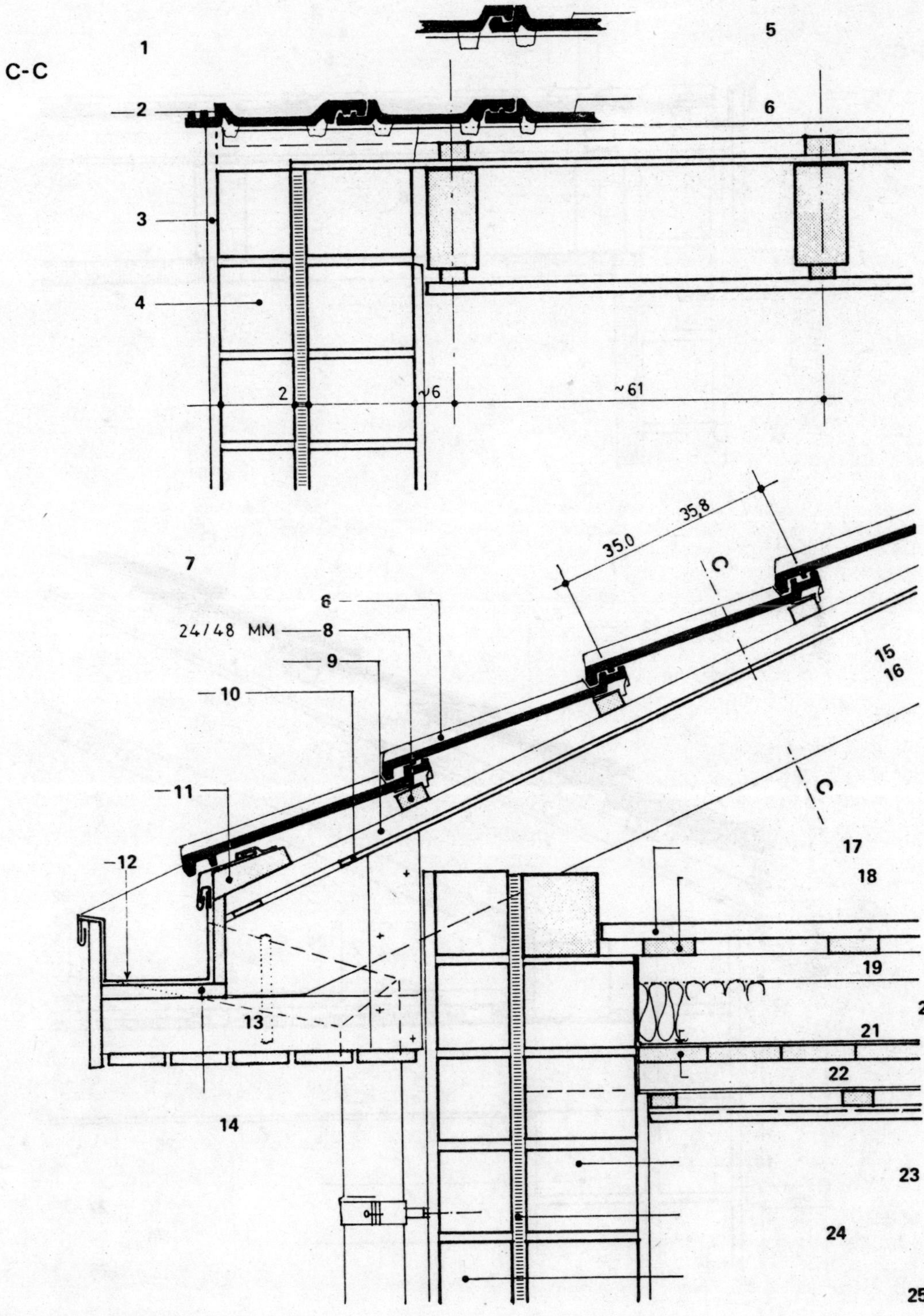

1 Verge detail
2 Tile . . . pointed in mortar
3 External rendering
4 Gable wall
5 Tile with single lapping
6 Tile with double lapping
7 Eaves detail
8 Battening
9 Counter-battening
10 Undercloak
11 Eaves board, conic
12 Box-gutter
13 Cleat
14 Fall board as gutter stiffening
15 Common rafter
16 Principal rafter
17 Board-floor (loft)
18 Slatted base
19 Beam
20 Insulation filling
21 Roofing-felt layer
23 Internal wall (cavity construction)
24 Insulation
25 External wall (cavity construction)

Plain-tile Single-lap Roofing

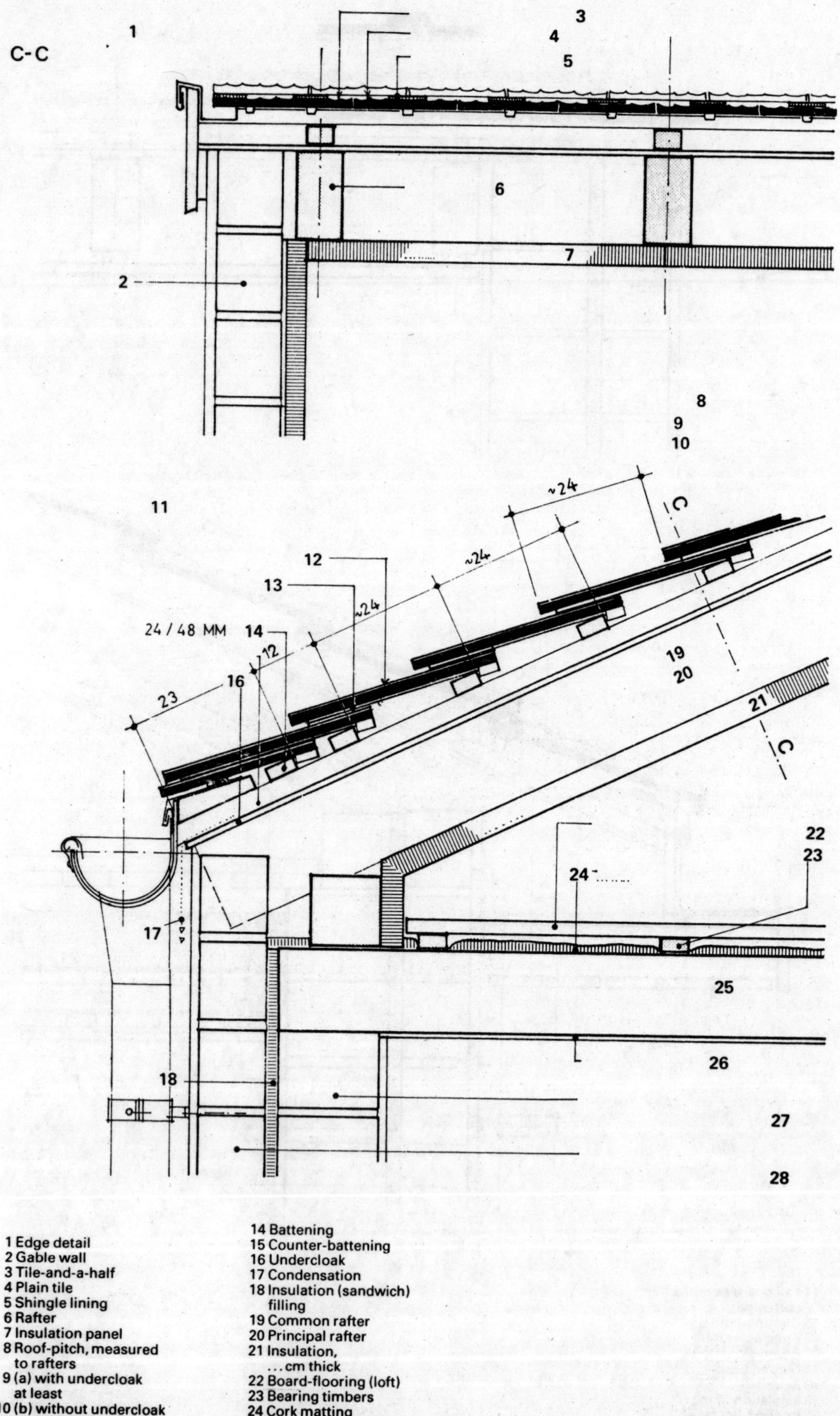

1 Edge detail
2 Gable wall
3 Tile-and-a-half
4 Plain tile
5 Shingle lining
6 Rafter
7 Insulation panel
8 Roof-pitch, measured to rafters
9 (a) with undercloak at least
10 (b) without undercloak
11 Eaves detail
12 Plain tile single lapping, . . . -section
13 shingle lining between tiles
14 Battening
15 Counter-battening
16 Undercloak
17 Condensation
18 Insulation (sandwich) filling
19 Common rafter
20 Principal rafter
21 Insulation, . . . cm thick
22 Board-flooring (loft)
23 Bearing timbers
24 Cork matting
25 Reinforced concrete ceiling
26 Plaster (ceiling)
27 Internal wall (skin)
28 External wall (skin)

1:10

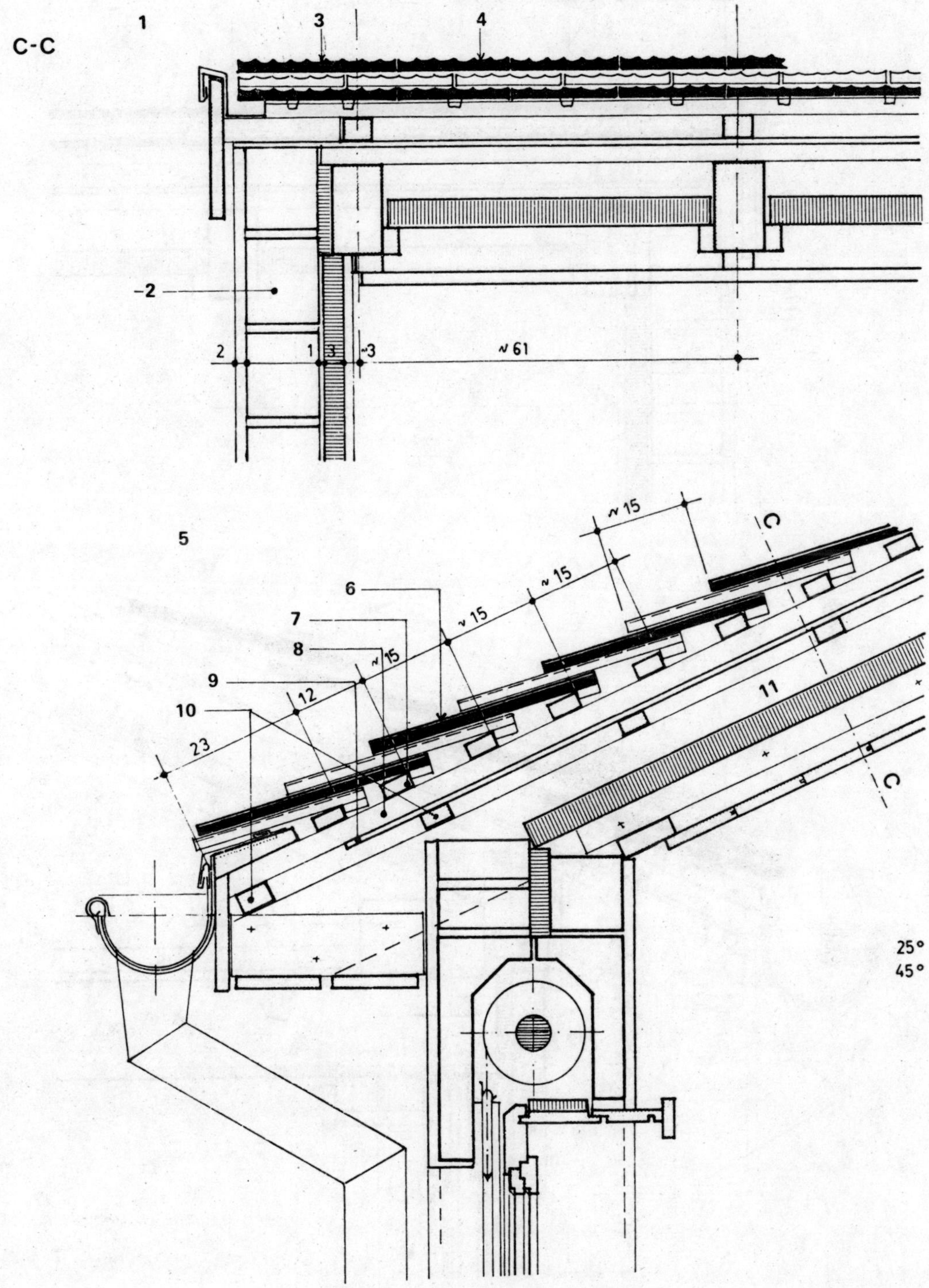

1 Verge detail
2 Gable wall
3 Tile-and-a-half
4 Plain (standard) tile
5 Eaves detail
6 Plain tile, double-lapping, . . . -section
7 Battening
8 Double battening
9 Undercloak
10 Counter-battening
11 Rafter
12 Pitch, measured to rafters:
a) with undercloak;
b) without undercloak

Plain-tile/"Crown" Roofing

1:10

C-C

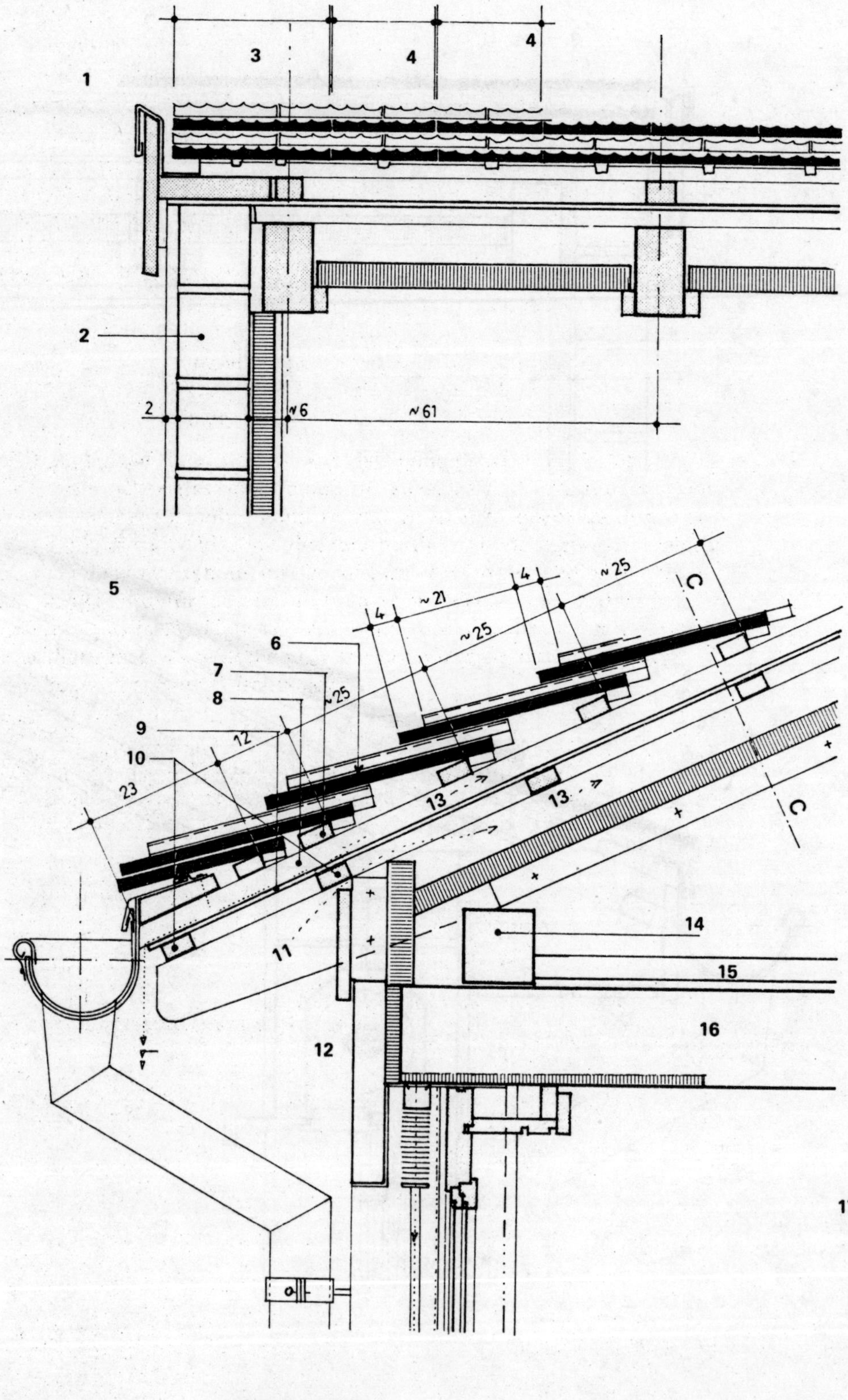

1 Ridge detail
2 Gable wall
3 Tile-and-a-half
4 Common rafter
5 Eaves detail
6 Plain-tile double-overlap roofing, ...-section
7 Battening
8 Battening
9 Undercloak
10 Counter-battening
11 Rafter foot, tapered
12 Condensation (water)
13 Air space
14 Wall-plate
15 Loft (floor)
16 Reinforced concrete ceiling
17 Pitch, measured to rafters: with undercloak, without undercloak

Asbestos slate roofing
The position of the building in conjunction with wind and weather conditions should be taken into account when using this type of roof covering. In particular the amount of rainfall and snow to be expected is important.
When the roof space is to be heated or in the case of large space, hall-type buildings, a continuous close-boarding layer or under-roof construction over the entire area is necessary, as well as insulation boarding. For horizontal coursed coverings with rafter spacing up to 70 cm, normal battening (24/48 mm) is sufficient. For wider spacings, double battening is to be recommended. The gauge of battens depends on the size of tile or slate used, and on the roof pitch. For a slope of 18°-30° the gauge is 18 cm; for 30-45° slopes, 20 cm; for slopes more than 45°, 22 cm. The spacing for the first setting out line is 2/5 more than the standard gauge, measured on plan on the rafters. In areas where heavy snowfall is normal the horizontal coursed single lap covering is not suitable because of its relatively low compressive strength. Roof coverings should always be carried out in the direction facing the main weather side.
With a double-lapped covering, 2 (or, in part, 3) thicknesses overlap. This form of roof covering is, therefore, compressively strong. The choice of tile or slate size depends on the height of the building, the roof pitch, and aesthetic considerations. (Sizes: 40 × 30, 40 or 60 cm, and 30 × 20 or 30 cm), etc. As the batten gauge varies from 11-25 cm, the precise lengths of joists should be obtained from a qualified craftsman.
To create an architecturally harmonious overall picture, visible metal sheeting or roofing should be avoided.

Single lap horizontal coursed roofing, eaves detail and plan of roof

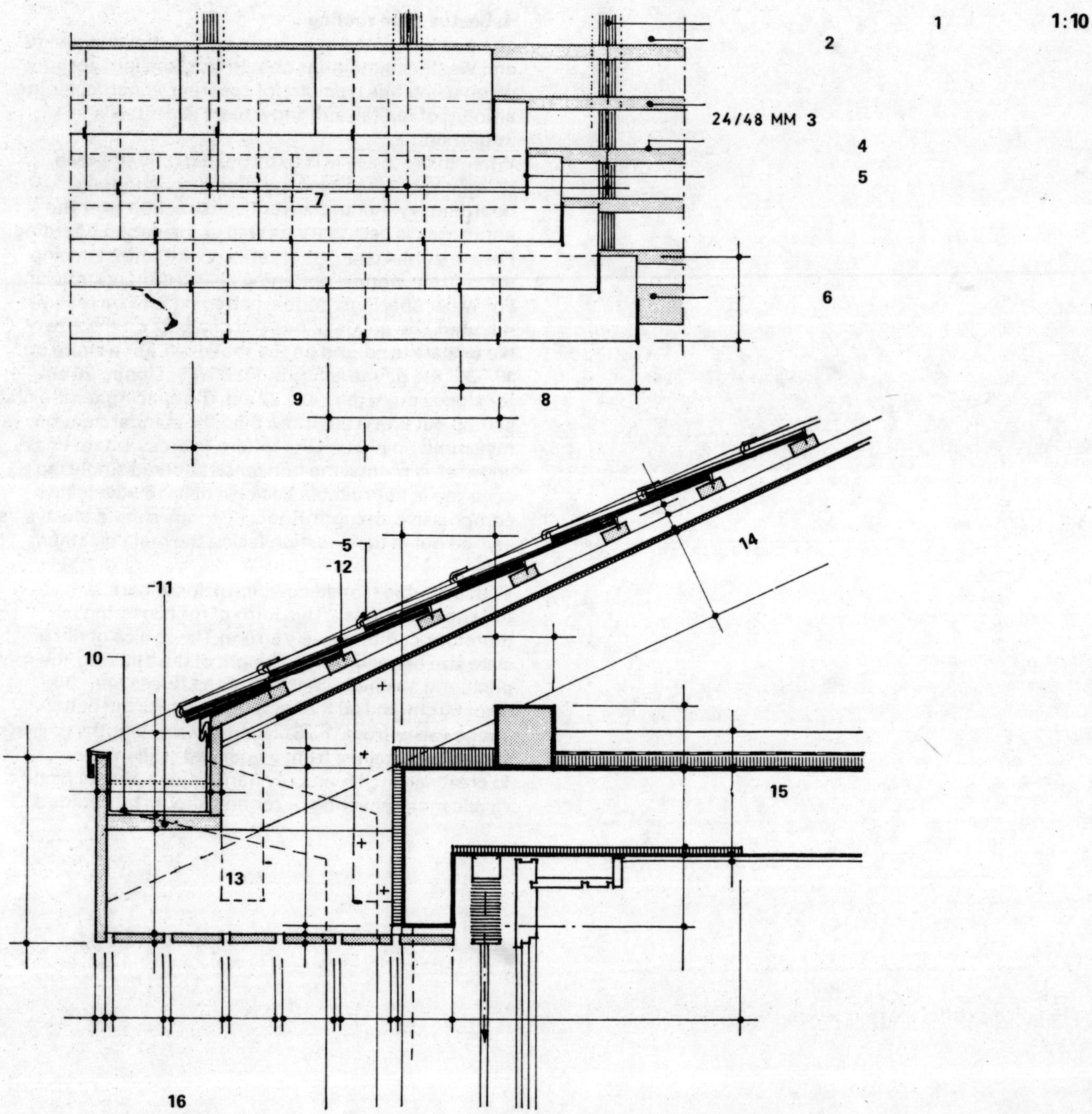

1 .../... mm
counter battens
2 Roof boarding
(sub-roof)
3 24/48 mm slate battens
4 Setting out line (gauge)
5 Fixing hook
6 Verge board
7 Rafter centres
8 Slate width
9 Plan of roof coverings
10 Box gutter
11 Sloping sole board
12 Slate
13 Fixing board
14 Normal rafters
15 Reinforced concrete slab
16 Eaves detail

Slate double lap roofing, eaves detail and plan of roof

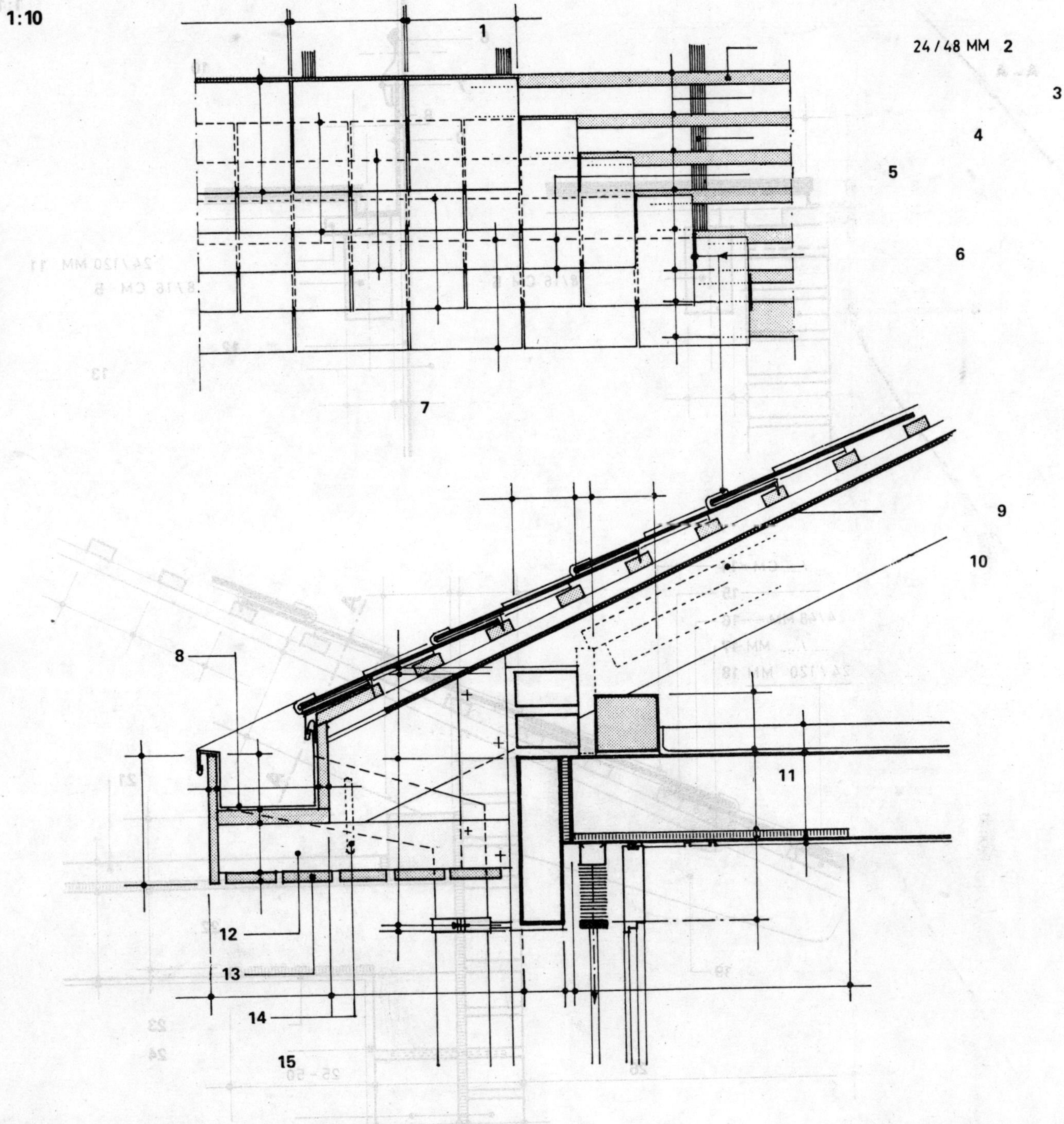

1 Slate width
2 Slate battens 24/48 mm
3 Gauge
4 .../... mm
counter battens
5 Double lap
6 Fixing hook
7 Plan of roof coverings
8 Box gutter
9 Roof lining
10 Insulation board
11 Concrete slab
12 Bracket
13 Soffit boarding
14 Dog
15 Eaves detail

Slating, double lap, edge and abutment details

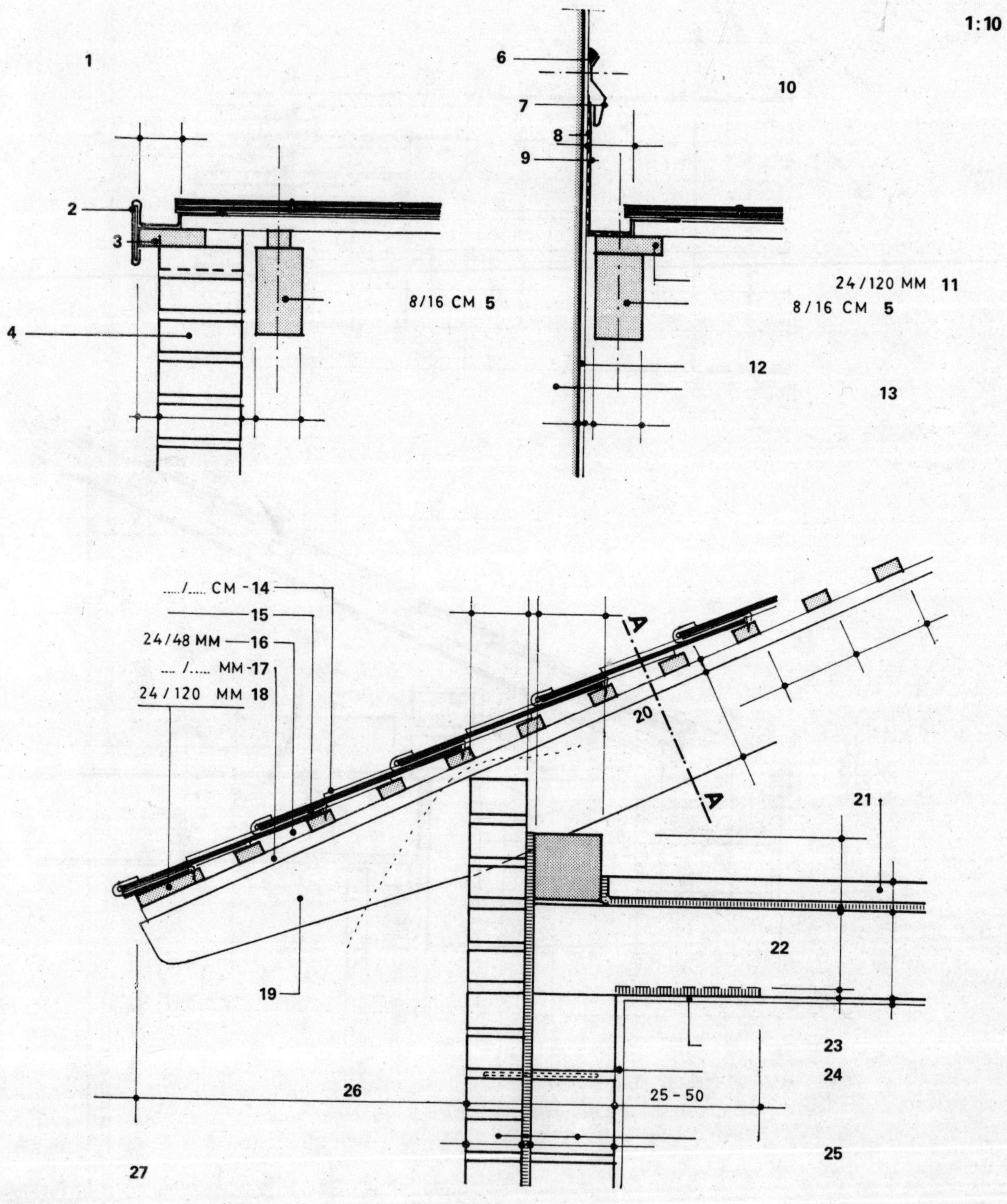

1 Verge detail. A – A
2 Metal flashing ... cm
3 .../... mm verge board
4 Facing brickwork
5 8/16 cm rafter
6 Sealing mastic
7 Covering strip 7-10 cm wide
8 Building paper underlay
9 Metal gutter lining
10 Detail at junction with upstand wall
11 24/100 mm bearing board
12 Plaster
13 Chimney
14 Roofing slates .../... cm
15 Slating hooks
16 24/48 mm roof battens
17 .../... mm counter battens
18 24/120 mm verge board
19 Tail of rafter, shaped
20 Ventilation
21 Floated screed
22 Reinforced concrete slab
23 Ceiling plaster
24 Wall plaster
25 Cavity wall
26 Eaves projection
27 Eaves detail

1:10

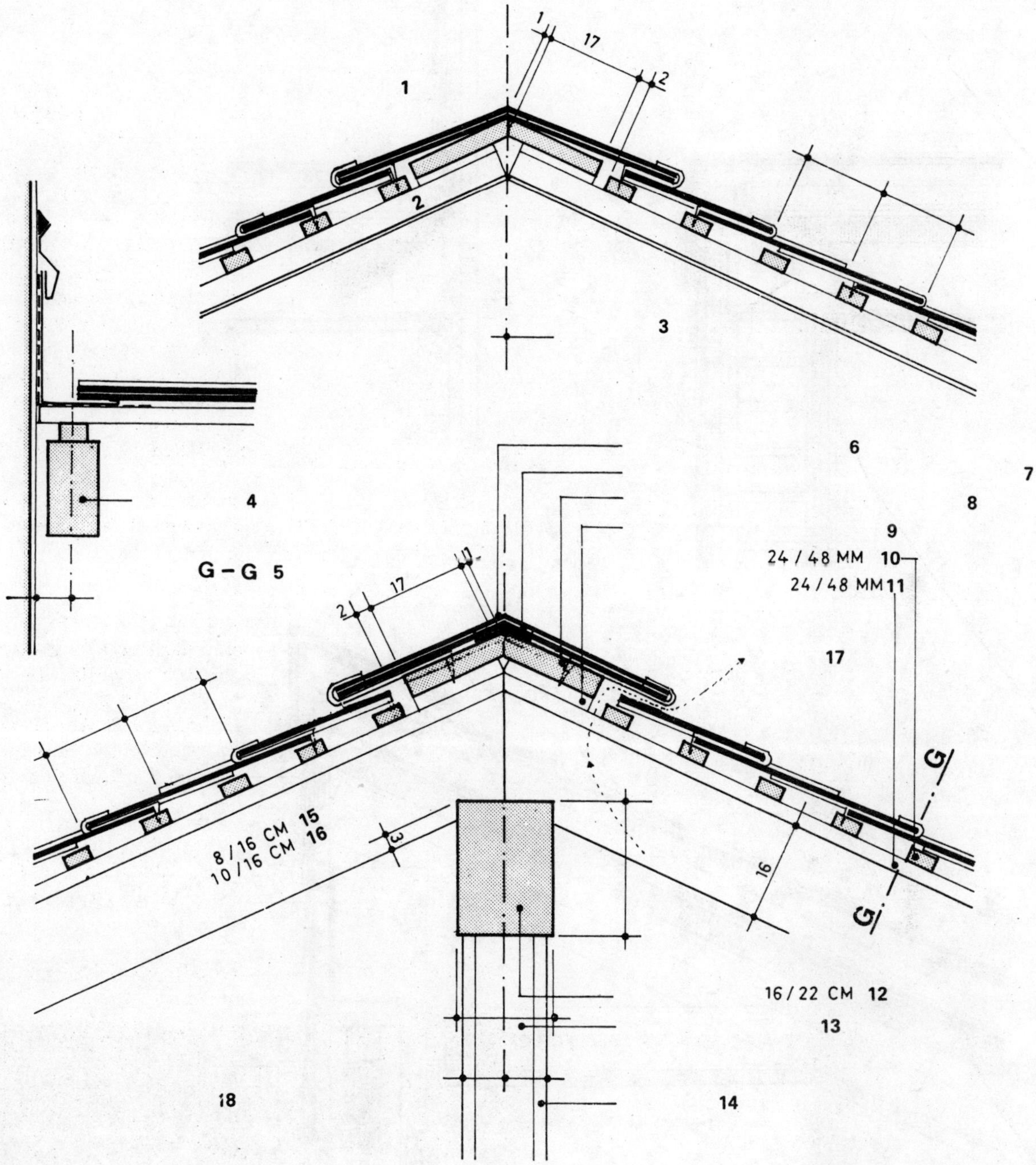

1 Ridge construction (not ventilated)
2 Double layer of battens
3 Ridge line
4 Rafter
5 Section G – G
6 Ridge angle tile
7 Distance piece 25/5/5 cm for each pair of slates
8 Bearing board 24/170/180 mm
9 Fixing piece 24-30/150 mm
10 24/48 mm roof battens
11 24/48 mm counter battens
12 16/22 cm ridge plate
13 Strut (brace)
14 Post
15 Normal rafters 8/16 cm
16 Principal rafters 10/16 cm
17 Ventilation
18 Ridge construction (ventilated)

Slating, double lap, alternative details

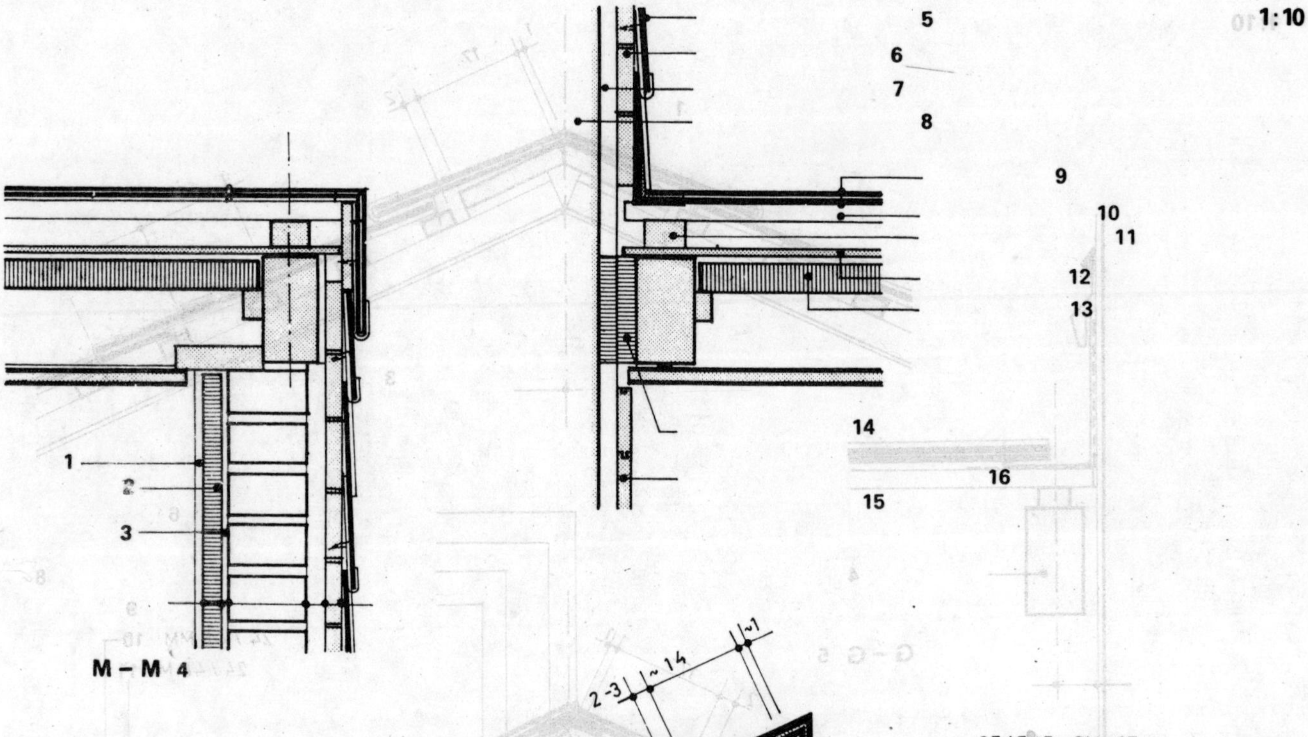

1 Plaster
2 Insulation
3 1 cm levelling plaster
4 Verge detail section M – M
5 Vertical slating
6 Vertical boarding
7 Grounds
8 Brickwork
9 Roof covering
10 Roof battens
11 Counter battens
12 Sub-roof boarding
13 Insulation boarding
14 Insulation strip
15 Horizontal wall boarding
16 Detail at junction with wall
17 Distance piece 25/5/5 cm
18 Bearing board 12/60-70 cm
19 Ridge angle tile
20 Vertical boarding, butt jointed; open expansion joint 1-2 cm
21 Purlin 16/22 cm
22 Fixing hook
23 Filling piece
24 Calculation of height: (Height of window × 4%) + 8 cm = height of opening, min. 16 cm
25 Window or door reveal
26 Ventilation
27 4/10 cm brace
28 Ridge detail of shed roof with ventilation

Corrugated asbestos cement (Eternit) roofing, edge and abutment details

1:10

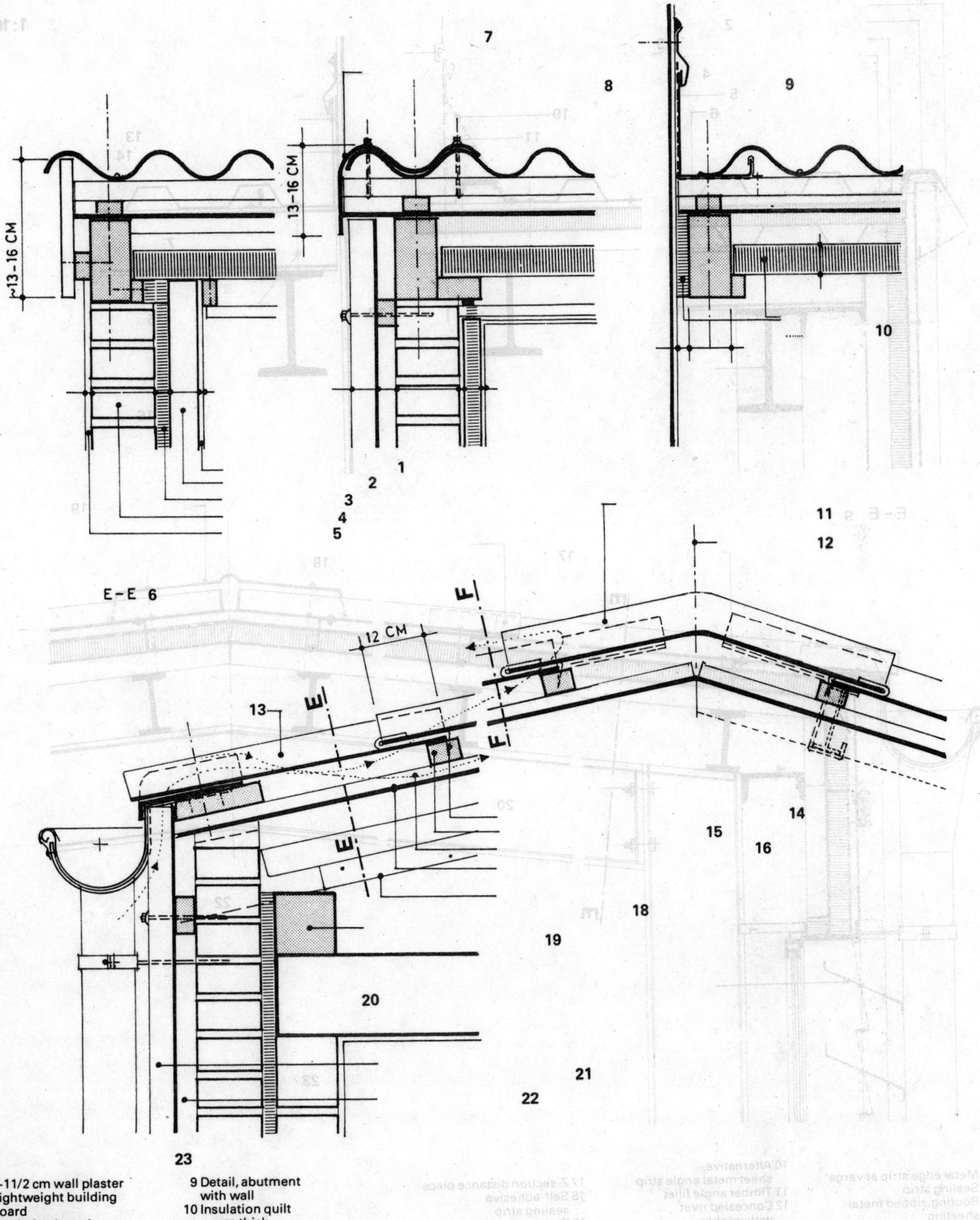

1 1-11/2 cm wall plaster
2 Lightweight building board
3 Insulation board
4 External wall
5 External rendering
6 Verge detail, section E – E
7 Verge detail, variation F – F
8 Verge closing piece (corrugated angle section at gable end)
9 Detail, abutment with wall
10 Insulation quilt ... cm thick
11 Ridge piece with ventilation space in corrugation
12 Ridge centre line
13 Corrugated sheet sizes: width 92 cm, lenght 62 cm
14 Fixing hook
15 Roof battens 40/60 mm

Insulated and non-insulated sheet metal ribbed roofing

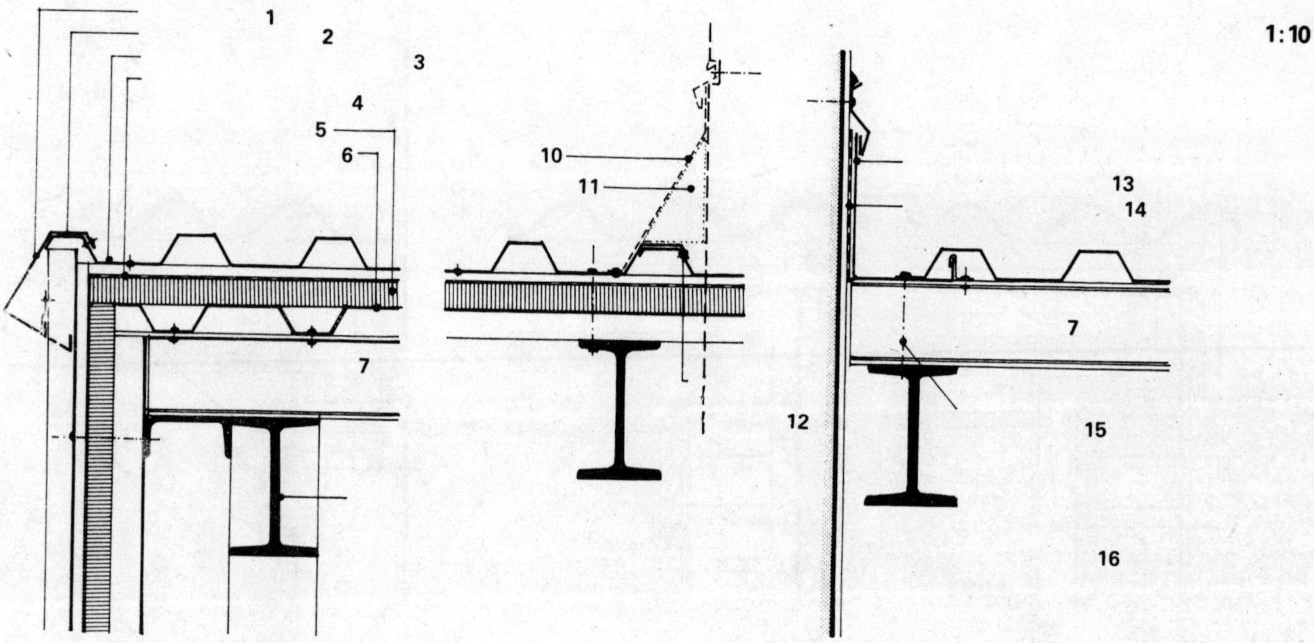

E-E 9

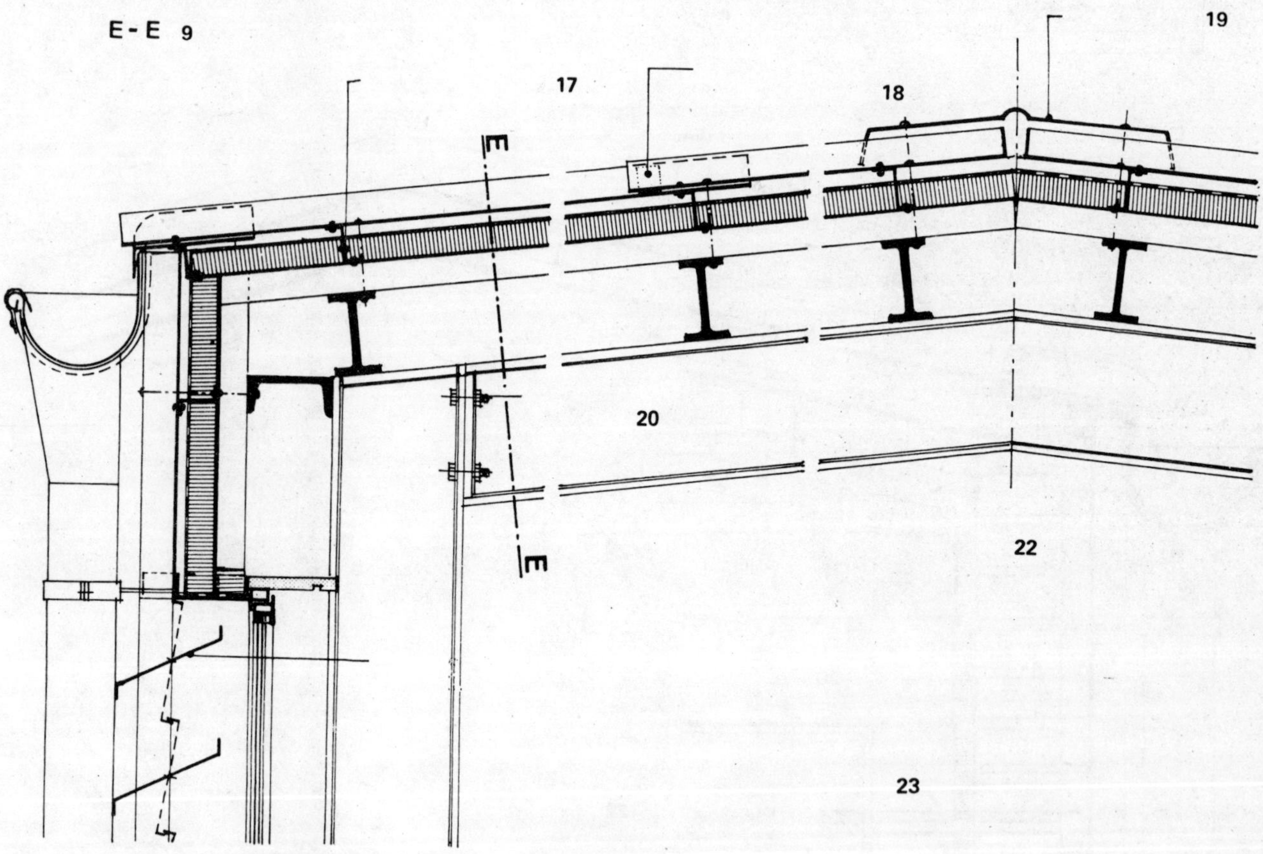

1 Metal edge strip at verge
2 Sealing strip
3 Roofing, ribbed metal sheeting
4 Impervious layer, felt or self-adhesive film
5 Thermal insulation
6 Ribbed metal sheeting, load bearing
7 Steel purlin
8 Steel I-beam bearer
9 Verge detail, section E–E
10 Alternative, sheet metal angle strip
11 Timber angle fillet
12 Concealed rivet with washer
13 Metal angle strip with junction at gutter
14 Protective layer of building paper
15 Tapping screw
16 Section through sheet metal ribbed roof (non-insulated)
17 Z-section distance piece
18 Self-adhesive sealing strip
19 Ridge covering piece
20 Screwed or rivetted
21 Solar shading louvres, adjustable
22 Ridge detail
23 Section through double layer ventilated roof with sheet metal ribbed covering

Bonded Flat Roof Covering

In this design, the slope must run toward the drains in order to avoid water pockets. All connecting and edge sheeting should be mounted on the roofing paper base.
Vapor barrier: cardboard with glass fiber insert, connections overlap 10 cm, heat bonded. Thermal insulation: one-layer blunt joint or rabbeted design (possibly two-layer laid in offset), covered with the necessary hot tar coatings. The thickness of insulation depends on the desired results. The dew point should be carefully noted!

As a rule, the sealing cover is 3 or 4 layers, of which one layer is inorganic. Cardboard layers should be heat-bonded to one another. The first layer should cover approximately one-third of the sheeting cover, the second layer the second third and the last layer the remainder.

The final protective covering consists of 2 cm of sand substrate and 2 - 3 cm gravel top layer.

Slabs or cement coating to support traffic. To support large continuous roof coverings, roof-covering ventilation is recommended.

Non-ventilated and ventilated roofs, constructional alternatives

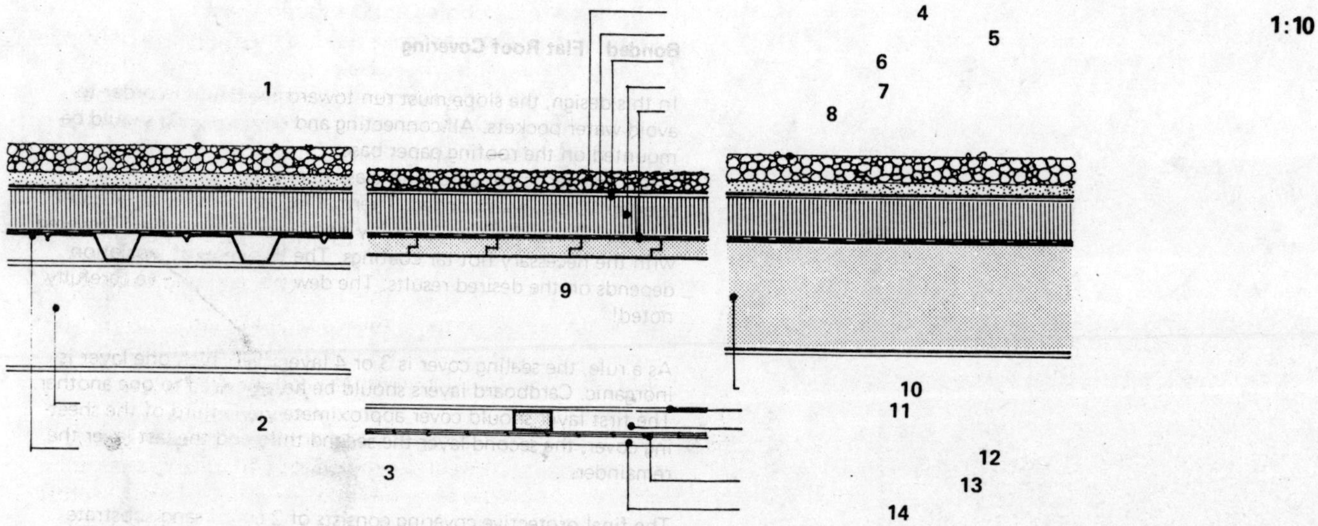

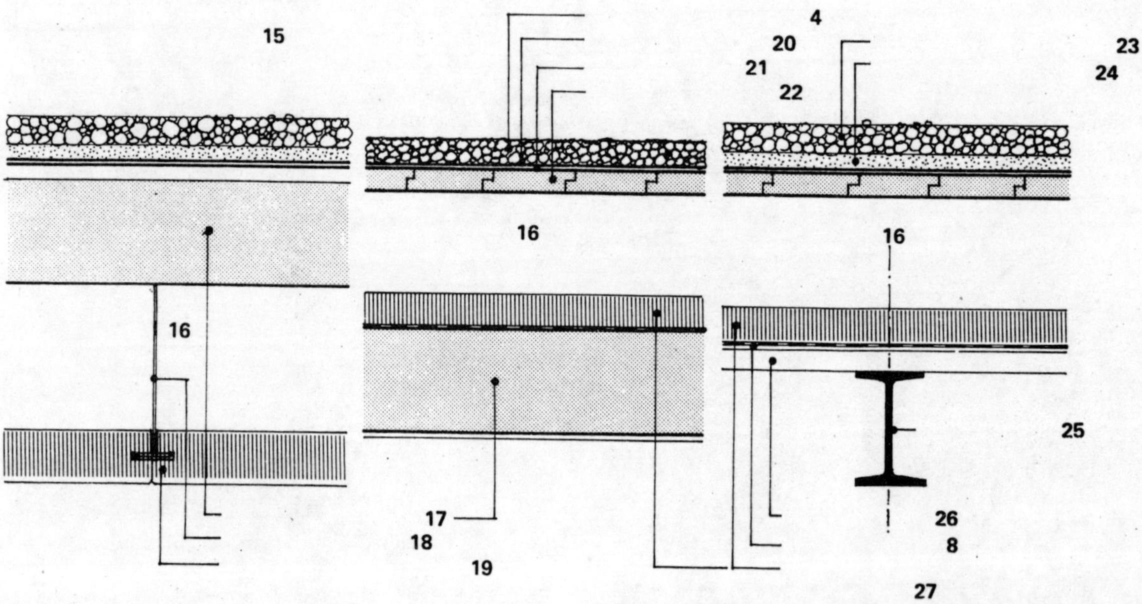

1 Non-ventilated roofs, constructional alternatives
2 Steel beam (side elevation)
3 Ribbed steel sheeting, profile according to span
4 Layer of bitumenized gravel
5 PVC sheeting (impervious layer)
6 Separating layer
7 Insulation board ... cm
8 Vapourproof membrane
9 Timber joists
10 Solid slab construction
11 Firrings
12 Studding 24/48 mm at 30 cm centres
13 Insulating reed mat
14 Ceiling plaster
15 Ventilated roof, constructional alternatives
16 Ventilated void
17 Reinforced concrete slab
18 Hangers
19 Insulation boarding ... cm thick
20 Impervious layer
21 Separating layer
22 Timber boarding
23 3 - 4 cm gravel
24 2 cm sand
25 Steel beam
26 Ribbed steel sheeting
27 Insulation quilt or board ... cm thick

Pavings to balconies and terraced areas

Great attention has to be paid to the question of impact sound insulation where balconies and terraced areas occur above habitable rooms. Insulation should be provided by two different materials. As a rule the quilting thickness represents about 1/3 of the total thickness of the insulation layer, which in turn is dependent on the amount of thermal insulation as well as on the impact sound insulation required. Experience shows that a floating floor layer forms an unstable sub-floor construction. For this reason an additional layer of concrete is unavoidable to facilitate an even distribution of loads. The use of concrete fulfills a double purpose, however, since it also acts as a protective layer.

Larger areas of protective concrete require wire mesh reinforcement. In areas exceeding 40 m² expansion joints should be allowed for. The choice of a separating layer system with bedding supports for paving helps to prevent the formation of puddles on the surface. Since, however, no system is perfect, it should be remembered that, if one jumps about on paving slabs with a hollow space beneath, a drum-like noise will be caused. In buildings with multiple-occupancy it is therefore recommended to lay concrete slab pavings in sand, an old and well tried method. The filtering layer should be of coarse, washed sand. Quartz sand is not suitable. Around drainage points a filter bed of gravel (3-8 cm diameter) is necessary, to prevent sand running into the drainage system.

The following examples show a number of constructional forms, – (with and without sheet metal connection pieces), – as well as moisture – impervious layers in PVC or felt sheeting.

Balcony and terrace paving details

1:20/5

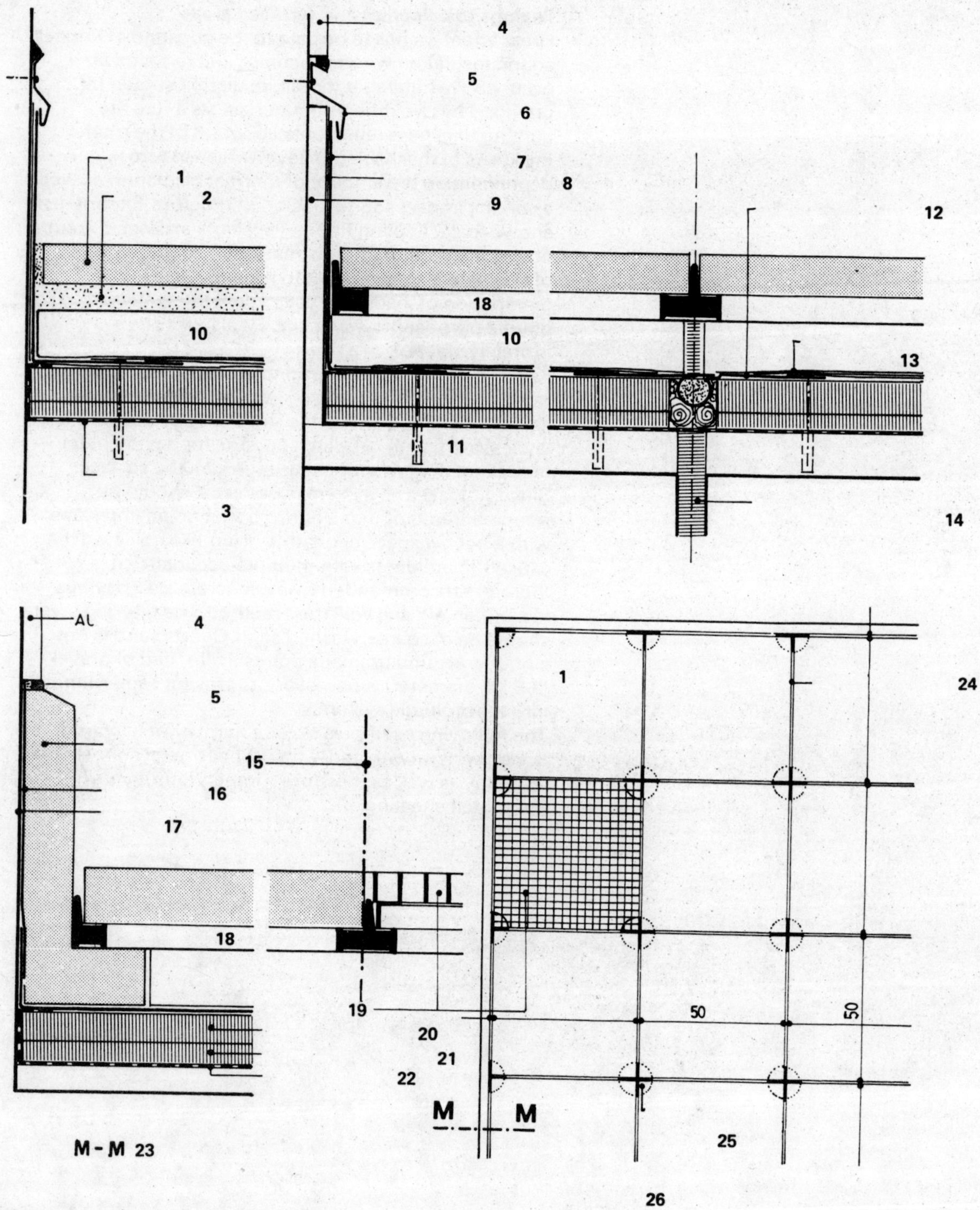

1 Concrete paving slab
2 Layer of sand
3 Reinforced concrete slab trowelled smooth, flat or to falls
4 External rendering
5 Elastic joint sealant
6 Cover strip
7 Sheet metal angle strip
8 Protective building paper
9 Screed
10 Protective concrete layer
11 Concret to falls
12 Metal expansion strip
13 Moisture-impervious layer (3-4 layers)
14 Expansion joint with insulation sheeting
15 Precast concrete upstand unit
16 PVC sheeting
17 Wall or upstand
18 Void
19 Fine mesh lattice grating
20 Insulation board 3 cm
21 Insulation quilt 1-2 cm
22 Vapourproof membrane
23 Detail M – M
24 Open joint 4-5 mm wide
25 Bedding supports for paving of vinyl plastic or rubber
26 Plan of slab paving

1:5

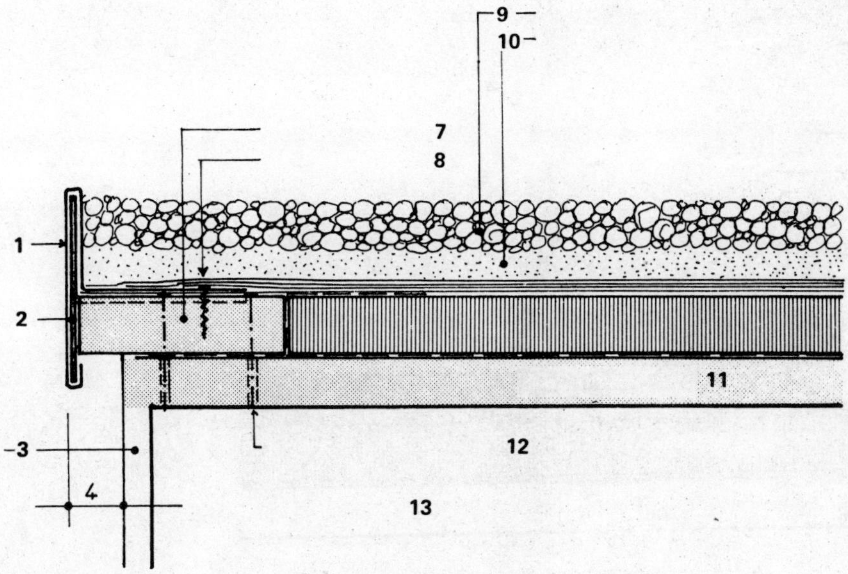

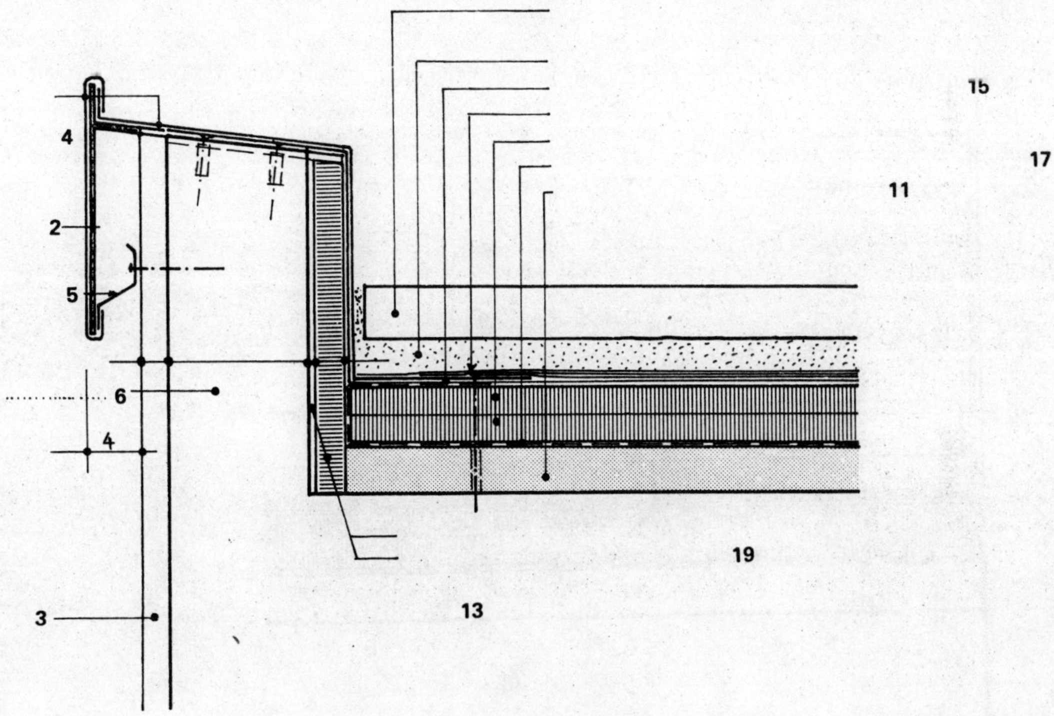

1 border sheeting of . . . 3 x folded
2 insertion bracket
3 facade plaster
4 edge sheeting of . . . two-part, 5 x folded
5 bracket strips
6 roof border of . . .
7 stop plank
8 wood screws
9 round gravel inlay 3-4 cm
10 sand bed base ~2 cm
11 cambered concrete 2 - . . . cm thick
12 patent stone screws
13 concrete floor
14 . . . panels . . . / . . . / . . . cm, type . . . (or cement coating)
15 cardboard base as sheeting protection
16 sealing layer . . . layers
17 insulation 1st layer of . . . cm, 2nd layer of . . . cm
18 vapor barrier
19 coating layer, . . . insulation panel . . . cm thick

Angle sheet metal/brickwork connections

1:5

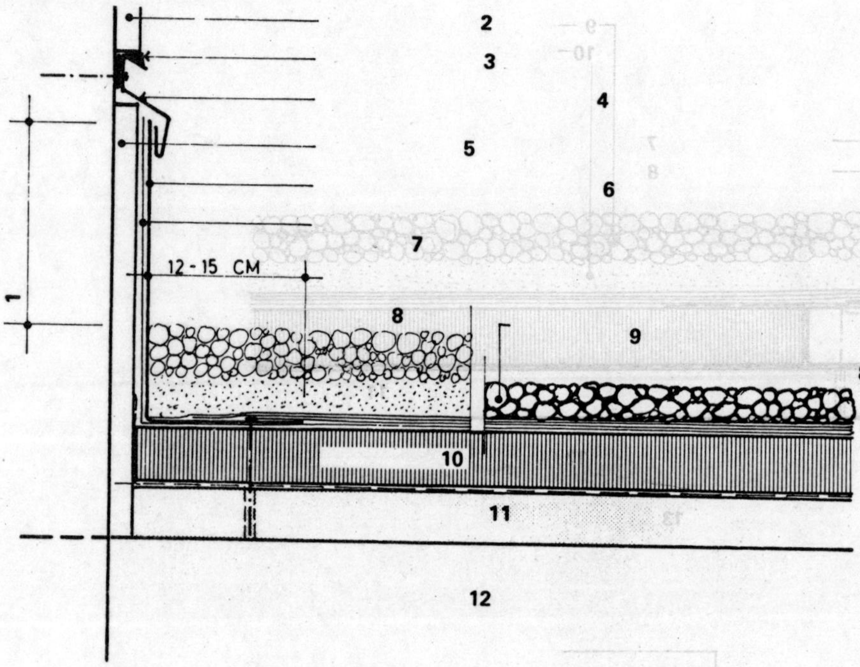

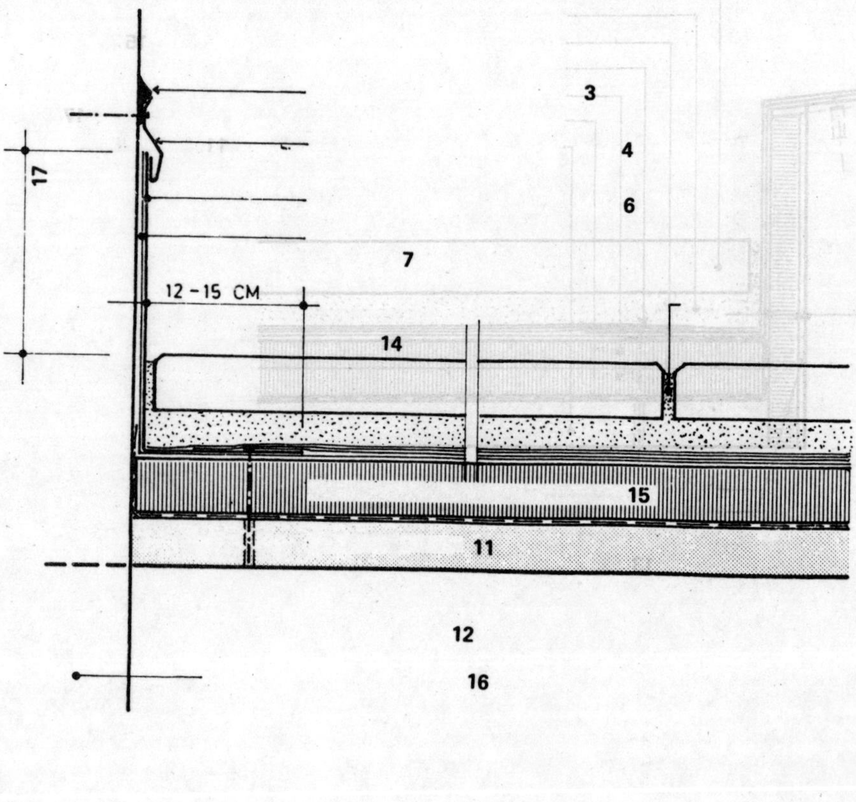

1 min. 15 cm
2 facade plaster
3 elastic joint cement
4 cover strips . . . cm, development
5 base plaster
6 angle sheet . . . cm, development
7 roofing layer as sheeting protection
8 not for walking traffic
9 gravel layer 2-3 cm thick asphalted
10 insulation
11 cambered concrete
12 concrete floor
13 joint sand floated in
14 roof, for walking traffic
15 insulation according to need
16 floor poss. restrained
17 min. 15 cm depending on situation

1:5

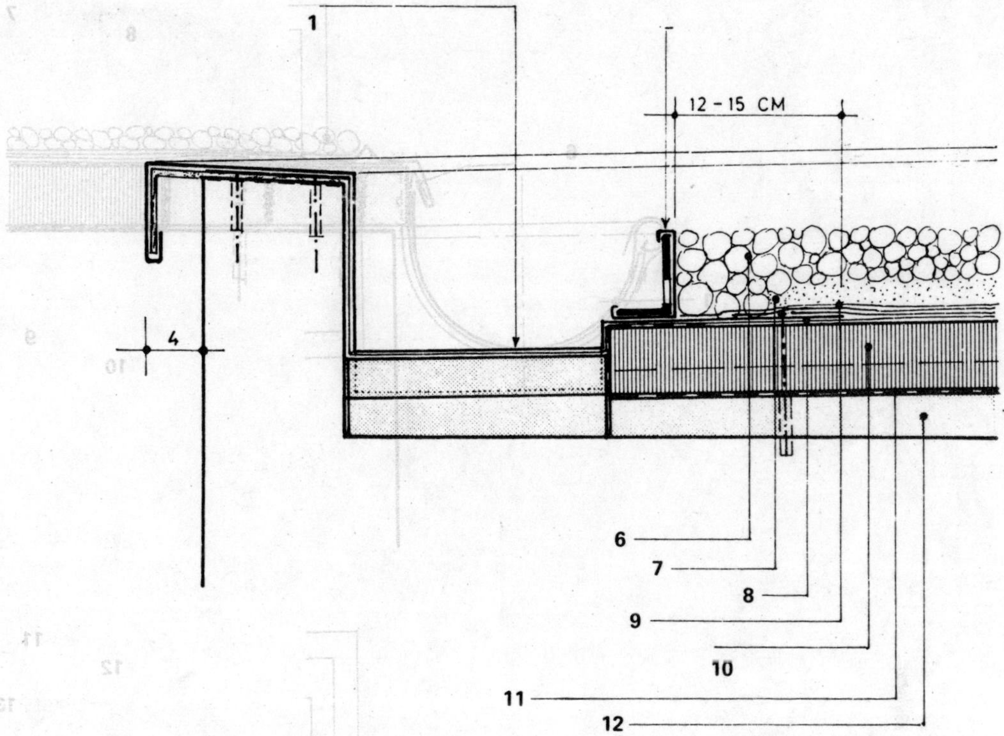

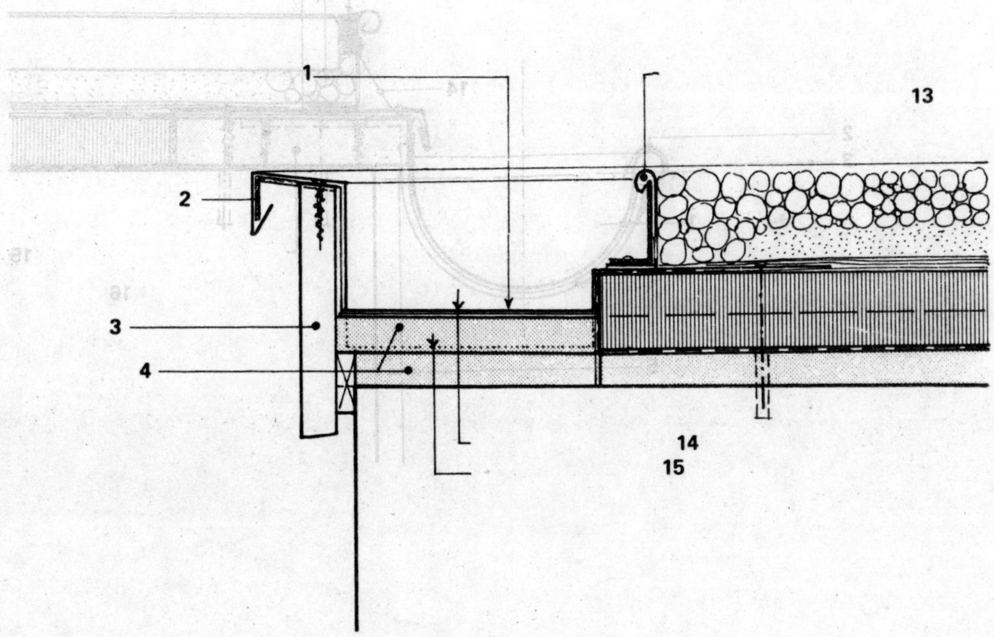

1 inside box trough, development . . . cm, 6 x folded
2 mounting bracket
3 finishing panel
4 cambered plank
5 perforated, squared standing border . . . / . . . / . . . mm and clamping flange
6 round gravel insert 4 cm
7 sand bed base 2 cm
8 cardboard base as sheeting protection
9 sealing cover . . .-layer
10 insulation panels, 1st layer of .. . cm, 2nd layer of . . . cm
11 vapor barrier
12 cambered concrete 2-8 cm
13 perforated, standing sheet metal with bead design and bracing square
14 highest point
15 lowest point

Projecting gutters

1:5

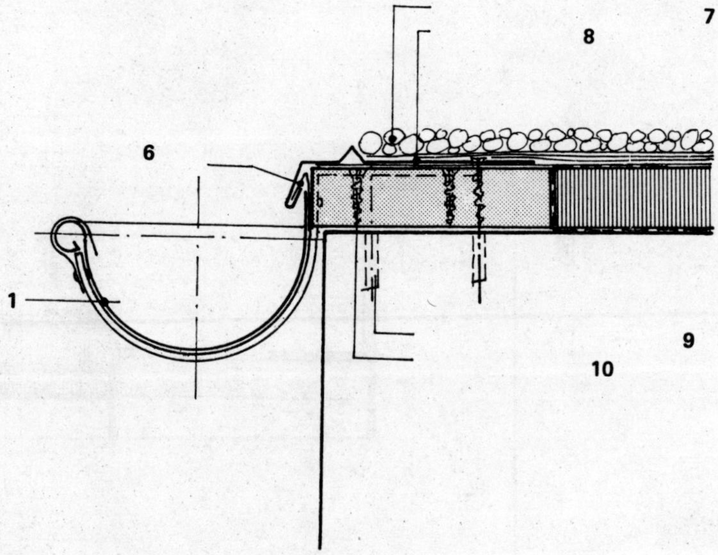

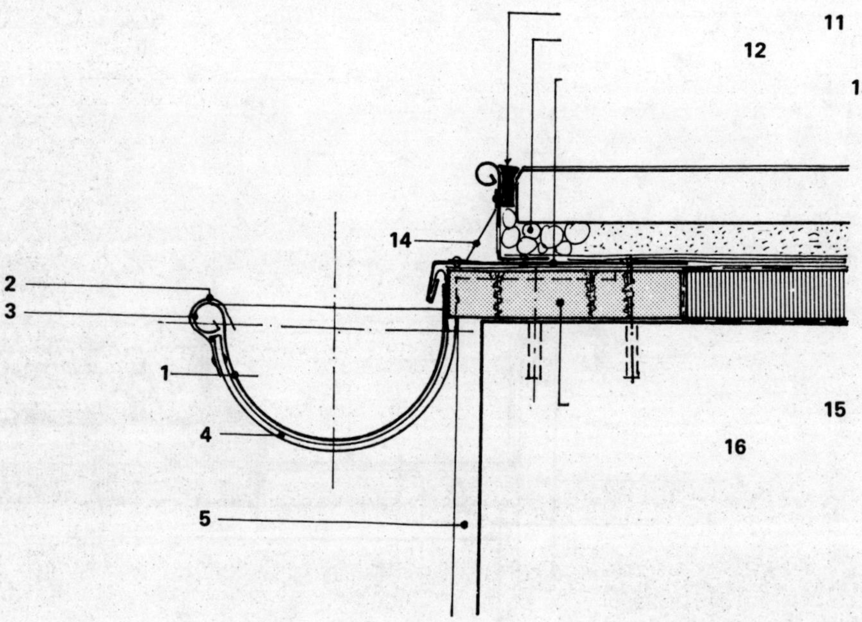

1 semi-circular front gutter, development . . . cm
2 bead flange
3 gutter collar
4 gutter hook cross section . . . / . . . mm
5 facade plaster
6 clamping flange
7 gravel cover 2-3 cm thick
8 inlet sheet metal
9 patent stone screw
10 wood screw
11 elastic joint cement
12 round gravel insert
13 inlet sheet, development . . . cm
14 standing sheet strut
15 cave board . . . / . . . mm
16 concrete floor

1:5

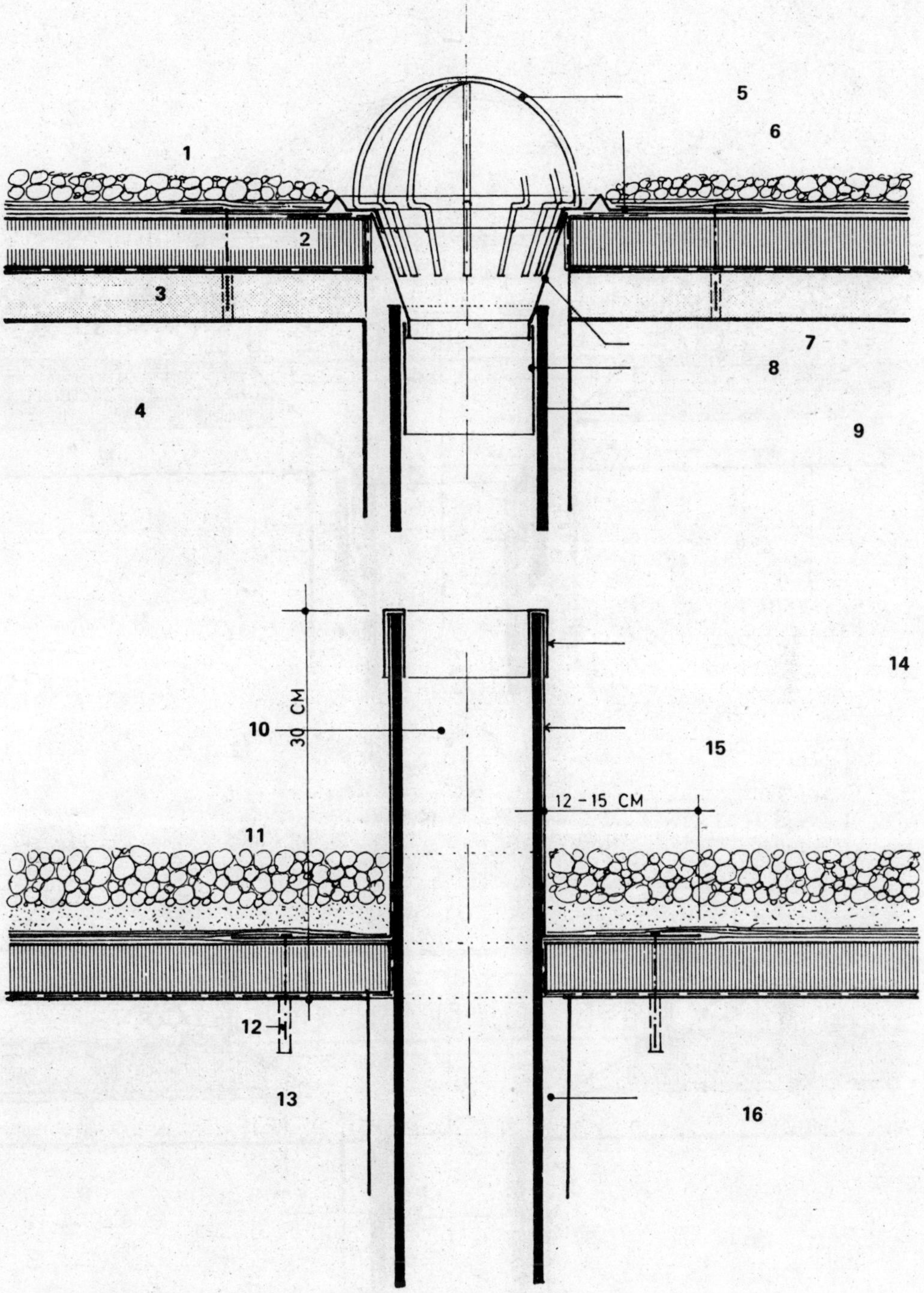

1 not for walking traffic
2 insulation according to needs
3 cambered concrete
4 concrete floor
5 leafed basket
6 base plates
7 inlet funnel
8 inlet ring
9 roof water drainage line of . ., Ø internal clearance . . . cm
10 vapor tube Ø . . . cm
11 roof, not for walking
12 patent stone screw
13 concrete floor, abraded
14 vent tube hood (edge bracket)
15 vent tube bracket angle sheet
16 silk braid fullering all around

1:5

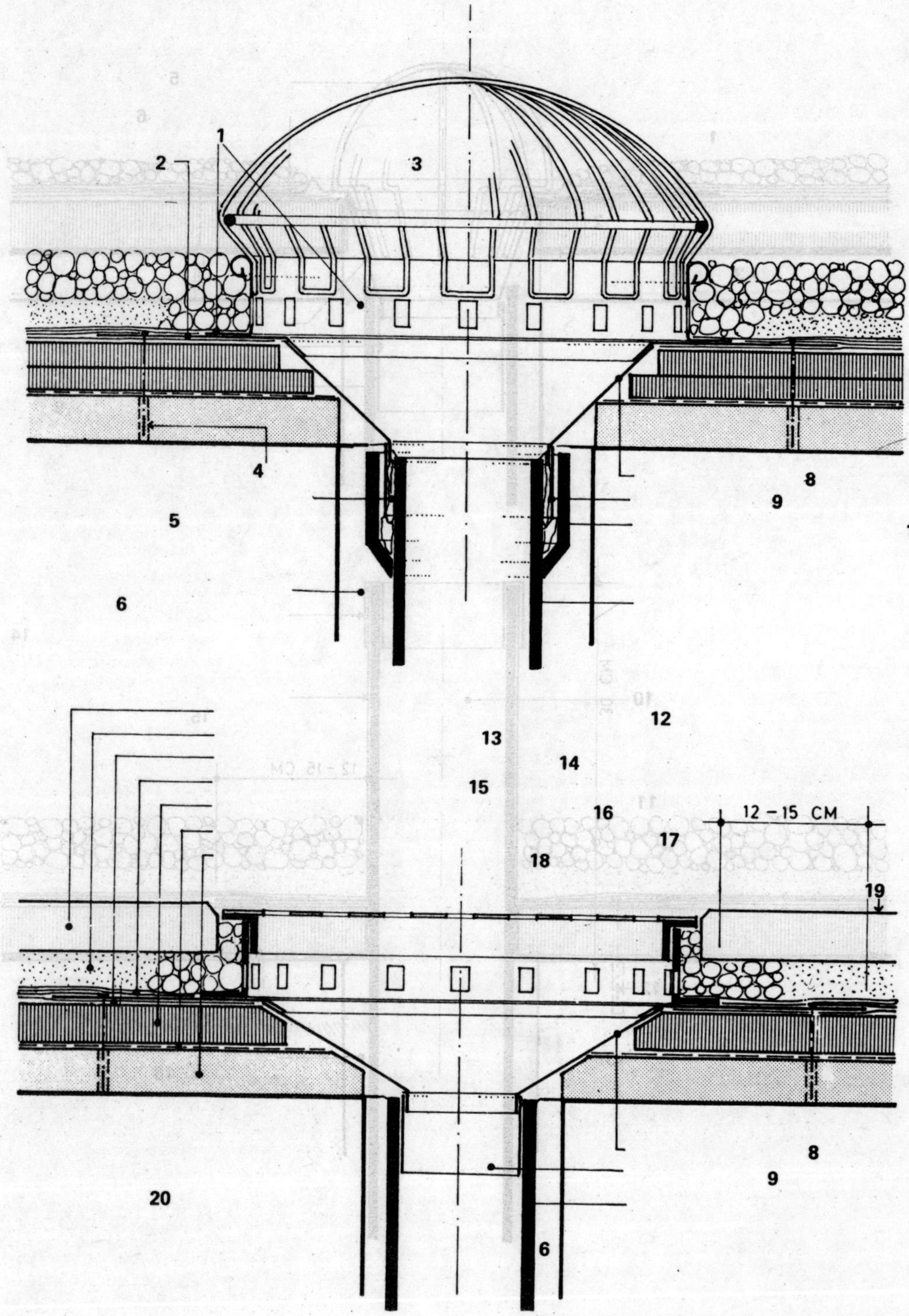

1 standing border, perforated
2 base plate
3 leafed basket
4 patent stone screw
5 tarred cord insert with lead wool calking
6 silk braid fullering all around
7 roof, not for walking traffic
8 inlet funnel
9 inlet ring
10 . . . sleeve welded on
11 roof water drainage line of . . , Ø internal clearance . . . cm
12 cement slabs . . . / . . . / . . . cm, type . . .
13 sand bed 2-3 cm thick
14 cardboard base as sheeting protection
15 sealing cover, . . .-layer
16 thermal insulation, . . .-layer
17 vapor barrier, cardboard with glass fiber insert
18 cambered concrete 2- . . . cm thick
19 roof, for walking traffic
20 concrete floor

1:5

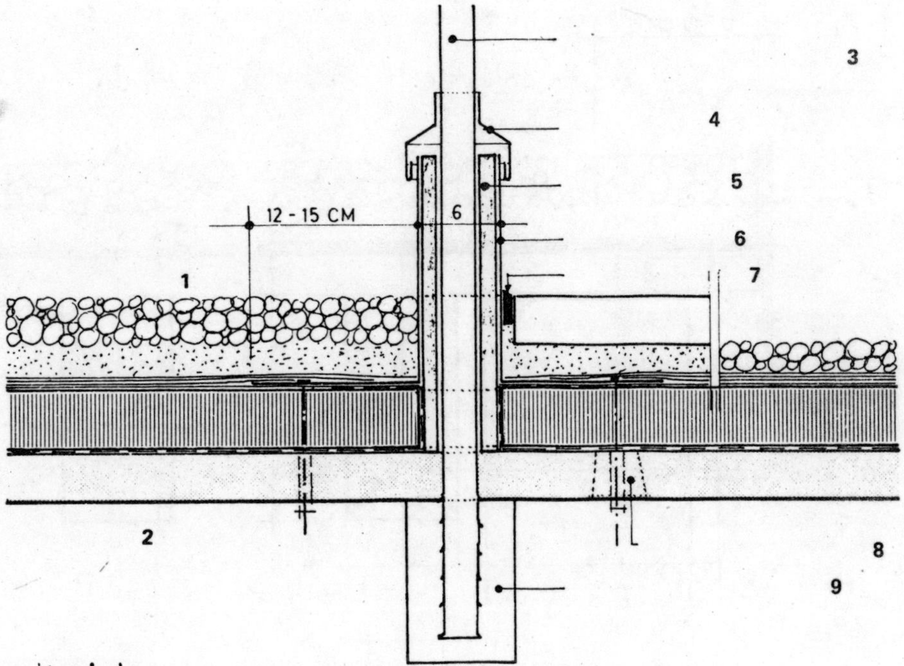

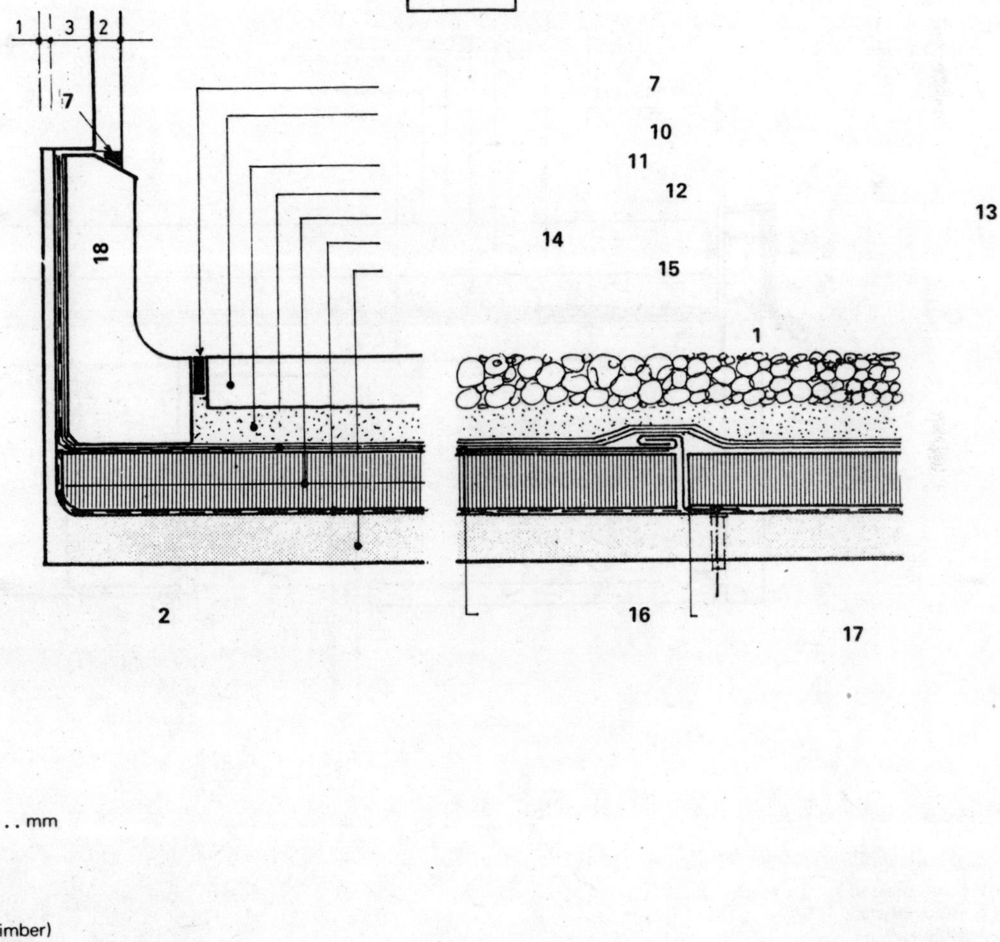

1 not for walking traffic
2 concrete floor
3 railing posts or supports . . . / . . . mm
4 sheet metal hood
5 insulating compound
6 angled housing
7 elastic joint cement
8 (earlier conical dowel-driving timber)
9 recess . . . / . . . / . . . cm
10 . . . panels . . . / . . . / . . . cm, type . . . (or cement coating)
11 sand bed 2 cm
12 sealing cover, . . layer
13 insulation 1st layer of . . ., . . . cm, 2nd layer of . . ., . . . cm
14 vapor barrier
15 cambered concrete 2-7 cm
16 . . . sheeting
17 Z-stud (bracket flange)
18 cement base

Border mountings, wooden substructure

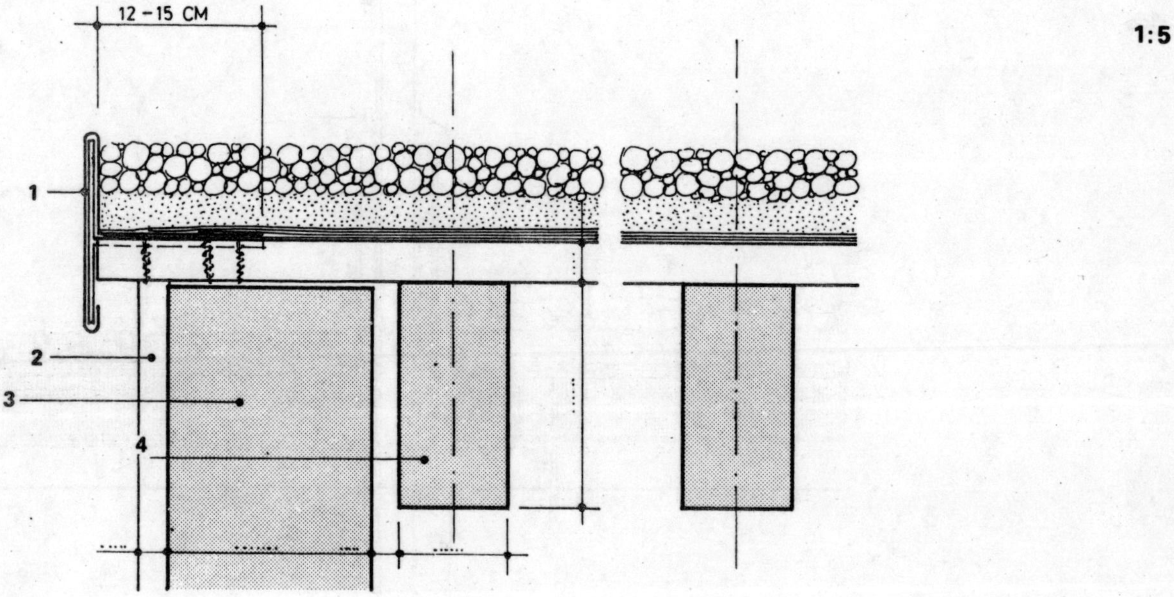

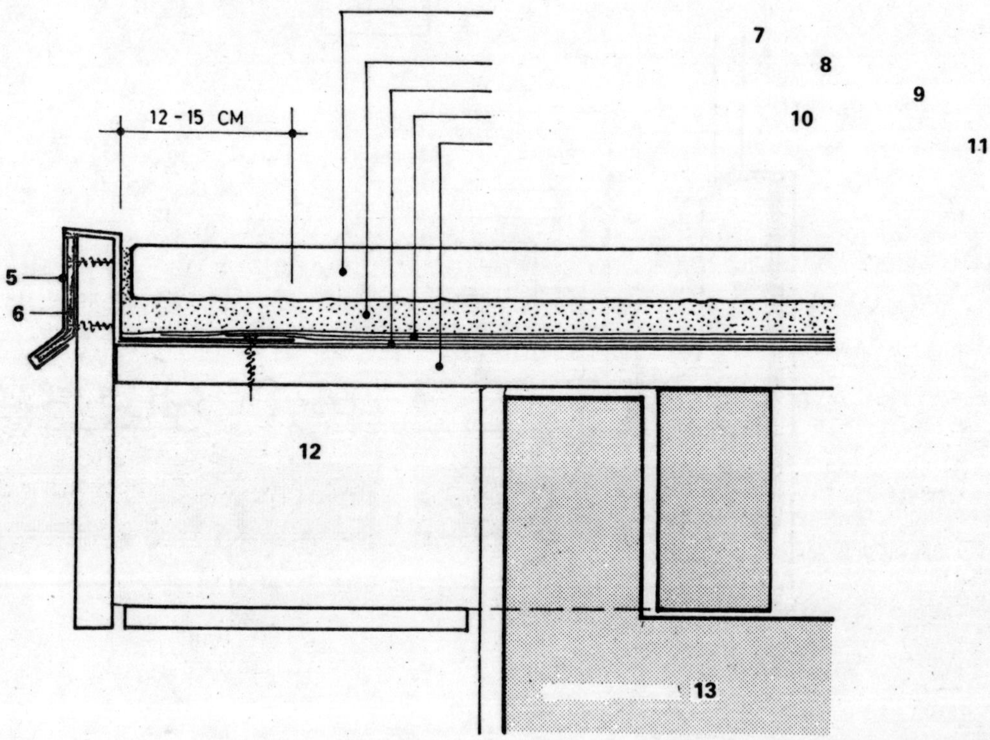

1 board sheet in . . . 3 x folded
2 facade plaster
3 gable wall
4 system of rafters or binders and joists
5 board sheet of . . . 5 x folded
6 mounting bracket
7 . . . panels . . . / . . . / . . . cm, type . . . or cement coating
8 sand base 2 cm thick
9 cardboard base as sheeting protection
10 sealing cover, . . .-layer
11 formwork of . . . wood 24 cm thick
12 dragon beam
13 gable wall

1:5

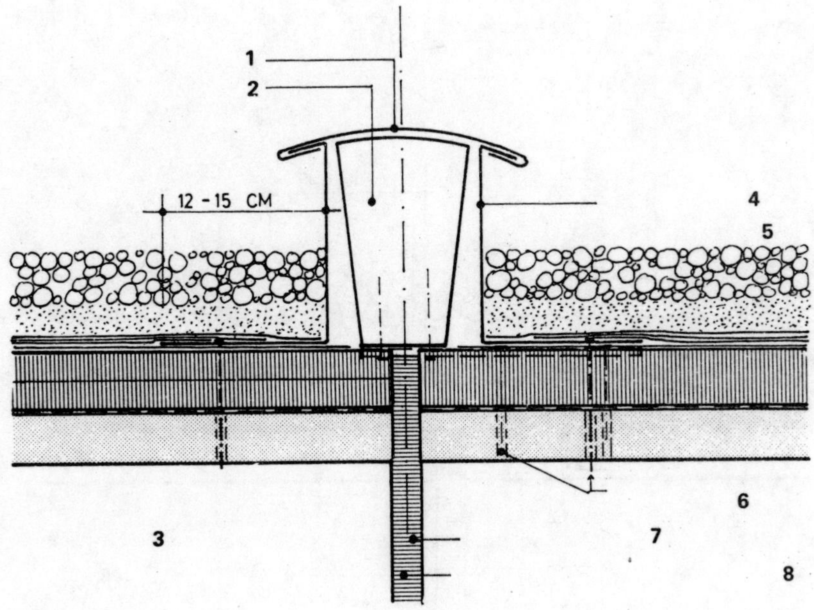

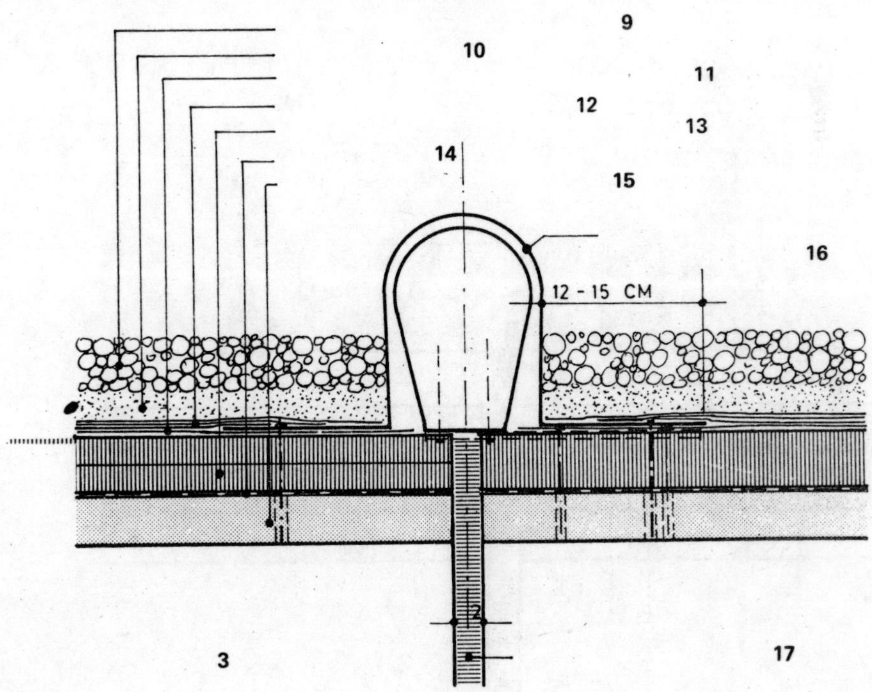

1 strip cover hood
2 conical wood strip . . . / . . . or . . . cm
3 concrete floor
4 angled sheet
5 roof, not for walking
6 patent stone screws
7 expansion joint
8 . . . insulation panel insert
9 round gravel layer 4 cm thick
10 sand bed 2 cm
11 cardboard base as sheeting protection
12 sealing cover, . .-layer
13 thermal insulation, . .-layer
14 vapor barrier
15 cambered concrete 2- . . . cm thick
16 dilatation sheet of . . . with upper bellows
17 . . . insulation panel

Expansion

1:5

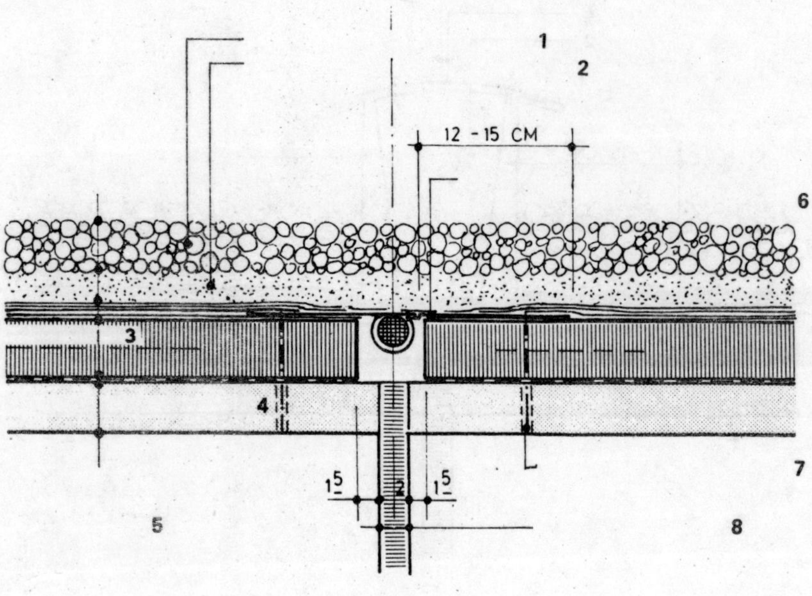

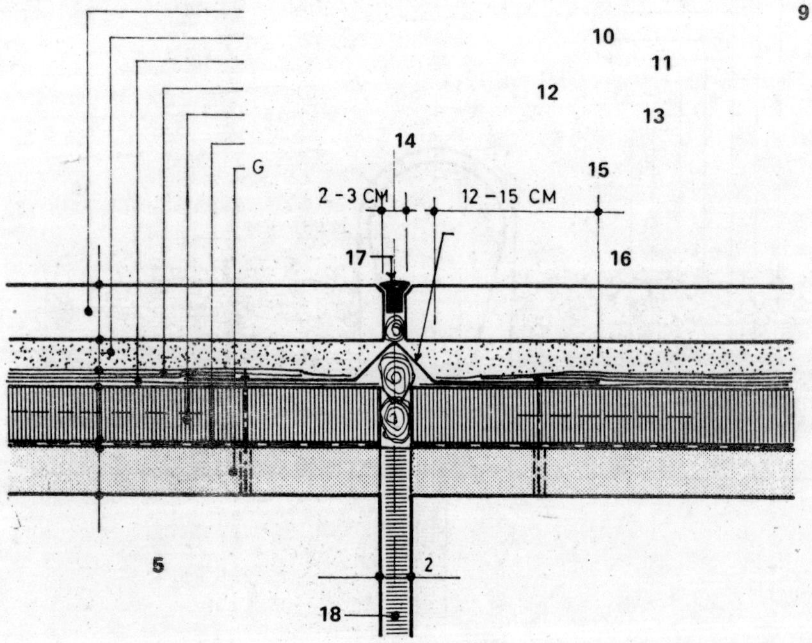

1 round gravel layer 3-4 cm
2 sand bed base ∿ 2 cm
3 insulation
4 cambered concrete 2-5 cm
5 concrete floor
6 dilatation sheet of . . ., spring sealed with . . . putty
7 patent stone screws
8 expansion joint
9 . . . panels . . . / . . . / . . . cm, type . . .
10 sand base 2-3 cm thick
11 cardboard base as sheeting protection
12 sealing layer, . . .-layer
13 thermal insulation, . . .-layer
14 vapor barrier
15 cambered concrete 2- . . . cm thick
16 dilatation sheet of . . . triangular spring
17 putty joint
18 . . . insulation panel insert

Chimneys for heating installations

The internal flue dimensions of a chimney depend on the boiler capacity, temperature of gases emitted, height, size and position of the chimney, and the dimensions of the bricks or blocks used. A square shape is the most usual form for brick chimney stacks as they are still common today. Rectangular forms are the second most common. The ideal shape would be a circular cross-section. Where high gas emission temperatures occur, which cause strong upward forces, the choice of the correct cross-sectional area is more important that the flue shape.

A basic rule is that chimneys should never be bonded to other brickwork, of whatever kind, if the development of cracks and the escape of exhaust gases is to be prevented. If chimney stacks are situated outside the external walls of a building, an insulation layer is necessary between flue and the outer skin of the stack to prevent condensation. Where a number of flues are built in parallel, they should always be constructed separately, so that expansion and contraction can occur freely from bottom to top. If the boiler is also periodically in use in summer to supply hot water or for other purposes, insulation to sides facing rooms is essential, if there is no parallel cold air flue for the full height of the stack, (approx. 1/2 × cross-sectional area of flue).

The chimney base, approx. 100 cm high, should be built solid in sand lime bricks, or cement paste blocks, (or, alternatively, the centre filled with a lean mix mass concrete, PC 100-150 N, [PC = Portland cement; N = normal]). The base can, of course, be wholly of concrete (PC 200-250 N).

In the case of central heating chimneys the first 6 m in height should be constructed exclusively of fireclay blocks, jointed with fireclay mortar. The remaining parts of the chimney should be of solid brickwork or special insulation blocks. All openings should be left during the course of erection, since subsequent breaking out loosens the jointing and reduces stability.

Brickwork chimneys should be constructed with staggered joints from course to course in a strong bond. They must be absolutely air-tight and cleanly pointed on the inside.

Additional costs can be avoided by having the responsible authorities conduct a pressure test on the chimney before the final cladding is in place. The base area to the core of chimneys built in special insulation blocks should slope inwards. Jointing should be as for brickwork stacks.

Changes of direction in the vertical course of the flue should be avoided, if possible. The flue connection should be so fixed that the outlet lies vertically above it. If, however, a change in direction is unavoidable, great care must be taken in its execution, and a brick support under the diagonal length will be necessary. The chimney cap should rest on the casing and be at least 3 cm from the core to allow for expansion. Coverings to flues can be omitted; they represent an unnecessary cost.

The height of chimneys, measured vertically from the outer surface of the roof covering should be at least:

100 cm for flat roofs,

100 cm for pitched roofs up to 30°. In problematic situations the chimney should be taken up 50 cm above the ridge.

50 cm where the chimney emerges through the ridge.

1:20

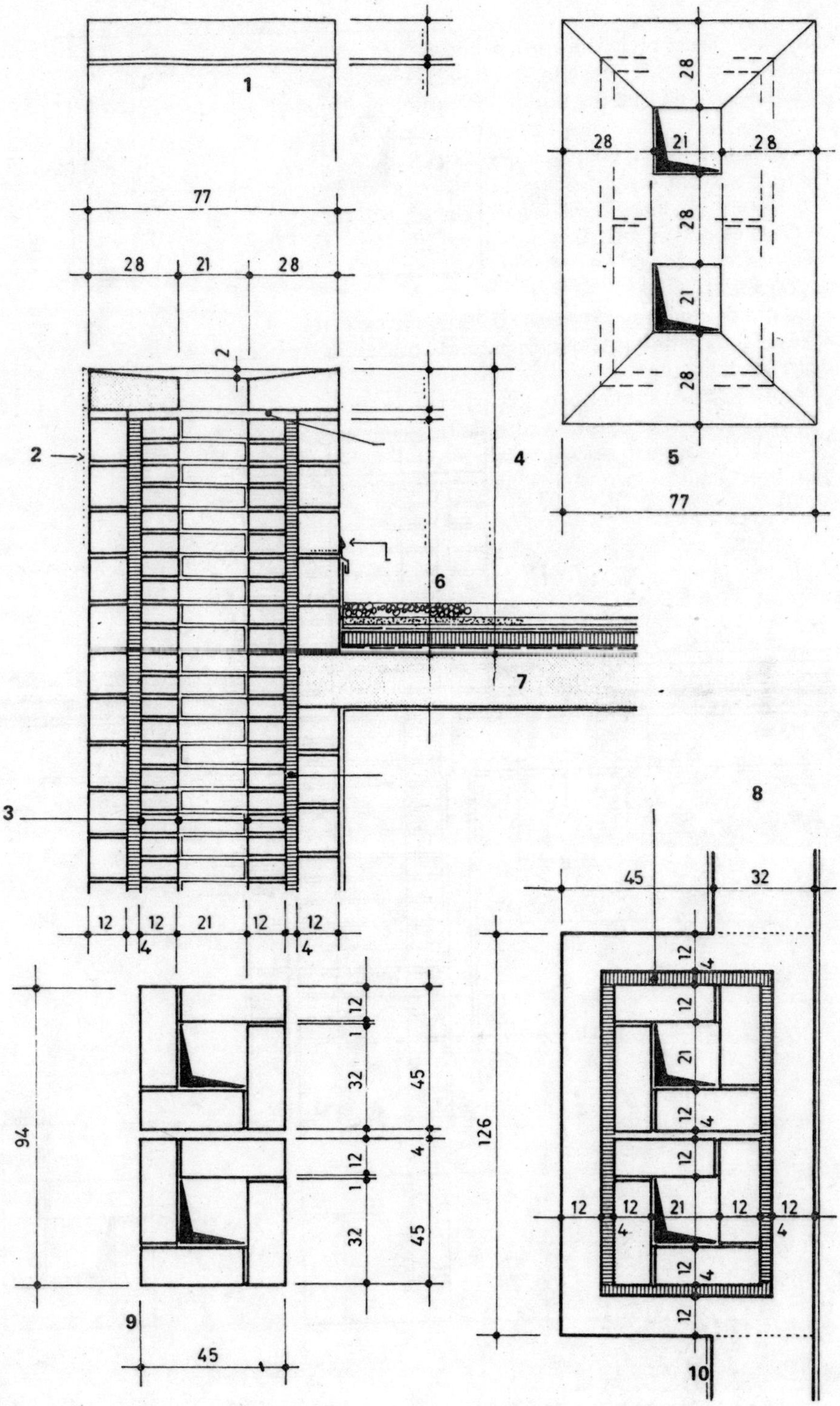

1 side view
2 variants: chimney cover sleeve size with plaster design
3 chimney flue freely dilatable throughout entire height
4 expansion joint height ∿ 3 cm
5 top view
6 elastic joint cement
7 concrete ceiling
8 mineral wool panel throughout as heat protection
9 layer 1, 3, 5, 7, etc.
10 layer 2, 4, 6, 8. etc.

Chimney head, one-flue

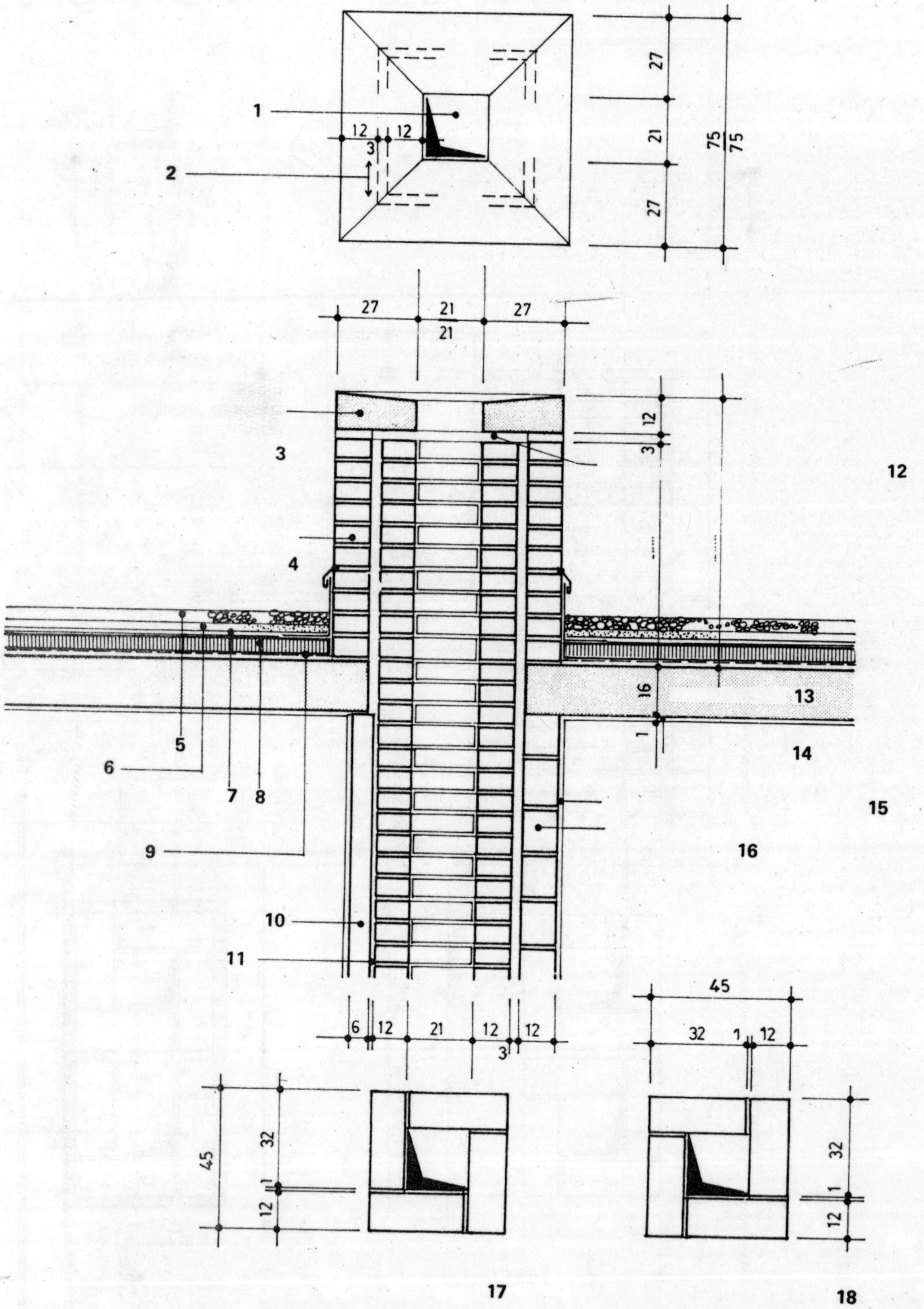

1 chimney flue, outlet opening cross section 21/21 cm
2 bearing surface
3 chimney cover plate reinforced concrete PC . . . B, exposed surface smooth
4 chimney casing in exposed . . . brick . . . cm thick
5 round gravel layer
6 sand bed
7 sealing cover, . . . -layer
8 . . . insulation, . . . -layer
9 vapor barrier
10 chimney casing with . . . lightweight panels
11 hollow space min. 1 cm
12 expansion joint, height ~ 3 cm
13 concrete floor
14 ceiling plaster
15 wall plaster 0.5-1.5 cm
16 supporting wall of . . . bricks
17 layer 1, 3, 5, 7, etc.
18 layer 2, 4, 6, 8, etc.

1:20

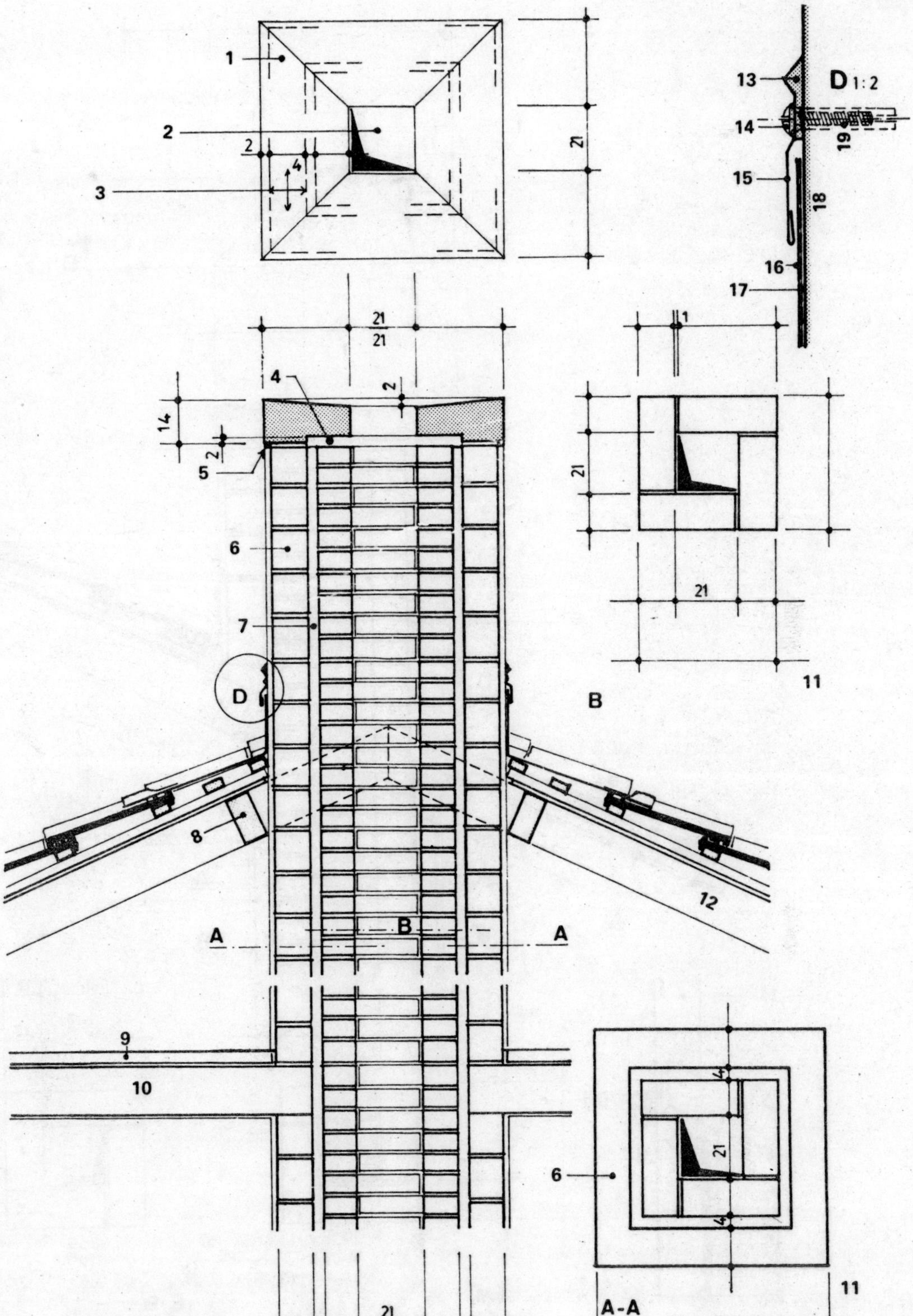

1 Chimney coping-slab, reinforced, exposed surfaces smooth
2 Flue opening
3 Bearing surface
4 Expansion joint, depth
5 Mastic joint-filling
6 Stack cladding in . . ., cm thick, from roof level
7 Insulation only with high flue-gas-temperatures (high-performance boiler)
8 Trimmer
9 Loft flooring
10 Reinforced concrete ceiling
11 Course (masonry)
12 Rafter
13 Plastic joint-infill
14 Round-headed screw
15 Masking (protective) strip
16 Angle plate
17 Underlining
18 Wall line
19 Patent screw (masonry)

170

Chimney Coping, mid-roof outlet

1:20

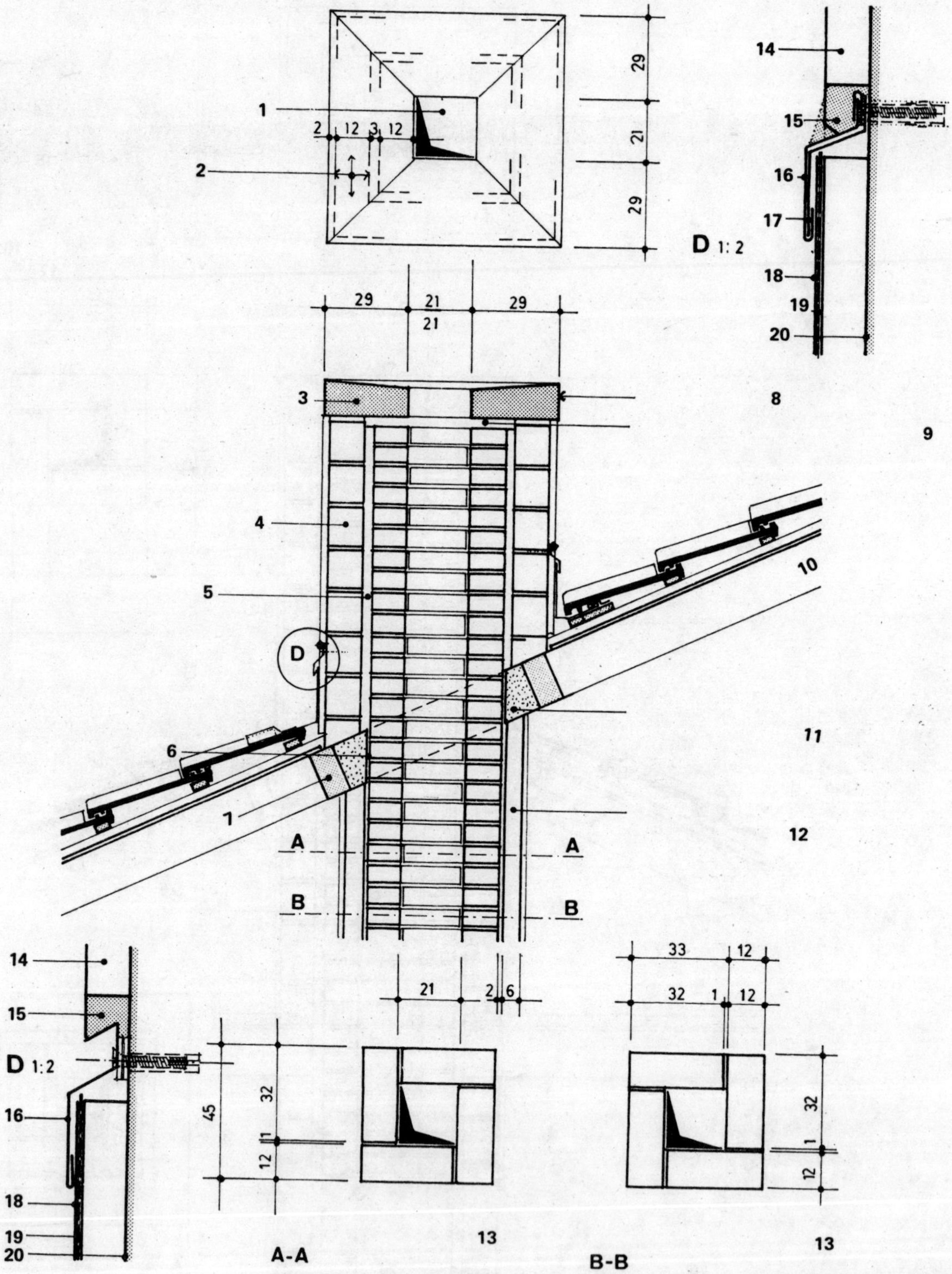

1 Flue (smoke-duct) cross-section, opening
2 Bearing surface
3 Chimney coping-slab, reinforced, exposed surfaces smooth
4 Stack cladding with, ...cm thick
5 Insulation only with high flue-gas temperatures (high-performance boiler)
6 Asbestos insulating joint
7 Trimmer
8 Smooth
9 Expansion joint, depth ~ 3 cm
10 Rafter
11 Flashing
12 Stack cladding with ...
13 Course (masonry)
14 Plaster rendering
15 Plastic joint-filling
16 Weatherstrip
17 Bracket
18 Angle plate
19 Underlining
20 Wall line (face)

20

Stairs

Flight width is based on the purpose of the stairs and local building codes. The same applies for staircase clearance width. As a rule, the headroom between flights should be at least 2 m if regulations do not stipulate otherwise. The free height is measured vertically from the front edge of the tread to the underside of the flight lying over it.

The tread ratio is derived from the dimension development – 63 or 64 cm – distribution over two rises + one run. The tread dimensions should be adapted to the requirements so that climbing is as effortless as possible.

Run depth is indicated primarily in full cm; the rise corresponds to the ratio of the dependent dimension to the difference in elevation between bottom and top step or, as the case may be, the difference in elevation of floors.

With regard to flight length, it is recommended that an intermediate landing – at least three to four times the tread depth – be installed after 8 to 12 steps.

The walking line is situated approx. 40-45 cm inside the handrail; thus, even with winding stairs, the desired dimension is achieved at the right place. It is advisable to number the steps consecutively from bottom to top. The railing (or handrail) should be at least 85 cm vertically over the front edge of the step, unless regulations stipulate the contrary.

These suggestions offer a good basis for finding the right solution.

It is essential to check the agreement between planned and carcass dimensions before beginning work on the stair coverings.

Staircase forms

1:100

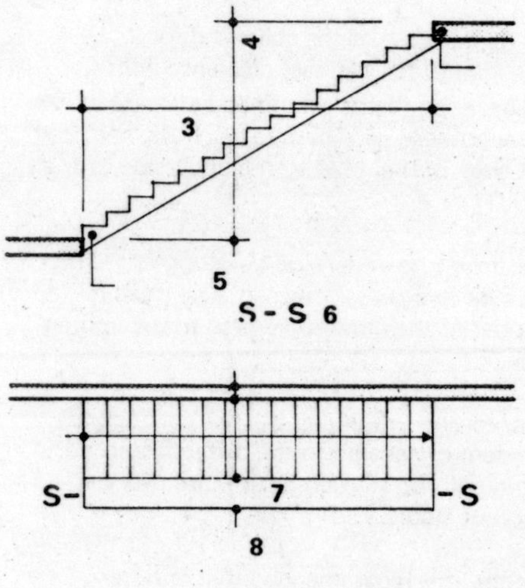

9

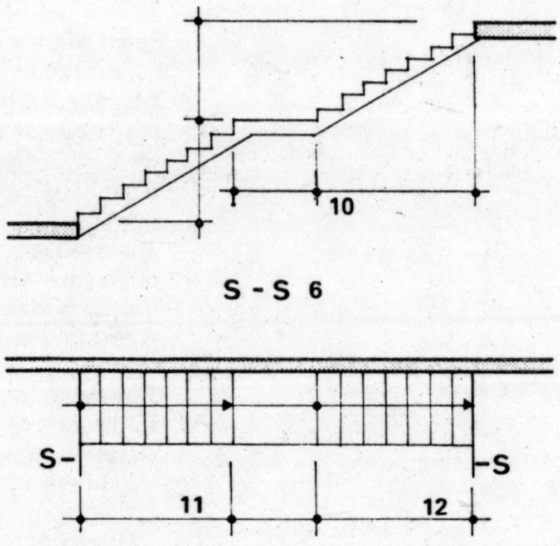

13

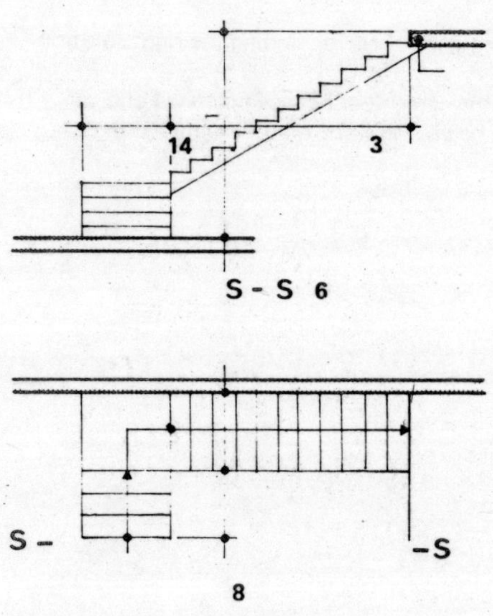

15

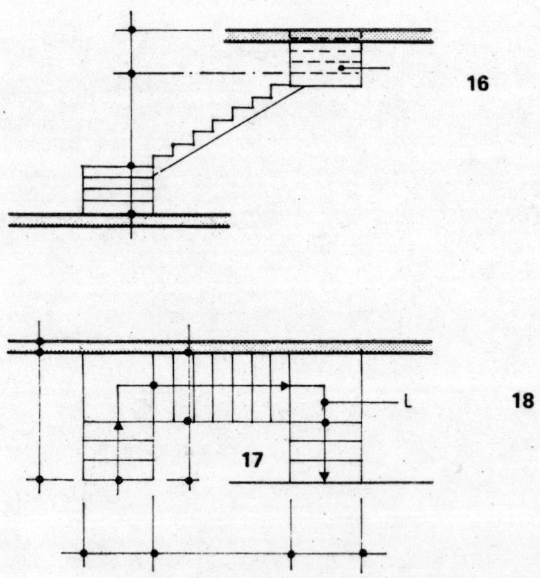

19

1 Floor landing
2 Top step
3 Length of flight
4 Rise of flight
5 Starting step (springing)
6 Section/elevation S–S
7 Stair well
8 Plan of staircase
9 Single flight straight staircase
10 Intermediate landing
11 1st flight
12 2nd flight
13 Straight staircase with intermediate landing
14 Flight width
15 Dog-leg staircase with quarter-space landing
16 Staircase soffit
17 Staircase light-well
18 Walking line
19 Three flight staircase with 2 quarter-space landings

1:100

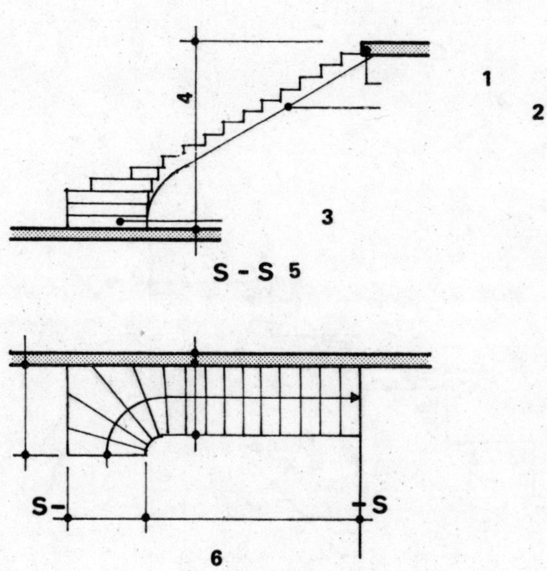

7

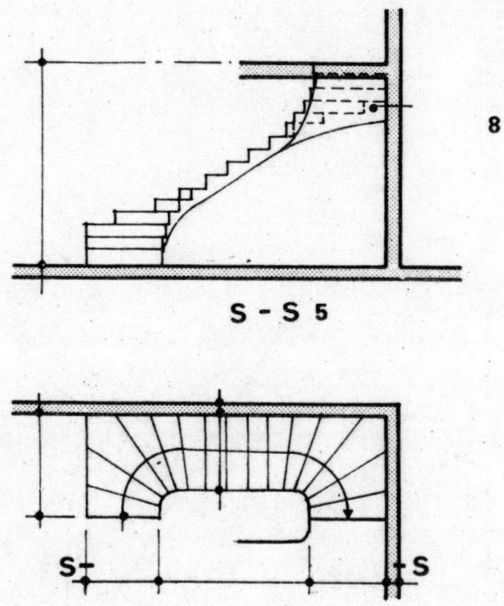

9

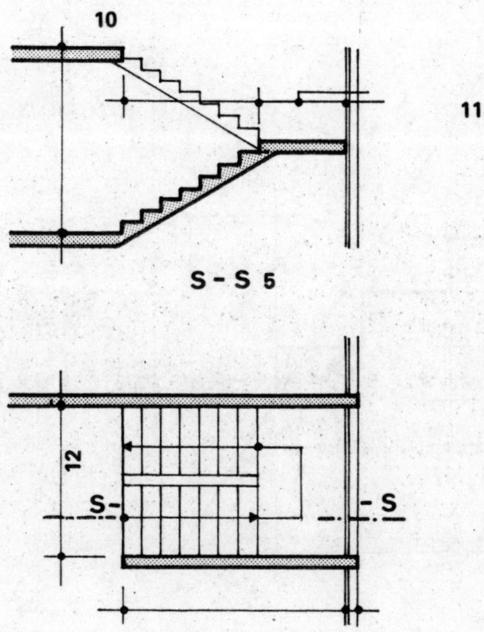

13

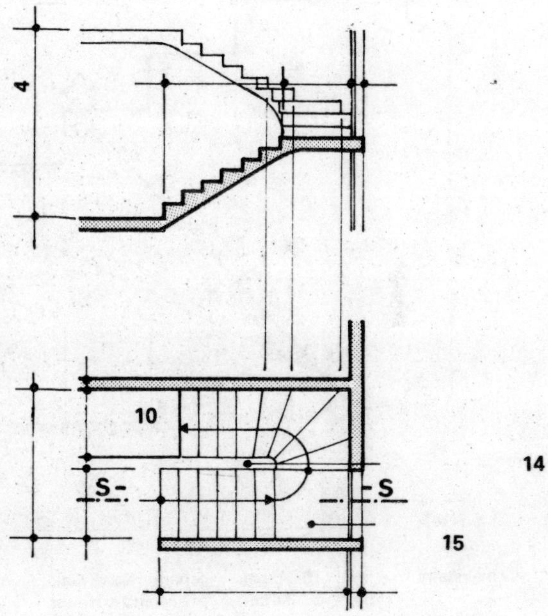

16

1 Top step
2 Flight of stairs
3 Starting step/springing
4 Rise of flight
5 Section/elevation S–S
6 Plan of staircase
7 Single flight staircase with winders at bottom
8 Staircase soffit
9 Single flight staircase with winders at top and bottom
10 Floor landing
11 Intermediate landing
12 Width of staircase
13 Two flight staircase with half-space landing
14 Stair well
15 Quarter space landing
16 Two flight staircase with quarter-space landing and winders

Tread ratio and plotting

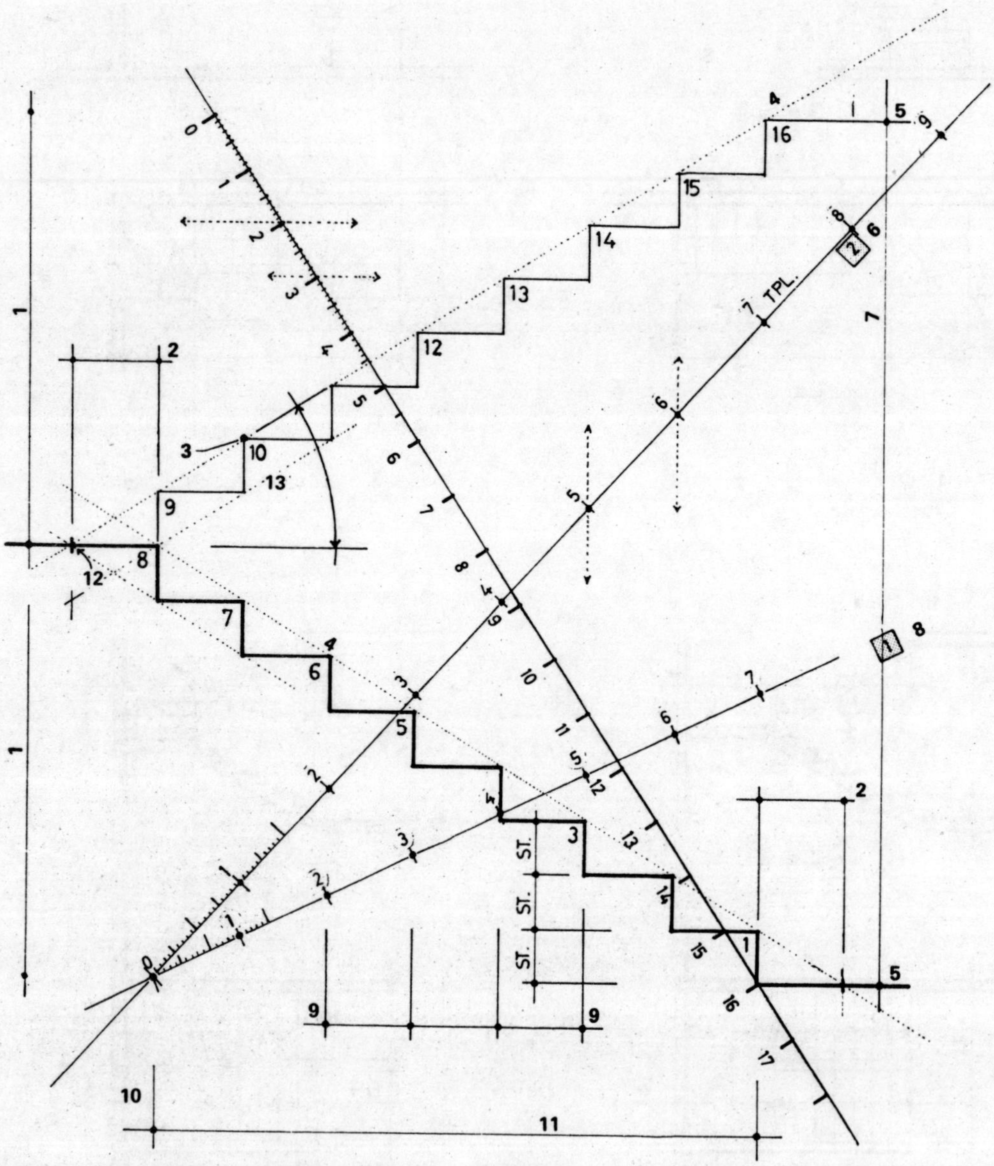

normal stairs	rise run	16-18 cm 27-31 cm	general residential, office and business buildings, etc.	rise angle approx. 35°
steep stairs	rise run	19-21.5 cm 20-25 cm	weekend and single-family houses as well as cellar and topping stairs	rise angle approx. 41°
open stairs	rise run	12-15 cm 33-39 cm	garden stairs	rise angle approx. 20°

1 stair flight height
2 tread width
3 intersection point = tread edge
4 rise line
5 landing
6 variant 2
7 storey height
8 division point line (TPL) variant 1
9 run
10 rise
11 stair flight length
12 starting point
13 rise angle (STW)

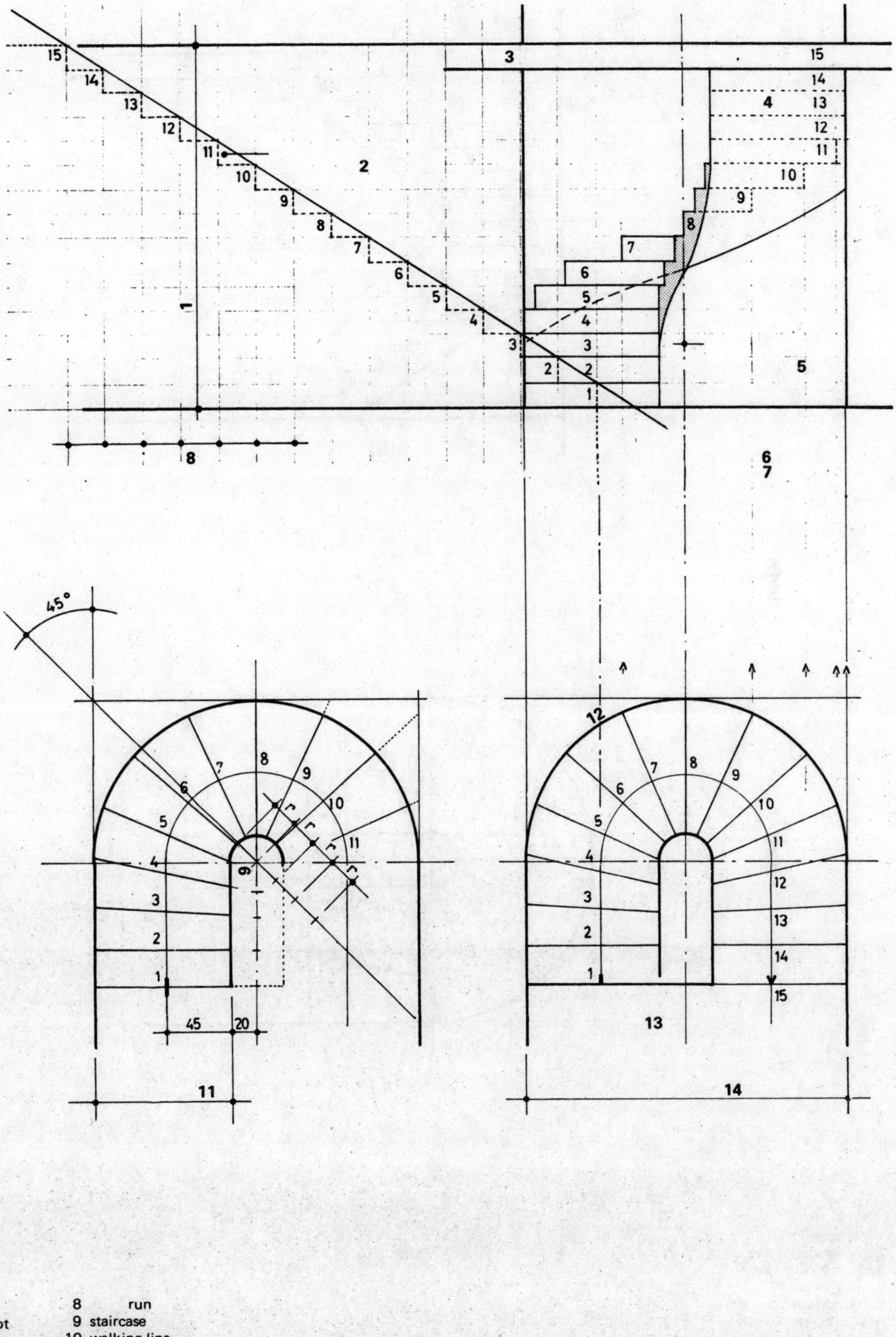

1 flight height
2 walking line plot
3 ceiling
4 underside of flight
5 axis of staircase
6 view toward rounding
7 wreath
8 run
9 staircase
10 walking line
11 flight width
12 rounding
13 plan
14 staircase width

Plots, single-flights with 1/2 turn

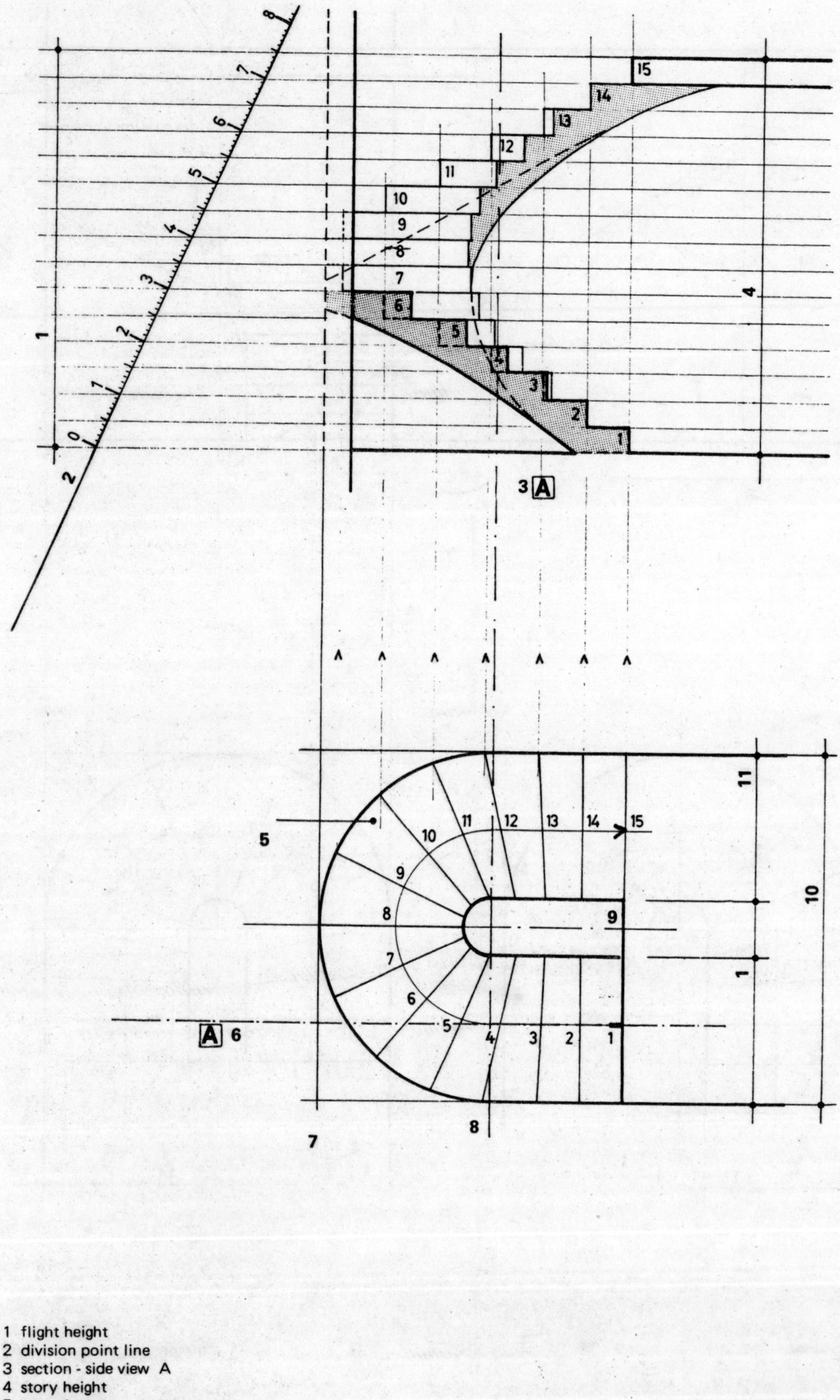

1 flight height
2 division point line
3 section - side view A
4 story height
5 turned steps
6 section line, side view A
7 run . . . cm uniform along walking line
8 plan
9 stairwell
10 staircase width
11 flight width

Steel staircases

In certain situations, where a purely industrial construction is required, staircases of steel are appropriate. In situations of increased fire risk and where the staircase is the only escape route, a steel staircase is not to be recommended.

Steel staircases should be treated with a rust-proof coating before finishings are applied, (or, better still, hot dip or spray galvanized). The final coating should be scratch- and impact-resistant. The cross-sectional size and form of the string will depend on the length between fixings or the width of flight, and on the type of use to which it will be subjected.

For industrial staircases, treads of close mesh grating, or checkered, channelled or perforated sheet metal are generally used. All-steel stairs are not suited to domestic situations, however, since they generate a great deal of noise. For this reason, treads are often manufactured that can be filled with concrete and covered with PVC or a fabric finish. Close-grain oak or beech treads are also a suitable solution. Where timber or steel grating are used for treads, setting screws are necessary for accurate parallel positioning.

In order to keep the transmitted sound within limits, the stair flight and landing bearings should be insulated with a suitable sound absorbing material.

Steel staircase and balustrade

1:20/1

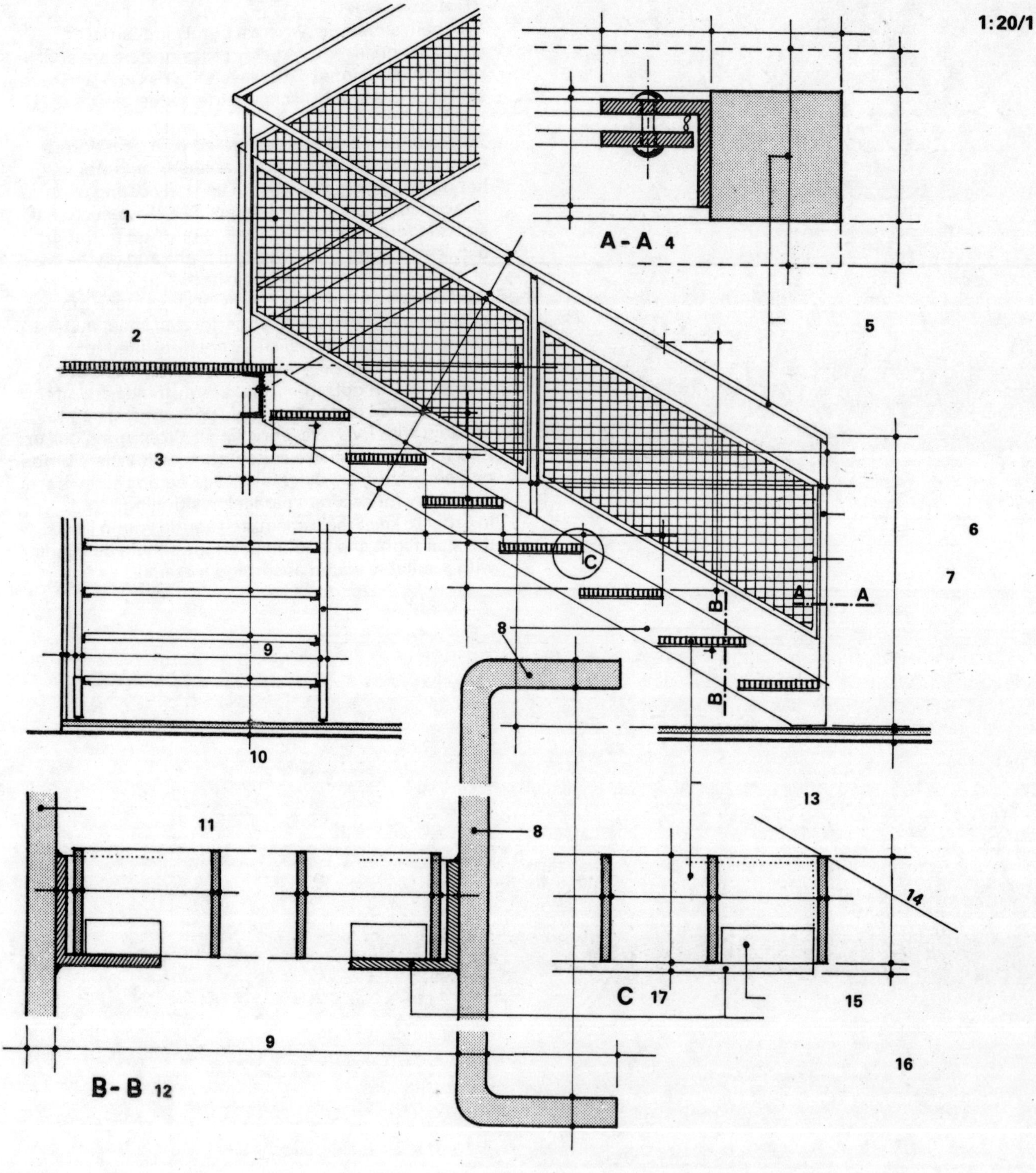

1 Wire mesh, (mesh spacings .../... mm; diameter ... mm)
2 Landing
3 Setting screw
4 Detail A–A
5 Handrail .../... mm
6 Post support .../... mm
7 W-section steel .../.../... mm
8 Open string .../.../.../... mm
9 Flight width
10 Elevation of flight
11 Wall string .../.../.../... mm
12 Detail B–B
13 Lattice grating .../.../... mm
14 Pitch line
15 Flange
16 Angle bearer .../.../... mm, seam or spot welded
17 Detail C

Steel staircase, treads with concrete filling

1:20/2

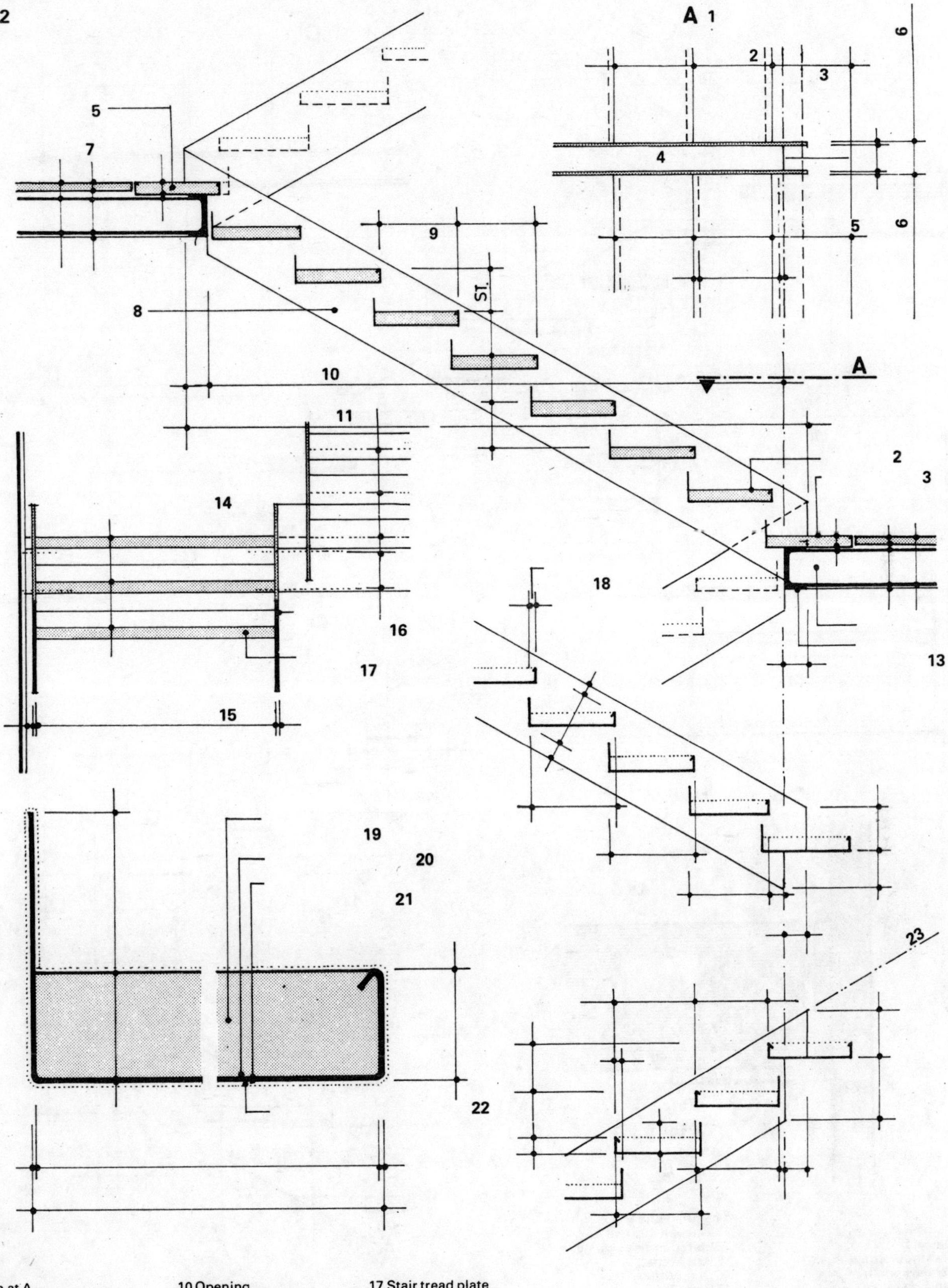

1 Plan at A
2 Starting step (springing)
3 Set back width of 1 tread
4 Stair well
5 Top step
6 Flight width
7 Landing
8 Open string
9 Going
10 Opening
11 Length of string
12 Reinforced concrete
13 U-section beam with rounded edges
14 Intermediate or floor landing
15 Flight width
16 Steel string . . . / . . . mm
17 Stair tread plate
18 Nosing dimension
19 Concrete PC 350 - 450 BN filling trowelled smooth
20 Bitumen coating
21 Sheet steel 2 mm thick bent to shape
22 PVC covering (optional)
23 Pitch line

Steel staircase with timber treads

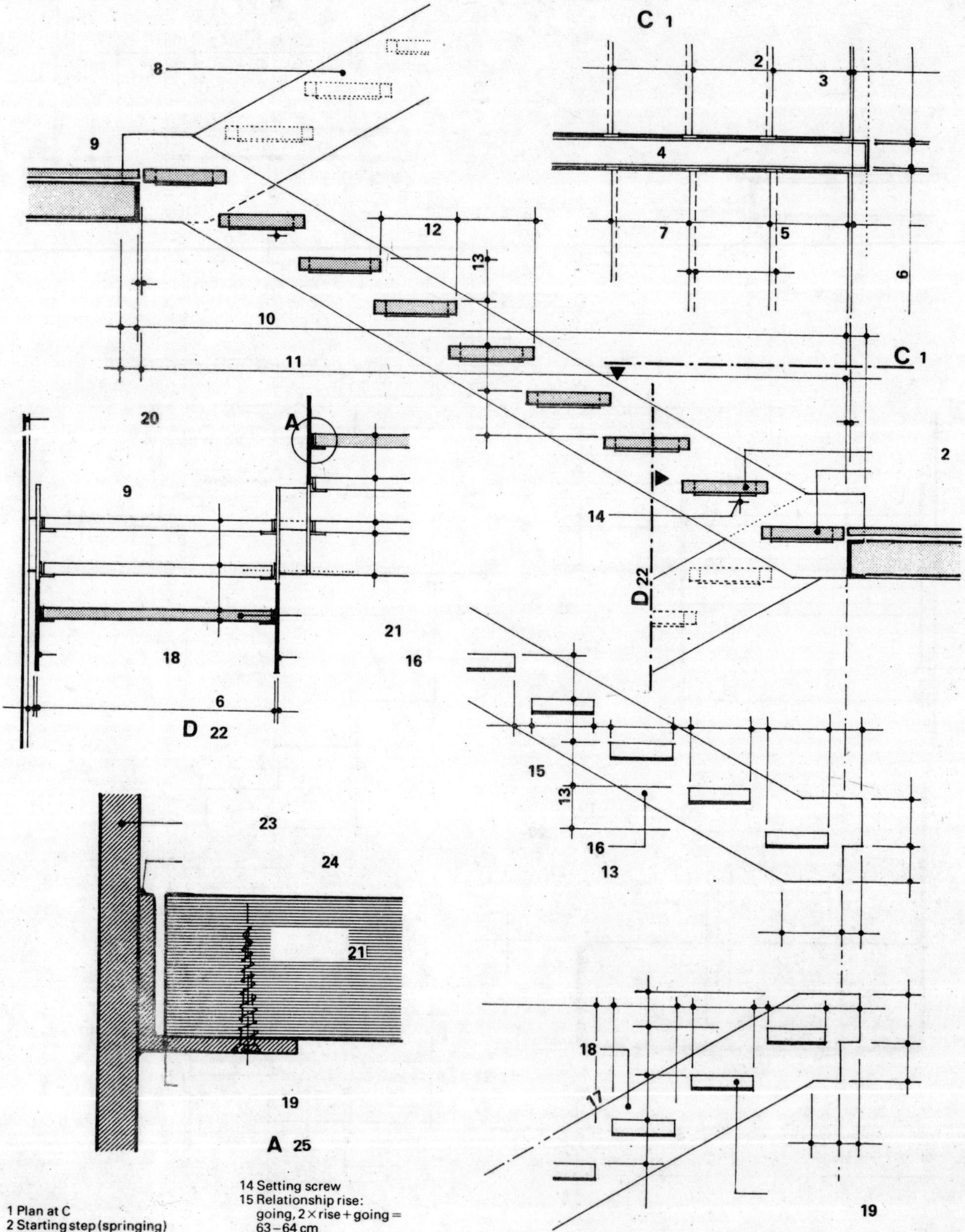

1 Plan at C
2 Starting step (springing)
3 Set back width of 1 tread
4 Stair well
5 Top tread
6 Flight width
7 Intermediate tread (flier)
8 Open string
9 Landing
10 Opening
11 9 × Going
12 Going
13 Rise
14 Setting screw
15 Relationship rise: going, 2 × rise + going = 63 – 64 cm
16 Open string
17 Pitch line
18 Wall string
19 Steel angle .../.../... mm
20 Wall plaster
21 Timber tread (... cm)
22 Section/elevation D
23 String
24 Welding seam
25 Detail A

Reinforced concrete staircases

The long life and fire safety implicit in reinforced concrete stairs are responsible for their having become virtually the only type of staircase used in building today. They can be poured insitu from site or lorry mixed concrete. The diagonal bearing slab usually has a minimum thickness of 10-12 cm and is reinforced and cast in a single process with the steps.
Where a large number of identical units is required, the choice, for economical reasons, is usually for staircase flights or step units in precast concrete. Normal reinforced concrete staircases are built in in two work stages, and the structural element serves as a staircase during building operations. The coverings to treads and risers are put in place shortly before completion of the building. Because concrete is not an optimal material from the point of view of sound insulation, staircase flights are either constructed using insulation slabs or kept clear of staircase walls. All bearing points of landings should be insulated with sound absorbing slabs or, better still, with insulation quilt.
More formal staircases are often clad with natural or artificial stone slabs. L-shaped angle units are most commonly used. The most commonly found types are to be found amongst the many examples given.
The impression of comfort can be enhanced by carpeting the finished steps.

Insitu concrete stair flights

1:20

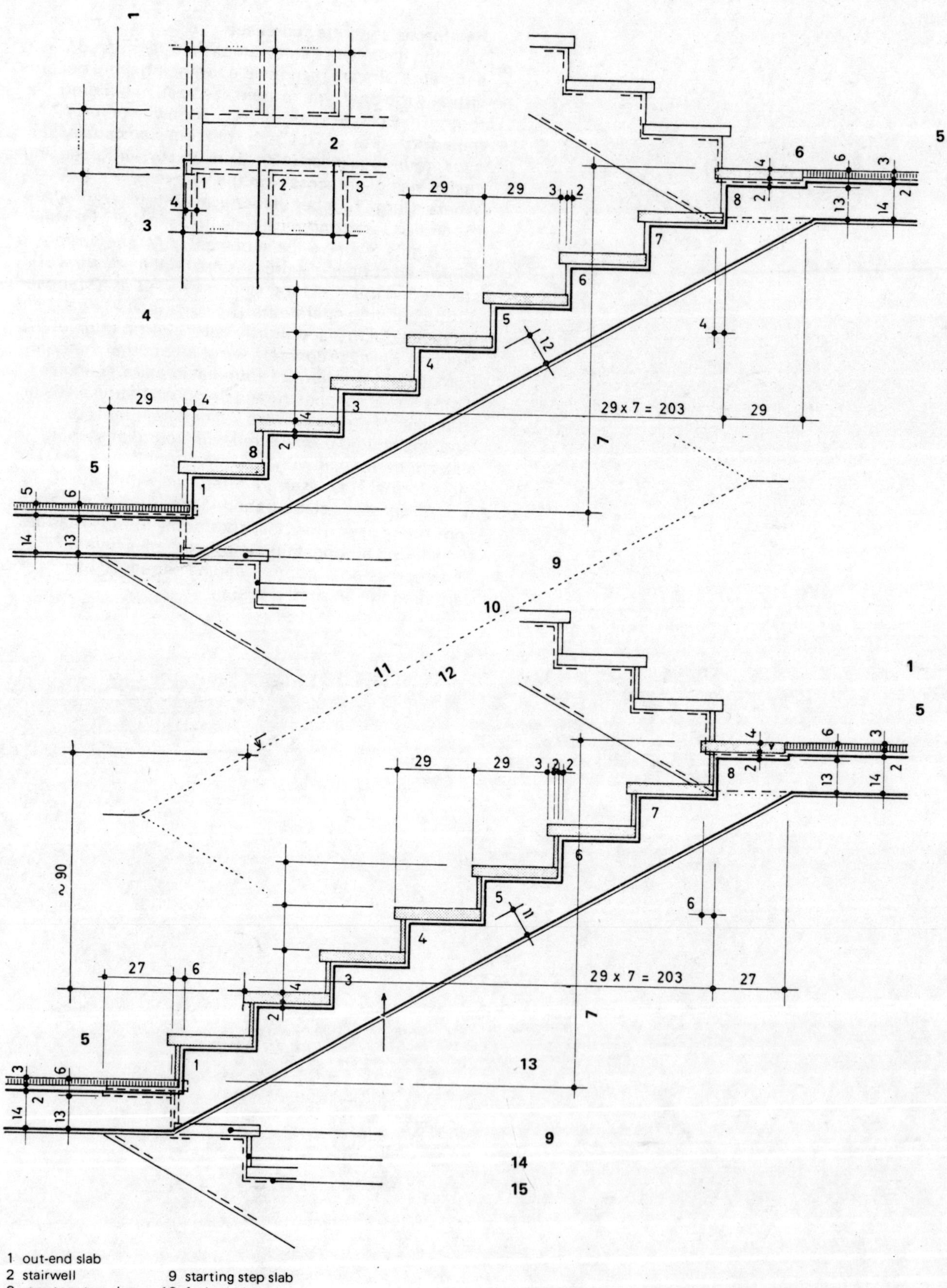

1 out-end slab
2 stairwell
3 step top, top view
4 rise
5 landing
6 out-end
7 flight height
8 starting step
9 starting step slab
10 facing side plastered
11 upper edge handrail
12 stair railing
13 cast-in-place concrete stairflight
14 riser slab
15 mortar bed

1:20

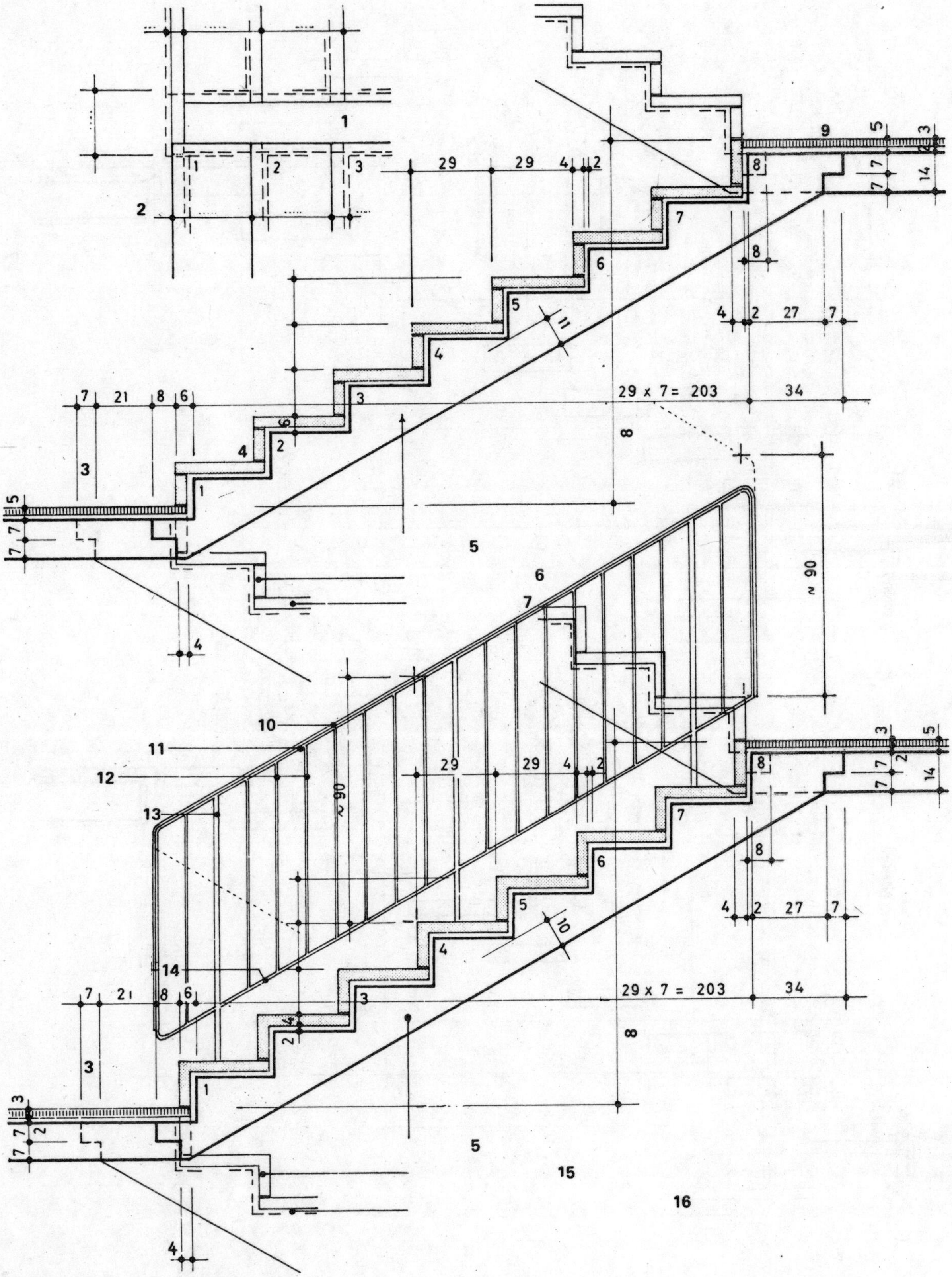

1 stairwell
2 tread, top view
3 landing
4 starting step
5 concrete element stair flight
6 riser slab
7 starting step slab
8 flight height
9 out-end
10 handrail section . . .
11 support rod
12 baluster
13 post support
14 foot traverse
15 angle step
16 mortar bed (lower layer)

Projecting tread slabs with railing variants

1:20

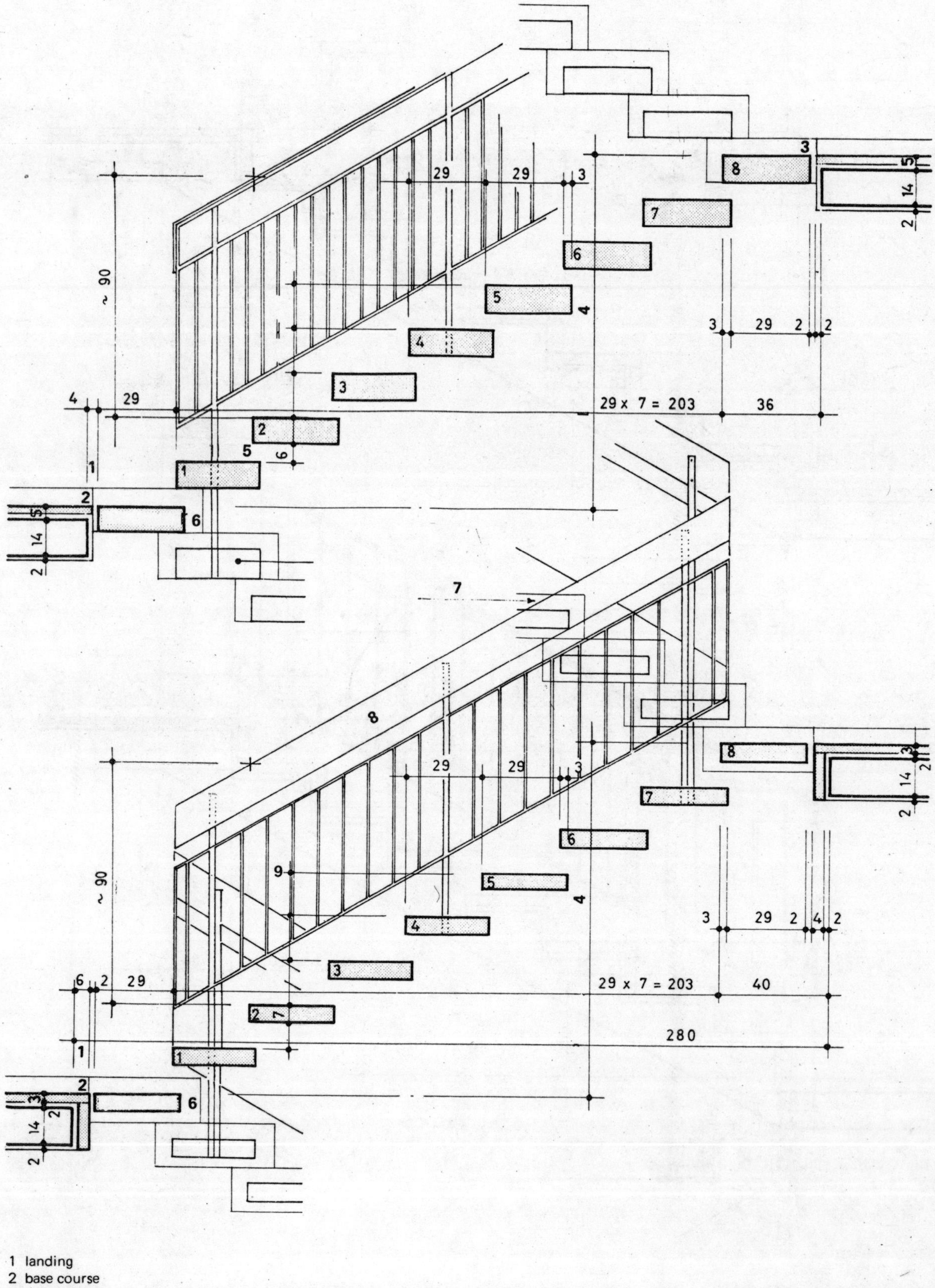

1 landing
2 base course
3 out-end
4 flight height
5 starting step
6 landing step
7 projecting tread slab with base piece
8 handrail beam
9 rise

1:20

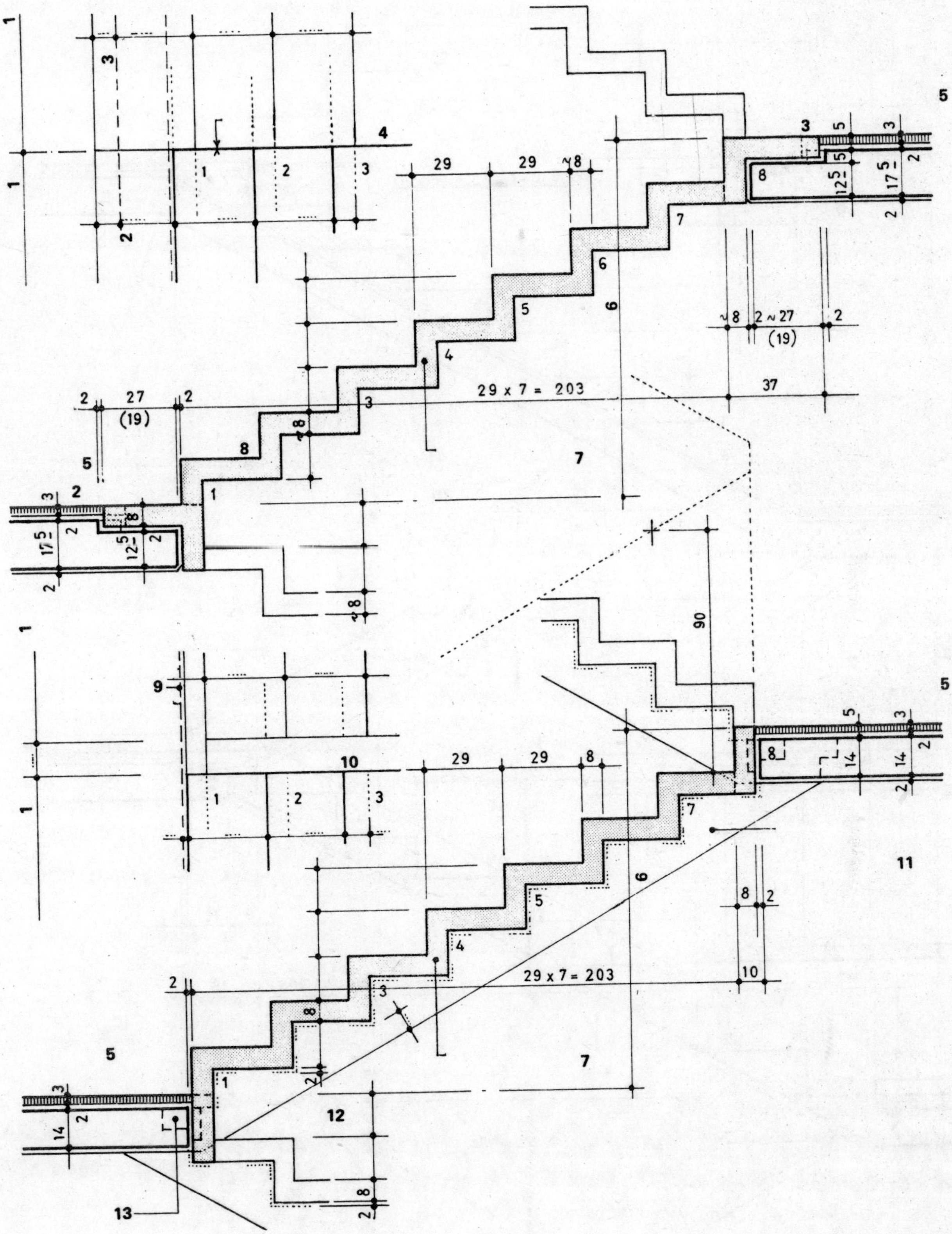

1 flight width
2 landing step
3 out-end
4 design without stairwell
5 landing
6 flight height
7 angle element - flight
8 starting step
9 stair landing line, unplastered
10 stairwell
11 rib supporting element, width . . . cm
12 rise
13 rib mounting

Ramp/string stairs with triangular steps

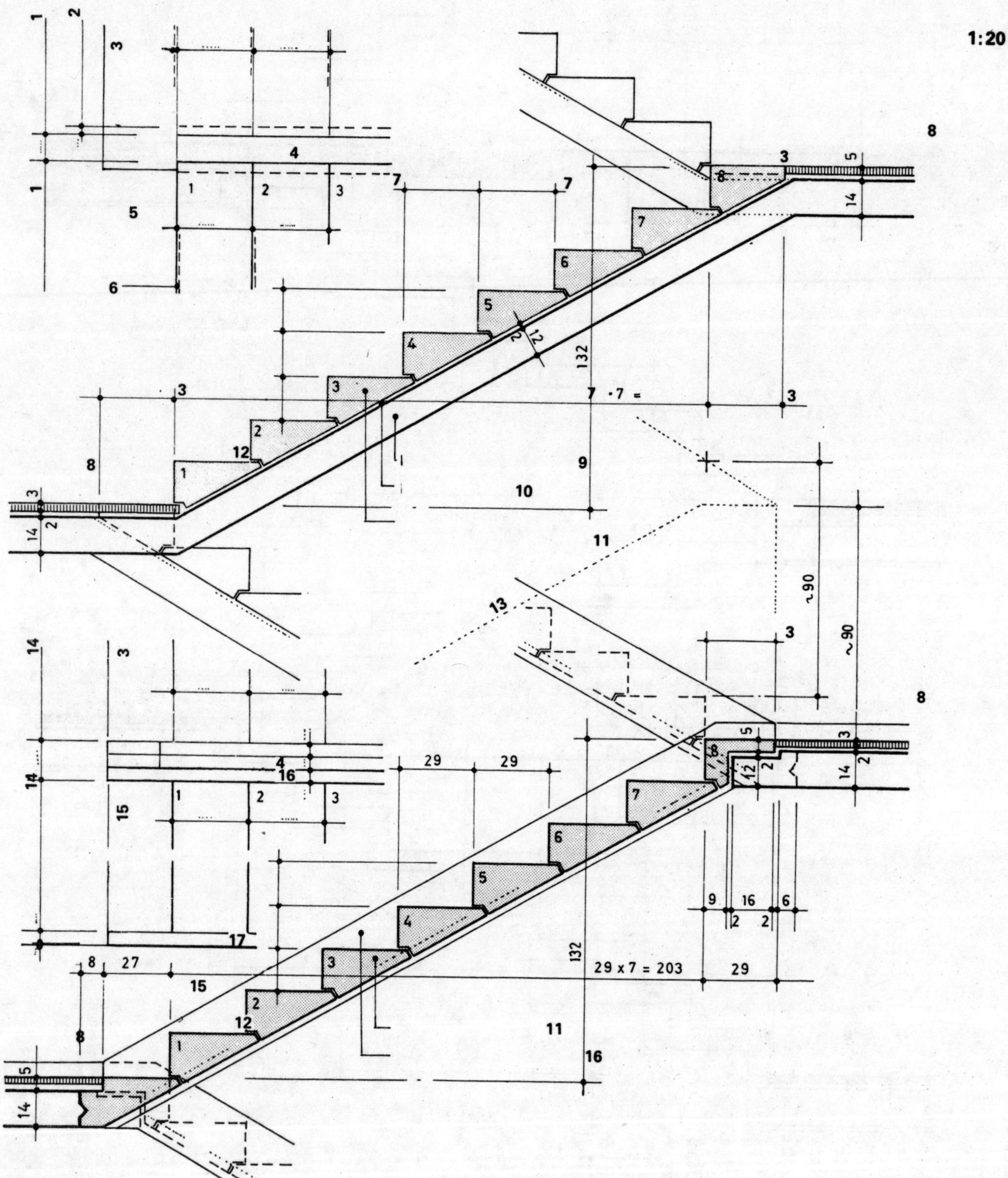

1 flight width
2 ramp width
3 out-end
4 stairwell
5 landing, top view
6 execution with or without batter
7 run
8 landing
9 flight slab (ramp)
10 mortar bed
11 crowbar tread, also called triangular step
12 starting step
13 handrail
14 string clearance
15 landing step
16 stairwell string
17 wall string

Stair flights, walking surface variants

1:20

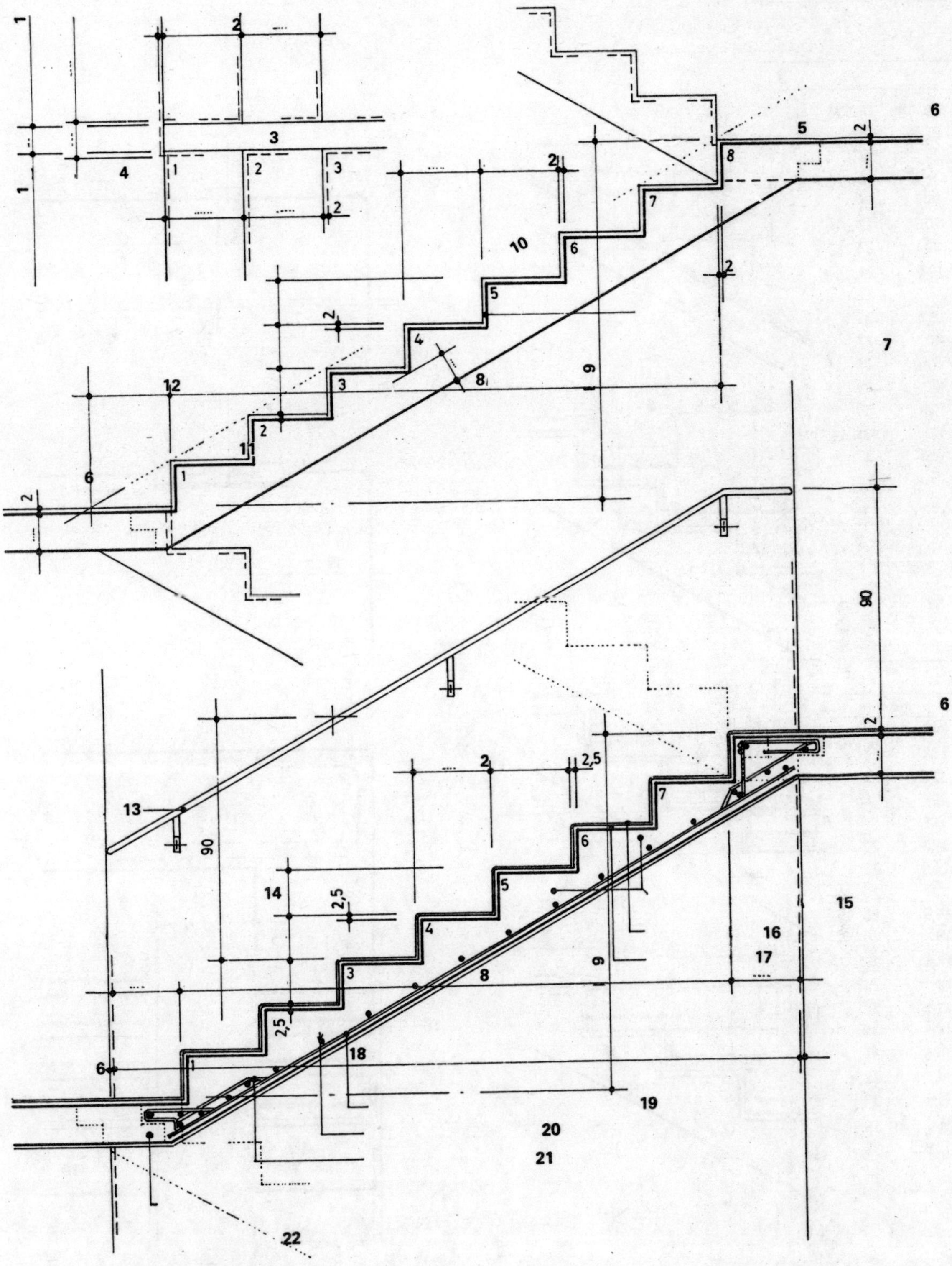

1 flight width
2 run
3 stairwell
4 tread, top view
5 out-end
6 landing
7 cement coating with . . . additive or armored concrete, manufact. . . .
8 flight length
9 flight height
10 rise line
11 starting step
12 tread width
13 handrail Ø . . . mm of . . .
14 rise
15 cast-in-place concrete or element flight
16 . . . covering
17 smoothing
18 masonry lining of stairwell
19 tensile steel (supporting reinforcement)
20 spreading reinforcement
21 bent-up reinforcement
22 stair flight support for element design

Stair footings, edge protection and tread ratio

1:20/1

1

2	3
23 CM	17 CM
22,5	18
22	19
21,5	20
21	21
20,5	22
20	23
19,5	24
19	25
18,5	26
18	27
17,5	28
17	29
16,5	30
16	31
15,5	32
15	33

1

2	3
23,5	17
23	18
22,5	19
22	20
21,5	21
21	22
20,5	23
20	24
19,5	25
19	26
18,5	27
18	28
17,5	29
17	30
16,5	31
16	32
15,5	33
15	34
14,5	35

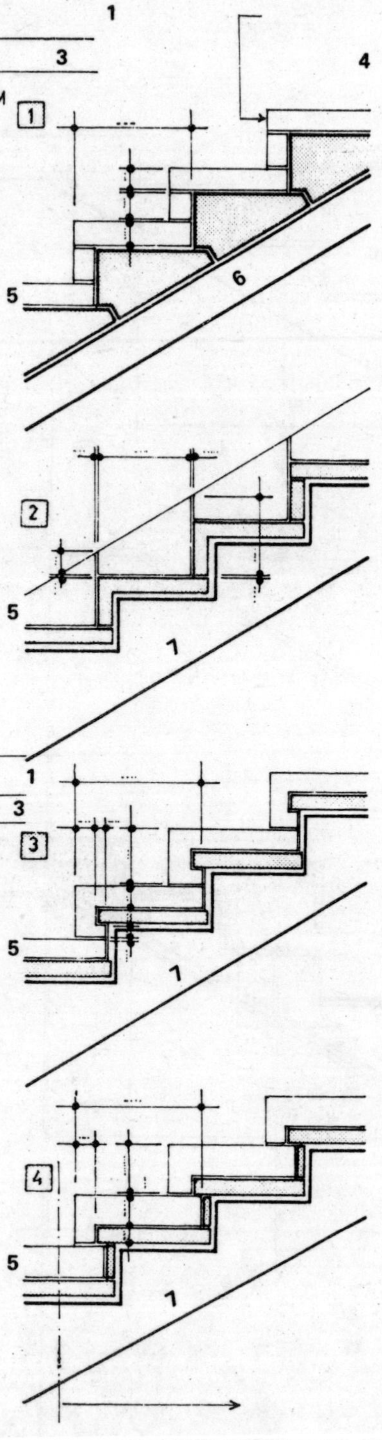

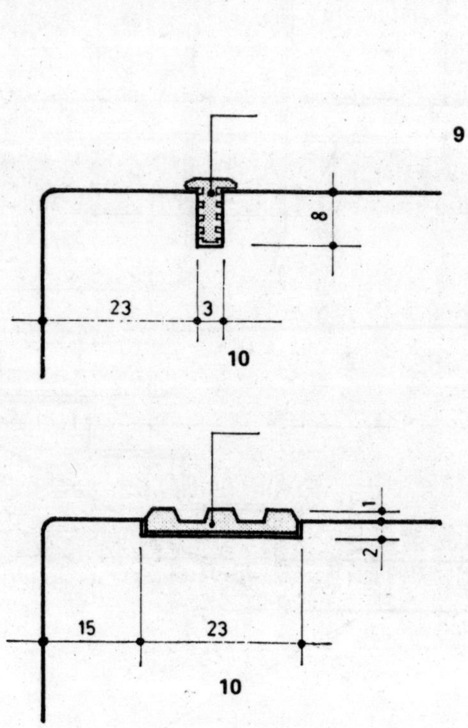

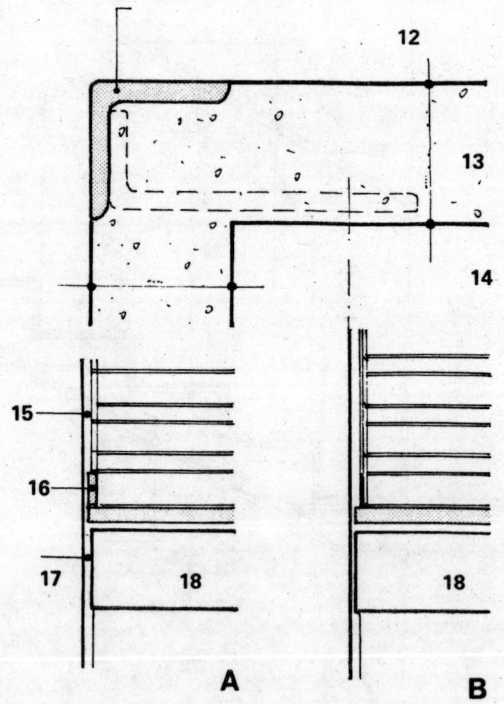

1 tread ratio for 63 cm development
2 rise
3 run
4 base course head treated same as surface
5 base course
6 flight slab (ramp)
7 stair flight
8 base course väriants 1,2,3 and 4
9 non-skid section No. . . .
10 tread edge
11 non-skid insert section No. . . . ribbed
12 angle edge of . . ., . . . / . . . mm
13 cement coating or armored concrete
14 step-tread
15 plaster
16 stair base course
17 distance approx. 1 cm
18 element flight
19 stair front view

Wooden Staircases

When selecting wood as the material for stairs, local fire regulations on the number of floors and building purpose are to be strictly observed.

Hard woods – oak or beech – should be used to assure long service life of the treads. However, if the treads are to be covered with linoleum, rubber or plastic (PVC), fir or pine is sufficient.

The type of wood selected must be well supported, narrow-circled, have a minimum of knots and be full-edged in machine-planed execution with chamfered (beveled) edges.

In general, stairs are treated naturally, varnished and lacquered (possibly with primer coat beforehand and graining with putty to match the tone of the wood).

String thickness depends on the mounting or flight length and the use of the stairs. The outer string is approx. 2 cm wider in cross section than the wall string.

The stair string at the wall connection is called the wall string, while the projecting string is called the outer or stairwell string. In order to keep the strings from shifting, they are held with locking screws in the desired position at the upper and lower ends and (with more than six steps) also in the middle.

The riser should not be grooved into the lower edge of the tread to prevent creaking in the joints. In order to prevent tread sagging, it is recommended that the riser be raised approx. 2 mm in the middle, also eliminating creaking in the tread mounting.
The underside of the flight can be faced as desired.

Wooden stairs without risers

1:20/2

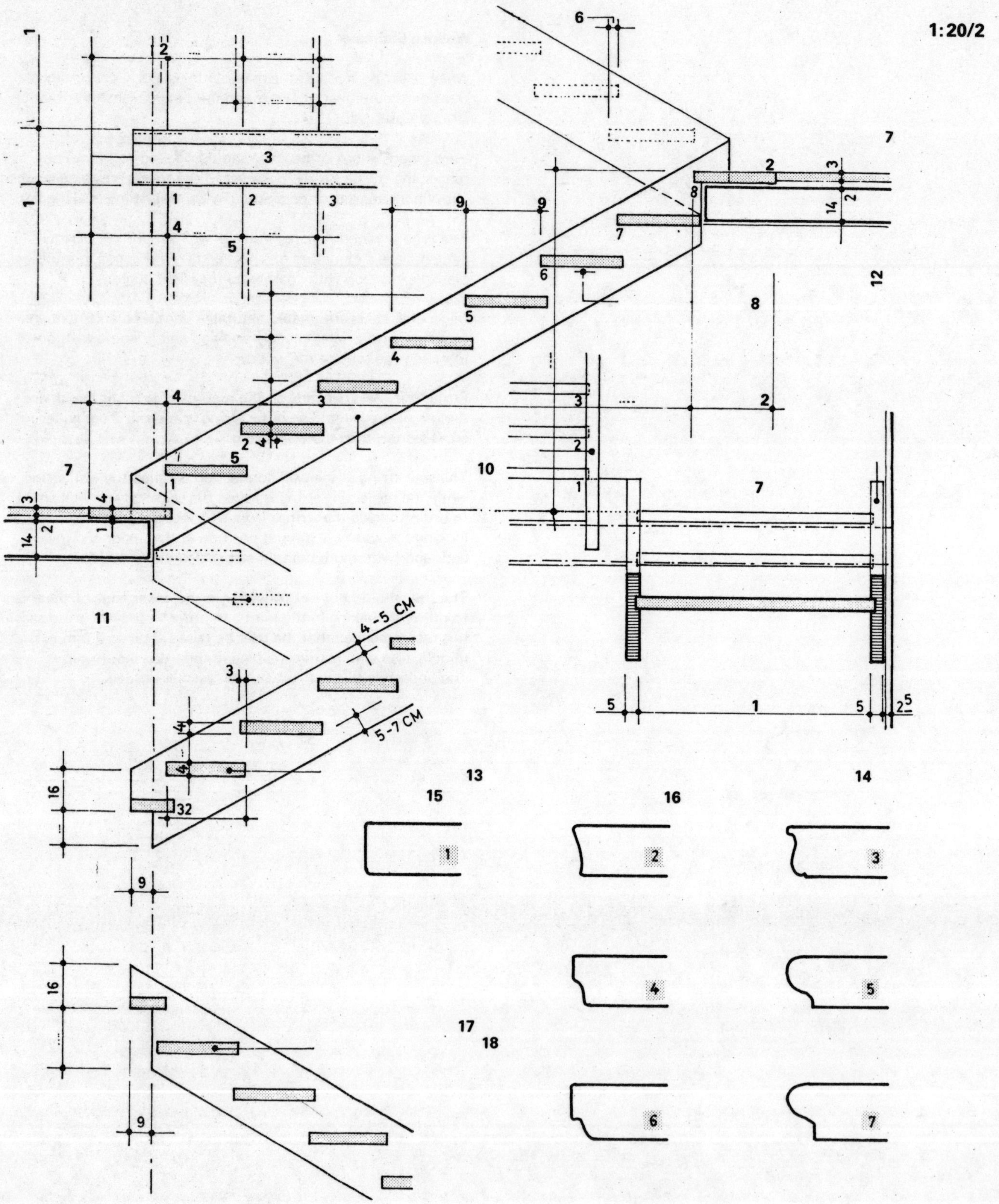

1 flight width
2 out-end
3 stairwell
4 flush step
5 starting step
6 tread overhang width
7 landing
8 locking screw
9 run
10 stairwell string (outer string)
11 . . . wooden tread 4/32 cm
12 wall string 5/32 cm
13 rabbet for tread fullering
14 tread front edge forms
15 a. chamfered
16 b. shaped
17 rabbet 4/32 cm
18 depth approx. 20-25 mm

1:20

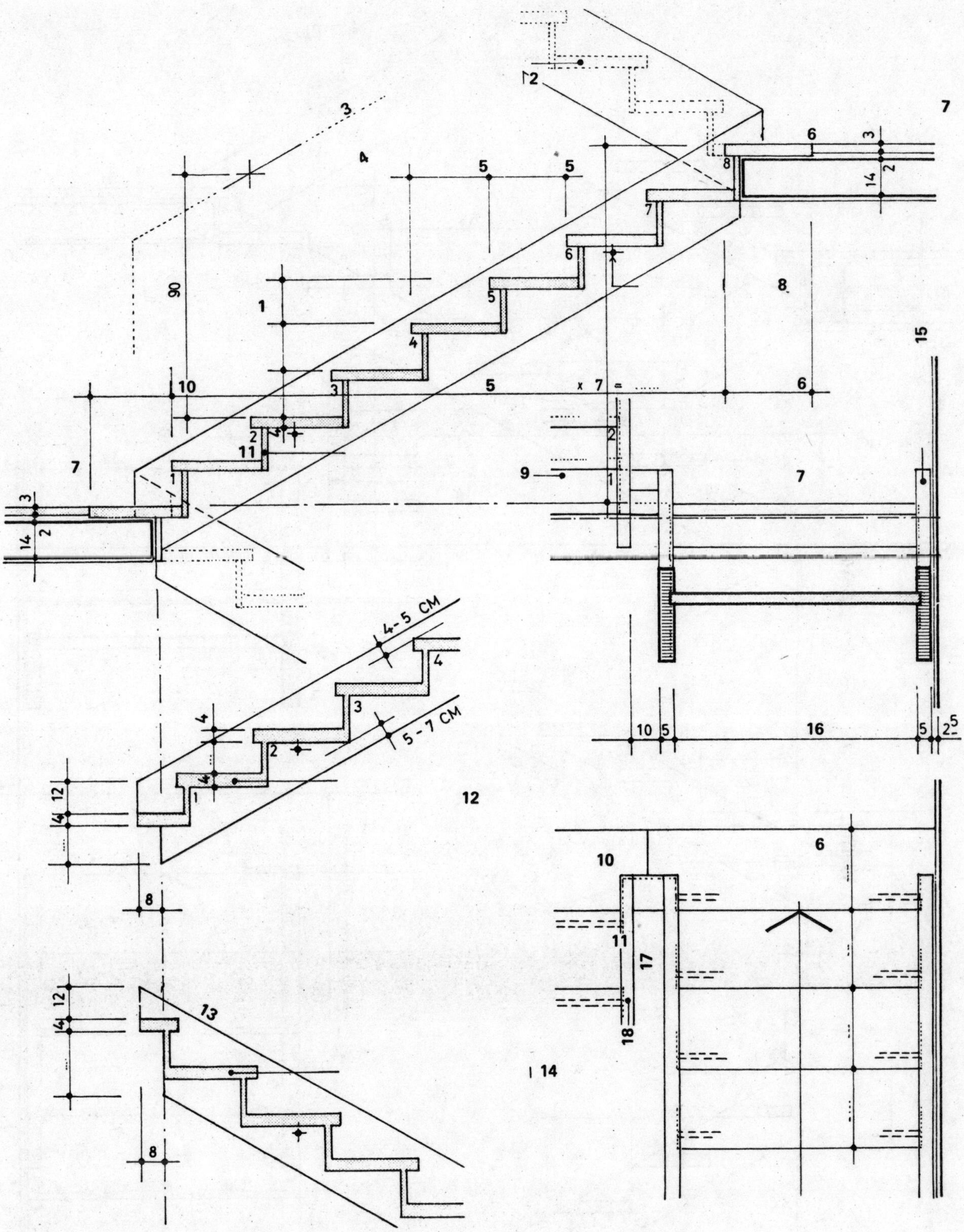

1 rise
2 . . . wooden tread . . . / . . . cm
3 handrail
4 stair railing
5 run
6 out-end
7 landing
8 locking screw
9 . . . riser . . . / . . . mm
10 flush step
11 starting step
12 rabbets for mortising
13 slope line
14 rabbet depth 20-25 mm depending on flight width
15 wall string
16 flight width
17 stairwell
18 stairwell string

wooden stairs without risers

1:20

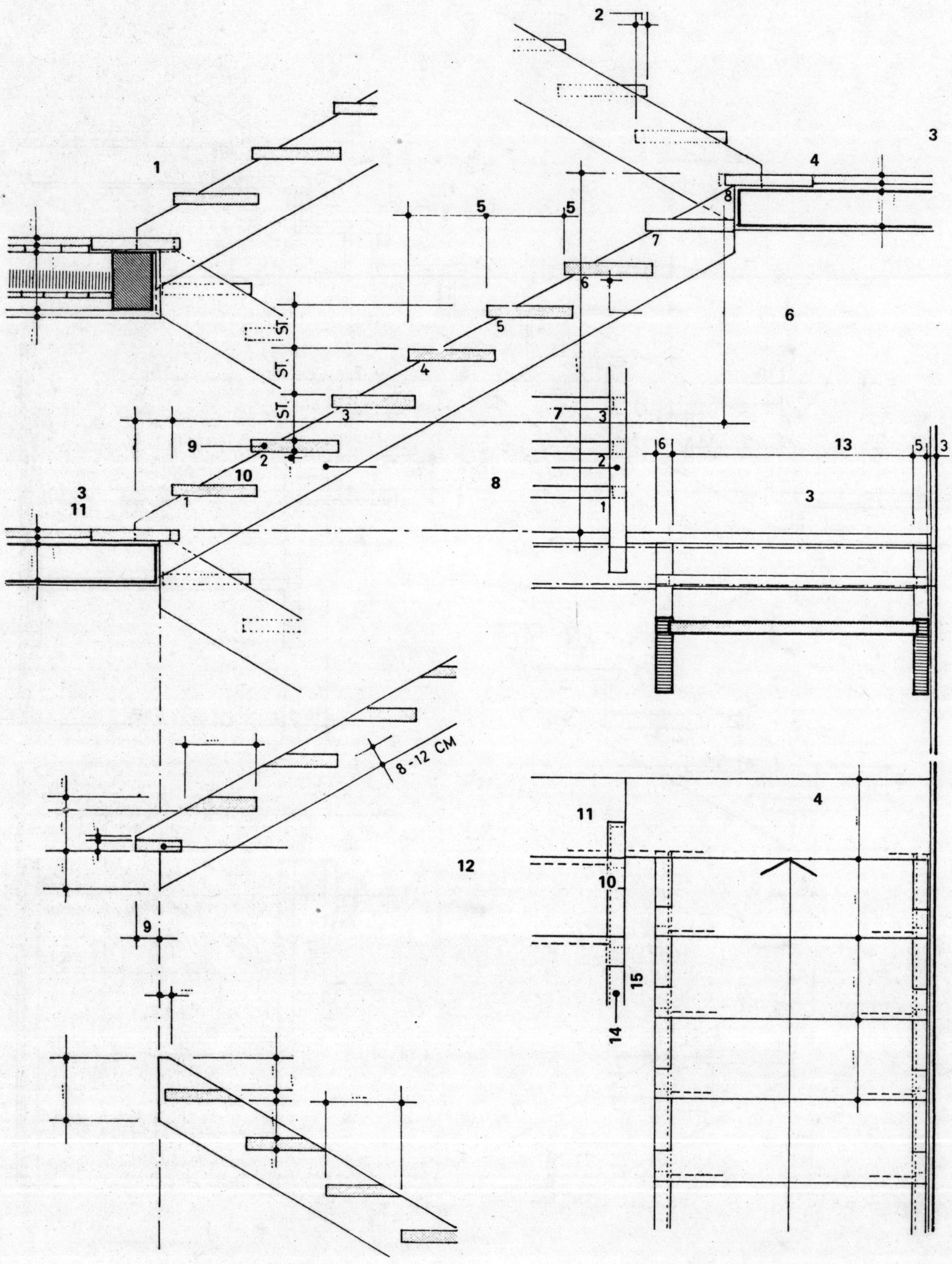

1 variant: connection at beam floor
2 tread overhang width
3 landing
4 out-end
5 run
6 locking screw
7 flight length
8 stairwell string (outer string)
9 . . . wooden tread . . . / . . . mm
10 starting stair
11 flush step
12 rabbet depth 20-25 mm depending on flight width
13 flight width
14 stairwell string
15 stairwell

1:20

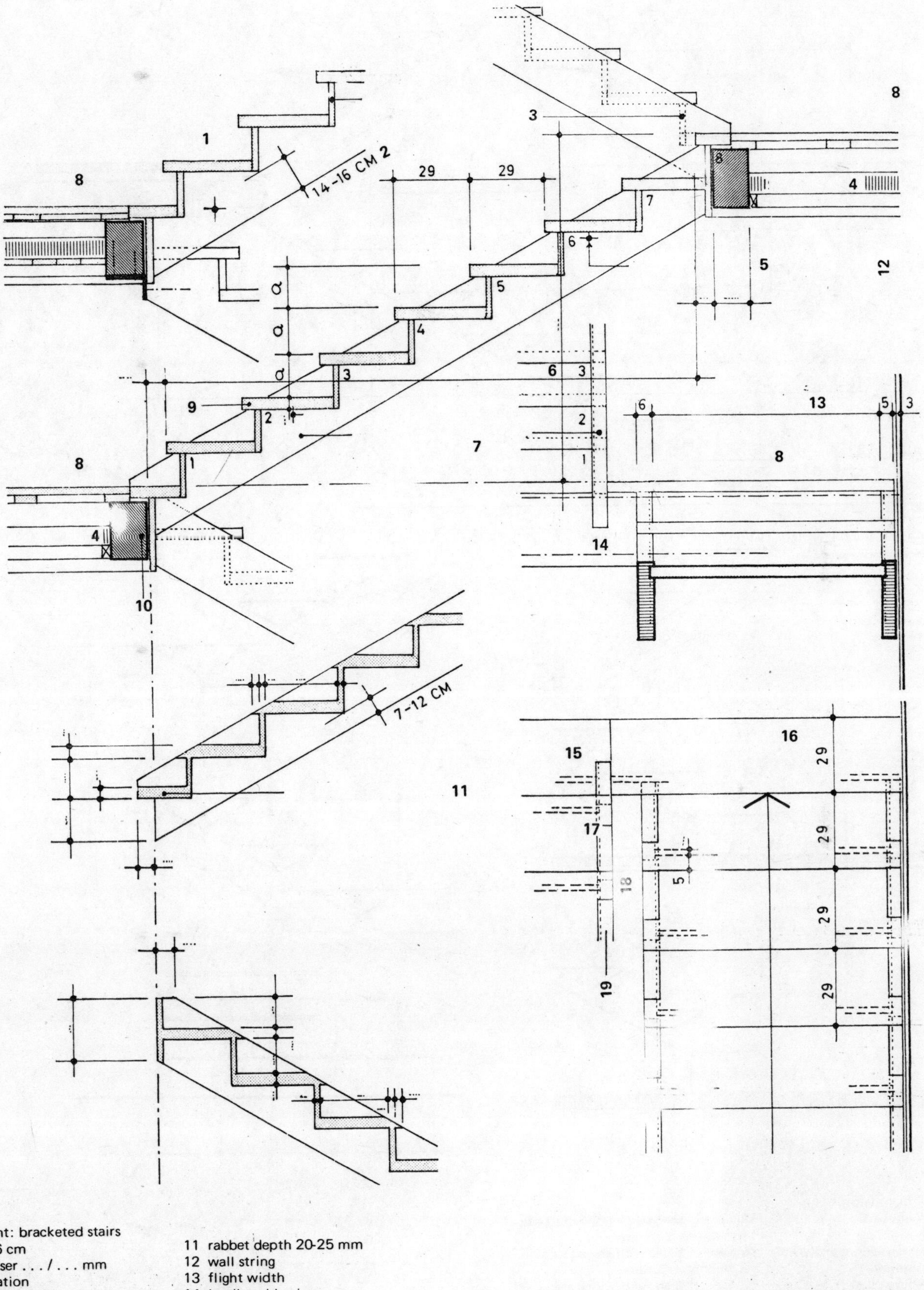

1 variant: bracketed stairs
2 14-16 cm
3 . . . riser . . . / . . . mm
4 insulation
5 locking screw
6 flight length
7 stairwell string (outer string)
8 landing
9 . . . wooden tread . . . / . . . mm
10 beam . . . / . . . cm
11 rabbet depth 20-25 mm
12 wall string
13 flight width
14 landing side view
15 flush step
16 out-end
17 starting step
18 stairwell
19 stairwell string

Wedge-tread wooden stairs

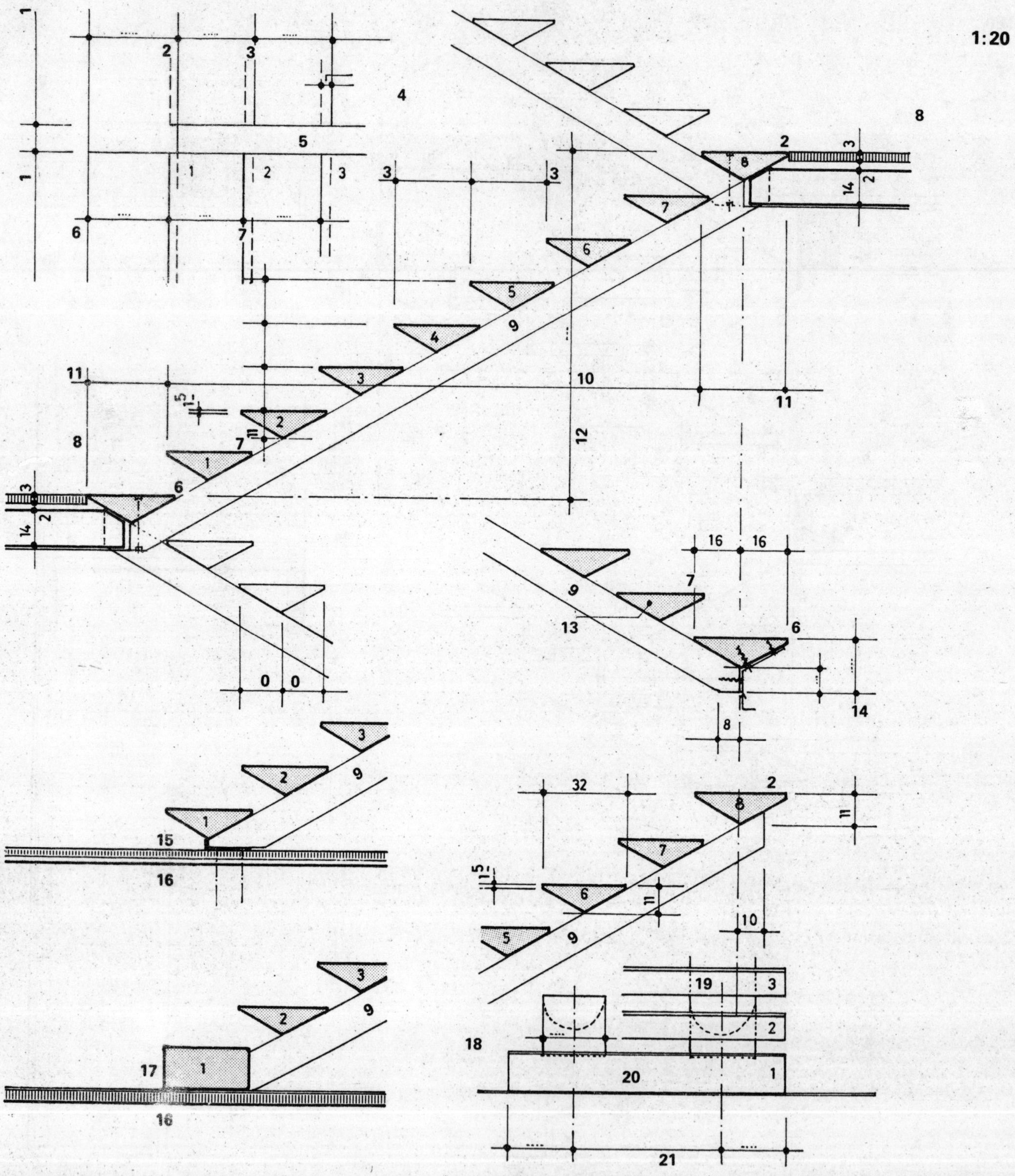

1 flight width
2 out-end
3 run
4 tread overhang width
5 stairwell
6 flush step
7 starting step
8 landing
9 supporting rib
10 flight length
11 width same as run
12 flight height
13 . . . wooden wedge-shaped tread
14 flat-iron 5/55 mm
15 base of flight with angled shoe
16 floor connection
17 base of flight with block step
18 . . . wood, string piece section width
19 side view
20 block step
21 center-to-center distance between ribs

Windows and Glazed Doors (Wood)

As windows and glazed doors (for balconies) are particularly exposed to the weather, the greatest care must be taken over correct design. The material used must be fine-grained, free from knots and well seasoned. To obviate structural defects the finished treatment must be known when deciding the type of wood. With natural treatment choice woods with high oil content can be used for painted effects white pine (whitewood), or a similar good class of wood is advisable so that the colour will not flake. As wood weather-bars are more susceptible to defects than efficient, they are generally omitted or replaced by a rain-repellant metal strip. Frames of more than 25 cm width must be glued. It is most important that timber elements after completion be immediately immersed in a transparent or white size or primer in the manufacturer's workshop. The following work must be carried out before the delivery or fixing of the windows and glazed doors: sills in place, lead stops provided, when necessary with a plaster finish. Nowadays the frames are almost exclusively secured to the linings (stops) with expansion screws so that all essential work can be carried out in one operation by a single sub-contractor. The lining is packed with putty or foam plastic. For filling and levelling frame connections to walls and soffits a type of silk fibre packing is needed, oakum caulking is not to be recommended because of staining and fading dangers. Paper should not be used owing to problems of vermin infestation.

Window opening forms

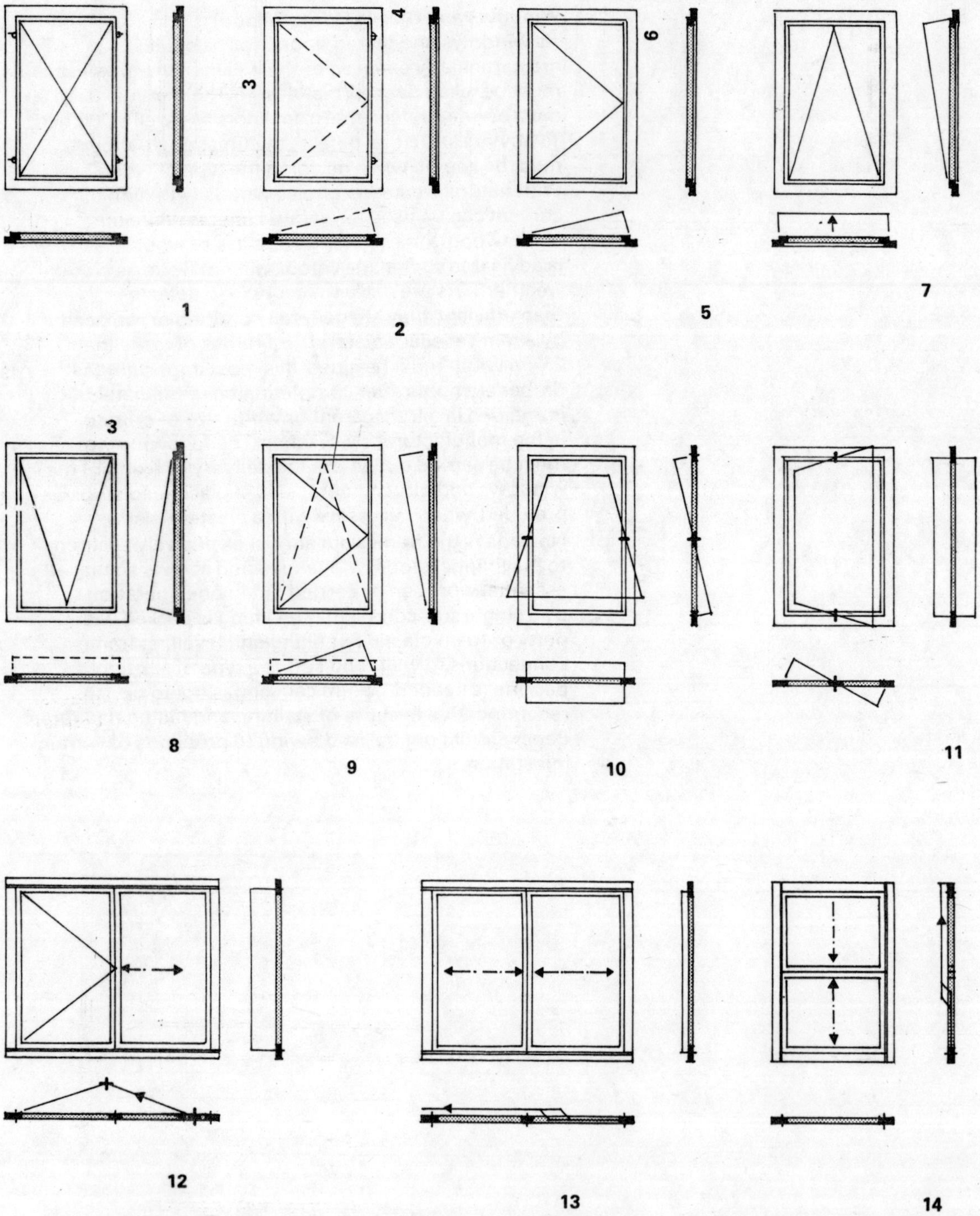

1 Casement, fixed light
2 Casement, fixed light, side hung for cleaning
3 Hinge edge
4 Closing edge
5 Casement, side hung
6 Opening edge
7 Bottom-hung inward opening casement
8 Top-hung inward opening casement
9 Side- and top-hung inward opening casement window (combined movement)
10 Horizontally pivotted window
11 Vertically pivotted window
12 Folding windows
13 Horizontally sliding windows
14 Vertically sliding windows (double hung sash)

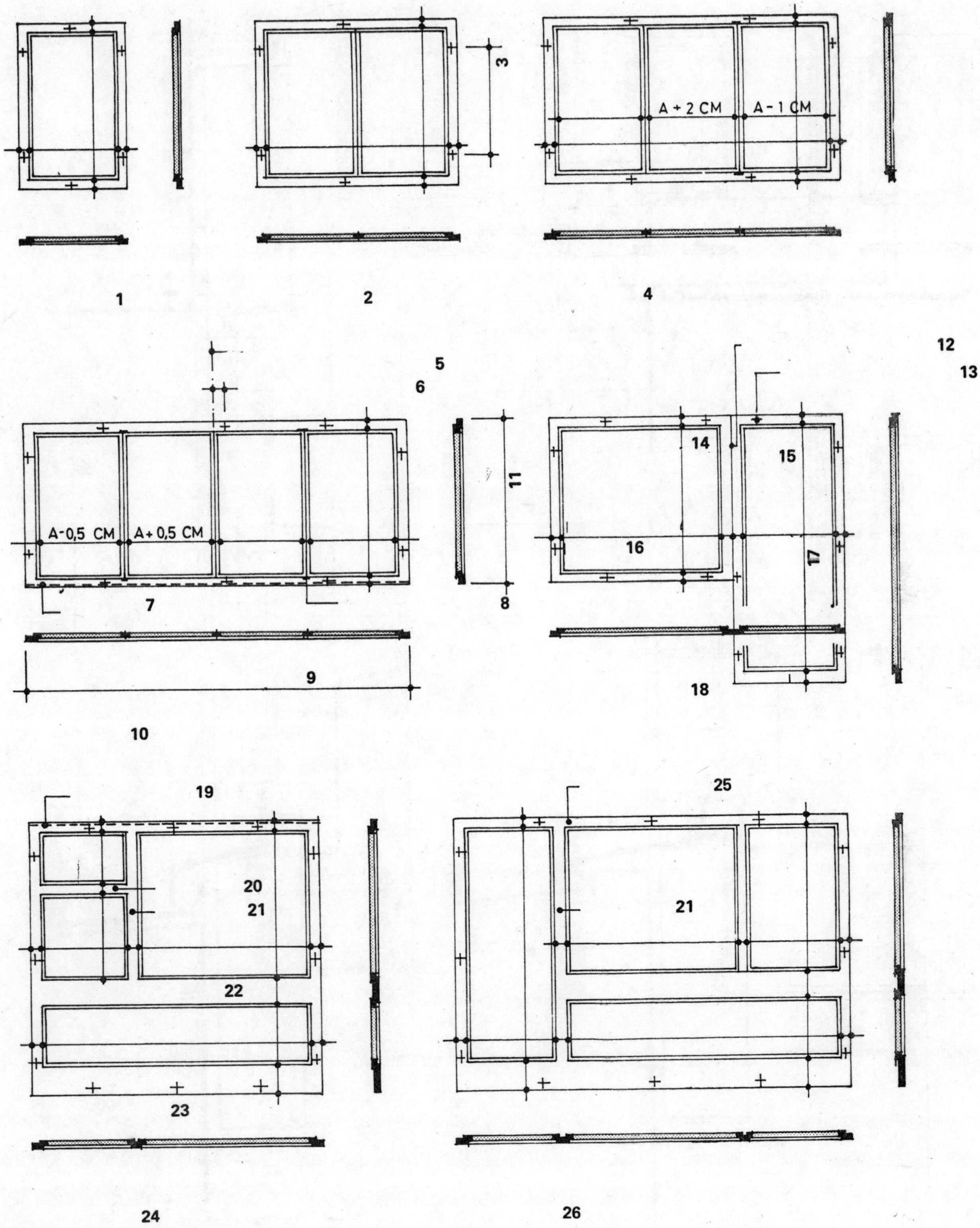

1 Casement, single light
2 Two-light casement
3 Spacing 80-100 cm
4 Three-light casement
5 Fixing line for ironmongery, espagnolette bolt
6 Spacing, min. 5 cm
7 Groove for sill
8 Pivot pin hinge
9 Overall width of window unit
10 Casement, 4-light
11 Overall height of window unit
12 Cross-tongued connection
13 Frame fixing
14 Window light
15 Balcony door
16 Width of casement opening
17 Height of door opening
18 Alternative, balcony door and side window unit
19 Groove for soffit lining
20 Transom
21 Mullion
22 Transom
23 External elevation
24 Window unit (4-light)
25 Outer frame
26 Window unit (4-light)

Single Window, construction details

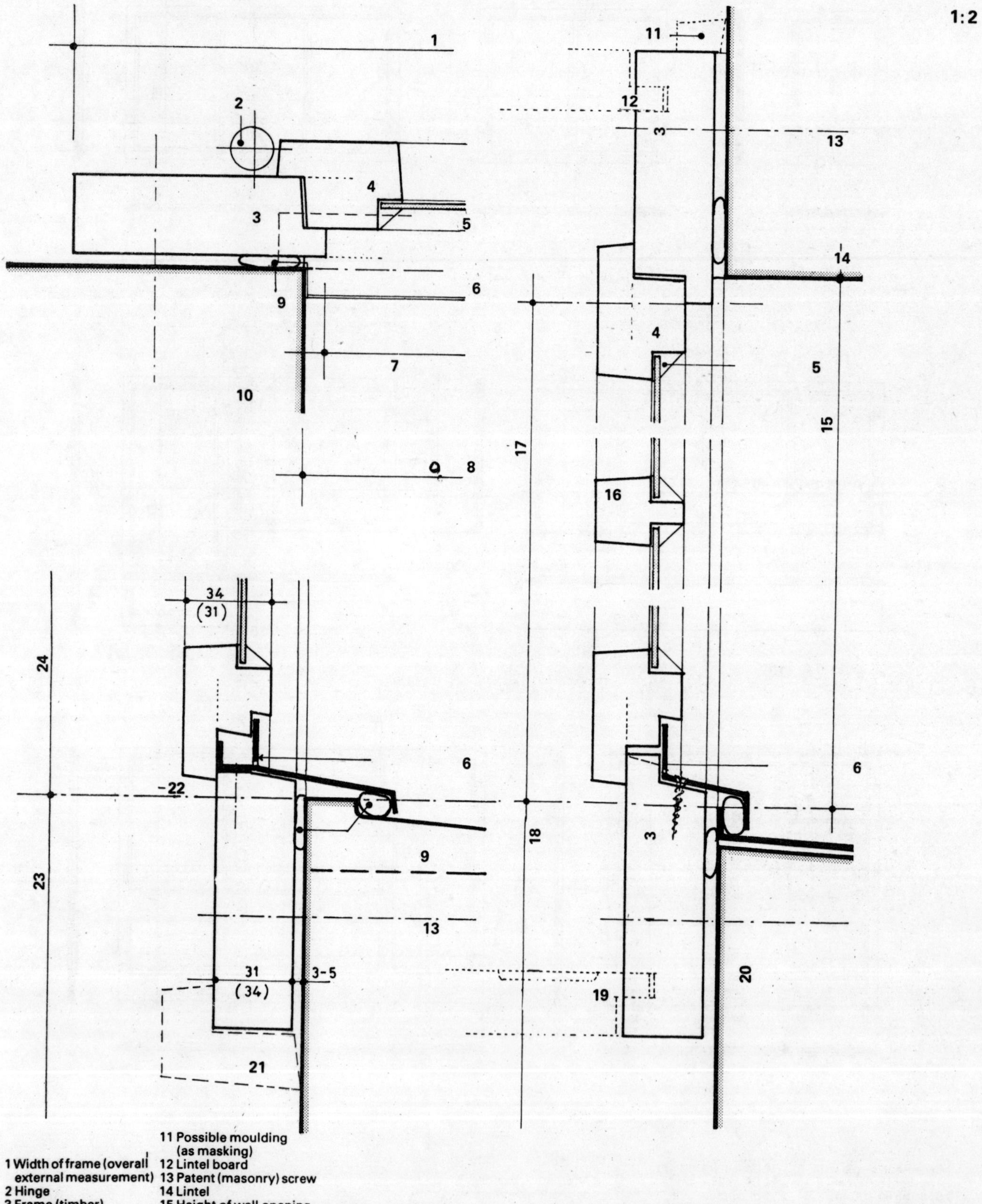

1 Width of frame (overall external measurement)
2 Hinge
3 Frame (timber)
4 Casement (timber)
5 Putty (rebate)
6 Water bar
7 Frame opening width
8 Width of opening between reveals
9 Putty sealing
10 Frame lining (side)
11 Possible moulding (as masking)
12 Lintel board
13 Patent (masonry) screw
14 Lintel
15 Height of wall opening, measured from top edge of threshold or sill
16 Glazing-bar
17 Height of frame opening, measured from top edge of sill or threshold
18 Window-breast (or threshold) height
19 Possible external sill
20 Breast
21 Possible moulding
22 Top edge of sill
23 Breast height
24 Window

1:20/2

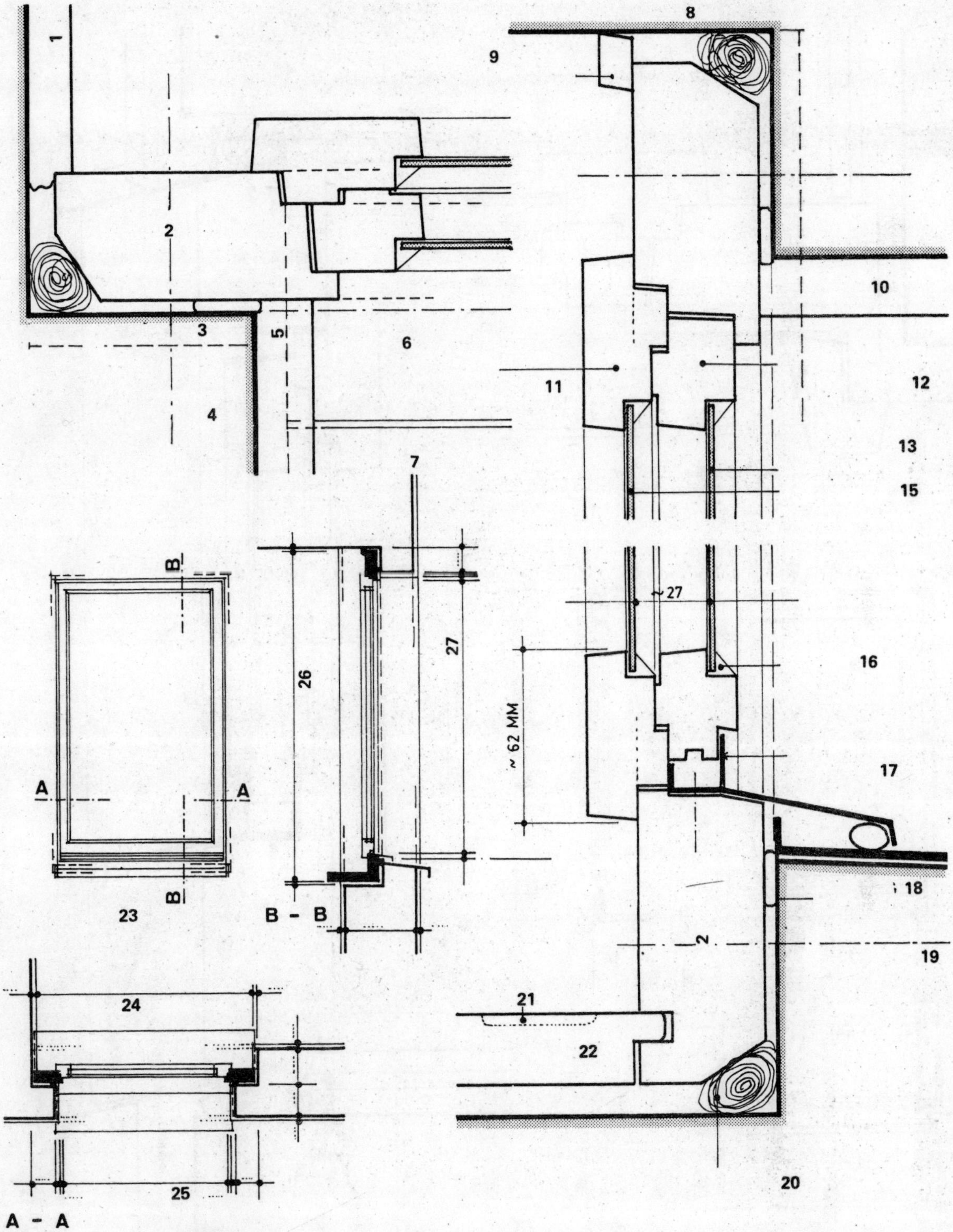

1 Plastering (wall or jambs)
2 Window-frame (timber)
3 Plaster infill
4 Frame lining (side)
5 Plaster (jambs)
6 Weather bar from above
7 Metal sill from above
8 Ceiling joint
9 Moulding
10 Plaster
11 Inside window-iining
12 Outside lining
13 Glazing
14 Outside
15 Inside
16 Puttying rebate
17 Weather bar
18 Putty sealing
19 (dry)-Patent (masonry) screw
20 Insulation
21 Condensation channel
22 Ledge
23 Elevation (from outside)
24 Overall external width of frame
25 Width of (window) light

Single Composite Window, variants

1:20/2

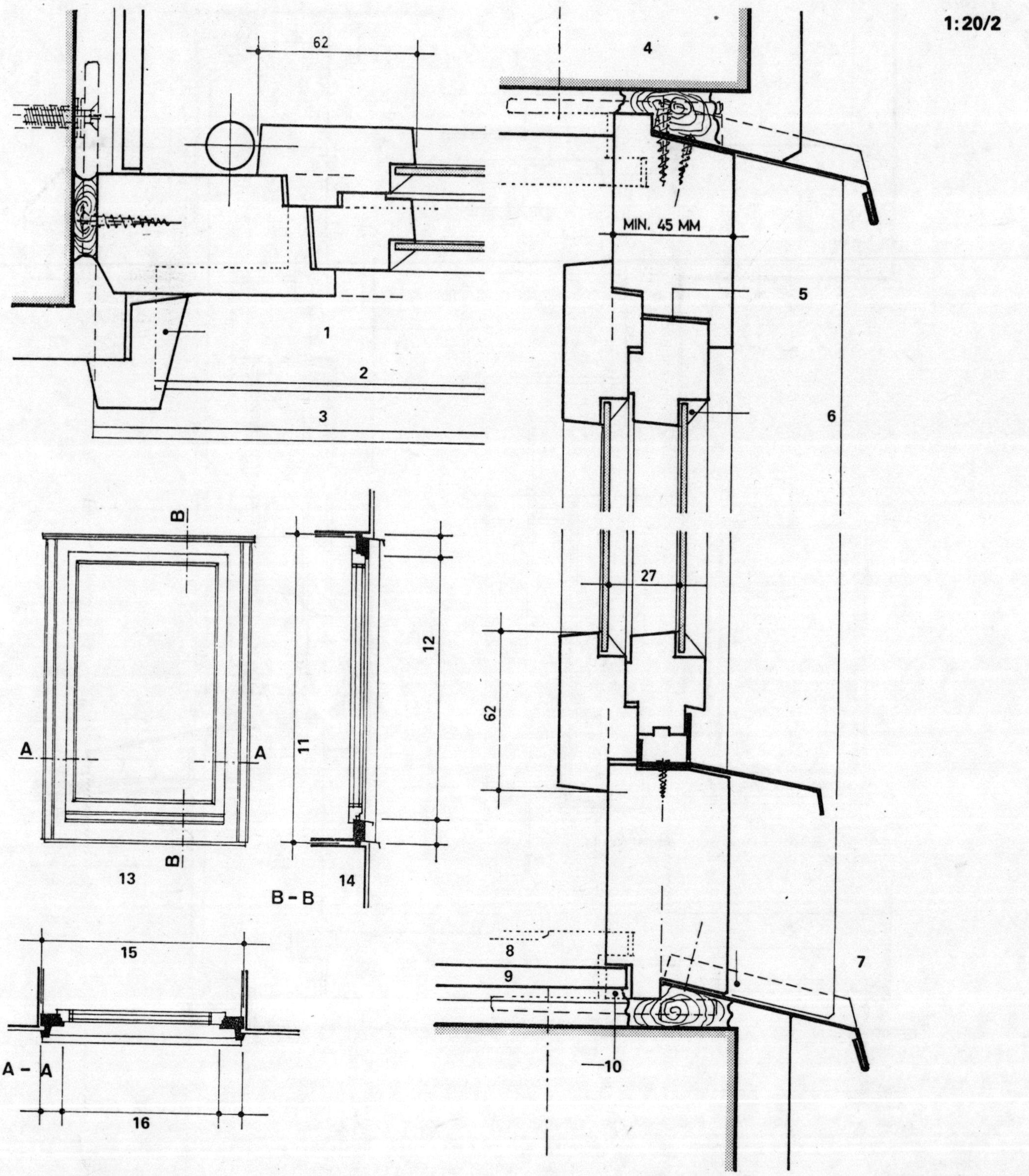

1 Moulding
2 Weather bar (strip)
3 Flashing
4 Lintel joint
5 Angle joint
6 Puttying rebate
7 Possible flange (at side)
8 Possible ledge
9 Slabs
10 Frame rebate for slab-joint
11 (Overall) external height of frame
12 Height of (window) light
13 Elevation from outside
14 Section
15 External width of frame
16 Width of (window) light

1:20/2

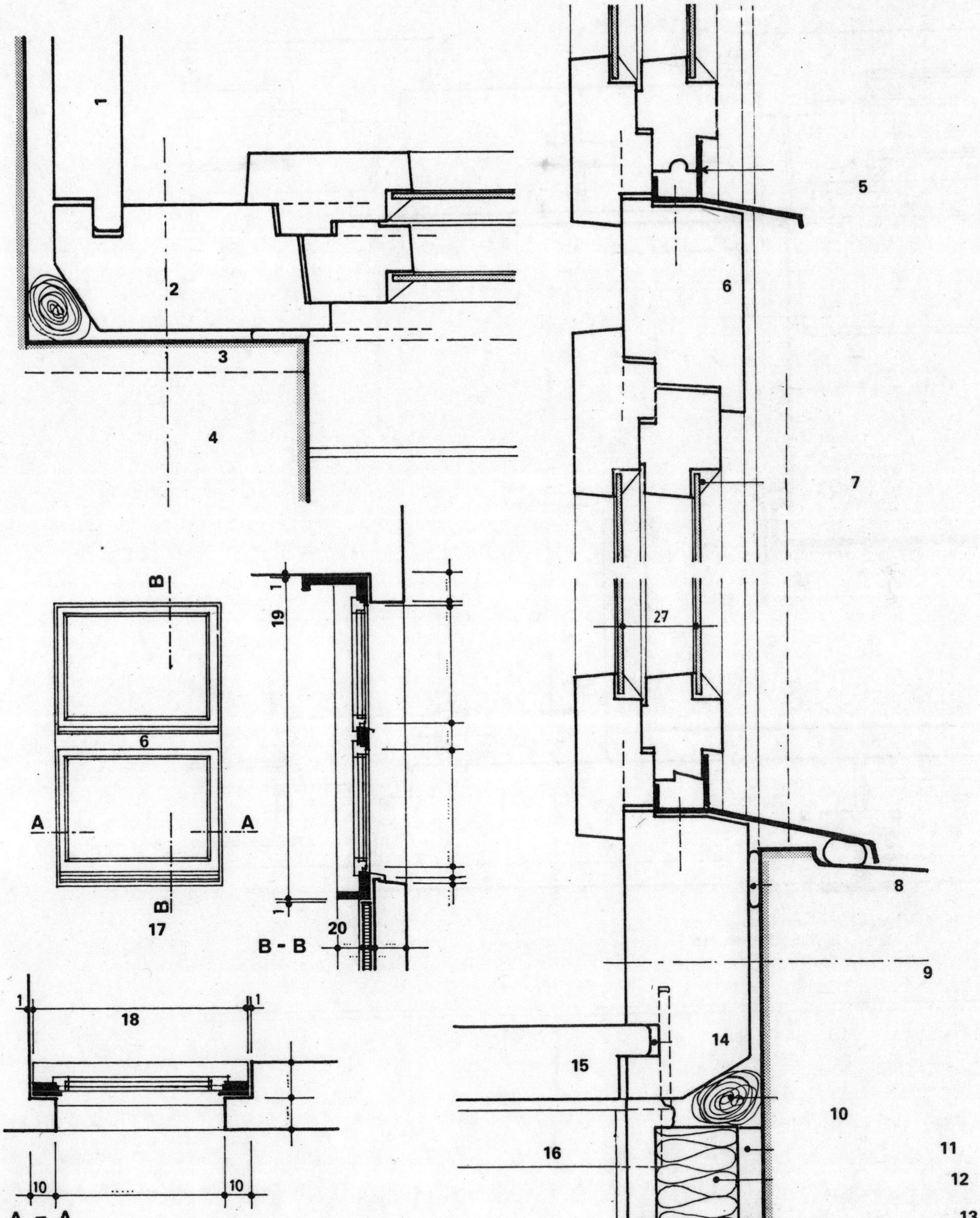

1 Window-lining
2 Window-frame (timber)
3 Infill plaster
4 Frame-lining (jambs)
5 Weather bar (strip)
6 Transom
7 Puttying rebate
8 Putty sealing
9 (Dry) Patent (masonry) screw
10 Insulating coil
11 Infill plaster
12 Insulating slab
13 Plasterwork (parapet)
14 Groove
15 Window-ledge
16 Patent or T-section steel-bracket
17 Elevation from outside
18 (Overall) external width of frame

Coupled Composite Windows

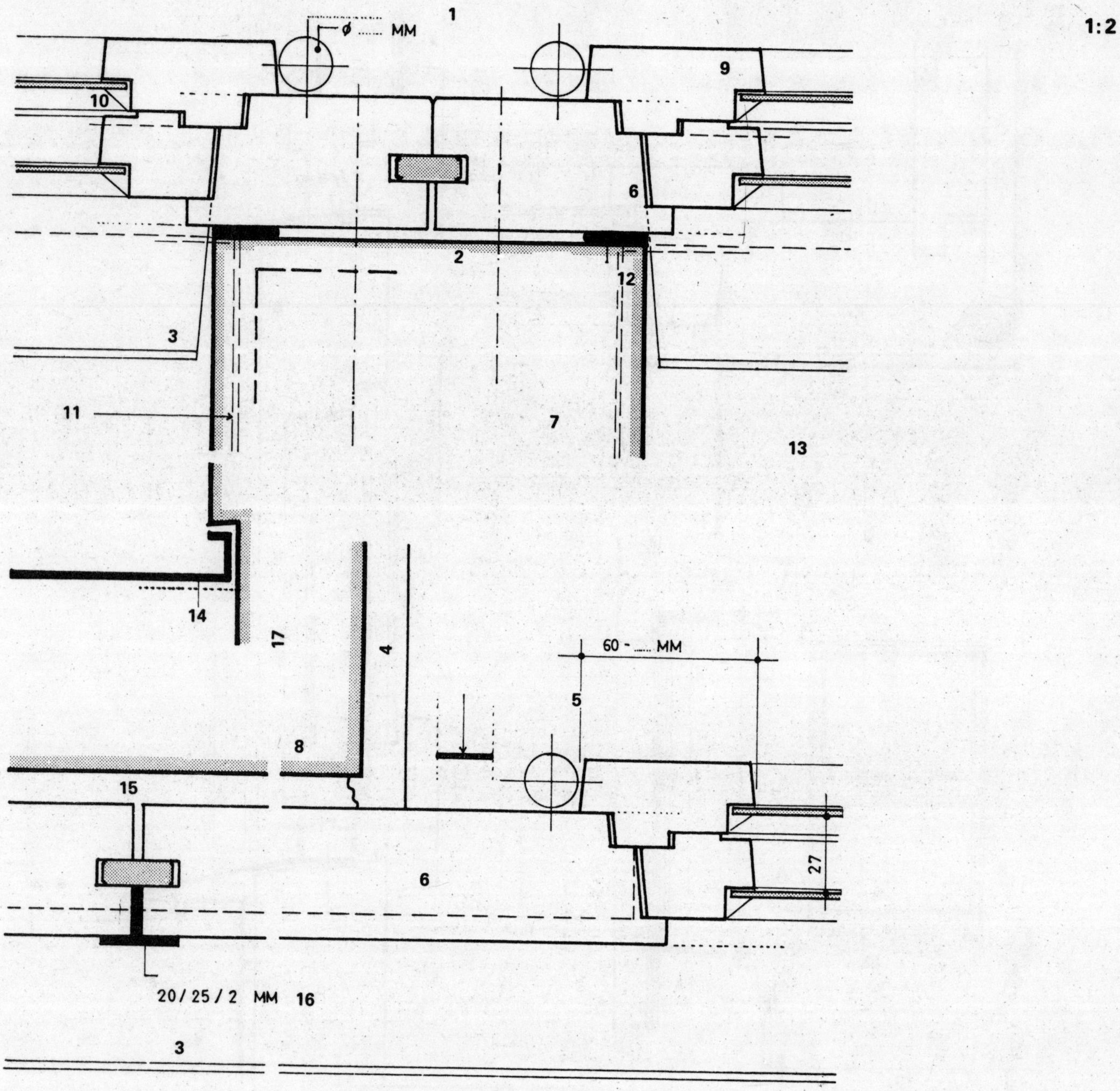

1 Hinge
2 Possible plaster infill
3 Weather bar
4 Wall plastering
5 Continuous hinge
6 Window- or door-frame (timber)
7 Pier- or external-wall-joint
8 Wall- or internal-pier-joint
9 Inside lining
10 Puttying rebate
11 Metal sill
12 Putty sealing
13 Metal window-sill or door-threshold
14 Section through metal window-sill
15 Distance piece
16 T-section (aluminium)
17 Pier joint

1:20/2

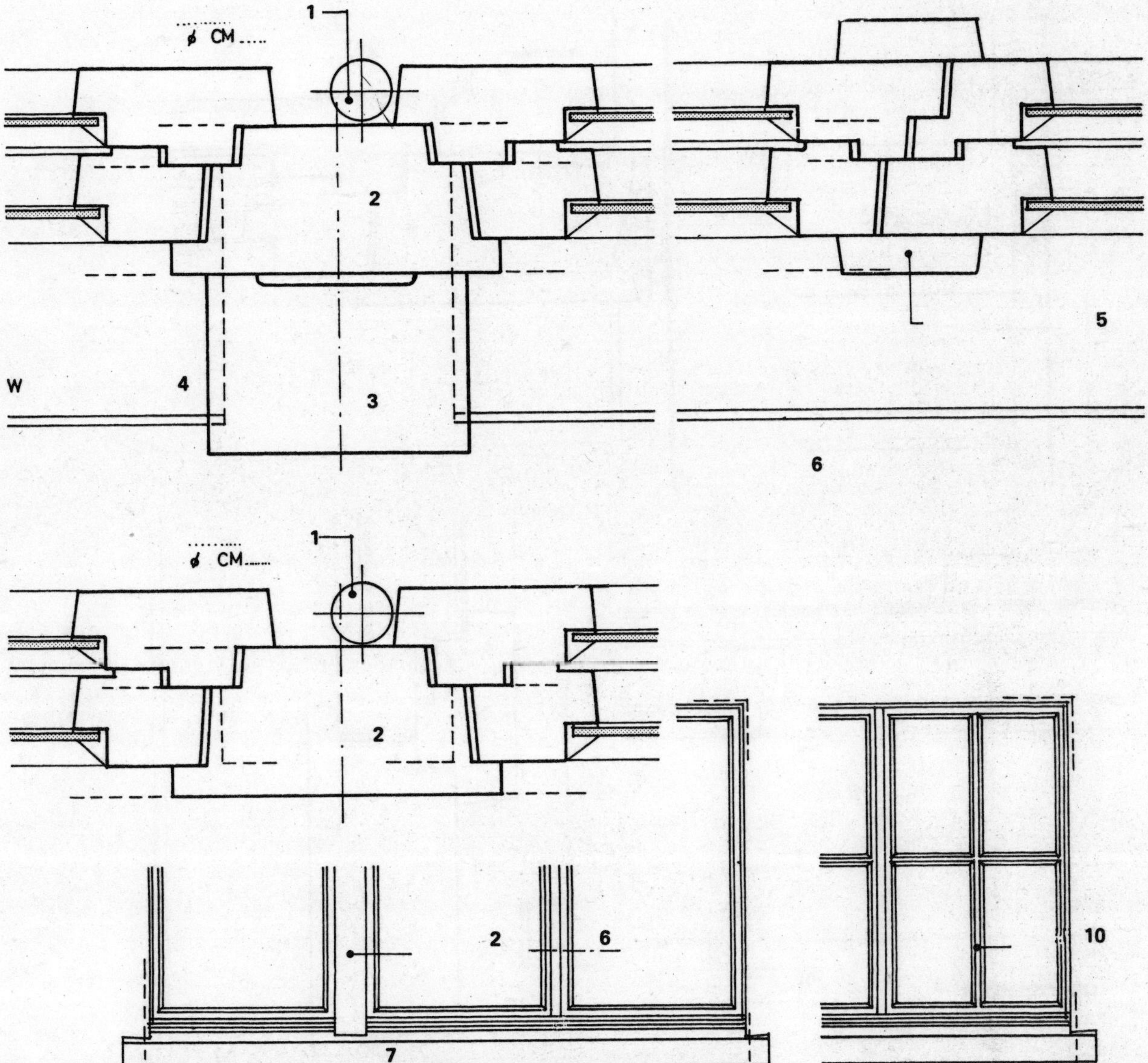

1 Hinge
2 Mullion
3 Mullion lining
4 Weather bar
5 Lining fillet
6 Middle section
7 Window-sill elevation
8 Window external elevation
9 Frame external measurement
10 Glazing-bar
11 Window with cross-bar

Composite Windows, fixing details

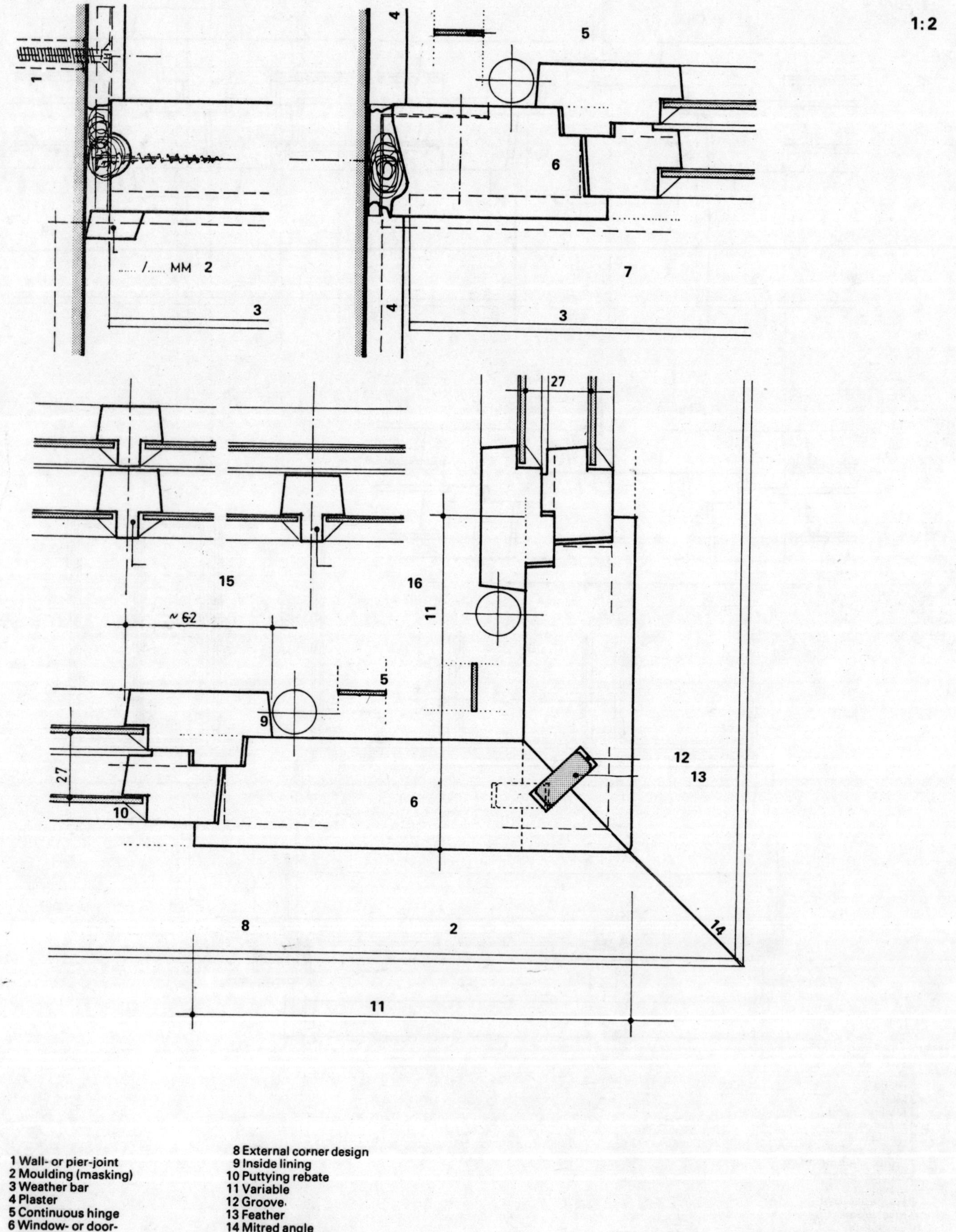

1 Wall- or pier-joint
2 Moulding (masking)
3 Weather bar
4 Plaster
5 Continuous hinge
6 Window- or door-frame (timber)
7 Jamb lining
8 External corner design
9 Inside lining
10 Puttying rebate
11 Variable
12 Groove
13 Feather
14 Mitred angle
15 Double glazing-bar
16 Single glazing-bar

1:20/2

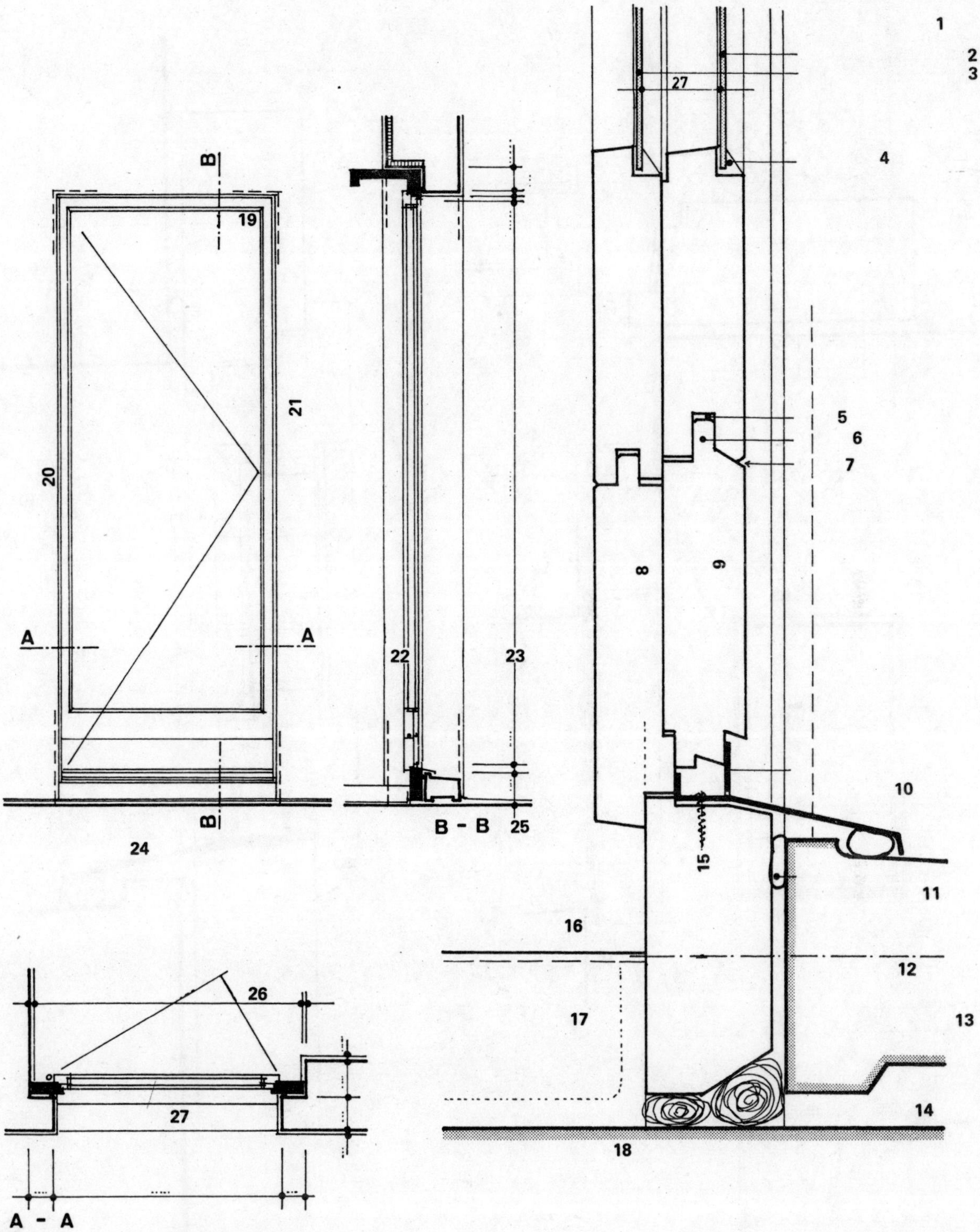

1 Glazing
2 Outside 6/4-glass
3 Inside 4/4-glass
4 Puttying rebate
5 Groove (recess)
6 Tenon
7 Chamfer
8 Inside lining
9 Outside lining
10 Weather bar
11 Putty joint or joint-covering fillet
12 Patent (masonry) screw
13 Door-sill (threshold)
14 Mortar bed
15 Door-frame timber
16 Flooring
17 Plaster (hard finish) floor
18 Floor joint
19 Double glazing
20 Hinge side
21 Closing side
22 Inside (room)
23 Outside
24 Elevation from outside
25 Section
26 Overall external measurement of frame
27 Threshold

Windows with toughened glass

1:20/2

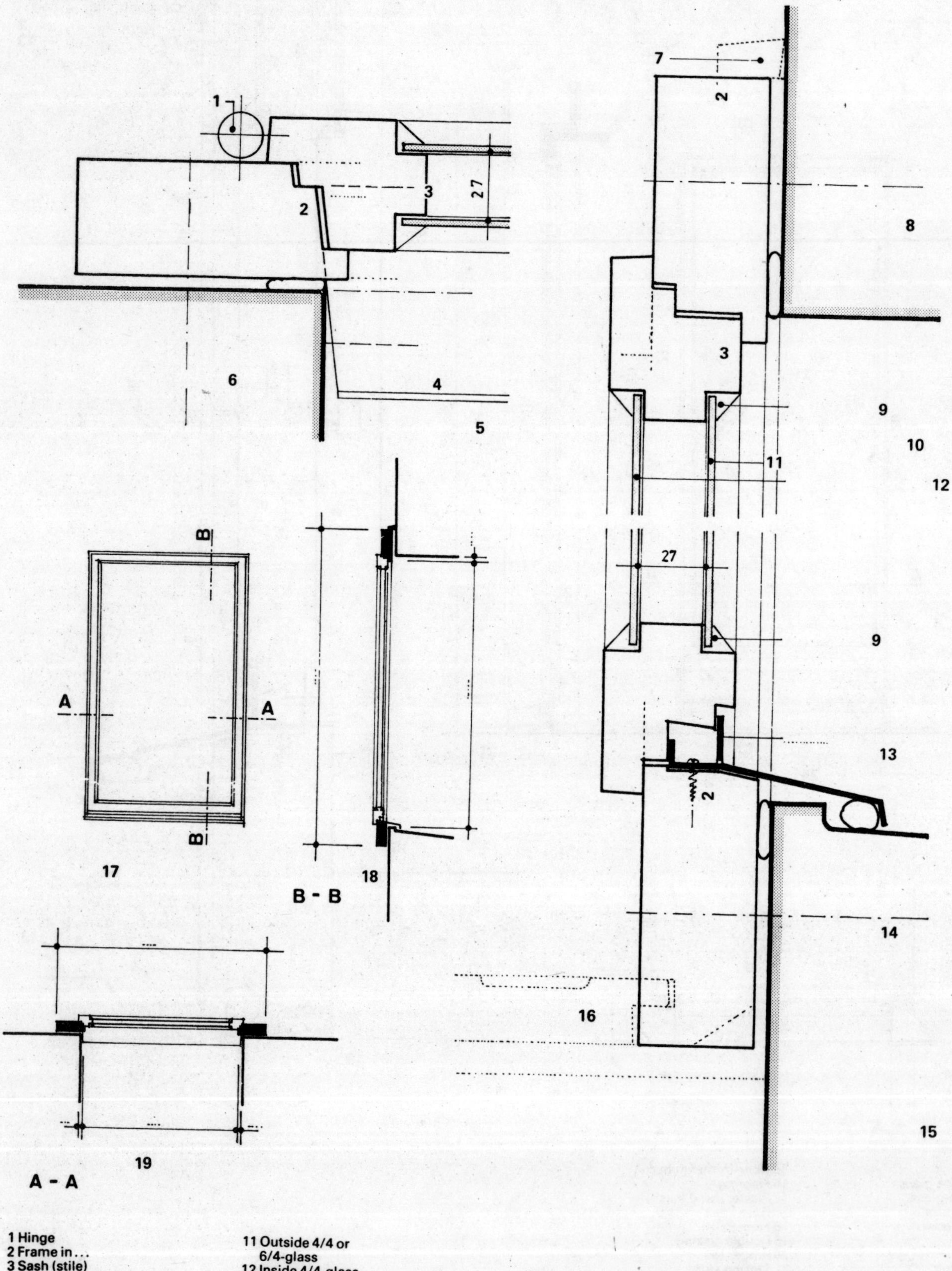

1 Hinge
2 Frame in . . .
3 Sash (stile)
4 Weather bar, from above
5 Sill, from above
6 Frame-lining (jamb)
7 Moulding
8 Lintel (head)
9 Puttying rebate
10 Glazing
11 Outside 4/4 or 6/4-glass
12 Inside 4/4-glass
13 Weather bar
14 Patent (masonry) screw
15 Window-breast (parapet)
16 Ledge
17 Elevation from outside
18 Section
19 Plan

1: 20/2

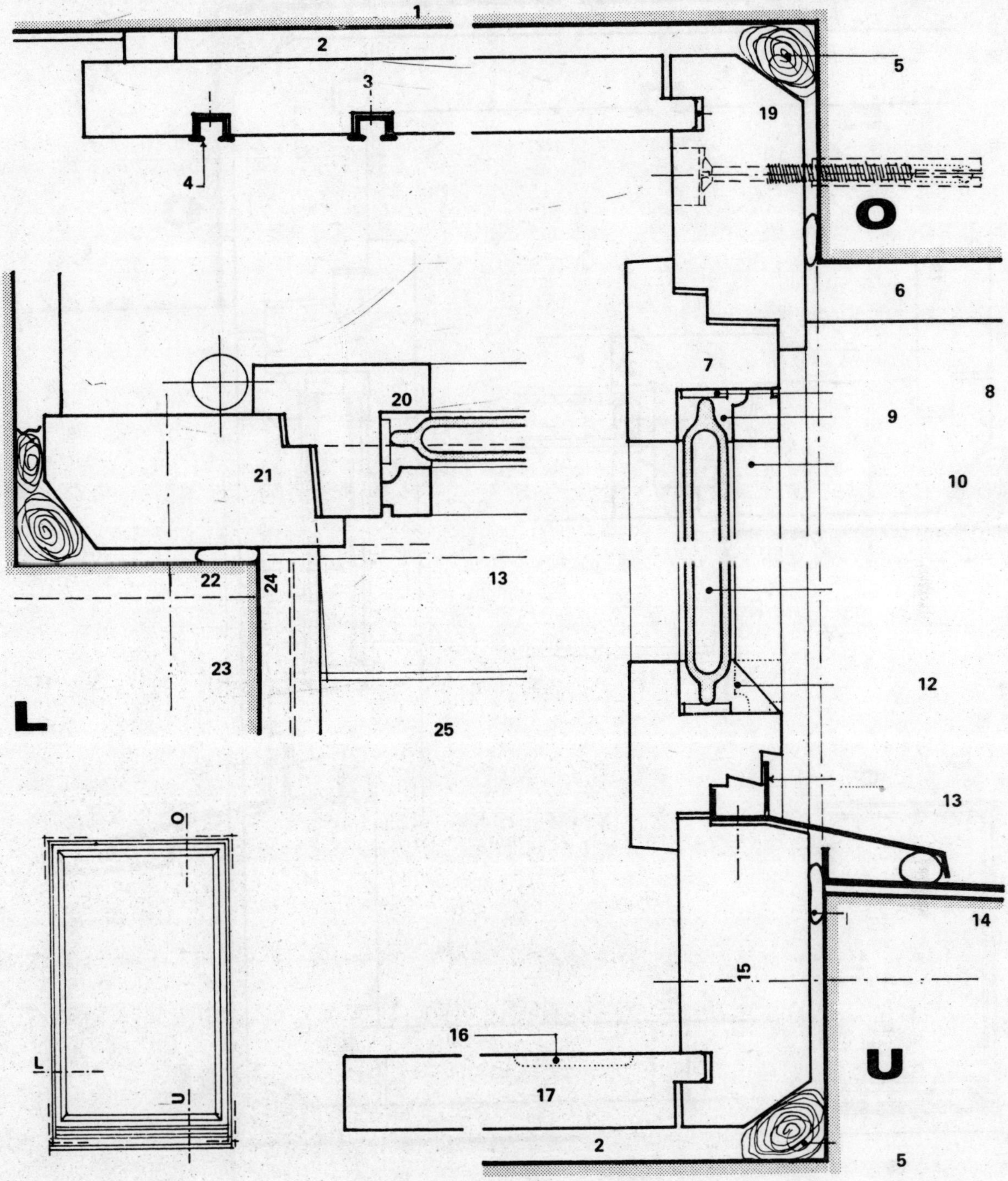

26

1 Ceiling fixing
2 Ceiling/floor joist
3 Curtain board
4 Curtain rail
5 Insulation
6 Plaster
7 Sash (timber)
8 Distance piece
9 Putty
10 Glazing fillet (wood)
11 Insulated glazing, rim heat-sealed, glass double throughout
12 Puttying rebate
13 Weather bar
14 Putty sealing
15 Window-frame (timber)
16 Condensation channel
17 Ledge
18 Window-breast
19 Groove (recess)
20 Timber sash
21 Window-frame in . . .
22 Possible plaster infill
23 Jamb lining
24 Jamb plastering
25 Metal sill, from above
26 Elevation of window from outside

Windows with rim-fitted insulated glazing

1:20/2

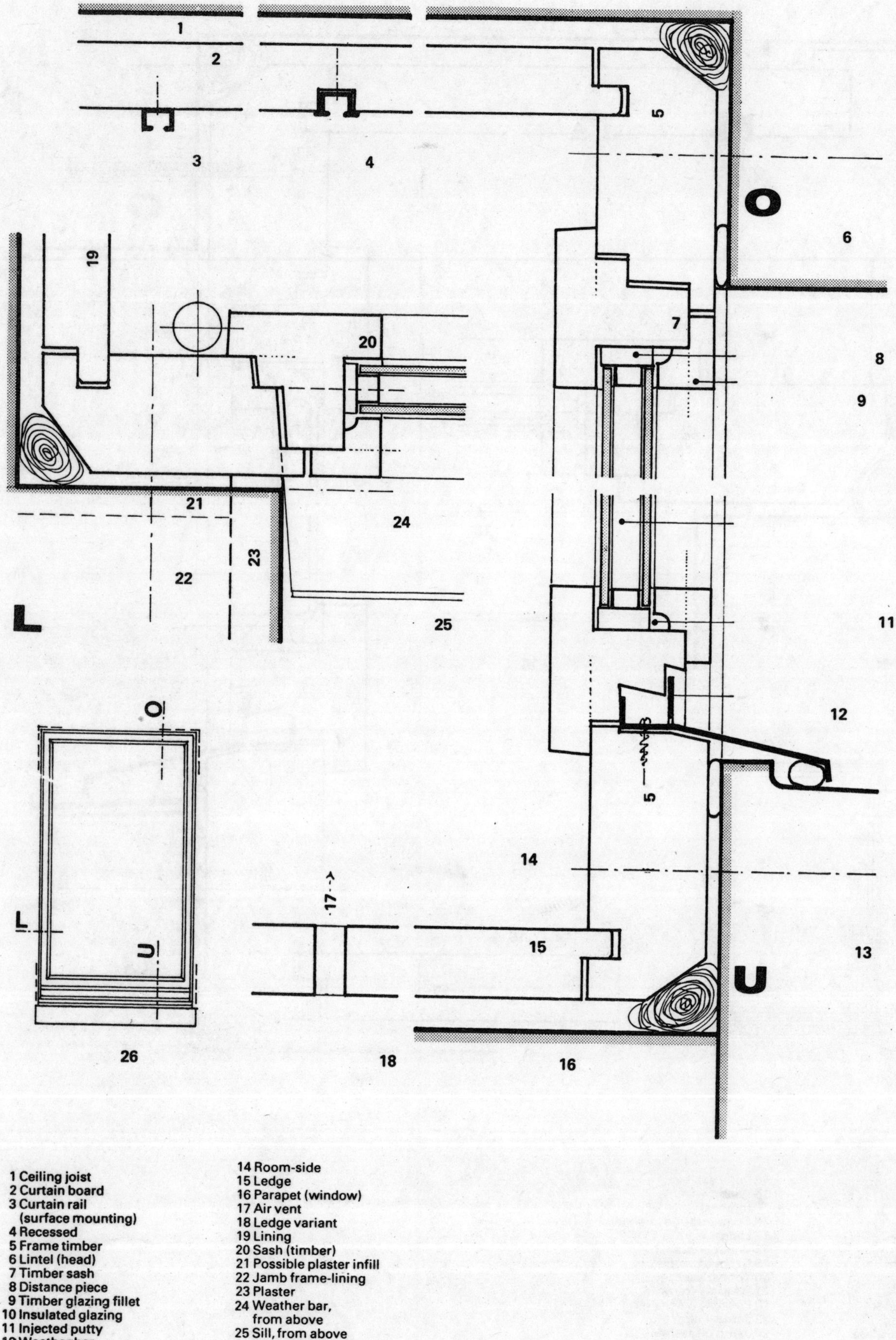

1 Ceiling joist
2 Curtain board
3 Curtain rail (surface mounting)
4 Recessed
5 Frame timber
6 Lintel (head)
7 Timber sash
8 Distance piece
9 Timber glazing fillet
10 Insulated glazing
11 Injected putty
12 Weather bar
13 Window-sill
14 Room-side
15 Ledge
16 Parapet (window)
17 Air vent
18 Ledge variant
19 Lining
20 Sash (timber)
21 Possible plaster infill
22 Jamb frame-lining
23 Plaster
24 Weather bar, from above
25 Sill, from above
26 Outside (window) elevation

1:10/2

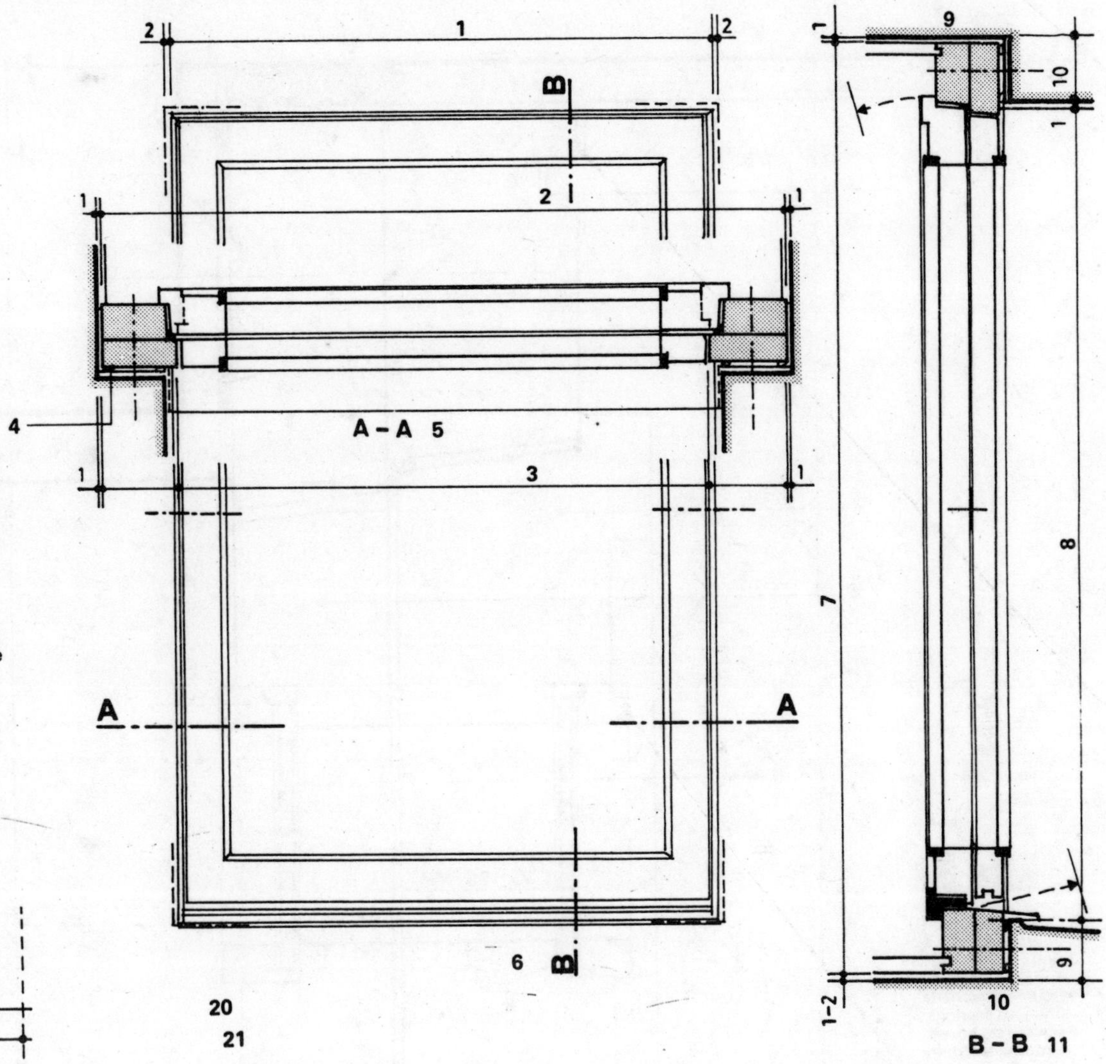

1 Clear width between plaster
2 Overall width of frame
3 Width of casement opening
4 Joint sealant or water stop
5 Plan A–A
6 External elevation of window
7 Overall height of frame
8 Clear height between plaster
9 Lintel
10 Parapet or apron wall
11 Section B–B
12 Glazing bead
13 Double casement (internal section)
14 Double casement (external section)
15 Double frame (internal frame)

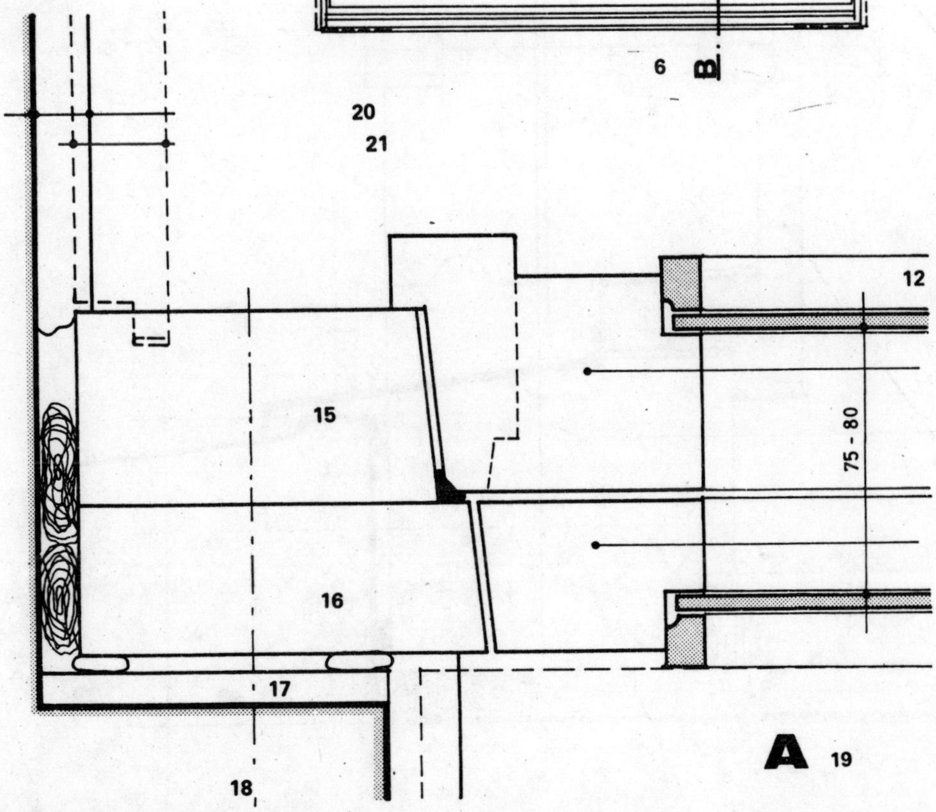

16 Double frame (external frame)
17 Levelling plaster
18 Frame reveal
19 Detail A
20 Plaster to reveal
21 Window lining

Pivot windows, section

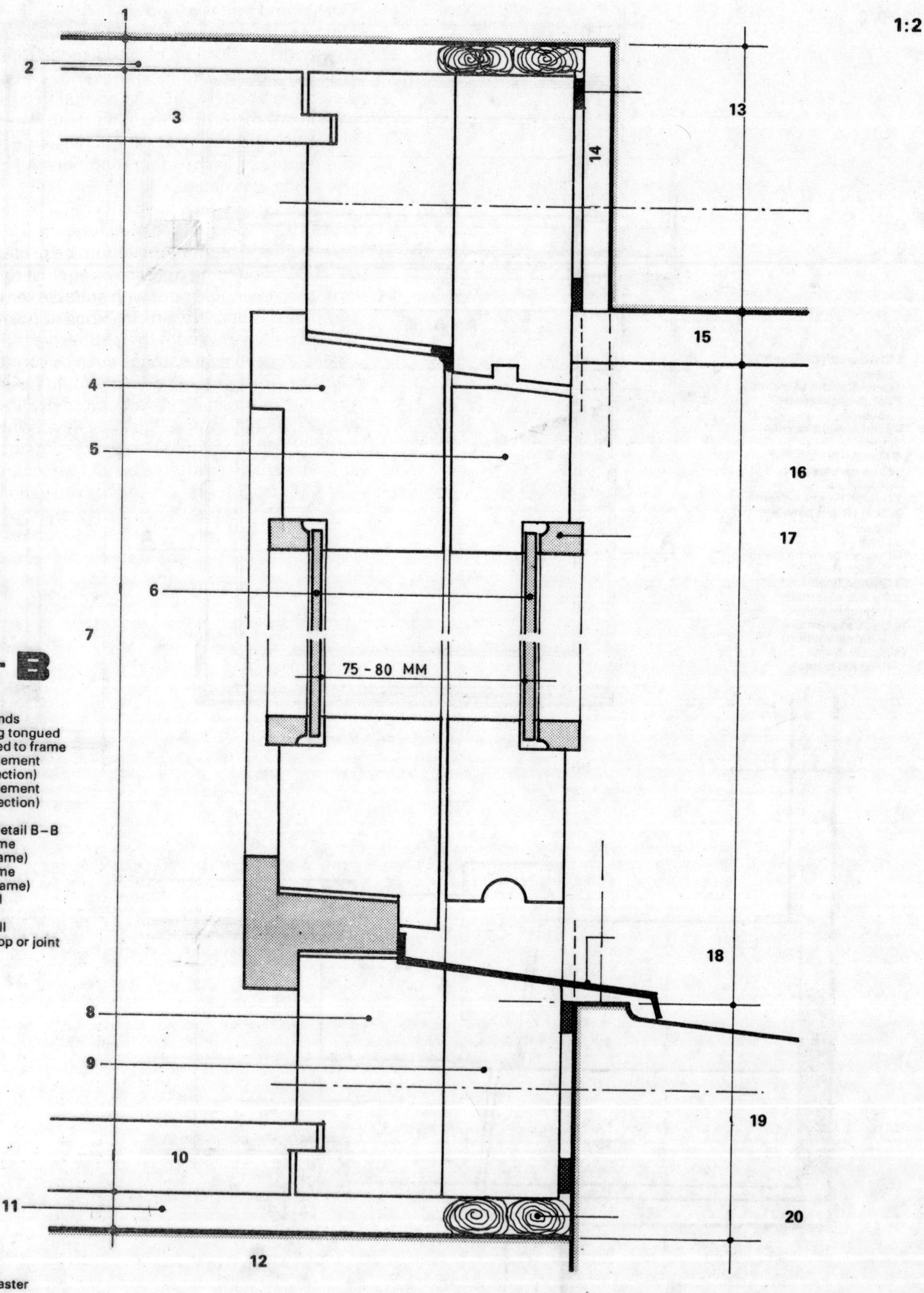

B - B

1 Lintel
2 Void/grounds
3 Soffit lining tongued and grooved to frame
4 Double casement (internal section)
5 Double casement (external section)
6 Glazing
7 Sectional detail B – B
8 Double frame (internal frame)
9 Double frame (external frame)
10 Window sill
11 Void
12 Parapet wall
13 Weather stop or joint sealant

14 Levelling plaster
15 Plaster
16 Window reveal
17 Glazing bead
18 Metal weathering strip
19 Window sill
20 Glass wool cord insert

Timber and metal windows

Lightweight metal (aluminium) casement sections are weatherproof and can be anodised to.make them virtually indestructible. Connections can be electrically welded, absolutely flat, with complete freedom from twisting or distortion, enabling clean and strong assembly. Glazing beads are of the same manufacture and treatment as the other members. All couplings should be concealed.

Insulation in window elements must be rot- and fire-proof and impervious to moisture.

All sections in aluminium should be protected for the duration of building operations against the action of lime, mortar and cement with suitable removable coatings or adhesive film. In exposed positions they should be covered with thick adhesive tape to protect against mechanical damage such as scratching, etc.

All fixing and coupling pieces should be connected in a unit construction system, so as to allow for silent expansion and contraction in all directions.

Where combined timber/metal casements are used, the metal sections should be situated on the weather side. Where all-metal casements are used, all sections should be insulated, to avoid the creation of a cold bridge and the formation of condensation. At closing edges sealing strips are essential. In the choice of window types, cost plays a considerable role.

Timber and metal windows with double glazing

1:20/2

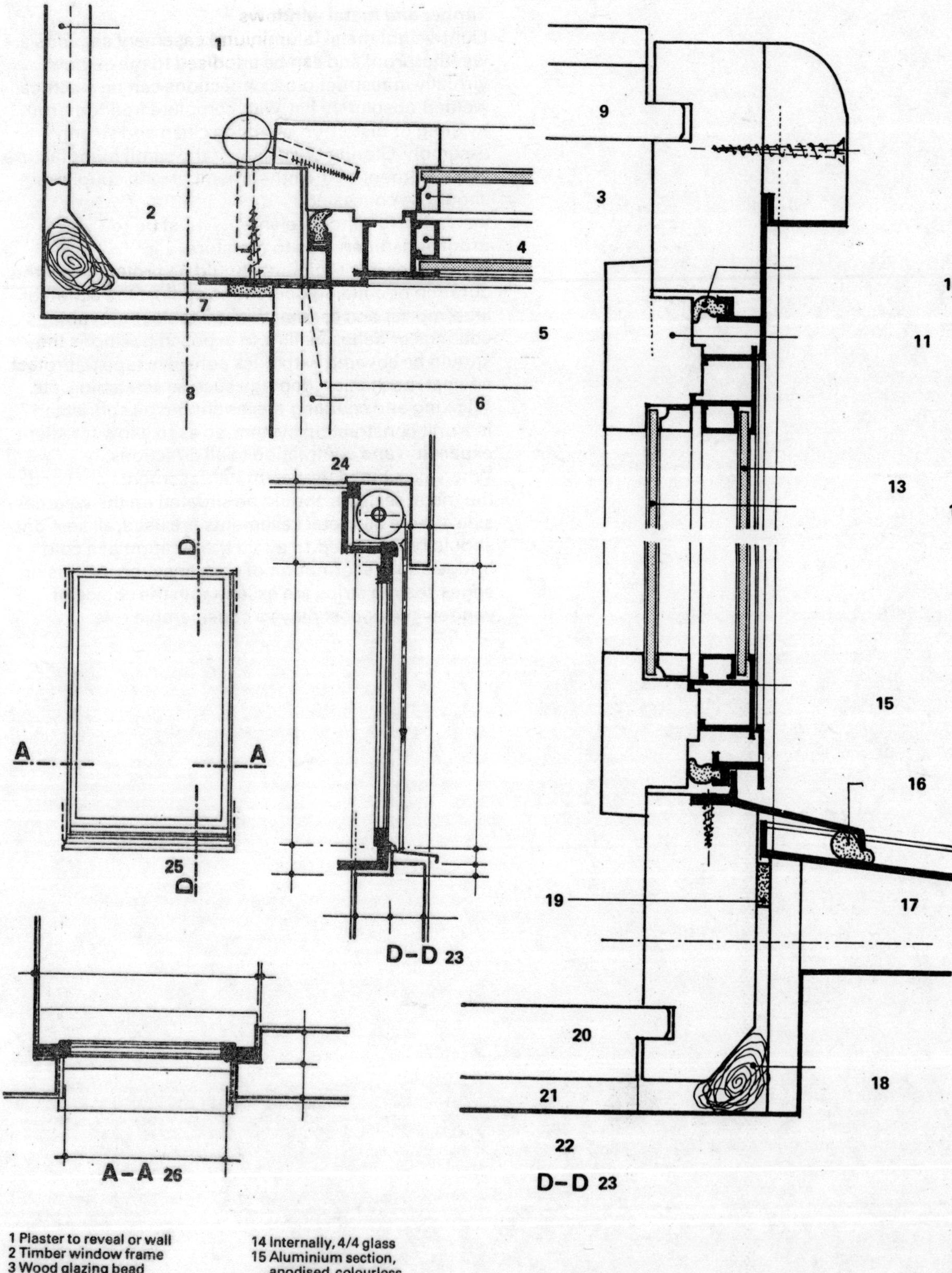

1 Plaster to reveal or wall
2 Timber window frame
3 Wood glazing bead
4 Metal glazing bead
5 Aluminium weather arm
6 Plaster to reveal
7 Levelling screed
8 Frame at reveal
9 Curtain board
10 Casement-frame sealing strip
11 Timber casement
12 Double glazing
13 Externally, 4/4 or 6/4 glass
14 Internally, 4/4 glass
15 Aluminium section, anodised, colourless
16 Sealing compound
17 Mortar bed
18 Glass wool cord
19 Jointing strip or mastic joint seal insert
20 Window sill
21 Grounds
22 Parapet or apron wall
23 Section D–D
24 Ceiling
25 External elevation
26 Plan A–A

Aluminium window construction system with patent double glazing (thermopane)

1:20/2

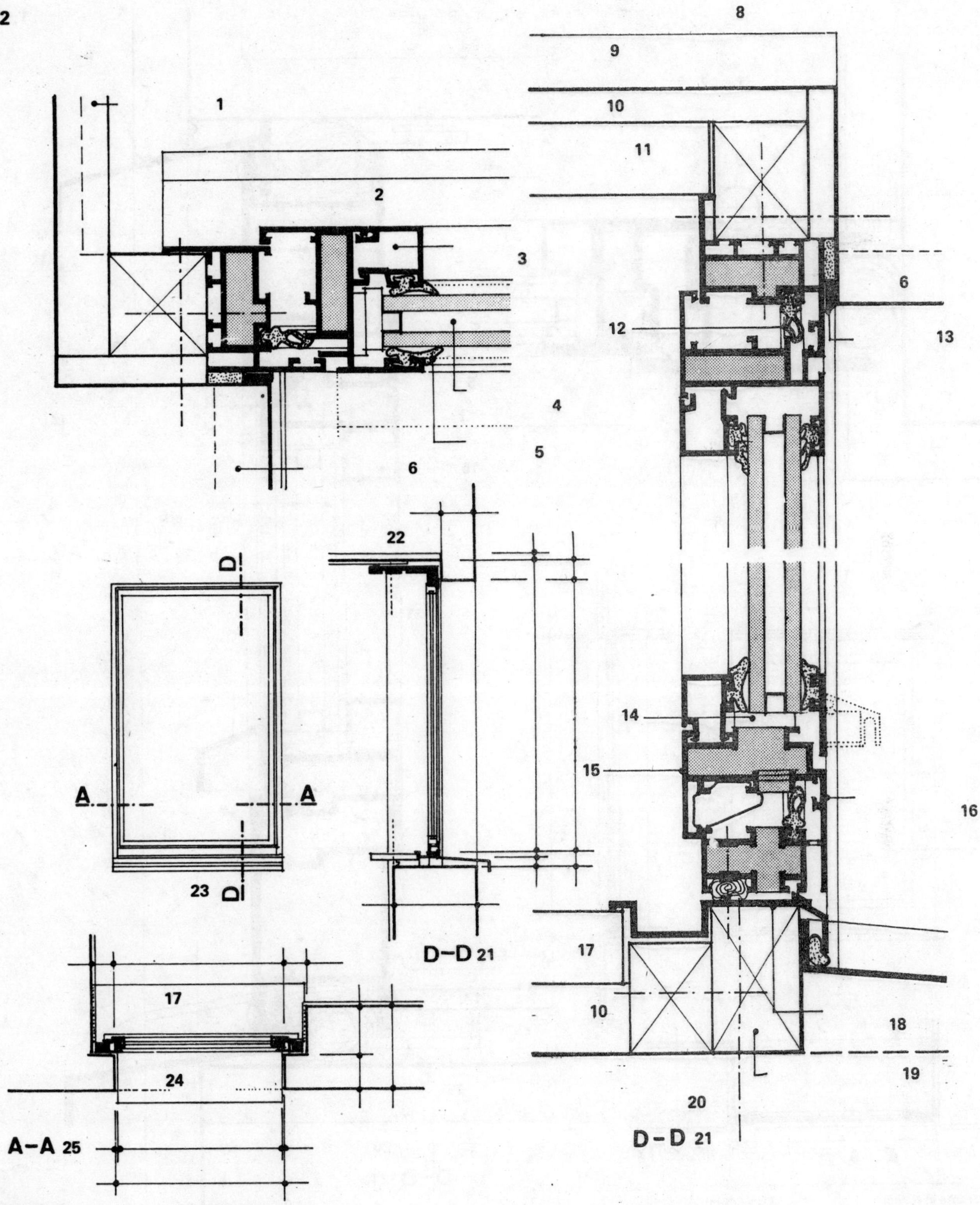

1 Wall plaster
2 Condensation channel
3 Glazing bead
4 Patent double glazing
5 Glazing strip
6 Plaster
7 Frame at reveal
8 Detail of abutment at ceiling
9 Insulation
10 Grounds
11 Soffit lining
12 Casement-frame sealing strip
13 Sealing compound
14 Distance piece
15 Casement section
16 Window frame section
17 Window sill
18 Sill connection piece
19 Fixing fillet
20 Parapet or apron wall
21 Section D–D
22 Ceiling
23 External elevation
24 Metal window sill
25 Plan A–A

Steel section windows with patent double glazing

1:20/2

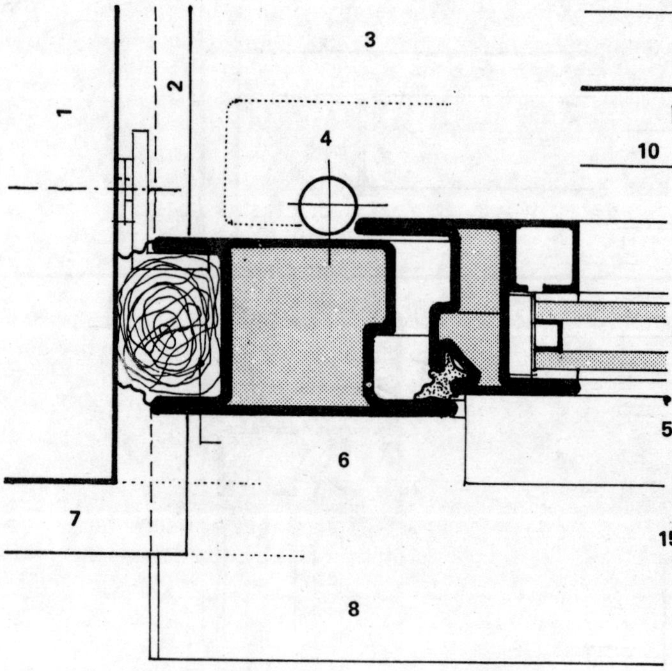

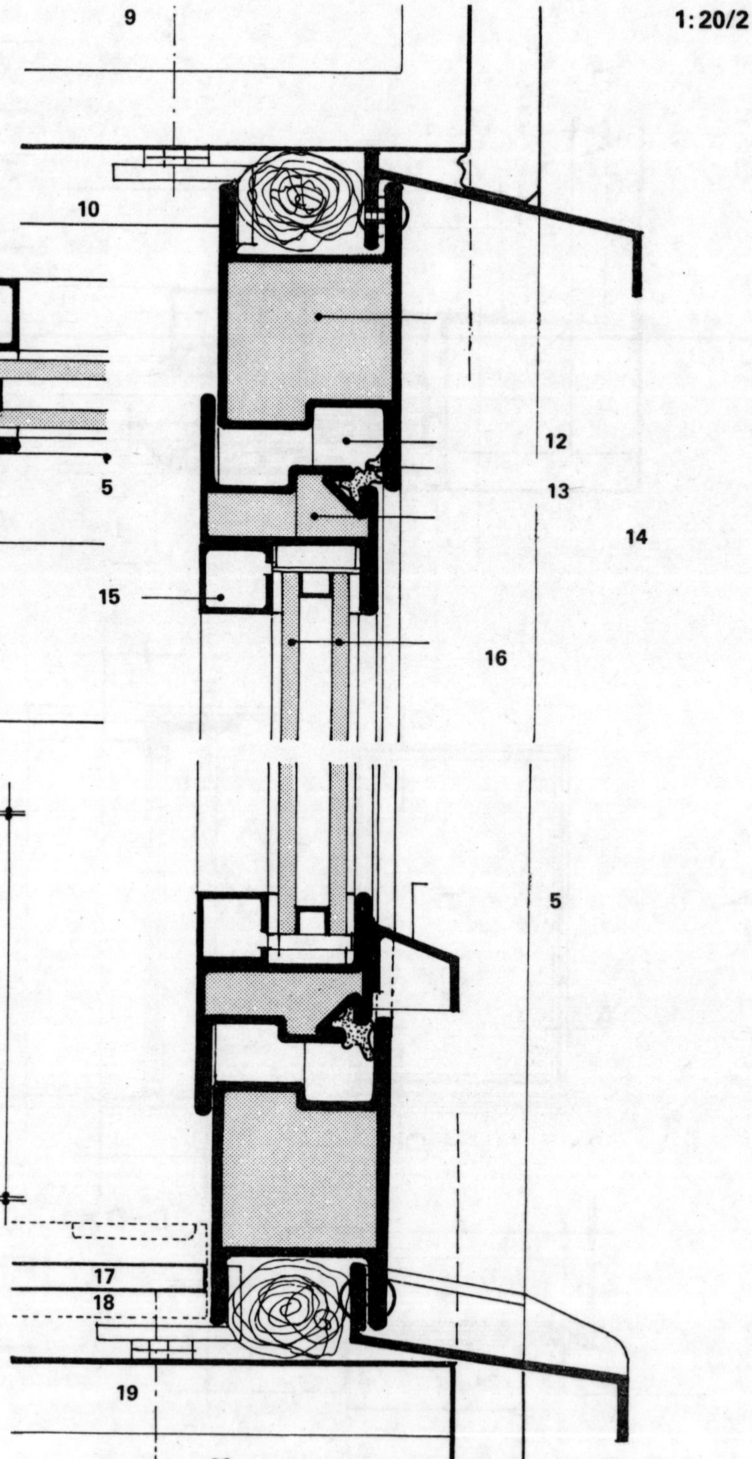

D–D 21

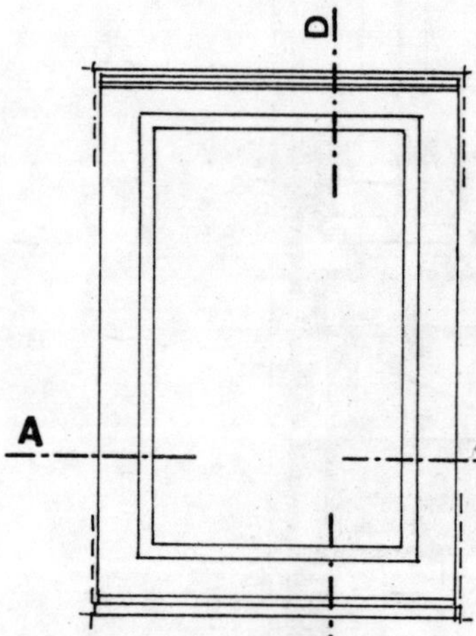

22

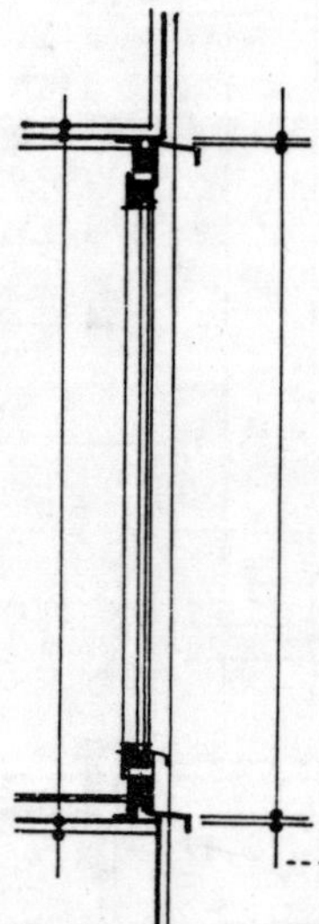

D- D 21

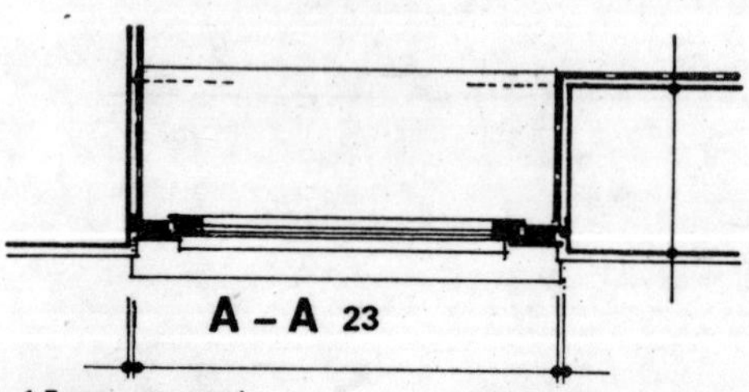

A – A 23

1 Frame at reveal
2 Wall plaster
3 Window sill on plan
4 Condensation groove
5 Metal weather arm
6 Glass wool cord insulation
7 Plaster
8 Weathered metal sill
9 Soffit
10 Ceiling plaster
11 Window frame section, insulated
12 Void
13 Casement-frame sealing strip
14 Casement section, insulated
15 Metal glazing bead
16 Patent double glazing
17 Tiles
18 Mortar
19 Insulation
20 Parapet or apron wall
21 Section D–D
22 External elevation of casement
23 Plan A–A

Plastic windows and doors
The production of good quality plastic windows and doors incorporating the latest technical information is guaranteed by constant supervision of the manufacturing process.
Corners of casements and frames are joined by butt welding. Where the windows are divided, glazing bars are inserted in the same way. Windows of large area should contain reinforcement pieces in the hollow section.
The material used must have the following properties: it should not distort; it must be inflammable, mechanically strong and colour-proof. It should also be proof against corrosion, rot and fluctuations in temperature, be insusceptible to ageing, and odourless. Furthermore, the plastic material must be insensitive to all common cleaning and washing agents such as caustic solutions and acids, as well as to paint or plaster droppings.
As in the case of metal windows, the glass panes are bedded in Neoprene glazing sections. The sectional form allows a conversion from simple to double glazing at any time.

Plastic windows, simple glazing or patent double glazing

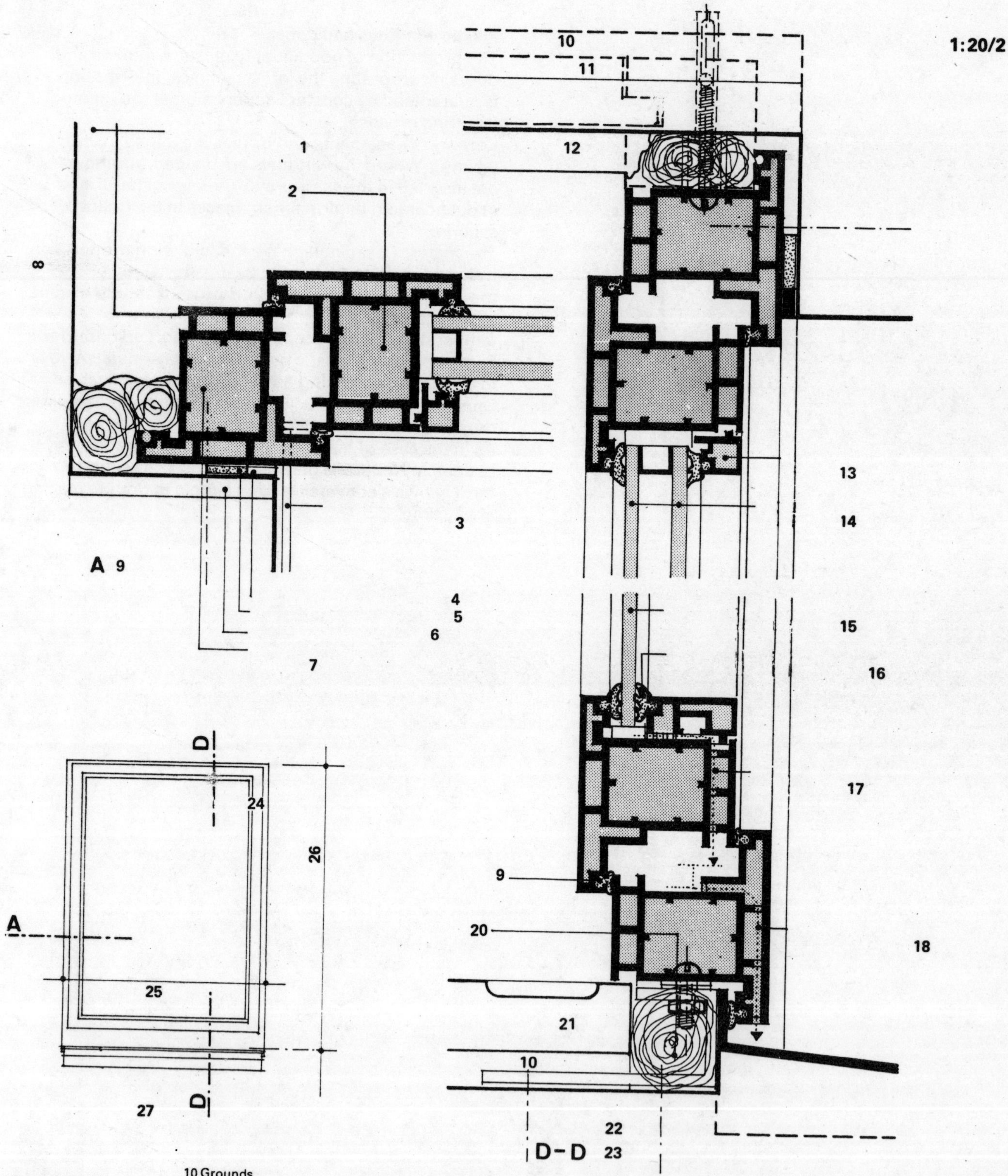

1 Plaster to wall or reveal 1,5 - 2 cm
2 Cellular casement section
3 Metal window sill, upstand
4 Elastic joint sealant
5 Foam rubber sealing strip
6 Levelling screed
7 Cellular window frame section
8 Frame at reveal
9 Detail A
10 Grounds
11 Curtain board
12 Ceiling plaster
13 Glazing bead
14 Patent double glazing
15 Alternative, single glazing
16 Glazing strip (e.g. Neoprene strip)
17 Drainage to glazing rebate
18 Drainage to frame rebate
19 Casement-frame sealant
20 Glass-wool cord insert
21 Window sill
22 Parapet or apron wall
23 Section D–D
24 Single or patent double glazing
25 Clear width beween plaster
26 Clear height between plaster
27 Window, external elevation

Roller Shutters, Venetian (slatted) Blinds, Folding Shutters

Wooden roll shutters: principally in fine-grained, knot-free, pine, for natural or painted finish.
Bars secured to flexible, but break-and-bend resistant, bands with special "hooks" at evenly spaced intervals.
Metal roll shutters: dovetailed hollow bars in aluminium, splinter-resistant, crack-and-scratch free, stove-enamelled. Bars joined solid to one another with chrome-nickel steel bands, even spacing of bars for good ventilation without possibility of looking through.
S-profile light-metal slats: riveted, slat to slat, with hinged bands.
Rolled and folded slats: slats in light metal, concave, flanged shape, stove-enamelled or given a scratch-and-crack resistant enamel coating.
Slats opened, closed and raised by guidebands.
Plastic rolling shutters: clipped together or chain-like type of assembly, in dyed-through, light-stable, finish.
High fire-resistance, dirt and insect resistant, non-reactive to cleaning agents. Bars adjustable for regulating light and air.
General: furling mechanism noiseless, wood rollers, metal from 2 m, rustless. Guide-bands built-in or exposed, depending upon type of slat or bar, storm-proof anchorage.
Folding (boxing) shutters: for painted finish generally pine, knot-free as far as possible. For natural finish pine or fir of first quality. Construction data: all joints with double tenons. Window/door shutters fixed with or without overlap fillets. Shutters in one or more parts.
Two angle-hinges to each leaf, perhaps with intermediate T-hinge straps or angle-bands. Shutter held in place by key-bolt system or automatic catch.

Roller Shutters, externally extensible

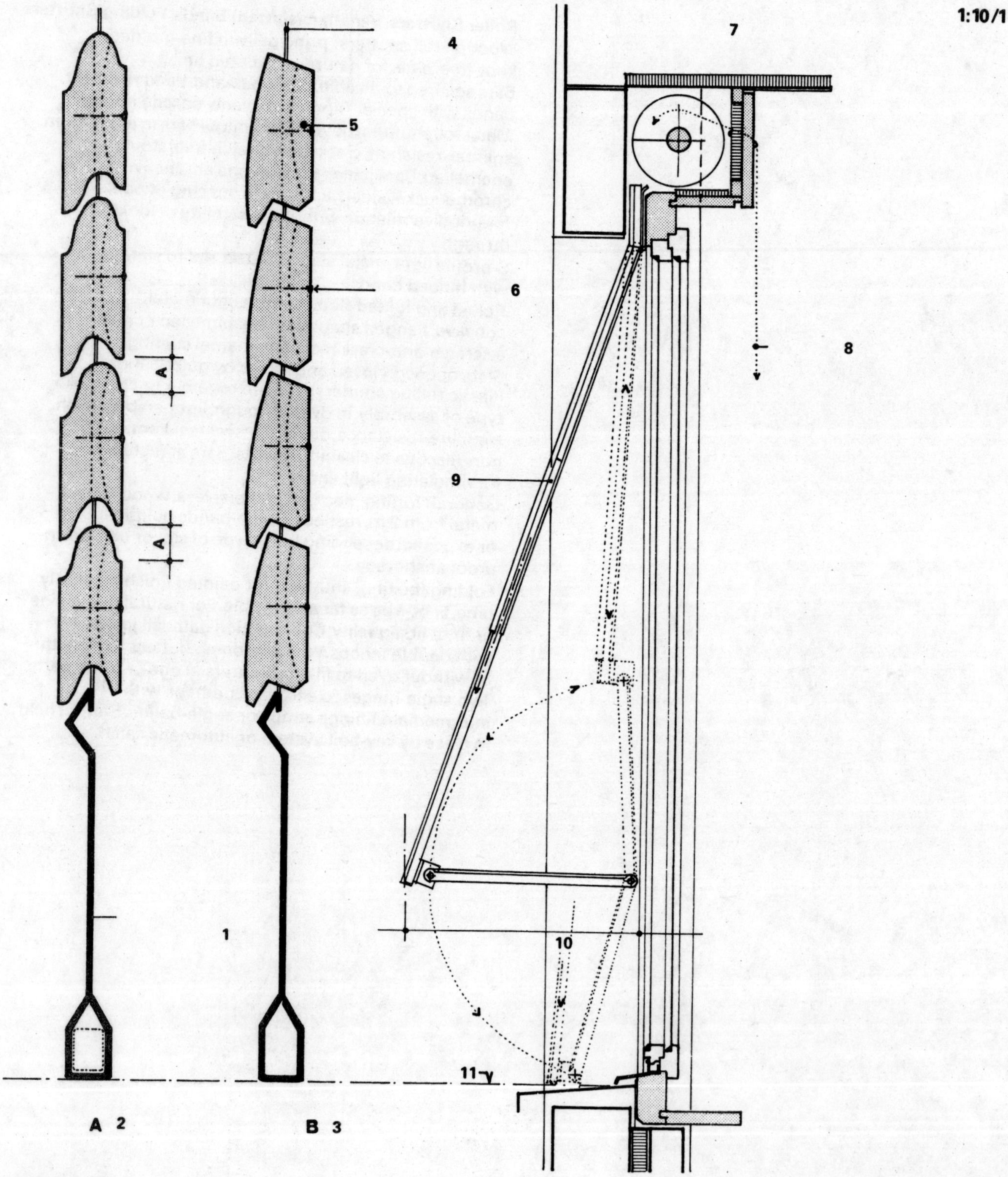

1 End piece (rail)
2 Variant A
3 Variant B
4 Hinge, corrosion-free
5 Pine lath
6 Special (slotted) grip
7 Concrete ceiling
8 Coil
9 Double guide-band
10 Maximum extension
11 Top edge of base element

1:10/1

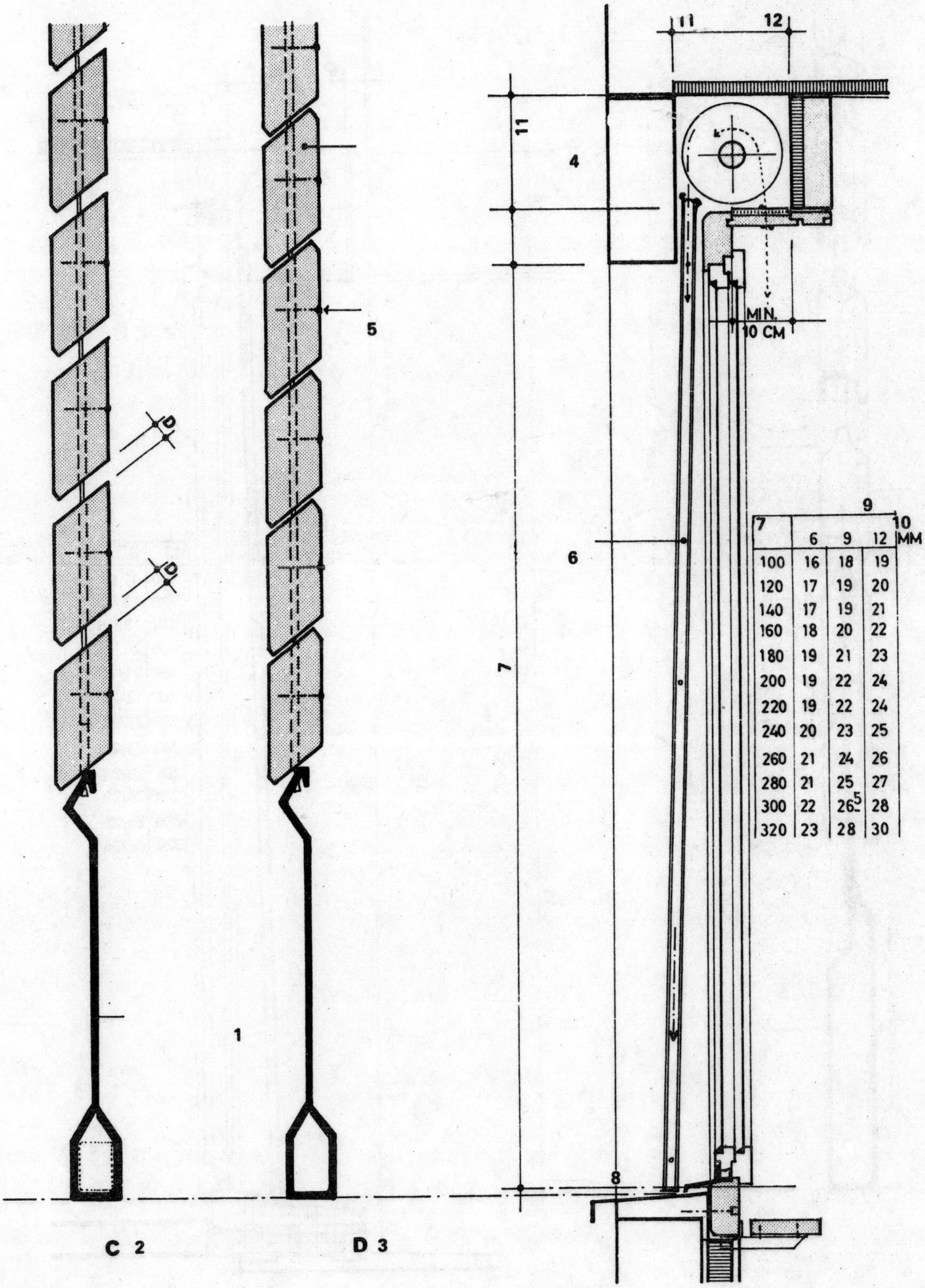

7	9			10
	6	9	12	MM
100	16	18	19	
120	17	19	20	
140	17	19	21	
160	18	20	22	
180	19	21	23	
200	19	22	24	
220	19	22	24	
240	20	23	25	
260	21	24	26	
280	21	25	27	
300	22	26.5	28	
320	23	28	30	

1 End piece (rail)
2 Variant C
3 Variant D
4 Pine prismal-lath
5 Special (slotted) grip
6 Guide-channel, fixed
7 Roll-shutter height = clear height of opening + 15 cm
8 Top edge of sill
9 Standard dimension
10 Lath thickness
11 Roll-shutter box
12 Internal measurement

Roller Shutters with aluminium hollow profiles

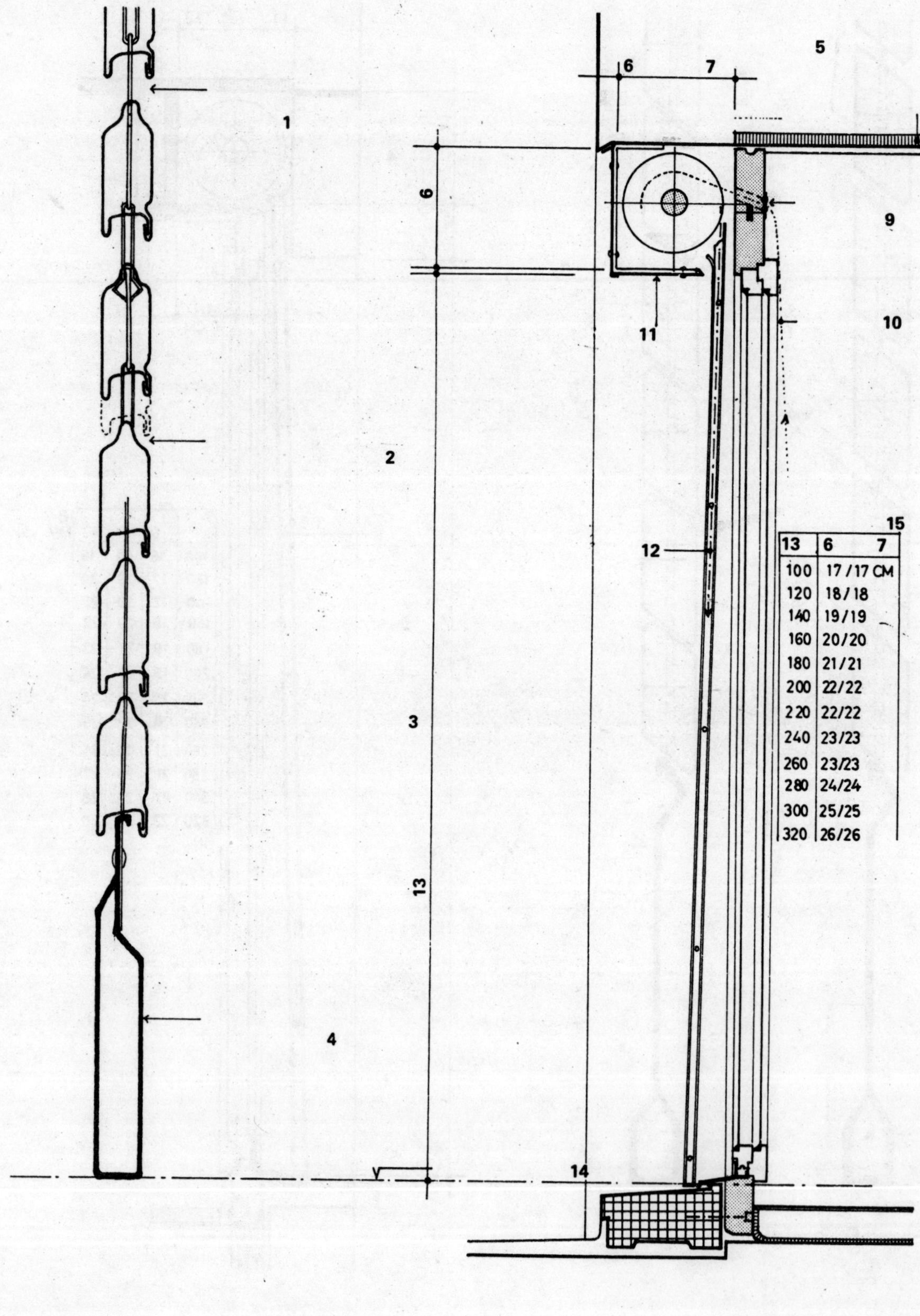

13	6	7
100	17/17 CM	
120	18/18	
140	19/19	
160	20/20	
180	21/21	
200	22/22	
220	22/22	
240	23/23	
260	23/23	
280	24/24	
300	25/25	
320	26/26	

1 Open, possibly with special chain profile
2 Closed, only every second lath
3 Fixed with hinge-joint
4 Hollow-profile end-piece
5 Ceiling joint
6 Roll-shutter box
7 Internal measurement
8 Insulation
9 Double coil-guide
10 Hoist webbing
11 Cover, removable
12 Guide-channel, fixed
13 Glazed-door, clear height of opening
14 Top edge of threshold

1:10/1

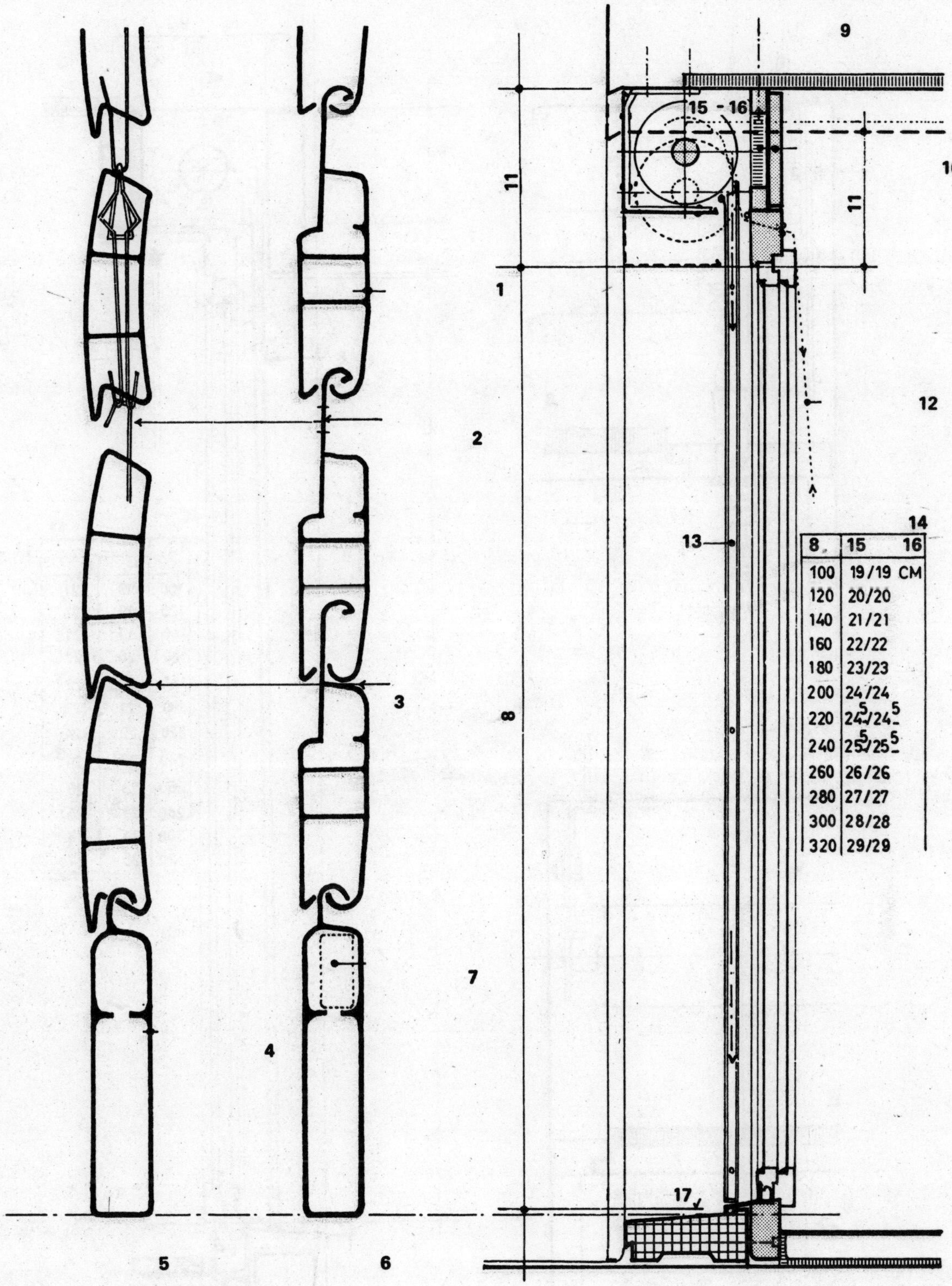

8	15	16
100	19/19 CM	
120	20/20	
140	21/21	
160	22/22	
180	23/23	
200	24/24	
220	$24^5/24^5$	
240	$25^5/25^5$	
260	26/26	
280	27/27	
300	28/28	
320	29/29	

1 PVC-lath
2 Open (light-air-aperture)
3 Closed
4 End-piece (rail) in . . .
5 Chain profile
6 Straight profile
7 Possible counter-balancing weight
8 Glazed-door, clear height of opening
9 Ceiling fixing
10 Cover (hood) removable
11 Height
12 Hoist webbing
13 Guide-channel, fixed
14 Standard measurement
15 Roll-shutter box
16 Internal dimension
17 Top-edge of threshold

Slatted Rolling Blinds, construction details

1:10/5

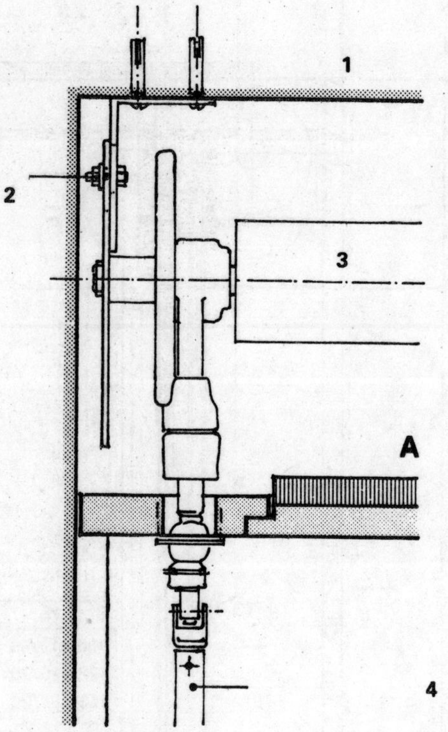

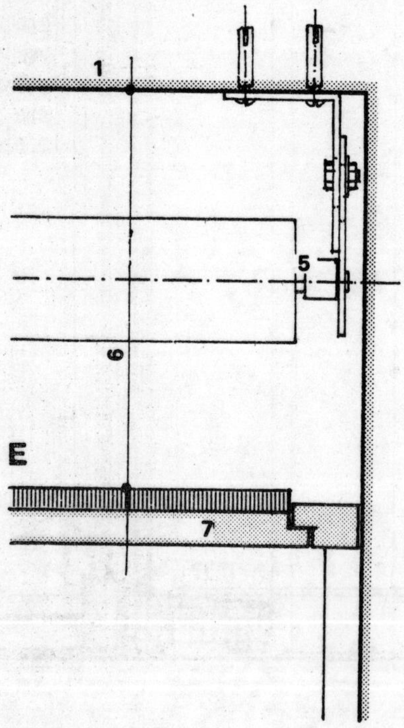

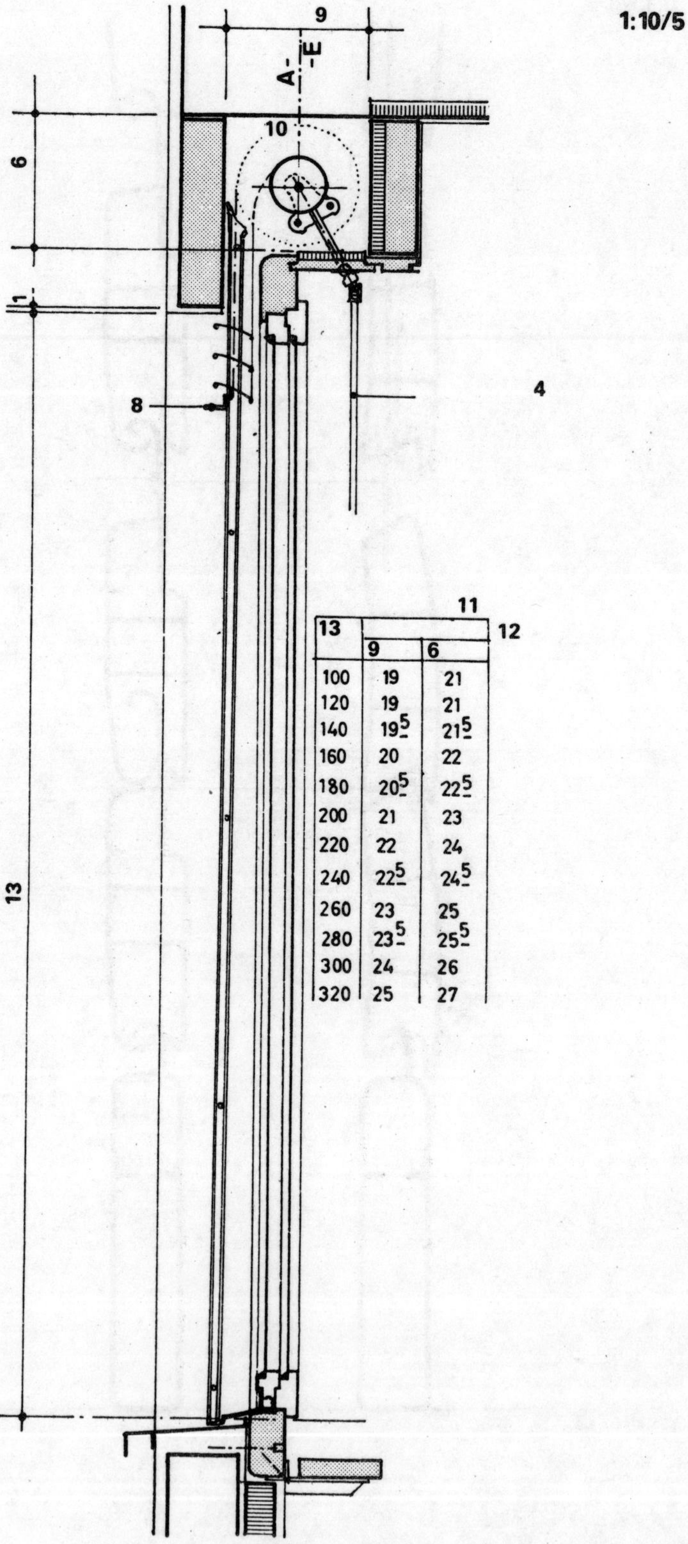

13	11 (12)	
	9	6
100	19	21
120	19	21
140	19^5	21^5
160	20	22
180	20^5	22^5
200	21	23
220	22	24
240	22^5	24^5
260	23	25
280	23^5	25^5
300	24	26
320	25	27

1 Lintel
2 Adjustable (slot)
3 Shutter roller
4 Crank (wind) rod
5 Shutter roller
6 Roll-shutter box, height
7 Roll-shutter cover
8 Stop-angle
9 Width
11 Standard measurement
12 Box size
13 Clear height of window

1:10/1

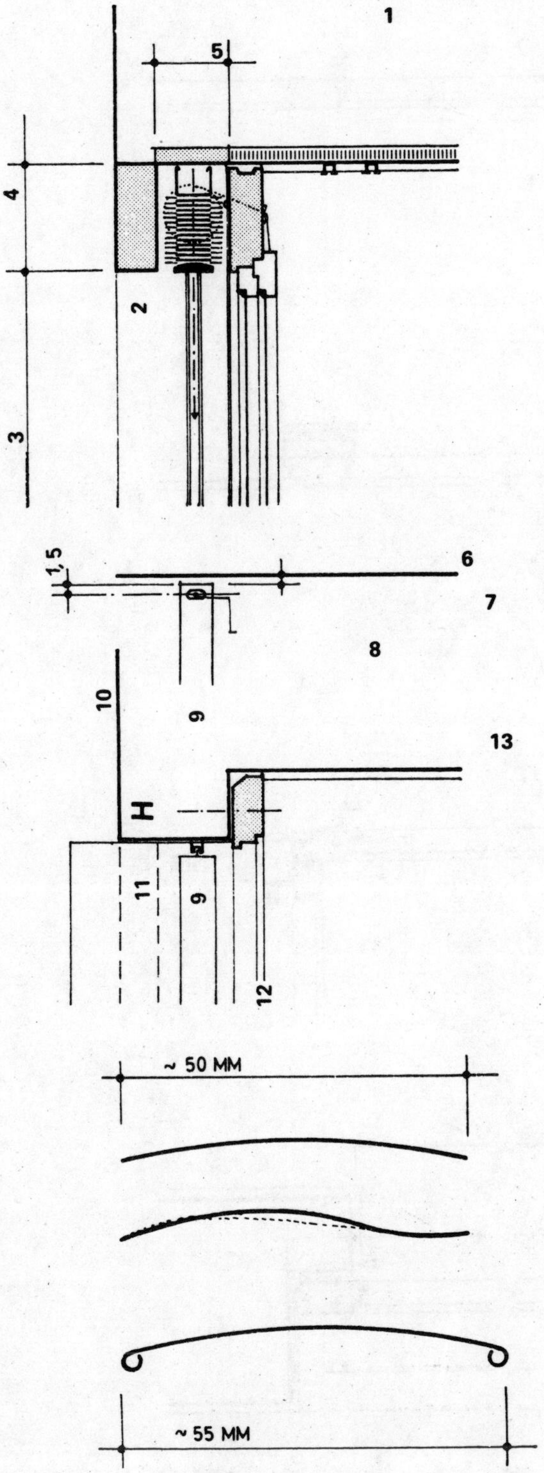

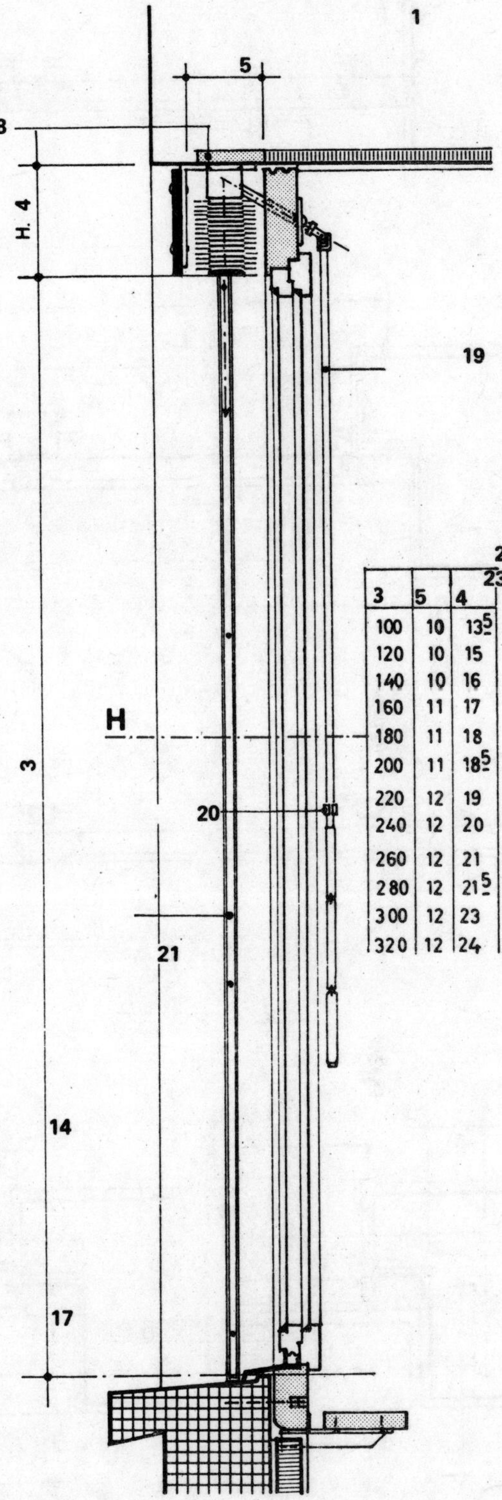

22, 23

3	5	4
100	10	13^{5}
120	10	15
140	10	16
160	11	17
180	11	18
200	11	18^{5}
220	12	19
240	12	20
260	12	21
280	12	21^{5}
300	12	23
320	12	24

1 Ceiling fixing
2 Jambs (external)
3 Clear height of window
4 Height
5 Width
6 Jamb- or wall-connection
7 Distance
8 Guide rod or cable
9 Slat
10 Sill or threshold, from above
11 Apron
12 Frame (timber)
13 Jamb- or wall-fixing detail
14 Slat types
15 C-type
16 S-type
17 Curled edges
18 Dowelled board
19 Crank(wind)-rod operation
20 Bracket
21 Guide-channel, fixed
22 Standard measurement
23 Lintel (head)

Roller Shutters, guide assembly

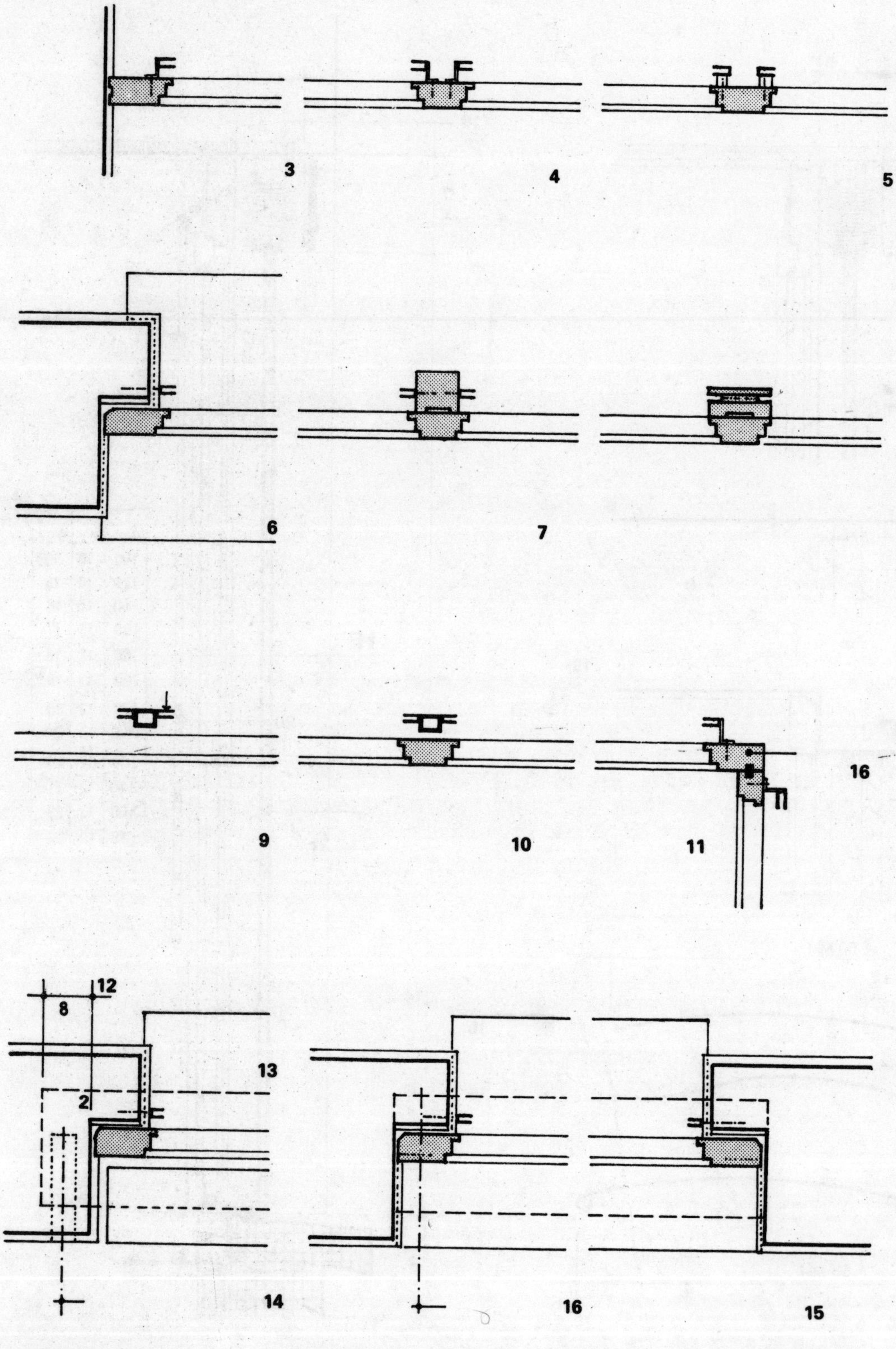

1 Guide-band (channel)
2 Roll-shutter box
3 With distance-angle
4 With distance-angle
5 With distance-angle
6 Guide-channel, surface-fixing, plaster mounting
7 Guide-channel surface-fixing, wood mounting
8 Guide-channel, concealed mounting
9 Guide-channel with 4-edge (sided) tube
10 Guide-channel with 4-sided tube
11 Corner (angle) mounting, variant
12 Min.
13 Window-sill or threshold
14 Operating spindle
15 Reverse

1:10

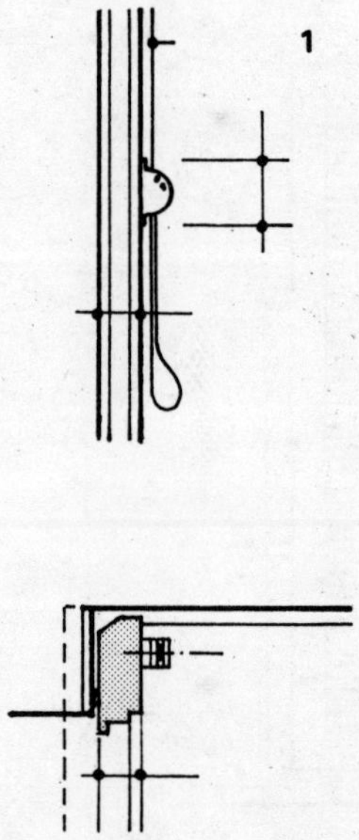

3

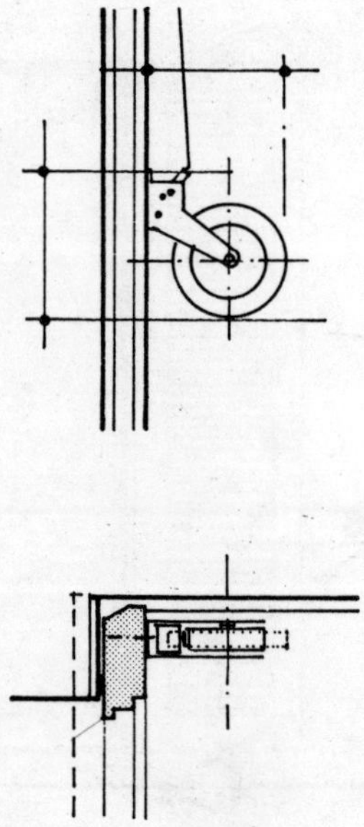

4

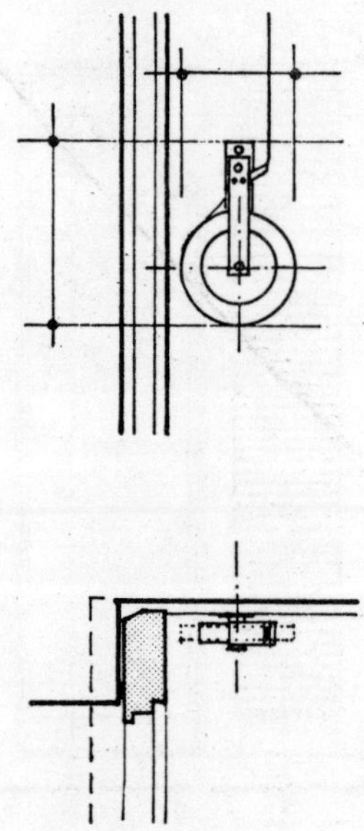

5

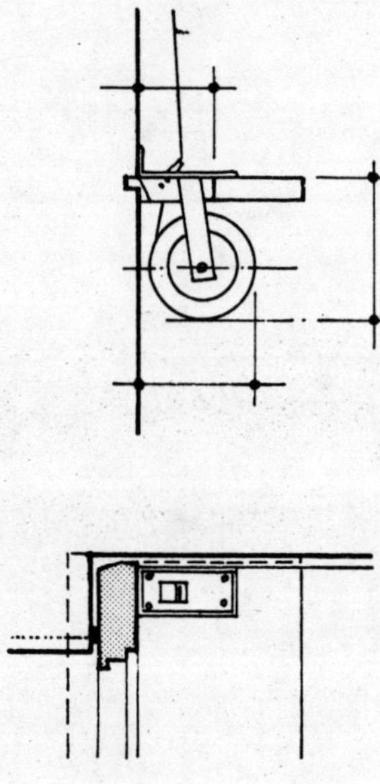

6

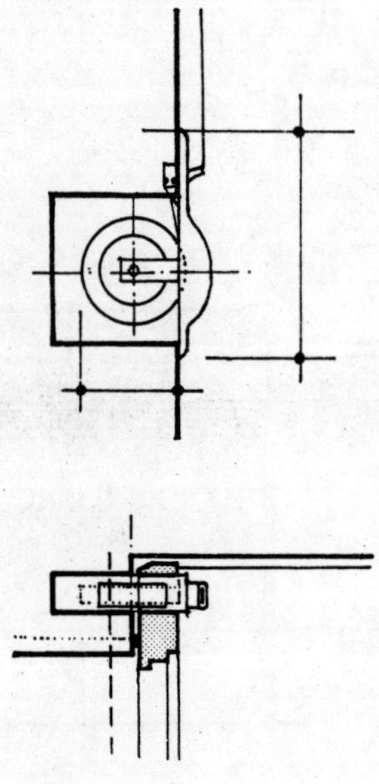

7

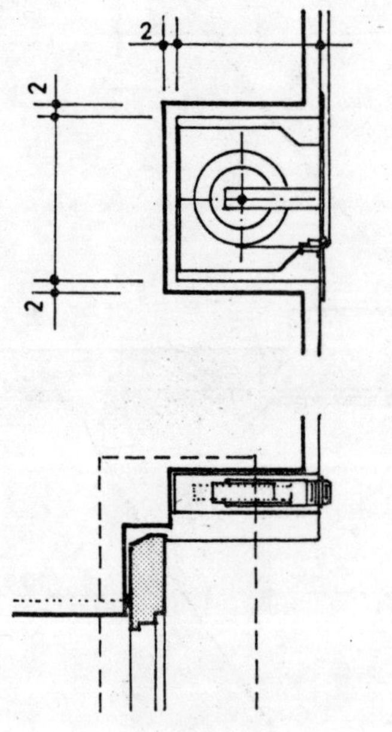

8

1 Hoist mechanism (webbing)
2 Frame (timber)
3 Hoist (webbing) clamp, mounted on frame
4 Bracket-coil, mounted on frame (possibly with pivot)
5 Hoist-winder mounted on jamb or wall
6 Hoist-winder under ledge
7 Hoist-winder 3/4 countersunk
8 Hoist-winder with wall-box, sunk mounting

Glazed-door Folding Shutters, types of opening

1:25

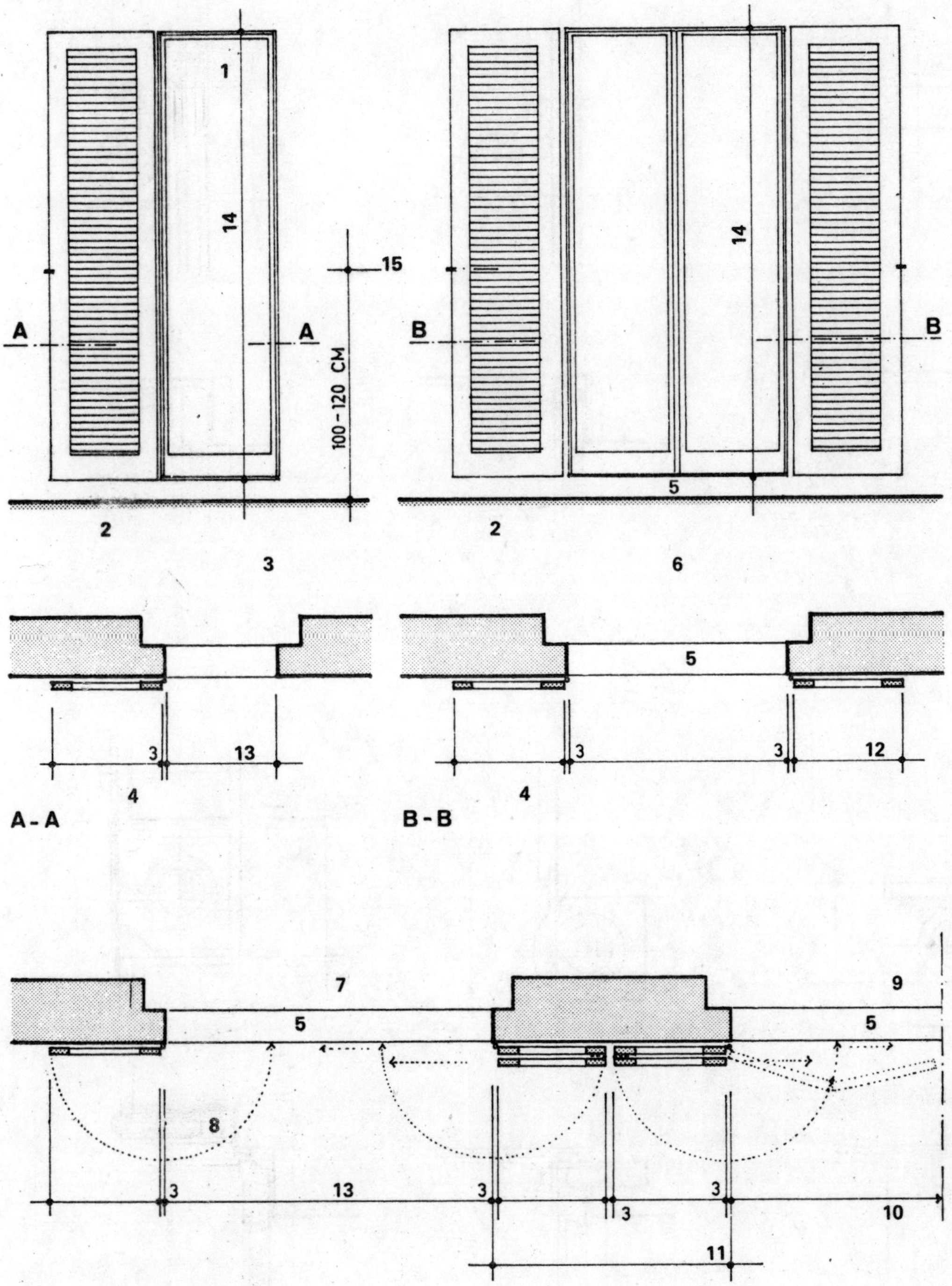

1 Balcony window (French window)
2 Elevation
3 Single-leaf shutter
4 Plan
5 Threshold
6 Two-leaf shutters
7 Three-leaf shutters
8 Plan variant
9 Four-leaf shutters
10 Door-axis distance
11 Minimum wall-width
12 Shutter measurement
13 Door measurement
14 Door-height – 1 cm = shutter measurement
15 Back-stay

1:25

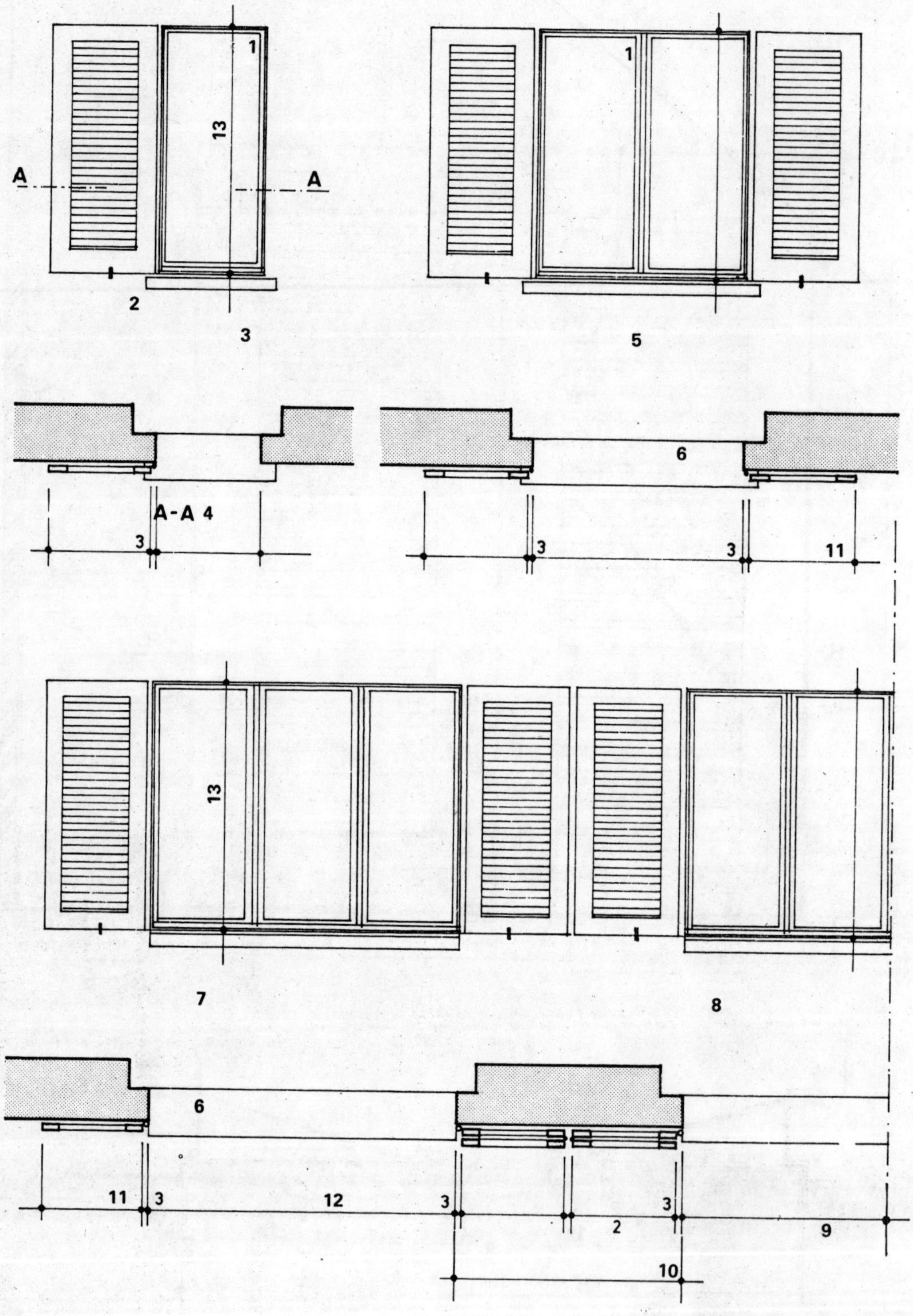

1 Window
2 Elevation
3 Single-leaf shutter
4 Plan
5 Two-leaf shutters
6 Window-sill
7 Three-leaf shutters
8 Four-leaf shutters
9 Window-axis distance
10 Minimum wall-breadth
11 Shutter measurement
12 Window measurement
13 Window height -1 cm = shutter measurement

Folding Shutters with fixed louvres

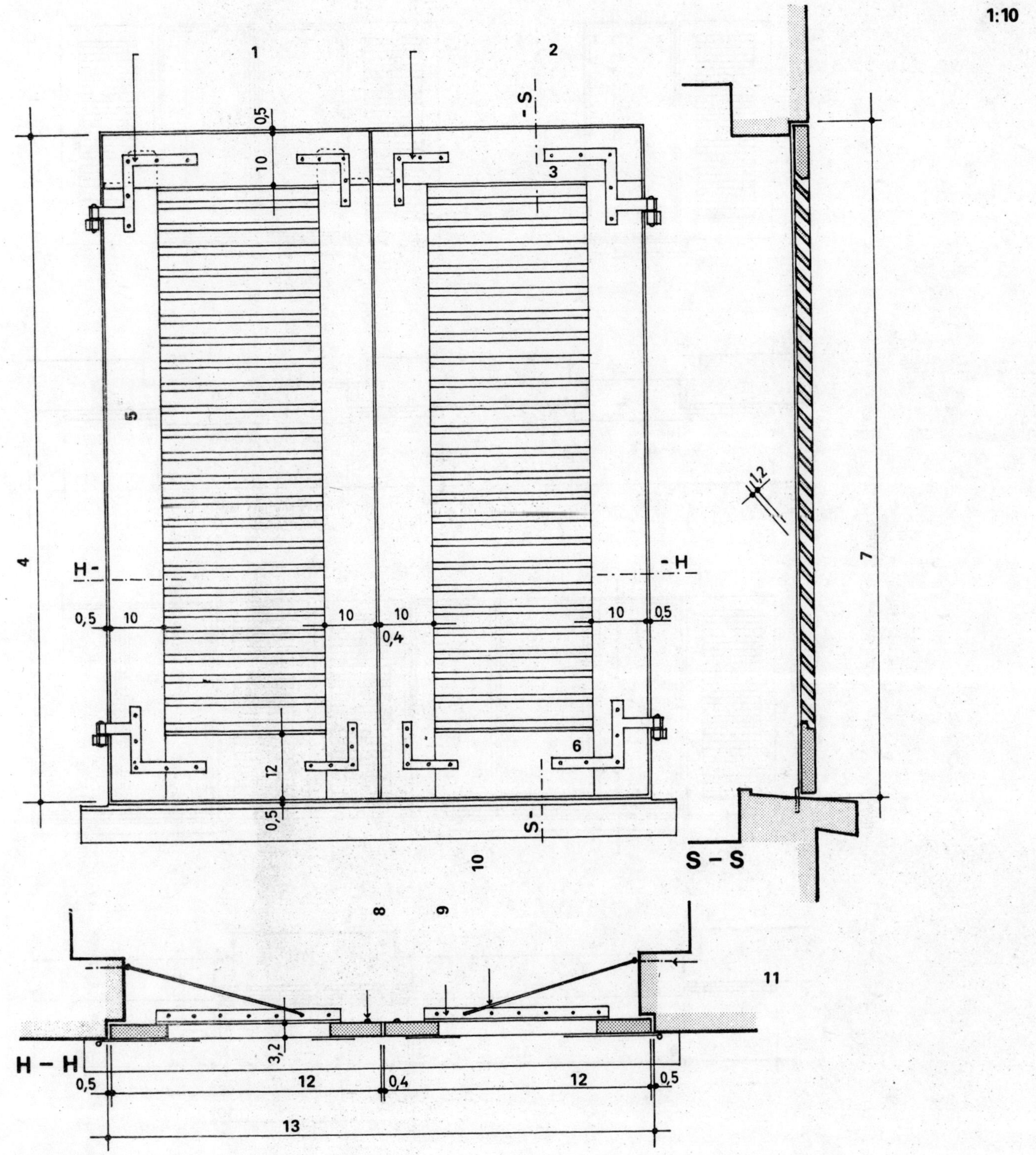

1 Angle hinge
2 Angle
3 Top rail
4 Shutter measurement – height
5 Hinge-rail
6 Bottom rail
7 Shutter-lining measurement-vertical
8 Lug
9 Ratchet
10 Locking bar
11 Eye-bolt
12 Shutter measurement – width
13 Shutter-lining – width

1:10

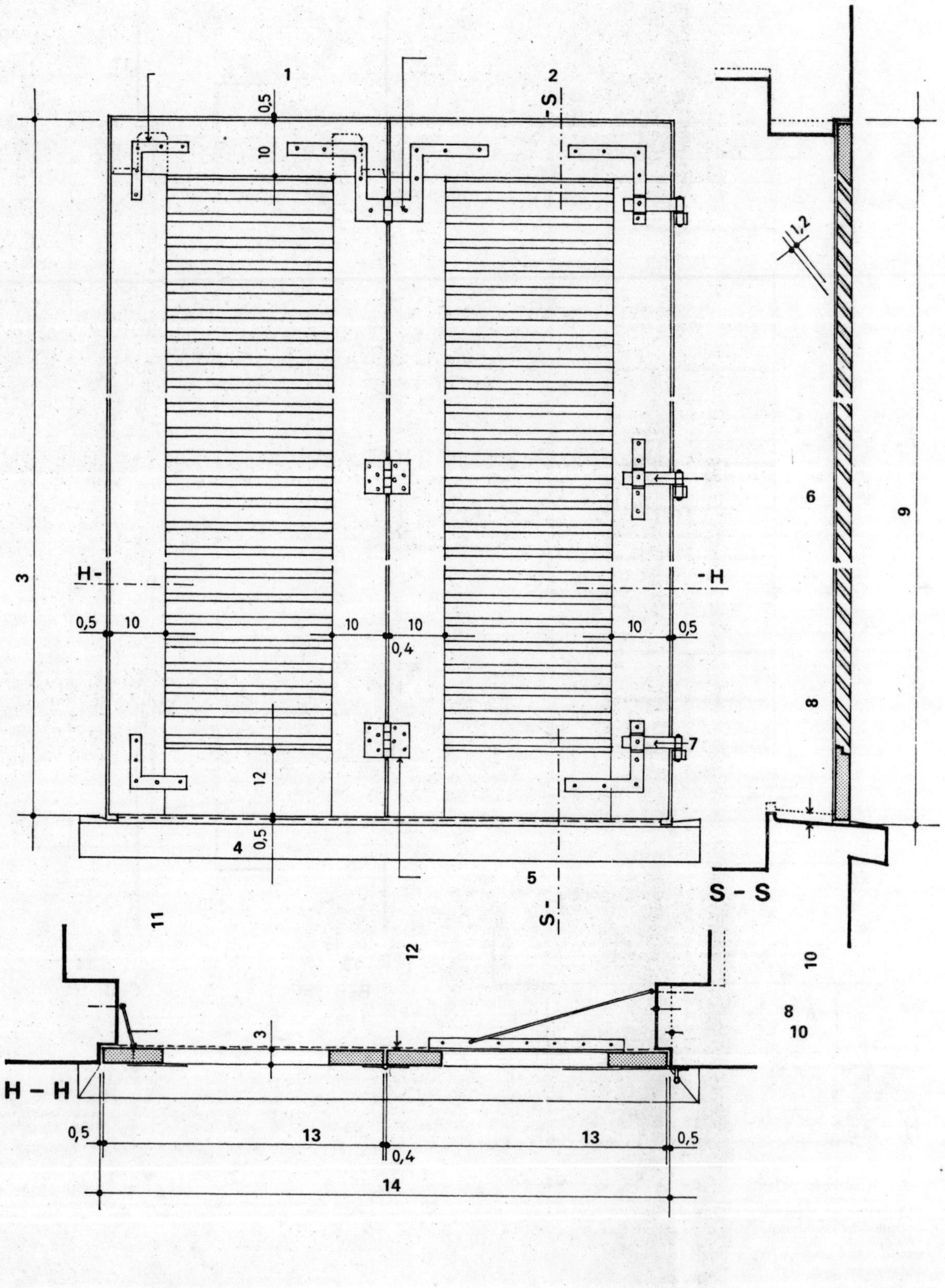

1 Angle
2 Angle-hinge
3 Shutter-measurement – height
4 Artificial-stone sill or threshold
5 Butt-hinge
6 Intermediate hinge
7 Angle-hinge
8 With rebate
9 Clear height
10 Without rebate
11 Fastening
12 Lug
13 Shutter measurement – width
14 Fillister- or clear-opening-measurement – width

Folding Shutters with adjustable louvres

1:10

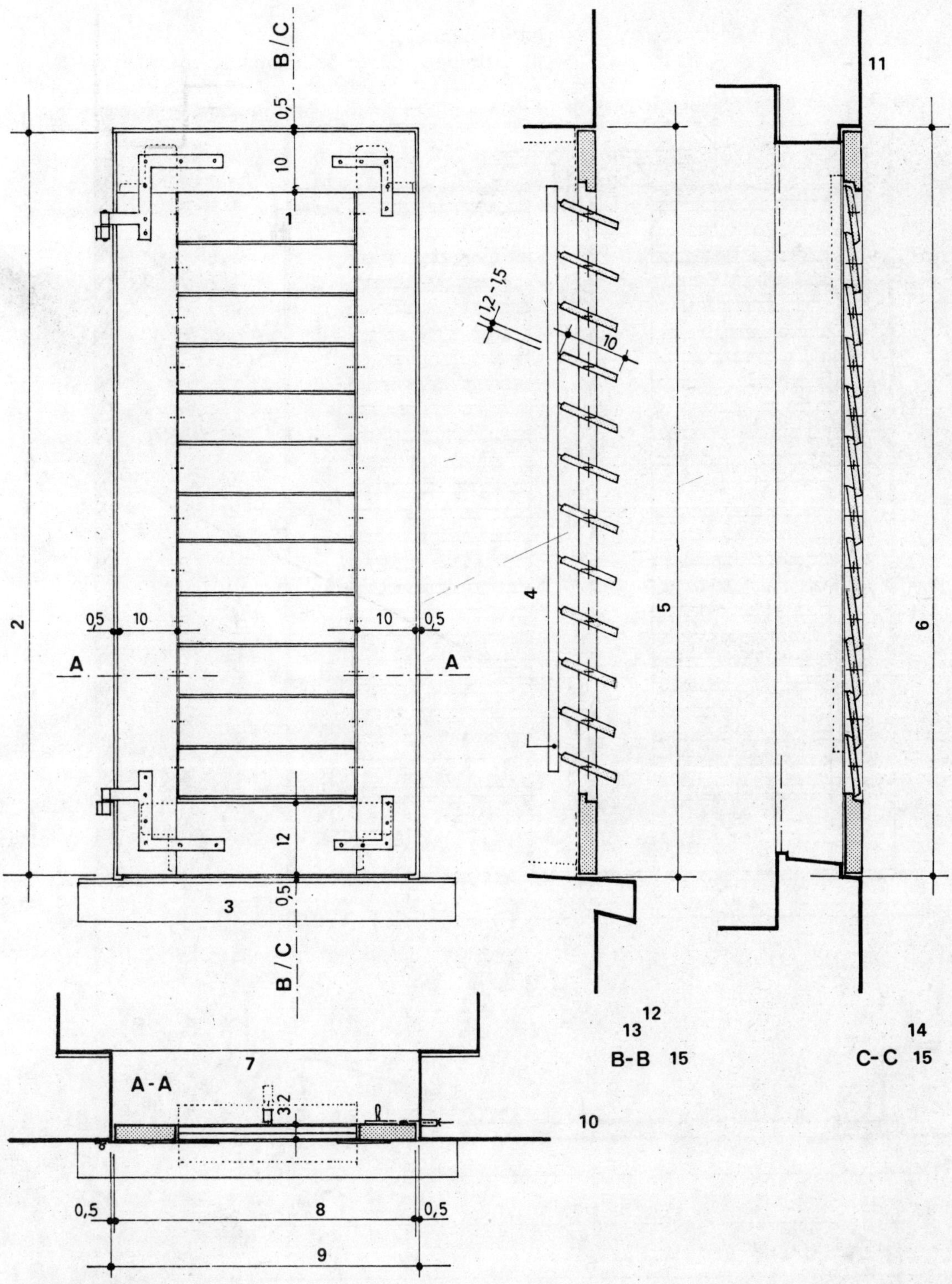

1 Louvre board, movable
2 Shutter measurement, height
3 Sill
4 Manipulating strip
5 Height of opening
6 Height of fillister
7 Plan
8 Shutter measurement, width
9 Width of opening
10 Bolt fastening
11 Lintel fixing
12 Louvres
13 Open
14 Closed
15 Section

Fabric blinds

The running line of blinds must be so constructed, that fabric and fascia bar remain straight and parallel in all positions, so that jamming and twisting cannot occur.

The guide tracks must be fixed to withstand gales, and the running of the blinds must be noiseless and smooth. Blind rollers of wood with metal end bearers; for lengths over 2 m a steel roller is necessary.

Drawing, return and working members should be rustproof.

The following quality of fabric is required:

Cotton fabric, colour fast, impregnated against fungus attack, should keep its shape and not react to extremes of temperature.

Synthetic fabrics should allow passage of air and have a cotton-like appearance; should be impregnated, resistant to decay, bird droppings and ultra-violet rays, colourfast, weatherproof and should keep their shapes.

Fabrics manufactured from glass fibres with PVC-coating should be transparent and allow passage of air; they should be colour-fast and rub-resistant, both in wet and dry states; non-combustible; of clean, durable and form-keeping quality; weatherproof.

Plastic sheet (PVC) with or without polyester base fabric: waterproof, rot-resistant and resistant to ultra-violet radiation; colour-fast.

Where synthetic materials are used, care should be taken to avoid odorous substances.

Roller blinds, forms of movement and fixing

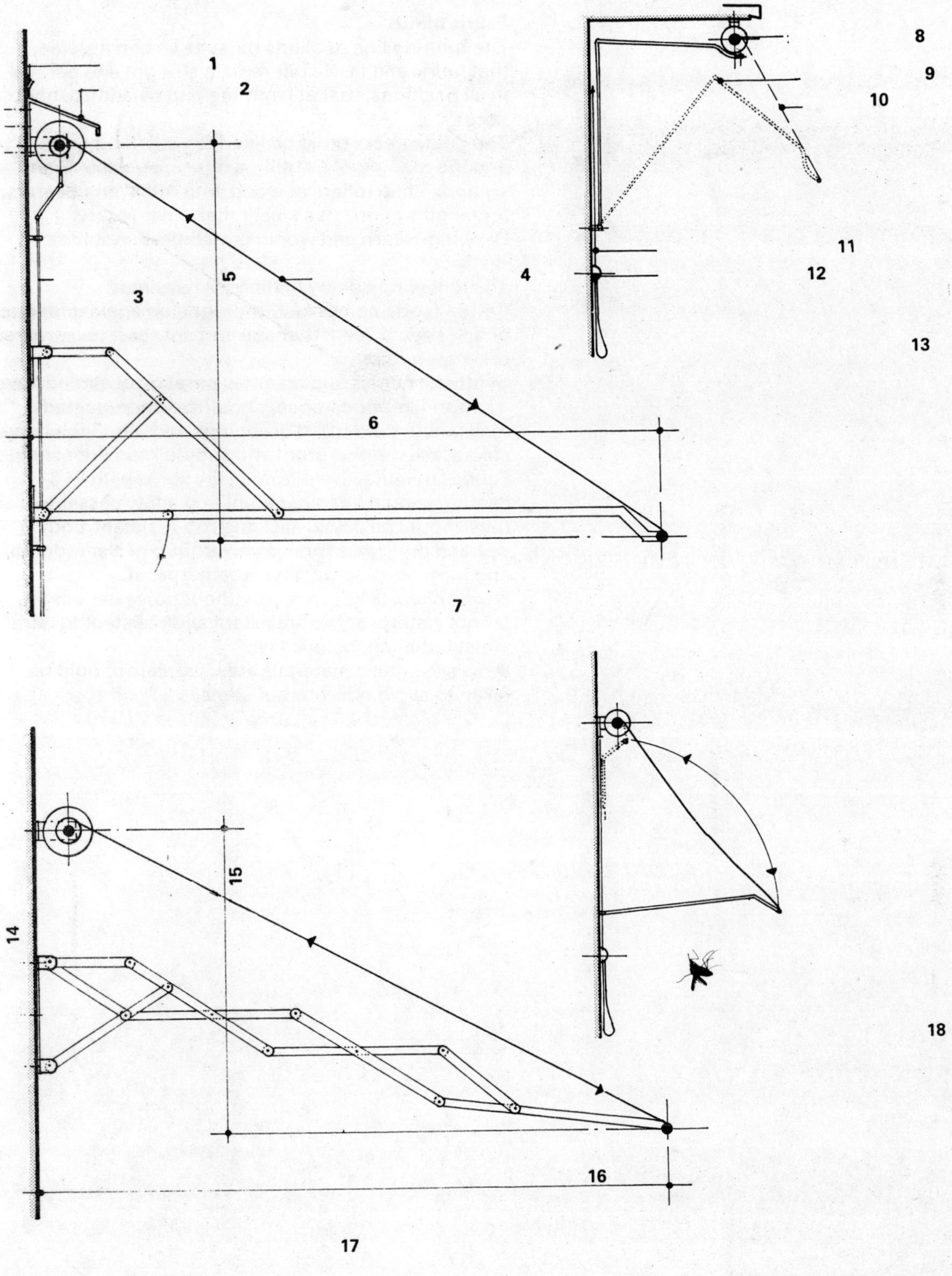

1 Mastic sealant
2 Sheet metal canopy
3 Winding rod
4 Sun-blind fabric
5 Height, at least 1/2 projection
6 Projection
7 Lever arm blind with straight adjustable extension arm
8 Blind roller
9 Extension arm
10 Fabric
11 Operating belt
12 Belt clamp
13 Sun blind with cranked extension arms
14 Line of wall or facade
15 Height, at least 1/4 projection
16 Projection, max 4.50 m
17 Blind with scissors-action arm
18 Sun blind with straight extension arms

Folding arm blinds, alternative types

1:10

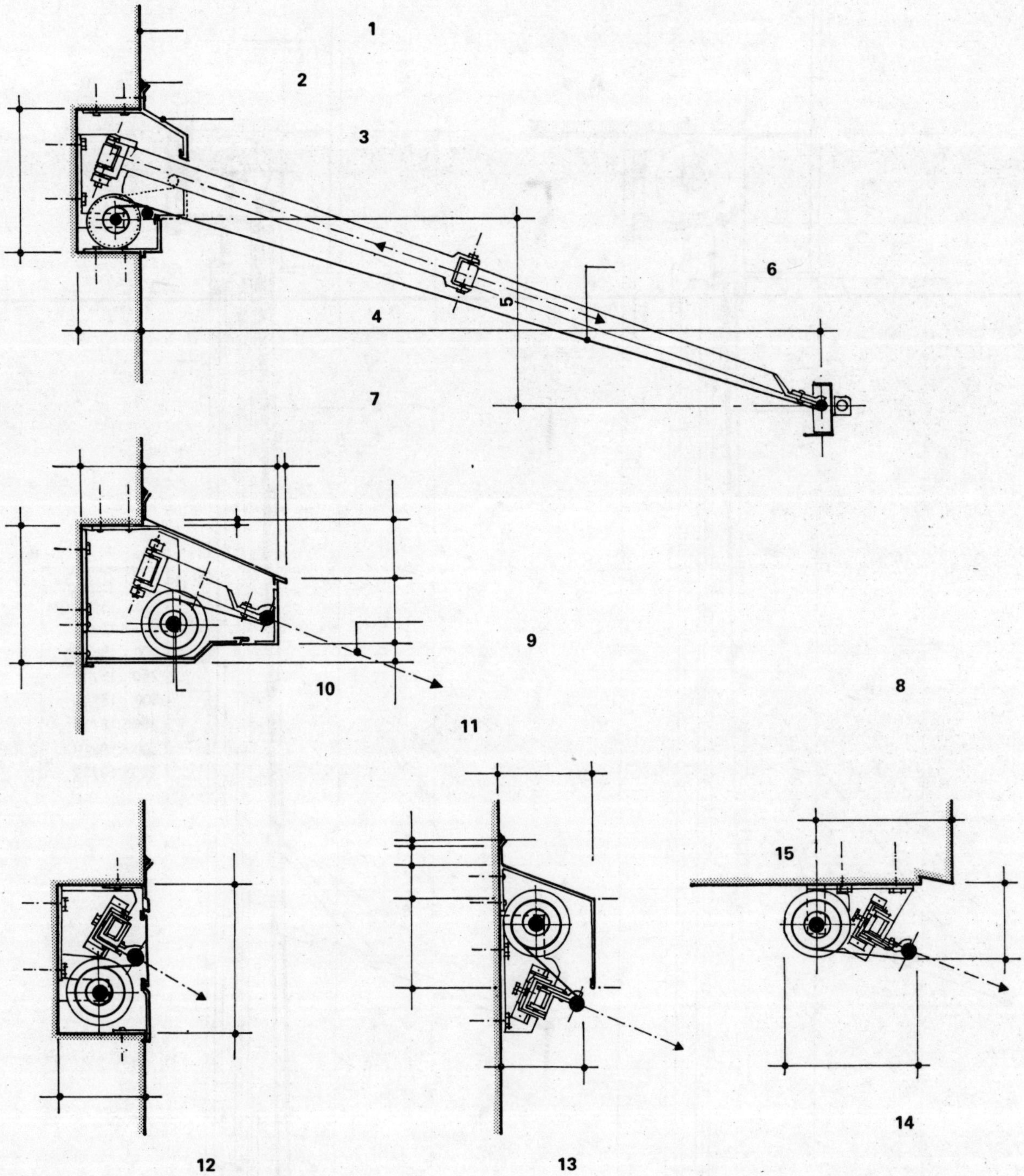

1 Line of facade
2 Mastic sealant
3 Sheet metal box canopy
4 Projection
5 Height of slope
6 Blind fabric
7 Folding arm blind, fitted in recess
8 Constructional alternative
9 Line of blind extension
10 Blind roller
11 Fixed to soffit of wall projection
12 Fixing in recees
13 Fixing to face of wall
14 Soffit fixing
15 Balcony or canopy roof

Window blinds, alternatives A and B

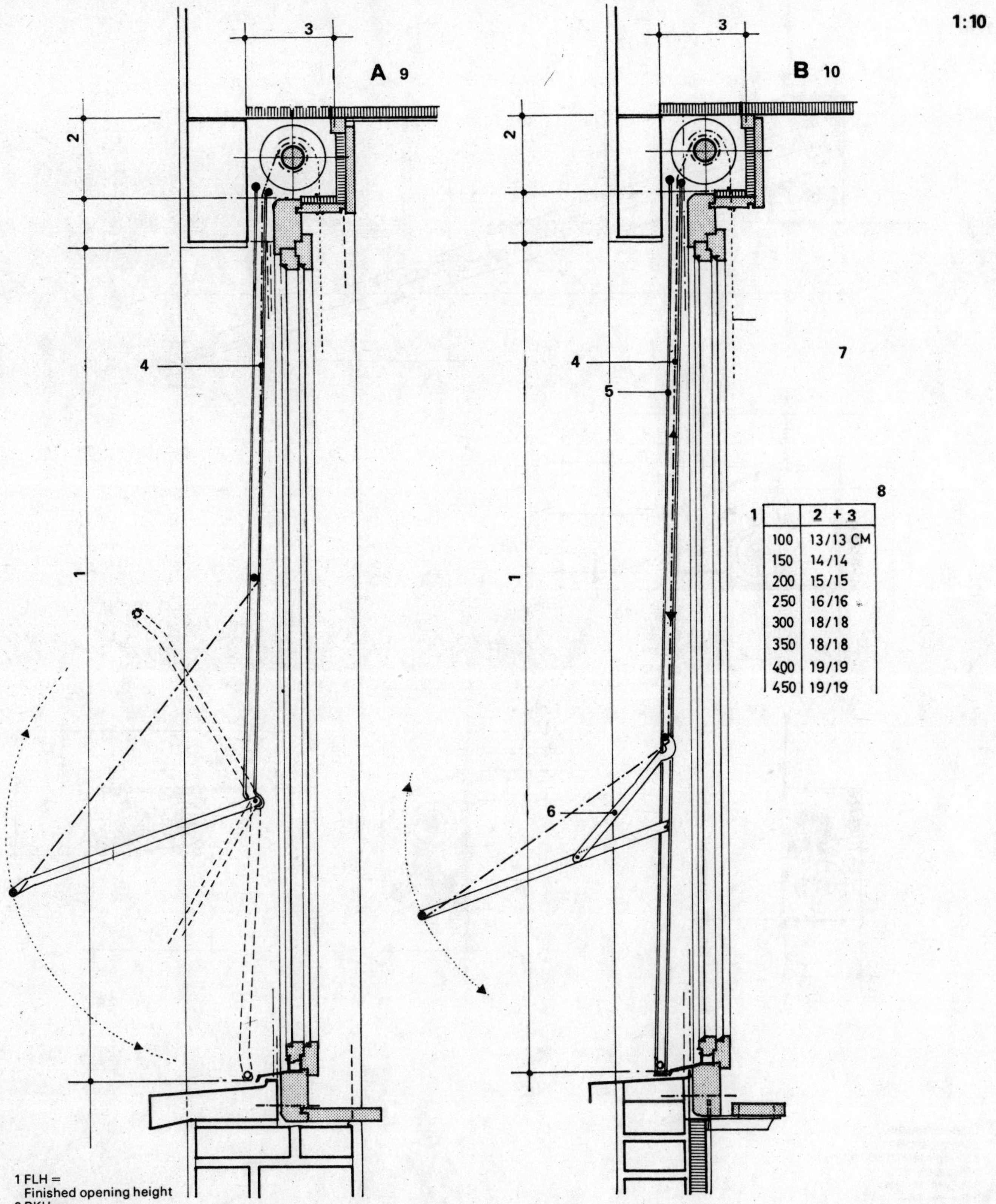

1	2 + 3
100	13/13 CM
150	14/14
200	15/15
250	16/16
300	18/18
350	18/18
400	19/19
450	19/19

1 FLH = Finished opening height
2 RKH = Height of blind box
3 RKB = Width of blind box
4 Blind fabric
5 Guide track
6 Automatic pivot
7 Belt pull or winding rod operation
8 Dimensions
9 Alternative A
10 Alternative B

Glass Bricks

Glass bricks must have the following properties: good light transmittance (diffuse light), acid resistant, unaffected by moisture, non-fading and non-staining, and high resistance to pressure and shock. Glass bricks used in walls must not be subjected to static loads. Unprotected wall areas should not exceed 12 m^2 – the panel height must not exceed 6 m and the width not more than 7.5 m.

Surface texture according to the type of brick, ribbed on one side or smooth on both sides; available as vacuum-hollow or solid bricks with a high insulation coefficient, not battered, not subject to condensation. Since glass bricks provide fire protection, they can also be used in fire-division walls depending on the regulations.

The bricks are to be laid with no breaks and no cracks, with surrounding expansion joints and are to be anchored against storms.

Joint width depends on field size (minimum 6 mm). The distribution and supporting reinforcement should be adapted to circumstances and make use of galvanized rods only. In the case of skylights, the joint width is based on the field span width as well as the anticipated load. If skylights are to support traffic, glass fiber or (chamber) cup bricks (topside with non-skid grooves) are recommended.

Joints in skylights should be sealed with long-lasting joint putty on the side exposed to weather; this putty seal must be watertight. Expansion joints should be used on all sides for rabbeted installation.

Glass brick wall

1:10/20

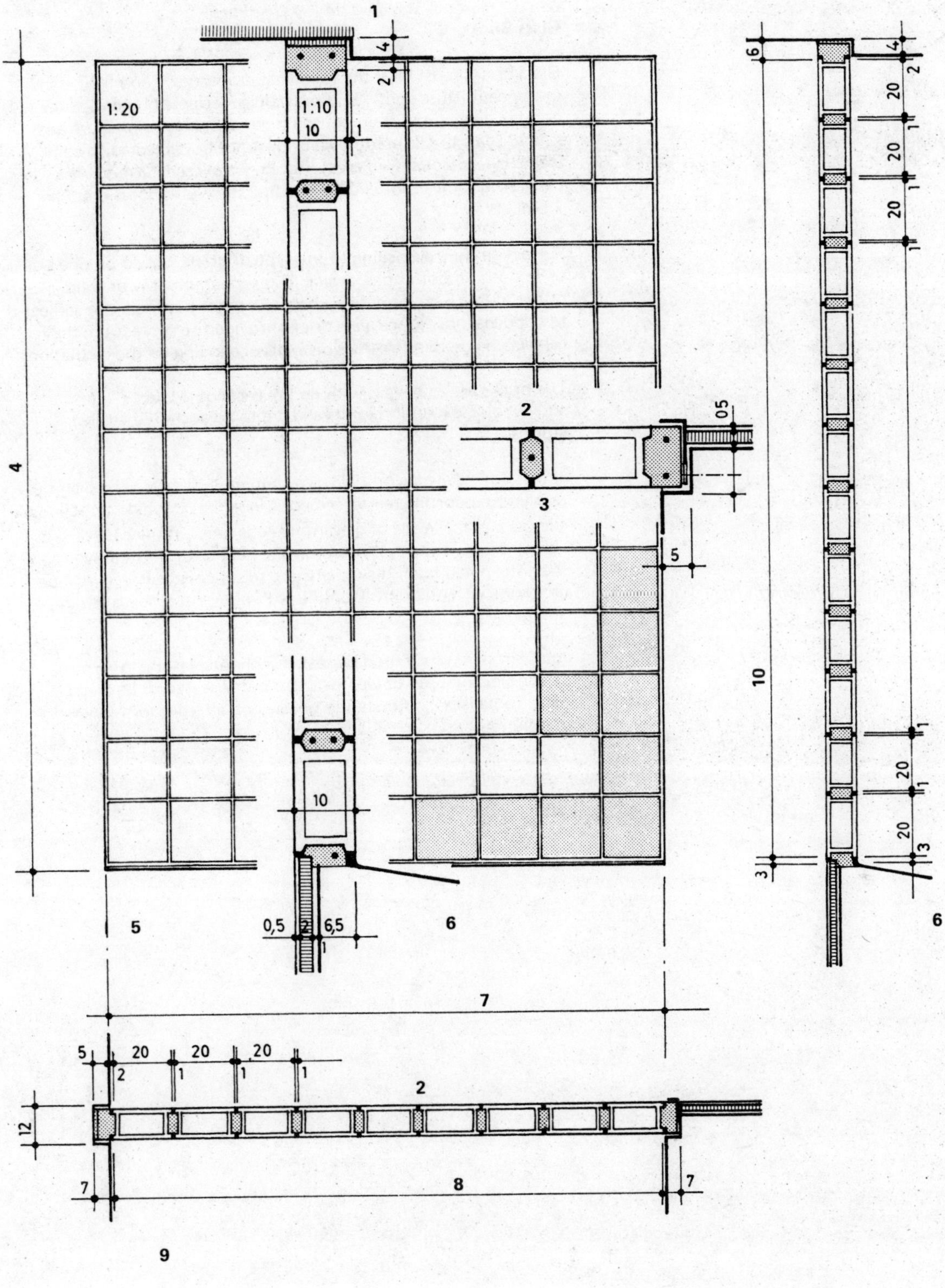

1 ceiling connection
2 interior
3 exterior
4 plaster headroom
5 side view
6 section
7 plaster - clearance width
8 panel clearance width
9 plan
10 panel headroom

Glass brick wall witn door mounting

1:10/20

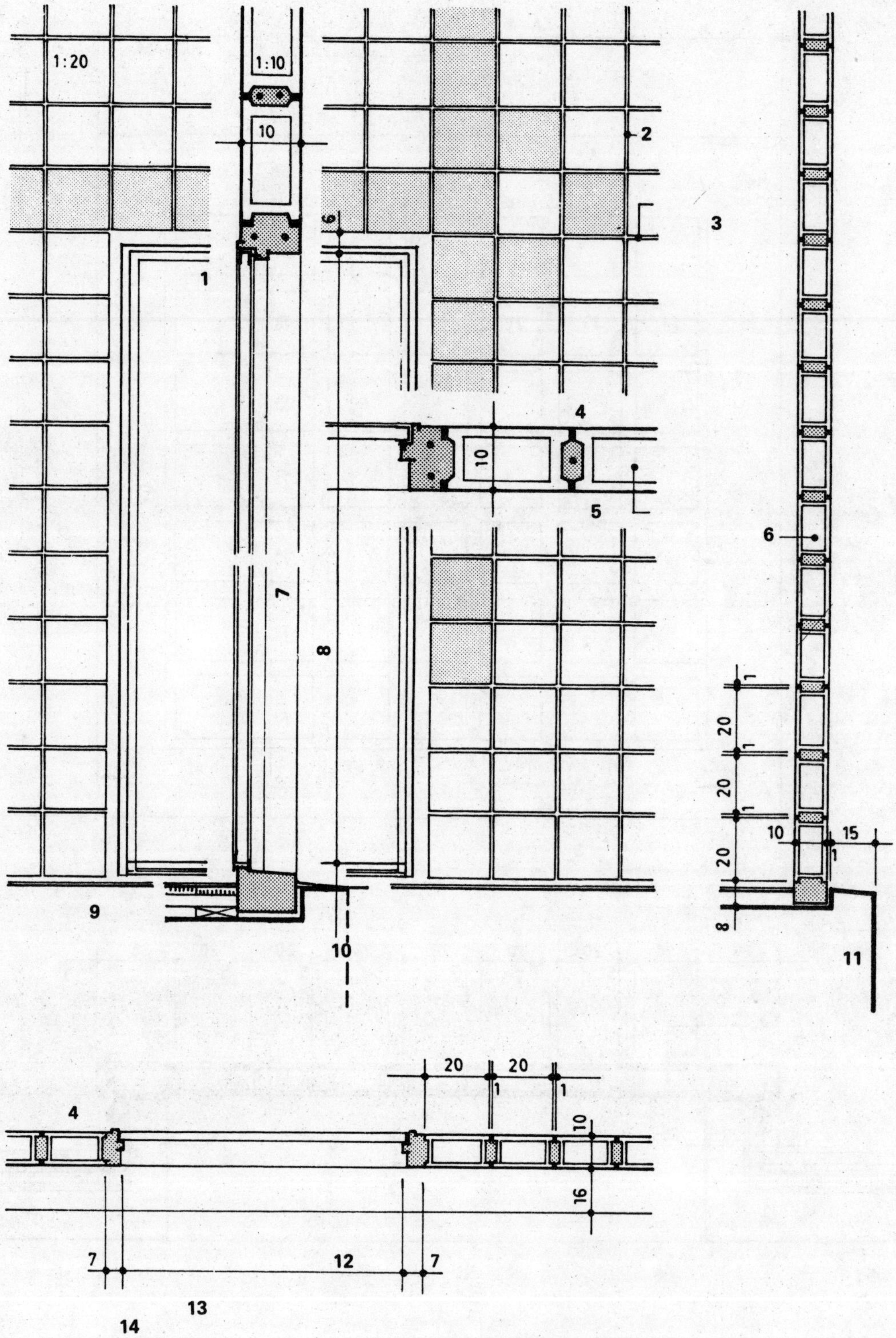

1 door
2 vertical joint
3 horizontal joint
4 interior
5 exterior
6 vacuum-hollow brick
7 cross section, scale 1 : 10
8 casing headroom
9 side view
10 floor connection
11 cross section
12 casing clearance width
13 horizontal section
14 (plan)

Skylight, laid, for walking traffic

1:20

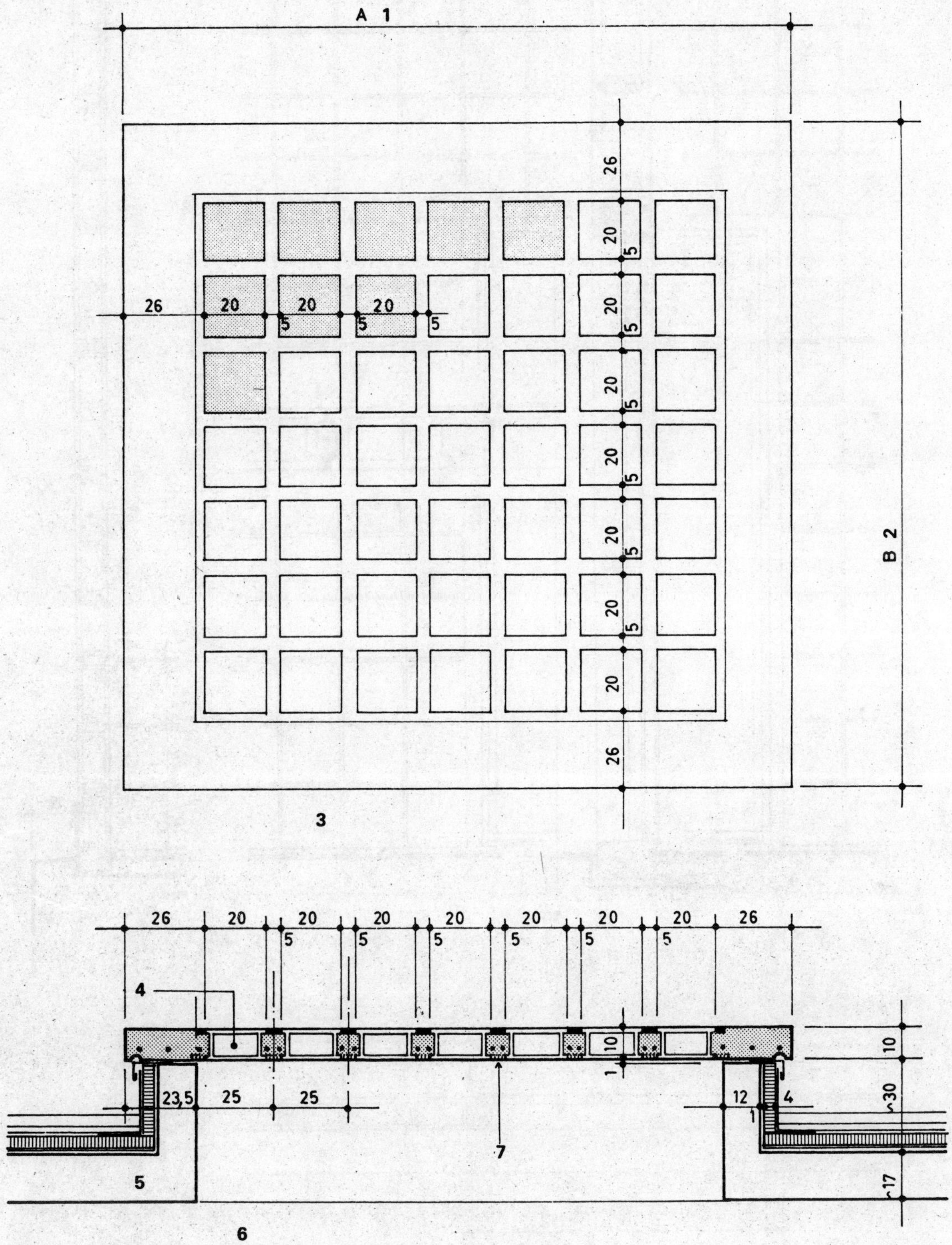

1 exterior dimension A
2 exterior dimension B
3 skylight top view
4 vacuum-hollow brick
5 solid ceiling
6 cross section, scale 1 : 20
7 poss. therm. insul.

Door Construction

The following door sizes (widths) are recommended: For baths, showers and WC's 60-70 cm, pantries/ kitchenettes 70-80 cm, large kitchens 80-90 cm, for double doors up to 130 cm, bed-room and office doors 80 cm, hospital doors, single or double, 110-130 cm wide, with two leaves the larger 80-90 cm. Cellar and service-room doors 80-90 cm, boiler-house doors 90-130 cm, for door sizes of more than 110 cm two leaves are preferable. Domestic entrance-doors 90-100 cm, for blocks of flats 100-110 cm.
Wherever heavier use is expected (schools, lecturehalls, shops etc.) the problem must be studied in relation to the appropriate number of door-openings, the choice of door-sizes and the type of construction. In addition the relevant legal provisions must be respected.
Door headroom amounts generally to about 200 cm. Housewives and the elderly and fragile like internal doors to be designed without floor rebates (door-sills). External doors are provided with a lower threshold of (as a rule) 3 cm.
For the most part nowadays flush doors faced with plywood with glued-in blocks are used (also hardboard, chipboard, etc.). Under present-day heating conditions solid doors are not recommended; but if desired, flush doors with semi-solid or solid cores, are suggested.
The depth of the door-lining depends on the type of lock and thickness of the door-leaf. The door-lock should be 100 cm from the floor.
The following work must be completed before fixing: with flush doors the interior plaster work, with framed doors a straight-and-true plaster finish round the wall opening. Frames and linings are fixed with bolts, blocked edges with ties.

Flush Door and Lining

1:25/2

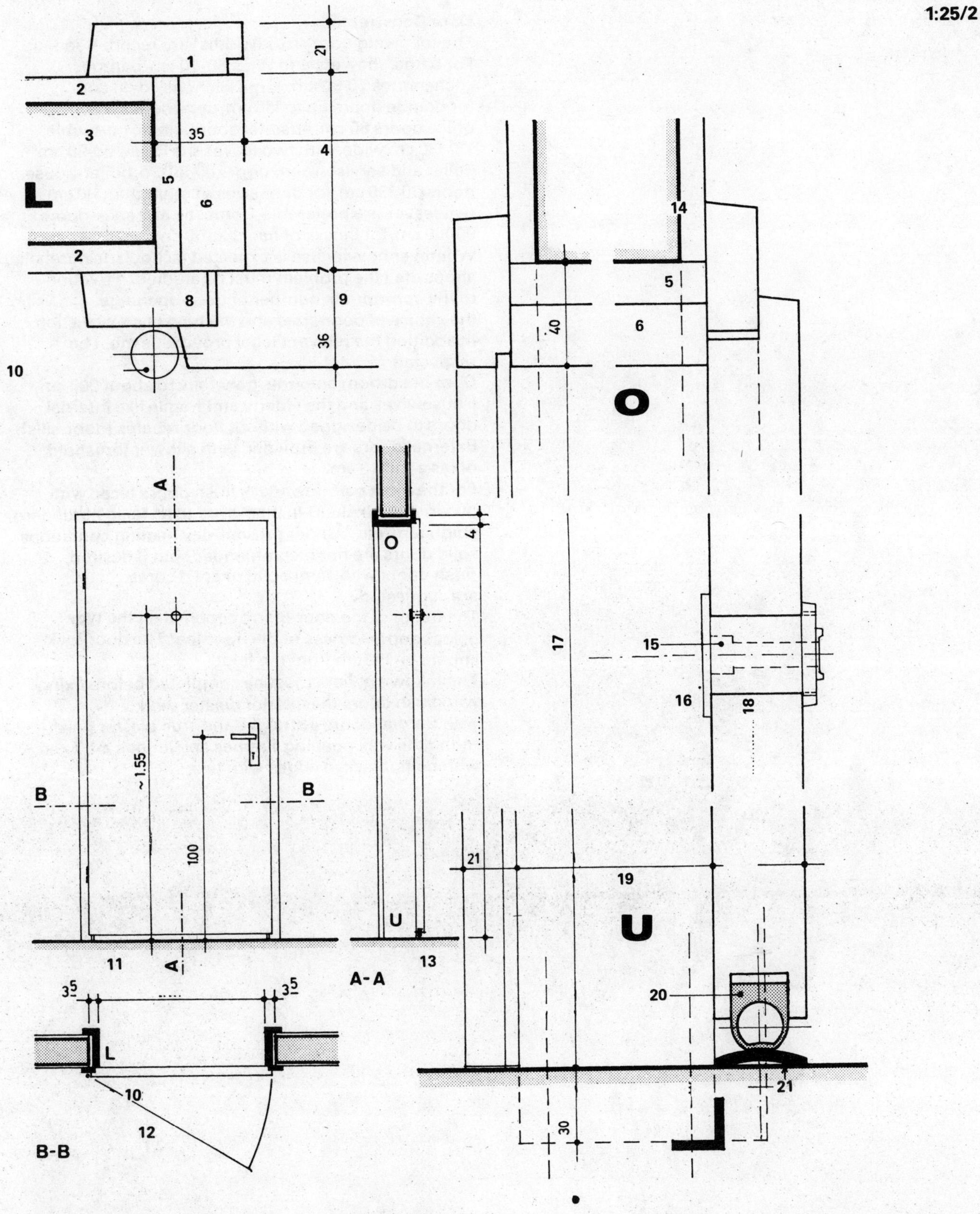

1 Ornamental lining
2 Plaster
3 Jamb detail
4 Width of opening of door case
5 Grounds
6 Lining (casing)
7 Lining depth
8 Rebated lining
9 Door (leaf)
10 Hinge, left
11 Elevation
12 Plan
13 Section
14 Lintel, detail
15 Peep-hole
16 Built-in at eye-level
17 Headroom
18 Door, flush plywood (or hardboard) facing, factory-made
19 Lining depth variable
20 Hollow-section rubber-sealing
21 Dished aluminium plate

1:2

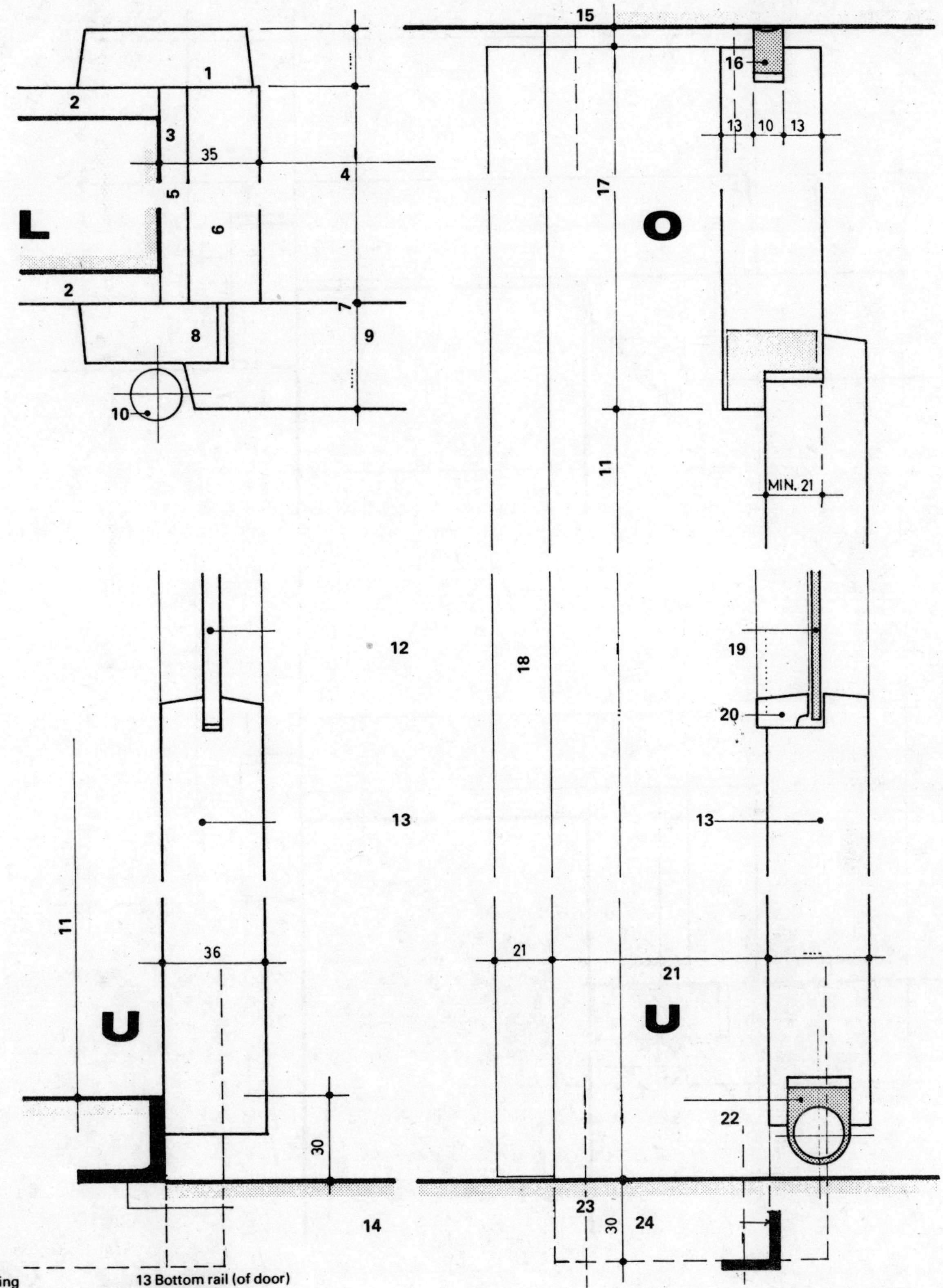

1 Ornamental lining
2 Plaster
3 Jamb detail
4 Width of door-case opening
5 Grounds
6 Lining (casing)
7 Lining depth
8 Rebated lining
9 Door
10 Hinge
12 Panel, dovetailed fixing
13 Bottom rail (of door)
14 Stop angle
15 Ceiling joint
16 Inserted fillet
17 Lintel, securely built-in
18 Ornamental lining
19 Glass, laid in putty
20 Beading
21 Lining depth, variable
22 Hollow section, rubber sealing
23 Floor joint
24 Angle, galvanized iron

Flush Door and Lining

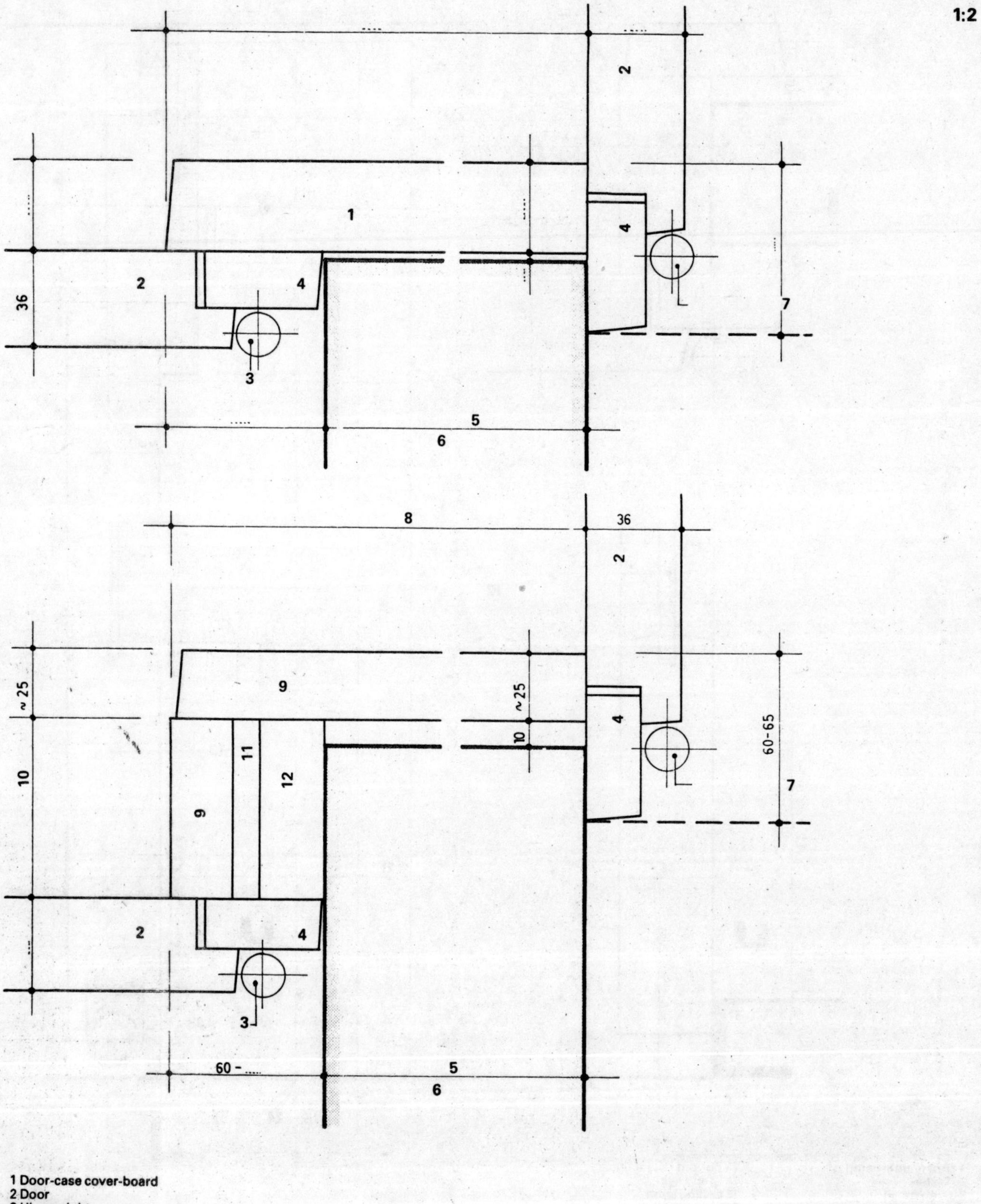

1 Door-case cover-board
2 Door
3 Hinge, right
4 Rebated lining
5 Thickness of wall
6 Variable
7 Hinge, left
8 Lining depth variable
9 Lining
10 Lining (casing) depth
11 Strap
12 Grounds

1:2

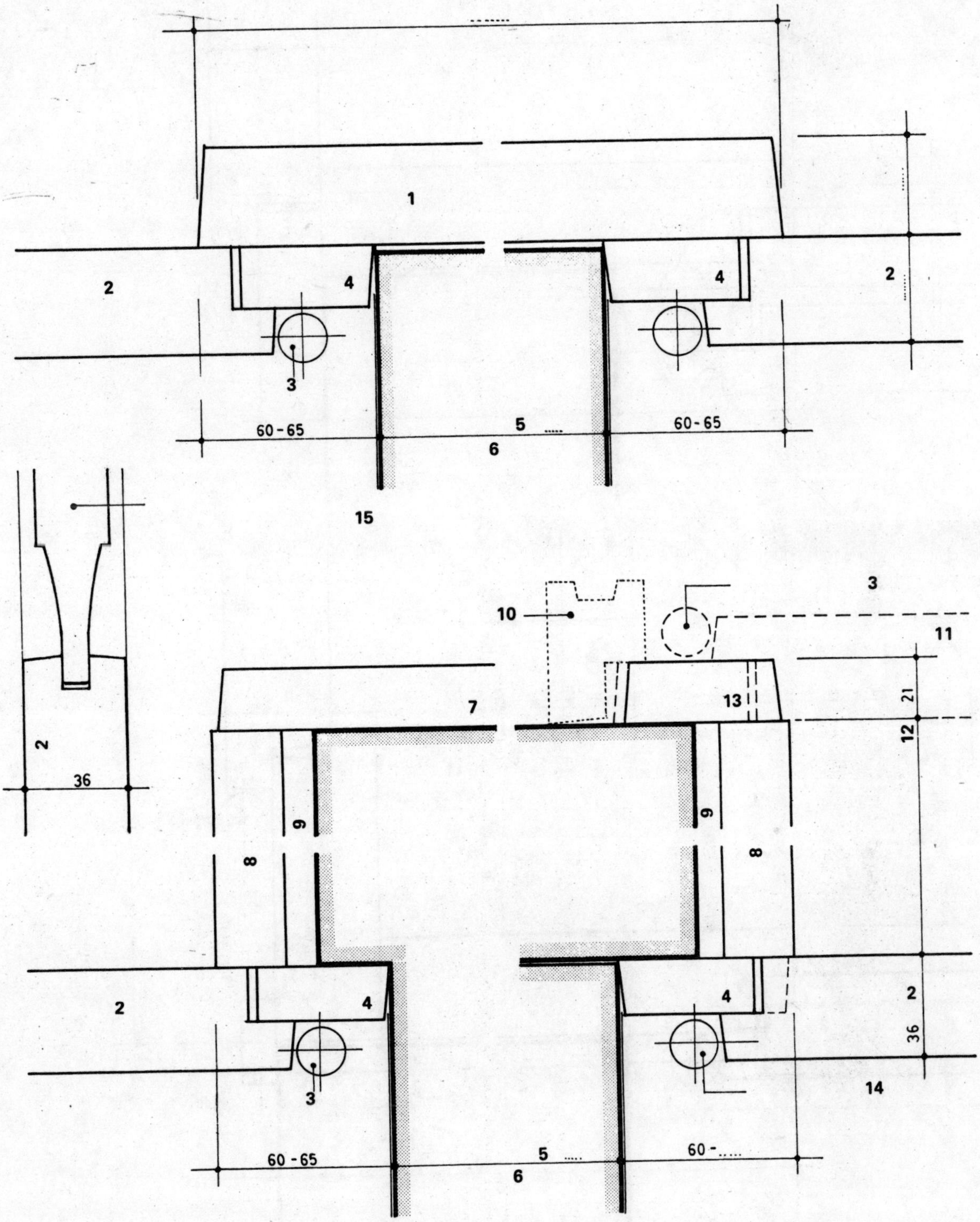

1 Door-case cover-board
2 Door
3 Hinge, right
4 Rebated lining
5 Thickness of wall
6 Variable
7 Cover board in
8 Lining
9 Grounds
10 Ornamental Moulding, grooved
11 Possible external door
12 Lining depth
13 Ornamental lining (architrave)
14 Hinge, left

Lining, type variants

1:2

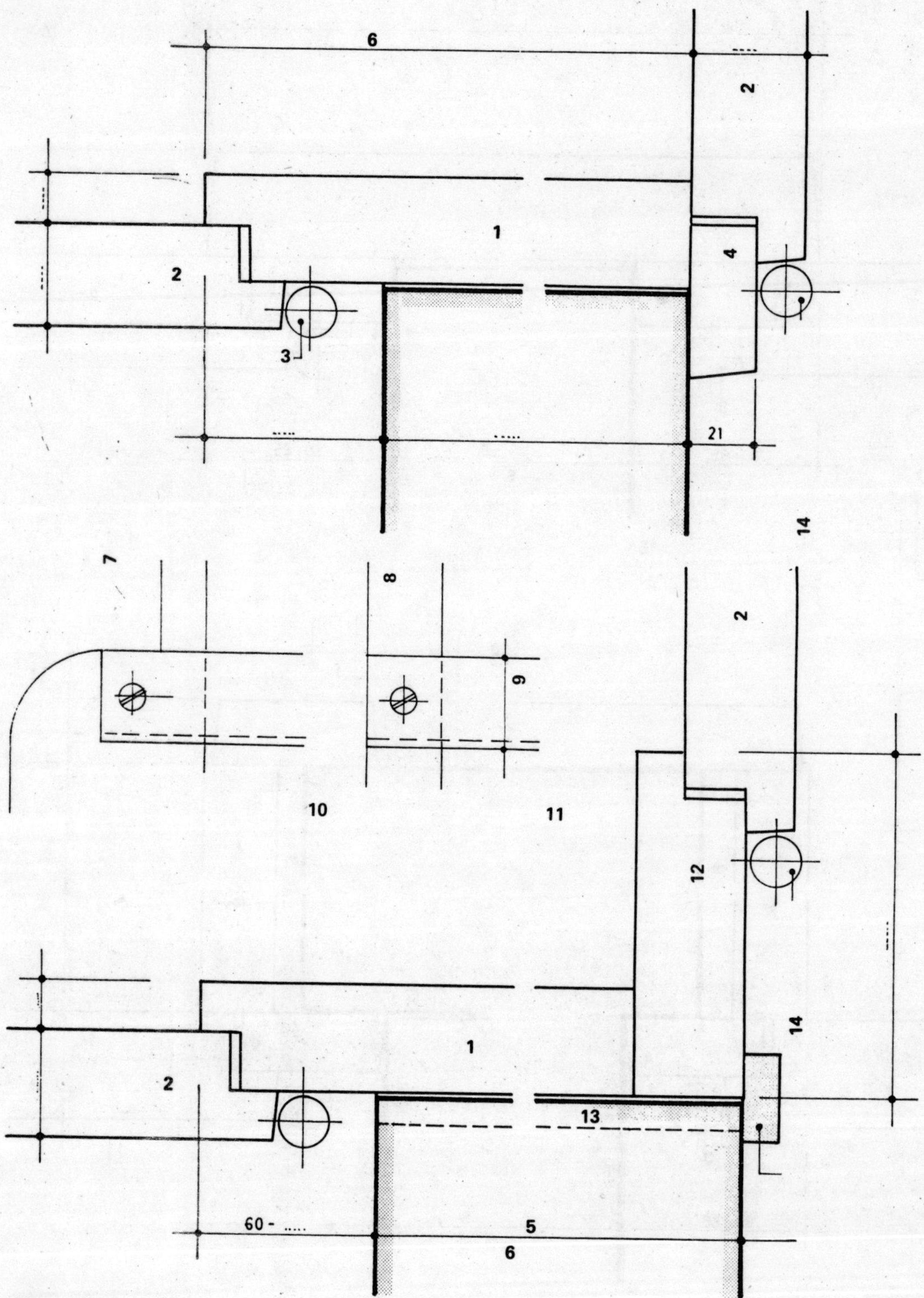

1 Door-case cover-board in...
2 Door
3 Hinge, right
4 Rebated lining
5 Thickness of wall
6 Variable
7 Frame
8 Lining
9 Angle height
10 Angle-iron in framed-door casing
11 Flush door with lining
12 Door-case board in...
13 Possible plaster-infill
14 Hinge, left

1:2

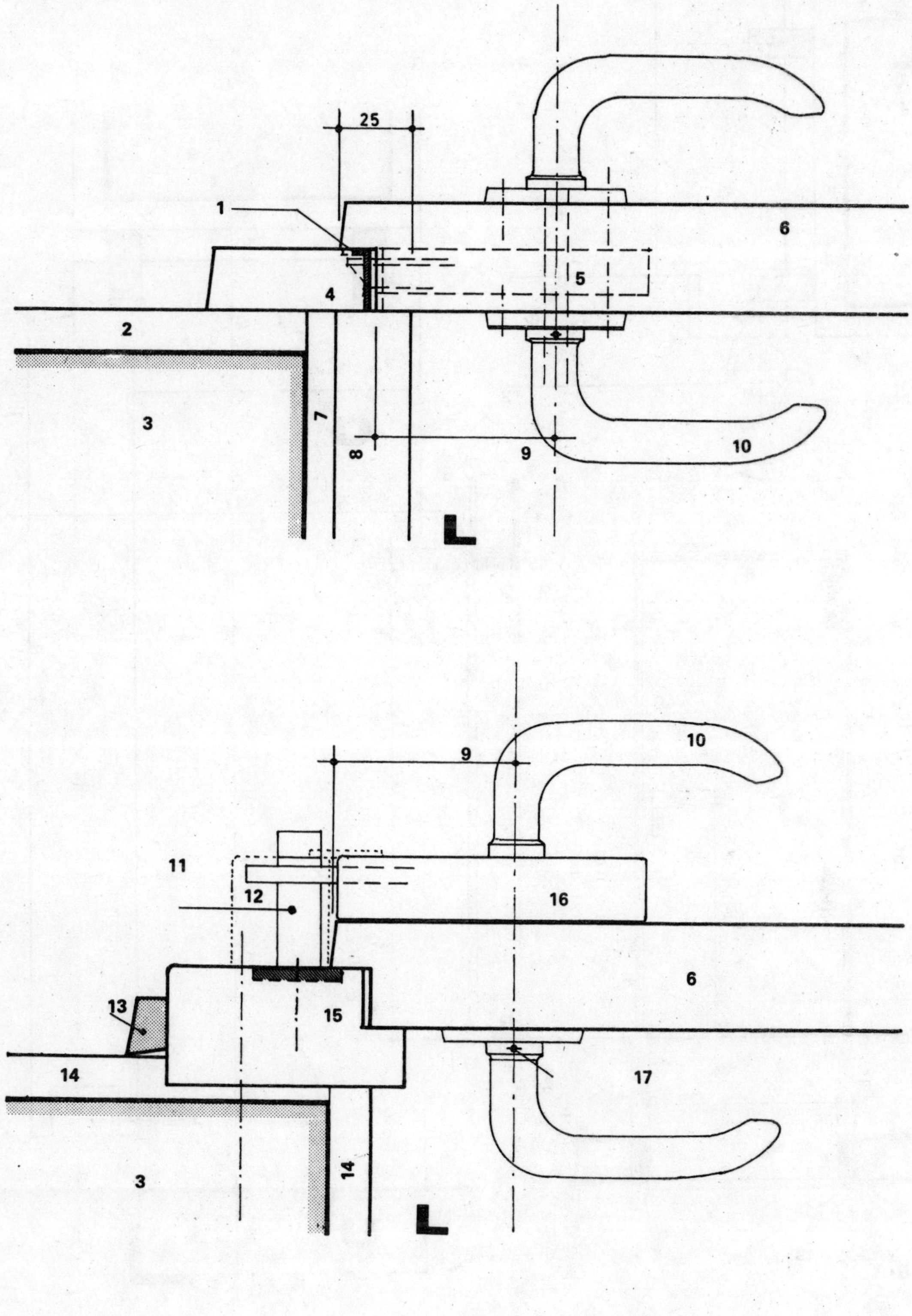

1 Striking plate
2 Plaster (wall)
3 Masonry
4 Rebated lining
5 Mortise lock
6 Door
7 Grounds
8 Lining
9 Latch measurement
10 Door-handle
11 Closer
12 Open or concealed
13 Moulding (planted)
14 Plaster
15 Door-frame
16 Rim lock
17 Turn

Flush Door, construction details

1:25/2

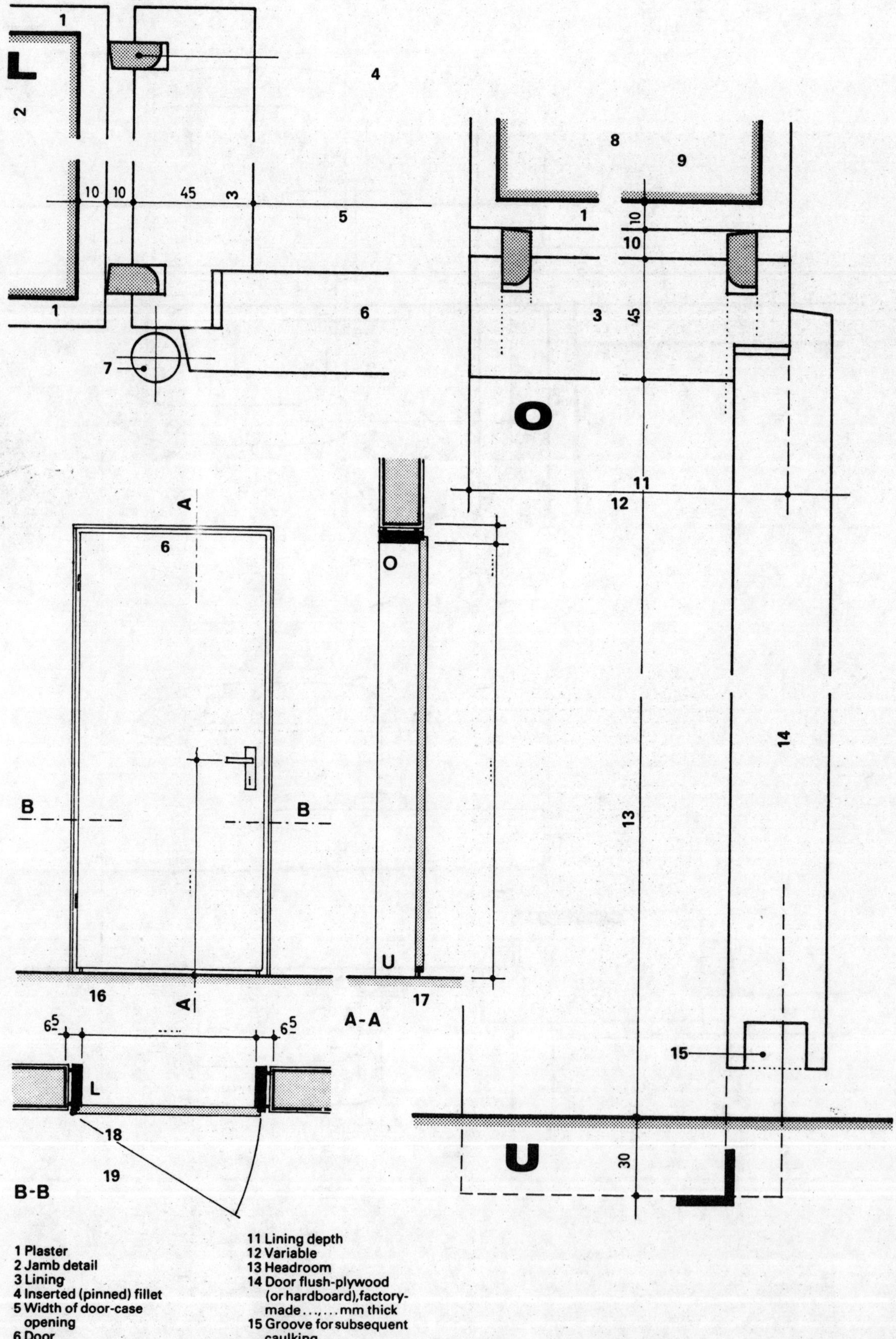

1 Plaster
2 Jamb detail
3 Lining
4 Inserted (pinned) fillet
5 Width of door-case opening
6 Door
7 Hinge
8 Lintel
9 Casing detail
10 Cavity
11 Lining depth
12 Variable
13 Headroom
14 Door flush-plywood (or hardboard), factory-made . . ., . . . mm thick
15 Groove for subsequent caulking
16 Elevation
17 Section
18 Hinge, left
19 Plan

1:2

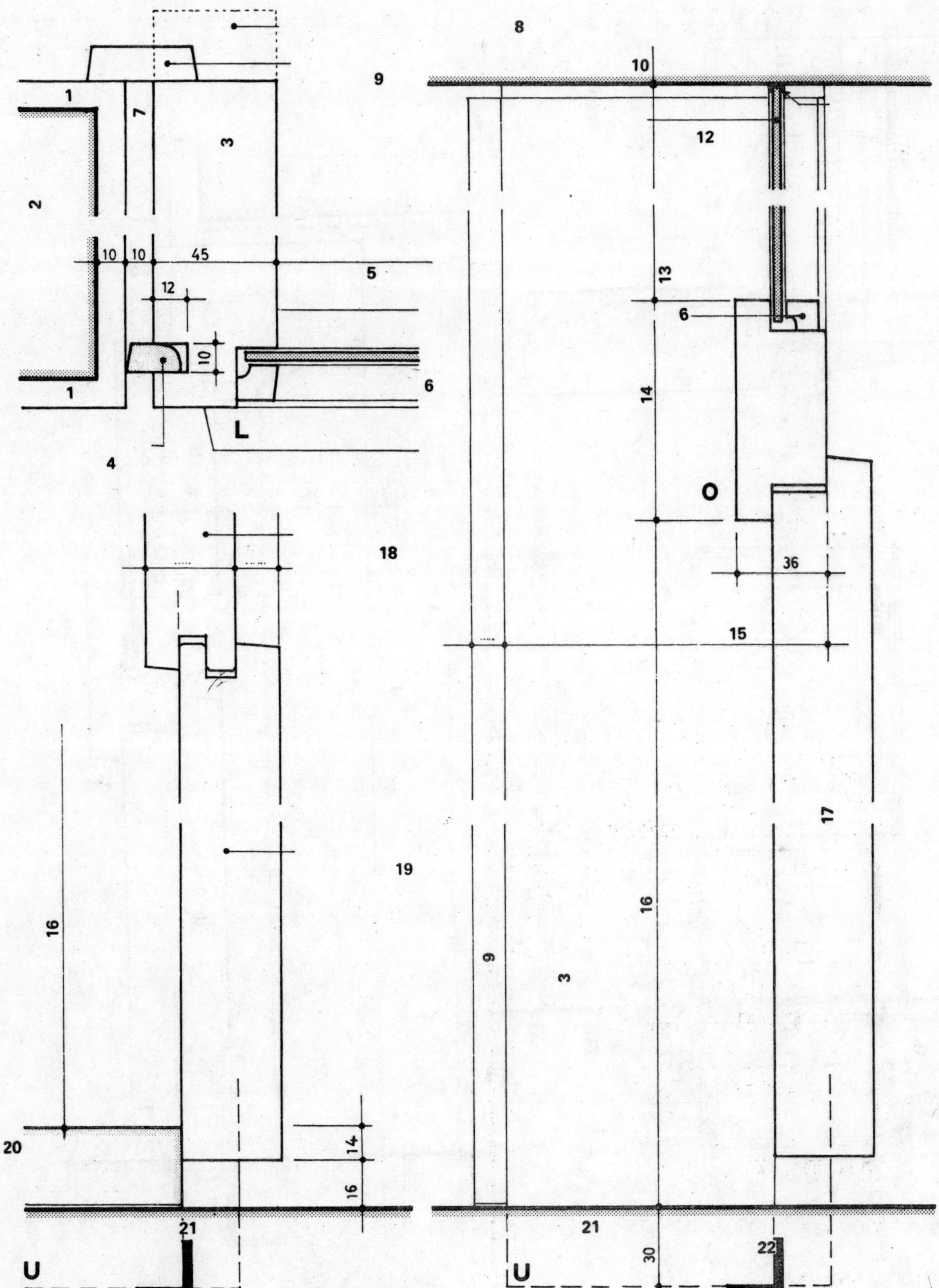

1 Plaster
2 Jamb detail
3 Lining
4 Inserted fillet (pinned)
5 Width of door-case opening
6 Glazing bead
7 Grounds
8 Possible lining-projection
9 Moulding
10 Ceiling joint
11 Sealing with . . .
12 Glass laid in putty
13 Fanlight
14 Frame
15 Lining depth variable
16 Headroom
17 Door, flush plywood (or hardboard), facing factory made . . ., . . . mm thick
18 Transposed filling element
19 Bottom rail (door)
20 Timber threshold
21 Floor joint
22 Angle, galvanized iron

Block-Frame Door, construction details

1:25/2

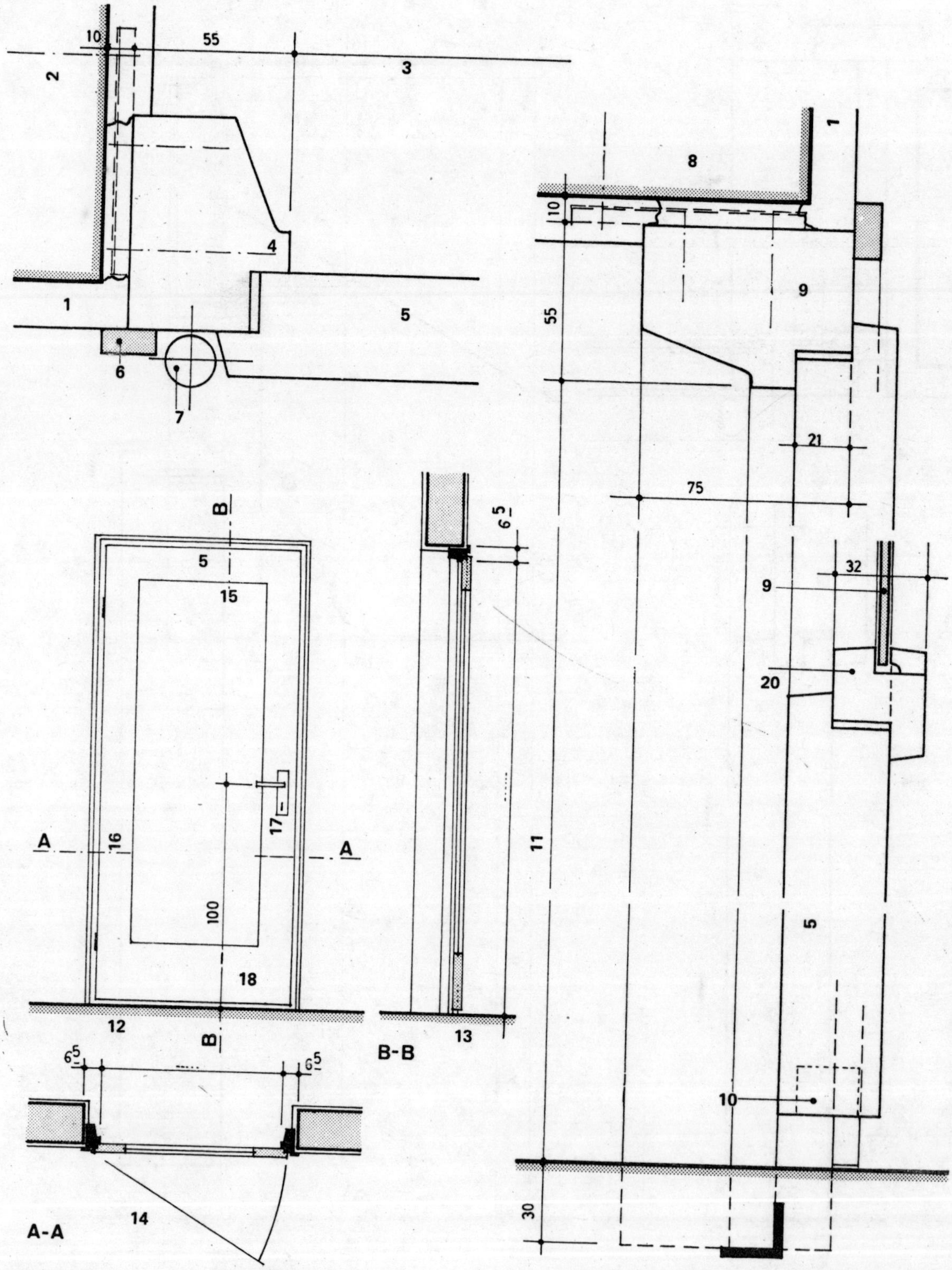

1 Plaster
2 Jamb casing
3 Clear width of frame
4 Wood screw
5 Door
6 Moulding (masking joint)
7 Hinge, left
8 Lintel casing detail
9 Block-frame
10 Groove for subsequent core
11 Headroom
12 Elevation
13 Section
14 Plan
15 Infilling
16 Stile
17 Stile (lock side)
18 Bottom rail
19 Glass laid in putty
20 Built-in element (for glass panel), at eve-level

1:25/2

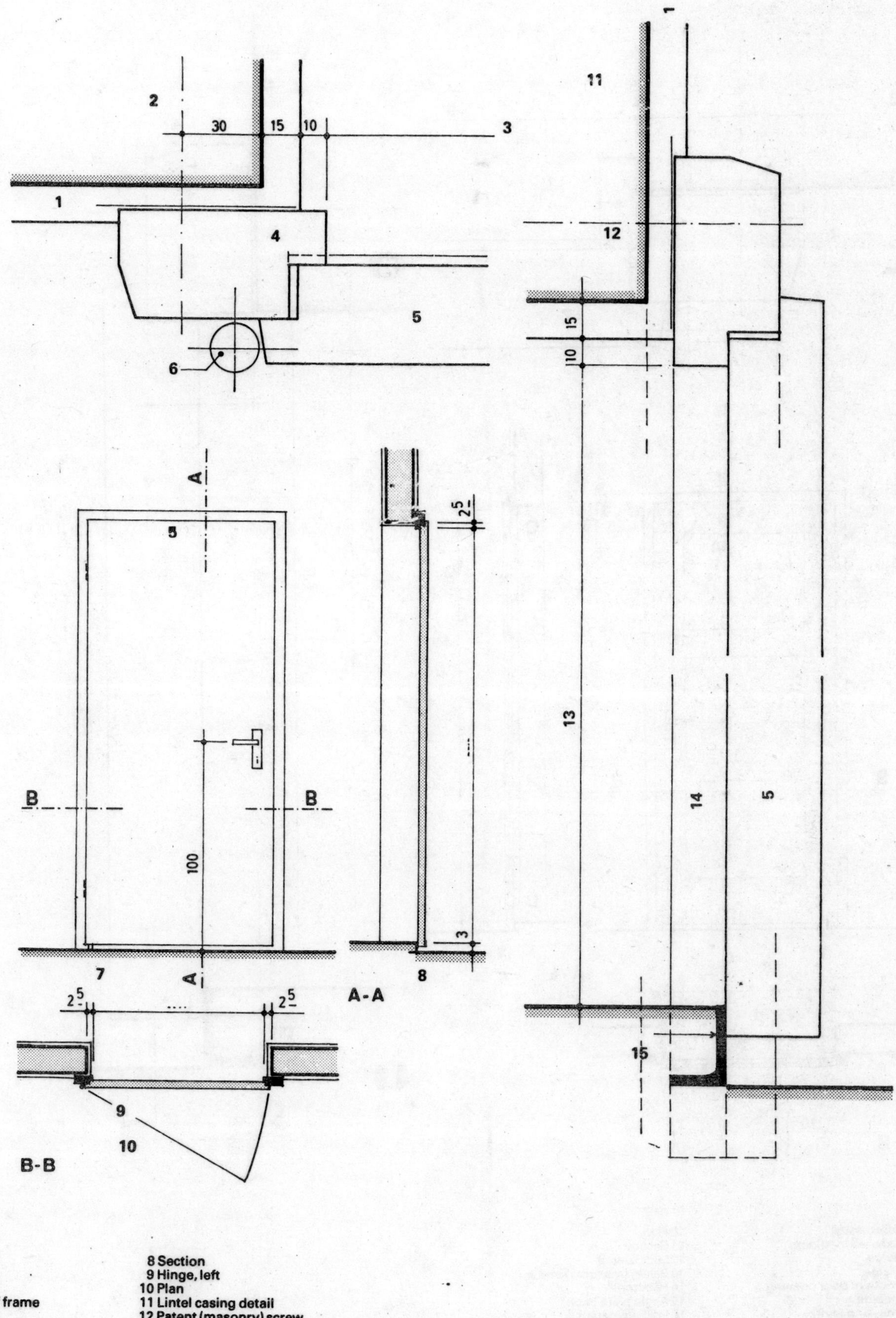

1 Plaster
2 Jamb casing
3 Clear width of frame
4 Frame
5 Door
6 Hinge
7 Elevation
8 Section
9 Hinge, left
10 Plan
11 Lintel casing detail
12 Patent (masonry) screw
13 Headroom
14 Frame
15 Angle lining (stop)

Panneled Framed Door

1:25/2

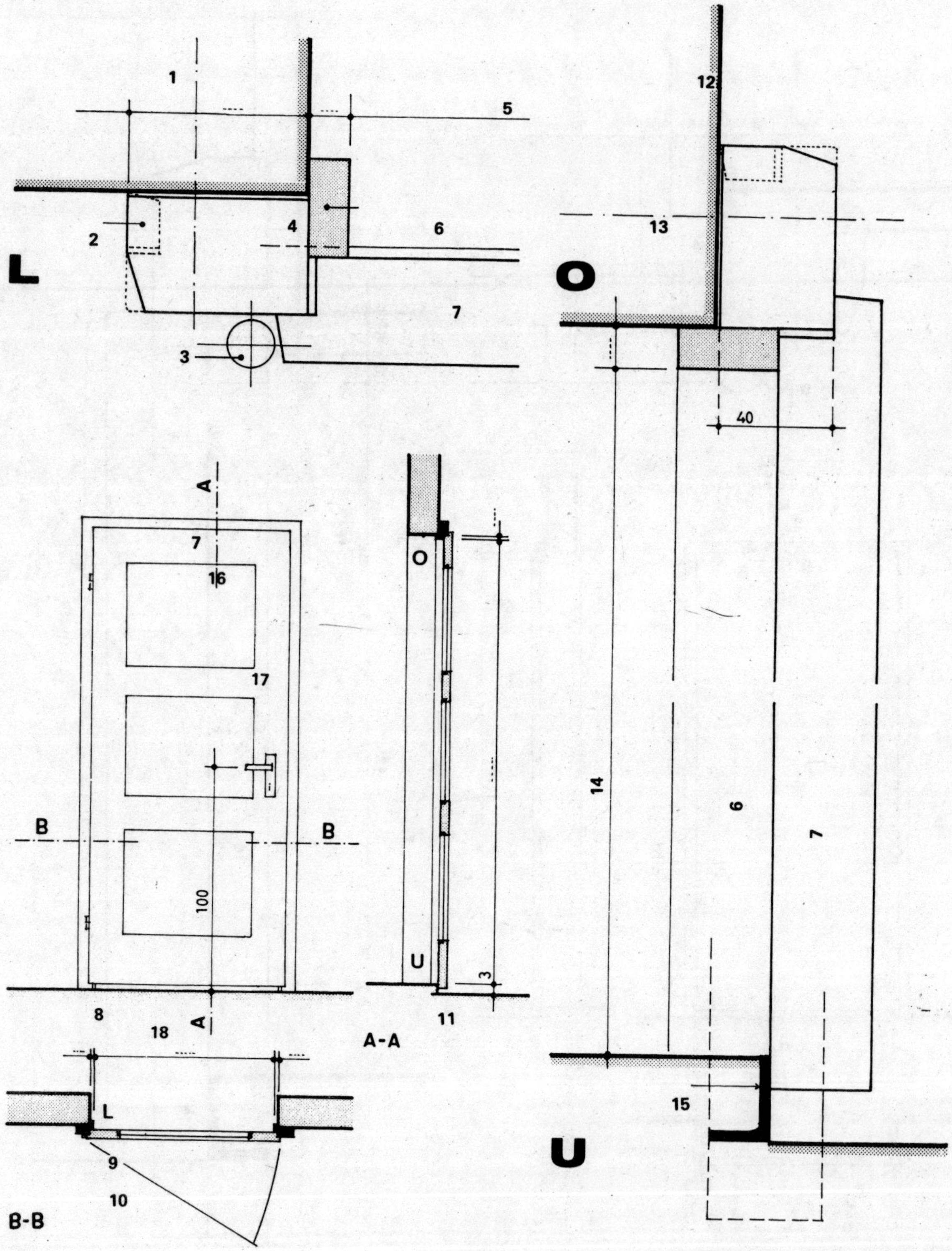

1 Jamb detail
2 Rebated moulding
3 Hinge
4 Frame
5 Width of door opening
6 Moulding (masking joint)
7 Door
8 Elevation
9 Hinge, left
10 Plan
11 Section
12 Lintel detail
13 Patent (masonry) screw
14 Headroom
15 Angle plate (stop)
16 Infilling (panel)
17 Intermediate rail
18 Framed (panelled) door

1:2

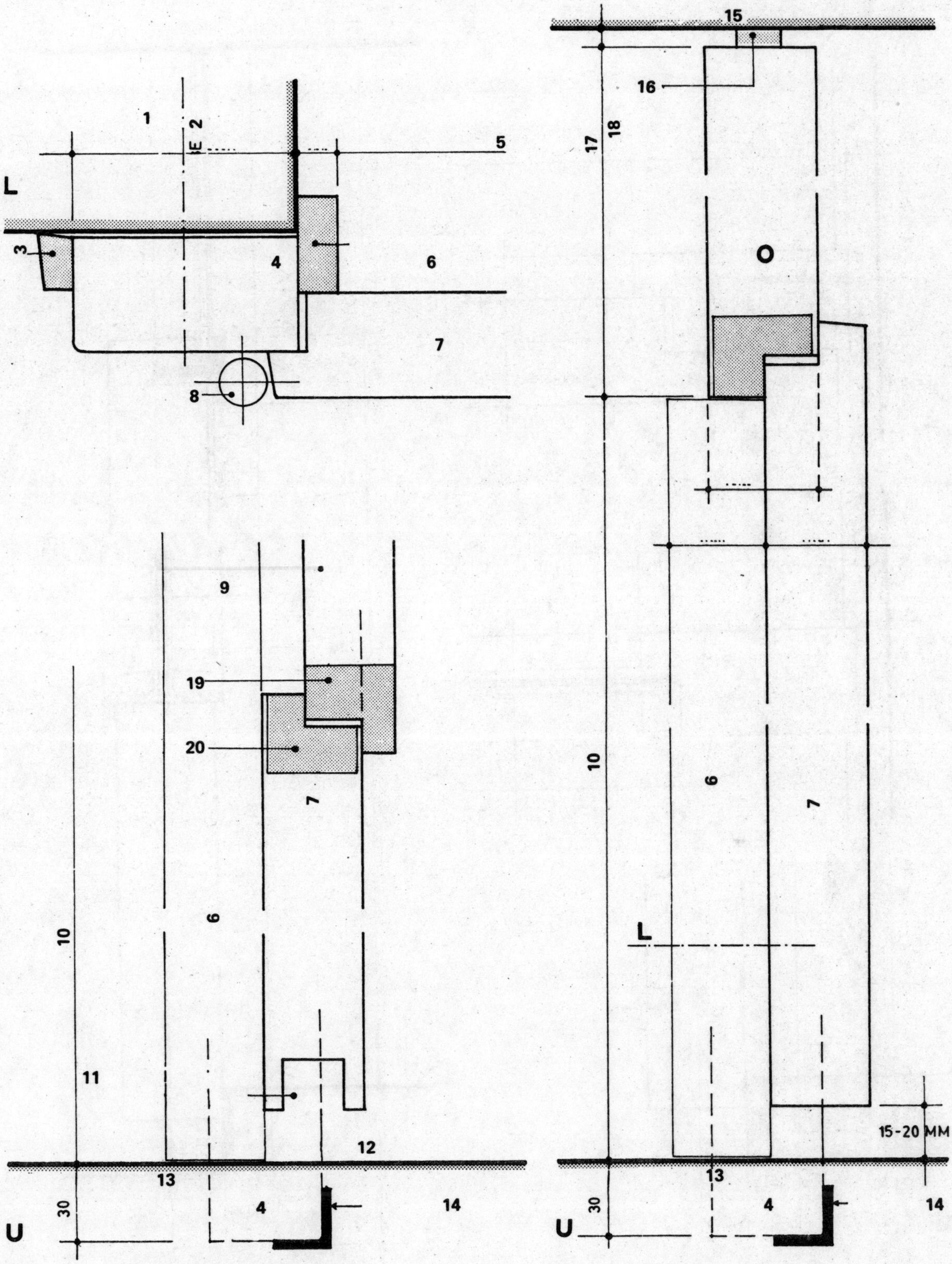

1 Jamb detail
2 Patent (masonry) screw
3 Moulding
4 Frame
5 Width of door opening
6 Moulding (masking joint)
7 Door
8 Hinge
9 Control element, built-in at eye-level
10 Headroom
11 Groove for subsequent core
12 Without stop
13 Floor connection (joint)
14 Angle
15 Ceiling joint
16 Felt caulking
17 Lintel (failure-proof fixing)
18 (Frame widening)

Framed Door, type variants

1:2

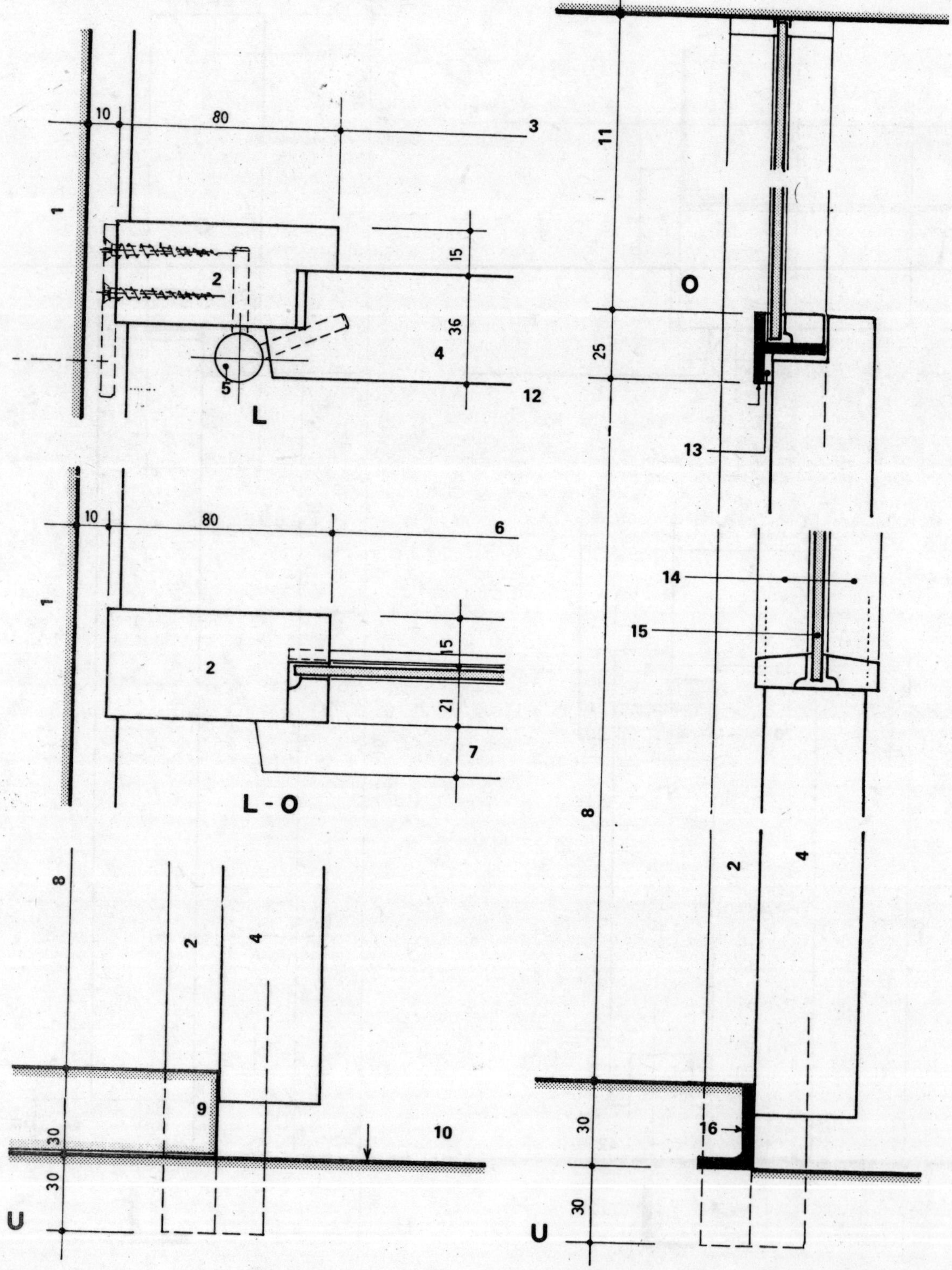

1 Wall lining detail
2 Frame
3 Width of door-frame opening
4 Door
5 Hinge
6 Width of (glass) light
7 Door from above
8 Headroom
9 Timber threshold
10 Flooring, top edge
11 Depth of (glass) light
12 T-section angle
13 Foam-plastic caulking
14 Glazing bars
15 Glass laid in putty
16 Angle (stop)

1:25/2

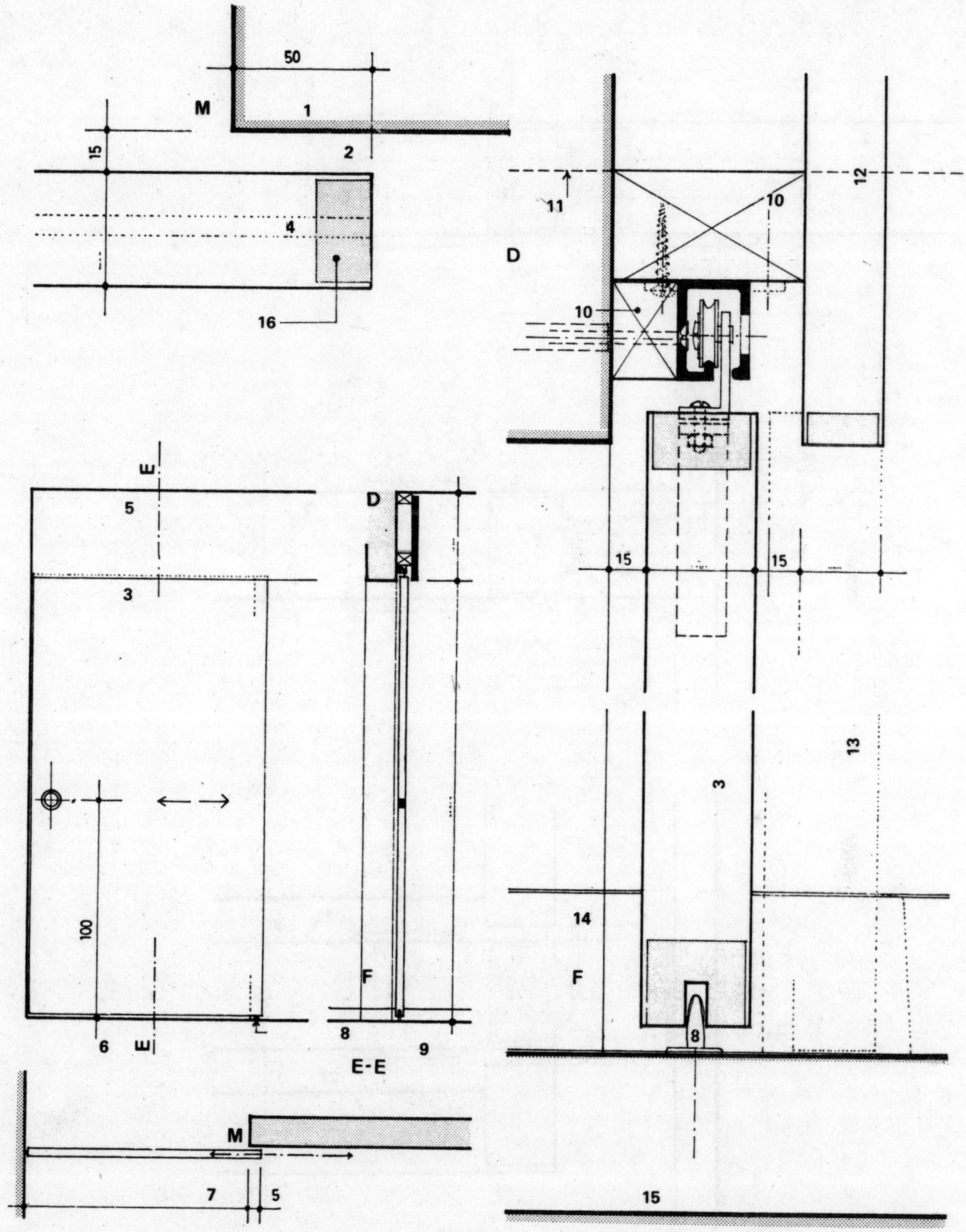

1 Wall
2 Cavity
3 Door
4 Groove
5 Fascia
6 Elevation
7 Width of opening
8 Track
9 Section
10 Distance piece
11 Ceiling joint
12 Demountable fascia
13 Jamb casing (optional)
14 Base
15 Mastic floor
(hard finish)
16 Glued-in block

Sliding Door, details

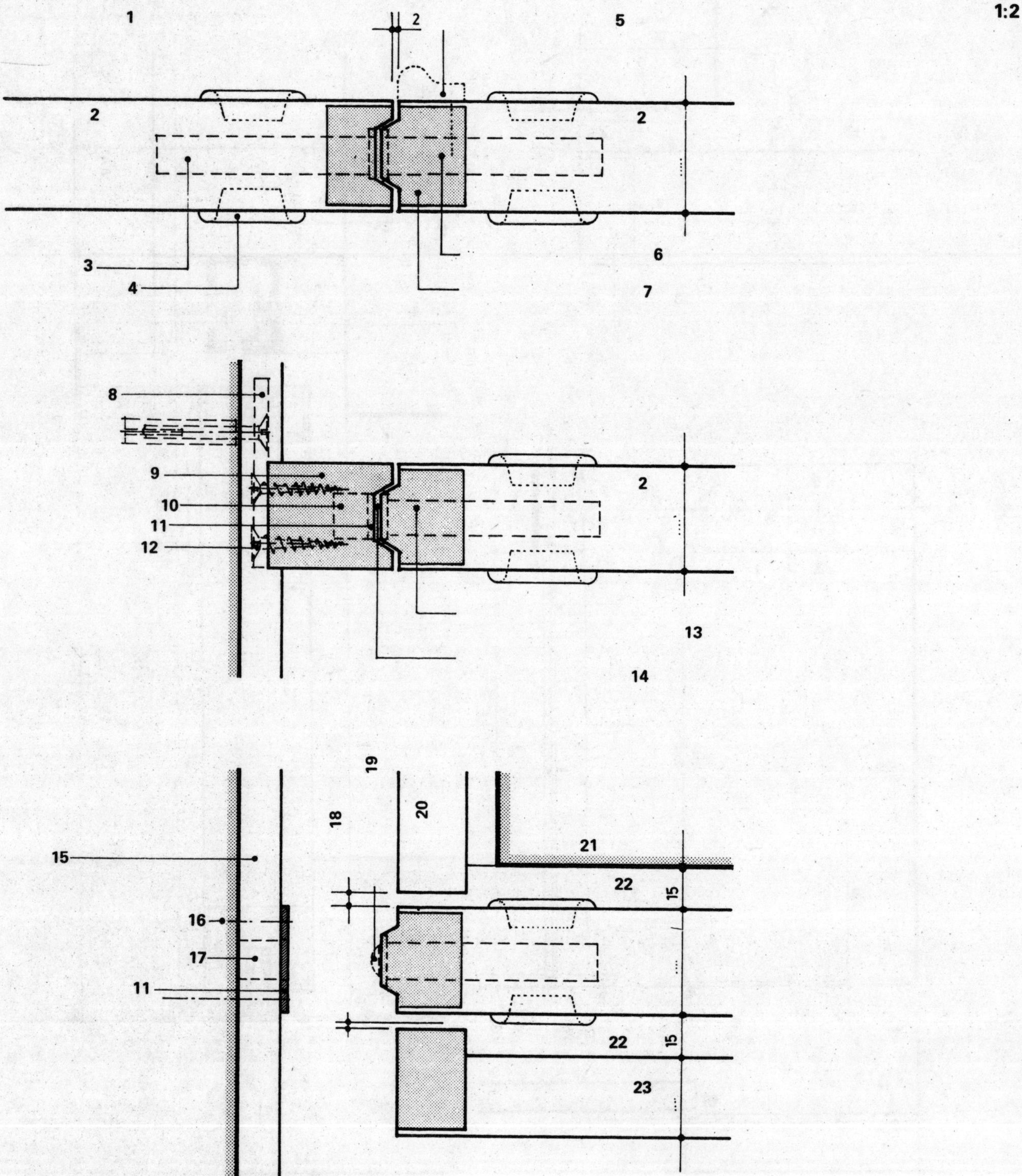

1 Middle section
2 Door
3 Sliding-door mortise dead lock
4 Recessed hand-grip
5 Possible moulded closer
6 Lock case
7 Glued-in or glued-round block
8 Flat
9 Casing
10 Lock opening
11 Striking plate
12 Wood screw
13 Sliding-door mortise lock with spring-grip
14 Check
15 Wall or jamb plaster
16 Patent (masonry) screw
17 Lock cut-out (channel)
18 Minimum
19 Rubber cushion
20 Lining
21 Wall
22 Cavity (space)
23 Masking element

1:25/2

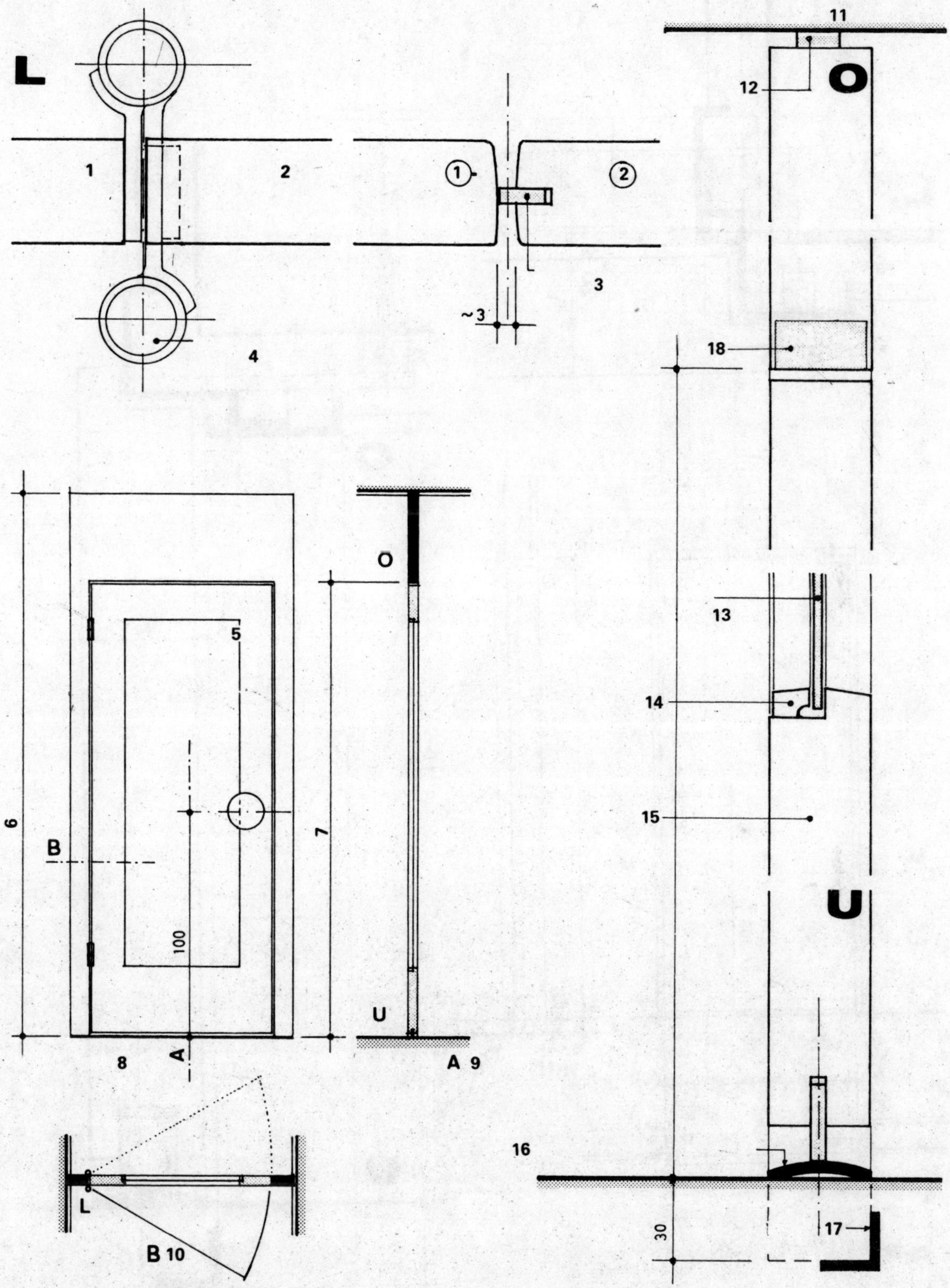

1 Frame
2 Door
3 Lipping
4 Swing-door hinge
5 Glass panel
6 Room height
7 Door height (head-room)
8 Elevation
9 Section
10 Plan
11 Ceiling joint
12 Self-adhesive sealing strip
13 Glass laid in putty
14 Glazing fillet
15 Bottom rail
16 Dished aluminium plate
17 Angle
18 Glued-in block

Metal Door with angle-lining and rebate-sealing

1:25/2

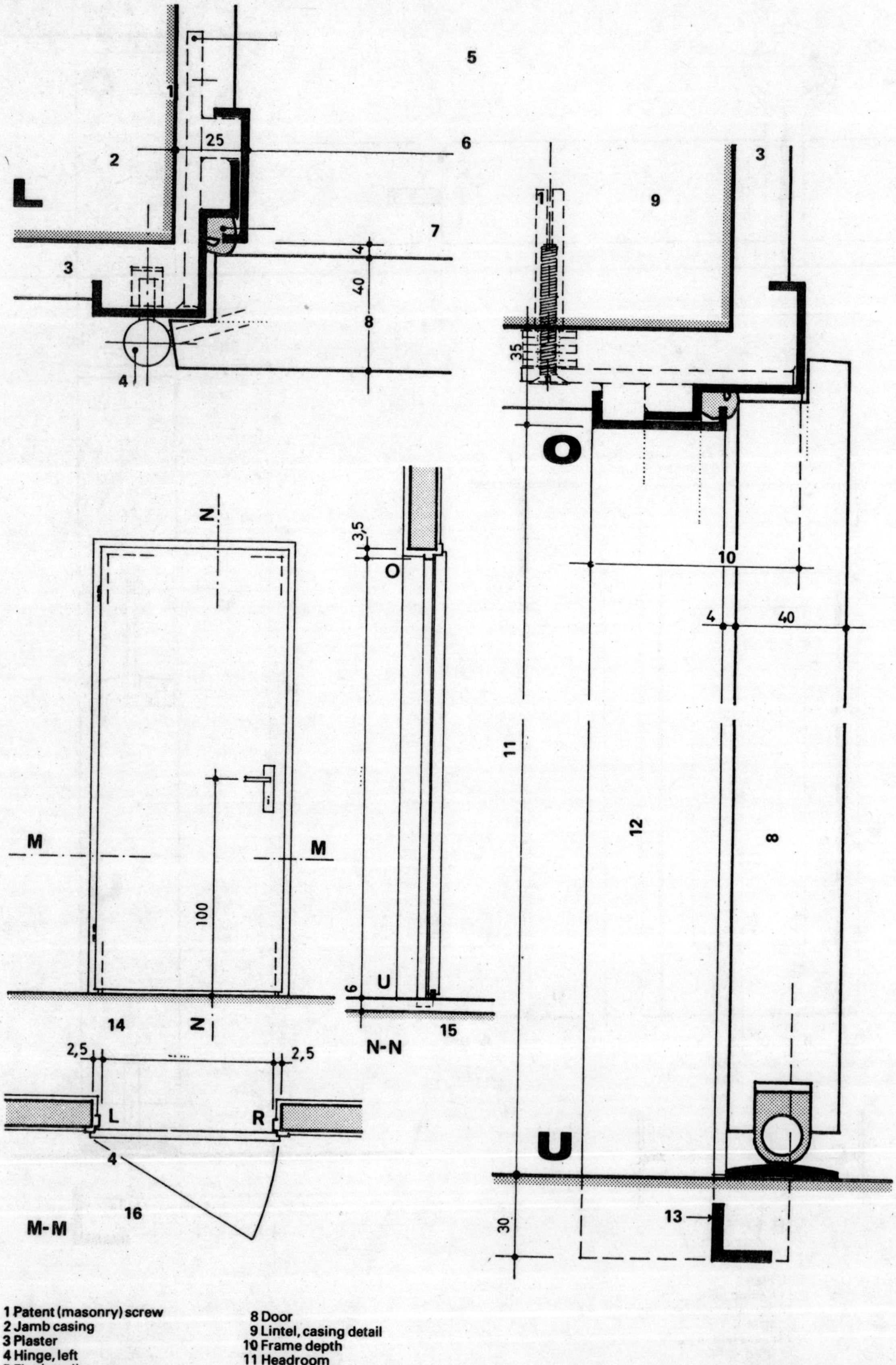

1 Patent (masonry) screw
2 Jamb casing
3 Plaster
4 Hinge, left
5 Flat (steel), welded to angle-frame
6 Width of door-frame opening
7 Cushion (caulking)
8 Door
9 Lintel, casing detail
10 Frame depth
11 Headroom
12 Angle-frame
13 Angle (plate)
14 Elevation
15 Section
16 Plan

1:25/2

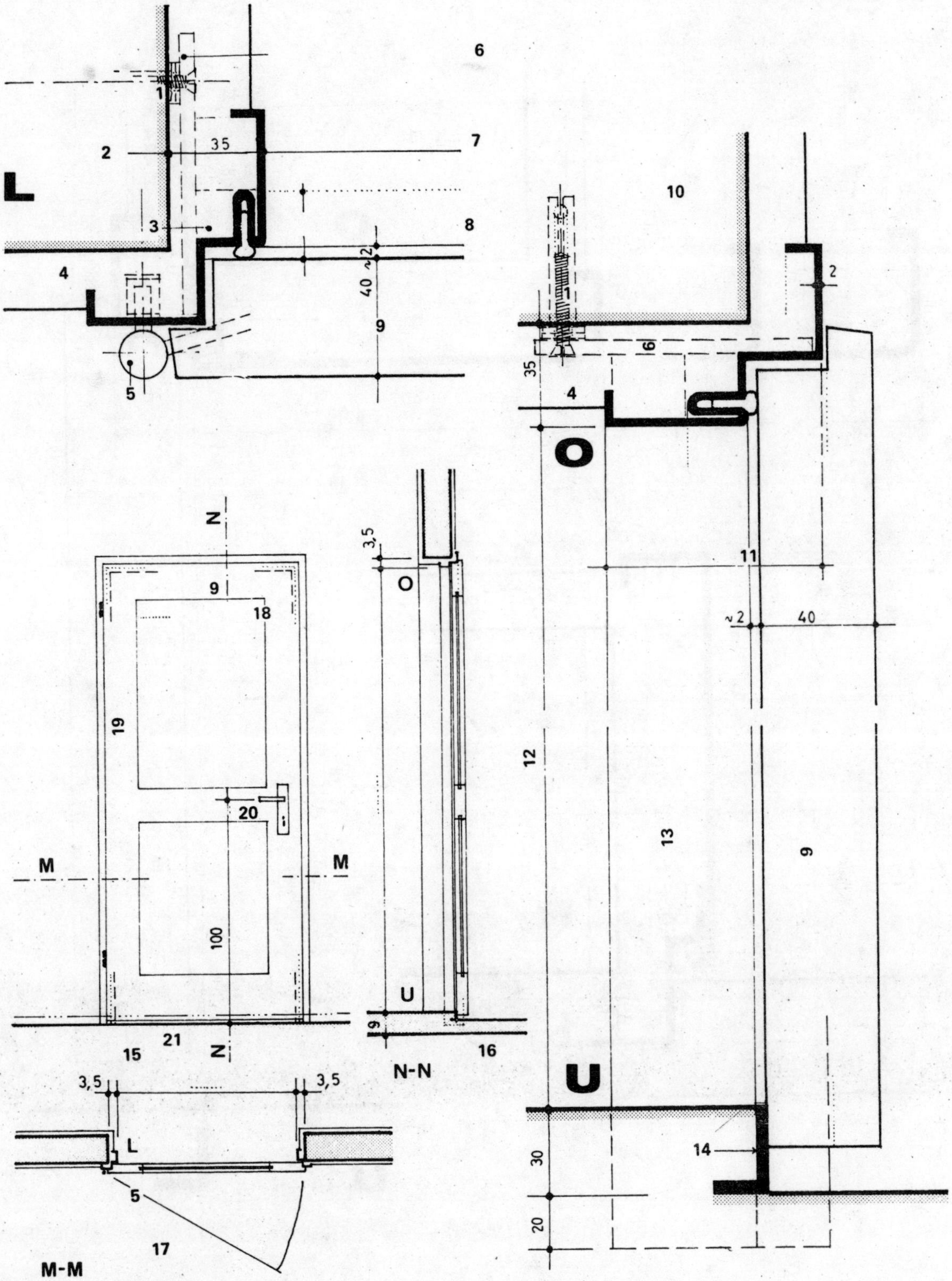

1 Patent (masonry) screw
2 Jamb lining
3 Possible grout
4 Plaster
5 Hinge, left
6 Flat (steel), welded to angle-frame
7 Width of frame opening
8 Threshold angle
9 Door
10 Lintel, casing detail
11 Frame depth
12 Headroom
13 Angle-frame
14 Lining angle
15 Elevation
16 Section
17 Plan
18 Door-infilling
19 Hinge-stile
20 Intermediate rail
21 Panelled door

Metal Door with full-width lining and rebate-sealing

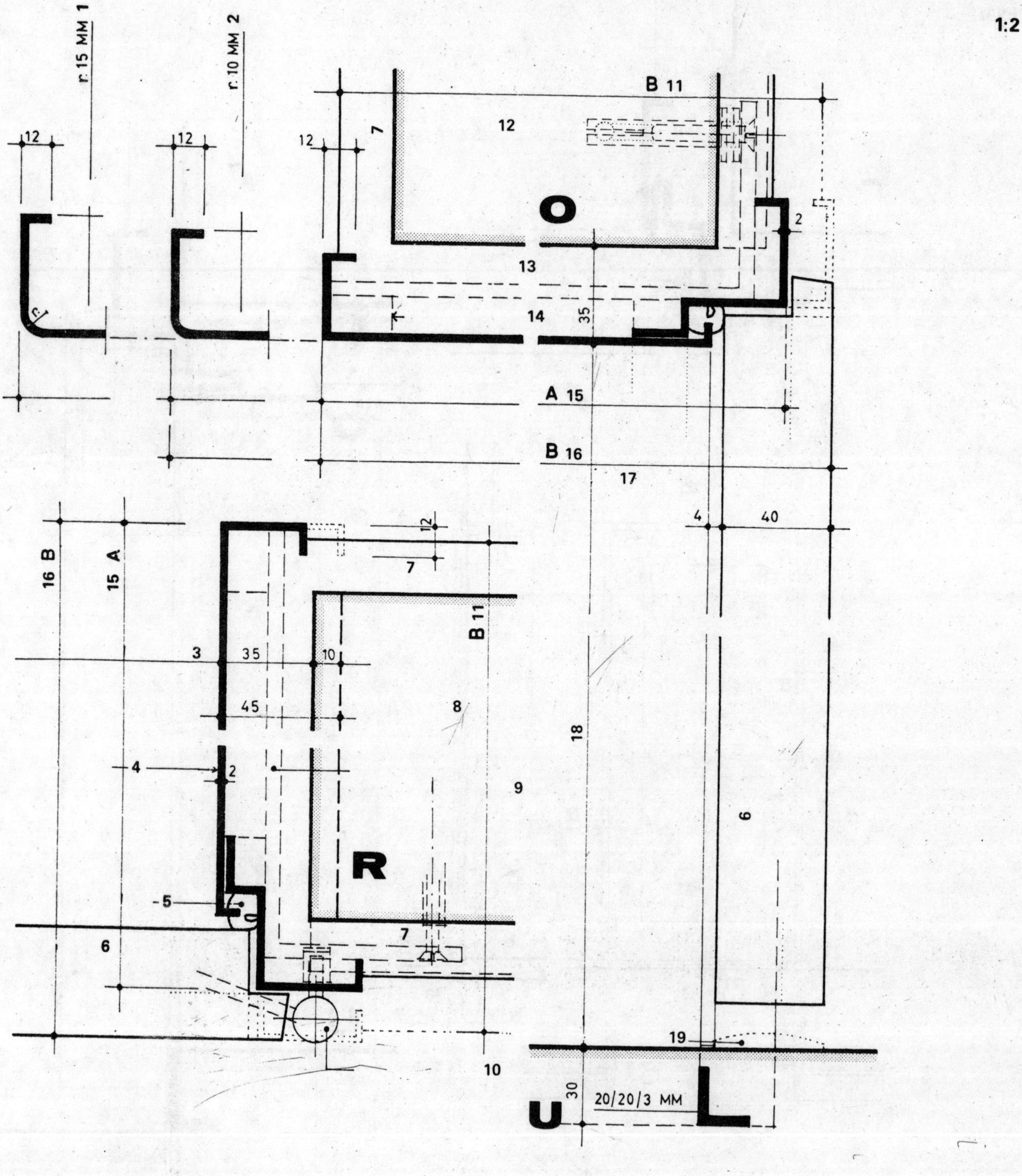

1 Variant
2 Variant
3 Width of frame opening
4 Complete framing
5 Sealing
6 Door
7 Plaster
8 Jamb lining detail
9 Flat (steel), welded to frame
10 Hinge, right
11 Plaster external measurement for (variant) B
12 Lintel, lining detail
13 Grout
14 Reinforcement
15 Frame depth variable
16 Frame dimension (variant)
17 For door without head
18 Headroom
19 Possible dished... -plate

1:25/2

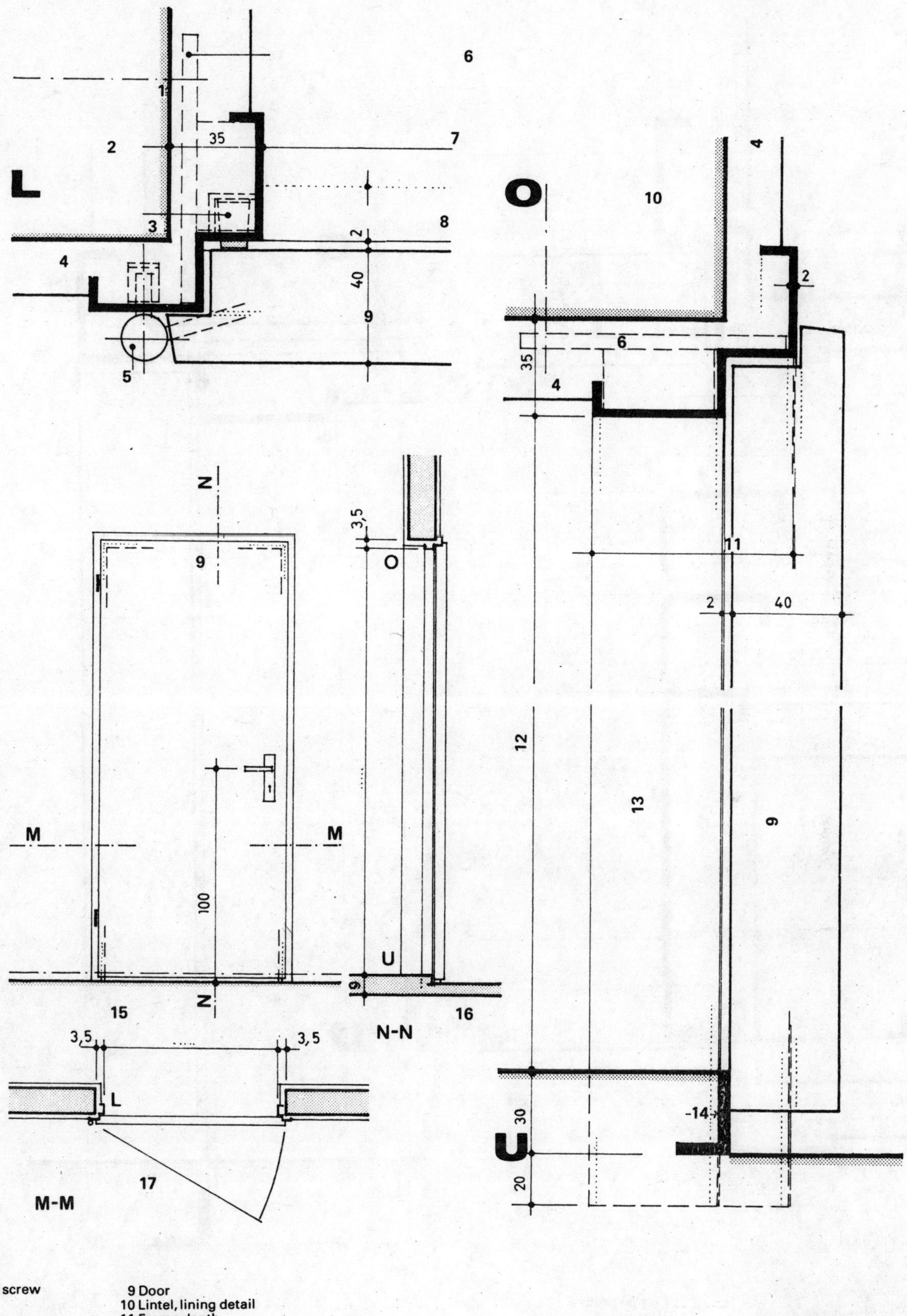

1 Patent (masonry) screw
2 Jamb lining
3 Rubber cushion
4 Plaster
5 Hinge, left
6 Flat (steel), welded to angle-frame
7 Width of frame opening
8 Threshold angle-plate
9 Door
10 Lintel, lining detail
11 Frame depth
12 Headroom
13 Angle-frame
14 Stop
15 Elevation
16 Section
17 Plan

Metal Doors with angle- and full-width-linings, variants

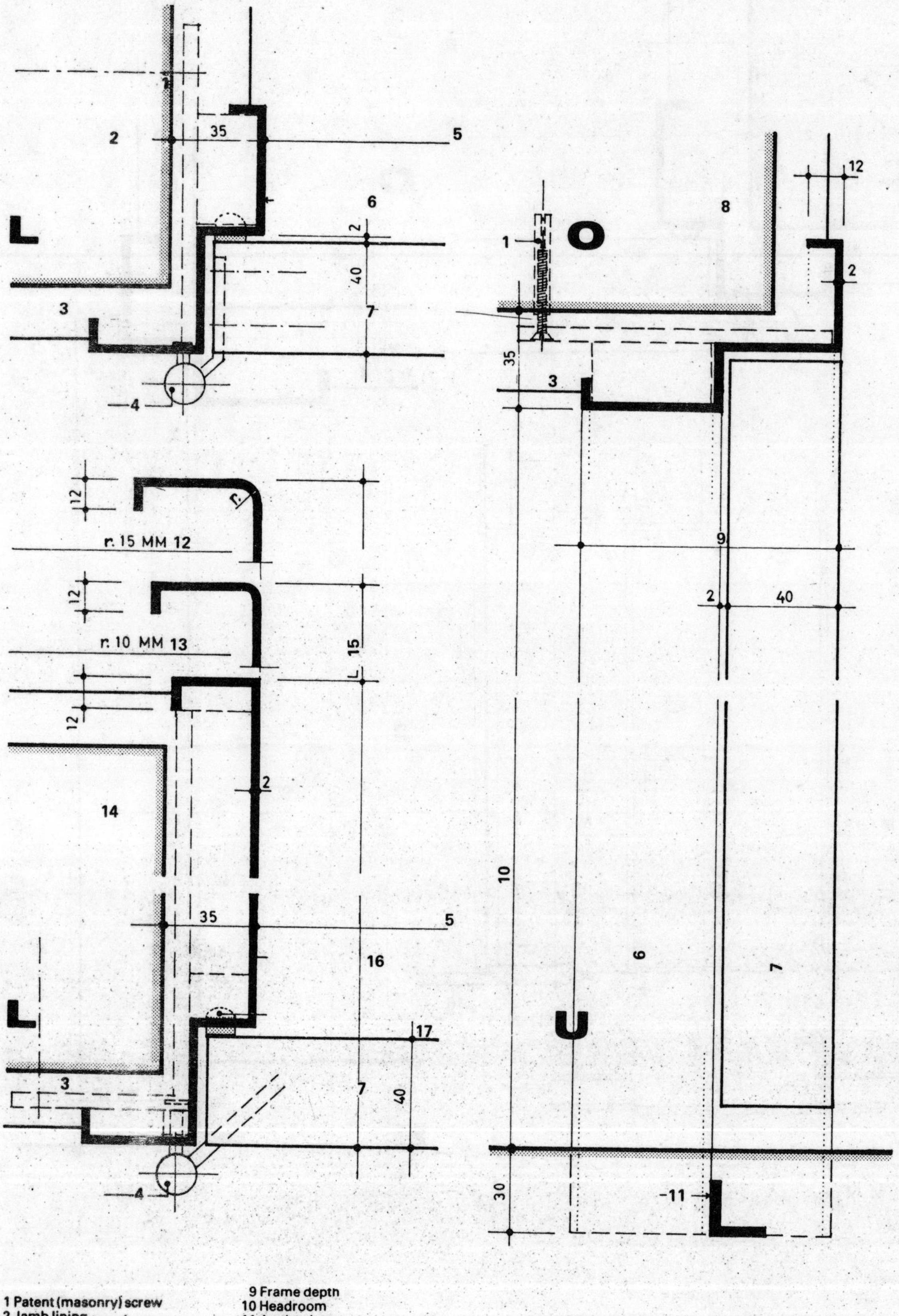

1 Patent (masonry) screw
2 Jamb lining
3 Plaster
4 Hinge, left
5 Width of frame opening
6 Angle-frame
7 Door
8 Lintel, lining detail
9 Frame depth
10 Headroom
11 Angle-plate
12 Variant:
13 Variant:
14 Jamb lining detail
15 Frame depth, variable
16 Complete framing
17 Rubber cushion

Metal Angle-frame Door without rebate-sealing

1:25/2

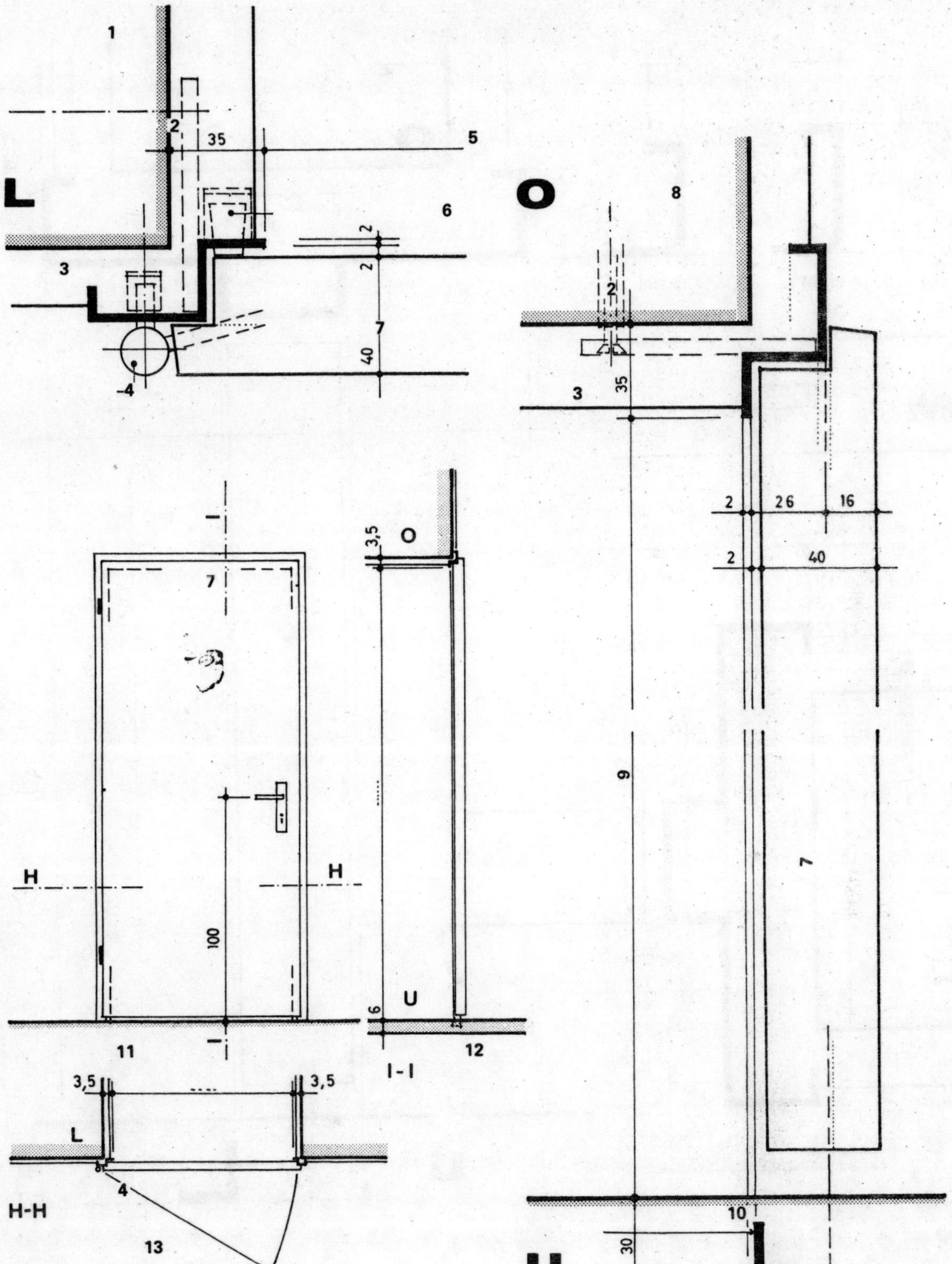

1 Jamb lining
2 Patent (masonry) screw
3 Plaster
4 Hinge, left
5 Width of frame opening
6 Rubber cushion
7 Door
8 Lintel, lining detail
9 Headroom
10 Stiffening angle-plate
11 Elevation
12 Section
13 Plan

Metal Linings for swing doors

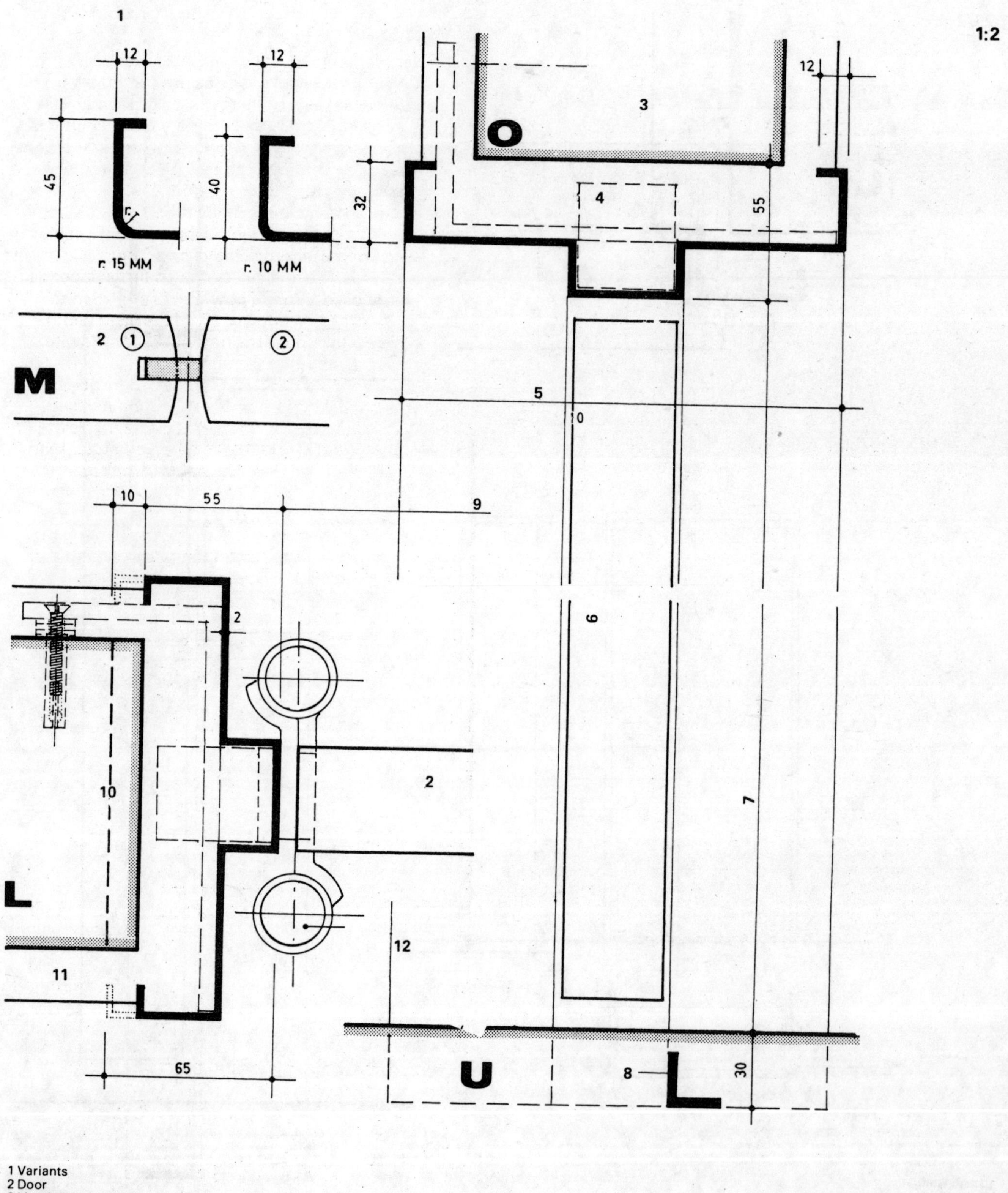

1 Variants
2 Door
3 Lintel, lining detail
4 Grout
5 Frame depth
6 Door with glass-infill panel
7 Headroom
8 Angle-plate
9 Width of frame opening
10 Jamb lining
11 Plaster
12 Swing-door hinge

Wall cupboards

All timber members must be well seasoned, knot-free, dry stored and delivered to site as pre-fabricated units. Care should be taken to avoid twisted growth timber, which is not suitable for use in joinery work, since it is subject to constant warping, depending on temperature and the moisture content of the air. All timbers to be built in must be primed before fixing.

Modern requirements have made the use of chipboard for cupboards recommendable. Lippings and nosings are however necessary to achieve clean, durable visible edges to boards. The thickness of the boards depends on the height used, varying between 19 and 25 mm.

Shelving: Thickness = approx. 2% of the clear width.

For rear linings to cupboards hardboard (or "Pavatex" board) ca. 4.5-6 mm thick is sufficient.

The divisions should be related to the proportions of the room. It should be remembered that built in cupboards constructed to precise dimensions utilize the recesses, corners and angles of a dwelling better than standard size cupboards or moveable furniture. Furthermore, built in furniture gives a flat or a house a personal touch.

Design: cupboard depth: 55-60 cm; clothes hanging space, shelving. Drawer space should also be allowed. In cupboards less than 40 cm deep telescopic hanging rails should be used.

Corner cupboard, elevation, sections, details

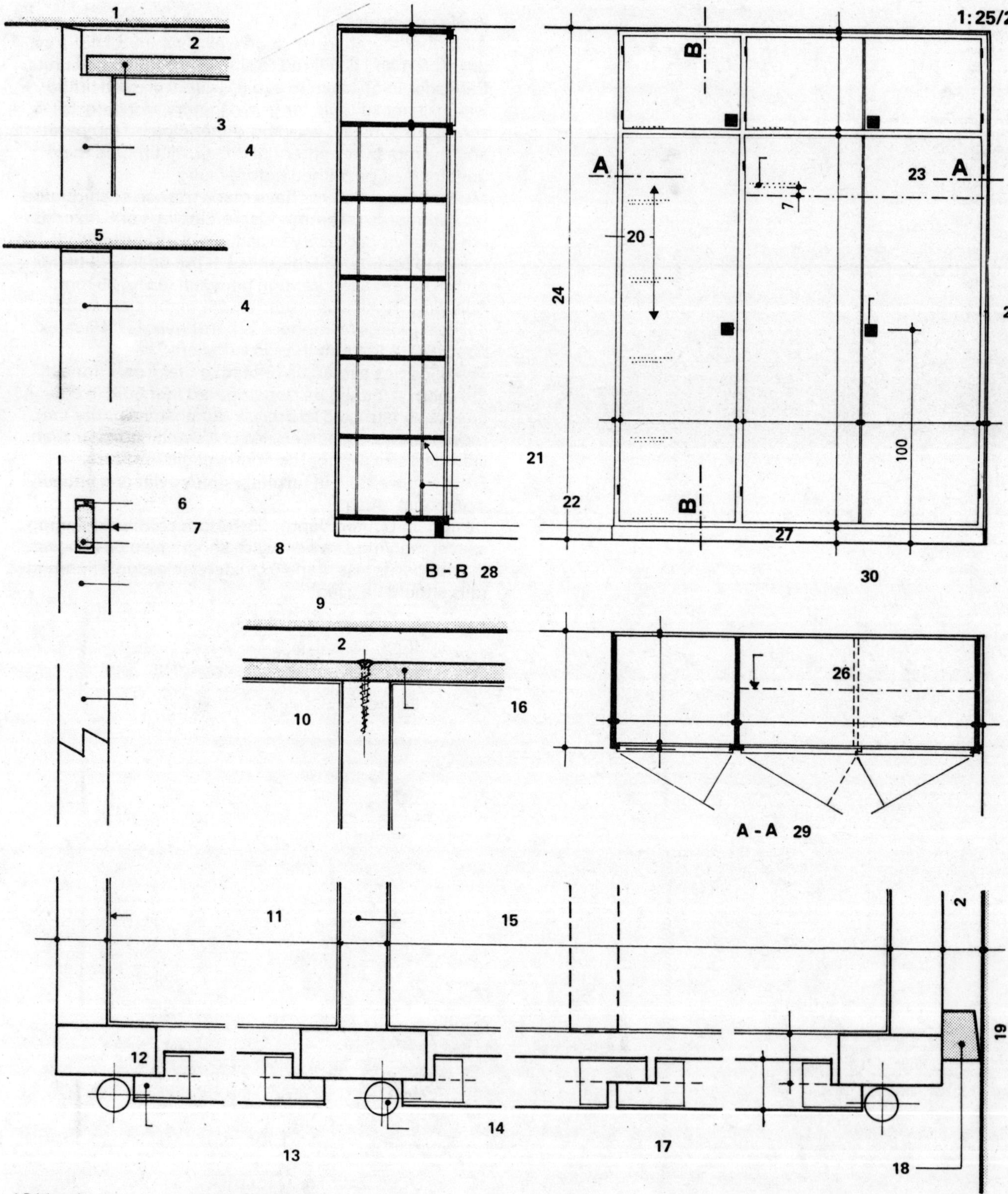

1 Brickwork
2 Void
3 Back, hardboard or plywood
4 Side
5 Wall plaster
6 Groove
7 Butt joint
8 Hardwood cross-tongue
9 Cupboard side cross-tongued and glued
10 Cupboard side with Z-lapped joint and glued
11 Line of shelving
12 Fascia framing
13 Cupboard door with rebated edge; chipboard with lippings
14 Door hinge
15 Division wall
16 Back
17 Cross-rebated meeting stiles
18 Shadow bead
19 Junction with wall
20 Adjustable shelving
21 Shelf bearer
22 Track for shelf bearers, let in
23 Fixed shelving
24 Height of opening
25 Height of handle or lock
26 Hanging rail
27 Plinth
28 Section B–B
29 Plan A–A
30 Elevation of built-in cupboard

Corner cupboard with alternative details

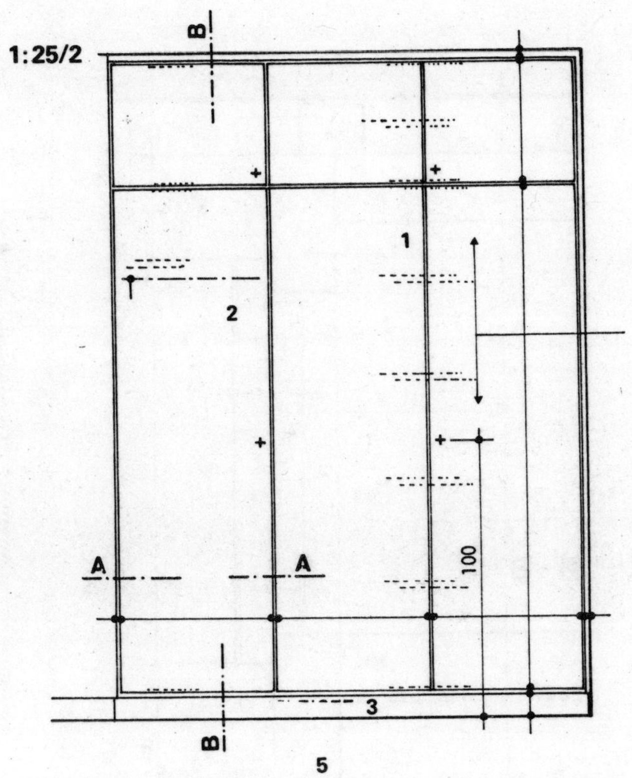

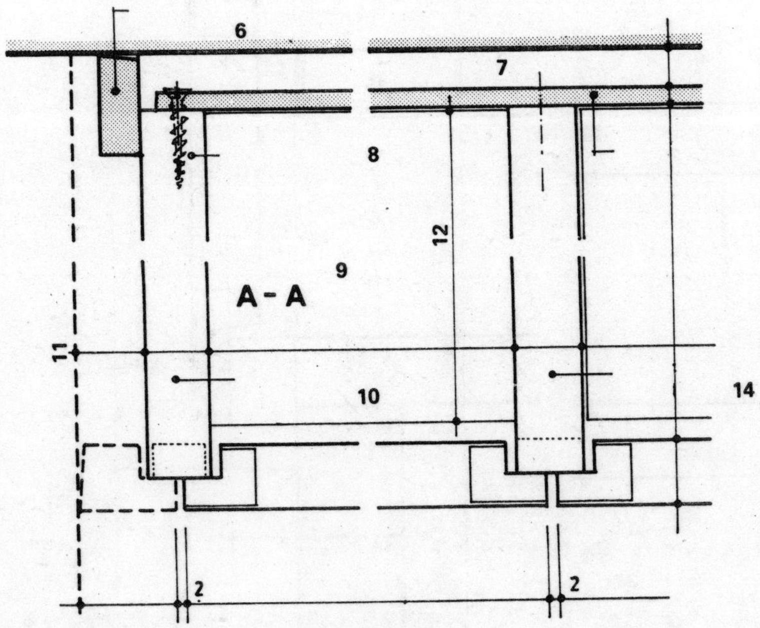

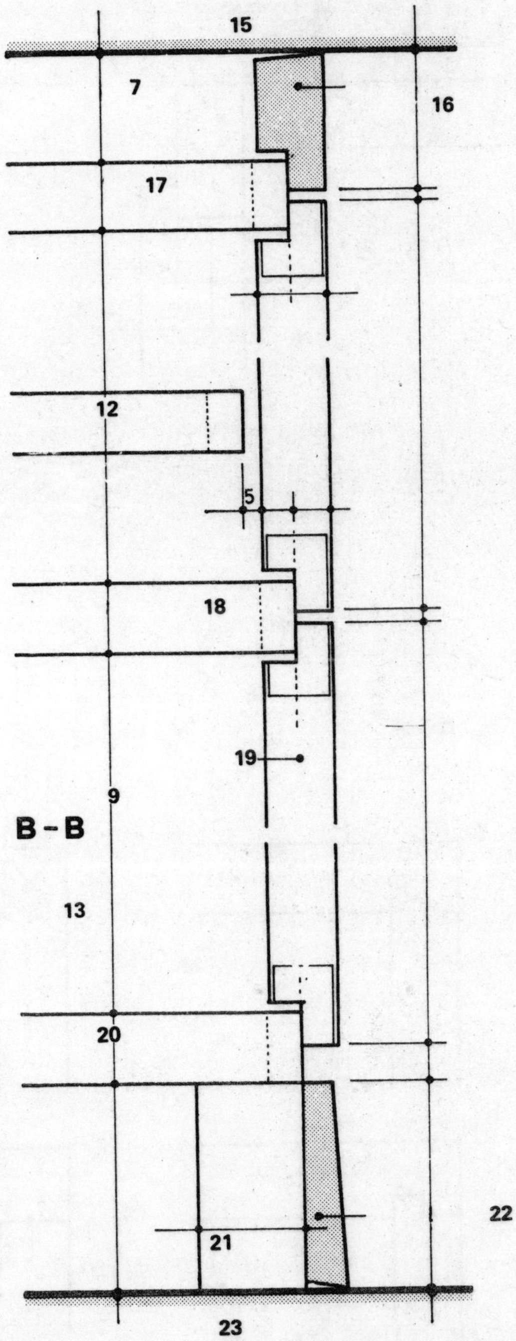

1 Small doors with concealed hinges
2 Hanging rail
3 Plinth
4 Adjustable shelving
5 Elevation of cupboard
6 12/30 mm architrave
7 Void
8 Side
9 Section A–A
10 Chipboard with lipping
11 Alternative, junction with wall
12 Shelving
13 Back, hardboard or fibreboard
14 Chipboard with lippings
15 Junction with soffit
16 Cover strip
17 Top
18 Intermediate floor
19 Door, with rebated edge
20 Cupboard floor
21 Plinth
22 Skirting
23 Plinth detail

Cupboard details

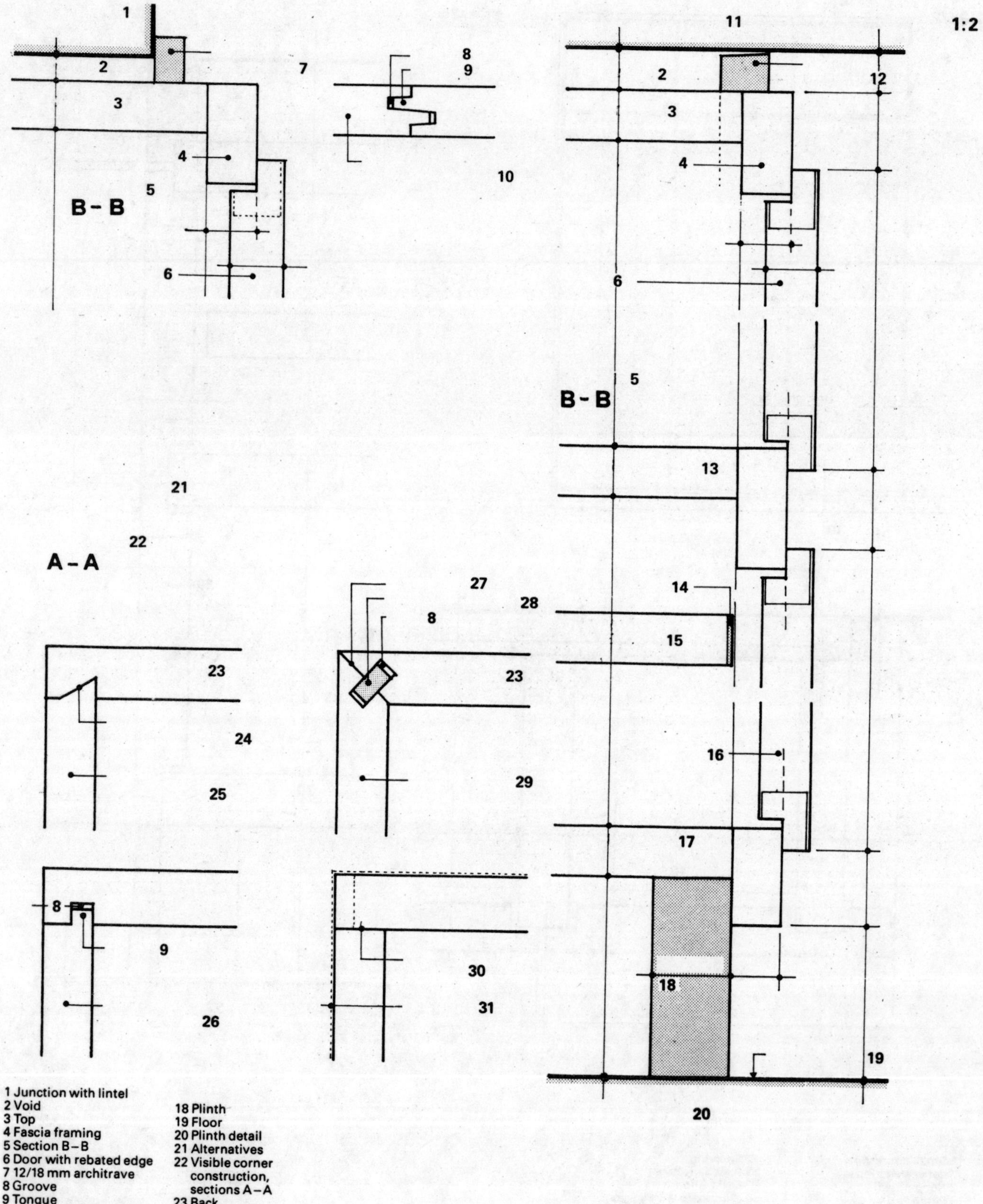

1 Junction with lintel
2 Void
3 Top
4 Fascia framing
5 Section B – B
6 Door with rebated edge
7 12/18 mm architrave
8 Groove
9 Tongue
10 Tongued and grooved comb joint
11 Junction with soffit
12 Shadow bead
13 Intermediate floor
14 Plastic edging
15 Adjustable shelving
16 Chipboard with lippings
17 Cupboard floor
18 Plinth
19 Floor
20 Plinth detail
21 Alternatives
22 Visible corner construction, sections A – A
23 Back
24 Splay-grooved
25 Side glued in
26 Side tongued and grooved (to rear)
27 Mitre
28 Hard wood cross-tongue
29 Side
30 Butt joint
31 Veneer

Corner cupboard for clothes and linen with details

1:25/2

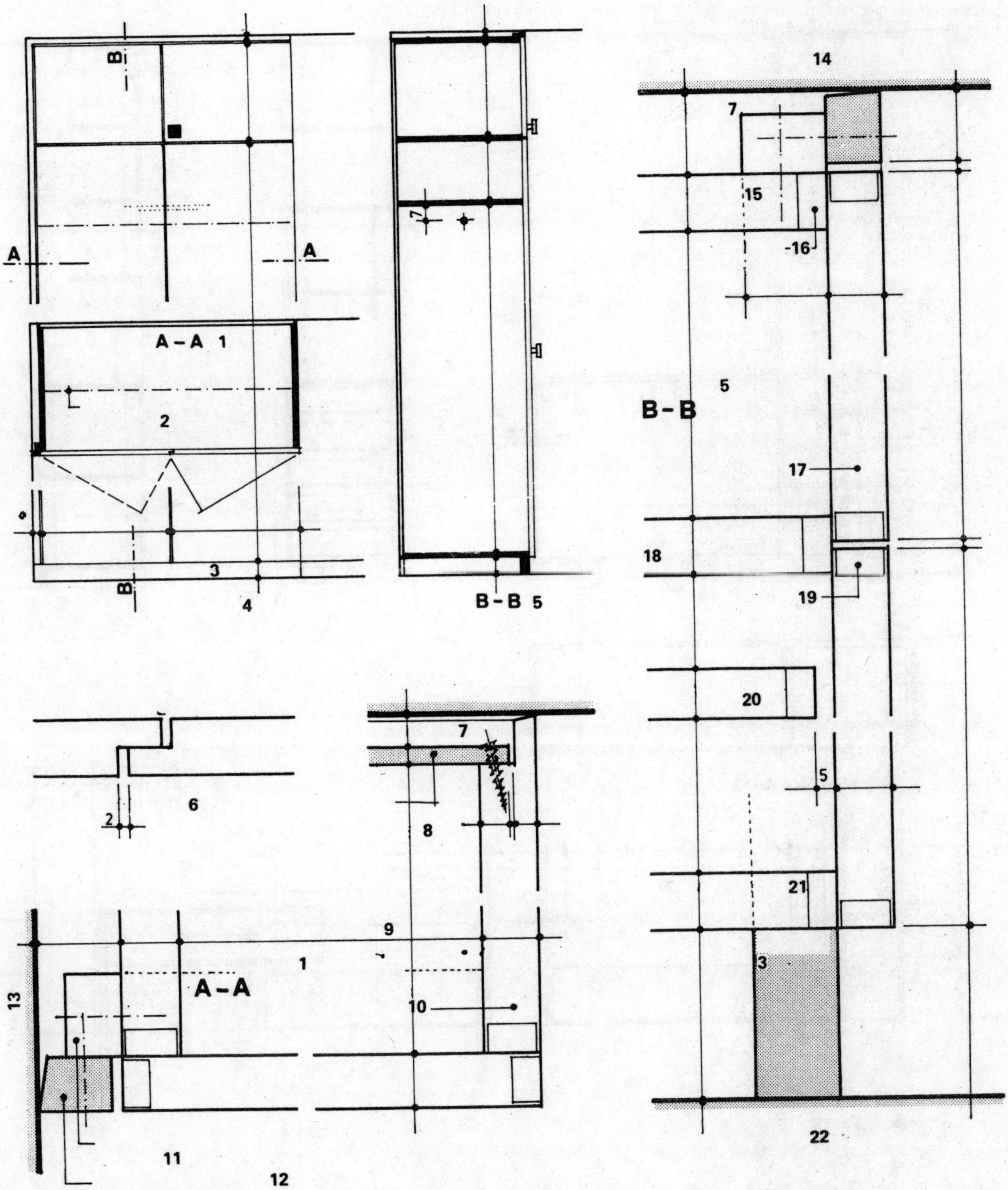

1 Plan A–A
2 Hanging rail
3 Plinth
4 Elevation of cupboard
5 Section B–B
6 Cross-rebated meeting stiles
7 Void
8 Back, hardboard or plywood
9 Internal dimension of cupboard
10 Cupboard side, chipboard
11 Fixing fillet
12 Cover strip
13 Junction with wall
14 Junction with soffit
15 Top
16 Nosing
17 Door, surface mounted
18 Intermediate floor
19 Lipping
20 Fixed shelving
21 Cupboard floor
22 Plinth detail

Floor-to-ceiling cupboard with additive elements

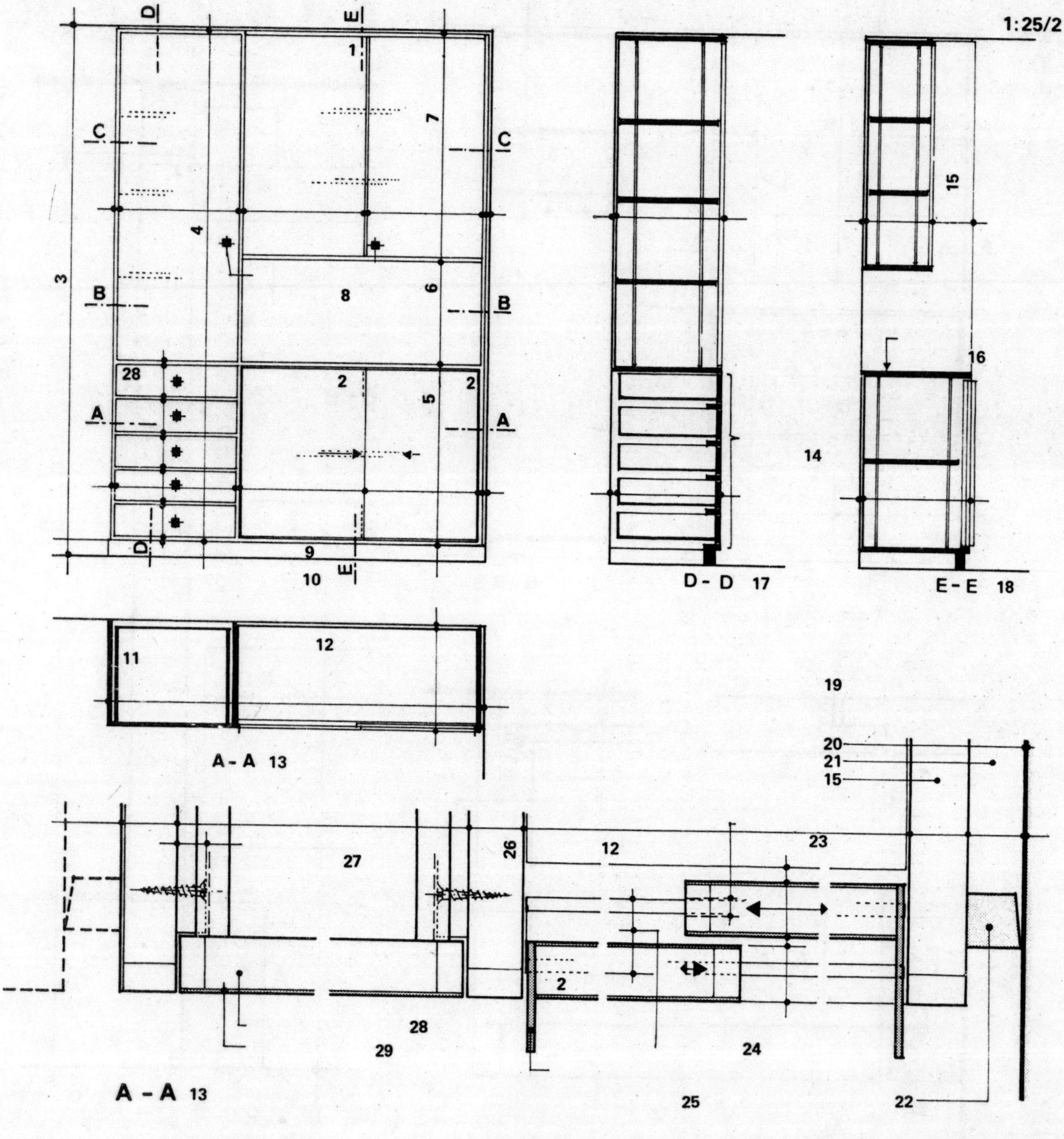

1 Side-hung door
2 Sliding door
3 Height of recess
4 Floor-to-ceiling cupboard
5 Lower cupboard
6 Recess
7 Top cupboard
8 Espagnolette bolt
9 Plinth
10 Wall cupboard elevation
11 Drawer
12 Shelving
13 Plan A–A
14 Chest of drawers
15 Side
16 Working surface
17 Section D–D
18 Section E–E
19 Wall fittings constructional alternatives
20 Line of wall
21 Void
22 Shadow bead
23 Continuous groove
24 Double guide tracks
25 Flat door grip 40/2 mm at hand height
26 Division wall
27 Hardwood drawer runner
28 Drawer fascia
29 Veneer

1:2

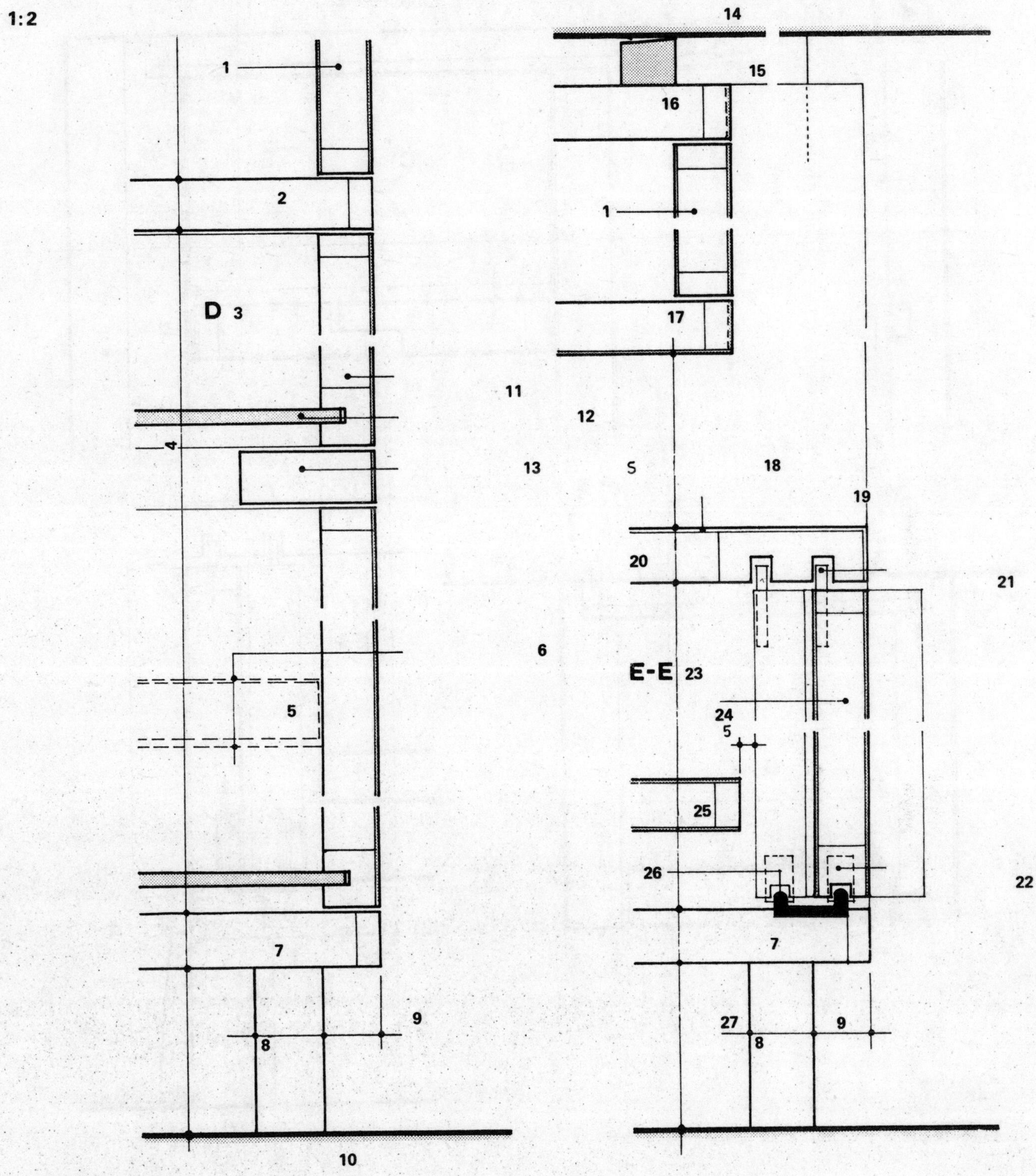

1 Small door with lipping
2 Intermediate floor
3 Section D
4 Height of chest of drawers
5 Drawer runner
6 Groove for runner
7 Cupboard floor
8 Plinth
9 Cupboard projection
10 Plinth detail
11 Drawer fascia
12 Drawer lining
13 Fascia strip
14 Junction at soffit
15 Shadow bead
16 Top
17 Exposed soffit
18 Cupboard recess
19 PVC lining
20 Work top
21 Strip grooved in
22 Plastic runner
23 Section E – E
24 Sliding door with veneered face
25 Adjustable shelving
26 Double door track
27 Void

Wall cupboards, alternative details

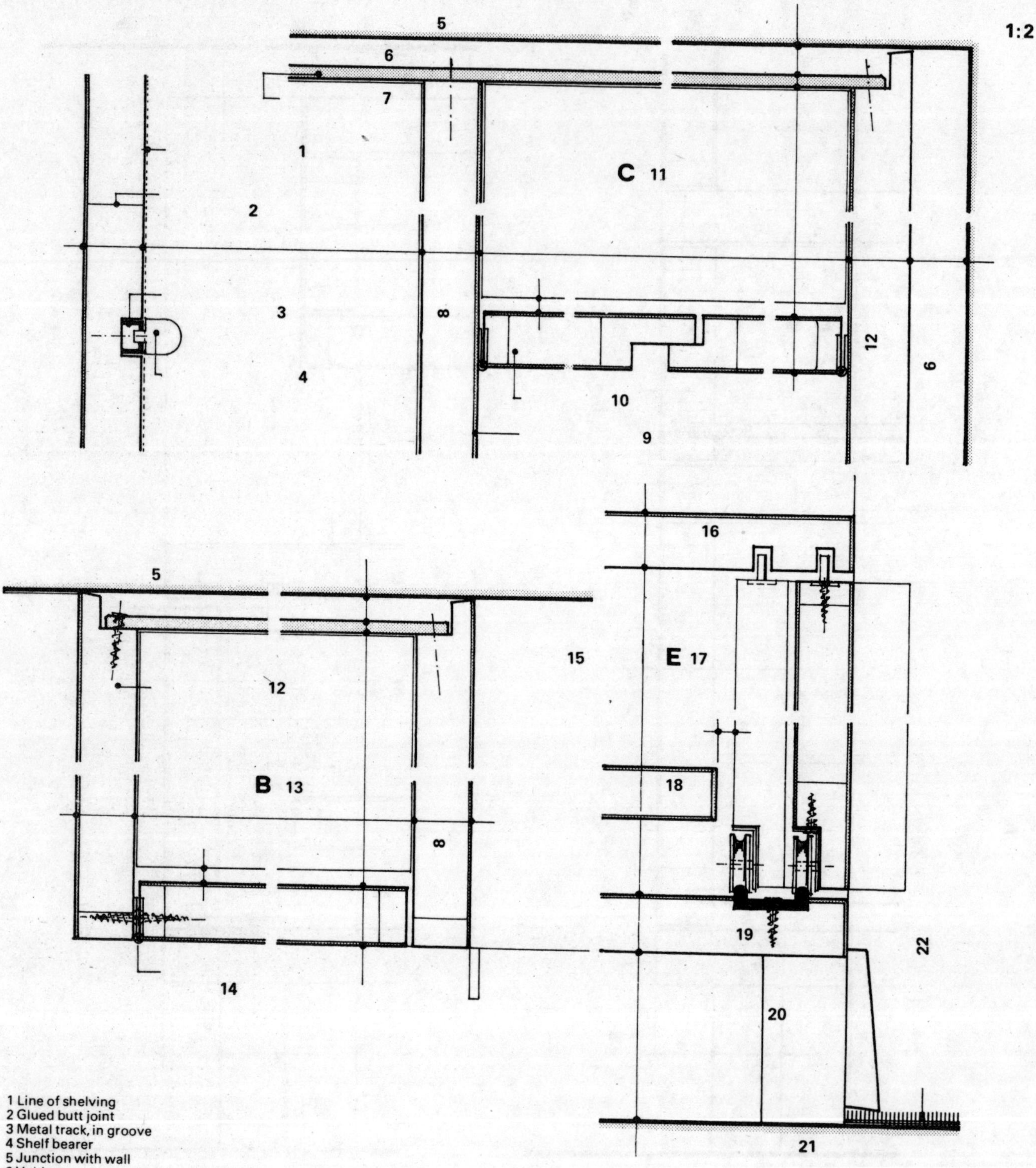

1 Line of shelving
2 Glued butt joint
3 Metal track, in groove
4 Shelf bearer
5 Junction with wall
6 Void
7 Back
8 Division wall
9 Veneer
10 Door
11 Plan C, top cupboard
12 Side
13 Plan B
14 Piano hinge
15 Plan of work top
16 Work top
17 Alternative, section E
18 Shelving
19 Cupboard floor
20 Plinth
21 Plinth detail
22 Carpeting

1:2

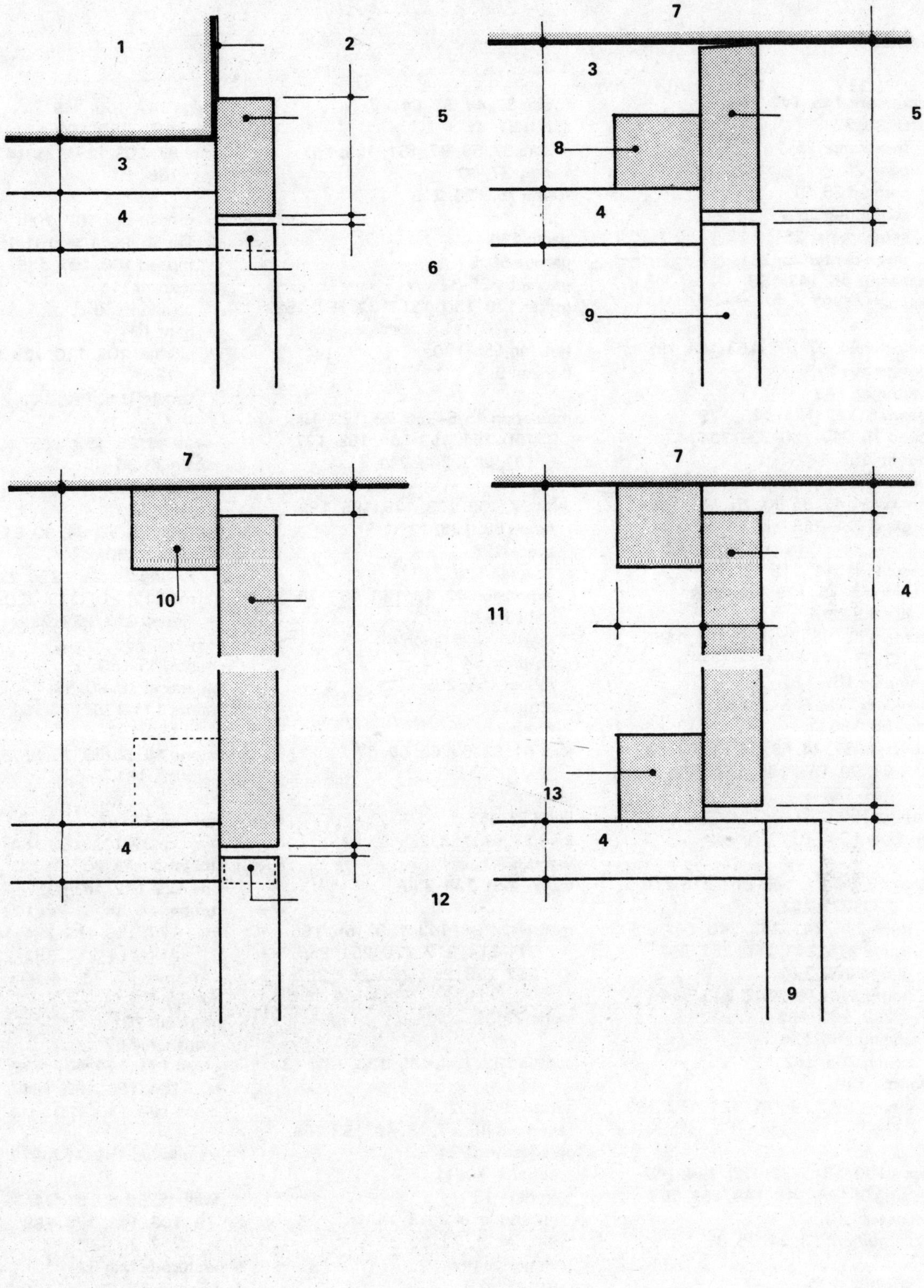

1 Junction with downstand beam
2 Wall paper
3 Void
4 Top
5 Architrave
6 Lipping
7 Junction with ceiling
8 Fixing fillet
9 Door
10 Shadow bead (fixing fillet)
11 Fascia, screwed
12 Lipping
13 . . . / . . . mm fixing fillet
14 Wood or chipboard fascia

Index